For Peter Lindsay —

To commemorate your final year at the
University of Alberta, and your impending
return to Australia.
With all best wishes —

Keith Moore

Edmonton September 1992

THE OXFORD
COMPANION TO
AUSTRALIAN
SPORT

THE OXFORD COMPANION TO AUSTRALIAN SPORT

EDITED BY

WRAY VAMPLEW
KATHARINE MOORE
JOHN O'HARA
RICHARD CASHMAN
IAN F. JOBLING

THE AUSTRALIAN SOCIETY FOR
SPORTS HISTORY
with assistance from
THE AUSTRALIAN SPORTS COMMISSION

Melbourne
OXFORD UNIVERSITY PRESS
Oxford   Auckland   New York

OXFORD UNIVERSITY PRESS AUSTRALIA
Oxford New York Toronto
Delhi Bombay Calcutta Madras Karachi
Kuala Lumpur Singapore Hong Kong Tokyo
Nairobi Dar es Salaam Cape Town
Melbourne Auckland Madrid
and associated companies in
Berlin Ibadan

OXFORD is a trade mark of Oxford University Press

National Library of Australia
Cataloguing-in-Publication data:

The Oxford Companion to Australian Sport.
ISBN 0 19 553287 2
1. Sports—Australia—Encyclopedias.
2. Sports—Australia—Biography.
3. Athletes—Australia—Biography.
I. Vamplew, Wray.
796.0994

Edited by Venetia Nelson
Cover designed by Sarn Potter
Typeset by Bookset Pty Ltd, Victoria
Printed by Impact Printing Pty Ltd, Victoria
Published by Oxford University Press,
253 Normanby Road, South Melbourne, Australia

FOREWORD

THE AUSTRALIAN SOCIETY for Sports History (ASSH) is proud to be involved in the first comprehensive presentation of sport in Australia. No other society for sport history elsewhere in the world has ever undertaken such a venture, so this is a pioneering effort. ASSH's origins are to be found in a Sporting Traditions Conference convened by Richard Cashman and Michael McKernan in July 1977 at the University of New South Wales in order to bring together academics who shared a common interest in the history of sport; however, the society was not formally created until the fourth Sporting Traditions Conference, organised by Richard Stremski and Bill Murray at the Melbourne Cricket Ground in May 1983. ASSH, which now boasts a membership of 400 academics and non-academics alike, publishes a *Studies in Sports History* series, a semi-annual journal (*Sporting Traditions*), and a regular *Bulletin*, all of which are important sources on the history of sport in Australia.

This particular project originated when Oxford University Press approached Richard Cashman, who then discussed the idea with John O'Hara and Wray Vamplew. As acting president and incoming president of ASSH respectively, they suggested that the Society itself might take on the task. That proposal was enthusiastically endorsed at the annual general meeting of ASSH in Sydney in July 1989 and was reinforced by the overwhelming response of ASSH members to a circular asking for their assistance.

An editorial board was established to oversee the project, and without their enormous effort this volume would not exist. Their three years of 'hard yakka' are praiseworthy not only for the magnitude of the accomplishment but also because they have performed the task on behalf of ASSH without any financial reward; the society, which is a non-profit, incorporated association, will use the royalties from this volume to continue to promote further research and study of sport. This has truly been a labour of love and dedication to a cause.

The few to whom the many owe so much are: Richard Cashman, who bore the heavy burden of the biographical entries; Ian Jobling, who collated the material on associations/organisations and also handled the illustrations; Katharine Moore, who supervised the selections on sports and sports venues despite the difficulties posed by her departure overseas in mid-1991; John O'Hara, whose arduous portfolio included competitions, trophies, medals, events, incidents, and miscellaneous material; and Wray Vamplew, who organised the vital thematic essays, supervised the production of the manuscript, and also served as first among equals rather than as editor-in-chief. In addition, each editor acted as a second reader for one of the other editors.

The editors consciously intended to avoid producing an Australian copycat version of Arlott's *Oxford Guide to Sport and Recreation*. One notable difference is the inclusion in this volume of a number of essays highlighting the economic, social, and political significance of sport in Australia; some of the themes examined are amateurism, betting, nationalism, and violence. Another difference was the decision generally not to deal with the rules of games and not to be simply an encyclopedia of sport. On the other hand, the book was not meant to be primarily an historical account, even though history is often necessary to give the background to Australia's sporting traditions. A final guiding principle was that women in sport should be given 'a fair go'.

Approximately 150 photographs, drawings, and cartoons span three eras of Australian sport and give special emphasis to issues like ethnicity, age, crowds, gender, trophies, and minor sports. Photographs often replicated elsewhere have been consciously omitted, of Bradman for example, while many of the illustrations herein have not been published before. The Australian Gallery of Sport in Melbourne was particularly helpful to the editor of this section of the *Companion*. The sources of the illustrations are listed on pp. 425–8.

There will probably be some controversy over the contents, or more likely the omissions, of this volume. To some extent these are a function of the overall space limitation and of the balance that the editors attempted to achieve between the various categories of entry. For example, the venues for sporting activities were necessarily restricted to a handful deemed to be of major significance, a decision which may annoy advocates of venues not so deemed. Similarly, the various competitions, medals, etc. are inevitably dominated by the major sports, but other, more catholic, entries provide some balance.

Virtually all sports that have been played in Australia are mentioned, from animal baiting to trugo to woodchopping, but chess and dancing were deliberately excluded as not being sport. Unfortunately, a few genuine sports like batinton, fives, hurling, and pétanque were omitted due to lack of sufficient information, and the editors could not secure knowledgeable writers to provide thematic essays on coaching, regionalism, and several other important aspects of sport.

Debate will also focus, undoubtedly, on the choice of Australia's first DLXXXV. A whole volume of cricket or football biographies could have been produced, of course, but the editors decided to spread biographical entries across many sports—albeit with due emphasis on the aforementioned most popular ones. Perhaps the most contentious omission will be the editors' decision not to deal with specific clubs because of the difficulty of 'drawing the line'; they instead concentrated on national sporting associations. All such organisations were contacted, though not all replied. At times therefore an association is dealt with by an entry on the sport itself, or in a biographical entry. Alternatively, some sports are only listed within their respective associations or in biographical entries, for example roller sports, indoor soccer, and darts.

The actual selection of material is somewhat idiosyncratic, influenced by what ASSH members offered to contribute and by the sporting predilections of the editorial board. The editors recognise the need for a companion to this *Companion*: it could be supplemented by one containing clubs and teams in various competitions, Olympic medallists, additional themes, and other space-restricted items, as well as by lists of champions, crowds, times/records, Test captains, premierships, Cup and Gift winners, etc. Suggestions along this line, or criticisms of this volume, should be addressed not to the editors but to the secretary of ASSH!

Editors alone cannot produce a book. Sincere thanks must go to the many members of ASSH who contributed material and to the officials of various sports associations who assisted by supplying information or entries. These contributions vary significantly in style and quality, but this was seen by the editors as a strength rather than a weakness. The names of the contributing authors are listed on pp. 423–4. It has not been possible for the editors to check every statistic and historical fact presented; the individual authors therefore remain responsible for any errors in the entries they submitted. On the other hand, the typists, Marie Baker and Barbara Triffett, can be thanked profusely and exonerated from any blame.

One member of the society, Greg Blood from the National Sports Information Centre, deserves special mention for his production of the extensive bibliography, which contains lists of books sport by sport. Although it excludes articles, the bibliography contains a guide to sporting periodicals and also indicates the major archival and library holdings in Australia for sports research. Thanks are also due to Gerald Crawford, who served for a short but intensive period as a Canberra-based research assistant in order to help fill in some of the gaps in the material, and to editorial assistant Janice Cameron, who prepared the final drafts of most submissions, assisted in the daunting task of cross-referencing, and also composed a few last-minute entries. Their employment was made possible by major sponsorship from the Australian Sports Commission and a grant from the Collingwood Football Club. The editors would also like to acknowledge assistance from their host universities of Flinders, Western Sydney, New South Wales, and Queensland (particularly the Department of Human Movement Studies).

Richard Stremski
President, ASSH

STYLE

HEADWORDS are given in bold. They distinguish 1. the names of sportspeople (in capitals); 2. the names of organisations, awards, events, venues, incidents, etc. (in capitals and lower case); 3. the names of racehorses and dogs (in italic capitals and lower case). The longer essays and all entries on the various sports are distinguished by a heading on its own line. The names of organisations, awards, etc. whose names begin a sentence at the start of an entry are not preceded by the article; neither are entries which start with a family or set of brothers or sisters. Nicknames are given after the full name, but not in bold or in capitals. Commonly used names that are merely abbreviations of a given name are not recorded as nicknames but are used at some point in the entry.

Each entry has below it the initials of its authors, whose names may be found in the alphabetical key after the bibliography. This volume does not use 'q.v.' within entries. Cross-references appear at the end of entries, in bold and with the same distinction between capitals and capitals/lower case. Only one given name appears in the cross-references except where a subsequent name, as in Adam Lindsay Gordon, is important to identify the person. The only cross-reference placed on its own as a separate entry is **Yabba**.

ABBREVIATIONS

THE FOLLOWING ABBREVIATIONS have been generally adopted, but are not used where the full name is of major significance to an entry.

ABC	Australian Broadcasting Commission (now Corporation)
ACB	Australian Cricket Board
ACT	Australian Capital Territory
AFL	Australian Football League (formerly VFL)
AIF	Australian Imperial Forces
AIS	Australian Institute of Sport
AJC	Australian Jockey Club
AM	Member of the Order of Australia
ASC	Australian Sports Commission
BEM	British Empire Medal
FA	Football Association
FIFA	Fédération Internationale de Football Associations
IOC	International Olympic Committee
MBE	Member (of the Order) of the British Empire
MCC	Melbourne Cricket Club
MCG	Melbourne Cricket Ground
NSW	New South Wales
NT	Northern Territory
NZ	New Zealand
OAM	Order of Australia Medal
OBE	Officer of the Order of the British Empire
PGA	Professional Golfers' Association
RSL	Returned Services League
SA	South Australia
SCG	Sydney Cricket Ground
SMH	*Sydney Morning Herald*
UK	United Kingdom
US	United States
USA	United States of America
VFA	Victorian Football Association
VFL	Victorian Football League
VRC	Victorian Racing Club
WA	Western Australia

A

Aboriginal and Islander Hall of Fame is a permanent photographic exhibition consisting of sixty-two black-and-white plates depicting more than one hundred Aboriginal sportsmen and women who have achieved national or international recognition. It was inaugurated in 1992. One hundred sets have been produced, of which sixty are housed by Aboriginal and Islander communities. The remainder have been deposited in major libraries, museums, and sporting galleries throughout Australia. The collection was a jointly funded project of the Aboriginal and Torres Strait Islander Commission and Macquarie University under the supervision of Professor Colin Tatz. Selection of the athletes for the gallery was by a panel of four Aboriginal and two non-Aboriginal sporting authorities. The Hall they chose includes representatives from twenty sports, emphasising the seldom acknowledged variety of Aboriginal and Islander contributions to Australian sport.

JO'H
See **Aborigines in Sport**.

Aboriginal Rugby League Test Players. When lay-preacher Lionel Morgan scored two tries as right-wing three-quarter in the second Test against France at the Brisbane Exhibition Ground in 1960, he was the first Aborigine to represent Australia in rugby league. An elusive speedster, Morgan retained his position for the third Test, in which he gave the final pass for Australia's only try. He toured England with Australia's 1960 World Cup team, scoring 3 tries in four games. Born at Tweed Heads, NSW, in 1938, Morgan played there before joining Brisbane club Wynnum-Manly in 1959. In fifteen appearances for Queensland from 1960 to 1963, Morgan collected 15 tries and 25 goals. He retired from club football in 1969. More than a dozen Aborigines and Pacific Islanders have followed Morgan into the Australian team, including captains Arthur Beetson and Mal Meninga.

TB
See **Aborigines in Sport**; **Aboriginal and Islander Hall of Fame**; BEETSON, ARTHUR; MENINGA, MAL; SIMMS, ERIC.

Aboriginal Sports Foundation, a body appointed to advise the Federal Minister for Aboriginal Affairs on the promotion and financing of Aboriginal sport, was created in 1969. Found-

ing directors were Pastor Sir Doug Nicholls (Australian rules and athletics), Lionel Rose (boxing), Darby McCarthy (horse-racing), Charles Perkins (soccer), Evonne Goolagong (tennis), Elley Bennett (boxing), Bill Dempsey (Australian rules), George Bracken (boxing), Syd Jackson (Australian rules), David Kantilla (Australian rules), Ian King (cricket), Wally McArthur (athletics and rugby league), Michael Ahmatt (basketball), Eric Simms (rugby league), and Reg Saunders (of military fame). From 1978 the foundation assumed full responsibility for the award and administration of grants to Aboriginal groups and individuals. Despite political and administrative bickering in the early 1980s, which resulted in its functions being absorbed by the Department of Aboriginal Affairs, the foundation achieved a significant rise in the profile of Aboriginal sport. It also assisted the development of the potential of individual Aboriginal sportspeople.

CT and PT
See **Aborigines in Sport**.

Aborigines in Sport

Aboriginal sporting achievement is exceptional. There has been much adversity, which has included the genocidal impulses of settler society, physical isolation, legal separation, social segregation, and every form of racial discrimination. Sport, wrote the late Ron Pickering, should be based on an ethos of play, competition, and opportunities being fair and equal for all. For Aborigines, there has been exclusion from competition, discrimination within it, and at times gross inequality of chances, choices, and facilities. Denial of competition takes two forms. One is structural: because of their place in the political, legal, economic, and social system, Aborigines very rarely have access to squash courts, ski lodges, and A grade golf courses. The other is institutional: on settlements and missions—where most Aborigines have lived, literally, no grass. Pools, gyms, courts, tracks, nets, coaches, physiotherapists, and scholarships are not part of Aboriginal vocabulary or experience, even today.

The phrase 'from plantation to playing field' encapsulates the history of black American sport. With the abolition of slavery and the passing of civil-rights laws came greater participation—and triumph. Aboriginal history has been the reverse. Sport, particularly cricket, flourished when there was relative freedom from legislative control—but so did genocide. Aborigines were to go from playing field to plantation or, rather, to institutions called settlements, missions, or pastoral properties. It was a long period of incarceration. As shown by the photographs in the Aboriginal and Islander Sports Hall of Fame, most achievement followed the abolition of special laws and the chance to escape isolation. During the 'freedom' period cricket was the only universal sport: football was barely organised and only corrupt boxing and professional athletics (pedestrianism) were 'avenues'. Remarkably, Aborigines played talented and enthusiastic cricket in an era which saw geographic isolation, rigid missionary control, settler animosity, poor diet, rampant illness and, of course, killing. In 1850 the Reverend Matthew Hale introduced cricket to Aborigines at Poonindie, near Port Lincoln in SA 'to train them in the habits of civilised life.' The team did well, winning all but one local match. This farming community even journeyed to Adelaide to play 'scholars of the Collegiate of St. Peter', a match, said the Anglican Bishop, which proved incontestably 'that the Anglican aristocracy of England and the "noble savage" who ran wild in the Australian woods are linked together in *one brotherhood of blood*'.

In the 1870s the Aborigines at Coranderrk in Victoria were successful farmers, musicians, politicians, Christians, and cricketers. The famous English naturalist H. N. Moseley went there in search of a platypus. The 'incorrigibly lazy' natives would not find him one. They were otherwise occupied: 'We found the cricket party in high spirits, shouting with laughter, rows of spectators being seated on logs and chaffing the players with all the old English sallies: "Well hit!", "Run it out!", "Butter fingers" etc ... The men were all dressed as Europeans; they knew all about Mr. W. G. Grace and the All-England Eleven ...' Cumeroogunga on the Murray River in NSW produced a wealth of professional runners, cricketers, and rules footballers. For the mission's founder, Daniel Matthews, cricket was 'an uncivilising activity'. His biographer wrote: Aborigines 'had discovered that their prowess in sport, particularly in cricket and running, gave them a passport to the white man's world, even to his respect and friendship'. Matthews tried to prevent this passage. Even a Spanish Benedictine monk saw cricket as a civilising force. In 1879, at New Norcia mission in WA, Abbot Don Salvado introduced the game to people he described as 'these poor creatures, so hideous to look at'. Coached only by a local grazier, walking 100 kilometres each way to

play in Perth and Fremantle, they were aptly nicknamed 'The Invincibles'.

Queensland settlers killed about ten thousand Aborigines between 1824 and 1908. Yet in the 1890s when Aborigines began playing cricket around Deebing Creek, near Ipswich, townspeople felt that 'every encouragement should be given to our ebony brethren', and came to watch the play. The Aborigines won major trophies and the Colonial Secretary—about to receive Archibald Meston's report on the need to stop the genocide—sent the Aborigines two bats 'in appreciation of their excellent behaviour and smart turn-out'. In the 1860s the sons of Victorian pastoralists taught their black labourers to play. A match was arranged between the Aborigines of the Lake Wallace district and the Melbourne Cricket Club. 'With the sympathies of the whole of the population of Melbourne behind them', and before 10 000 spectators at the Melbourne Cricket Ground on Boxing Day, 1866, 'these children of the forest' (as the *Age* called them) lost by 9 wickets. Amid talk of skulduggery and exploitation, and certainly with much illness among the players, hotelier Charles Lawrence agreed to coach an Aboriginal team to tour England. The team landed in May 1868, the first Australian cricketers to go abroad. They played forty-seven matches for nineteen draws, fourteen wins, and fourteen losses. Mulvaney and Harcourt's *Cricket Walkabout* celebrates this tour.

But here the 'fairy tales' ended. Legal and physical separation were under way. Poonindie closed in 1895. Coranderrk Aborigines fought bitterly and successfully to prevent their farmland being taken by jealous white neighbours, but the (new) 'forced assimilation' policy—ensuring that 'half-castes' left the reserves —meant the loss of their harvesters. Similarly Cumeroogunga's population dwindled from 394 to 134. Queensland and WA were busy implementing a different philosophy, that of protection/segregation. Chief Protector Roth began isolating Ipswich men, despatching them far and wide: they were 'malcontents' who had 'evidently been too much encouraged in competition with Europeans in the way of cricket matches ... and have been treated socially far above their natural station in life'. The same philosophy put an end to New Norcia's cricket in 1905. Victoria's Aborigines Welfare Board came to office in 1869: had it been a year earlier, the English tour would never have occurred.

The decades of 'freedom' saw great cricket from two 1868 heroes: Johnny Mullagh and Cuzens. One comment on their English performances was that they 'were in all-round capacity not only the backbone of the side, but some of the ribs as well'. Cuzens played for Victoria against Tasmania in 1866; Mullagh played for

Victoria against Lord Harris's English touring team in 1879. The Mullagh Oval at Harrow, now defunct, was society's tribute to this 'virtuous exemplary man'. The prince of the many black pedestrians was Charlie Samuels. The Queenslander ran 136 yards in 13.2 seconds and 300 yards in 30 seconds in 1886. In 1888 he clocked the generally unbelievable time of 9.1 seconds for 100 yards. Acclaimed as Champion of Australia, the *Referee* described him as 'one of the best exponents of sprint running the world has ever seen'. Other notables were Patrick Bowman, the Carrington Cup winner in 1887, Alf Morgan, Larry Marsh, Bobby McDonald, inventor of the crouch start in sprinting in 1887, and Bobby Kinnear, winner of the Stawell Gift in 1883.

The new century saw legal restrictions, very limited sports opportunities, and two controversial right-arm fast bowlers: Jack Marsh and Albert (Alec) Henry. Both played Sheffield Shield matches between 1901 and 1904. M. A. Noble, the NSW selector, deemed Marsh 'not to have class enough' to play for Australia. He meant colour, not calibre, since many rated Marsh the fastest and best bowler in the country. Both died sadly: Marsh was kicked to death in a street in Orange; Henry was removed to Barambah (now Cherbourg, Queensland) 'for loafing, malingering and defying authority' and then to Yarrabah, in the remote north, to die at 29. Jerry Jerome's Dalby (Queensland) employer gained him exemption from repressive Aboriginal laws. This 'weirdly constructed native' began boxing at 33 and won the Australian middleweight crown in 1913, the first of sixty-two professional titles to be won by Aborigines. He was considered a 'trouble-maker' by the administration—for 'inciting all other Aborigines to refuse to work unless paid cash for it'. He died, penniless, at Cherbourg in 1950. Only boxing and professional running were really accessible to Aborigines. Tom Dancy (Queensland) won the premier race, the Stawell Gift, in 1910, as did Lynch Cooper (Victoria) in 1928. Cooper also won the World Sprint Championship in 1929; his winnings put him beyond the reach of the paternalistic Welfare Board.

Cumeroogunga in NSW produced great athletes and political activists, including the Cooper, Onus, Briggs, and Nicholls clans. Doug Nicholls won the Warracknabeal and Nyah Gifts in 1929. In the former race he won £210 in 12 seconds over 120 yards; the entire mission income that year, from all sources, was £1164! Doug boxed in Jimmy Sharman's tents; he then tried out for Carlton, only to be told that because of his colour he smelled. He played fifty-four games for Fitzroy between 1932 and 1937, alongside such 'giants' as Haydn Bunton and 'Chicken' Smallhorn. The 1930s saw the beginnings of the great black boxers, the hungry fighters. Ron Richards (Queensland) was national champion in three divisions; he beat Gus Lesnevitch, long-reigning world light-heavyweight champion, and lost twice to the immortal Archie Moore. His life was tragic, plagued as it was by managerial exploitation, too many fights, police harassment, racism, and alcohol. At this time another important trend began: brothers Dick and Lyn Johnson were the first Aborigines to play rugby league for NSW (1939–45). In the 1930s controversial fast bowler Eddie Gilbert was revered by the Queensland crowds. When he bowled Bradman for a duck in a Shield game, 'the Don' wrote that this spell was the fastest bowling he had ever seen. Gilbert always needed permission to play and to travel interstate. He died in a mental institution.

Restriction and discrimination continued during and after the war. Ten years after Nicholls, Australian rules admitted two players: Eddy Jackson for Melbourne (1947–52) and the one man who matched Nicholls' talents, Norm McDonald. A professional boxer, runner-up in the 1948 Stawell Gift, McDonald played in five Grand Finals for Essendon! Dave Sands (born Ritchie) of NSW was the best of six boxing brothers. Holder of Australian titles in three different divisions and Empire middleweight champion, he is rated by some boxing historians with Les Darcy as one of Australia's two greatest fighters. Many considered him capable of beating the current champions Randolph Turpin and Sugar Ray Robinson. He died in a truck accident, aged 26. Boxing was still the quickest avenue to money, social mobility, and a modicum of social acceptance. At this time Elley Bennett (Queensland) won the Australian bantam and featherweight titles, and Jack Hassen (Queensland) the lightweight championship. George Bracken (Queensland) was a superb national lightweight boxing champion in this period and Gary Cowburn (NSW) held an amateur and two professional titles. Another South Australian, Wally McArthur, exported himself to English rugby league, where he played 165 first-division games, scoring 611 points. This was also the era of one of the greatest rules men of all time, Graham 'Polly' Farmer, who was to revolutionise modern football with his accurate handpassing. If Aboriginal men had little access to sport, women had even less and Faith Thomas (SA) became an important role model when in the 1950s she was selected to play cricket for Australia against England. She was the first Aboriginal sportswoman of note to emerge.

The 1960s was a better decade for Aborigines. A sense of guilt and atonement was abroad, with the media calling for radical changes in behaviour and attitude. Many restrictive laws were modified, though not abolished. More Aboriginal champions emerged over a greater variety of sports. In some respects it was to be the beginning of a (literal) golden era. Two gold medals were won by Aborigines at the Perth British Empire and Commonwealth Games in 1962: Percy Hobson (NSW) in the high jump and Jeff Dynevor (Queensland) in bantamweight boxing. Michael Ahmatt (NT-SA), John Kinsella (NSW), and Joe Donovan (NSW) wore the green and gold at the 1968 Mexico Olympics for basketball, wrestling, and boxing respectively. Two Queenslanders established notable 'firsts': Lionel Morgan played Test rugby league and Lloyd McDermott played Test rugby union. Another 'first' was Cheryl Mullett (Victoria), who twice represented Australia in international badminton. Aborigines began to blossom in WA rules competition, with men of the calibre of Ted ('Square') Kilmurray, Barry Cable, and Syd Jackson. Between 1954 and 1974 NT Aborigines were effectively 'wards of the state', yet Billy Dempsey was able to move to a fine rules career in the West and David Kantilla could leave Bathurst Island, home of the Tiwi people, to play rules for SA. Such mobility was exceptional, but so was their playing ability. 'Darby' McCarthy (Queensland) broke through a rigid colour bar in the racing industry, and became a popular and much-revered jockey, while 'Artie' Beetson (Queensland) and Eric Simms (NSW) became legends in league. Ian King (Queensland) followed the fast-bowling traditions of Alec Henry and Eddie Gilbert, and Brian Mansell rode his way into many records as Australia's first (and only) Aboriginal cyclist. Perhaps the high-water mark of the decade was Victoria's Lionel Rose winning the world bantamweight title from 'Fighting Harada' in Tokyo in 1968. As *Sports Illustrated* put it, for Aborigines from the Todd River in Alice Springs to Redfern in Sydney, he 'represented a hope that their own futures might rise beyond futility'. In late 1991 a television film, aptly titled *Rose Against the Odds*, was praised by the serious press: Rose was hailed as 'a national treasure'.

Repeal of special legislation began seriously from 1973 onwards. Controls did not disappear overnight, nor did sports facilities appear either. It is not surprising that Aborigines in remote Australia turned to such an accessible and inexpensive sport as darts. Ivy Hampton (NT) and Horrie Seden (Queensland-NT) represented Australia in Pacific and World Cup competitions. Tony Mundine (NSW) and Hector Thompson (NSW) had illustrious ring careers, culminating in fights for world titles. The football codes had become more tolerant and an astonishing number of Aborigines, quite disproportionate to their population numbers,

began to emerge in first-division rules in WA, and in league in NSW. Maurice Rioli (NT) became a rules hero in the NT, WA, and Victoria, and Larry Corowa (NSW) was awarded the MBE for his achievements in league. By 1991, fourteen Aborigines had played Test league for Australia and five Aborigines had amassed forty-six union tests between them. Torres Strait Islander Danny Morseau played twenty-seven basketball matches for Australia and Harry Williams (NSW) took the field on seventeen occasions for Australia's Socceroos.

Evonne Goolagong-Cawley (NSW) is undoubtedly the greatest Aboriginal sports achiever. In the 1970s a black girl from the outback entered the realms of tennis to win seventeen State titles, three Australian singles, an Italian, French, and South African open and, to crown her glory, the Wimbledon singles in 1971 and again in 1980. Her tennis, wrote critic Rex Bellamy, 'was so beautiful that at times it chilled the blood'. With Evonne came enlightenment. Mark Ella achieved the hitherto unthinkable: in a 'silvertail' sport like rugby union, he not only played twenty-six tests for Australia but captained the national side on nine occasions. There were more: Mal Meninga, a member of the South Sea Island community in Queensland, played thirty-one tests for Australia including twelve as captain, and Steve Tutton captained the national volleyball side from 1983 to 1985.

A broader, more tolerant 'participatory democracy' in sport began in the mid-1980s. Adam Schreiber (NSW) was a world-ranked junior squash-player who turned professional; May Chalker (WA) captained the WA women's golf team; Marcia Ella, Nicole Cusack, and Sharon Finnan played netball with great distinction for NSW and for Australia; Erin Vickery (Victoria-Queensland) and Debbie Norford (Queensland) played touch football for Australia; and Greg Lovell (Tasmania) won forty-five Australian and sixteen world wood-chopping titles. The 1990s began with even greater hope: an Aboriginal teenage girl, Cathy Freeman (Queensland), emerged as a sprinter and won a gold medal in the sprint relay at the 1990 Auckland Commonwealth Games, while an Aboriginal teenage boy from the West, Karl Feifer, went to The Netherlands in 1991 and won five medals at the World Championships for the Disabled. Both were acclaimed as national celebrities.

CT

See **Aboriginal and Islander Hall of Fame**; **Aboriginal Rugby League Test Players**; **Aboriginal Sports Foundation**; AHMATT, **MICHAEL**; **BEETSON, ARTHUR**; **Boxing**; **CAWLEY, EVONNE**; **Cricket**; ELLA **Brothers**; FARMER, GRAHAM; FEIFER, KARL; GILBERT, EDDIE; JEROME, JERRY; McCARTHY, RICH-

ARD; MENINGA, MAL; MULLAGH, JOHN-
NY; NICHOLLS, Sir DOUGLAS; PERKINS,
CHARLES; RICHARDS, RANDELL; ROSE,
LIONEL; SAMUELS, CHARLIE; SANDS, DAVE;
SIMMS, ERIC; WILLIAMS, HARRY.

ADAMS, PHILLIP, OAM (1945–), a
farmer from Forbes, NSW, has had outstanding
success in pistol shooting at the Commonwealth Games. In three appearances from 1982
to 1990 Adams collected fourteen medals, sur-
passing the record of Mike Wenden for the
most medals achieved in these Games. Adams,
who was Australian Free and Air Pistol Champion in 1988, appeared in the 1984 and 1988
Olympics and has achieved a tenth place in the
world championships. A laconic character with
a high media profile, he has done much to
publicise the fun and discipline involved in
target shooting.
RC

ADAMSON, LAWRENCE ARTHUR
(1860–1932), born Isle of Man, grew up in the
privileged world of the English upper class.
After attending Rugby he read classics at Oxford University. He came to Australia in 1887
for health reasons to take up a post at Wesley
College, Melbourne. He was persuaded to
become sportsmaster in an attempt to revive the
flagging interests of the boys for sport. An
astute blend of improved training methods and
the adoption of rituals and codes of privilege
proved successful and Wesley enjoyed continuous sporting success up to the First World War.
Appointed headmaster in 1902, Adamson was
passionate in his support of team games and
amateurism, promoted the cause of character
formation, and the production of Christian
'gentlemen'. He revived the military cadet
corps in the school and celebrated Empire Day
in considerable style.
RC†
See **Amateurism**.

Adelaide Cup Run at Flemington. From
June 1884 on-course betting, whether via book-
maker or totalisator, was made illegal in SA.
Off-course betting had already been banned.
The result of this was the virtual cessation of
racing in the colony and the winding up of the
SA Jockey Club. However, entries for the 1885
Adelaide Cup, the premier event in the SA
racing calendar, had been accepted and to save
face and financial embarrassment, the SAJC
arranged to have the race run at Flemington in
Victoria. For the record, the Cup was won by
Mr E. W. Ellis's 4-year-old, *Lord Wilton*, ridden
by T. Sanders.
WV

Adelaide Oval is a picturesque sporting arena
with St Peter's Cathedral rising behind an elegant Edwardian scoreboard and Moreton Bay

fig trees at its northern end, the Mount Lofty
Ranges to the east, and nearby city skyline to
the south. The ground consists of 6.07 hectares
and includes four grandstands and grass banks;
the playing surface is 165 × 117 metres, a rare
true oval. In the 1880s the playing field was
surrounded by an asphalt bicycle track and
the SA Bicycle Club held regular meetings
before audiences of several thousand. As a
cricket ground Adelaide Oval is internationally
famous. The playing area was ploughed, levelled, and planted in 1871 and the formal opening took place on 13 December 1873 with a
match between British and colonial-born players. In 1873–74 a SA team played an England
eleven containing W. G. Grace, and a year later
its first intercolonial match was played against
Victoria. Adelaide Oval was the sixth Test
match venue in 1884; forty-eight tests have
been played there to the end of 1990. Australia
has won twenty-one, lost thirteen, and drawn
fourteen of these games. Three women's Test
matches have also been played at the ground
and of these Australia has won one, lost one and
drawn one. The record attendance for a Test
match was 50 962 on 14 January 1933 when
hostile followers howled abuse at English captain Douglas Jardine and his fast bowler Harold
Larwood, after the Australian captain Bill
Woodfull was felled during a bodyline attack.
The highest individual score in a Test match
was Donald Bradman's 299 not out against
South Africa in 1931. Perhaps the most remarkable all-round achievement in first-class cricket
was also performed at the ground when George
Giffen scored 271 runs in a single innings and
took 16–166 in a match against Victoria in
1891–92. Both Bradman and Giffen have
grandstands named after them.

Although the oval was developed primarily
for cricket, Australian rules football has been
played there since 1878. South Adelaide Football Club has been a permanent tenant of the
ground but other clubs to have used it as a
home ground include Adelaide, West Adelaide,
Port Adelaide, and Sturt. The initial interstate
match was played against the VFA in 1880 and
international matches were first played against
an English team led by cricket entrepreneurs
James Lillywhite and Arthur Shrewsbury in
1888. Australian National Football Council
Carnivals, including teams from several States,
were held at the ground in 1911, 1930, 1953,
and 1969, and a National Football League Carnival was staged in 1980. The first SA Football
Association Grand Final was held in 1889. The
record attendance for football is 62 543 at the
Port Adelaide–Sturt Grand Final in 1965.
BW
See **Bodyline**.

Aerobatics
Following the Second World War, the only

aerobatics flown in Australia were by ex-air force personnel in Tiger Moths with occasional use of Wirraway and Harvard aircraft. By the late 1960s, a group of aerobatics enthusiasts organised an Australian National Aerobatic Championship held at La Trobe Valley. Following the success of this meeting, the Australian Aerobatic Club (AAC) was formed in Melbourne in 1970, with G. A. 'Peter' Lloyd as inaugural president. In 1972 a group of six members of the AAC decided to participate in that year's World Aerobatic Championships in France. There they were introduced to the versatile Pitts aircraft, which revolutionised the sport in Australia and directly contributed to its increased popularity. The administration of the sport improved at this time as well, with State and national championships being organised, programmes being developed for training judges, pilots, and coaches, and the AAC being incorporated in NSW. In the 1980 World Championships Australia won a bronze medal in the team championship, and in 1984 a bronze medal went to Frank Fry for his individual performance in the known programme at the World Championships in Hungary.

KM*

Aerobics

In Australia the term aerobics is used synonymously with exercise to music, aerobic dance, or dance exercise, and refers to the aerating of the blood through continuous rhythmic exercise. Its origin can be traced back to the late nineteenth century. Modern aerobics became popular in the USA in the 1970s with such innovators as Jackie Sorensen and Hollywood personalities such as Jane Fonda and Richard Simmons. At first Australian aerobics was heavily calisthenic and exercise-based, but by the late 1980s it had taken on more of the American emphasis on dance. As a result of these cross-cultural influences there has been a gradual sophistication of aerobics to include a variety of class styles and formats (e.g., low impact, cardio funk, circuits, new body, step workouts, single-peak, multi-peak, etc.). In a fairly short time aerobics has established a strong base in health and fitness clubs, community recreation programmes, employee health and fitness settings, and in schools. The first instructor training programmes began in the early 1980s with State Government agencies overseeing accreditation. In 1987 the Fitness Leader Network was established and has been instrumental in formalising the aerobics industry through a newsletter, workshops, annual conferences, and other services. Most States have equivalent regional organisations. Aerobics has quickly become entrenched not only as a very popular fitness activity but also as a new form of competitive sport. Competitive

aerobics began in the mid-1980s and a national championship is held annually. In June 1990 Australia was represented at the First World Aerobic Championship in San Diego, California.

RB*

See **Calisthenics and Physical Culture**.

AHMATT, MICHAEL (1942–83?), brewery technician, born Darwin, played his entire basketball career from Adelaide. He represented SA for ten years and also amassed an amazing 588 first-class games for South Adelaide. A great ball-handler and passer, he made his mark as the most outstanding player in Australia's 1964 Olympic team in Tokyo, which achieved a creditable ninth place. He represented Australia again at the 1968 Mexico Olympics. In 1969 Ahmatt became an enthusiastic member of the newly created Aboriginal Sports Foundation. Revered by his peers and the crowds, he retired in 1979; at the age of 40 he died of a heart attack. Ahmatt and Danny Morseau, a Torres Strait Islander, are the only two indigenous Australians to have played basketball for Australia.

CT and PT

See **Aboriginal Sports Foundation**; **Aborigines in Sport**.

AIF Rugby Union Football Team was selected from the AIF in 1919 to compete for the King's Cup as part of the post-war activities. It was one of the finest teams ever to represent Australia, with an outstanding record: during the Cup matches they lost just once, to England 3–0. They won several additional matches throughout England and Wales and on their way home defeated Natal 34–3. On arriving home a promotional tour of Queensland and NSW was arranged. The talented and battle-hardened team of 'diggers' easily won all the tour matches, including three against the Australian fifteen.

PH

Ajax (1934–?), a thoroughbred racehorse by *Heroic* out of *Medenham*, bred in NSW, was only once unplaced in forty-six starts. He had thirty-six wins but ironically is best remembered for one defeat: at odds of 40 to 1 on he was beaten by *Spear Chief* in the Rawson Stakes at Rosehill in 1939 after eighteen successive victories. Restricted chiefly to weight-for-age racing, he nevertheless won the Newmarket Handicap as a 3-year-old carrying 9 stone, and he won the second of his three VATC Futurity Stakes with 10 stone 6 pounds. In 1938 at Randwick he equalled the Australasian record for 1 mile. Trained by Frank Musgrove and usually ridden by Harold Badger, *Ajax* was retired to stud in 1941 before being exported in 1948 to the USA.

AL

1 Aborigines playing cricket, Point Macleay, SA, 1870s.

2 Johnny Mullagh was a leading player in the Aboriginal
cricket team that toured England in 1868.

3 Aboriginal professional athlete Charlie Samuels ran 136 yards in 13.2 seconds in 1886, the fastest time recorded in Australian professional athletics to that time.

4 Aboriginal badminton–player Cheryl Mullett, of Victoria, represented Australia in international competition.

AKHURST, DAPHNE (1903–33), born Ashfield, Sydney, was a champion schoolgirl tennis-player. She won the first of her five Australian women's singles titles in 1925 when only 21. Her strength, athleticism, and attacking technique did much to enhance women's tennis. She teamed with Jim Willard to win the Australasian mixed doubles titles in 1924 and 1925 and also won the Australian women's doubles titles, with Sylvia Harper. Akhurst formed part of the first women's team to tour England, and although hampered by a recurring knee injury, she reached the quarterfinals of Wimbledon. She won the 1926 Australian women's singles title. Akhurst was ranked third in the world by the end of 1928 when she reached the quarterfinals of the French singles title and the semifinals of the Wimbledon singles. In the same year she added the Australian singles, doubles (with Esna Boyd), and mixed doubles titles (with Jean Borotra) to her imposing record. After winning the 1930 Australian singles and doubles, she curtailed her competitive career after marriage to Roy Cozens in February 1930. She died when only 29.

VO'F
See **Lawn Tennis**.

ALCOCK, HENRY UPTON (1823–1912), born Dublin, a promoter and maker of billiard tables, played an important part in popularising billiards. He studied cabinet-making before moving on to the billiard-table trade. After emigrating to Melbourne in 1853 he set up a business using local timbers and slate from old houses. Within ten years his factory occupied almost an entire block and produced three tables a week. Alcock organised a series of tours by British professionals, including world champion John Roberts Senior, who was impressed with his tables. A few years later the young Duke of Edinburgh added his endorsement, which ensured financial success for Alcock & Co. Oddly enough Alcock never mastered billiards himself, although he built thousands of tables and even wrote books on how to play the game.

GC*
See **Billiards and Snooker**.

ALDERMAN, TERRY (1956–) steadily matured in the 1980s as one of the finest seam and swing bowlers cricket has known. With a relaxed run up and a very straight approach he became known for securing a high proportion of lbw (leg-before-wicket) decisions. His Test career had two major setbacks. When fielding in the Perth Test against England in 1982, he dislocated his shoulder trying to tackle an intruder; later he was banned from Test cricket for two years for joining the Australian 'Rebel' tours to South Africa in 1985–87. The only

bowler to take forty wickets in a Test series twice (42 at 21.26 in 1981 and 41 at 17.36 in 1989), Alderman was largely responsible for Australia regaining the Ashes in 1989.

KM-H
See **Cricket**.

ALDERSON, Sir HAROLD GEORGE (1890–1978) was a long-serving sports administrator. He had a lifelong association with the NSW Rowing Association from 1918 to 1978, serving as secretary, chairman, and president (1970–78). Alderson was best known as a prominent Olympic and Commonwealth Games administrator. He managed the Australian team to the 1936 Berlin Olympics. A dedicated believer in amateurism, Alderson was critical of the excessive nationalism and quasi-professionalism at those Games, arguing at the time that Australia should withdraw from the Olympics to concentrate on the less tainted British Empire Games. President of the Australian Olympic Federation from 1946 to 1973 he helped Melbourne secure and make a great success of the 1956 Olympics.

RC

All Australia Netball Association (AANA). Netball was known as women's basketball in its early years and it was not until 1970 that the title All Australia Netball Association was adopted. Associations had been established in most States by the mid-1920s. The initiative for the formation of a national organisation came from both Queensland and NSW following the introduction of an interstate competition for a trophy donated by Prouds of Sydney in 1926. The meeting which led to the formation of the All Australia Women's Basket Ball Association (AAWBBA) was held in Sydney in August 1927. Some of the decisions taken at that meeting were that contests would be held annually in each State in rotation and that it would be preferable to play interstate 'carnivals' on grass courts. Even at this stage there was an acceptance of a uniform set of rules of the game of basketball for use throughout Australia. The AAWBBA always had the desire to foster international links but differences in rules between countries hindered progress. England, the USA, NZ, and Australia all played their own code of rules and it was not until 1938 that the first international match was played between Australia and NZ. A reluctance to compromise on the various rules and the outbreak of the Second World War delayed further progress. AAWBBA/AANA has initiated and contributed to the policies and programmes of many government and corporate sports bodies. Alongside the development of sponsorship, competition, resource development, and coaching and umpiring accreditation there has been a corresponding development in research, particularly in the areas related to team preparation for match play. There has been a very close relationship between AANA and the AIS, with netball selected as one of the eight foundation sports in 1980. Recent restructuring of AANA, together with the fact that male players may now become affiliated members, augur well for the association's continuing development.

DH and IJ

See **Basketball**; BENZIE, GWEN; **Netball**.

All Golds. The remarkable athlete George W. Smith returned to NZ from the 1905–6 All Black British tour so impressed with the northern union (later renamed rugby league) that with young Wellington forward Arthur H. Baskerville he organised a team to play that code in England. Sarcastically labelled the 'All Golds', Baskerville's team was persuaded by entrepreneur James J. Giltinan and cricketer Victor Trumper to travel via Sydney and play three games against local disaffected rugby union players. The matches (under union rules as no one knew the northern rules), held at Sydney Showground in August 1907 and all won by the visitors, were a financial success sufficient to encourage the Australian dissidents to form the NSW Rugby League and start their own competition in 1908. The 'All Golds' had a successful tour, winning the Test series, but unfortunately Baskerville contracted pneumonia on the way home and died in Brisbane aged 25 years.

TB

See **Giltinan Shield**.

ALLAN, TREVOR, OAM (1926–), born Sydney, showed immense talent as a schoolboy rugby player. After competing for the Gordon Club he played the first of fourteen Tests for Australia against NZ at Dunedin in 1946. Selected vice-captain of the 1947–48 Wallabies, he took over as captain when Bill McLean broke his leg and led Australia to wins over England, Scotland, and Ireland. He captained Australia with further success against the Maoris and All Blacks in 1949 before switching to rugby league in 1950. After playing five seasons with the English club Leigh, he played two seasons for North Sydney. A tall, debonair centre, Allan was one of the great players of his era: a fine positional player, an incisive runner, and a deadly tackler. He was a respected rugby commentator for the ABC and was awarded the OAM in June 1991 for his services to rugby union.

MC

ALLEN, MONIQUE (1971–) became Australia's most successful gymnast. After winning a gold medal for vault at the 1980 NSW championships, she became junior national champion in 1984 and 1985 and senior national champion in

1988, 1989, and 1991. Allen has won fourteen apparatus medals including five gold at international competitions, and achieved the highest-ever Australian ranking (twenty-fifth) in the all-around in the 1989 world championships. She was the senior member of the first Australian women's team to win gold at the 1990 Pacific Alliance and was silver-medallist in the all-around at the 1990 Commonwealth Games. She has achieved distinction through the Advance Australia Award and her appointment to the Review Committee for Women's Sports. Coached by Ju Ping Tian, Allen has been resident at the AIS since 1984.

KO'B

ALSTON, ADRIAN (1948–), born Preston, England, began his soccer career as an apprentice professional with Preston North End at the age of 15. He joined South Coast United (Wollongong) in early 1968. Spells followed with St George, Safeway United (Wollongong), Luton Town, Cardiff City, Tampa Bay (USA), and Canberra City. A serious knee injury forced his retirement in 1978. Known as 'Noddy' for his aerial prowess, the 6-foot, rangy Alston was also known for his close ball control, shielding ability, and thoughtful positioning. Such qualities were best exhibited during the 1974 World Cup when top performances as an isolated striker led to a $65 000 transfer to English first-division club Luton Town. In all, Alston made sixty-two appearances for Australia between 1968 and 1977, scoring 17 goals.

PM

Aluminium Cricket Bats. During the Perth Test match against England in the 1979–80 season, Australian fast bowler Dennis Lillee legally, but controversially, used an aluminium bat (in which he held a commercial interest). He had previously used the bat without incident against the West Indies. England captain Mike Brearley successfully remonstrated to the umpires that Lillee's bat would damage the ball. When the umpires and his captain ordered Lillee to use a conventional wooden bat instead, he reacted petulantly by flinging his aluminium bat away and delaying the match. Since 1980, the laws of cricket have specifically required that the bat be made of wood.

DS

Amateur Pistol Shooting Union of Australia (APSUA) was established at the 1956 Olympic Games because it was found necessary to have a national body which would be recognised by the then Australian Olympic Federation and the International Shooting Union (UIT). In January 1956 the Tasmanian, Victorian, and SA pistol-shooting associations established APSUA's predecessor the Amateur Pistol Shooting Association of Australia, with the immediate objective of entering a team in those Olympic Games in Melbourne. NSW and the ACT were affiliated later in 1956, Queensland and WA joined in 1963, and the NT in 1967. The first Australian championships, with matches contested in the free pistol, rapid fire, and centre fire, were held in Hobart in January 1958 and have been held annually ever since. Standard pistol and ladies' match (later called sport pistol) were added in 1968, air pistol in 1970, and junior match in 1975. National championships have also been conducted by APSUA in black powder and service pistol since 1977, metallic silhouette since 1987, and action pistol since 1989. Australian pistol-shooters have competed in every Olympic Games since 1956 except for Moscow in 1980; the first Olympic medal was a bronze, won by Patti Dench in Los Angeles in 1984. APSUA has regularly sent teams to world championships since 1958 and the Commonwealth Games since Jamaica in 1966.

JP and IJ

See **ADAMS, PHILLIP**; **Australian Clay-target Shooting Association**.

Amateurism

The belief that money and sport are in various ways incompatible has had a long, tortuous, but gradually waning influence on the growth of sport throughout the world. Amateurism was the main item on the agenda when Pierre de Coubertin called his first international Congress of Sport at the Sorbonne in 1894, with the intention of proposing the re-establishment of the Olympic Games. Nearly eighty years later, Australian historian Bill Mandle could still claim that 'the problem of whether a man should make his living out of playing a game is still a live issue in the philosophy of sport'. Indeed, in the practical world of sport in 1992 there is still agonising about payments for players at the highest levels of rugby union. Further, it seems that Australia, of all the countries prominent in international sport, has been the slowest to accept openly the various sporting roles as paid occupations. While it is not surprising that Australia inherited the amateur ideology from Victorian England, it is perplexing that Australia has been so slow to follow even England down the path to professional sport, and has maintained a kind of schizophrenia about the excesses and attractions of the North American professional sports of football, basketball, and hockey. Even more, it is a curious paradox that, as John Daly, Australian Olympic coach and sports historian, has argued, although Australians have seemed to regard winning as their national sport, it is only fairly recently that they have been prepared to recognise the financial consequences of the commitment necessary to achieve sporting excellence. Stoddart, in his analysis of Austral-

ian sport, *Saturday Afternoon Fever*, says that 'the public has slowly moved from a stiff intolerance of pay for play (despite the evidence of long-term practice) to a reluctant acceptance of the professional'.

For a number of reasons it is difficult to describe clearly the nature of this change and to explain why Australia has taken so long to embrace fully professional sport. First, as Mandle has reminded us, we lack accurate historical analyses of the development of many Australian sports, particularly about the ideas and roles of the administrators. What is known suggests significant differences between sports because they are subject to different pressures and constraints. The financial considerations for spectator sports like Australian rules football, rugby union, rugby league, and cricket seem quite different from those for Olympic sports such as track and field and swimming, because the sources of funds are different. The differences in timing, the continued existence of professional and non-professional forms, the influence of television and of international competition increases the likelihood that generalisations will lack substance. Some sports like athletics, boxing, and sculling were professional from the beginning, with amateur forms emerging later. Other sports such as hockey remain amateur, while others like rugby have developed different forms. Some sports moved gradually to professionalism while others, particularly cricket, emerged abruptly amid controversy, while basketball and soccer started abruptly but in a planned way. Second, it seems that often the disputes are only superficially about money: they are really about what sport is, who controls it and for what purposes. They therefore draw on complex sets of moral, educational, psychological, and social values, many of which remain unstated because they are taken for granted by their proponents. Third, there seems, in many instances, to have been a difference between rhetoric and reality. The dispute was not so much between proponents of different practices but rather between practice and ideal. This adds to the complexity of any analysis because of the difficulty of knowing what counts as evidence. For these reasons one needs to be tentative in making generalisations about the amateur–professional debate in Australian sport. It would perhaps be more profitable to follow Mandle and take particular sports, isolating particular problems such as why Australia did not follow the English practice of distinguishing 'gentlemen' and 'players' in cricket.

It might reasonably be claimed that in the development of Australian sport there has been, before the late 1970s, a reluctance to treat sport openly as an acceptable form of work, because it is essentially a recreation—and Australians place a peculiar emphasis on recreation. There is a consequent reluctance to accept coaching and sports administration as paid occupations, and a reluctance by government and business openly and directly to support athletes representing Australia in international competition. In so far as each of these practices can be seen to have contributed to the success of many other countries in international competition, Australia's reluctance to embrace professionalism whole-heartedly is perplexing in view of the rather narrow-minded obsession with winning. Throughout the history of international sport, Australia's sporting successes have loomed large in the country's self-concept, yet it was not until the 1970s, when dissatisfaction with recent international performance had developed, that the move towards a generally more professional approach was urged because early successes had been, it seemed, 'in spite of the system'. Australia's approach was seen to be amateur in two senses. One of these is at the bottom of the various forms of the amateur–professional debate. It is the sense of 'amateur' which Australia inherited as part of its conceptual luggage from Victorian England. In the words of John R. Tunis, a sports watcher popular in America in the 1930s, the amateur spirit is, in essence, 'the feeling that you're doing something just because you want to do it'. The amateur performs for the love of the activity (the word means 'one who loves') and is thereby receptive to its influence and wants to do it well. This is of course to be distinguished from the derived sense of 'incompetent' or 'unskilled', which has no place in the debate. The notion of the amateur as someone who performs the activity for its own sake is the anchor of the amateur ideology which de Coubertin made a central part of the Olympic philosophy of sport. In this philosophy sport for its own sake is the source of the educational and moral values which give sport its lofty purpose. Although this seems like an instrumental view of sport, it is important to realise that the alleged benefits come only when sport is not pursued as the instrument of those or any other benefits: the benefits to character and body come when excellence in sport is pursued as an end in itself. The only demands to be met are those which arise from the internal logic of sport as sport. Accordingly, an understanding of amateurism in this sense requires an understanding of the nature of sport itself, and disputes about amateurism usually have at their core different views of what sport actually is. In turn, disagreement about what sport actually is often leads to disputes about what is valuable and important in sport. This fusion of fact and value arises because sport is what we make it, and opponents approach the debate with the assumption that 'sport' refers to something good (in their terms) and that the term should be reserved for that use. Disputes about amateurism therefore come to reflect differences in social and moral values held by different cultural and socio-economic groups, because sport fits differently into their view of the world. For example, a proponent of the amateur ideology who valued sport for its moral and physical benefits in the education of the young is not likely to agree about payment of athletes with someone who sees sport primarily as a source of fun and entertainment. Michael McKernan in his contribution to *Sport in History* has provided an illuminating illustration of the debate in his analysis of the relationship between sport and recruiting in Australia for the First World War.

In contrast to the amateur is the professional who, from the amateur viewpoint, pursues sport as a paid occupation and is thereby subject to considerations other than those internal to the sport. As a result, the professional athlete is less open to the influence of the sport itself and may also be forced to confront conflicts which arise as a result of pursuing two different goals: excellence in sport and earning a living. Conflicts are all the more likely to arise as earning a living for the most part depends on the sport being an entertainment, and this may produce demands which are in conflict with the demands of excellence in the sport. The financial consequences of losing may lessen the willingness to dare, or worse, increase the pressure to cheat or to disregard the ideals of sportsmanship. So it is asserted that the use of sport for extrinsic purposes lessens its educational value, compromises the pursuit of excellence, and jeopardises moral values. The central form of the debated connection between sport and money is of course the pursuit of sport as paid employment. The definition of the amateur adopted by the Victoria Amateur Athletic Association during the 1890s shows, however, that more than 'pay for play' is involved:

> one who has never competed for a money prize, staked bet, or declared wager, or who has not knowingly and without protest competed with or against a professional for a prize of any description or for public exhibition, or who has never taught, pursued or assisted in the practice of any athletic exercise as a means of livelihood or for pecuniary gain.

For those who espouse the ideology of amateurism in such terms, any kind of associations of money with sport, direct or indirect, is regarded as undesirable. Typical reasons for rejecting the professional were well stated by one Australian champion of amateurism in 1896 just before a group of Australian rules football clubs broke away from the Victorian Football Association to form the Victorian Football League and follow the professional route of using gate money to pay players. Ian Turner and Leonie Sandercock in their history of the VFL, *Up*

Where Cazaly?, quote from a speech of T. S. Marshall attempting to explain the decline in the number of players and spectators at matches in 1895 and 1896. He saw the main cause as 'thriftless spongers' who were playing the game for money.

> The game is ostensibly played for exercise and healthful recreation. But in reality there is, to the knowledge of delegates, a percentage in nearly all teams—and the percentage is yearly increasing—of men whose absence from the field would be a benefit, and whose presence is due solely to the fact that their connection with the game affords them facilities for leading idle and worthless lives. These men are in every way a menace to the sport, and it is on account of their degrading influence that parents who have the moral well-being of their sons at heart find themselves compelled to prohibit them from playing. Exception ought certainly to be taken to players who live on the game, and whose language and demeanour, both on and off the field, are discreditable to themselves and to the clubs in whose ranks they appear. Something must be done towards weeding such men out.

The passage is instructive because it illustrates the assumptions which typically led to the denigration of professionalism. Because games are essentially recreation, people who do nothing else (i.e. do not have a 'proper' job) lead 'idle and worthless lives'. Such people, not surprisingly, also display discreditable language and demeanour which keep away fine young men who would otherwise benefit from the game. It is the 'moral well-being' of the players which is placed in jeopardy by association with those who are prepared to do nothing else but live off the game. Marshall was referring also to a practice which was covert and in breach of the VFA's rules. He described the undesirable players in this rather oblique way because there were strong suspicions that clubs were breaking transfer rules and attracting players through under-the-table payments and other financial help. Thus, even in the early stages of organised sport, clubs were responding to the competitive pressure which naturally encourages professionalism. The desire to flourish in the sport and win was undermining the lofty principles of amateurism from the beginning. In this case, in the words of Sandercock and Turner,

> the Victorian Football League was born—and with it came formal recognition that football was no longer a game for the pleasure of a handful of gentleman amateurs but had become an entertainment for many thousands of predominantly working class supporters, provided by men who were rewarded in one form or another for their services.

Mandle notes, however, that payment to players was not authorised until 1911, and then only as compensation for 'broken time'.

The inexorable pressure towards professionalism in a competitive system, resisted by the conservative attempts to maintain the amateur philosophy, led over the years to an increasing sophistication in ways of financially supporting athletes without paying them openly. Pressures were greatest in those sports with spectator appeal and significant gate money, because players increasingly felt entitled to a share as their sporting commitments increased. Television increased the pressures by increasing the money and the pressures to win, because of the links between sponsorship and success. The conflicts between the traditional and the commercial, the amateur and the professional views of sport usually simmered quietly, with a period of 'shamateurism'—the popular name for the status of the amateur athlete who was financially supported in some covert way. Many writers have rightly decried the hypocrisy of sport at such stages, as it professed the amateur rhetoric but operated covert professional practices. Two institutionalised ways of meeting the conflicting requirements overseas, the sports scholarship, widespread in the USA, and the 'state amateur' in the Communist countries, were sneered at from the tenuous purity of Australia's amateur approach. At the same time, some Australian athletes had taken jobs which allowed time for training. In the late 1970s cricket burst into professionalism with a flourish in the Packer affair, and the public debate ranged widely over questions of who should control what and who was entitled to what. About the same time the Federal Government initiated a stronger commitment to international athletes in the face of recent lack of success at the Olympic Games. This was accompanied too by moves to establish the AIS, to train coaches, and to move the administration of sport away from the 'kitchen table'. Internationally also, the Olympic movement began to loosen the financial constraints on the Olympic athlete, as it recognised the realities of modern competitive demands and the requirements of the international media. Because Australia had been as scrupulous as any country in adhering to the letter and spirit of the Olympic rules, albeit grudgingly in the face of overseas practices and overseas success, the new concessions contributed to a more comfortable acceptance of the relentless pressure towards professionalism.

In the absence of the necessary historical studies we can only speculate about the reasons why Australia in general has been slow to accept the ideas of athlete, coach, and sports administrator as paid occupations in some sense. A number of factors seem sufficiently plausible to be worthy of investigation. For example it would be helpful to know more about the ideas of the sports administrators throughout the development of the various sports. Except in some sports which have been self-consciously working-class, it seems likely that many administrators would have had class connections with England which would have meant they were involved with the amateur ideology. Many teachers and principals of schools could be expected to be similarly inclined.

A second promising area to explore is the concept of the Australian hero. If it were true that the Australian notion of the hero is one of 'the battler' struggling against the odds, the opposite to the 'tall poppy', then this would not fit with the idea of sportsman as paid entertainer—as 'show-pony', despised by the battler. Stoddart sees Sieben's 200 metres butterfly victory at the Los Angeles Olympic Games as 'being in the classic Australian mould—the unknown battler defeating the recognized champion'. Similarly the teams-pursuit cyclists were 'battlers' overcoming the technological disadvantage of inferior bikes. Mandle offers evidence from the 1890s which indicates the aversion of the Australian cricketers to being classed as professionals because of the Australian attitude to entertainers. Studies of Australian sporting heroes as battlers or entertainers may help us understand not only Australia's sporting development but also the Australian identity.

Although the battle has been protracted, it would seem that in the last decade of the twentieth century it is over. Even though not all sports have been able to make the transition, the precedents have been set. In 1990, an Australian academic in visual arts and media studies, Bruce Wilson, was able to state that 'the changing nature of sport is presented by the media as a form of natural evolution. So natural have these transformations appeared that they have been largely accepted by the fans'. Further, writing of the development of the two major codes of football in Australia he concludes that 'so thorough is the appropriation of football by the ideology of business that football administrators have come to accept that what is desired by commercial forces is also in the best interests of the game'. There are now teams in private ownership, trading of players, players' associations, sports marketing, and all the trappings of commercialism. Sources of funding have multiplied from the gate takings and members' subscriptions and voluntary fund-raising to include sponsorship (which is now a business relationship much removed from patronage), product endorsements, advertising, State and Federal Government assistance, TV broadcasting rights, gambling and alcohol sales, corporate boxes, and product marketing. Not all sports have access to all sources. At the same time, in the other world of financial support for sport, we find the House of Representatives Standing Committee on Finance and Public Administra-

tion concluding in their report '*Going for Gold*' that the Commonwealth has an essential responsibility for the funding of the pursuit of excellence by Australia's élite athletes, but that funding should 'concentrate on those sports where Australia has established it can be internationally competitive'. However, the number and type of sports to be supported at the élite level should be the subject of regular review and the review should take account of established international performance indicators. It is but a short step to calculating the cost of a gold medal and then choosing the cheapest. Professionalism has come and the future lies with those sports which can either attract spectators, particularly on television, or win gold medals which do not cost too much. For the rest, the future promises much to watch, and our own games to play, for fun, as always.

RJP

See **Athletics**; BEAUREPAIRE, FRANK; **Golf**; HARDWICK, HAROLD; **Jack Affair**; **Rowing: Intercolonial Regattas**.

America's Cup yacht race derives from a race around the Isle of Wight, to and from Cowes, in 1851. The race was held as part of the festivities associated with the Great International Exhibition to celebrate the British Empire and its industrial power. In such context it was ironic that the US boat *America* defeated fourteen British boats. The Hundred Guinea Cup awarded to the victor was given, by the *America*'s syndicate, to the New York Yacht Club, with a deed which invited match-race challenges from other yacht clubs. As the cup had no name it became known as (the) *America*'s Cup. Organised competitive sport was still in its earliest state: the New York Yacht Club (NYYC) was the first such club in the USA and had been in existence for only seven years. For the next 132 years the NYYC defeated all challengers, until 1983 when it was beaten by Alan Bond's Australian business syndicate representing the Royal Perth Yacht Club in their fourth challenge. Sir Frank Packer had mounted the first of his three unsuccessful Australian challenges in 1962. His involvement, like Alan Bond's win or Sir Thomas Lipton's five unsuccessful English challenges, and Harold Vanderbilt's three successful defences for the USA, marks the Cup as a key site for competition over national and personal prestige.

PJ

See *Australia II*; BEASHEL **Family**; BERTRAND, JOHN; HARDY, **Sir** JAMES; LEXCEN, BEN; **Sailing and Yachting**.

ANDERSON, JAMES OUTRAM (1894–1973), born Enfield, Sydney, won the NSW men's open singles title in 1914 after winning the Victorian schoolboys' singles tennis championship. In 1919, when again NSW champion, he played the first of fifteen Davis Cup ties, between 1919 and 1925, teaming with Gerald Patterson to win the title for Australasia against the British. His major tennis triumph came in 1922–23 when he defeated in five sets the American Wimbledon champion, William 'Little Bill' Johnston, who had never lost a Davis Cup tie. Ranked third in the world, Anderson won the Australian singles titles in 1922, 1924, and 1925 and the doubles, with Norman Brookes, in 1924. He was twice a Wimbledon semifinalist and won the men's doubles, with Randolf Lycett, in 1922. Anderson, who was known as 'the Greyhound', had a hard, flat and shoulder-high forehand, though his backhand was less reliable. He was described as 'tall, ungainly, and taciturn', yet generous in acknowledgment of his opponent's good shots. Anderson declined to represent Australia in 1924 when the Lawn Tennis Association of Australia refused to provide adequate reimbursement. He turned professional in 1926 and became a tennis coach. He died in Gosford.

VO'F

See **Lawn Tennis**.

ANDERSON, PHILIP GRANT, OAM (1958–), is undoubtedly the best-known Australian professional road cyclist currently on the world circuit. Rising to number one in the world rankings in 1985, Anderson has finished in the top ten of the Tour de France on five occasions. He came to international prominence riding his first Tour in 1981, when he briefly snatched the tour leader's yellow jersey from five-time winner of the event Bernard Hinault. Born in London, Phil Anderson grew up in Melbourne where he began competitive cycling as an amateur with the Hawthorn club. In 1978, he won a gold medal at the British Commonwealth Games in Edmonton, Canada. Turning professional shortly afterwards, Anderson moved base to Europe, where he has lived since. His major professional wins have included the Tour de Suisse, and the Tour de Romandy. Despite fame in Europe (where he was nicknamed 'Le Skippy' early in his professional career), Anderson's achievements have largely failed to capture the public imagination in Australia—to which he returns regularly. His sporting achievements were, however, recognised by the Australian government with the award of the OAM in 1987. Anderson has remained a consistent performer on the international circuit for more than a decade, concentrating his efforts on one-day events and stage wins. In 1990 his professional earnings, including endorsements, were estimated at $525 000.

JS

Animal-baiting

Early British immigrants, both convict and free, brought with them to Australia traditionally popular blood sports. These included cock-fighting, bull-baiting and running, throwing at cocks, and dog-fighting. In bull-baiting, the participants tethered the animal to a stake and tortured it; they similarly staked a rooster to the ground and stoned it to death. In bull-running, a crowd of youths chased bulls through a town. Cock-fighting and dog-fighting were, of course, competitions, usually to the death, between especially trained and bred animals. All these sports occurred in NSW by 1810. Although some British immigrants brought a popular workers' tradition of blood sports with them from the old country, others were reformers who imported ideas about legally ending these sports. These reformers were usually part of the newly emerging middle class, many of whom came from an evangelical background which encouraged them to advocate what they termed 'humanitarian' reform. In essence, they wanted to create new types of behaviour for the working class so that they would be more dependable workers and more moral citizens. Middle-class employers, often evangelicals themselves, felt that these workers not only must be well-disciplined employees during working hours, but that their private lives must conform to the middle-class ideals of self-restraint and moral behavior. This meant the elimination of traditional recreations, such as animal baiting. Blood sports often took place at or near a public house. Suppression of the sports and their most popular venue often went hand in hand as many of these reformers also advocated temperance. This reform movement succeeded in England by 1835 with the passage of the Cruelty to Animals Act which outlawed blood sports. This Act effectively suppressed most public animal-baiting by 1840. In Australia, some forms of blood sports such as bull-running had disappeared in the early 1830s, but many such sports continued to exist. James Mudie gave evidence to the House of Commons Select Committee on Transportation in 1837 about the continued existence of blood sports in Australia. In NSW, as late as 1845, cock-fighting attracted crowds of 400 and purses of £100. The Sydney edition of *Bell's Life* continued to advertise challenges between owners of fighting dogs and to report the results of these matches in the 1840s. Australian lawmakers enacted legislation outlawing such sports in the 1840s, but cock-fighting at least was quite common into the 1870s when it declined in popularity at the same time as the new spectator team sports, such as Australian rules football, appeared. Nevertheless, some brutal animal sports have continued covertly, and a recent Senate Select Committee on Animal Welfare has inquired into greyhound-racing and the practice of greyhound 'blooding', in which cats, rabbits, and possums are still used as animal baits.

TD

See **Coursing; Public-house Sports**.

Ansett 'Horse of the Year' Awards are voted on by the members of the Australian Racing Writers' Association at the end of each racing year and are sponsored by Ansett Airlines. This prestigious award for racing excellence was inaugurated in 1976–77 when it was won by the 3-year-old filly *Surround*. Competition has been formidable over the years, with horses of the quality of *Sovereign Red*, *Dulcify*, *Strawberry Road*, *Vo Rogue*, and *Our Poetic Prince* missing out.

WAE

Anti-Football League, founded in 1967, was the brainchild of Melbourne journalist and writer Keith Dunstan. After he placed a small article in two Melbourne newspapers, several thousand people pledged support and requested cloth badges of the league's symbol, a square football. Club membership entitles holders to car stickers, cloth badges, and regular information on the club's subversive activities. All money raised by the league (up to $50000 annually) goes to the Multiple Sclerosis Society. Activities have included public burning and burying of a football, skywriting over football matches, and the annual non-event day in September. On the day before the Grand Final in September invitations are sent out to over a hundred thousand people not to attend a non-football match at the ground. Tickets entitle the holder to stay away from the non-match and all other matches throughout the season. The police are asked not to control the non-crowds, and football writers are invited not to turn up. At the close of the season the annual Wilkie Medal is awarded to the citizen who has done most against the game during the year.

GC*

ANTONIE, PETER THOMAS (1958–), born Melbourne, is one of Australia's most durable and versatile rowers, with a career extending across three decades. He was three times a member of a winning Penrith Cup crew for lightweight fours (1977–78 and 1984), he stroked a winning King's Cup crew (1988), and he also won the Australian sculling championship (1991). He is the only rower to achieve victories in these three national events. Between 1977 and 1990 Antonie rowed at thirteen world championships, winning the lightweight single sculls (1986), gaining silver medals in the lightweight fours (1977) and lightweight eights (1983), and a bronze medal in the lightweight fours (1978). He was Commonwealth Games Lightweight Single Sculls Champion in 1986.

SB

See **Rowing and Sculling**.

Applied Sports Research Programme (ASRP). The National Sports Research Centre (NSRC) was established in 1983 to cater for the scientific needs of sport through the provision of information services and research funding. The centre's Applied Sports Research Programme is the avenue through which sports can endeavour to find solutions to practical problems. ASRP bridges the gap between sport and sport science, encouraging researchers, coaches, and administrators to work together more closely. Projects funded through ASRP cover a wide range of sports sciences including physiology, biomechanics, history, sociology, psychology, medical equipment, and motor learning. Selection of projects for funding depends on their potential to provide practical results for use by coaches and administrators. ASRP has grown in importance and has attracted increased funding and a greater awareness of its potential; evidence of this is provided in a comparison of funds made available by the Australian Sports Commission which shows an increase from $75000 in 1983 to $325000 in 1991. The availability of funds for research has led to a growth in the number of sports governing bodies which have established research committees. All sports also have the opportunity to publicise their areas of research needs in the annual publication, *Sports Research Needs*, which is produced by the NSRC. This booklet is sent to all educational institutions and other sports research institutions to encourage potential researchers to work in practical and applicable areas. Completed research is published in various forms: a technical report pertinent to sports scientists is produced by the researcher as well as a report which provides readily accessible information for the coach and/or administrator; in addition, resources such as videotapes and coach education materials are produced where appropriate.

JD, KT, and IJ

See **Sports Science**.

Archer (1856–72), a thoroughbred racehorse (by *William Tell* out of *Maid of Oaks*), winner of the first two Melbourne Cups, was foaled at T. J. Roberts' Exeter Farm near Nowra in NSW. The bay horse was trained and raced by Étienne de Mestre. After winning races at Randwick in 1861, *Archer* was taken by ship to Melbourne and won the Cup by six lengths in a field of seventeen. In his second Cup win he carried 10 stone 2 pounds; only *Carbine* has won with more. His entry for the 1863 Cup was disallowed for late arrival. He was twice placed in Australasian Champion Sweepstakes, and won other events at Randwick. After injury he was retired to stud at Braidwood in 1865.

AL

See **DE MESTRE, ÉTIENNE**; **Horse-racing**; **Melbourne Cup**.

Archery

Bows and arrows were used by primitive hunters at least 10000 years ago but, possibly because of the efficiency of the boomerang, were unknown in Australia before white settlement. In Victoria in the 1840s a London-born publican, Wilbraham F. E. Liarchet, organised several sporting attractions, including archery, for participation by patrons of his Brighton Pier Hotel, while the first public exhibition of archery was reported at Emerald Hill in South Melbourne in 1855. The following year the Governor of Victoria demonstrated the sport's popularity with the gentry by acting as tournament director of the State's first major archery competition. Several archery clubs were formed in SA and Victoria in the 1850s but virtually disappeared between the 1880s and the mid-1920s when the sport enjoyed renewed popularity and clubs were formed around the country. Both men and women compete in modern archery, which has several disciplines including target, field, clout, and flight. 'Target' involves shooting at a fixed, upright target from various specified distances; in 'field' competition the targets are superimposed on animal figures; 'clout' requires the archer to shoot arrows high in the air to fall on a target marked out on the ground; the object of 'flight' is to fire arrows over very long distances. Plans to establish an Archery Association of Australia (AAA) came to fruition in 1948. This body then affiliated with the Fédération Internationale de Tir de l'Arc (FITA) which allowed the AAA to send teams to world championships. The first team went to Sweden in 1965 where the Australian champion Hans Wright finished seventh. Until recently Australia's success in international competition had been modest, but in August 1991 Simon Fairweather won a gold medal in the world target competition. In national competition Del Roache has excelled, winning the national title ten times between 1959 and 1970 and on one occasion winning all five ladies titles at a NSW championship.

JC* and AB†

See **FAIRWEATHER, SIMON**.

ARMSTRONG, DUNCAN (1968–   ), born Brisbane, was sent to the 1988 Seoul Olympics primarily as a 400 metres swimmer. He finished second at that event to East Germany's Uwe Dassler. It was in the 200 metres event, however, that he raced to swimming immortality when he beat Anders Holmertz of Sweden and Matt Biondi of the USA in a new world-record time of 1 minute 47.25 seconds. A gold-medallist at the age of 20, Armstrong was another product of the mercurial coach Laurie Lawrence.

RH and MH

See **Swimming**.

ARMSTRONG, WARWICK WINDRIDGE (1879–1947), born Kyneton near Melbourne, was a cricketer whose aggressive approach, single-minded disposition, and towering stat-

ure were likened by contemporaries to the British cricket hero W. G. Grace. Armstrong was famous for his uncompromising and persuasive manner on and off the playing field and his career was notable for controversial and abrasive relations with players and officials. Neville Cardus described him as 'Australian cricket incarnate'. Armstrong played fifty tests between 1902 and 1921 including ten as captain for an unbeaten record of eight successive wins and two draws. The gregarious Armstrong became a successful whisky merchant after his retirement from cricket and died a wealthy man in Sydney.

DM

See **Cricket**.

Arnold Medal. From 1904 to 1978 the respective winners of the Tasmanian Football League and the North Tasmanian Football Association played off for the title of Tasmanian State Premiers. From 1953 until the competition's dissolution in 1979 the best and fairest player in the intrastate game was awarded the Weller Arnold Medal.

MH*

ARNOLD, RICHARD ALDOUS (1849–1923) and **WILLIAM MUNNINGS MONTAGU** (1851–1919), rugby administrators, were born at Stradbroke, Paterson River, in NSW, and attended St Mark's Collegiate School. Richard was also a pupil at Rugby in England in the early 1860s. Their father, William Munnings Arnold, was a member of the NSW Parliament from 1856 to 1875. Both sons became public servants assisting the NSW Parliament, though Monty later became a stockbroker. The brothers, who believed in the precepts of 'Muscular Christianity', became involved with the influential Wallaroo Football Club from its inception in 1870 and between them served in most of the major positions of the Southern Rugby Football Union (founded in 1874) and the NSW Rugby Football Union (renamed in 1892) in the period up to the First World War. They had an important role over four decades in the development of rugby football in Sydney and led the resistance to the introduction of Australian football in the city. They were opposed to the introduction of a district competition in Sydney, but when it began they joined the North Sydney Club. Along with J. J. Calvert the brothers were influential in the 1907–8 split in the rugby code. Monty Arnold ensured that the role of the Wallaroos, his brother and himself, would be recognised by publishing a short article on the history of the game from 1829 to the 1880s in *Old Times*. His version of events was accepted until recently, when some of its historical accuracy was questioned.

TH

See **Muscular Christianity**; **Rugby League**.

AROK, FRANK (1932–), born Kanizsa, Yugoslavia, was Australia's longest-serving soccer coach who led the Socceroos from 1984 to 1990. After his playing career was cut short by injury at the age of 24, he became, with the Novi Sad club, the country's youngest-ever first-division coach and was on the coaching panel that prepared Yugoslavia for the 1962 World Cup. He initially came to Australia to coach St George Budapest in 1969, the first of three separate and successful spells with that club which in turn propelled him to unique status in Australian soccer. His modern coaching methods, fiercely competitive nature, and flamboyant personality made him a dominant figure in the Australian game, leading to his appointment as national coach. He coached Australia in ninety games including forty-eight full internationals. High points of his reign were the 4–1 defeat of world champion Argentina in 1988 and a place in the last eight in the 1988 Olympic finals, arguably the biggest success achieved by Australia at senior level. Above all he will be credited with being responsible for Australian soccer developing its own playing style in the mid- to late 1980s.

LM

Art

Many aspects of Australian life, including pastimes, games, and sports, have been recorded in paintings since the beginning of European settlement. In the early years painting depicted the leisure activities of Australians which were largely spontaneous, sporadic, and required a low level of organisation, such as walking, dancing, picnics, boating, and bathing. The Australian fascination with aquatic activities began not long after settlement; picnics at the beach, digging in the sand, and paddling in the water were all popular, and numerous artists painted such scenes: Frederick Terry, *Watson's Bay* (c. 1852–59); Henry Burn, *Brighton Beach* (1862); Nicholas Shiels, *Clovelly Beach* (1885); and Tom Roberts, *Holiday Sketch at Coogee* (1888). Throughout the twentieth century Australians became more active on the beach and developed equipment and vessels which enabled them to participate in a wide range of aquatic activities. Paintings of the beach and a broader range of aquatic activities of the twentieth century include Charles Meere, *Australian Beach Pattern* (1940); Miriam Moxham, *The Bathing Pool* (n.d.); Jeffrey Smart, *Surfers Bondi* (1963); Alan Lee, *Pinke Zinke* (1978); an anonymous painting entitled, *Sculling race on river, Dent Royal Hotel*; Walter Withers (n.d.), *Yachts off Williamstown*; and Edith Holmes, *Summer Holidays* (1950).

Several painters depicted the development of sport as it became a more institutionalised and organised activity throughout the latter half of the nineteenth century. Hunting was an early activity of the colonists which was used to supplement the meagre food supplies and give variety to a monotonous diet. Many of the native animals were swift, so rural settlers owned kangaroo dogs for running down kangaroos, as depicted in Edward Roper's *Kangaroo Hunt in the Australian Bush* (n.d.), and emu, as in B. S. Moro's *Emu Hunting* (c. 1850). Hunting developed into a popular sport, no longer just for food, and a variation of the traditional British hunt developed. Dingoes were substituted for foxes but in time foxes, fox hounds, and deer were imported. Several paintings depict the development of these refinements in hunting on horseback, including the *Meet of the Melbourne Hounds at St. Kilda* by an anonymous artist (c. 1873), and Arthur Esam's watercolour, *Merri Creek Hunt and Locals* (n.d.). Hunting was one of only a few active sports which included women as participants; Frederick Woodhouse's *Hunting in Victoria* (1907) is one which provides pictorial evidence of equestriennes riding side-saddle and astride. Septimus Power, regarded as one of Australia's greatest painters of horses, has captured the significance of the hunt for both sexes in his *Out with the Hounds* (1923).

Woodhouse and his son, Frederick Junior, were both widely acclaimed as animal painters, especially Melbourne Cup winners, but many artists captured the evolution of this popular activity from the early race meetings which involved a few horses on makeshift tracks: Benjamin Duterrau, *New Town Race Course* (1836); George Row, *Victorian Race Meeting near Sunbury* (1858); and J. M. Skipper, *Race-course, Adelaide, South Australia* (1840). The sport grew rapidly and the following paintings depict this development: Frederick Woodhouse, *The Second Melbourne Cup, 1862—the Start*; A. T. H. Lyttleton, *Adam Lindsay Gordon Steeplechasing at Flemington, 7 November 1868*; H. J. Ryan, *Flemington Racecourse from the Footscray Side of Salt Water River* (1880); and Carl Kahler, *Derby Day at Flemington* (1886). Of course, there are still 'bush' race tracks around this vast country and Pro Hart has captured the nature of these rural meetings; two of his paintings are *Race Course Painting* (1968) and *St. Patrick's Day Races* (n.d.). Russell Drysdale's *Saddling Up at Coen Races* (1953) features horses and jockeys; this relationship is also depicted in Robert Dickerson's Degas-influenced *Jockey in the Straight* (1969), Sam Fullbrook's *Jockey, horse and aeroplane* (1976), and Stuart Reid's *Phar Lap* (n.d.).

Cricket flourished in the colonies. One of the earliest paintings was *A Cricket Match in Hyde Park, Sydney*, painted by John Rae in 1842. T. H. Lewis's watercolour of Hyde Park— *The Old Days of Merry Cricket Club Matches*, although painted in the same year as Rae's, presents a contrast because it is of a well-organised match which has attracted a significant number of spectators. Early intercolonial matches were captured in lithographs by S. T. Gill and Cuthbert Charles Clarke. It seems likely that Gill was the artist who painted in watercolour *The Grand Cricket Match: All England Eleven Versus Twenty-Two of N.S.W. Contest in the Outer Domain of Sydney, Jan. 29th, 30th, 31st and 1st Feb., 1862*. This inaugural game was depicted from within the covered grandstand which accommodated a cross-section of colonial society. Beyond the players can be seen the brightly coloured tents in the refreshment areas. Cricket was an activity used by missionaries throughout Australia to 'educate' Aborigines about the culture of the British. John Michael Crossland's *Portrait of Nannultera, A Young Poonindie Cricketer*, painted in oil in about the mid-nineteenth century, shows an Aboriginal lad dressed in European clothes wielding a bat. The extent of cricket's popularity for participants of all ages and levels of performance is illustrated in Russell Drysdale's *The Cricketers*. Drysdale was born in England but came to Australia as a child and showed a great ability to relate his experiences of people and places through his paintings. In this painting the bowler delivers the ball to the batsman who is located against a brick wall, probably that of a hotel in a rural town. Fred Williams's *Cricketer* (1955), although painted in London, clearly depicts the concentration of an Australian beneath the baggy green cap. Of course there are many paintings of cricket; a large range may be seen at the Australian Gallery of Sport and the Melbourne Cricket Club Museum at the Melbourne Cricket Ground. Donald George Bradman has been the subject of many portraits; several are on display in the Bradman Museum in Bowral, NSW, and include a copy of a portrait by R. Hannaford (the original hangs in the Long Room at Lords), a commissioned portrait by Bill Leak (1989), and another by Allan Fearnley.

Boxing, for much of the nineteenth century, was an underground activity until bare-knuckle bouts were superseded in the 1880s by the use of gloves and the introduction of the Marquess of Queensberry rules. S. T. Gill's two watercolours of McLaren's Boxing Saloon in Main Road, Ballarat, in 1854 and 1855 provide an interesting insight into this activity in at least one location. In both paintings the boxers are wearing gloves and the venue is certainly not 'underground'. Nancy Kilgour's realistic portrayal of the bout *Ron Richards versus Fred Henneberry at the Rushcutter's Bay Stadium* depicts a similar scene almost a century later: an enthusiastic and intense crowd awaiting the outcome. The legitimacy and significance of this sport throughout the twentieth century is further depicted in Donald Friend's pen and ink and wash on paper entitled *The Pugilist* (n.d.).

The influence of Britain on sport in Australia is evident, particularly in the evolution of football, with both rugby and soccer being played throughout the latter half of the nineteenth century. The introduction of an Australian code of football is attributed to MCC members T. W. Wills and H. C. Harrison, who drew up a set of simple rules. This code of rules was adopted by the Melbourne Football Club in 1859; portraits of Wills (c. 1920) and Harrison (1870), painted by Sir John Longstaff and W. Handcock of NZ, respectively, hang in the Australian Gallery of Sport and Olympic Museum. A colourful and modern depiction by Arthur Streeton entitled *The National Game* (1889) captures the popularity of this sport. Dorothy May Braund's painting of a highly stylised Geelong player in mid-air, entitled *Leap*, provides a different perspective.

S. T. Gill was a prolific artist and, in addition to his many paintings of balls, boxing, horse-racing, and cricket, his 1867 watercolour entitled *A Bowls Match* now hangs in the Melbourne Bowling Club. Many different physical activities and sports have been depicted in paintings. John Brack has painted skaters, gymnasts, and ballroom dancers; Russell Drysdale has depicted netball in *Basketball in Broome* (1958), which again illustrates the significance of missionaries and their use of sport in educating the Aborigines; while the great portrait artist Sir William Dargie's painting of tennis player Margaret Court is a tribute both to a great athlete and to a significant sport in Australia.

IJ

See **BURNS, PETER**; **Drama**; **Film**; **Literature**.

ASHTON, JAMES (1899–1973), **ROBERT** (1902–77), **GEOFFREY** (1904–) and **PHILIP** (1906–) were all born in Sydney and after schooling lived on the family property at Binda in NSW. They played from 1926 as a team for the Goulburn Artillery Polo Club, with James captain, Philip number one, Geoffrey number two and Robert as 'back'. Between 1928 and 1939 they won five Countess of Dudley Cups. In England in 1930, with Australian ponies, they won sixteen out of twenty-one matches, reached the final of the Champion Cup, and were rated a 26-goal team; they also played in the USA. Returning to England in 1937, they beat the British Army at Aldershot, and, with R. Skene replacing Philip, won the coveted Champion Cup at Hurlingham. Rated no higher than 7-goal players, the Ashtons' skill and team-work enabled them to beat higher-rated teams; they were unbeaten 'off the stick' in Australia in eleven years.

GW

See **Polo**.

Athletics

When Australia was settled by the British,

typically English sports in vogue at the time were translated to an antipodean setting. Steeplechasing, hunting, and horse-racing were the activities of the élite (or those who aspired to gentry status) and the colonial upper-class used these symbolic but exclusive display sports to indicate their position in the new society. The sports of the lower orders were those of low organisation requiring only energy or physical strength and little or no equipment. Athletic sports like boxing or footraces (walking/running) were organised by entrepreneurial colonial tavern-keepers. In keeping with British traditions, these activities offered impromptu sporting entertainment for a drinking and gambling clientele wherever groups of ordinary folk congregated. Old English sports like the high leap, putting-the-stone, wrestling, and running over various distances (and sometimes over sheep hurdles) allowed members of a community to identify with a local champion and gamble on the result. There were other tavern sports like quoits and skittles, but 'athletic sports' could cater for family groups and were deemed respectable, whereas quoits and skittles were usually tavern-yard activities and not appropriate for women or children.

Foot-running, or pedestrianism as it was then known, was a feature of the earliest sports meetings in colonial Australia. Matches of ability attracted much attention and large crowds. Often head-to-head contests, they were sometimes made more complex and amusing by conditional rules (for example, each entrant to carry a jockey). The extraordinary pedestrian William Francis King, or 'The Flying Pieman' as he became popularly known in Sydney in the 1840s, carried animals across his shoulders as dead weights when he walked from Campbelltown to Sydney in 8 hours and from Sydney to Parramatta in just under 7 hours. The usual contests simply matched two 'peds'. The *Adelaide Register* carried the following notice on 12 November 1845: 'The advertiser challenges to run any person in the Colony for any distance being not less than a mile for the sum of £20 at the Adelaide Races in January next— W. G. Lambert.' Lambert, licensee of the Club House Hotel in Hindley Street, had been a well-known ped in England before emigrating to SA. Widespread interest in 'locomotives' like Lambert and King encouraged the sport, and prize-money attracted famous peds from all over the world: Tom Malone and Frank 'Scurry' Hewitt from Ireland, Harry Hutchins and Albert Bird from England, and Lou Myers from America. These 'champions of the world' came to Australia in the nineteenth century to compete against local athletes. When public enthusiasm for such contests was at its peak in the 1870s the winner of such contests could earn a great deal of money.

Tales of sharp practices such as mismeasuring distances and not trying against local champions after being paid appearance money gradually reduced the popularity of professional athletics in Australia. In their place amateur athletics were advocated as 'healthy, manly *and moral*' activities and were sponsored by influential eminent citizens who sought to counteract the appeal of the professionals to an easily distracted working class. In Adelaide it was a group of the 'colonial gentry' (Morphett, Kingston, Hawker, Bundey, and Ayres) who formed the Adelaide Amateur Club in 1864 (the first in Australia) and encouraged the working class to do likewise in Port Adelaide. The pattern was similar in other colonies. In 1867 John Gregory Harris defeated Colden Harrison for the amateur title of Australia. H. C. A. Harrison, recognised as 'the father of Australian Rules Football', was the amateur champion of Victoria from 1859 to 1866. In his autobiography *The Story of an Athlete* (1918–19), Harrison described the interest in races between crack runners. When he defeated Lambton Mount, 'hero of Ballarat', in a series of races (100 yards, quarter-mile, and quarter-mile over hurdles) 'hundreds of people drove all the way from Ballarat'. Harrison's winning times of 10.5 seconds and 50.25 seconds for the 100 yards and quarter-mile respectively were excellent given the year (1861) and the fact that the races were run on spongy turf. When Harrison won the quarter in just over 50 seconds it was considered a world record! Harrison was one of a group of élite citizens, including Professor Irving, M. Byrne, W. J. Hammersley, A. Hardcastle, W. Levy, and R. J. Wardhill, who established the amateur sport of athletics in Melbourne under the auspices of the MCC.

The Amateur Athletic Association of NSW was formed in 1887. Richard Coombes, an English pedestrian of some note, was one of those who met in Sydney to 'take over management of amateur athletic sports in this colony'. He was to be president of the Association for over forty years (1894–1935) but became even better known as 'the father of amateur athletics in Australia'. The colonial organisation of athletics in NSW was, however, preceded by the establishment of the Sydney Amateur Athletic Club in 1872. The State Governor, Sir Hercules Robinson, was patron and the club boasted nearly one hundred 'Muscular Christians'. The first meeting of the club was attended by the Governor and Sir James Ferguson, visiting Governor of SA, who was able to report on the success of amateur athletics in Adelaide and its influence on the working class (the Port Adelaide Club had been formed in 1870). While SA witnessed the establishment of the first amateur club in Australia, it was NSW which first organised clubs into an interactive and supporting association under the guidance of Coombes. Victoria followed in 1891, Queensland in 1895, Tasmania in 1902, and SA in 1905. WA formed an association in 1905 but it was disbanded in 1908 and did not reform until 1928. The first Australasian Track and Field Championships were held in Melbourne in November 1893; NSW, Victoria, and NZ were the only teams competing. After the third championships were conducted at the SCG in October 1897 an intercolonial conference took place, chaired by Richard Coombes, and a committee was formed to draw up rules for an Amateur Athletic Union of Australasia. Coombes was elected president and Edward S. Marks honorary secretary-treasurer; both men held these positions until 1934. NZ withdrew from the AAUA in 1927.

Before the formation of the AAUA, the Olympic Games were held in Athens in 1896. Australia had one representative, Edwin Flack, who had travelled with members of the London Athletic Club to contest the middle-distance events. He won both the 800 (2 min 11 sec) and the 1500 metres (4 min 33.2 sec), entered the marathon, and played in the tennis doubles with Englishman George Robertson.

Flack was perhaps the greatest of Australia's Olympic representatives but there have been many other success stories. Gold-medal athletes at the Games have included Flack (1896), Nick Winter (1924), Jack Metcalfe (1936), John Winter (1948), Marjorie Jackson (1952), Shirley Strickland (1952–56), Betty Cuthbert (1956–64), Herb Elliott (1960), Glynis Nunn (1984), and Debbie Flintoff-King (1988). Of course there have been some near misses, athletes of great talent and world fame who did not win gold at the Olympics but are notable nonetheless. John Landy, Ron Clarke, Raylene Boyle, Lisa Ondieki, Ric Mitchell, Decima Norman, John Treloar, Pam Ryan, Peter Norman, Marlene Mathews, and Gary Honey can be included in this group. John Treloar, Decima Norman, and Raylene Boyle each won the sprint double at a British Empire/Commonwealth Games. Rob de Castella became a national hero after wins in the 1982 Commonwealth Games marathon and the World Championship marathon in Helsinki in 1983.

In the professional ranks, two athletes are still revered: Arthur Postle, 'The Crimson Flash', and Jack Donaldson, 'The Blue Streak'. Postle set world records for sprint events from 50 yards (5.1 seconds) to 200 yards (19 seconds). He was reputed to be the fastest human alive in 1906 when he defeated R. B. Day of Ireland on the Kalgoorlie goldfields. Record crowds were attracted to all his races. Donaldson rivalled Postle in events over 100 yards and in South Africa in 1910 he defeated Postle and American champion Charles Holway in the 100 yards in 9.38 seconds—a new world record. It was not until 1948 that this time was beaten. Donaldson was called the 'Carbine of Running' and assumed legendary hero status. His 130 yard world record lasted until 1951. At Stawell, site of the legendary Stawell Gift, Donaldson is still spoken of as the greatest of all professional athletes.

One of the most significant features of the twentieth century has been the emancipation of women from a solely domestic role, giving them the opportunity to engage in a wide variety of social activities previously not available or considered not appropriate for them. Participation in competitive sport by Australian women has been a phenomenon of the recent past, since the 1920s and 1930s. Participation in sport offered women an attractive form of self-assertion. Old questions of impropriety and lack of femininity were challenged by newer fashionable arguments of improved health through regular exercise. Australian women followed the overseas trend towards sporting involvement.

The transition from a private, domestic individual life to a public, active, communal one did not occur without opposition. Sport, for example, was considered a male domain and involvement in competitive sport by women was seen as out of the ordinary. But there were young women who were brave enough and who were encouraged by parents or siblings to participate in competitive sports. After the 1924 Olympics in Paris it had been decided that in future Games there would be athletic events for women. In 1926 three events for women were included in the NSW State Championships (75 yards, 100 yards, and 4 × 110 yards relay). Edith Robinson won both sprints. She repeated this success in 1927 and 1928 and was selected as a member of the Australian team for the 1928 Olympic Games in Amsterdam. She was the first Australian woman athlete to represent her country, and she ran second in her heat of the 100 metres and third in the semifinal. Other States provided competition for women athletes following the NSW pattern. SA included a race for women in the 1928 State championships and Victoria a women's relay race in one of its interclub meetings a year later. That same year Queensland conducted three events for women: 100 yards, 4 × 100 yards relay and a three-legged race! Women in Tasmania were allowed to compete at men's meetings in 1930, but it was not until 1939 that a women's athletic association was formed. The WA Women's Amateur Athletic Association was established in 1936.

Women held their first national championship in Melbourne in January 1930. Four States—NSW, Victoria, Queensland, and Tasmania—were represented and the talented Chrissie Dahm won the 100 yards national title. The national Women's Athletic Union was formed in 1932. For fifty years the two groups, men and women, operated athletics separately, but in the early 1980s they combined to form one union; that union operates today as Athletics Australia.

While men's and women's athletics (formerly 'amateur athletics') have combined of late to conduct events, the professionals have preserved their own Athletic League, with each State conducting its own programme of events. Major meets like the Easter Stawell Gift in Victoria attract professionals and are part of a national circuit. Athletics Australia conducts a calendar of special meets in each State that mirrors, in a small way, the European Grand Prix circuit. Little Athletics provides opportunities for Australian schoolchildren to begin track and field at an early age and caters for children up to the age of 14.

JAD

See **Athletics Australia**; BOYLE, RAELENE; CAIRD, MAUREEN; CERUTTY, PERCY; CLARKE, RON; COOMBES, RICHARD; CUTHBERT, BETTY; DE CASTELLA, ROBERT; DONALDSON, JOHN; DOUBELL, RALPH; ELLIOTT, HERBERT; FLACK, EDWIN; FLINTOFF-KING, DEBBIE; HOGAN, HECTOR; JACKSON, MARJORIE; KILBORN, PAM; KING, WILLIAM; LANDY, JOHN; MARKS, ERNEST; MATTHEWS, MARLENE; METCALFE, JACK; MONEGHETTI, STEPHEN; NICHOLLS, **Sir** DOUGLAS; NORMAN, DECIMA; NORMAN, PETER; NUNN, GLYNIS; ONDIEKI, LISA; POLLOCK, JUDITH; POSTLE, ARTHUR; ROWLEY, STANLEY; SAMUELS, CHARLIE; SAXBY, KERRY; STAMPFL, FRANZ; **Stawell Gift**; STRICKLAND, SHIRLEY; **Sydney to Melbourne Run**; WINTER, ANTHONY; WINTER, JOHN; YOUNG, CLIFF.

Athletics Australia is the national co-ordinating body for athletics. The Amateur Athletics Association of Australasia was formed in Sydney in 1897 with original membership comprising NSW, Victoria, Queensland, and NZ. The founding president and secretary were Richard Coombes and E. S. Marks, respectively, both of whom retained their positions until 1934. All early organised athletic events were for male competitors only; it was not until 1926, when the NSW men's association included women's events in their State championships at Manly, that women became recognised officially. NZ withdrew from the national body in 1927 and the name was changed to the Amateur Athletic Union of Australia (AAUA). The Australian Women's Amateur Athletic Union was founded in 1932 and it was not until 1978 that the men and women amalgamated. The word 'amateur' was dropped in 1982 and the current name, Athletics Australia, was adopted in 1990. Outstanding and long-serving administrators in

addition to Coombes and Marks include Doris Magee who was women's secretary from 1937 to 1940 and 1942 to 1978 and Arthur Hodsdon as men's secretary from 1947 to 1974. Athletics Australia works closely with the ASC, the AIS, the Australian Coaches Association, Little Athletics, and also veterans' and professionals' associations to promote and develop the sport for men and women of all ages.

PJ* and IJ

See **Athletics**.

AUSSI Masters Swimming, originally constituted as the Australian Union of Senior Swimmers International (AUSSI) in September 1975, has as its purpose the encouragement of adults, regardless of age or ability, to swim regularly in order to promote fitness and improve general health. The first 'masters'-style event in Australia was conducted at the Harbord Diggers' Club in May 1971. In March 1974 a 45-member team of US Masters Swimmers visited Australia for a carnival which was held at the Heffron Pool in Sydney. In October that year a meeting was held which formed the Australian Masters Swimming Association (AMSA), and the first national championships were held in March 1975. National swims have been held annually and AUSSI is an active supporter of the biennial Australian Masters Games. AUSSI played an important part in the formation of Masters Swimming International (MSI) in 1983 and many Australians have held, and currently hold, office in this international organisation. AUSSI has conducted three international swim meets: the Pan Pacific Masters Championships in Sydney in 1981 and 1983; and the Second FINA/MSI World Masters Swim at which 4000 swimmers (3000 from overseas) competed in Brisbane in 1988. This event has the record of being the world's largest swimming meet. AUSSI has 6300 members in 154 clubs affiliated with eight branches in each State and Territory in Australia. Its management and operation have been acknowledged by the Australian Sports Commission and Australian Swimming. AUSSI is a member of the Confederation of Australian Sport.

IW and IJ

Aussie Sports Programme, inaugurated in 1986 and funded by the ASC, is a national strategy to increase and diversify sports participation for children throughout Australia. Offered to all children in their last three years of primary school it has been seen as an ideal introduction to organised sport. The programme was developed by sportspeople, educators, government representatives, coaches, and administrators to become the first child-based national sporting programme in Australia. It centres around existing adult-sized games like cricket, baseball, and hockey scaled down to 'kid-sized' games. In some cases the rules are changed along with the playing area and in many cases the equipment is different. This enables children to experience all aspects of a game and to enjoy the rewards of making regular hits, runs, and kicks not necessarily prevalent in adult games. The games give all children, regardless of sex or size, a chance to play and improve their skills. An important responsibility of the programme is a code of conduct aimed at reducing the emphasis on 'win at all costs' and promoting the principles of good sporting behaviour.

GC*

See **Children**.

Austral Wheelrace (also known as Austral Wheel Race) is Australia's oldest, most prestigious professional track-cycling contest. Originally organised by the Melbourne Cycling Club, the Austral received its official title in 1887, although the club had staged a similar event in 1886. The early Australs attracted large crowds to the MCG. The 2 mile handicap was witnessed by 30 000 spectators in 1898. In 1892 and 1895 the winners collected the substantial amount of £200, thus ensuring a competitive contest. At other times the prize-money was less than the amount won through betting; this led to a number of scandals, almost killing the sport. Austral winners have included many of Australia's leading cyclists, such as former world champions Gordon Johnson, Sid Patterson, Steele Bishop, Tassie Johnson, Danny Clark, and Stephen Pate. Although contemporary Australs have lacked the capacity crowds of the 1890s, the event has maintained its reputation as Australia's premier professional track race. Several thousand witnessed the 1991 event when Stephen Pate created history as the first rider to start behind the scratch mark and win.

DRS

See **Cycling**.

Australia II, a yacht from the Royal Perth Yacht Club, finished ahead of the American boat *Liberty* in the final race of seven to take out the 1983 *America*'s Cup. A bald description of the win could read: 'On 26 September 1983 a WA business syndicate headed by a British-born entrepreneur won a series of races between two technology-laden 12-metre sailing hulls'. But this would fail to convey the extraordinary response to *Australia II* and its winged keel. The entrepreneur, Alan Bond, became a cultural hero; the designer of the boat, Ben Lexcen, became a household name; and the winged keel became a symbol of Australia's entry into the high-tech era. Australia's Prime Minister at the time, Bob Hawke, declared the win to be 'one of the greatest moments in Australian history'.

PJ

See *America*'s **Cup**; BEASHEL **Family**; BERTRAND, JOHN; HARDY, Sir JAMES; LEXCEN, BEN; **Sailing and Yachting**.

Australian Basketball Federation. In 1927 Victoria was the first Australian State to establish a basketball association: the members were from the Military, the Church of England, the Presbyterian Church, and the YMCA. SA formed an association in 1936 and NSW followed soon after in 1938. The Second World War disrupted the development of basketball, but associations were formed in the remaining states (Queensland, WA, and Tasmania) after hostilities ceased. A National Federation of Basketball, however, had been formed in 1939. It became known as the Amateur Basketball Union of Australia but did not become fully effective until the first Australian championships were held in Sydney in 1946. In 1949 Australia became the fifty-second affiliated member of the International Amateur Basketball Federation. In December 1982 the national governing body of the sport became the Australian Basketball Federation Incorporated.

JS* and IJ

See **Basketball**; BURGE, IVOR.

Australian Blind Sports Federation (ABSF) was formed in Sydney in 1977 when a group of people from Queensland, NSW, Victoria, and WA met to form a steering committee. The Australian Blind Cricket Carnival had been conducted annually for some time before this, since 1952. In February 1978 the National Sports Association of and for the Blind was formed and it sought support from the Australian National Council of and for the Blind (ANCB). Later that year the association met to select the Australian team for the Olympics for the Disabled to be held in Holland in 1980; from this meeting came the idea of a national championship at the same time as the Olympic trials. After several years of work on a constitution, ABSF was formed in January 1980 and the first Australian championships were held in Melbourne; these championships have rotated in the capital cities since that time. Three sports which were in the first ABSF championships and which have continued on a regular basis are athletics, swimming, and lawn bowls; other sports which have been introduced are goalball (1981), tandem cycling (1982), powerlifting (1983), indoor bias bowls (1984), and swish (a modified form of table tennis in which the net is replaced by a board placed above the table below which the ball must travel) (1984). The ABSF has always had three eye-classifications for legally blind competitors, and recently the International Blind Sports Association extended the international classifications system to the 6/60 limit with the possibility of those with field-of-vision problems of 20 per cent or less being eligible for this type of competition.

ABSF representatives have participated in many international competitions since 1977 in world championships and Olympic Games. The ABSF is affiliated with the Australian Paralympic Federation, the Australian Olympic Committee, the Australian Confederation of Sport for the Disabled, and the Confederation of Australian Sport. The AIS, through the ASC, provides scholarships for athletes with disabilities as well as providing funding assistance for the Sport Talent Encouragement Plan (STEP): the ABSF has a strong focus on youth and junior events. In addition to the member State associations, three sport-specific national associations have become members of the ABSF: the Australian Blind Cricket Council (1952), the Australian Blind Cricketers Association (1980), and the Australian National Goalball Association (1989).

IF* and IJ

See **Australian Deaf Sports Federation**; **Australian Sport and Recreation Association for Persons with an Intellectual Disability**.

Australian Bowls Council (ABC) controls the sport for almost 300 000 male bowls-players. What has become the largest lawn-bowling association in the world was established in NSW in October 1880 and, as the other five States formed their own associations soon after, it became necessary to create a national body, the ABC, on 22 September 1911. The ACT and the NT were admitted as full members in 1989. In recent years the sport has attracted sponsorship, which has influenced the number of professional bowlers, and an increase in the number of teenagers has probably arisen because of the sport's inclusion in many secondary schools.

AM* and IJ

See **Australian Women's Bowls Council**; **Lawn Bowls**.

Australian Clay-target Shooting Association. Australia's first registered clay-target club was established through the efforts of a small band of shooters who decided in 1926 that they preferred to shoot clay birds rather than live ones. After several months of shooting in a quarry behind the ICI factory in West Footscray, a suburb of Melbourne, the Nobel Clay-Bird Club was formed after a meeting held on 9 September 1927, at 380 Collins Street, Melbourne. Between 1926 and 1936 numerous clay-bird clubs were formed and became affiliated with the Gun-Clubs Association of Victoria, which was a live-bird shooting body with headquarters at the original Melbourne Gun Club at Tottenham. In 1936 the Clay-Target-Shooters' Association of Victoria was formed; this was followed by the formation of the Australian Clay-Pigeon Trap-Shooting Association (ACPTSA). Immediately after the war clay-target shooting suffered the effects of both gun and ammunition shortages, but the 1950s saw a great expansion. The inclusion of a two-person team in international trench shooting for the first time at the 1956 Olympic Games in Melbourne gave a great impetus to the sport. At the 1973 World Moving-Target Championships, staged by the Melbourne Gun Club, Australia won bronze medals in the trench team event. Since 1974 Australia has sent both trench (target-release machines located in a trench in front of the shooter) and skeet teams to world championships and has been relatively successful. The sport is now controlled by the Australian Clay-Target Association, with associations in all States, 295 registered clubs and 8000 registered shooters. A national championship tournament in the disciplines of international- and standard-trap, and in skeet competition, is staged each year.

GB* and IJ

See **Amateur Pistol Shooting Union of Australia**.

Australian Council for Health, Physical Education and Recreation (ACHPER), which was formerly known as the Australian Physical Education Association (APEA), is a national association for professional people who are committed to promoting healthy life-styles. A 1954 meeting of representatives from State physical education associations unanimously agreed to form a national association. The meeting also agreed that the Victorian Physical Education Association should consign its *Physical Education Journal* to APEA, and the council of APEA appointed A. W. Willee as its first editor. The inaugural president was Dr Fritz Duras. Initially the focus of APEA was on physical education, and membership included physical education teachers in schools and lecturers in tertiary institutions. As physical education broadened in its scope to include other areas related to the promotion of active and healthy life-styles, it was decided that APEA should follow trends from North America and change the name to include the three disciplines of Health Education, Physical Education, and Recreation. At present ACHPER represents an affiliation of State and Territory branches with the national organisation. National convenors are appointed in seven major areas: Health Education, Physical Education, Recreation, Sport, Dance, Community Fitness, and Movement Sciences. ACHPER is active in the following areas: policy formulation and the creation of public awareness of major issues both through the political process and the media; continuing education and professional development of members; information dissemination; initiating, fostering, and supporting research; and undertaking special projects aimed at creating community awareness about healthy living.

5 Charles Perkins, a former soccer player and an active campaigner for black rights, was responsible for founding the Australian Aboriginal Cricket Association, and for its 1988 tour of England.

6 Michael Ahmatt, an inaugural member of the Aboriginal Sports Foundation, represented Australia in basketball at both the 1964 and 1968 Olympic Games.

7 Amateur rowers competed for the Briscoe Trophy, which was first awarded at the 1882 Melbourne Regatta to the winner of the Senior Fours, an event for 'Non-Manual Labourer Amateurs'.

8 Adelaide Archery Club, 1876.

9 The starters in the 100 yard race at the 1896 Queensland Amateur Athletic championships. Left to right: R. C. Rule (Rockhampton), J. Keiver (Rockhampton) and W. Cartwright (Sydney).

10 Athletics were administered for many years by Richard Coombes (President), E. S. Marks (Honorary Secretary) and W. B. Alexander (Honorary Treasurer), through the Amateur Athletic Union of Australasia.

11 The 'Fun Run' has become a significant event for people of all ages. These are entrants in 'The *Sun* Superun', Melbourne, April 1990.

12 Early this century clay-target and other shooting events became popular activities, and retailers sought to capitalise on the need for appropriate clothing and equipment.

That the Victorian Rifle Association in General Meeting assembled this Twenty Sixth Day of February 1897 desires to place on record its Appreciation and Admiration of the Generosity and Public Spirit displayed by

David Syme, Esq.

in undertaking to pay the Whole of the Expenses of a Team of Riflemen to proceed to England to represent the Colony of Victoria in the Matches of the National Rifle Association at **Bisley** and in the Imperial Rifle Matches and other Public Functions connected with the Celebration of the Long and Glorious Reign of her Most Gracious Majesty Queen Victoria and that this Resolution be engrossed on Parchment attested by the Signatures of the Proper Officers of the Association and Presented to Mr Syme as a Memento of his Loyalty and Patriotism in making a Splendid Contribution to the Public Demonstrations of a World Wide Empire in honour of its Beloved Sovereign

13 This address expressed the appreciation of the Victorian Rifle Association of David Syme's sponsorship of a team of riflemen to the Imperial Rifle Matches at Bisley in 1897.

Initiatives of ACHPER include the Daily Physical Education Programme which is the first comprehensive curriculum for daily physical education for Australian primary and junior secondary schools; Jump Rope for Heart which is a joint educational and physical fitness programme undertaken with the National Heart Foundation; the Australian Health and Fitness Survey; the Australian Health and Fitness Award Scheme; the Health Education and Lifestyle Project; Recreation in Nursing Homes; and the conduct of Physical Education Week in all States. ACHPER Publications, widely recognised as one of Australia's leading mail-order houses, publishes the quarterly *ACHPER National Journal* and, in conjunction with the Australian Sports Medicine Federation, the *Australian Journal of Science and Medicine in Sport*. ACHPER also works co-operatively with the Australian Sports Commission. Membership of ACHPER at present exceeds two and a half thousand.

EM and IJ

See **BLOOMFIELD, JOHN; DURAS, FRITZ; Government Policy**.

Australian Cricket Board (ACB) is the controlling body for cricket throughout Australia and is responsible for the staging of interstate and international matches. These matches include Tests and one-day internationals, the Sheffield Shield competition between States, and the interstate one-day competition. The ACB also organises youth international tours, under-19 and under-17 national championships, the Cricket Academy (based in Adelaide since 1989), Kanga Cricket throughout Australian primary schools, and Cricket A–Z in secondary schools. The first national organisation for cricket was the Australasian Cricket Council which existed from 1892 to 1900 and attempted to assume control from strong colonial bodies such as the Melbourne Cricket Club and the NSW Cricket Association. The Australian Board of Control for International Cricket was formed in 1905 and combined with England and South Africa to become one of the founding members of the Imperial Cricket Committee, under the jurisdiction of the Marylebone Cricket Club at Lord's. This body later became the International Cricket Conference and, in 1989, the International Cricket Council; it comprises all the world's cricket nations. The ACB came into existence under that title in 1973 after a reorganisation.

IMcD and IJ

Australian Croquet Association. Following the national croquet championships in Brisbane in 1949, representatives of the participating States met to form the Australian Croquet Council (ACC) which was to conduct the Australian championship and interstate events, represent Australian croquet in England and other countries, and promote the sport nationally. The ACC met annually until 1987 when the name changed to the Australian Croquet Association.

CF and IJ

See **Croquet**.

Australian Curling Association (ACA). Curling is a game of Scottish origin which may be likened to lawn bowls on ice; curling stones are slid a distance of approximately 36 metres into circles painted on ice. The Curling Club of Australia, the first in this country, was established by expatriate Scots at the 'Glaciarium' in Melbourne in 1933. The club's inaugural president was the renowned tennis-player Norman Brookes. The club lasted until 1939 and curling virtually disappeared until the ACA was established in 1984; its headquarters are at the Olympic Ice Rink in Oakleigh, which is the last remaining full-size rink in Melbourne where one can curl. In 1986 the ACA developed international links by becoming affiliated with the Royal Caledonian Curling Club in Scotland and being accepted as a member of the World Curling Federation. The ACA's first international match was against a visiting Canadian navy delegation in 1986 and this event led to the establishment of an annual invitation bonspiel (tournament) which commenced in 1988. The second curling club was established in Brisbane in 1991.

DJ* and IJ

Australian Cycling Federation (ACF). It was really only after the formation of the Melbourne Cycle Club on 1 August 1878 that there was regular bicycle racing in Australia. Although the Melbourne Bicycle Club no longer exists, the Sydney Bicycle Club, the second to be formed, still flourishes as a successful businessmen's club. The ACF was not formed until the turn of the century; this body became affiliated with the Union Cycliste Internationale (UCI) in August 1903, becoming the ninth national body to be recognised. The control of amateur cycling is vested in the ACF (professional cycling is controlled by the Australian Professional Cycling Council). Membership exceeds seven and a half thousand, with associations in all States and the NT. The ACF is affiliated with the Australian Olympic Council, Australian Commonwealth Games Association, UCI, and the Federation of International Amateur Cycling.

MW and IJ

See **Cycling**.

Australian Deaf Sports Federation (ADSF). Interstate sporting competition for the deaf in Australia began with a cricket match between NSW and Victoria soon after the First World War. Competition gradually expanded to include tennis and table tennis. By the end of the

Second World War most States were participating in more than one sport at what had become known as deaf sports carnivals. At one such carnival in Adelaide in 1954 a meeting of welfare superintendents, delegates from each State, and representatives of the three Australian deaf sports associations—cricket, tennis, and table tennis—decided to form an appropriate national deaf sports organisation, the ADSF. Its task was to control all aspects of interstate deaf-sports competition. It was ten years later that the first Australian deaf games were staged in Sydney. These games have been held every three years since then. Membership of ADSF comprises deaf organisations for the following sports: badminton, basketball, bowling, women's bowling, indoor carpet bowls, cricket, darts, golf, netball, soccer, squash, swimming, table tennis, tennis, and tenpin bowling. ADSF also comprises the ACT Deaf Sports Club, NSW Deaf Sports Association, Queensland Deaf Sports Association, Victorian Sports Association of the Deaf, SA Deaf Sports and Social Club, Tasmanian Deaf Sports Club, and the WA Deaf Recreation Association. The ADSF is a member of the Comité Internationale des Sports des Sourds, the Australian Olympic Committee, and the Confederation of Australian Sport. Athletes have represented the ADSF at World Games for the Deaf since 1965 and at the Winter Games since 1975.

AB* and IJ

See **Australian Blind Sports Federation**; **Australian Sport and Recreation Association for Persons with an Intellectual Disability**.

Australian Federation of Amateur Roller Sports. The international body which controls roller skating, the Fédération Internationale de Patinage à Roulettes (FIPR), was founded in 1924, and by 1936 rules had been established for competitions in speed skating, rink hockey, and artistic skating and dancing. The development of the sport in Australia was interrupted by the outbreak of the Second World War. Australia became a member of the international body in 1952, but in June 1956 was suspended from the newly named body (Fédération Internationale de Roller Skating—FIRS) for non-payment of outstanding fees. The Roller Skate Rink Operators Association (RSROA) was formed in 1958 and in 1965 the Australian Federation of Amateur Roller Skaters (AFARS) was created when a motion changing the constitution of the RSROA was accepted. However, many arguments and disagreements ensued, so in 1966 it was agreed that the RSROA would remain as a separate body. AFARS became a member of FIRS in 1967; it changed its name, but not its acronym, to the Australian Federation of Amateur Roller Sports in 1989. AFARS has hosted the following world championships: in 1975 the Artistic

Championships in Brisbane, and in 1986 the Speed Road Championships in Adelaide and the Artistic Championships in Sydney. AFARS representatives in international competition have an excellent record; Australia was ranked number one in the world in 1989 in speed skating and has also performed well in artistic competition. Roller hockey was a demonstration sport at the Olympic Games in Barcelona in 1992 and Australia earned the right to compete against eleven other nations. In 1989 Australia and NZ formed the Oceania Confederation of Roller Skating under the presidency of Ivan Martin; the first Oceania Championships were held in NZ over Easter 1992.

IM and IJ

Australian Gallery of Sport and Olympic Museum. The Australian Gallery of Sport and Olympic Museum is funded by the Melbourne Cricket Club and by private sponsors. It is Australia's first national multi-sport museum and gallery and is situated at the Melbourne Cricket Ground. The Gallery of Sport was built with funds provided by the Victorian and Federal governments and the Melbourne Cricket Club, and was opened on 22 November 1986, the thirtieth anniversary of the 1956 Melbourne Olympic Games opening ceremony. The gallery's permanent collection focuses on selected sports including Australian rules football, cricket, cycling, hockey, boxing, lacrosse, rowing and yachting. Major temporary exhibitions on various themes are also held. The Olympic Museum contains artefacts, information and photographs from all modern summer Olympic Games, with the emphasis on Australian involvement. The museum also displays Olympic medals, costumes, sports equipment and documents.

Australian Gymnastic Federation (AGF). Before 1949, when the Australian Gymnastic Union (AGU) was formed, gymnastics was organised through clubs in NSW, Victoria, and Queensland. The dominant clubs in that period were the Sydney YMCA, and the Wesley Collegians and YMCA in Melbourne under coaches Bonnie Frank and Alf Lorbach respectively. The first Australian championships, for men only, were held in 1950. The AGU was first represented in international gymnastics at the Olympic Games in Melbourne in 1956 when artistic gymnastic teams for men and women took part, but women did not participate in the Australian championships until 1959. The AGU became the Australian Amateur Gymnastic Union in 1968 and evolved into the AGF in 1977. Incorporation of this body in 1981 coincided with the centenary celebrations of the Fédération Internationale de Gymnastique (FIG), with which the AGU had affiliated in 1954. Affiliations of the various gymnastic organisations throughout Australia occurred as follows: 1949 Victoria, Queensland, and NSW; 1955 WA; 1956 SA; 1969 ACT; 1970 Tasmania; 1981 NT. Rhythmic Sportive Gymnastics officially came within the AGF in 1977. Although the AGF's constitution claimed jurisdiction for sports acrobatics and the federation assisted with inquiries and liaised with their international body, sports acrobatics in Australia formed a separate national association. In keeping with FIG's international statutes, the AGF has now accepted responsibility for the development of general gymnastics, which is the participation/recreation discipline. A real improvement in the standard of performance in this sport has occurred since Australian gymnasts were included in the first intake of the AIS in 1980. There are over fifty thousand registered gymnasts in Australia.

PB* and IJ
See **Gymnastics**.

Australian Hockey Association (AHA). Hockey clubs were formed in Adelaide in 1900, Perth in 1902, and in Sydney and Melbourne in 1906. Various States formed hockey associations in the first decade of the new century (Victoria and NSW in 1906 and WA in 1908). The First World War halted progress but the sport was back in full swing again in 1919; Queensland's association was formed in 1921 and Tasmania's in 1934. The first visit to NZ by an Australian team in 1922 emphasised the need for a national body, a need which prominent NSW and Victorian officials had discussed as early as 1912; the AHA was established in 1925.

BC and IJ
See **Hockey**.

Australian Institute of Sport (AIS) was established in Canberra in 1981 as a central sports institute where the best athletes in the country could be trained using modern sports science and experienced coaches. After the halcyon days of the 1950s and 1960s when Australian sportsmen and women ranked high in international competitions, there had been limited success. Aussie tennis-players were being replaced at the top level by Europeans or Americans and, on a broader front, Australians did not win a gold medal at the 1976 Olympics. The divisive debate surrounding the participation of Australian athletes in the Olympic Games in Moscow in 1980 brought the situation of élite athlete support (and success) to a head, resulting in the Fraser Government's proposal for the establishment of a sports institute in Canberra.

The AIS was built in the suburb of Bruce alongside the national stadium. It was dubbed from the beginning 'the gold-medal factory', indicating its primary function in the Australian sporting environment. Within five years it was a splendid institute with facilities unmatched anywhere in the world. A sport science course was established at the Canberra College of Advanced Education to cater for athlete scholars, and other educational institutions in Canberra provided access for the nation's sporting élite so that they could combine sporting excellence with career training. Seven sports were included in the new institute: athletics, basketball, gymnastics, netball, swimming, tennis, and weightlifting. Don Talbot, expatriate swimming coach, was the first director of the AIS and the best coaches in the country (and outside) were sought as mentors of the 150 young athletes who attended the institute in its first year. Criticism of the location of the AIS and the narrow range of sports there was overcome by decentralisation. State sports institutes were established and other sports added, notably hockey in Perth, cycling and cricket in Adelaide, squash and diving in Brisbane, and rugby in Sydney; rowing and water polo were added to the Canberra sports.

Controversy over 'means and ends' has troubled the reputation of the AIS since its inception. It has been criticised for taking too much of the national sport budget each year, of being too élitist, and too selective in its sports. Decentralising its sports and encouraging the development of State sports institutes has deflected much criticism, and success in national arenas has justified the expense. However, implications of drug use to achieve some of that success has tarnished the image of élite sport in Australia. The AIS convinced the Senate Inquiry into Drugs and Sport and the Australian sporting public that use of ergogenic aids by some of its athletes were isolated incidents and contrary to its code of ethics. Random drug tests of all scholarship holders at the AIS is now obligatory.

The AIS has been in existence for over a decade and its efficacy and influence can now be judged. Success in the 1990 Commonwealth Games assured the nation that it is influential in producing champions. Coaching methods have been improved and the sports medicine staff are used as a resource by the nation's élite when they are injured. Talent identification schemes are in place, often initiated in Canberra, and that talent is developed through sport camps. The AIS provides a national focus and an inspiration for élite athletes.

JAD
See **Amateurism**; COLES, ALLAN; DE CASTELLA, ROBERT; **Government Policy**.

Australian Ju-jitsu Association (AJ-JA) was officially constituted by the State ju-jitsu associations of Queensland, WA, Victoria, SA, and NSW at a meeting held in Queensland in 1985; Tasmania and the NT have joined since then. The aim of the AJ-JA is to promote the art of ju-jitsu throughout Australia on a traditional, competitive, and self-defence basis. The AJ-JA is affiliated with the World Ju-jitsu Federation.

BB and IJ

Australian Karting Association (AKA). Karting in Australia developed rapidly in the late 1950s with the advent of 'motorised' go-karting in America and by 1961 the AKA had been established. There are more than eighty karting clubs throughout Australia, each affiliated with State associations. Small automobiles, formerly known as 'go-karts', with drivers from as young as 7 years to the elderly, race in tests of speed and endurance nearly every weekend of the year. Annual championships in each state culminate in national championships which have been held every Easter since the first in 1964 in Seymour, Victoria. There are three forms of karting: sprint, bitumen, and dirt-track racing, as well as superkart racing. AKA junior and senior drivers have a proud record of performance in international competition and world championships.

KS* and IJ

Australian Kendo Renmei (AKR). Kendo, or Japanese fencing, is the oldest martial art in Japan and developed over seven hundred years ago. It was introduced into Australia with the founding of the Sydney Kendo Club in 1966; there were earlier forms of kendo in various parts of Australia before that but these were not authentic kendo. The Sydney Kendo Club became affiliated with the International Kendo Federation in 1972. The first All-Australian Kendo Championships were held in Melbourne in 1975 and the first official Australian kendo team competed in the fourth World Kendo Championships in Sapporo, Japan, in 1979. Since 1975 the Japan Kendo Federation has assisted greatly with the advancement of the sport by sending instructors to Australia to assist its promotion and development. By 1979, kendo clubs had been formed in all States and Territories of Australia. In 1981 the AKR began offering coaching courses at various levels through the Confederation of Australian Sport Coaches Assembly and there are now twenty-six accredited coaches promoting and teaching kendo by the approved method.

SN and IJ

Australian Ladies' Golf Union was established in 1921. Foundation States were NSW, Victoria, and WA; Tasmania joined in 1923, Queensland in 1924, and SA in 1925. The major championships held in Australia are the Australian Ladies' Amateur Championship, the Australian Junior Championship, the Australian Senior Championship, the Australian 72-Hole Stroke Championship, the Gladys Hay Interstate Championships, and the Junior Interstate Series. Australia also participates in the Commonwealth Tournament, the Espirito Santo World Championship of Women's Golf, the Queen Sirikit Cup, and the Tasman Cup for both senior and junior golfers. Teams are also sent to international tournaments in Great Britain, Europe, NZ, and Canada.

VJ and IJ

See **Golf**.

Australian Mountain Bike Association (AMBA). Mountain bikes were used in Australia in the early 1980s following the trend of the USA. By 1984 a club by the name of 'Fat-Tyre Flyers' had been formed in Victoria to cater for an increasing number of off-road cyclists. In August 1984 the first Australian Mountain Bike Championships were held around the town of Sofala in NSW and this inaugural event was used to gauge the level of interest in the sport throughout Australia. More than fifty entrants contested over a 79 kilometre course of bitumen, fire trail, fire road, and river crossings. After a series of meetings over the ensuing years, the AMBA was formed in January 1988 and it affiliated with the Australian Cycling Federation in November of that year. Australia competed in the World Mountain Bike Championships in 1989. Ben Monroe won the Junior Downhill World Title and shared top-ten placing with Travis Temme in the hill-climb and cross-country events. The Suntour Mountain Bike Grand Prix Series was introduced in 1990 and in 1991 more than five hundred registered competitors took part in a seven-round series, culminating with the 1991 national championships. There are more than thirty affiliated clubs around Australia, with members participating in both competitive and social mountain-bike riding. There are no State governing bodies; all administration is national. Internationally, AMBA is affiliated with the International Mountain Bike Commission and the Federation of International Amateur Cyclists.

GN and IJ

Australian Olympic Committee (AOC). Australia's involvement in the Olympic Movement may be traced to the International Athletic Congress at the Sorbonne in Paris in 1894 which was called by Baron Pierre de Coubertin to discuss amateurism and the revival of the Olympic Games. The minutes of the Victorian Amateur Athletic Association (VAAA) of 13 March 1895 state that at that congress 'Mr. C. Herbert, Hon. Sec. of the English AAA, officially represented this Association'. In some documents there is also reference to a 'Norman Jones' being present as a representative of the VAAA, but there is no mention of this gentleman in either the minutes of the VAAA or the

NSW Amateur Athletic Association. Further evidence that Herbert was the sole 'representative' of the athletic world in Australia may be determined from a report from 'Harrier', who wrote in the *Australasian* in August 1894: 'Among those present were Mr. C. Herbert (secretary of the British AAA and the official delegate of the Victorian AAA)'. The International Olympic Committee (IOC) was formed at the conclusion of the congress. Leonard Cuff of NZ, although unable to attend in person, had sent a letter of support to de Coubertin and he became the first IOC member in Australasia.

Richard Coombes, in an article in the *Referee* in January 1894 written under the pseudonym 'Prodigal', included the preliminary programme of the 1894 Congress which included Item 8—the re-establishing of the Olympic Games. In July 1895 'Prodigal' pleaded that 'If Australasia is to be represented at these [1896 Olympic Games] it is about time something in the shape of a pow-wow was decided upon'. Fortunately, Melbourne distance runner Edwin Flack won the 800 and 1500 metres track events at Athens in 1896, thereby establishing representation by Australia at the first Olympic Games. Coombes became an ardent supporter of the Olympic Games and replaced Cuff as the IOC member in Australasia in 1905. During a visit to Melbourne in May 1911 he broached the matter of establishing an Olympic committee there and suggested it should be a permanent body which would create an Olympic fund, select and approve representatives, and act in conjunction with similar bodies in the other States and NZ. The Victorian Olympic Council was formed at a meeting held at the Amateur Sports Club in Melbourne in September 1911.

By the beginning of 1913, Olympic councils had been formed in NSW, Tasmania, Victoria, and NZ, and Coombes reported in February of that year that the IOC was under the impression that an Australasian Olympic Council had been formed but that there was no such organisation. This was probably because such an organisation had been proposed at a conference in Wellington, NZ, in December 1911; the proposal had been rejected not because the various delegates were averse to the idea but because it was felt, as 'Argus' wrote, that the time was not yet ripe for such a council.

The Australian Olympic Council came into being at a meeting in Melbourne in January 1914 of representatives from the various Olympic councils: Victoria, NSW, Tasmania, Queensland (September 1913), and NZ. Although there was no Olympic body in SA, it was clear that there would be one soon, so it was decided to allow the two representatives voting rights. The title of the organisation was a major question. The 'Australasian Olympic Council' was submitted but was opposed by the NZ representatives, who considered that as the Dominion of NZ was a component part of the new body this title would be incorrect. Eventually, despite NZ's opposition, it was resolved that the title should be the 'Olympic Federation of Australia and NZ' as this would give the dominion an opportunity to join in the future. NZ successfully applied to the IOC in 1919 to become a separate National Olympic Committee, and Australian athletes who took part in the Olympic Games in Antwerp in 1920 were chosen by the Australian Olympic Federation (AOF). The AOF became known as the Australian Olympic Committee at the General Assembly in May 1990. The new title brought the AOC into line with the National Olympic Committee designation of other Olympic nations. The changes in the constitution also created a structure which was sports-based and in line with the IOC Charter which provided more direct input by the national sports governing bodies throughout Australia. At the same time, the restructuring recognised the ongoing contribution of the State Olympic councils whose nominees will, from 1993, be entitled to two executive positions.

The AOC comprises affiliated sports (those included in the summer and winter Olympic Games), recognised sports, and associated bodies; it has a particularly good relationship with the Australian Sports Commission, which was the principal provider of funds during the four years of the XXVIth Olympiad which culminated in the Barcelona Olympic Games, and the contribution of the Australian Institute of Sport as Technical Advisor to the AOC has been of particular significance. The objectives of the AOC are numerous, but the principal aim is to develop and protect the Olympic Movement in Australia in accordance with the Olympic Charter.

IJ

See **ALDERSON, Sir HAROLD**; **COOMBES, RICHARD**; **EVE, JAMES**; **Olympic Games**; **PATCHING, JULIUS**.

Australian Professional Rodeo Association (APRA). Rodeos have become increasingly popular throughout Australia since the beginning of the twentieth century, but it was not until towards the end of the Second World War in 1944 that the Australian Rodeo Club was formed in SA. Its rules were based on the American Cowboys Turtle Association which had been formed after a riders' strike at the Boston Gardens Rodeo in 1936. The NSW Rough Riders Association was also established in 1944. The magazine *Hoofs and Horns*, started by R. M. Williams and Lance Skuthorpe Junior to promote this arena sport, carried a notice advising that a meeting would be held in Sydney on 31 December 1944 with the intention of forming the Australian Rough Riders Association (ARRA). At that meeting representatives of the riders met with those of the Royal Agricultural Society (RAS) of NSW because it was the latter organisation which was the power behind the promotion of rodeos. The RAS did not concur with the requests of the riders, who wanted organised rodeos with standard rules, a panel of competent judges, and insurance coverage for injured contestants. However, the ARRA was formed in 1945 and competitions in saddle and bareback bronc-riding, bull-riding, bulldogging, and roping have been successfully staged at Australian championships. The ARRA changed its name to APRA in 1988.

PP and IJ

Australian Recreational and Sport Fishing Confederation (ARSFC). Throughout the nineteenth century opportunities to fish in Australia were limited by transport and by the necessity of most anglers to construct all their own equipment, but the ranks of anglers grew steadily. The first known amateur fishing club was formed in Victoria in 1867 and by 1907 the NSW Fisheries Department had published a guide for anglers in that State. Between the wars and following the development of motorised vessels and factory-produced fishing tackle the sport prospered. It is estimated that at present 4.5 million Australians fish at least once a year and there are more than eight hundred thousand keen anglers. Visitors to Australia in 1990 who fished exceeded sixty-eight thousand. The ARSFC was formed in 1984 to represent the interests of anglers and of their clubs and associations across the nation. The Australian Anglers Association and the Australian National Sport Fishing Association represent the interests of the general angler who fishes both inland and at sea; the other bodies cater for more specialised interests such as the following: Native Fish Australia, dedicated to the preservation of Australia's native species; the Fresh-Water Fishermen's Assembly, anglers dedicated to trout fishing; the Game-Fish Association of Australia, for those interested in pelagic marine fish such as marlin and tuna; the Australian Underwater Foundation, fc: spearfishers; and the Australian Casting Association, for promoting casting techniques. State and Territory fishing advisory councils were established to liaise with their respective governments on recreational fishing matters.

TB* and IJ

Australian Rugby Football League (ARFL). The Australian Rugby League Board of Control was formed in 1924 and became the ARFL in 1984. It controls national and international competition through associations in the NT and

every State in Australia except Tasmania. The Norfolk Island Rugby League is also affiliated with the ARFL. Australia was a foundation member of the International Rugby League Board which comprises Great Britain, NZ, France, and Papua New Guinea.

RAA and IJ

See **Rugby League**.

Australian Rugby Football Union (ARFU). Eighty years elapsed from the beginning of rugby football as an organised game in Australia until there was national co-ordination of the sport. It seems strange that for so long Australian rugby officials, even after the Australian team won a gold medal in the 1908 Olympics in London, did not have the foresight to form a national body. The controlling International Rugby Football Board (IRFB) which consisted of the four home unions of England, Wales, Ireland, and Scotland, was formed in 1890. It was not until 1926, however, that Australia was given an indirect form of representation on the board: delegates were appointed to the London-based Rugby Football Union (RFU) and those Englishmen reported on rugby in Australia and elsewhere around the world. England Test breakaway L. G. 'Bruno' Brown was one of those delegates. When Brown was elected president of the RFU in 1947–48, his appointment coincided with the offer of the IRFB to admit Australia, NZ, and South Africa as full members. But to secure IRFB membership Australia needed to form a national body and it was Brown who urged that all States be represented on the ARFU no matter how weak they were. The ARFU was formed in November 1949 with a constitution which was heavily weighted in favour of the NSW Rugby Union, which had 5 votes while Queensland had only 2. In 1989 new ground was broken and the Queensland Rugby Union was given an extra vote on the ARFU Council together with a vote given to the NT Rugby Union. The ARFU has been responsible for several initiatives in Australian and international rugby, including the establishment of the World Cup which was launched in Australia and NZ in 1987. The ARFU has also begun the changes in tour allowances and in the revamping of Regulation Four which now permits players to receive material reward for non-playing rugby activities such as the writing of books, public appearances, and speeches. In 1991, former Test referee and ARFU president Dr Roger Vanderfield was appointed president of the IRFB.

GC# and IJ

Australian Rules Football
Australian rules evolved as a new football code during the third quarter of the nineteenth century in Melbourne. From 1859 to 1877 it was

largely a Victorian game, and it continued to be known as Victorian rules—or Melbourne rules—until the 1880s. The most durable myth concerning the origins of Australian rules football is that it derives from Gaelic football, even though the latter was codified well after the Australian game. Unidentified forms of football had been played by Irish soldiers in Sydney in 1829 and by Victorian goldminers in the early 1850s, but these games probably resembled the ones played in English, Irish, and Scottish villages for centuries. They contributed nothing to the origins of Australian rules. Neither did the early schoolboy games played in Melbourne. A plaque in Yarra Park outside the MCG commemorates the match played there between Scotch College and Melbourne Grammar in August 1858 as the first organised game of football in Australia between schools or clubs (even though a match was played two months earlier between Melbourne Grammar and St Kilda Grammar). These historic schoolboy matches were not uniquely Australian, but were modelled on the football played in the English public schools, especially Rugby.

In between the schoolboy matches of June and August 1858 a man who umpired both games, Thomas Wentworth Wills, wrote a letter to a new sporting weekly, *Bell's Life in Victoria*. In his letter Wills, who had returned to Melbourne in December 1856 from seven years' schooling at Rugby, suggested that a men's football club be formed. Wills was an outstanding cricketer who could not abide six months without games in the winter, and he even suggested a rifle club as an alternative to football for sharpening the eye and tuning the reflexes. Shooting would not do much for general fitness, but it did accord with a prominent new concern, namely, promoting a sense of manly courage. Whereas Wills had tried with little success to promote football in 1857, his efforts were well received a year later when they had the added impetus of the new creed of Muscular Christianity, for *Tom Brown's Schooldays* was being avidly read in Melbourne in 1858.

After a handful of games among Melbourne cricketers and others in 1858, formal rules were delineated in May 1859. The seven men who formulated the first rules were all members of the Melbourne Cricket Club. Four of them served on its committee between 1858 and 1861, and several had played football in the British public schools. They had attended a variety of schools, but two of them (J. B. Thompson and W. J. Hammersley) did share a Cambridge University connection. Thus they emulated the Trinity College meeting of 1848 when they consciously perused the rules of Eton, Harrow, Winchester, and Rugby in May 1859 in order to create their own compromise. The codification of Australian rules in 1859

grafted Harrow and Winchester concepts on to Rugby's by determining that handling was permitted at any time, but that the man with the ball could run no further than was needed to kick the ball, i.e. two or three yards. If the ball was cleanly caught from a kick, the man who marked could take a free kick (without interference from opponents). Apparently for the sake of keeping the game simple, the founders postulated no offside rule; this facilitated the development of a more open style of play since team-mates as well as opponents could mark the ball. Perhaps as a concession to those who feared too much handling, throwing the ball was banned from the start. This eventually led to the unusual Australian method of handpassing, where the ball is held in one hand and punched with the closed fist of the other. The key innovation that made Australian rules unique was formalised in 1866 when a new rule once again allowed running with the ball (after a technical prohibition since 1860). However, the runner was required to touch the oval-shaped rugby ball (used exclusively after 1867) to the ground or bounce it every five or six yards. This rule ironically was designed to restrict the very fleet of foot, some of whom had been running up to forty yards with the ball, albeit illegally, before kicking it. One such harrier, H. C. A. Harrison (a cousin of Thomas Wentworth Wills) was delegated the task of writing the 1866 set of rules—which were thought to be the original until the 1859 rules were discovered in the early 1980s. Despite the re-enforced emphasis on handling, the rules were amended in 1874 so that goals had to be kicked rather than the ball carried through the goal-posts (which were seven yards apart, without a crossbar). Another rule change that year penalised players if they continued to hold the ball when tackled; holding an opponent, when he was not in possession of the ball, had been prohibited in 1859.

One of the most noteworthy features of Australian rules was that it tamed the most brutal aspects of rugby. Hacking and tripping—the aspects of play most likely to lead to serious injury—were banned in 1859; 'rabbiting' (stooping in order to up-end an opponent) and 'slinging' (throwing an opponent to the ground) were disallowed in the mid-1870s. Climatic arguments (less rainfall and harder grounds in Melbourne) have been posited to explain the Victorian city's propensity for a more open, flowing game in contrast to Sydney's preference for rugged, unadulterated rugby. The more likely explanation is that Australian rules, though based on rugby, was modified as an off-season pastime for middle-class cricketers. As J. B. Thompson declared, 'Black eyes don't look so well on Collins Street.' Blackened eyes and hacked shins were especially unsuitable for middle-class cricketers who could not afford injury-induced leisure time in the Antipodes. Even with these modifications, the Australian game in its first few years still bore a close resemblance to rugby and was commonly referred to in the local press as a variant of that code. Physical strength remained the single most important component of the game for the first decade or two, and newspaper commentators regularly compared competing teams in terms of average weight—a key factor in determining the outcome of scrimmages.

The new code was not played much by workers for its first twenty years because the lower classes did not have enough leisure time, nor could they afford to purchase a leather-encased pig's bladder. Village football had been a game played largely by peasants and handcraft workers, but not until the 1880s and 1890s with the advent of professionalism—and the gradual extension of the Saturday half-holiday from government offices and banks to include tradesmen and shopkeepers—did the lower classes participate in Australian rules football. What made Australian rules the people's game almost immediately, however, was that it was played in open parklands. This meant that for its first two decades there was no admission charge to watch the game, contrary to cricket and many other sports. The initial parkland venue of Australian rules was responsible not only for its popularity but also for much of its early development. The playing area was originally rectangular, for example, and did not become oval until the game shifted on to cricket grounds in the late 1870s and 1880s. Large parklands allowed for considerable length and width of playing area. Length was unlimited until 1866 when a maximum of 200 yards was imposed; width was restricted to 150 yards in the same year. The size and shape of the field helped make play essentially defensive. This defensive outlook continued to dominate Australian rules for two decades after a shift to oval fields eliminated the depth of forward pockets. Since goals were at a premium for the first half-century of Australian rules, incessant scrimmages were a common defensive tactic in the second half of the usually low-scoring, therefore close, games. Until 1869 the first team to score two goals won the match, regardless of whether it took two hours or two days. High marking, like high scoring, did not become a notable feature of Australian rules until the game moved out of the parklands in the 1880s and on to the cricket ovals, where there were no gum trees to restrict long or high kicks. Even then, the 'little mark' (after the ball had travelled only two or three yards) was a common means of moving the ball from a forward pocket toward the front of goals. The move to enclosed arenas coincided with charging the growing number of specta-

tors, including a substantial proportion of women. By the early 1870s crowds of 2–3000 at football matches were common, and occasionally as many as 10 000 watched. To realise the significance of these numbers, it is worth noting that only 2000 people watched the Football Association Cup in London in the mid-1870s. By 1880 when the FA Cup attracted 6000 spectators, 15 000 had already attended a football match in Melbourne, while 34 000 saw South Melbourne play Geelong in 1886.

In May 1877 seven of the Victorian clubs— Melbourne, Carlton, St Kilda (formerly South Yarra), Hotham (later North Melbourne), Albert Park (later South Melbourne), Geelong, and Barwon—formed the Victorian Football Association (VFA) in order to regulate the game throughout the State and to promote intercolonial matches. Simultaneously, the SA Football Association was established; it adopted the Victorian code, even though a soccer-style game had been prevalent in Adelaide two years earlier. Sydneysiders, however, consciously resisted a game that had originated in Melbourne, and rebuffed Victoria's proselytising activity. NSW's retention of rugby decisively swayed its northern neighbour towards that code for the sake of intercolonial competition, even though Victorian rules had prevailed in Queensland schools and football clubs until the early 1880s.

The VFA's limited success in spreading Australian rules football was matched by its inability to balance conflicting interests between its weaker and more powerful clubs. Most of the weak clubs attracted few spectators and small revenues, especially during the depression of 1893–95, and were consequently critics of the clandestine professionalism which was prevalent among most of the stronger clubs as they competed for success. Despite strenuous resistance by VFA secretary T. S. Marshall, the examples of England's Football Association (which accepted professionalism in 1885) and Rugby League (which was founded in 1895 largely over this issue) secured the future of professionalism in Australian rules football and foreshadowed the gradual demise of the VFA.

Making the game viable, commercial, and appealing to spectators was the main reason for founding the Victorian Football League (VFL) in 1897 by the eight clubs with the largest followings. Melbourne, Essendon, Geelong, Collingwood, South Melbourne, Fitzroy, Carlton, and St Kilda broke away from the VFA because they did not want to 'carry' the economically unviable clubs. Although the VFA continued to exist and took in new members to make up for the clubs which had left, the far more powerful VFL dominated Australian rules both in Victoria and throughout Australia. In order to make it more attractive to those who were paying to watch, the new VFL immediately altered the game, which was still very slow in the mid-1890s. Behind posts, originally twenty yards either side of the goal-posts, had been added in the 1870s as a defensive stratagem. Whenever the ball passed between a goal-post and a behind post, it could be cleared with a free kick. After 1897 each behind counted as a point (goals were henceforth worth 6 points). The tallying of behinds reduced the probability of a draw in low-scoring matches and the consequent reliance on defensive scrimmages. Two other modifications in 1897 were designed to speed up play and eliminate congestion. The number of players on the field was reduced from twenty to eighteen per side (a substitute, or nineteenth man, was first allowed in 1930, and a second substitute was permitted on the bench in 1946; until 1978, however, they could only replace injured players and could not be freely interchanged). Second, the 'little mark' was abolished; henceforth, a kick had to travel at least ten yards in order to be marked. The resultant longer kicking added to the high marking and made the game even more distinctive, open, and appealing as a spectacle. With the advent of the stab pass (a low-trajectory kick) in 1902 systematic play of an offensive nature was entrenched, and goal-scoring steadily increased.

By 1906 the game had progressed to the point where an Australian National Football Council (ANFC) was created to regulate interstate movement of players through clearances and permits. Although the ANFC organised interstate matches to determine a national Australian champion, the annual carnivals to find a winner were usually contests to see who came second to Victoria. Both the ANFC and its successor, the National Football League, have been controlled by the VFL, which has invariably determined the rules and served as a model for Australian rules nationally. Nonetheless, WA and SA, in particular, have maintained significant State competitions and have produced many outstanding players. A national competition finally materialised in the 1980s, but only under the aegis of Victorian football. In 1982 a team from South Melbourne played its home games in Sydney as a prelude to a full move there a year later. In 1987 two new interstate teams, Brisbane and West Australia, were created—the former by drafting existing VFL players, the latter by drawing mostly upon WA players. Thus, the twelve-team VFL was expanded into a fourteen-team national competition, and in 1990 the VFL altered its name to the Australian Football League. In 1991 an Adelaide-based team, the Crows, also entered the competition.

RS

See **Adelaide Oval**; **Amateurism**; **Arnold Medal**; BALDOCK, DARRELL; BARASSI, RON; BEAMES, PERCIVAL; BLIGHT, MALCOLM; **Boags Cascade Medal**; BROWNLOW, CHARLES; **Brownlow Medal**; BUNTON, HAYDN; BURNS, PETER; CAZALY, ROY; **Coleman Medal**; **Colliwobbles**; COVENTRY, SIDNEY; DYER, JACK; FARMER, GRAHAM; FARMER, KENNETH; **Field Trophy**; FITZGERALD, LEONARD; **Footscray Football Club Community Fights Back**; **Gardiner Medal**; **Grant Memorial Trophy**; **Grogan Medal**; HAFEY, TOM; HARRISON, HENRY; HICKEY, REGINALD; JESAULENKO, ALEX; KENNEDY, JOHN; KERLEY, DONALD; **Law**; LEE, WALTER; **Liston Trophy**; **Literature**; LUKE, KENNETH; **Magarey Medal**; MATTHEWS, LEIGH; MCCRACKEN, ALEXANDER; MCHALE, JAMES; MCNAMARA, DAVID; MINOGUE, DANIEL; **Morrish Medal**; **Mulrooney Medal**; MURRAY, KEVIN; **National Australian Football Council**; NICHOLLS, Sir DOUGLAS; PAGE, PERCY; **Phelan Medal**; PRATT, BOB; REYNOLDS, RICHARD; RICHARDS, LOUIS; ROBRAN, BARRIE; **Sandover Medal**; **Simpson Medal**; SKILTON, BOB; **Smith Medal**; **Smith Memorial Medal**; SMITH, NORMAN; **St Bernard's Disqualification**; STEWART, IAN; **St Kilda's Premiership**; **Strikes and Industrial Disputes**; **Tassie Medal**; THURGOOD, ALBERT; **Tied Grand Finals (VFL)**; **Titus Award**; TODD, JOHN; **Unionism**; **VFL Grand Final 1946**; **VFL Park**; **Victorian Amateur Football Association**; **Wander Medal**; WHITTEN, TED; WILLIAMS, FOSTER; WILLS, THOMAS; WORRALL, JOHN.

Australian School Sports Council (ASSC). School sports associations (primary and secondary) have been established in some States for over one hundred years. NSW celebrated its Centenary of School Sport in 1989, while the primary association in Victoria was established early in the century. Interstate school sporting competitions based on selected representative teams can be traced back to the 1920s in Australian football and netball. Rapid expansion occurred in the 1970s, creating a need for some organising body to co-ordinate these exchanges. The Australian Primary School Sports Association and the Australian Secondary Schools Sports Federation (ASSSF) were formed. In 1981 the ASSC was established to act as the parent body for all school sport and as the focal point for an expanding organisation. The organisation was formed, conducted, and supported by teachers who took the initiative and then sought the approval of their respective departments of education. The feature of being teacher-driven is still the strength of the respective state schools sports councils and the ASSC. Their affairs are conducted by the people most concerned with the conduct of school sport. The first national executive director was appointed in 1984 after receipt of a grant to the ASSC from the Australian Sports Commission. As its affairs became more involved, and as more teachers required leave to participate in its activities, the Conference of Directors-General of Education took an interest in its activities; a committee of review was appointed in 1986 to report on its activities and make recommendations on streamlining the development and delivery of school sport in Australia. The committee's report endorsed the role of the ASSC as the major co-ordinating body and recommended that the three national school sporting associations (ASSC, Australian Public School Sports Association, and ASSSF) be reconstituted as one body, namely the ASSC. George Hay became the inaugural president. The endorsed aims of the ASSC following the review included providing a forum for discussion and agreement about sports competition between States; developing and making recommendations about sports policy to directors-general of education; co-ordinating and monitoring interstate competitions; acting as the authorising body for international school sport; and acting as a lobby and a focus for Australian school sport. The ASSC has agreed on policies on such issues as competition, conduct of events, and codes of behaviour for players, teachers, coaches, parents, spectators, administrators, officials, and the media. In 1991 the Conference of Directors-General commissioned a review of the place of interstate sporting competitions in school sport; the report issued in September 1991 indicated that 'interstate sporting competitions do have a place in contemporary school education'.

GH* and IJ

See **Children**.

Australian Ski Federation (ASF). The establishment of a national skiing federation was first considered in 1926, but it was not until 1932 that the Australian National Ski Federation (ANSF) was formed, its founding members being the Ski Council of NSW, the Ski Club of Victoria, and the Tasmania Ski Council. The ACT, through the Canberra Alpine Club, became affiliated in 1939 and in 1985 SA joined through the SA Skier's Federation. The ANSF affiliated with the Fédération Internationale de Ski (FIS) soon after. The ANSF's initial responsibilities were international relations, national championships, national team rules, and national proficiency tests, although these tasks were usually delegated to one State. The first interdominion championship was contested in 1936 between Australia and NZ; this was a most significant event because it was the first international ski competition in the southern hemisphere. Australia hosted its first international ski competition in 1937 with competitors from NZ, Austria, USA, and Australia. During the period 1940–44 ANSF was not operative, except that it resigned from membership of FIS because of the perception that this international body was dominated by Nazism. ANSF reaffiliated with FIS after the war. Australia first took part in the Winter Olympics in 1952 and a team has been sent to every Winter Olympic Games since. The first FIS-sanctioned international competitions to be held in Australia were in 1969. A new constitution was adopted in 1976 and the name was changed to the ASF. The first World Cup of Skiing to be held in Australia was conducted at Thredbo in 1989 and in 1991 Australia's first long-distance Worldloppet cross-country race was conducted at Fall's Creek in Victoria. After a comprehensive review in 1990, the ASF is undertaking an extensive restructuring which will affect the federation and constituent State bodies.

MS* and IJ

See **Skiing**.

Australian Soccer Federation (ASF). The first administrative soccer body in Australia was the Anglo-Australian Association in Melbourne in 1884, with the first colony-wide organisation being the NSW British Football Association which began in 1898. Both these bodies applied to the English Football Association (EFA) for direct affiliation, which was granted and led to the EFA providing development grants to promote the game in Australia. Football Association (Australia) was established in October 1923 and clubs around Australia became affiliated through their district associations. But many breakaway soccer organisations were formed over the next forty years because of dissatisfaction with the standard of administration within the code. The last of these breakaway bodies eventually became the ASF, which was established following a mass exodus in 1957 from the Australian Soccer Association Limited by clubs unhappy with the progress being made by soccer in Australia. Every major club gradually joined the revolt and the ASF was formally established in 1961. The ASF manages all aspects of the soccer code of football including its marketing, promotion, development, and all international activities. Members of ASF include every State and Territory association as well as amateur, junior, and women's soccer organisations.

PK and IJ

See **Soccer**.

Australian Society for Sports History (ASSH) was formed at the fourth 'Sporting Traditions' Conference, held at the MCG in July 1983. The broad objectives of the society are to promote discussion and research on sporting traditions with special reference to Australia and to organise meetings and publish materials to advance interest and scholarship in this area. Colin Tatz was the first president of ASSH and Wray Vamplew was the inaugural editor of its journal, *Sporting Traditions*, which first appeared in November 1984. ASSH emerged out of the biennial Sporting Traditions Conferences, first held at the University of NSW (1977 and 1979) and at La Trobe University (1981).

RC

Australian Society of Sport Administrators (ASSA) was formed in 1983 under inaugural president Gus Staunton. It views administration as the pivotal point of Australian sport and believes that in order to improve the standard of sport in Australia it is important for both salaried and honorary administrators to belong to a professional association. The society aims to advance the quality of sports administration by providing resource information and direction for further education and training, and opportunities for the exchange of knowledge and ideas. Membership is open to sport administrators, academics and public servants employed in sport-related occupations, and tertiary students engaged in studies in sport, recreation, leisure, and similar subjects. Student members are eligible for the annual ASSA Scholarship. *Sportsnetwork* is the quarterly national journal of ASSA and is distributed widely throughout Australia directly to members, and to other interested organisations and institutions. ASSA has eight State chapters providing services to members in many areas. Formal education courses developed by ASSA for its National Accreditation Scheme for Sport Administrators (NASSA) are conducted in most States. These NASSA courses are conducted in liaison with the various State Government departments of sport, Technical and Further Education colleges, universities, and local councils in order to avoid duplication of effort and to maximise the use of resources.

HK

Australian Sport and Recreation Association for Persons with an Intellectual Disability (AUSRAPID) was formed in September 1986, the work of an action committee which had arisen from the Recreation Project undertaken by the Australian Association on Mental Retardation (AAMR). The committee comprised representatives from State departments of recreation and sport and delegates from AAMR, the Special Olympics, and State associations concerned with recreation and sport for people with intellectual disabilities. The aim of AUSRAPID is to provide greater sporting and recreational opportunities for people with an intellectual disability by fostering family and community awareness of their needs, by co-ordinating the services which provide such opportunities, and by encouraging governments to allocate funds for AUSRAPID's programmes. All States and the ACT have associations which are affiliated with AUSRAPID. Associations were formed in each State as follows: 1982 SA; 1983 Queensland, NSW, and WA; 1985 Tasmania, the ACT, and Victoria. At first AUSRAPID was dependent on funds contributed by State associations; then it received support from the Australian Society for the Study of Intellectual Disability and from the Federal Government through the National Committee on Sport and Recreation for the Disabled. In 1988 AUSRAPID became a member of the International Sports Federation for Persons with Mental Handicap, thereby providing opportunities for élite athletes to participate in international competition. In 1988 the ASC became the principal funding agency for AUSRAPID.

Links with national recreation and governing bodies of sports have been instrumental in encouraging the integration of people with intellectual disability into the activities of these generic bodies, which include All Australia Netball Association, Athletics Australia, Australian Swimming, Australian Gymnastics Federation, and Australian Tenpin Bowling Congress. An Australian team travelled to Harnosand, Sweden, in 1989 to compete in the first World Championships in Athletics and Swimming for Mentally Handicapped Persons. Since the inception of AUSRAPID several State associations have changed their titles. In recent years AUSRAPID has become a member of the Australian Confederation of Sports for the Disabled, and was an inaugural member of the Australian Paralympic Association. AUSRAPID is involved with the selection of the first Australian team to compete in a Paralympics, at Madrid in 1992.

ML and IJ

See **Australian Blind Sports Association**; **Australian Deaf Sports Federation**.

Australian Sports Commission (ASC). The establishment of a sports commission to provide a more co-ordinated approach to sports development in Australia was a platform in the Australian Labor Party's 1983 election policy. The ASC was established initially as an office in the Federal Department of Sport, Recreation and Tourism in September 1984 and eventually as a statutory authority from July 1985. Its primary objectives are to maximise funding for sport from the private sector, to provide leadership in the development of Australia's performance in international sport, and to increase the level of participation in sport by the non-élite. The ASC raises and administers funds through the Australian Sports Foundation, assisting sporting associations, élite athletes, and various working parties, as well as sponsoring development programmes and research projects such as the *Oxford Companion to Australian Sport*.

JO'H

See **Applied Sports Research Programme**; **Australian Council for Health, Physical Education and Recreation**; **Government Policy**.

Australian Sports Drug Agency. In 1985, following the pioneering survey conducted by the Australian Sports Medicine Federation, the Federal Government established the National Programme on Drugs in Sport (Anti-Drugs Campaign) under the control of the Australian Sports Commission. As a first step against the widespread use of drugs, shown by the survey to be at all levels in Australian sport, the programme provided expert advice, initiated a drug-detection scheme, produced educational materials, and established links with similar agencies in other countries. In 1988, after a review, it was decided that the Australian Sports Drug Agency should be established as an independent statutory body. The Australian Sports Drug Agency Bill passed through Parliament on 21 December 1990. The agency is now responsible for the development and conduct of all components of the drug detection programme in Australia, the development and implementation of educational programmes, international liaison, research, and the provision of advice to the government. The agency's office is in Canberra.

RJP

See **Drugs**.

Australian Sports Medicine Federation. Central to the development of sports medicine in Australia has been the Australian Sports Medicine Federation which was formed in 1963 by the amalgamation of the Australian Sports Medicine Association and the Australian Federation of Sports Medicine. The former sprang out of the medical arrangements for the 1956 Melbourne Olympics; the latter began in 1961 as a NSW breakaway group who felt that the association was overly dominated by Victorians. Eventually it was acknowledged that Australian sports medicine, barely established as it was and with insufficient trained personnel, could not afford two rival bodies and a merger was organised. At first membership was restricted to medical graduates, with provision for a further 10 per cent being drawn from suitably qualified non-medical graduates. Over time, however, membership has broadened and now the roll of about four thousand includes not only medical practitioners but health care professionals such as dentists and physiotherapists, sports scientists including exercise physiologists and physical educators, and also athletes and coaches. It thus covers a wide range of activities related to sport including diet and nutrition, physical and mental preparation for sport, health education for active participants, and the treatment and rehabilitation of activity-related injuries.

WV

See **Drugs**; **Sports Medicine**.

Australian Surfriders Association (ASA). The first surfriders' association was established in 1963 by five well-known surfing identities of that era: John Witzig, Bernard 'Midget' Farrelly, Snow McAllister, Rodney Sumpter, and Bob Evans. Initially based in NSW, its main purpose was to develop a national competition for selecting a team of surfers to challenge internationally. This was achieved in 1964 when the first Australian titles and the first world surfing titles successfully ran consecutively at Manly Beach, Sydney. These events in 1964 were also significant because all States were represented at the national titles and a meeting of State delegates was convened which resulted in the formation of the ASA. From that year, annual general meetings of the ASA were held in conjunction with the national titles until 1987 when it was decided to hold future annual general meetings six months before the titles so that rule changes could be more effective. In the 1980s the ASA developed steadily, especially with funds generated from several major surfing events; for example the ASA Victorian branch conducts the Bell's Beach Easter Classic, which has become the world's longest-running pro event and is rated as a Triple A professional event on the world circuit. The ASA has hosted three world titles since its inception: Manly in 1964; Bell's Beach in 1970; and Gold Coast in 1982. As one of forty-two member nations comprising the International Surfing Association (ISA), ASA annually selects teams in open and youth (scholastic) areas for international competition. ASA now represents more than thirty-five thousand competitive and recreational surfers throughout Australia, providing competition at regional, State, national, and international level. It is also responsible for junior development/safety and coach education programmes. With the support of the Australian Sports Commission, national co-ordinated programmes such as coaching accreditation, administration, judging, and development seminars are conducted. Since 1985 the ASA have conducted polls and presented awards to the Australian Surfing Hall of Fame.

CC* and IJ

See **FARRELLY, BERNARD**; **Surfing**.

Australian Swimming Incorporated is the central body which co-ordinates and controls the activities of all State and Territory swimming associations as well as those of water polo, diving, synchronised swimming, AUSSI masters swimming, and the Australian Swimming Coaches Association. From 1862 to 1909 there was no central controlling body and the Australasian swimming championships were conducted under the terms of an agreement entered into between the swimming associations of NZ, NSW, Victoria, Queensland, and WA. The NSW Amateur Swimming Association decided in 1908 that the time was opportune to establish a central controlling body for the sport. In 1909 a conference was held in Sydney with James Taylor as chairman at which delegates from NSW, Queensland, Victoria, WA, and SA were present; the outcome was the formation of the Amateur Swimming Union of Australia (ASUA). Foundation members were NSW, Victoria, and SA; Queensland, Tasmania, and WA joined the union in 1913. ASUA has been an affiliated member of the Fédération Internationale de Natation Amateur since 1909, and jurisdiction over the affiliated associations and their members in Australia is vested in Australian Swimming Incorporated, its name since 1985.

SA* and IJ
See **Swimming**.

Australian Tenpin Bowling Congress (ATBC). In late 1961 and early in 1962, under the guidance of Walter Rachuig, an executive director of the American Bowling Congress, Australian tenpin bowlers met in several major cities throughout Australia to organise and elect office-bearers in area associations with the aim of creating a national association. Committees were established in Melbourne, Brisbane, Newcastle, Broken Hill, Wollongong, and Sydney. The ATBC was duly formed at a meeting in Sydney. Two bowling manufacturing companies, AMF and Brunswick, assisted Rachuig in his travel to Australia and he fulfilled expectations through his assistance in the formation of various area associations making up the ATBC. His contribution to Australian tenpin bowling has been commemorated since 1963 through the annual Walter Rachuig Trophy which is awarded at the three-day national championships. The first ATBC national championships were held in Sydney in 1962, with forty teams competing at Rushcutter Bowl. These championships now attract more than three thousand entries and usually take up two bowling centres for over two weeks. The ATBC's strength lies in the commitment of hundreds of honorary workers in its affiliated associations around the country. Some other associations were formed in Brisbane, Sydney, and Melbourne as a result of a 'split' in 1977, but although these bodies are not recognised as official administrative arms of the sport, they nevertheless perform their function of serving members in many similar ways to the ATBC. The ATBC receives State and Federal Government grants following its acceptance in 1965 as the official affiliated body with the Fédération Internationale des Quilleurs (FIQ). The FIQ charter allows participation by ATBC bowlers in Asian zone and world championships and other FIQ-approved tournaments such as the American Machine and Foundry Bowling World Cup.

SJ and IJ
See **Tenpin Bowling**.

Australian Tertiary Education Sports Association (ATESA) evolved in three separate stages over twenty years from 1968. The initial impetus was the organisation of an annual athletics carnival held over several days and combined with an unusual event called the Wakehurst relays. The latter had a team format where in each event the winning performance was the combined score of individual scores, that is, the winning high-jump performance might have been a score of 4.08 metres which was derived from the sum of the two individual scores of 1.9 metres and 2.18 metres. The idea of this format was to ensure a larger number of competitors; it also gave the opportunity for a team of good competitors to challenge a team with one excellent competitor and average supporting participants. These carnivals were hosted initially by the Australian School of Pacific Administration and were held for several years at the Narrabeen Lakes in Sydney. Gradually other sports were added to the programme: aquatics was introduced in 1975 and women's and men's gymnastics in 1979. These competitions took place between students at colleges of advanced education and were hosted by the Australian College of Physical Education in Sydney, but then they began to be rotated throughout the States. The Australian Colleges of Advanced Education Sports Association (ACAESA) was formed following a meeting of team managers who attended the Intercollegiate Championships in Sydney in 1978. The championships in Adelaide were the first to be held under the banner of the newly formed ACAESA and a record number of twenty-four colleges representing all States in Australia was in attendance. ACAESA introduced the concept of Summercol and Wintercol—annual events including sports which were normally played in those seasons. A competitive team attending the Intercols would normally have a squad of 150 participants. In 1989 the name ACAESA was changed to ATESA to reflect the changing status of the members, some of which had amalgamated with universities while others had been accredited with university status. The executives of both ATESA and the Australian University Sports Association have been meeting for several years with the aim of consolidating the administration of those bodies which organise university sport. The final stage of this process was completed in March 1992 when both organising bodies of university sport dissolved and reconstituted as one body called Australian Universities Sports Federation.

TC and IJ

Australian Underwater Federation (AUF) is the national sporting organisation for all underwater activities in Australia. It arose from a gathering of skindiving enthusiasts at Long Reef, NSW, in April 1946 which formed the Underwater Spear Fishermen's Association of NSW. The name was changed to the AUF in December 1966. Most of the early activities were related to spearfishing: there were even attempts to have this activity included as a demonstration sport at the 1956 Olympic Games in Melbourne. Rules were also being formulated at this time for the inaugural Aqua-Lung Championships of Australia to allow competition using scuba (self-contained underwater breathing apparatus). Finswimming was recommended for inclusion in AUF National Titles in 1968 and underwater hockey (formerly known as octopush) was included in 1974. Through its three committees—sport, technical, and scientific—the Australian Underwater Federation monitors standards, diving instruction, safety, equipment, photography, accidents, sports competition, and scientific applications of diving in various sports. Through its Project Sticky-Beak it collects information on all diving incidents regardless of their significance and supports research and collection of data on diving-related problems. This enables it to represent the diving community in matters such as poor equipment design, substandard instruction, the recreational diving industry, and problems that may arise in dealing with government and private enterprise.

GB* and IJ

See **Skindiving and Spearfishing**.

Australian Universities Sports Association (AUSA) represents the sports union or equivalent organisation in every university in Australia. The history of AUSA can be traced from its inception in 1921 when the universities of Adelaide, Melbourne, Sydney, and Queensland decided that an umbrella organisation should be instituted to foster sport among all universities in Australia. Its main purpose is to organise and govern sport between member universities, provide effective communication with the broader sports community, and increase public awareness and support in university sport. AUSA establishes its policy through an annual meeting of its council, which is comprised of a delegate from each member association or union. A 1989 review of AUSA has resulted in changes in administration and sport delivery. A five-member board of directors is elected annually to implement council policy under four main areas: planning and development, marketing, competitions, and finance. Recently AUSA implemented a new sports structure involving approximately forty-five sports organised into regional, national, and international competition. Competition is based on regional conferences where all university teams compete. Successful teams at these conferences then compete at national level. AUSA also offers opportunities for student athletes and teams to compete overseas in international student competitions such as the World University Games (Universiades) or World Student Championships. AUSA has close links with Australia's national sports governing bodies, the ASC, and the AIS. AUSA's membership will be expanded following the awarding of university status to many more tertiary institutions and the amalgamation of others. In March 1992 AUSA and ATESA dissolved and reconstituted as one body called the Australian Universities Sports Federation (AUSF) which services over four hundred and fifty thousand members of Australian universities.

PK and IJ

The Australian Way of Sport
Australian sport as we know it has evolved from the mixture of games, traditions and ideologies brought here after white settlement from various countries and cultures. The most popular sports, cricket, rugby, soccer, tennis, golf, horse-racing and so on, came with the original white population from Britain, along with strongly held ideologies such as amateurism and the character-building properties of games, both of which persisted as motivating forces for decades. In more recent times America has contributed its games, such as basketball, and its sporting practices as well: tackle counts and cheerleaders in rugby league, and general show biz in basketball. Many other countries have contributed to Australian sporting culture: gymnastics emanated from Germany, calisthenics from Sweden, and surfboard-riding from Polynesia. Sports invented in Australia are by comparison relatively few; Australian rules football is the one major sport developed in this country. Australia can also claim to have invented speedway and to have created a few minor sports such as trugo.

There are many myths about the Australian way of sport. Keith Dunstan has argued that Australians have a unique passion for sport, though it is doubtful whether Australians are any more obsessed than North Americans or the populations of any number of other industrialised societies. Others have claimed that Australian sport is egalitarian and a great leveller, ignoring how much sporting traditions have been shaped by race, class, and gender—Australian sport has, for instance, always been more accessible to men than to women. There is also the myth that Australian sporting performance is exceptional. While this has been true in some periods, such as the 1950s, it has been less true at other times.

Although much of Australian sporting culture has been borrowed, the different physical environment and society in which it has taken root has given rise to a distinctive Australian culture of sport. While Australian sport may not be quite as unique as many Australians believe, there is an identifiable Australian way of sport. Many examples of this distinctiveness can be provided. Barry Andrews has pointed out that there is a rich stock of Australian sporting language, citing, for instance, the statement that a batsman could 'safely tug four bits off the deck at the WACA without fear of getting rissoled for a gozzer by a guzunder'. Australia has developed its own tradition of irreverent barracking and barrackers in which a particular Australian humour is manifest—cutting down the pretentious to size. Sports arenas and venues have particular features and even an Australian ambience. Cricket grounds in Melbourne are far larger for instance than their English equivalents. Bay 13 at the Melbourne Cricket Ground and the Hill at the Sydney Cricket Ground developed their own crowd cultures before they were dismantled. Other events, such as surfing at Bell's Beach, the Sydney to Hobart yacht race, and the City to Surf Fun Run make use of the particular Australian environment. There are also distinctive techniques and ways of approaching sport which have developed in Australia such as the Australian 'crawl' in swimming and the tradition of open or 'running' rugby. The greater bounce of Australian wickets has given more encouragement to leg-spin bowling in cricket than is the case in England. Australia also has a rich tradition of sporting heroes and heroines, each of whom has expressed some aspect of Australian popular culture. Because of Australia's colonial heritage Australians have always set great store on heroes and heroines who have defeated the mother country, particularly on its own ground. As a small player in world politics great emphasis has also been set on success over the might (and often what is viewed as chicanery) of the USA, whether it be in the Davis Cup, yachting, or boxing.

There are a number of historical reasons why sport has become a central element of Australian culture. European settlement of Australia coincided with the eighteenth-century expansion of sporting culture in Britain, when it became more fashionable and popular then ever before. Many sports, such as cricket, horse-racing, golf, boxing, and pedestrianism, became better organised at this time. Many great British sporting institutions, such as the Marylebone Cricket Club, the Royal and Ancient Golf Club, and the Jockey Club, were founded in the eighteenth century.

Organised sport was also an integral part of the Australian social landscape during the decades from the gold rushes to the First World War, critical decades in terms of Australian cultural formation and the emergence of Australian nationalism. This was the era when small towns expanded into pulsating cities, when new communities were created in country towns and suburbs, and when a larger network of primary, secondary, and tertiary institutions emerged. Many influential Australians—politicians, educators, clergymen, social thinkers, and businessmen—believed that sport could play an important role in an emerging Australian culture. They patronised sporting clubs, allocated prime land for sporting venues, preached the value of sporting participation, and articulated the ideals which underpinned sport. They encouraged the games revolution and the development of sport as a mass entertainment industry from the 1850s onwards. Many of Australia's great sporting traditions and clubs date from 1850–1914, such as the Melbourne Cup, the beginning of Test cricket, and the Stawell Gift. The nexus between sport and community was established in a myriad ways. The Collingwood Football Club, for example, provided a focus for an emerging working-class suburb, while the Royal Sydney Golf Club provided an expression for those who regarded themselves as establishment Sydney.

Possibly Australia's greatest contribution to world sport has been in aquatic sports. The climate, together with the existence of many attractive beaches and waterways, has provided important incentives for developments in this arena. Australian scullers, many of whom learned to row on fast-flowing coastal rivers, dominated world sculling for some decades in the later nineteenth century, producing a succession of world champions. Australia was also one of the leading nations in the rise of competitive swimming, which took off around the turn of the century, with Australia winning the first Olympic swimming event for women in 1912. Imported British attitudes towards the beach and the sea have been greatly modified in Australia. Bathing machines and manufactured entertainment beside the beach and on piers were discarded in the first decade of the twentieth century when the cult of surf bathing and sun-tanning became popular. Australia developed its distinctive surf lifesaving clubs and traditions. Australia has continued to play a leading role in surf culture: Australian men, and more recently women, were prominent in surfboard-riding and the Ironman event from the 1970s.

While it is evident then that much of Australian sporting culture has been imported, and traditions and techniques will continue to be borrowed, it has always been substantially modified and adapted to suit Australian needs. Australia has developed a rich sporting culture of its own which has been closely interwoven into the fabric of broader Australian culture.

RC

See **Amateurism**; **Australian Rules Football**; **Bell's Beach**; **Ethnic Influences**; **Gender**; **Ironman**; **Rowing and Sculling**; **Speedway**; **Surfing**; **Surf Lifesaving**; **Swimming**; **Sydney to Hobart Yacht Race**; **Trugo**.

Australian Women's Bowling Council (AWBC) had its inaugural meeting in Sydney in 1947 with representatives from the six State bowling associations. The first AWBC applied to the British Empire and Commonwealth Games Association for the admission of women bowlers in the games of 1958 and 1962 but were unsuccessful; women were, however, included in the Commonwealth Games in Brisbane in 1982. The AWBC promoted the idea of forming the International Women's Bowling Board, the first meeting of which was held in NSW in December 1969, with Australians being elected as president and secretary. The AWBC has approximately one hundred and fifty thousand members who belong to 2200 clubs.

MF and IJ

See **Australian Bowls Council**; **Lawn Bowls**.

Australian Women's Cricket Council (AWCC). In 1905 delegates from over twenty clubs formed the Victorian Ladies' Cricket Association, with Vida Goldstein as founding president. Unfortunately this association disbanded during the First World War although it had been responsible for the staging of the first interstate matches. State women's cricket associations re-formed after the war: Victoria in 1923, NSW in 1927, Queensland in 1929, and SA and WA in 1930. The AWCC was formed in 1931. Founding affiliates were NSW, Victoria, and Queensland; SA and WA affiliated in 1934.

The AWCC was established to promote and regulate the development of women's cricket throughout Australia. It initiated the first Australian championships, staged in Sydney in 1931 between NSW, Victoria, and Queensland. In 1934 the first international series was held when England accepted the invitation of the AWCC to tour Australia. Since that time, the AWCC has conducted open-age national championships, hosted international touring teams and staged the fourth World Cup. Membership has varied since the AWCC's inception: although it was a founding member, the Queensland Women's Cricket Association disbanded in 1962 and did not rejoin until 1976. The ACT and Tasmania did not establish associations until 1977 and 1982 respectively, although Tasmanian women had been playing cricket since the early part of this century. The AWCC was actively involved in the 1984–85 introduction of Kanga Cricket into primary schools as it realised the advantages which could be gained from introducing cricket to girls in the early years.

ES* and IJ

See **Cricket**; **Women's Cricket—First Test**.

Australian Women's Soccer Association (AWSA). Formed in Sydney in 1974 when five teams from NSW, northern NSW, WA, Queensland, and Victoria met for the first national championship, AWSA now consists of nine members. Each member is responsible for the organisation of its local and State soccer competitions for females over the age of 12. AWSA is affiliated with the Australian Soccer Federation, the Oceania Women's Football Confederation, and the Confederation of Australian Sport. It now holds national championships annually for each of its three age divisions (under-16, under-19, and open). The first international appearance by an Australian women's soccer team was in 1978 when the senior team competed in the first World Women's Invitation Football Tournament in Taiwan. Since then Australian teams have taken part in numerous international competitions and Test series against NZ. The national senior team was ranked eighth in the world in 1990. There are more than thirty thousand females playing soccer in organised competitions throughout Australia at district, school, and tertiary institutions.

KD, HR, and IJ

14 A cheer-squad at the Collingwood versus Melbourne Australian Rules match, 20 April 1992.

15 Barracking is enhanced at AFL games with huge banners extolling the virtues of the respective teams.

16 Australian Rules Football quickly became a popular spectator sport, and by 1883 there was a reversible grandstand at the MCG to accommodate the crowds that watched the matches on an adjacent oval.

17 Arthur Streeton's painting, *The National Game* (1889),
is a colourful and modernistic depiction of football.

18 The art of S. T. Gill, such as his 1854 watercolour,
McLaren's Boxing Saloon, Main Road, Ballarat, highlighted
the sporting activities of Australians in the middle of the
nineteenth century.

19 The Australian Gallery of Sport and Olympic
Museum, Australia's first national multi-sport museum, is
situated at the MCG.

20 The Olympic Museum contains displays of Olympic costumes, sports equipment, documents and medals.

B

BACHLI, DOUGLAS WILLIAM, MBE (1922–), born Albert Park, Victoria, was a remarkable golfer who within two years of beginning his game at Royal Canberra had a handicap of 5. He won three Victorian amateur titles, one Queensland amateur, and numerous State foursomes titles. His major achievements were winning the Australian amateur in 1948 and again in 1962, then the crown jewel, the British amateur, in 1954, the first and only Australian player to do so. He beat the great American Bill Campbell 2 and 1 at Muirfield. He was in the Australian team that won the inaugural Commonwealth teams event at St Andrews in 1954 and was a member of the national team which won the Eisenhower Cup at St Andrews in 1958. He regards his 'finest streak of golf' as the first 9 at Royal Sydney. As defending champion, he was playing Harry Berwick in the third round of the Australian amateur in 1949. His card read: 3–3–3–3–4–2–4–3–4 = 29. This record remains intact.

CT

Badminton

Badminton was first played in Australia in the Army Drill Hall at Fremantle, WA, in 1900. From its beginning as a leisure activity, badminton grew as a sport and was most popular in church groups, especially the Congregational and Church of England denominations in both WA and Victoria: the high-ceilinged church halls were an ideal venue. Despite the intervention of the First World War, associations continued to be established, especially in metropolitan areas. In Victoria the main metropolitan associations soon after the war were Church of England, Congregational, Methodist, Presbyterian, Central, Footscray-Williamstown (later Western Suburbs), and Northern Districts. Victorian championships were held in 1924 and by the mid-1920s WA and Tasmania had State associations. In 1932 Victoria brought all their associations under the umbrella of the Victorian Badminton Association and removed sexism by calling all those who participated 'players'. The first interstate game was played in 1929 in Melbourne between Victoria and Tasmania and these contests continued until 1935 when the Australian Badminton Association (ABA) was formed, with Reginald Ede Clendinnen as president. The interstate competition is now played between all States for the Clendinnen

Shield. Australia made its first overseas tour in 1938 to NZ and won the Whyte Trophy; Australia has won most of these biennial trans-Tasman encounters. Australia's performances in international competition have been creditable since it began participating in events conducted by the International Badminton Federation. The greatest success was in the 1986 Commonwealth Games, when a gold, silver, and bronze medal were won. Australia has been notable in its involvement in the administration of the International Badminton Federation, with Roy Ward being vice-president since 1979 and editor of *World Badminton*.

RW and IJ

BAKER, REGINALD LESLIE ('Snowy') (1884–1953), born Sydney, acquired his nickname because of his blond hair. An all-round sportsman excelling at rugby union, swimming, athletics, and water polo, it was as a boxer that Baker made his name. After taking up boxing in 1902 he was NSW amateur middleweight champion by 1905. In 1906 he won the Australian amateur middleweight and heavyweight titles on the same night. Baker was unable to compete in the British 1906 championships due to pneumonia but boxed in the 1908 London Olympics. He lost a closely contested fight to J. W. H. T. Douglas, later better known as an English cricketer. In partnership with his younger brother William Harald, Baker subsequently became a sports entrepreneur when they bought the Sydney Stadium and promoted boxing. The tall and handsome Baker then went to Hollywood to further a budding film career. Although he appeared in a few movies, he achieved more success as a coach and instructor. He died in Los Angeles.

GC*

BALDOCK, DARELL JOHN (1938–), born East Devonport, Tasmania, played 119 games with St Kilda between 1962 and 1968, captaining the famous team which won St Kilda's only premiership in 1966. Only 179 centimetres tall and weighing 84 kilograms, Baldock played at centre half-forward and was one of the game's classiest players. He seemed to be a magician who had the ball on a string and who made opponents appear foolish and inept. Baldock must be one of the most skilful players never to have won a Brownlow Medal, finishing equal second in 1963 and 1965. He coached

St Kilda for sixty-two games between 1987 and 1989 for eighteen wins and forty-four losses.

BD

Ballooning

The first recorded successful ascent in Australia was made in 1871 by Thomas Gale and John Allen in Sydney. Vincent Patrick Taylor (also known as 'Captain Penfold') completed dozens of ascents around the country before the First World War. The Australian Ballooning Federation now co-ordinates the sport nation-wide, and regular meetings are held between March and October in Victoria, SA, NSW, and WA. Peter Vizzard of NSW has won the world hot-air balloon championship, and the main domestic competitions are held at Canowindra, NSW, at Easter, and the Seppeltsfield Meeting in the Barossa Valley each May.

KM

BANNERMAN Brothers. Described as a 'pocket Hercules', Charles Bannerman (1851–1930) was a diminutive right-hand batsman who scored Test cricket's first century, in the first Test in Melbourne in 1877. Born at Woolwich, Kent, he was rated by English captain James Lillywhite as the world's greatest player behind W. G. Grace. Famed for his aggressive and, at that time, unfashionable front-foot play, Charles was lionised by the colonial press and became the first 'star' of Australian cricket. His career was both dramatic and short-lived. Apparently unable to cope with public adulation he vanished from Test cricket after just three matches. He died of heart failure in Sydney. Charles's last Test in 1879 was Alexander Chalmers Bannerman's (1854–1924) first. Born in Sydney, 'Alick' Bannerman was a serious and conservative man with a reputation for bluntness on and off the field. According to W. G. Grace, Alick's dour and stonewalling approach 'vexed the soul of every bowler who opposed him'. His career proved more durable than that of his more famous older brother: he played twenty-eight Tests, including six tours to England. He died at his home in Paddington, Sydney.

DM

BARASSI, RON (1937–) is one of the best-known names in Australian football. After his father was killed in the Second World War, Ron was brought up in the home of Norm Smith, who had played football with the Melbourne club and who went on to become one of the most successful coaches in the VFL in the 1950s and 1960s. Smith became Barassi's substitute father and mentor. Barassi played under-age football with Melbourne and played his first senior game in 1953 at the age of 17. While not originally the most gifted footballer in the club, his physical strength, tactical skills, and enor-

mous powers of concentration lifted him above the rank of ordinary and eventually into the realm of genius. He went on to become club captain, club champion, and interstate representative. Barassi was such a central figure at Melbourne that when he transferred to the Carlton Club in 1965 he was accused of treachery. As captain-coach, and later coach only, at Carlton, he led them to two premierships. Barassi transferred to North Melbourne in 1973 and confirmed his legendary status by coaching the club to its first premiership in 1975 and another in 1977. Barassi is thought to have created the running game, which involved frequent handballing to players running past, on any part of the ground. The tactic was in opposition to the conventional mark-prop-kick game in which handball was viewed as a defensive strategy, moving the ball only when tackled.

RS

BARBERIS, VERDI ('Vern') (1928–), born Victoria, was Australia's first Olympic medallist in weightlifting, gaining the bronze medal at the 1952 Olympics in the 67.5 kilogram class. At the Commonwealth level Barberis also excelled, achieving a bronze medal in the 1950 Auckland Games and then gold at Vancouver in 1954. He concluded his representative international career at the 1956 Melbourne Olympics, placing eleventh. This placing was primarily caused by the need to establish his career as a schoolteacher and principal, which naturally forced him to downgrade his training level significantly. The Australian records set by Barberis in the early 1950s stood unchallenged until finally broken in 1975. He later contributed to the administration of the sport, serving for a term as president of the Australian Weightlifting Federation.

MN

BARHAM, PAMELA (née SMITH) (1937–) arrived in Australia from NZ in 1976 as an experienced international netball player, coach, and administrator. She was the Australian netball coach in 1982, 1985 and 1986. In 1984 she initiated a national network of information and assistance for netballers with an intellectual disability, and the first carnival for this group was held in Brisbane in 1986. Barham is noted for her contribution to numerous research projects in netball and with coaching programmes at State, national, and international levels. She was awarded the All Australia Netball Association Service Award in 1990.

IJ

BARNES, SIDNEY GEORGE (1916–73), born Charters Towers, Queensland, was a talented batsman who played thirteen Tests for Australia between 1938 and 1948. His final average of 63.05 remains one of the highest in

Australian Test history, and his fifth wicket partnership of 405 with Donald Bradman against England at Sydney in 1946–47 is still an Australian Test record. He was also a fearless fielder, and sustained considerable injury in 1948 when fielding close to the bat. Barnes made his first-class debut for NSW in February 1937. A complex character, he often antagonised authorities with his behaviour, and was eventually forced out of first-class cricket. He subsequently wrote on the game with some acerbity, and died at Collaroy.

RF

Barracking. To barrack, meaning, in British usage, to jeer at or taunt, is a word familiar to all Australian sports spectators. Scholars have debated its origins, pointing variously to English, French, Irish, and even Australian Aboriginal roots, but its practice is very much Australian. To a Briton the word has connotations which are unsporting or ungentlemanly, suggesting the ridicule of an opponent or loser. To Australians barracking is seen as an integral part of the enjoyment of spectating. Australians do not barrack *against* their opponent, generally they barrack *for* their team—providing a form of participation in the game. Occasionally they will barrack the referee, especially when they feel that their team is not being given a 'fair go'. In cricket and football crowds and even in racecourse grandstands barracking is sometimes almost a competitive sport in its own right, with participants attempting to outdo each other in comments designed to amuse the crowd as much as to give vent to their emotions. In this sport Australia's all-time champion was the Balmain 'rabbito' Stephen 'Yabba' Gascoigne.

JO'H
See **GASCOIGNE, STEPHEN.**

Baseball

Baseball in its modern form was developed in the USA from the 1830s to the 1860s, although the complete rules and the practice of players wearing gloves did not emerge until the 1890s. Baseball derived from a traditional game in England known as rounders, and in the 1860s the New York version replaced cricket as the summer game in America. Early settlers in Australia may also have played rounders, but variants of the American game were certainly played intermittently in Australia, mostly by Americans; games were held in Melbourne in 1857 and in Sydney and Melbourne in the early 1880s. Baseball really began in Australia after Spalding's tour of December 1888 when two American professional teams played exhibition games in Sydney, Melbourne, Adelaide, and Ballarat. From early 1889 cricketers had regular matches in Sydney, Melbourne, and Adelaide and the game has been played by enthusiasts

ever since. The first intercolonial matches, between SA and Victoria, were played in April 1889 in Melbourne. In 1897 an Australian team, including two Adelaide men and the rest from Melbourne, toured the USA but their standard was not good enough to attract interest and the badly organised tour was a financial and sporting disaster. This tour, funded by an Adelaide man, led to competition in that city being abandoned until 1908, and Melbourne did not fully recover until 1904. In Sydney, however, an eight-club competition began in 1899. Annual matches between NSW and Victoria commenced in 1900 and from 1910 became three-cornered contests when SA baseball was revived. This annual carnival was enhanced from 1934 when the Claxton Shield was donated. WA, where the game started in 1935, competed for the Shield from 1937; Queensland first entered the competition in 1939.

Before the First World War the game's rapid growth was helped by much-publicised 'international' games in Sydney and Melbourne against teams from the visiting American Fleet in 1908, and a tour by the New York Giants and the Chicago White Sox in 1914. Schoolboy baseball started in Sydney in 1908 and the first interstate schoolboy match was in 1912 between NSW and Victoria. By this time the game was widely played in both primary and secondary schools. The war thinned the ranks of players and temporarily ended the interstate series. There was a split in Melbourne between those clubs which played before the major football matches and those which did not, and in Sydney over a recently started summer competition. The game continued to be played, however, and expanded rapidly after the war there were regular visits by American warships and in 1928 by Stanford University. A Japanese team toured in 1919, a Japanese ship's team played in 1924, and Japanese residents in Sydney formed a team. Some Japanese men played in club sides and one pitched for Victoria against NSW in 1922. In the 1930s the game expanded. It was played in the major cities by hundreds of teams. There were city-wide club competitions, district competitions, and business-house teams; most larger country towns had competitions, and many schools played.

Baseball for women and girls emerged in Australia after the Great War and continued until after the Second World War. For some years from 1923 there was a competition between private girls' schools in Melbourne, and women's baseball seems to have flourished in the early 1930s. In October 1931 the NSW Women's Baseball Association held its first field day, with events which included accuracy and distance throwing, and circling the bases, as well as other sporting events. Nine teams were represented, some district-based (Drummoyne,

St George, Fivedock and Cumberland), while some were from companies, for example Arnott's, David Jones, and Nestlés. In 1933 a NSW women's team played games in Queensland and then toured Victoria. There was debate at this time about whether the women should play in trousers or skirts. The skirt got in the way of pitchers who threw underarm but the NSW team, whose pitcher threw overarm, preferred to play in trousers. In 1934 an interstate carnival was held in Sydney between teams from Queensland, Victoria, and NSW, and was won by the home team. All was not harmonious, however, for in 1934 in Brisbane the Kelvin Grove Women's Athletic Club resolved to exclude baseball from its activities and to sell the equipment on the grounds that baseball was not a women's game. The captain of the club's team, Miss Lyons, announced that she would resign from the committee and the club and join another club where she could play baseball. Women's baseball continued for some years; there were eleven teams in the 1939 Melbourne competition and there was still a league in the city in 1947. The emergence of softball seems to have replaced women's baseball, although individual women played in men's teams in the 1970s and 1980s.

During the Second World War, although the Claxton Shield was suspended, the game received a boost in 1942–44 from the presence of American servicemen who played representative games before large crowds against State sides and entered local competitions. After the war the men's game continued to expand steadily and it was estimated in 1953 that there were over seven hundred teams and ten thousand players in Australia. Regular night baseball started in Adelaide in 1952, but Sydney experiments in the same summer were not followed up. A Japanese team began a tour in November 1954 but RSL protests led to its being abandoned after games had been played in Sydney.

Baseball, which had gained its initial Australian appeal because cricketers believed it would complement their main game, was mostly played in winter, although summer games had been played since the 1890s and a summer competition flourished in Sydney from 1913 to the late 1930s. In the 1960s as cricket seemed to be losing its dominance as a summer sport, summer baseball was started in most centres and in 1973 the game was declared by its governing body to be a summer sport. Most ordinary club baseballers also played cricket and many outstanding State and Australian cricketers from the 1890s were also leading baseballers; the list runs from Trumper and M. A. Noble to Kippax, Ponsford, Harvey, O'Neill, and Border. Bradman recommended the game to cricketers but did not play himself. The switch to summer baseball has, not surprising-

ly, divided the players and created separate summer competitions and equally strong continuing winter leagues.

Summer baseball and more night games in the 1970s and 1980s were accompanied by efforts to raise the standard of play by developing international contacts and importing American coaches and players. Australia made its first international appearance in 1978 at the World Series in Italy and a team toured the USA and Canada in 1981. Federal funding in 1980 helped the appointment of an American as the first national director of coaching. Australia is active in the growing international amateur baseball movement which will see the sport admitted from 1992 as an official Olympic event. There was also a boom in the junior ranks with the introduction of tee ball, a simplified game without a pitcher, for primary school children, and also many competitions for teenagers. By 1990 there were perhaps 300 000 junior and 150 000 registered adult baseball players in Australia.

The sport operated under the control of the Australian Baseball Council from 1912 to 1978 (with a hiatus from 1933 to 1936), when the ruling body changed its name to the Australian Baseball Federation (ABF). There was a major split in 1988–89 in the ABF when it attempted to launch a national league in a style similar to that of soccer and basketball. Three States withdrew from the national body and in 1989 the Claxton Shield series was aborted. A national league was launched in the summer of 1989–90 and although attracting disappointing publicity and little public support in the first season, was encouraged by receiving a $500 000 sponsorship from Pepsi-Cola to help the eight-team league into the 1990–91 season.

Baseball in Australia may never satisfactorily solve the dilemma of its relationship with the traditional national game, cricket. It is perhaps also doomed to suffer neglect from the media. However, if it can avoid the administrative rows and disunity which have marred its history, it may yet enjoy a greater and more enthusiastic following. It may be helped in the future by finance and players from major American baseball clubs which may rather belatedly follow Spalding's early missionary efforts.

BM

See **Claxton Shield**; **Ethnic Influences**; **SPALDING, ALBERT**.

Basketball

Basketball was invented in 1891 at the YMCA Training School in Springfield, Massachusetts, and reached Australia approximately a decade later through YMCA clubs. At first the sport was regarded as a social activity, with a variety of rules being in use, and it was not until Dr Ivor Burge of Queensland published a set of standardised rules in 1929 that the sport began to move away from being the preserve of church and youth groups. During the 1930s the creation of city-based associations signalled its emergence in Australia as a sport, though a minor one. There was, however, enough following to warrant the formation of the Amateur Basketball Union of Australia (later the Australian Basketball Federation, and then Basketball Australia) in 1939, designed to co-ordinate these local activities. In 1947 Australia affiliated with the Federation of International Basketball Associations.

Until this time basketball made little impact on a society long nurtured on the sports inherited from Britain. The mild climate and the wide spread of population both played a part in the slow growth of indoor sports. The most important venues were church, YMCA and army drill halls, as well as primitive outdoor courts: few schools possessed a gymnasium, and local councils did not see any need to build the sports halls that have sprung up in the decades since. In the post-war period, important social changes began to have an impact. The presence of US servicemen and the regular pastoral visits of young male Mormon missionaries (who used the game to make contact with young male players) had an impact on playing and coaching standards, especially in Victoria and NSW. In SA the influx of European immigrants, particularly from the Baltic republics, had similar beneficial results: most of Australia's team at the Melbourne Olympics were recently naturalised immigrants. Despite Australia's modest showing in finishing twelfth among fifteen nations in 1956, the sport gained unprecedented attention, with all games sold out. An important consequence was the establishment of Melbourne's Albert Park complex in 1958, and this long remained the spiritual home of the sport, leading directly to the dominance of Victoria in its development. Even so, few still played: Victoria, for example, had only 1500 registered players at the time of the Melbourne Games.

The emergence of strong clubs saw an increase in participants, a steady improvement in facilities, and a push for national competitions. In 1946 the first interstate championship was played, but later the desire for a season-long competition saw the creation in the mid-1960s of the South Eastern Conference, featuring teams from Victoria, SA, NSW, and Tasmania. Dominated by one Melbourne club, and plagued with money worries, the conference was abandoned, being replaced in 1970 by the Australian Club Championship, which was played over a few days at one location. In country areas basketball grew in popularity—perhaps faster than in the cities—due largely to the intertown competitions that were established, such as in Gippsland and along Tasmania's north-west coast. Women

played the sport, but the pervasiveness of netball (long called 'basketball') kept women's basketball (often called 'international rules') in the shadows. As basketball grew in popularity this gradually changed, and the adoption of the name 'netball' in 1970 lessened public confusion over the two sports. The Women's Club Championship began in 1973.

The basing of competitions on strong local clubs was the model for the creation of the National Basketball League (NBL, 1979), and the Women's National Basketball League (1981), both of which soon came to include teams from all six States and the ACT. These became the premier competitions, encouraging the development of strong teams outside Victoria and SA. Both leagues were dominated by capital-city teams, but the emergence of the South Eastern Australian Basketball League (men) and the Women's Basketball Conference in the 1980s gave regional centres such as Grafton, Ballarat, and Mount Gambier the chance to participate in strong competitions.

As interest grew, there was an improvement in facilities; the old tin sheds of the pioneer days were replaced. In the NBL, for instance, some clubs were able to use large stadia built for various purposes, while others such as Brisbane and Gold Coast used custom-built facilities. Such developments were mirrored in country centres such as Albury, which began to build first-rate stadia. With these improvements in accommodation came a steady increase in spectator support. In the early days of the NBL crowds had remained small, but from the mid-1980s this began to change rapidly, partly due to increased media coverage, the performance of national teams at the 1984 and 1988 Olympic Games, the television coverage of American matches, the increasingly sophisticated publicity efforts of the clubs, and a growing determination of many parents to keep their children away from the perceived violence of the football codes. The enormous shift in public regard was confirmed in the spectacular degree of attention paid to Andrew Gaze's performances while playing US college basketball in 1988–89.

Mirroring the changes at the élite level, junior basketball flourished, with sharp increases in the number of children seeking to play the sport; the ACT, for instance, had 114 registered teams in 1981 and 335 by 1990. Most juniors played in intersuburban or intertown competitions, but there were many carnivals which enabled youngsters to represent their clubs in different parts of the country. Australian championships at under-12, -14, -16, -18, and -20 levels were contested by all States and the ACT.

After the 1956 Games Australia entered all Olympic competitions, though not always managing to clear the hurdle of the qualifying tournament. In their efforts to lift Australian basketball standards, administrators long felt the need to offset the country's geographical isolation, and to this end the widespread use of American imports at all levels of the sport was a controversial way in which Australian players became exposed to overseas skills. Regular participation in international carnivals, overseas tours by national and club teams, and invitations for overseas teams to tour this country also worked to lift both Australia's playing standards and its international basketball profile. The standard of Australian basketball slowly improved until it came to be regarded as very much one of the second-tier nations, just behind the leading nations such as the USA, USSR, and Yugoslavia. In the World Championships the women achieved a fourth place in 1979 and the men a seventh place in 1982. At the 1988 Olympic Games both men's and women's teams achieved a fourth placing, with the women being only a point away from a gold medal playoff.

SB

See **AHMATT, MICHAEL**; **Australian Basketball Federation**; **BURGE, IVOR**; **CHEESMAN, JENNIFER**; **Ethnic Influences**; **GAZE, ANDREW**; **GAZE, LINDSAY**; **MAHER, ROBYN**; **Netball**; **PALUBINSKAS, EDDIE**; **SMYTH, PHIL**; **STAUNTON, ROBERT**; **Unionism**; **WATSON, KENNETH**.

Bathing Costumes Controversy. By the first decade of the twentieth century, competitive swimming costumes for both men and women were skirtless, sleeveless, short-legged, and made of finely knitted wool or even transparent silk —but these costumes were only worn within the confines of the swimming pool. On public beaches a much greater coverage of late Victorian flesh was demanded. The first decade of the century saw the authorisation of daylight beach bathing and consequently a whole new set of official dress regulations—and controversial infringements. Men, many of whom had previously swum naked, were now required to wear shoulder-to-knee costumes, preferably with trunks over the top; and for women, a two-piece set of short-sleeved tunic and knee-length drawers was the minimum prescribed. Segregation of the sexes on beaches was also practised widely, and some local councils, most notably Manly in 1906, even tried to force male bathers to wear skirts over their one-piece costumes. Despite the official restrictions, the press of the time contained many reports of scantily clad young men swimming before admiring female audiences, and of young women parading the beaches in mid-thigh-length, low-cut tunics, with waists tightly corseted and belted.

VRW

Battle of Brisbane. Australia, beaten 8–6 in the ferocious first Test of the 1932 rugby league series against England, was determined to win the second at the Brisbane Cricket Ground on 18 June and keep alive its chance of regaining the Ashes. In a rugged struggle, celebrated as the 'Battle of Brisbane', the home team led 10–0 at half-time. Then hooker Dan Dempsey left the field with a broken wrist; 19-year-old centre Ernie Norman was off and back three times with concussion; lock Frank O'Connor and scrumhalf Hec Gee suffered bad cuts; and five-eighth Eric Weissel tore ankle ligaments. With other injuries, the battered Australians at times had only ten men playing. England scored twice to trail only 10–6 and, close to full time, looked certain to do so again until Weissel got the ball and hobbled sixty metres to create a try for Gee, converted by Sid Pearce. Australia's 15–6 victory was in vain, however, as England won the third Test 18–13 and retained the Ashes.

TB

See **WEISELL, ERIC**.

BAUMGARTNER, LEOPOLD (1932–), born Vienna, played for numerous soccer clubs before joining F. K. Austria in 1953. He represented Austria in 1948–49 (under-18s) and 1955 (senior B team). Club tours included South America (1954) and Australia (1957). The lure of a better life-style enticed Baumgartner to Sydney club Prague 1958–59. He played for Canterbury, South Coast, Apia-Leichhardt, and Hakoah from 1960 to 1964. He coached all the above teams except Canterbury and later Croatia, Polonia, and Yugal-Ryde. He was captain-coach of NSW 1960–63 and played for Australia against Everton in 1964. Dubbed 'The Professor', Baumgartner was an extraordinarily skilful and intelligent centre-forward. A masterful dribbler with immaculate ball control, his finest hour was leading a youthful Canterbury to an upset victory over Prague in the 1960 Grand Final. Known also for his fiery, volatile temperament, Baumgartner was a difficult player to handle. On the field, however, he had few peers.

PM

BEACH, WILLIAM (1850–1935), born England, learned his sculling in the Illawarra district of NSW. His early career did not suggest any ability out of the ordinary, but a steady improvement in skill and strength saw him able to defeat Edward Trickett for the Australian title in 1884. Shortly thereafter Beach amazed the Australian sporting world by convincingly winning the world championship from the seemingly invincible Ned Hanlan of Canada, and from this moment, Beach's heroic status was assured. Six successful title defences, including two against Hanlan, and final retirement as unbeaten champion, merely confirmed his special place in Australian sporting legend. A sense of how his contemporaries saw his achievement is gained from the fact that in 1886 he returned to Sydney from races in England to public receptions with the Governor and Premier of

NSW and the Lord Mayor of Sydney, and massive crowds packed the streets 'as far each way as the eye could reach' to see him pass by. Beach earned much respect for his modesty and honesty in a sport which attracted many 'sportsmen' of doubtful repute. In the Illawarra, where he worked as a blacksmith, he remained a hero until his death. At his funeral Sir Joynton Smith spoke for many: 'there has never been a man who ... made a better name, and left a better character for sportsmanship and courage, than Bill Beach.'

SB

See **Rowing and Sculling**.

BEAMES, PERCIVAL JAMES (1911–) represented Victoria in both cricket and football and was an outstanding sportswriter with the Melbourne *Age*. He captained Victoria in cricket (1945–46), scored three centuries, and 1186 runs (average 51.56). In football he was selected to play for Victoria eleven times, played 213 games with Melbourne, kicked 327 goals, was captain-coach for three seasons (1942–44), and played in three VFL premierships (1939–41).

NS

BEASHEL Family were prominent in 18-foot class sailing over three generations. **Dick 'Rocko' Beashel** was a champion skipper in the class in 1908 and his son, **Alf**, was one of the founders of the Eighteen-Foot Sailing League. His son, **Ken** (?1936–), a Sydney boat-builder, was twice world champion skipper in this event in boats of his own design: he won on *Schemer* in 1963 and on *Daily Telegraph* in 1968. Ken Beashel participated in *Australia II*'s victory in the *America*'s Cup in 1983 as supervisor in charge of maintenance. A third generation of the family, **Colin Beashel**, who was a member of the crew of *Australia II* as a mainsheet trimmer, had the difficult task of climbing the mast to lash a broken headboard in place in the second race. Earlier, in 1981, Colin Beashel, along with Phil Roy Tutty and Phil Smidmore, had won the world championship in the 5.5 metre keel yacht class at Nassau. Colin Beashel also took part in the 1984 Olympics, finishing eleventh in the Star class.

RC#

BEAUREPAIRE, FRANK (1891–1956), born Melbourne, had a swimming career unique in his era in that he competed in three Olympics, won six medals and set fifteen world records. Beaurepaire won three national titles in 1908 and was selected to compete in the Olympic Games in London, where he won a silver medal in the 400 metres and bronze in the 1500 metres. Using his modified trudgen stroke, he dominated world distance swimming for the next two years. In Europe in 1910 he set four world records and won seven English titles. It seemed that he would sweep all before him at the 1912 Olympics in Stockholm, but unfortunately he became a victim of swimming officialdom when he lost his amateur status in 1911 because he was employed as a swimming instructor by the Victorian Education Department. The Great War also robbed Beaurepaire of further Olympic success. After the war he was reinstated and continued his Olympic career at the 1920 Antwerp Games where he won a silver medal in the 4 × 200 metres relay and a bronze in the 1500 metres. In 1924, aged 33, he repeated this feat at the Paris Olympics. Beaurepaire became a successful businessman and Lord Mayor of Melbourne. He was knighted in 1942 and was a chief promoter of Melbourne's Olympic bid. He died on 24 May 1956 before he could realise his final Olympic goal of seeing the Games hosted in his own city.

PH

See **Olympic Games 1956 (Melbourne)**; **Swimming**.

BEECHEY, NORM (1932–), born Melbourne, was the first national hero of the touring-car era in Australian motor racing, and had a major influence on its development. He had his first race in 1953 and built his fame on spectacular, forcefully driven Holdens from 1958. He was the first Australian to apply the racing potential of high-performance American sedan cars, and both his Australian Touring Car Championships (1965 and 1970) were in cars powered by American V8s. He effectively retired at the end of 1972.

GH

See **Motor Racing**.

BEETSON, ARTHUR (1945–), born of Aboriginal parents at Roma, Queensland, played his first and last metropolitan rugby league games with Redcliffe in Brisbane, but in Sydney played for Balmain, Eastern Suburbs, and Parramatta, captaining Easts to premierships in 1974–75. He represented Queensland on three occasions and NSW seventeen times. He played fourteen Tests and fourteen World Cup matches for Australia in 1966–77. He built great bonds of loyalty and friendship as captain or coach, often leading Australian teams between 1973 and 1977. His captaincy inspired Queensland's victory in the first State of Origin match in 1980; he then coached the team to eleven wins from sixteen games in this series between 1981–84 and 1989–90. Initially a centre, Beetson became a second-row forward, then prop. He was an uncompromising, at times ferocious, defender, but even more, his explosive running, balance, and remarkable strength in clearing the ball to supports made him one of Australia's greatest attacking forwards.

SJR

See **Aboriginal Rugby League Test Players**; **Aborigines in Sport**.

Bell's Beach, several kilometres from Torquay on the south coast of Victoria, was the site of Australia's first professional surfing contest in 1973. 'Discovered' in 1961 by the Torquay boat crew, Bell's celebrated its thirtieth anniversary as a competition venue in 1991 when Pauline Menczer and Barton Lynch were awarded the 'Golden Bell' as winners of the annual Easter contest. Bell's is renowned for Australia's biggest surf (up to 6 metres), when the swell pushes from the west. It is bounded by Winkipop Point (eastern end) and Barnfather's Bluff (western end). The beach faces south-east. Winkipop is at the north end of Bell's Beach near the top car park. At the bottom end of 'Winky' is 'Lowers', which is surfed at Easter, along with Southside and Centreside. It requires at least a medium tide for good surfing. Bell's Beach itself has a powerful south-west swell; the offshore wind is a north-wester. There are two reefs: Rincon (best when the swell is small) on the inside, and another in the middle of the bay. Centreside and Southside are the two reefs around to the south from Bell's, within walking distance of Rincon. The seafloor is of rock, sand, and seaweed, forming a bowl. 'The Bowl' breaks at its best with low tides and medium-to-large swell.

Ground swells and offshore winds traditionally provide fine surfing conditions for the annual Easter rally. For the first six years of the Bell's contest giant waves were its trademark; not until 1968 was the surf down. That year Bob Evans, 'father' of Australian surfing, declared Bell's Beach as the best competitive surfboard event of the surfing year. Bell's was the venue for the 1970 world amateur championships. In 1971 it was set aside for conservation, and is now a surfing recreation reserve. It is the headquarters of surfing manufacturers and sponsors —Rip Curl, Piping Hot and Quiksilver—as well as board manufacturers. It is also the site of a government-backed Surfworld Museum (which includes a Surfing Hall of Fame and the offices of the Australian Surfriders Association). In 1973 Bell's hosted Australia's first professional event, and in 1976 American Jeff Hackman became the first non-Australian to win the Bell's Classic. In 1981 it was the scene of the biggest surf encountered in an Australian contest. At Bell's in 1987, 16-year-old Australian Nicky Wood became the youngest winner of a professional event. Other renowned winners include Nat Young, Paul Neilsen, Gail Couper, Michael Petersen, Terry Fitzgerald, Mark Richards, Simon Anderson, Cheyne Horan, Tom Curren (USA), Margo Oberg (USA), Damien Hardman, and Tom Carroll.
CD

See **Surfing**.

Bell's Life in Sydney and Sporting Reviewer (1845–71), *Bell's Life in Victoria and Sporting Chronicle* (1857–68), and *Bell's Life in Adelaide and Sporting Chronicle* (1861–62) were all modelled on *Bell's Life in London and Sporting Chronicle* (1822–86). The Australian *Bell's* each focused on some general news with a long leader on a serious political subject to leaven the main body of sporting news. The masthead of the journal was adorned with a large open eye and the legend *Nunquam Dormio*, 'I never sleep'. The papers sold for sixpence and were read by members of all classes. A distinctive feature of *Bell's Life* was the verse forecast of important races, as exemplified by Adam Lindsay Gordon's *Hippodromania*, originally published in *Bell's Life in Victoria*, which unsuccessfully predicted the results of the 1866 and 1867 Melbourne Cups. In 1868 the *Bell's Life in Sydney* readership had become mainly pastoralists and stockbrokers. After some changes of ownership the paper was incorporated into the *Sydney Mail* in October 1871.
GC*

BELSHAM, VICTOR COLIN, AM (1925–), has influenced squash, both nationally and internationally, through his roles as president of the Squash Rackets Association of Australia and national president and national representative for Australia on the International Squash Rackets Federation from 1976 to 1984. During this period he effected major innovations in the administration of the game within Australia by amalgamating the men's and women's associations and by encouraging the State bodies to take a more active role in management. Internationally he was influential in creating the rule changes which replaced the amateur/professional status of competitions with open events. He has been elected a life member of the Australian Squash Rackets Federation (1985) and of the Queensland Squash Rackets Association (1984). Before emigrating to Australia in 1961 he represented NZ as a rugby league player (1948–49); he was an international rugby referee from 1957 until 1961 and played for, selected, and managed Auckland representative cricket teams. He was also an active squash-player from 1961 until 1986.
KT

BENAUD, RICHIE, OBE (1930–), born Penrith, NSW, was an outstanding cricket all-rounder: an explosive bat, brilliant gully, fine leg-spinner with a fluent high over-the-shoulder action, and attacking captain. He learned the art of leg-break bowling from his father Lou, a Sydney grade cricketer. Although he played his first Test at the age of 21 it was some time before he made his mark. Thrust into the captaincy in 1958, the flamboyant Benaud proved a bold and decisive captain whose enthusiasm on the field was contagious. He was an imaginative leader who played with more buttons of his shirt undone than any previous player: Benaud was aware that image and style were crucial ingredients of sport. Benaud's greatest achievement was his contribution, along with that of (Sir) Frank Worrell, to the memorable and celebrated West Indies tour of 1960–61 which gave the game sparkle and aggression. He also engineered a daring victory at Manchester in 1961 when he exploited the rough, taking 6–70, turning almost certain defeat into an extraordinary victory. He was the first to make 2000 runs and take 200 wickets in Tests. Benaud made a smooth transition into cricket commentary where he became an authoritative face and voice of the game. He played a prominent role in the Packer 'revolution', which was in many ways an extension of his approach to the game. He has been the author of a number of cricket books. His brother John (1944–), who played three Tests for Australia, became a prominent Sydney journalist.

IH

See **Cricket**.

BENZIE, GWEN, AM (1914–), was secretary-treasurer of the All Australia Netball Association (AANA) for many years from 1950 to 1978. Her dedication and leadership were major reasons why AANA was held in high esteem by government and Australian and international sporting organisations. Her influence on the development of netball within Australia is paralleled by her contribution to the International Federation of Netball Associations (IFNA). She represented Australia at the inaugural meeeting of IFNA in 1960, was honorary secretary from 1963 to 1967, and vice-president from 1971 to 1975. Mrs Benzie holds AANA Service and Umpires Awards, was awarded an IFNA Service Award in 1983, and became a Member of the Order of Australia in 1978.

DH and IJ

See **All Australia Netball Association**; **Netball**.

Bernborough (1939–60), a thoroughbred racehorse by *Emborough* out of *Bern Maid*, was bred by Harry Winten and foaled near Dalby in Queensland. He was sold as a foal at foot with his dam to John Bach, who subsequently sold him to Albert Hadwen. When Bach's father Frank was disqualified by the Queensland Turf Club (QTC) in January 1941 concerning the ring-in of a horse at Albion Park racecourse, the ownership of *Bernborough* was queried. The QTC refused to accept that it was John rather than Frank Bach who had bought the horse, or that the sale to Hadwen was genuine; consequently the club rejected the horse's entries for Brisbane races. The independent South-West Queensland Racing Association was the only body to accept his nomination, so from January 1942 until July 1945 *Bernborough* did all his racing at

Clifford Park, Toowoomba, where he won eleven of his twenty starts. He was then sold to Sydney owner Azzalin Romano and trained by Harry Plant. Unplaced at his next start, *Bernborough* then commenced an unbroken sequence of fifteen wins in top races in Sydney, Brisbane, and Melbourne, ridden in all by Athol Mulley. The horse's characteristic withering run from towards the tail of the field made him an instant idol of the crowds. Unplaced under the burden of 10 stone 10 pounds in the 1946 Caulfield Cup, *Bernborough* broke down a fortnight later at Flemington. Saved for stud, *Bernborough* was sold to MGM boss Louis B. Mayer and was sent to Kentucky where he was an outstanding success.

AL

See **Horse-racing**.

BERRY, KEVIN JOHN (1945–), born Sydney, was from a working-class family. He came under Don Talbot's influence in 1958, and made the Olympic team in 1960 at the age of 15, swimming a heat of the medley relay and coming sixth in the final of the 200 metres butterfly. In all, he broke twelve world records—in the 110 yards, the 220 yards, and the 200 metres butterfly—and won nine Australian championships. He won three gold medals in the 1962 Perth British Empire and Commonwealth Games, in the 220 yards and the 110 yards butterfly and as a member of the 4 × 110 yards medley relay. At the 1964 Tokyo Olympics he broke the world and Olympic record in winning the 200 metres butterfly in 2 minutes 6.6 seconds, and received a bronze medal in the 4 × 100 metres medley relay.

RH and MH

BERTRAND, JOHN EDWIN, OAM (1946–), born Melbourne, was the skipper of *Australia II*, the yacht which captured the *America*'s Cup in 1983. He grew up on the beach-front at Chelsea, near Melbourne, and at the age of 7 began sailing with his brother Lex. As a junior he sailed with success in Sabots and VJs. He was spotted by Rolly Tasker in 1962, after winning the National VJ championship in Perth; Tasker suggested him to Jim Hardy as a potential *America*'s Cup crew member. He sailed in this contest in 1970, 1974, and 1980 before becoming skipper in 1983. Bertrand's connections with the *America*'s Cup dated back to his great-grandfather who worked as an engineer on Sir Thomas Lipton's British Cup challenges. Bertrand brought many skills to sailing. He wrote a thesis on the aerodynamics of 12 metre sails and also achieved a master's degree in ocean engineering. After being runner-up in the 1972 world championships, Bertrand came fourth at the Munich Olympics when his craft in the Finn dinghies was becalmed. He won a bronze medal at the 1976 Olympics, was chosen for the 1980

Games before the sailing team withdrew, and represented Australia in the Admiral's Cup in 1973 and 1977. Bertrand has been Australian champion in the following classes: lightweight Sharpie (1968), Soling (1972–73, 1978–79, and 1979–80), Finn dinghies (1975–76), and International Etchells (1991). He was Ampol Australian Yachtsman of the Year in 1977 and 1983, was awarded the OAM in 1984 and was inducted into the Sport Australia Hall of Fame in 1985.

AMJ

See *Australia II*.

BETHWAITE Family produced three world champions in yachting. **Julian** and his sister **Nicky** won the Cherub dinghy class in 1976. Julian, with a crew of Peter Warner and Tim Halles, later won the world title in the 18-foot skiff class in 1991 on Sydney Harbour. **Mark** had the distinction of achieving world champion status in two classes, Soling and 24-foot, in 1982. The Victorian helmsman participated in the 1972 and 1976 Olympics, finishing eighth and ninth respectively in the Flying Dutchman dinghies.

RC#

Betting on Sport

Sport and gambling are, and always have been, related concepts in the minds of Australians. The essence of sport is competition and wherever there is competition there are winners and losers, the two prerequisites for gambling. For most people gambling is more readily associated with the racing sports, particularly horses and dogs, but other sports have an equally long history as the objects of betting. The volume of betting on the non-racing sports in Australia is impossible to estimate because most of it is illegal. Nevertheless, every week, particularly during the winter months, millions of dollars change hands on the results of sporting contests. Football, because of the intensity of the loyalties it stimulates, is the object of the largest amount and greatest variety of betting, but few sports, if any, are completely free from its influence. Even the gentle sports, such as croquet, while not subjected to organised betting, do involve occasional bets among the players.

In early colonial Australia disposable income was a rare commodity and, initially at least, organised sport was even rarer, so sports betting was not a prominent feature of society. That began to change after about a decade, with the opening of a billiard room for the NSW military officers in 1802 and the emergence of cock-fighting in 1804. Within another few years pedestrianism, boat-racing, and boxing had all become regular features of colonial life. Equally important was the concept of the sporting challenge, which was limited only by the imagination of the betters. In 1811 one man won a challenge by riding from Sydney to Parramatta and back on the same horse in less than 4 hours and 45 minutes. He completed the forward journey in 2 hours and 10 minutes and the return trip in 2 hours and 11 minutes to collect a fifty guinea bet. In the same week another man won a 'considerable sum' when he carried another man over a distance of 50 yards, defeating an opponent who ran 100 yards unencumbered. Such challenges provided entertainment for spectators and speculators, but it was boxing which, apart from horse-racing, quickly became the favourite sport of the serious punter. Pugilism was less popular with colonial officials because of the disorderly behaviour it promoted, both during and after the match. Events thus had to be arranged in secret and publicised by word of mouth. However, the contests seldom remained secret from the magistrates and the constabulary, though the latter often allowed the matches to finish before they dispersed the crowd. In this way they began the Australian police tradition of looking the other way where sports betting is concerned.

Betting was not illegal in colonial Australia; the only real concern of officials was the behaviour of the crowds. When organised team sports began to emerge, however, the role of gamblers in them and the possibility of corruption did become a matter for public discussion. While newspapers published the odds on rowing and yachting races, billiard and boxing matches, athletics and animal-baiting, they also published comments critical of betting on cricket and football games. The controversies which surrounded the NSW v. Victoria cricket match in 1876, cycling's Austral Wheelrace in 1899 and 1901, and a football game at Balmain in 1902 were but a few examples which contributed to the debate over the 'evil' of gambling around the turn of the century. These events helped to discredit the gamblers, leading, in the first decade of the twentieth century, to the suppression of gambling on all sports other than horse-racing. Even on racing, betting was restricted to the racecourse. The suppressive legislation proved ineffective. It was impossible to police in a country which had developed a propensity to gamble as a part of its national character. Wherever sport was played bets were made. Now, however, the betting was less public and so it was less likely to offend the sensitive. The politicians soon realised the futility of their attempts to separate sport and betting and throughout the rest of this century they have been more concerned with finding ways of allowing sports betting while maintaining official supervision and minimising the dangers of corruption.

Over the last decade this search has gained momentum, with State governments motivated further by their need for increased revenue. The governments have also been influenced by the plight of bookmakers whose numbers and turnover have dwindled in the context of increased legalised gaming and the appearance of punters equipped with computers. Bookies have lobbied successfully in some States for the right to take bets on football matches directly from the racecourse. State-controlled Totalisator Agency Boards have also expanded their off-course betting operations to include sports betting. Although the various forms of Footy TAB have been the main focus of the TABs' sports-betting operations, yacht-racing and one-day international cricket matches have been experimented with in Tasmania, motor racing in NSW and other sports elsewhere. In Victoria the TABELLA operation provides regular betting opportunities on a range of sports, although it is restricted to a single betting venue and has not yet gained the degree of acceptance accorded 'Sports Books' in American casinos.

In most States legislation now permits governments or officials to authorise betting in TABs or with on-course bookmakers on almost any sport. Expansion of 'permission' has been limited by the unwillingness of some sports administrators to risk having their sports associated with charges of corruption, or by the lobbying of existing gambling operators who fear a reduction of their turnover due to the increased competition. Legal forms of sports betting also remain limited in their popularity because of the TABs' concentration on exotic betting forms and on special events and because the on-course bookmaker's operations are hampered by their racecourse venues and the limited betting time allowed. As a consequence, most sports betting in Australia continues to take place illegally. Big-betting football supporters in all States and Territories have little difficulty in finding each other. Factories and offices run their tipping competitions and fund-raisers sell their football cards without giving a thought to the possibility of prosecution. Other sports have a smaller betting turnover but the general pattern is the same. The office or factory 'bookie' is always available to frame a market if required. Similarly, supporters of an opposing team can always be persuaded to 'put their money where their mouths are'.

Sports betting in Australia has never rivalled the public prominence or equalled the turnover volume of gaming or the betting on racing. In NSW the Footy TAB operation turned over $14 million in 1990 but this was less than 2 per cent of the total turnover in Australia's eight TABs. It pales by comparison even with the gross profit of the two casinos in Tasmania, which in 1989/90 was $41 million. Although there are a significant number of big, and even semi-professional, operators, the typical sports better is the sports fan who expresses loyalty to 'the team' by betting on it to win. In this way a financial element is added to the contest, enhancing the sport and allowing the fan to become a participant who is affected by the outcome.

JO'H

See **Horse-racing**.

BEWSHER, BILL (1924–) was one of the founding members of Melbourne University Mountaineering Club. He made the first ascent of Federation Peak in Tasmania (1950) and pioneered climbing in Antarctica. He convened the first 'search and rescue' organisation within the Federation of Victorian Walking Clubs in 1959, and in 1969, played a leading role in establishing the Bushwalking and Mountaincraft Leadership Certificate and the associated training programme.

EH-S

Biathlon
This Olympic sport combines the endurance of cross-country skiing and the accuracy of smallbore (.22 calibre) rifle shooting. In 1976 the International Biathlon Congress, through the Union Internationale de Pentathlon Moderne et Biathlon (UIPMB), extended an invitation through the Australian Olympic Federation and the Australian Modern Pentathlon Union to establish the biathlon in Australia. These organisations, along with the Australian Ski Federation, Victorian Ski Federation, and representatives of the Australian army, formed a steering committee. Inspections to locate a suitable venue for the sport resulted in the choice of Mount Stirling, near Mount Buller in Victoria. The Victorian Biathlon Association was formed at a public meeting in April 1977, and the first events were conducted in July of that year with participants from NSW, Victoria, the ACT, the Royal Military College (Duntroon), and the Army Apprentices School. An equipment grant of five rifles, skis, poles, and rollerskis from the UIPMB greatly assisted the establishment of the sport. Australia entered a team of four in the UIPMB World Championships in Australia in 1978. With the increased popularity of Mount Stirling as a recreation area, it became apparent that the biathlon range was no longer in a suitable spot, so a new venue was found at Whiskey Flat. This location has been improved greatly with the extensions of ski trails, the erection of huts, and the installation of automatic targets before the visit by the Norwegian National Biathlon Team.

A biathlon team has represented Australia in international competition every year since 1978, except at the 1980 Olympics. Australian biathletes' performances have improved greatly, especially since 1985 when they have had support from the ASC and the AIS. Women's Biathlon World Championships were held for the first time in 1984; Australia was represented by Kerryn Pethybridge, who later gained fourth place in the World Championships of 1990. Women's biathlon was included on the Winter Olympic Games programme in 1992.

AP* and IJ

Billiards and Snooker

The game of billiards, which originated in Europe in about the fourteenth century, was imported to NSW by officers of the British regiments stationed in the colony. It was probably first played about 1795 and soon became so popular among the officers that they built their own billiard room. The game became even more widespread when the purchase of tables 'on time payment' became possible in the early years of the nineteenth century. But the main impetus for the popularity of the game came from enterprising publicans who erected billiard salons as part of their premises and were able to offer full-sized tables and all equipment in pleasant, well-lit surroundings. The concentration of the game in hotels meant that it became a predominantly male pastime; it also led to the development of an unsavoury reputation, as players were able to drink while competing and also bet on the outcome of contests. Challenge matches for large sums between individuals or teams were reported in Sydney in the 1830s. During the 1840s many billiard clubs were formed in Sydney and some exponents were able to set themselves up as teachers. A similar pattern emerged in other colonies. The game was introduced in Victoria in the late 1830s and quickly became popular in many Melbourne hotels and clubs, where contests for purses over £100 soon became common. By the mid-1840s hotels in Adelaide, Perth, and many country centres were also equipped with tables.

The chief impetus for the development of billiards in Australia came from a small Melbourne workshop in the early 1850s. The development and manufacture of tables had been steadily improving in England and other parts of Europe during the first half of the century, and colonial manufacturers adapted these techniques. They were led by an Irish immigrant named Henry Upton Alcock, who used the skills he had acquired in the trade to set up a table-manufacturing business in Fitzroy in 1853. He used local and Tasmanian timber, cloth imported from England, and local slate to build tables of exceptional quality. A great part of his success was the design of his tables, which were constructed in a way that enabled them to be dismantled and transported anywhere in the colony or to be used as dining tables when not used for billiards. Local manufacture of tables resulted in the opening of a thriving export market and ensured a steady supply of tables to an increasing number of billiard halls in Melbourne. It also facilitated the

establishment of tables in private houses and clubs such as the MCC, where members could compete in tournaments or play at their leisure. As in many other sports in the colonial era, social divisions and paradoxes emerged in the setting in which billiards was played and the manner in which the game was conducted. At one end of the social scale there were those gentlemen (and ladies) who played in private houses and exclusive clubs; at the other end were those who learned the game in hotels and billiard halls, gambled heavily on the outcome, and were generally regarded as not respectable. In an effort to boost sales of his tables both locally and for export, Alcock promoted many professional contests and exhibition matches during the 1860s. The Australian colonies became regular ports of call for players who billed themselves as 'professional champion of the world' and who were matched with local champions at large venues such as Melbourne's Theatre Royal. Matches were held over a number of sessions, each of which was played up to a set number of points—usually 750. A match would be won by the first player to reach an agreed total, often 18 000 points. A typical match would last over a number of days and the champion player would often give his opponent a start of several thousand points. In the late 1870s the purse for a major match was often in excess of £500, with considerable side betting by onlookers and participants.

In 1881 the first Professional Billiards Championship of Australia was held in Sydney, attended by over two hundred spectators who paid high admission fees and gambled heavily on the matches. However, the lack of a controlling body in Australia meant that subsequent matches generally depended on challenges between players. Other championship matches followed during the 1880s, including the 'Native Born Championship of Australia' held in Melbourne in 1887. The purpose of this contest was to break the domination over the game by Englishman Harry Evans. It was easily won by Fred Lindrum, and signalled the start of a powerful influence on Australian billiards exerted by the Lindrum family. During the 1890s the game was affected by two trends which were to occur again during the 1930s. The first concerned the rules. As with all evolving sports in the colonial era, the rules were regularly under review by controlling bodies, which in this case were located in England. Restrictions were placed on certain strokes, which limited the effectiveness of some players and resulted in players sometimes refusing to take part in tournaments which were conducted under the revised rules. For instance, the restrictions placed on the 'spot stroke' in the late 1880s curbed the scoring of Fred Lindrum and were also disliked by Charlie Memmott, the player who dominated the game through-out the 1890s. As a result, there were two 'Australian Championships' for some years, one where spot strokes were legal and the other where they were not. The second trend was related to economic conditions. As depression engulfed Victoria in the 1890s there was less money available for leisure activities such as the hire of a billiard table for a few hours, and the game declined. However, many players (in-cluding the Lindrum family) moved to the WA goldfields, where numerous salons were estab-lished. As the effects of the Depression less-ened, the game boomed again, particularly in Sydney. Full employment meant more money available for recreational activities; at the same time, playing the game became cheaper as many tables were installed in new social clubs, and the public billiard halls were forced to drop their prices in order to compete with the new venues. At the top level, many English champions were still visiting Australia for tours of major cities and regional centres. During these tours, which were generally sponsored by table manufactur-ers, publicans, and owners of sporting news-papers, the visitors competed against local champions and rising players, such as the young Walter Lindrum. Players were able to earn considerable income from the tours and were able to supplement their earnings by gam-bling on the outcome.

Participation in the sport of billiards was badly affected by the First World War, although the popularity of championship matches re-mained high. During the middle of the war years, the prodigious play of Walter Lindrum had ensured that he was the greatest scoring phenomenon in Australian billiards, and crowds continued to flock to his matches. By the early 1920s billiards had returned to its pre-war par-ticipation levels, new billiard rooms were estab-lished in all capital cities and country centres, and a number of players were able to make a modest living as professionals. During the 1920s Walter Lindrum completely dominated Aus-tralian billiards, amassing large scores (both breaks and averages) in the way that Bradman was soon to emulate on the cricket field. But one effect of this phenomenon was to reduce interest in contests at the top level, as other Australians were not in Lindrum's class and the English players were reluctant to visit Australia and face him. The 1930s Depression had a further dampening effect on the game. Crowds could no longer afford to pay to see top-class matches or exhibitions. Many firms could not afford the outlay for sponsorship, and those that could expected that tournaments and tours would be conducted on their terms. Further restrictions on scoring were introduced in the early 1930s by the Billiards Association and Control Council (BA&CC), a British-based group of amateur players with the power to determine how the professional tournaments should be conducted. The changes were based on the premise that the high scores prevalent in the game were causing a fall in spectator numbers and that changes to the rules would provide closer contests which would bring the crowds back. An alternative view was that crowds loved to see high scores and became extremely excited at the prospect of seeing a world record break, but could no longer afford the price of admission or the hire of a table. Further controversy raged when Lindrum be-came the World Professional Billiards Cham-pion in 1933 and wished to defend his title in Australia, much to the chagrin of the BA&CC. The title was eventually defended in Melbourne in 1934, by which time support for the sport was starting to decline seriously. The drop in popularity and patronage was accelerated by the Second World War, when many billiard rooms closed due to lack of players.

The decline of billiards continued in the post-war years, largely due to the preference of players for snooker, which is also played on a billiard table but uses a variety of coloured balls with different point values. Snooker was claimed to have been invented by the billiard table manufacturer Alcock and Frank Smith, a Sydney professional, in Melbourne in 1887, but it is more likely that it was developed in India in the mid-1870s by army officers experimenting with different-coloured balls. It was gradually exported over the next decade. During the 1920s snooker featured in many of the billiard tournaments of the day but generally as an adjunct to the main game, as it was regarded by players such as Lindrum as inferior to billiards. Its popularity increased enormously in the 1930s, probably due to the expertise displayed by Horace Lindrum in match play and the fact that snooker games were of relatively short duration—an attractive feature for players with little money in a depression. It was also easier to master than billiards, which was felt by some to account for its booming popularity in post-war Australia. It maintained a steady following in hotels, clubs, and billiard halls throughout the 1950s and 1960s, before receiving a huge impetus in the late 1960s when Eddie Charl-ton organised the first Australian professional snooker championship for more than thirty years and then became the World Professional Snooker Champion. Charlton's rise to success coincided with the televising of top-level snooker matches. Snooker is a sport which provides excellent television viewing and the game in-creased enormously in popularity, participa-tion, and purse as a result of televised matches in the 1970s and 1980s.

RG

See **ALCOCK, HENRY; CHARLTON, EDDIE;**

LINDRUM, HORACE; LINDRUM, WALTER; MARSHALL, BOB.

BJELKE-PETERSEN, CHRISTIAN, born Denmark, arrived in Hobart in 1892 and opened his first Institute of Physical Culture. He brought from Europe the latest ideas in medical gymnastics, massage, and treatment with electricity, impressing both the medical world and education authorities. With his brother Johannes, larger institutes were opened in Melbourne and Sydney. His younger brother Harald, fresh from courses in Europe and North America, joined his brothers in the expanding business. Christian was appointed director of physical training for the Defence Department of the Federal Government, and during the First World War was chief inspector of physical training to the military forces. The Bjelke-Petersen Physical Culture movement continues today, concentrated in NSW. Girls are now the only participants.

RO

See **Calisthenics and Physical Culture**.

Black Sunday. At around 3 p.m. on Sunday, 6 February 1938, five people drowned in heavy seas at Bondi Beach, Sydney. A further three hundred were rescued by around seventy surf lifesavers. Thirty-five swimmers were brought back to the beach unconscious and another thirty required medical assistance. The tragedy occurred when a set of three monstrous waves created a huge backwash, sweeping bathers off a sandbar. Many swimmers panicked. Casualties would have been greater had not three teams of lifesavers been preparing for a surf race, with a relieving surf patrol about to take over the beach watch. Seven belt reels were used in the rescue but most of the lifesavers performed their heroic feats without a line. That only five people died further enhanced the reputation of the lifesaving movement and the 'bronzed Anzac' tradition.

PM

See **LAIDLAW, AUB**.

BLIGHT, MALCOLM (1950–) was an adornment to Victorian and SA football for North Melbourne and Woodville respectively. His brilliant skills enabled him to lead the goal-kicking in each competition, as well as win both a Brownlow and a Magarey Medal. Blight demonstrated his ability to turn a game in spectacular fashion, engineering a famous victory over Carlton, which was sealed by his three goals in the final 5 minutes. The last of these was kicked, after the siren, from seventy metres, and passed through post-high. In 1975 Blight played in North Melbourne's first premiership team, and on retirement showed innovative flair while coaching Geelong to their first VFL Grand Final in twenty-two years.

DS

BLOOMFIELD, JOHN, OAM (1932–), left his native NSW to study at the University of Oregon and returned to Australia in 1974 to become head of the Department of Physical Education at the University of WA, establishing an excellent department specialising in exercise and sport science. As the first professor in the area Bloomfield played an important role in establishing and reviewing similar departments in other tertiary institutions of Australia. His 1973 report for the Australian government, *The Role, Scope and Development of Recreation in Australia*, was influential. Bloomfield has been co-chairman of the ASC (1987–89) and chairman of the AIS (1985–89). He was the first non-medical president of the Australian Sports Medicine Federation. He has achieved numerous honours: WA Citizen of the Year, the OAM (1982), and life membership of the Australian Council for Health, Physical Education and Recreation.

IJ

See **Australian Council for Health, Physical Education and Recreation**.

Boags Cascade Medal. Originally called the W. H. Gill Memorial Trophy on its inception in 1925 as an award to the best and fairest player in the Tasmanian Football League (TFL), the trophy changed its name to the Wilson Bailey Trophy from 1927 to 1929 before it became the William Leitch Medal in 1930. Between 1935 and 1941 the name was changed again, to the George Watt Memorial Medal. The TFL was suspended in 1942 and when it recommenced in 1945 the best and fairest award again became the William Leitch Medal. With the amalgamation of three leagues in 1987 the award became known as the Boags Cascade Medal, with sponsorship from both the northern and southern Tasmanian breweries.

MH*

Bocce

Bocce was first introduced into Australia by immigrant families from Europe, especially Italians, in the early 1900s and was played in backyards, streets, and parks of inner suburbs. The word is Italian for 'bowls'. In the game players try to place their bowls as near as possible to the target bowl (boccino); it can be contested by two players, or in teams of two, three, or four. Following the immigrant wave of the 1950s, families grew up around the sport and it became a part of their social culture. When ethnic social clubs were built, bocce courts were incorporated and it became a fully fledged competitive sport in the 1960s. The Victorian Bocce Federation was established in 1967, followed by the WA Federation in 1969. The first National Bocce Championships began in 1970 and the Bocce Federation of Australia (BFA) was formed in 1971 with branches in all States. An application for affiliation with the

Fédération International des Boules was accepted in 1974 and Australian players, participating for the first time in the international bocce arena, came eleventh in the fours events at these championships at Val-Les Bains in France. Melbourne hosted the third world doubles championship in 1979, the first time such an event had been held in the southern hemisphere, and the success of this event led to a significant increase in the number of participants in the sport—now estimated at 13 000 competitive players. Melbourne again hosted the sixth world championship with the addition of the world throwing championship in 1985, and in 1988, with seven countries competing, the twenty-fifth World Junior Bocce Championship. Australia has performed admirably in world doubles and fours championships since 1974, its best result being in 1988 when third place was gained from twelve participating countries. The standard of bocce play has improved greatly since the BFA introduced coaching accreditation courses in the late 1980s. The BFA believes bocce's future development in Australia lies in the expansion of the sport in the schools and more regular competitions for the younger players.

RC* and IJ
See **Ethnic Influences**.

Body-building

Many people involve themselves in body-building through weight training for reasons of self-esteem, personal image, fitness, or sex appeal. Sportspeople also participate to improve their on-field performances. But body-building is a sport in its own right, with the aim being to produce a body closest to a prescribed conformation. Events are divided into weight divisions and usually comprise both compulsory standard poses as well as freestyle posing.

JC*
See **FRANCIS, BEV**.

Bodyline. The term 'bodyline' was probably coined by cricketer John Worrall and popularised by a sub-editor of the Melbourne *Herald* as a cost-saving abbreviation of the phrase 'on the line of the body'. It describes short-pitched, fast bowling directed at the body of a batsman, with the field placed predominantly on the leg-side. Its invention is attributed to Douglas Jardine, the English captain in the 1932–33 series against Australia. Jardine is said to have conceived it as the only method by which the prodigious run-scorer Donald Bradman could possibly be contained, but it was used in Test matches against other Australian batsmen. Its chief executant was Harold Larwood, a mild-mannered but fearsomely fast professional bowler, who was in no position to deny his captain's instructions. The use of this form of attack had an extremely hostile reception, especially in the third Test match played at Adelaide in January 1933. Both Bill Woodfull, the Australian opening batsman,

and Bert Oldfield, the wicket-keeper, were hit severe blows. The injury to Oldfield, a blow on the skull, led to disturbances in the Adelaide crowd, and strong accusations of bad sportsmanship against the English captain.

The Australian Board of Control took it upon themselves to send a telegram to Lord's, expressing their concern about the damage that bodyline was causing to British–Australian relations. The Marylebone Cricket Club countered this with a testy reply, indicating its full confidence in the England captain. Jardine himself seemed unperturbed, and relentlessly pursued the bodyline attack in subsequent tests. Eventually, England won the Ashes series by four games to one. The English tactics left a nasty taste in the mouths of Australians, and any disinterested lover of the game of cricket must surely deplore them. Short-pitched, fast bowling has continued to plague the game, causing ill-feeling whenever it is employed, and endangering batsmen's lives.

JNT
See **BRADMAN, Sir DONALD**; **Cricket**; **WOODFULL, BILL**; **WORRALL, JOHN**.

BONIS, EDWARD TASMAN (1907–90) played mainly as a rugby hooker—he was dubbed the 'Prince of Hookers' after the 1933 South African tour—appearing for his native Queensland forty-three times and for Australia in twenty-one rugby Tests. An all-round athlete, he was an excellent sailor, cricketer, and swimmer. He established an Australian record by playing twenty-one consecutive Tests before being replaced by the redoubtable Alby Stone. His main regret was never touring the British Isles. He made a significant and continuing contribution to rugby at the State and national levels, coaching Queensland and being an Australian and Queensland selector.

RH and MH

BONWICK, JOHN HENRY (1934–) was a founding member of the Sydney Speleological Society in 1954. Bonwick designed and built innovative equipment for speleological purposes throughout his life, making a great contribution to the Australian capacity for cave exploration. He discovered the Chevalier Cave at Jenolan, and has explored hundreds of other caves. His children, Mark and Vicki, are today leaders in the younger generation of speleologists.

EH-S

Boomerang-throwing

The pastime of boomerang-throwing is believed to have started many thousands of years ago with some groups of the Australian Aboriginal people. Contrary to popular belief, not all Aborigines knew about the returning boomerang. Its development in these early days seems to have been confined to the eastern States of Australia. More recently, most of the activities and development in boomerang-throwing have occurred at the local level. People interested in throwing boomerangs often met at the local oval, and threw boomerangs together, just for the fun of it. Over time, these people decided to codify rules of competition, and establish a direction for the sport. This gave rise to the formation of a national governing body in 1969. This body, the Boomerang Association of Australia, now develops rules for competition and encourages throwers to share their knowledge with others interested in the activity. It also provides a means for Australian throwers to communicate directly with boomerang-throwers around the world in an effort to make the activity more enjoyable for all concerned. State and national championships are held each year, and in 1988 an International World Boomerang Throwing Cup was held in Barooga, NSW, attracting teams from Australia, the USA, France, West Germany, Switzerland, Holland, and Japan.

JG

BORDER, ALLAN, AM (1955–), born Cremorne, NSW, became Australia's most prolific batsman, with over 9000 Test runs by 1991. He also held a string of Test records: the most fifties and the most catches in Tests, the most consecutive Test appearances, and captaining Australia in most Tests. He is the only batsman to have hit 150 runs in both innings of a Test. He made his Test debut as a player in 1978–79. His elevation to the captaincy in 1984–85 occurred at a difficult time: Australia had lost the first two Tests against the West Indies and Kim Hughes had resigned as captain after a teary farewell. Although Border set a fine example to the team, frequently rescuing the side with determined innings, the Australian performance remained lacklustre. Border was so disappointed that he threatened to resign as captain. He at last achieved some results when his side triumphed, unexpectedly, in the Reliance World Cup in India in 1987. This was followed by the 4–0 Ashes triumph of 1989—he was only the third captain to regain the Ashes in England—and the 3–0 thrashing of England in Australia in 1990–91. A left-hand bat, a fine player of spin, and a more than useful left-arm spin bowler, Border has always been a popular captain and a fine ambassador both of cricket and of Australia, particularly in India and Pakistan. He has represented NSW, Queensland, and Australia with distinction and was named Australian of the Year in 1990.

KM-H
See **Cricket**.

BORTHWICK, PATRICIA (1926–), born Sydney, has won a record-equalling four Australian Women's Amateur Golf Championships, an unprecedented six NSW amateur titles, and has ten international appearances to her credit. The former hairdresser's career has been plagued by injury and illness. Badly burnt when she was 2, she was unable to attend school for ten years. Later, in an effort to keep her away from the surf, her parents bought her a set of golf clubs. Borthwick won her first NSW title in 1948 and toured Britain in 1950 and South Africa in 1953 as an Australian representative. She won her Australian titles on four different courses, her final victory being achieved after an eighteen-month absence due to hepatitis.

GC*

BOSISTO, GLYN DE VILLIERS, MBE (1899–), born Gawler, SA, is the only man to win four successive Australian titles in lawn bowls from 1949 to 1953 (the event was not held in 1950) and dominated the sport to such an extent in the 1940s and 1950s—winning at one stage sixty-eight successive championships—that he was dubbed the 'Bradman of Bowls'. In all he played for Australia, NSW, and Victoria on 256 occasions. Bosisto twice skippered the winning fours in the Australian championships (1951 and 1957) and won the Victorian State singles on five occasions. He represented Australia at two British Empire and Commonwealth Games (1954 and 1958). He was awarded the MBE in 1977 and inducted into the Sport Australia Hall of Fame in 1985.

RC

BOTHA, WENDY (1965–), born South Africa, but a naturalised Australian, is a surfer with a strong, powerful style. She has placed consistently well in competition, both amateur and professional. She won four South African amateur titles and after turning professional in 1985 was placed seventh in the world ranking in that year. She has had numerous victories in her professional career and has won the world champion title three times, in 1987, 1989, and 1991. As well as surfing, her interests include cycling, tennis, table tennis, horse-racing, and drumming. She supports health and environmental causes and coaches at surf clinics.

MV

Boxing
Prize-fighting—bare-knuckle combats to exhaustion organised by wealthy patrons and watched free by the gambling fraternity—originated in urban London. It was codified in 1743 by John Broughton, the English champion. His rules permitted any action except for eye-gouging and hitting a fallen opponent. This sporting tradition was transplanted to the Antipodes. The first recorded Australian prize-fight was between convicts John Parton and Charles Sefton on 8 January 1814. Parton triumphed in 90 minutes of hard fighting over fifty rounds—a round concluding when one

21 *Australia II*'s winged keel, a key factor in its success during the 1983 *America*'s Cup, became a symbol of Australia's entry into the high-tech area.

22 The Australian Sports Medicine Federation has been instrumental in the prevention, treatment and rehabilitation of sports-related injuries. Former prime minister Bob Hawke narrowly escaped injury in this incident.

23 Aussie Sports, funded by the Australian Sports Commission, is a national strategy to increase and diversify sports participation by children. T-Ball is an example of how it has modified the adult sport of baseball/ softball into an appropriate activity for young children.

24 Baseball was an activity enjoyed by many cricketers in Sydney, Adelaide and Melbourne from the early 1890s.

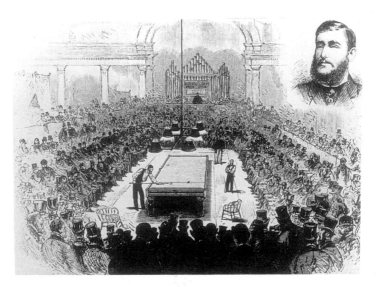

25 A billiards match at Athenaeum Hall, Melbourne, June 1876, between English champion, Mr Roberts, Jr, and Mr Albers of the Theatre Royal Billiard Saloon.

26 Reginald 'Snowy' Baker was an all-round sportsman, but it was mainly as a boxer that he made his name.

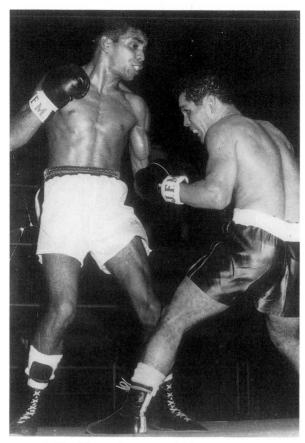

27 Lionel Rose, a bantamweight, became the first Aborigine to win a world boxing title when he beat Fighting Harada in Tokyo in 1968.

28 Boxing promoter Hugh D. McIntosh built a temporary stadium for the 1908 title fight at Rushcutter's Bay, Sydney, and the 20 000 spectators set an attendance record.

29 A highlight of boxing in Australia was the staging of the world heavyweight title fight between the black American, Jack Johnson, and the Canadian, Tommy Burns.

man was knocked down. Prize-fights were held at secluded Sydney venues from the 1820s, but details are sketchy as the police and press disapproved. The *Sydney Gazette* argued that such sinful and barbaric old-world pursuits were unsuited to a new society. Contests were enlivened by native-born v. immigrant antagonisms. John Kable, John Cuppitt, Bill Sparkes, and George Hough were prominent native-born fighters. Thousands watched Englishman Isaac Read defeat Hough in 98 minutes in Middle Head bushland in 1847. Prize-fighting flourished on the goldfields as entertainment-starved diggers paid to watch gloved exhibitions from John 'Black' Perry and other imports, and serious bare-knuckle contests. The world's longest fight was fought at Fiery Creek in 1854 when James Kelly defeated Jonathon Smith in over 6 hours, much of it marked by stares and sparring. Labouring-class prize-fighters, managed by discreet patrons such as bookmakers, publicans, graziers, and professional men, fought on until the decline of the prize-ring in the 1870s. Official surveillance intensified after 1860, aided by increased police efficiency and the rise of middle-class respectability. In 1877 Jem Mace, the former British champion, arrived to box exhibitions and proselytise the new Marquess of Queensberry Rules and the use of gloves. These rules prohibited kicking, holding, throttling, hair-pulling, and gouging—all tricks of the prize-fighter's trade. Mace persuaded Larry Foley, the Australian champion, to adopt gloves and the Queensberry Rules. Foley used his charisma and his gymnasiums to disseminate scientific Queensberry boxing. The death of prize-fighter Alec Agar in Sydney in 1884, and the gaoling of his black American opponent for one year, virtually ended the prize-ring: most future fights were gloved boxing matches. The introduction of entrance fees, from which boxers could be paid, in the 1880s also curbed the influence of patrons—the Fancy, as insiders called them.

Boxing gained some official acceptance by the 1890s as gymnasiums openly taught boxing and held matches. The fans also avidly read of the overseas exploits of Australian professionals Peter Slavin, Albert Griffiths who was Australia's first world champion (featherweight, in 1890), Bob Fitzsimmons, and Jamaican-born and honorary Australian Peter Jackson. Competing ideologies of the sport also matured. Proponents argued that boxing underpinned national defence, manliness, and physical and mental development, while the respectable claimed it encouraged brutality, gambling, and other base passions. Hugh D. McIntosh's promotion of the Jack Johnson–Tommy Burns world heavyweight title fight in Sydney in 1908 symbolised new directions in boxing. This fight, won by the black American Johnson over

the Canadian Burns, shattered the colour bar, introducing interracial competition into championship events. The 20 000 people at the newly built Rushcutter's Bay Stadium set an attendance record, heralding regular promotions and mass boxing audiences. The fight was also filmed, enabling millions to view it ever since. Simultaneously, travelling troupes boxed in tents about the countryside, gaining access to agricultural shows as their respectability increased. Jimmy Sharman's troupe was the most famous and enduring, surviving from 1912 to 1971. The tent-fighters fought exhibitions and those who accepted the challenge 'Who'll Take a Glove?'. The tents were proving grounds for young boxers and graveyards for old ones. The life was hard but provided camaraderie and a living. All were treated equally, a novelty for the Aborigines among them; their presence gave a racial edge to the fighting which raised interest and increased the takings.

Stadiums Ltd, headed by John Wren, monopolised professional boxing from the 1920s, to the sport's eventual detriment. Overseas boxers and locals Tommy Uren, Billy Grime, and Hughie Dwyer initially enlivened the scene. However, a lack of imports, and a return to smaller stadiums and corrupt practices in the Depression debased the sport. Yet Ron Richards, Fred Henneberry, Jack Carroll, and others provided plenty of action. Richards led an Aboriginal assault that netted Aborigines 15 per cent of Australian professional titles between 1930 and 1980, despite their being only 1 per cent of the population. Vic Patrick, Tommy Burns, George Barnes, and Aboriginal boxers Dave Sands, Elley Bennett, and Jack Hassen were the drawcards of the 1940s. The occasional ring death—notably that of Archie Kemp in 1949—led to repeated calls for a control commission, but all efforts foundered on Stadiums Ltd's monopoly. Boxers gained workers' compensation in 1952. The toothless Australian Boxing Federation emerged in 1967 along with other ineffective controlling bodies.

Boxing declined from the 1940s due to rising affluence and competing diversions. Yet paradoxically Australian world champions emerged: Jimmy Carruthers (bantam, 1952), Lionel Rose (bantam, 1968), Johnny Famechon (feather, 1969), and Rocky Mattioli (light-middle, 1976). Boxing revived temporarily, inspired by Rose, Famechon, and weekly boxing telecasts in 1968. Surveys in 1973 revealed that 300 000 people in Melbourne and Sydney—10–15 per cent of viewers—watched boxing on late-night television. Of those Melbournites watching Channel Seven's 'TV Ringside' (considered the best of the three boxing telecasts), approximately 56 per cent were men, 34 per cent were women and 10 per cent were children under 18. Its compère, Merv Williams—Queensland middleweight champion of 1922 and boxing writer for the *Sporting Globe* since the 1940s—thrilled audiences with his colourful commentary. Television consolidated the century-old Sydney–Melbourne dominance of boxing. Of the 241 promotions in 1973 involving 727 boxers, all but twenty were staged at Festival Hall Melbourne or League Football and RSL clubs in the Sydney–Newcastle area. TV boxing ended in 1975 because the available talent was overexposed. The high profile of televised boxing stimulated renewed concern about the sport, and in 1973 the National Health and Medical Research Council (NHMRC) investigated the health and regulatory aspects of boxing. It reported a recent British study that one in six boxers surveyed suffered brain damage. The NHMRC itemised dementia, impaired memory, mood swings, spasticity, and ear and eye damage, among boxing injuries. It listed eighty-eight known boxing deaths in Australia since 1893, sixty-one of them between 1910 and 1939. The NHMRC recommended stringent medical recording and examination, and accreditation of all boxing personnel. A Federal interdepartmental committee in 1974 unsuccessfully recommended a boxing commission with wide regulatory powers; Victoria and NSW created control boards in the 1980s, but the sport still needs strong Federal regulation.

Boxing in the 1980s experienced a cyclical low. With the demise of tent and TV boxing, and of Stadiums Ltd in 1975, there were no 'showcases' and no substantial promoters to foster new talent. Women's boxing was tried by a Melbourne promoter in April 1979 but it fizzled since the sport at large saw it as an ill-advised oddity. However, Australian boxing recently produced four world champions: Lester Ellis (junior-light, 1985), Barry Michael (junior-light, 1986), the brilliant Jeff Fenech (bantam, 1985; superbantam 1987; feather, 1988), and Jeff Harding (light-heavy, 1989). After 200 years Australian boxing still refuses to take the final count.

RB

See **BAKER, REGINALD**; **Burns–Johnson Fight**; **CARROLL, JACK**; **CARRUTHERS, JAMES**; **DARCY, LES**; **Drama**; **FAMECHON, JEAN**; **FENECH, JEFF**; **FOLEY, LARRY**; **GRIFFITHS, ALBERT**; **JACKSON, PETER**; **JEROME, JERRY**; **McINTOSH, HUGH**; **MILLER, WILLIAM**; **PALMER, AMBROSE**; **PATRICK, VIC**; **RICHARDS, RON**; **ROSE, LIONEL**; **SANDS, DAVE**; **SHARMAN, JIMMY**; **Stadiums Limited**; **WILLIAMS, MERVYN**.

BOYD, ESNA (1901–62), born Melbourne, contested seven Australian open tennis singles finals. Boyd is often remembered as having been runner-up for the first five opens. Yet when she did win the 1927 crown she may have

been fortunate, as the favourite Daphne Akhurst had been forced to withdraw. The following year Akhurst returned Boyd to her runner-up status. Boyd, who had a powerful flat forehand but weak backhand, was chosen in 1925 as a member of the first Australian women's team to tour Europe. Later she emigrated to Scotland as Mrs Robertson but returned briefly in 1932 to win her sixth Victorian singles title.

HCJP

See **Lawn Tennis**.

BOYLE, RAELENE (1951–   ) reached the finals of the 100 and 200 metres at three successive Olympics from 1968 to 1976. She was selected for the 1980 Olympics but withdrew after the Australian government boycott appeal. Boyle won three Olympic silver medals, the first in Mexico at the age of 17 when she equalled the 200 metres world record of 22.7 seconds. She won her other two medals in Munich. In a fifteen-year athletic career she won the sprint double at the 1970 and 1974 British Commonwealth Games, a string of six Australian titles for each event, and was a member of the 1975 4 × 200 metres relay team which set a world record. Boyle was Australian flag-bearer at the Montreal Olympics where she finished fourth in the 100 metres and was controversially disqualified from the 200 metres final when she was alleged to have broken twice. After switching to the 400 metres she won the Australian title in 1980 and the gold medal at the 1982 Commonwealth Games where she also gained a silver medal anchoring the 4 × 400 metres relay.

GC†

BRABHAM, Sir JACK, OBE (1926–   ), born Sydney, was a gifted racing driver and a practical engineer. He applied his skills with a distinctive blend of caution and confidence to become one of the most broadly accomplished drivers in the history of the sport. After winning two Australian speedway titles in his first three seasons he turned to road racing in 1952, investigated professional European road racing in 1955 and has not been a full-time Australian resident since. He complemented perfectly the informal and innovative London racing-car manufacturer Cooper, and together they conquered Formula One, winning the world championships in 1959 and 1960. With long-time Australian associate Ron Tauranac, Brabham opened his own racing-car factory in 1961, finding immediate success in minor formulas. Using new F1 engines built in Australia by Repco, Brabham won his third championship in 1966 and was a very close second to team-mate Denny Hulme in 1967. He retired from active racing in 1970 ('too early', he later said), and sold his share in the Brabham racing team, although he has retained his many global business interests in motor sport, the motor trade, and aviation. He was awarded the OBE in 1966 and was knighted in 1979. The three sons of Jack Brabham—Geoffrey, Gary, and David—became racing drivers but have yet to achieve the international status of their illustrious father.

GH

See **Motor Racing**.

Bradley Report. In late 1989 the Australian Soccer Federation (ASF) commissioned Dr Graham Bradley to produce this management review from which recommendations would come to make the administrative set-up of soccer more effective and the game more marketable to the general Australian sporting public. Bradley emphasised that soccer needed to broaden its support base beyond its current ethnic niches, or it would never fully realise its potential. The report was published in May 1990 with most of its recommendations adopted by the ASF. Its most notable points included the restructuring of the National Soccer League (NSL) and the ASF voting system; the creation of a Board of Commissioners and several specialist committees overseeing development, and internal and international competitions; and the requirement that NSL club status be based on satisfying an established set of criteria rather than purely on playing strength.

PK

BRADMAN, Sir DONALD, AC (1908–), born Cootamundra but brought up in Bowral, NSW, became Australia's most successful cricketer. Small (170 centimetres), and slight (65 kilograms), possessing a wonderful eye, nimble feet, and great concentration, Bradman was a self-taught cricketer. He achieved genuine stardom in 1930 when, on his first tour to England, he astonished the cricket world with a string of huge scores including 309 not out in a day in the Leeds Test. Bodyline bowling was introduced in Australia in 1932–33 to curb his phenomenal run-making. The physical and symbolic attack on Australia's greatest hero during a time of rising Australian nationalism and economic depression aroused deep emotions. Shunning established methods, Bradman embarked upon a creative and adventurous counter-attack which was partially successful. In statistical terms his Test career remains unique: an average of 99.94; a century in every third innings; the most double centuries; and the only person to score two triple centuries. He was also the only person to succeed twice in scoring 1000 runs in English first-class cricket before the end of May. Bradman towered above his contemporaries like a colossus. Despite his extraordinary achievements, Bradman has been the object of criticism. Some have suggested that he was a ruthless run-making machine, but he possessed a wide range of strokes, scoring at an extremely rapid rate. Others have suggested that his public reserve represented an aloofness. Bradman has had to cope with greater sustained public interest than any other Australian. The fascination with 'The Don' did not diminish with his retirement from cricket in 1949: a continuing stream of books, albums, videos, and radio tapes along with the opening of the Bradman Museum at Bowral have maintained his legendary status. Bradman was exceptionally successful as captain, administrator, and businessman. He is the only Australian who has been knighted for his services to cricket.

IH

See **Bodyline**; **Cricket**; **Sport Australia Hall of Fame**; **Squash Rackets**.

BREASLEY, ARTHUR EDWARD ('Scobie') (1914–), born Wagga Wagga, NSW, was apprenticed as a jockey at the age of 12 to local trainer S. H. Biggins. His nickname was a jocular reference to the leading trainer and ex-jockey James Scobie, whose achievements he in time eclipsed. Moving to Melbourne the following year, Breasley rode his first metropolitan winner in 1928, and in 1930 won the AJC Metropolitan on *Cragman* for his master, P. B. Quinlan. Breasley reached the peak of his Australian form during the forties with four successive Caulfield Cup wins (1942–45) and victory in other major races including the Victoria Derby and Oaks, Sydney Cup, and Epsom Handicap. In 1950 he visited England and was an instant success. After a visit home in 1952 (when he won his fifth Caulfield Cup), he returned to England. He recovered from a serious fall in 1954, and two years later became the senior jockey for Sir Gordon Richards's stable. By 1957 he had become the leading jockey in England, an achievement he repeated from 1961 to 1963. He recorded more than two thousand wins in his English career alone. These included the English Derby of 1964 on *Santa Claus* and a second Derby on *Charlottown* in 1966. He also rode *Ballymoss* to win the 1958 Prix de l'Arc de Triomphe in Paris. Retiring from riding in 1968, aged 54, Breasley began a new career as a trainer, and won the 1972 Irish Derby with *Steel Pulse*. He relocated his stables in 1975 to Chantilly in France until 1977, and then trained briefly in New York. He retired to the Bahamas.

AL

See **Horse-racing**.

British Empire and Commonwealth Games 1962 (Perth). Perth hosted the seventh Games from 22 November to 1 December and Prince Philip, president of the overseeing British Empire and Commonwealth Games Federation, presided at the opening ceremony. A model suburb was built at Wembley Downs to house the ever-increasing number of competitors, and almost £4 million was spent on preparations for the Games, much of it for international standard sports facilities. The event marked the first occasion on which Perth held a major international sporting festival. Just over one thousand competitors representing thirty-five countries engaged in athletics, bowls, cycling, rowing, swimming and diving, boxing, fencing, wrestling, and weightlifting. Men's events continued to dominate the programme, with women eligible to compete only in athletics, aquatics, and one event in fencing. The Australian women's team collected forty-two medals, and the men ninety-seven; swimmers dominated the place-getting, with Murray Rose and Dawn Fraser gaining four gold medals each, Ian O'Brien three, and Kevin Berry three. A record 225 000 spectators watched the events live over nine days of competition, and witnessed the emerging excellence of the Africans in selected sports, particularly distance running.

KM

See **Commonwealth Games**.

British Empire Games 1938 (Sydney). Staged as part of the 150th anniversary celebrations of the founding of a European colony in Australia, the Games were held in Sydney from 5 to 12 February. Six hundred competitors and officials representing fifteen countries took part in seven sports. The organising committee was headed by E. S. Marks, with James Eve as the energetic honorary secretary. The first athletes' village to be built at an Empire Games was established at the Royal Agricultural Society Showground; the men stayed there, while the female competitors were housed in hotels near King's Cross. Track and field athletes found the grass track at the SCG very fast, with virtually every Empire Games record being tied or broken. WA track star Decima Norman won five gold medals, a feat still unmatched in Commonwealth Games athletics. Australian wrestlers claimed six out of seven weight divisions, and the cyclists and rowers won most of the gold medals in their events. Females were restricted to competition in athletics, and swimming and diving; Australia's team of thirty women gained fifteen gold medals, eight silver, and six bronze. The 124-strong men's team achieved twenty first, twenty-three second, and twenty-nine third places.

KM

See **Commonwealth Games**.

Broadcasting

Radio has had a marked influence on the development and popularity of sport in Australia, with a sports broadcast coming before the nation's first station went to air officially. Amalgamated Wireless Australasia Limited began experimenting with radio transmission in early 1923 and broadcast a description of *Kunjolio's* win in the Grand National Steeplechase at Mel-

bourne's Flemington racecourse in July of that year. Regular race descriptions began in March 1925 through 3LO Melbourne and 2FC Sydney, and although they proved immensely popular with the public, many sporting bodies were fearful of their impact. Race clubs at first banned commentators from the courses, forcing broadcasters to call from trees outside the tracks or towers erected in the front yards of nearby homes. As sports descriptions were popular and helped to sell wireless sets and licences, they became the most common actuality broadcasts. Station owners were also in favour of them, for they were cheaper to produce than performances, where artists demanded payment. 2BL Sydney introduced the first football commentary in July 1924 with a broadcast of the rugby league final between Balmain and South Sydney. It also began giving scores and commentary (though not continuous description) of cricket during the first Test match between Australia and England in December 1924. 5CL Adelaide is credited with providing the first ball-by-ball cricket descriptions in Australia during the second Test in January 1925. Radio has played an important role in the coverage of sport, and in so doing has influenced the sporting preferences of Australians. The immediacy of radio and the greater mobility of the population means that radio can not only co-exist with television but can demand an increasing share of the available listening and viewing audience.

JMcC

See **McGILVRAY, ALAN**; **Media**; **NOBLE, MONTAGUE**.

BROCK, PETER (1945–), born Melbourne, was recruited by the newly formed Holden Dealer Team in 1969 in only his second season and helped start the Holden v. Ford rivalry which was to dominate two decades of Australian motor racing. A born racer, he quickly added polish and became one of sport's best known personalities. His racing fortunes have been closely tied to Holden's, his three Australian Touring-Car Championships (1974, 1978, and 1980) and nine Bathurst endurance-race victories between 1972 and 1987 all coming in Holden cars.

GH

See **Motor Racing**.

BROCKHOFF, JOHN DAVID (1928–), rugby coach, was a leading exponent of ten-man rugby, based on a strong forward platform and a kicking five-eighth. After attending Scots College, Brockhoff played for Sydney University and Eastern Suburbs, playing ten Tests for Australia. When Brockhoff was appointed national coach Australian rugby was at a low ebb, with only seven victories in the preceding thirty-six Tests. While national coach from

1974 to 1976 Brockhoff had some notable achievements including a draw against NZ and a series win against England. Returning to coach Australia in 1979, he achieved his greatest triumph when Australia defeated NZ 12–6— the first victory over NZ in Australia since 1934. After stepping down as national coach, Brockhoff became involved in the administration of the Sydney University Club as well as supporting the development of the Sydney district competition so that it catered for the city's developing suburbs—an issue that has still not been resolved.

TH

BROMWICH, JOHN EDWARD (1918–), born Kogarah, NSW, was a dour tennis-player who was a perfectionist. From the age of 5, hitting a ball against a wall, Bromwich developed double-handed groundstrokes on both sides and persisted with a double-handed service until the age of 13. He hit his forehand left-handed but served right-handed. Coming to prominence in the late 1930s, Bromwich established himself as a great craftsman doubles-player, winning the Australian men's doubles eight times with his perennial partner, Adrian Quist, from 1938 to 1950. During the Second World War he served in New Guinea, where he contracted malaria; nevertheless he played some of his most momentous Davis Cup matches in the immediate post-war period. Bromwich was runner-up in the Wimbledon singles in 1948 and winner of the doubles in 1948 and 1950; he won the US doubles in 1939, 1949, and 1950. In Davis Cup doubles he only lost one rubber out of twenty-two from 1937 to 1950. Bromwich was a great favourite with galleries for his tenacity in long rallies, his unorthodoxy, his ball control and placement, his loose-strung racket, and his rueful self-admonition on the court. In the mid-1950s he retired from full-scale competition to run a newsagency at Bacchus Marsh in Melbourne.

GK-S

See **Lawn Tennis**; QUIST, ADRIAN.

BROOKES, Sir NORMAN ('the Wizard') (1878–1968), born Melbourne, was the first to place Australian tennis in the forefront of world tennis by winning the 1907 Wimbledon men's singles and by his key role as player in nine Davis Cup ties and as a playing and non-playing captain of Australasian and Australian Davis Cup teams from 1905 to 1950. His left-handed and swinging serve, his controlled low volley, his anticipation, and his ability to analyse his opponents made him a formidable player. Bill Tilden described Brookes as '*the* greatest tennis brain in the twentieth century'. Brookes played a large part in Australasia's first winning of the Davis Cup in 1907 and in the memorable first Davis Cup Challenge in Australia in 1908 when

the skill and tenacity of the Australasian players in beating the Americans was first brought home to the Australian public. His last Davis Cup appearance as a player was in 1920, by which time he had played a total of twenty-two Davis Cup rubbers in challenge rounds. He continued playing at the highest level, however, reaching the final sixteen in the Wimbledon men's singles in 1924 at the age of 47. Brookes, who had come to tennis from a privileged and much-travelled background, went on to serve as Davis Cup captain until 1950, continuing thereafter as Davis Cup selector. He had become president of the Lawn Tennis Association of Australia in 1926, retiring from that position only in 1955, having wielded greater power in the conduct of Australian tennis than any other figure.

GK-S

See **Australian Curling Association**; **Lawn Tennis**; **Tennis Australia**.

Broomball

Broomball is a six-a-side team-game played with a broom (a stick with a rubber paddle-shaped end) and an inflated rubber ball on an ice rink. Players wear soft-soled sports shoes, padding, and a compulsory helmet. The rink measures 61 × 26 metres and is surrounded by barrier boards; the object of the game is to hit the ball with the broom into the goals at either end of the rink. A game is divided into two periods, each of 20 minutes' playing time. The normal line-up of players is a goalkeeper, two defencemen, and three forwards—the centre-men and two wingers. The game was first played in 1911 in Canada and is now played in several countries around the world. In 1981 it was introduced to Australia, with Canberra organising the first league. The sport grew quickly and in 1983 was being played in four States and the ACT. The ACT team, the ACT Animals, have won seven of the ten national championships. Australia has been represented overseas in 1988 on a goodwill tour to Canada. In late 1991 Australia sent two teams to the inaugural World Broomball Tournament held in Victoria, British Columbia, Canada.

GC*

BROWN, DAVID MICHAEL (1913–74), was Australia's leading rugby league footballer in the 1930s. His parents ran the surf-sheds at Sydney's Bronte Beach. Brown played rugby union at Waverley Christian Brothers' College, and entered Eastern Suburbs first grade in 1930. After the sudden loss of his hair, from 1932 he played in a distinctive leather headpiece. Under his captaincy Easts was the dominant team from 1932 to 1936. A try-scoring centre three-quarter and place-kicker, Brown toured England in 1933; his tour record of 285 points has not been surpassed. His 1935 record of 285 points in Sydney competition stood until 1978. In 1936 he captained Australia against the touring Englishmen. He then played three seasons in England for Warrington, at a record fee, returned to lead Easts to victory again in 1940, and retired the following year.

CC

See **Rugby League**.

BROWN, JOYCE (1938–) represented Victoria in netball from 1958 to 1963 as wing attack and goal attack and captained the victorious Australian team in the first World Netball Championships in 1963. She coached Australia to world titles in 1972, 1983, and 1991 and was national director of coaching for All Australia Netball from 1980 to 1983. Brown was inducted as an associate member of the Sport Australia Hall of Fame in 1989. She was a board member of the AIS (1984–86) and the Confederation of Australian Sport (1988–90).

IJ and PB

See **Netball**.

BROWNE, IAN ('Joey') (1931–), born Melbourne, learned to ride a bicycle as a small child but did not take up competitive cycling until he was 16. Unusually tall and solid for a cyclist (186 centimetres, 85 kilograms), Browne was tenacious, logical, and perhaps introspective, and had a long cycling career. He pulled off an upset win (with Tony Marchant) in the 2000 metres tandem cycling event at the 1956 Olympics. Although he reached his peak in 1956 he took part in two more Olympics and won a gold medal in the 10 mile race at the 1958 British Empire and Commonwealth Games and came third in the 1000 metres sprint at the next Games in Perth in 1962. He later became involved in cycling administration.

RH and MH

BROWNLOW, CHARLES (1861–1924), born Geelong, Victoria, made a great contribution to Australian rules football which has been acknowledged by the annual awarding of the Brownlow Medal. After playing football with North Geelong, Brownlow joined Geelong in 1879. He played for the club for thirteen years, was captain in 1884, was a member of six premiership sides and was coach from 1892 to 1914. He was, in addition, secretary of the combined football and cricket clubs from 1884 to 1917. He served Geelong for thirty-three years and was the club's delegate to the VFL for twenty years. Brownlow was one of the founding fathers of the VFL in 1896, serving as vice-president and as a delegate to the Australasian Football Council. He was responsible for introducing many important changes to the game.

SB*

See **Brownlow Medal**.

Brownlow Medal. The most prestigious award in Australian rules football was introduced in 1924 to commemorate the service to the sport of former Australian National Council president, Charles Brownlow. The medal is presented to the fairest and best player in AFL (formerly VFL) minor round matches. Voting for the Brownlow Medal has been done in various ways but has always been decided by field umpires. Until 1931 only one vote was awarded per game but, after a three-way tie between Stan Judkins, Alan Hopkins, and Harry Collier, a 3–2–1 voting system based on first, second, and third preferences, was introduced in the following season and retained until 1976 when the two-umpire voting system was introduced. The latter method lasted for only the 1976 and 1977 seasons. Since then field umpires have conferred to determine joint votes. At one time when players finished with equal votes the winner was decided by countback, but from 1980 such players were acknowledged as joint medal winners. In 1990 the AFL awarded Brownlow Medals retrospectively to players who had lost on count-backs. There have been several multiple winners of the award, with Haydn Bunton senior, Dick Reynolds, Bob Skilton, and Ian Stewart each successful on three occasions.

BW

See **BROWNLOW, CHARLES**.

BUCKINGHAM, BEVERLEY (1965–) won the 1981–82 Tasmanian jockey's premiership with sixty-three wins while still an apprentice, becoming the first woman to top the jockeys' list in any Australian State. Apprenticed to her father, she began riding in races in October 1980, little more than a year after New Zealander Linda Jones had become the first woman to win a race open to men and women riders in Australia, at Doomben in Brisbane, on 7 May 1979. Buckingham was by far the most successful woman jockey over the next few years, but found opportunities much more restricted after moving with her family to Victoria in 1989.

AL

Bulimba Cup. From Queensland rugby league's early days, matches were played between the south-eastern cities Brisbane, Toowoomba, and Ipswich. In 1925 a local brewery donated the Bulimba Cup for the contests and, in a round-robin of home and away matches, it was won that year by unbeaten Toowoomba who fielded nine current or future Australian representatives. The games became valuable trials for the Queensland selectors and were highlights of the season. However, as Brisbane began to dominate in the 1960s, interest died and the competition lapsed after 1972 when

Brisbane won for the nineteenth time. Toowoomba had been successful in sixteen years and Ipswich in eleven.

TB

BUNTON, HAYDN (1911–55), born Albury, NSW, is regarded by many discerning critics as the greatest, and one of the most graceful, Australian rules football players. In seven seasons of VFL football Bunton won three Brownlow Medals—the first to do so—and went within a whisker of a fourth. Although recruited to Fitzroy in 1930, the VFL refused to grant him a permit until 1931. He was an instant success, winning Brownlows in his first two seasons. As a rover-cum-centre with amazing stamina, Bunton appeared to be all over the field winning possessions. He was the leading goal-kicker for Fitzroy twice, was three times captain, and was coach in 1936. He represented Victoria fifteen times. Bunton became captain-coach of Subiaco, WA, in 1938 and won three Sandover Medals in four years. After playing again with Fitzroy in 1942, he played for Port Adelaide and later coached North Adelaide. He became a senior umpire in SA, officiating in the 1946 Grand Final. Bunton played 213 games and kicked 438 goals in three States. He was killed in a road accident at Gawler in SA at the age of 44.

SB*

BURDON, ALEXANDER (1880–1943) achieved fame when he broke his collarbone while playing rugby for NSW and received no compensation from rugby authorities. The Burdon incident helped focus attention on a long-standing dispute between the old guard of the NSW Rugby Football Union and new groups which had come into the game. It was the spark which led to the 1907 split in Sydney rugby. Burdon, who played for the Sydney and Glebe clubs, was selected as a forward for NSW in 1901 and played twenty-four games for his State. He toured with the first Australian rugby league team to Britain and played in two Tests. He was later a selector for NSW and Australia.

TH

See **Rugby League**; **Rugby Union**.

BURGE, Dr IVOR C., MBE (1906–), returned to Victoria from Springfield College, USA, to become director of physical education at the YMCA in Melbourne in 1928. He became the founding director of physical education at the University of Queensland in 1941, retiring as head of department in 1971. Burge was awarded life membership of the Australian Physical Education Association (now ACHPER). He has been credited with introducing basketball to Australia as well as founding the Queensland and Victorian basketball associations, and being co-founder of the Australian Amateur Basketball Union. He was also prominent as a square-dance caller.

IJ

See **Basketball**.

BURGE, FRANK ('Chunky') (1894–1958), born Darlington, NSW, was one of rugby league's outstanding try-scoring forwards. A fast, powerful and long-striding player, Burge redefined lock-forward play by breaking quickly from the scrum to run with the backs. He scored 141 tries for Glebe in the Sydney competition between 1911 and 1922 (including eight tries in one first-grade game) and on the Kangaroo tour of England in 1921–22 he scored 33 tries. A punishing tackler and a competent goal-kicker, he was the complete footballer. Burge first played for NSW in 1912 and represented Australia in nine Tests against England. He was captain-coach of Grenfell (1924–25) and St George (1927–28). His three brothers also gained representative honours in football: Peter, a union/league international, Albert, a union international, and Laidley, who played rugby league for NSW. He died in Sydney on 5 July 1958.

MS

Burns–Johnson Fight. This sensational fight took place on Boxing Day 1908 at the open-air Sydney Stadium between black American Jack Johnson and the current World Heavyweight Boxing Champion, white Canadian Tommy Burns. Twenty thousand men (and several disguised women) watched, while thirty thousand disappointed spectators gathered outside. People crowded post offices around Australia to hear progress reports and many thousands more viewed the fight film afterwards. The first-ever black–white encounter for the heavyweight crown was seen as a symbolic race war by a racially conscious Australian community. Jack Johnson, the first of a line of flamboyant black boxers to challenge white racial ideas and marry white women, added to the drama. Burns, like previous white champions, initially drew the 'colour line' against Johnson but the smell of Hugh D. McIntosh's £6000 'win or lose' offer for a Johnson fight opened the championship to blacks. Johnson (185 centimetres tall), considered the best-ever heavyweight by many, beat Burns (170 centimetres tall) in a bitter fight marked by Johnson's deliberate humiliation of Burns. The police stopped the punishment in the fourteenth round.

RB

BURNS, PETER CHARLES (1866–1951) was known as 'Peter the Great' and was one of the most outstanding Australian rules footballers of all time. Burns came from Ballarat Imperial Football Club to play for South Melbourne (1885–91 including four premierships) and then Geelong (1892–1902). After retirement he remained at Geelong to serve as timekeeper for a further forty years. He was a key player for Victoria and was captain in 1899. Burns was of medium build and played as a follower-cum-rover alternating as full back. His life-sized portrait in South Melbourne uniform, now hanging in the Geelong Club rooms, is possibly the best ever painted of an Australian rules footballer.

NS

BURRIDGE, PAM (1964–) is a former competitive swimmer from Newport Beach, Sydney, who has surfed from an early age. She entered her first competition at the age of 13 and in 1979, 1980, and 1981 she won the NSW titles. She was national women's champion in 1980, and choosing that year to turn professional, finished among the top eight women surfers in the world. Since then she has travelled the world to compete and has won or placed well consistently in most competitions. In her ten years of professional surfing she has always been among the top ten world ratings and has been runner-up to the world title four times. In 1990, she won the world title, clinching the result with her victory at Sunset Beach, Hawaii. She combines her competitive career with her interests of modelling, recording music, and public relations work.

MV

See **Surfing**.

Bushwalking

During the nineteenth century some Australian athletes competed in walking races over long distances in rugged country. One of the clubs formed for this activity, the Melbourne Amateur Walking and Touring Club, established in 1894, also embraced what is now known as bushwalking, and became the first such club in Australia. Speed walking gradually diminished in popularity, and finally disappeared. Further bushwalking clubs formed, while the establishment and growth of the Scout and Guide movements also fostered interest in bushwalking. Some clubs became linked with the conservation movement and under the influence of individuals like Myles Dunphy of Sydney took a leading part in the fight to extend the Australian National Park system. The main change in the nature of bushwalking arose in the 1930s when Paddy Pallin of Sydney started the design and manufacture of lightweight equipment for walkers. Early walkers had carried their food and equipment in a bushman's swag and on longer ventures had used packhorses. The 1930s Depression saw a remarkable boom in the popularity of hiking and bushwalking. The railways, in conjunction with various media companies, operated mystery hikes which attracted thousands of participants. Many new clubs were formed, often with a large membership, and the biggest, the Smile-Away Club, numbered many thousand enthusiasts. In the 1960s bushwalking clubs played the main role in the Swedish sport of orienteering coming to Australia, and they also fostered the growth of rock-climbing in this country. Then, in the 1970s, the 24-hour walks of some clubs led in turn to the new sport of rogaining, which is a test of navigation skills somewhat like orienteering but taking place over a continuous 24-hour period, often in fairly wild country.

EH-S

See **BEWSHER, BILL; CROLL, ROBERT; DUNPHY, MYLES; EMMETT, EVELYN; PALLIN, FRANK; WATERS, WILLIAM; WEINDORFER, GUSTAV**.

BUTCHER, WENDY (1949–) made her hockey debut for WA at the age of 16 in 1965. In the same season she was chosen for the Australian team and remained a fixture in the side until retiring in 1974. Usually playing at right-half, her greatest assets were a high work rate and outstanding ball skills. An excellent anticipation and great positional sense contributed to her success in setting up her team's forward play. Butcher made a come-back in 1978 as Wendy Pritchard and captained WA in her final season, 1980. She played in thirteen Australian championships, winning eleven, including six in a row between 1965 and 1970.

RQ

C

CAIRD, MAUREEN (1951–) became the youngest Olympic track and field winner when she won the 80 metres hurdles in Mexico in 1968 at only 17 years and 19 days. An athlete of great courage, she created an Olympic record which will remain forever on the books, because the event was increased to 100 metres at the next Games. An outstanding junior, Caird won the Australian junior 80 metres when only 15 and a mere 44.5 kilograms. She retained her title in 1967 (setting a junior record of 10.6 seconds) and again in 1968 and 1969. While Caird will be remembered best for her hurdling feats, she was also Australian junior champion in the pentathlon (1967) and the long jump (1968). In addition she set two world records over the new 200 metres hurdles distance in 1969 while still a junior. Caird battled recurring stomach pains and a succession of leg injuries until her premature retirement in 1972, but still managed to win her first senior national titles in 1970 when she defeated arch-rival Pam Kilborn in both 100 and 200 metres hurdles, gaining selection for the Edinburgh British Commonwealth Games. After successfully defending her national 200 metres title she won a berth to the Munich Olympics but announced her retirement when mystery stomach pains were diagnosed as cancer.

GC†

CALDOW, MARGARET (née JACKSON), BEM (1941–) played netball for Victoria in open competition from 1961 to 1979 and was captain for eight of these years. Caldow first represented Australia in 1962 and played in the inaugural World Netball Championships in England in 1963. She was captain of the Australian teams which won the world championships in 1975 and 1979, thereby becoming the only player to have competed in three victorious world champion teams. She was awarded the British Empire Medal in 1977, was voted Victorian Sportswoman of the Year for 1977–78, and became an inaugural inductee of the Sport Australia Hall of Fame in 1985.

IJ and PB

Calisthenics and Physical Culture

In the mid-nineteenth century, physical culture developed quickly in Europe, the USA, and Australia as a physiologically sound and beneficial regimen of exercise for what was seen to be a weakened urban population with no access to the healthy activities of country life. Its various forms proliferated swiftly; most were designed for the indoors and limited spaces and used portable apparatus. The movement was adopted by many groups for their own purposes: by private schools to stiffen the sinews of boys who would come to rule the Empire; by the Church through notions of 'Muscular Christianity'; and by the various eugenics movements of the last hundred years. It has since spawned a multitude of variations from Olympic gymnastics to body-building and calisthenics.

Physical culture was practised in Australia from the 1850s. It was sufficiently established for Gustav Techow to publish his *Manual of Gymnastic Exercises* in Melbourne in 1866. It was immediately seen by women as a suitable form of exercise which did no damage to any notions of femininity and respectability, and was introduced in Melbourne in 1879 by two enterprising Englishwomen, Harriett Elphinstone Dick and Alice Moon. They provided classes in most of the city's private girls' schools. From their work developed the unique form of Australian calisthenics which includes a range of exercises set to music deriving directly from their nineteenth-century originals: free exercises from the Swedish Ling method; figure marching and rod exercises from Germany; Indian club-swinging which came via England; folk dancing from Europe; and, added in this century, rhythmic dancing from the Delcroze method of the French, and modern jazz ballet from America. These have all survived due to the central role of the competitions run by the Royal South Street Society, Ballarat, since 1903. Teams ranging from small church-based clubs up to prestigious State teams have since competed in four age groups and five grades, and now average 3000 girls a year. Boys also competed until the Second World War broke the continuity. About 30 000 girls are annually engaged in calisthenics in Victoria alone, and clubs like Clifton, Regent, and Minerva/Merinda have existed continuously for fifty years. What Australian rules football has been for boys, calisthenics has been for girls, and the two have spread over the same geographic areas of the continent—SA, WA, and Tasmania, with less growth to the north. The sport is now nationally organised. In NSW, the dominant form is Bjelke-Petersen physical culture, introduced first in Hobart in 1892 by the Dane Christian Bjelke-

Petersen. 'Calisthenics' is from the Greek words for beauty and strength and refers to exercises to develop health and gracefulness.

RO

See **BJELKE-PETERSEN, CHRISTIAN; DICK, HARRIETT; FELTHAM, ENID; HOPTON, VERA.**

CAMPBELL, KEITH (1931–58), motor-cycler, born Prahran, Melbourne, was Australia's first world champion in any form of tarmac racing. After competing on the famous Isle of Man circuit in 1951 and 1952, he joined the 'Continental Circus' in 1953. By 1956 he had become one of the most successful private entrants in Europe. After victory in the 1956 Swedish 350 Grand Prix he secured a contract with Moto Guzzi and became their team leader. He became Motorcycle World Champion in the 350 cc category in 1957, winning the Dutch, Belgian, and Ulster Grands Prix. Combining a great determination with a laid-back personality and a dry sense of humour, he was very popular with his contemporaries. Campbell was killed on 13 July 1958 at Cadours in France after losing control of his machine when it hit a patch of oil in a 500 cc race.

DC

Campdrafting
This sport probably had its beginnings at the Tenterfield Show in 1885. Clarence Smith of Boorook Station is credited with its origin. Confined to the eastern States, the sport is conducted in association with rodeo. The contest in campdrafting lies in the ability of riders and their horses to drive a selected beast around a pegged course. A herd of cattle is held in a suitable area known as a camp, and the horse and rider ride into the herd to select the required beast (drafting). Until recently there were no official rules governing the sport, but a method of scoring a competitor out of a hundred has now been established by the Bushman's Carnival Association of NSW. Several hundred regular drafts are held each year with the largest attracting up to a hundred contestants. The two drafts which hold premier place in Australia are the Warwick Gold Cup and the Risdon Cup which are both held at Warwick in Queensland.

GC*

CAMPESE, DAVID (1962–) is a flamboyant full back or winger whose trademark 'goose step' and elusive running have helped to make him the leading try-scorer in international rugby union, with 46 tries to his credit at the end of 1990. Campese is Australia's most capped player, with sixty-four Tests and, along with Simon Poidevin, holds the world record for most appearances against one country. Both have played twenty-one Tests against the All Blacks. After coming to prominence through

ACT and Australian under-21 sides, he made his Test debut on the 1982 tour of NZ. Although Campese has been involved in many great tries, his solo effort against the Barbarians at the end of the 1988 short tour of England and Scotland, when he used defenders like a slalom course, must rank as one of the best. Campese spends the winter playing for Randwick in the Sydney club competition and the off-season playing in Italy. He will be remembered as one of the most exciting runners in the game. Campese, who scored 6 tries, was the star player in Australia's 1991 World Cup victory.

GC†

Canoeing
Competitive canoeing is divided into five categories: canoe sailing, flat-water racing, slalom and wild-water racing, canoe polo, and marathon racing. The Australian Canoe Federation (ACF) was formed in September 1949 at a meeting initiated by NSW and comprised that State, Victoria, and SA. There was considerable support for its formation because an association was needed to support canoeing at the Olympic Games which were to be held in Melbourne in 1956. Application for membership of the International Canoe Federation followed soon after. Canoeing was a great success at the Olympic Games, with the event being held at Lake Wendouree, Ballarat. Australia gained a bronze medal in the kayak pairs 10 000 metres event. Throughout the 1970s the ACF organised seven distinct working parties to cover the main administrative and activity interests: racing, slalom, marathon, touring, sea touring, canoe polo, and the Board of Canoe Education. Australia has performed well at international events, especially the Olympic Games and at International Canoe Federation World Championships. In his exceptional career Dennis Green won sixty-four Australian championships, competed in five Olympic Games, and carried the national flag in the opening ceremony at Munich. Much of the credit for Australia's improved performance at the élite level can be attributed to the inclusion of canoeing as a sport based at the Australian Institute of Sport in Queensland.

JM and IJ

See **GREEN, DENNIS; HOWARD, ARTHUR.**

Carbine (1885–1914), a champion thoroughbred racehorse and stallion, was born at Sylvia Park stud farm near Auckland in NZ. His sire, *Musket*, and dam, *Mersey*, had both been imported from England by the NZ Stud Company. The bay colt was sold as a yearling to a former jockey, Dan O'Brien. *Carbine* was unbeaten in five starts in NZ as a 2-year-old, and was sent to race in Australia. In late 1888 O'Brien sold him to Melbourne owner and breeder Donald Wallace, and *Carbine* was trained thereafter by

Walter Hickenbotham. At the age of 3 *Carbine* won nine of thirteen starts, stamping himself as a champion with a courageous win in record time in the 1889 Sydney Cup carrying 12 pounds over weight-for-age (championship weights). He won the race again in 1890. After carrying an injury when second to *Bravo* in the 1889 Melbourne Cup, *Carbine* won nineteen of his next twenty-two starts. His triumph was in winning the 1890 Melbourne Cup in a record time against a record field (thirty-nine) carrying a weight (10 stone 5 pounds) which has never been equalled. An idol of the crowds, *Carbine*'s complete race record was thirty-three wins and nine placings from forty-three starts. At stud at Bacchus Marsh in Victoria, from 1891 to 1894, *Carbine* was an immediate success: his first crop included *Wallace* who became a top performer and later one of Australia's most successful sires. *Carbine* was sold in 1894 for 13 000 guineas—an Australian record for many years—to the Duke of Portland and was shipped to England. At first regarded as a disappointment in England, *Carbine* justified his status as champion by siring *Spearmint*, winner of the 1906 Derby at Epsom. A son and a grandson of *Spearmint* also won the Derby. *Carbine*'s blood lines had an enormous influence throughout the thoroughbred world.

AL

Cardigan Bay (1956–?), foaled in NZ and gelded when only 5 months, became harness racing's first $1 million prize-winner. His first win, at his fifth start, was as a 3-year-old. In 1963 *Cardigan Bay* won the final of the Inter-Dominion Series and the NSW Summer Cup off 24 yards as well as the Lady Brooks Cup in Melbourne off 36 yards. He also won two Auckland Cups and a NZ Cup over 2 miles off a 54 yards handicap in a time of 2 minutes 2 seconds, creating a world record for 13 furlongs. Bought by an American syndicate for $100 000 in 1964, *Cardigan Bay* went on to win thirty-seven races in North America. By the time of his retirement in 1968 he had achieved eighty wins, twenty-five seconds, and twenty-two thirds from one hundred and fifty-four starts. As part of the conditions of his sale, *Cardigan Bay* was returned to NZ where his arrival was celebrated by the issue of a special postage stamp in his honour.

GC*

CARDWELL, VICKI (née HOFFMAN) (1955–), born Adelaide, later a resident of Melbourne, is one of Australia's greatest female squash-players, having won one world title, four British Opens and twenty other national events in seven countries. After winning the Australian women's amateur title in 1978, she turned professional. She won the Australian women's open event five times between 1979 and 1984 and teamed with Pakistani Hiddy Jahar in 1980, to win the Audi Team World Cup. She won the first of four successive British Opens in 1980. She captured the women's open world championship in 1982, defeating fellow Australian Rhonda Thorne in straight sets. On giving birth to her son Joshua in 1985, Cardwell retired from world tournaments but was still ranked among the top Australian players.

KT

See **Squash Rackets**.

CAREY, SAMUEL WARREN (1911–), born Campbelltown, NSW, trained as a geologist and became interested in the caves of northern NSW while a student. During the Second World War, as Captain Carey, he trained Australian commandos in the caves of Mount Etna, Queensland, so that they might fight in the caves of the Pacific Islands. After the war he was appointed professor of geology at the University of Tasmania and there convened the meeting which established the Tasmanian Caverneering Club, Australia's first organised speleological group, and the model for others throughout Australia.

EH-S

See **Caving**.

CARLILE, FORBES (1921–), born Melbourne, has the distinction of having represented Australia at Olympic Games both as competitor in modern pentathlon (Helsinki 1952) and as coach of the Australian swimming team (London 1948, Melbourne 1956). He also coached the Dutch team at the Tokyo Games in 1964. Forbes Carlile was a pioneer in the field of scientific training techniques. His experimental work with Professor Frank Cotton at Sydney University from 1947 to 1955 gave Australian swimmers of the period a winning edge.

PH

See **Sports Science**; **Swimming**.

CARROLL, JACK (1907–78), born Arthur Hardwick at Kensington, Victoria, became Australian welterweight title-holder in 1928, also holding the title from 1933 to 1938. After victories over top imports, he was ranked number one world welterweight contender from 1936 to 1937. An awkward fighter who could switch hands readily and cut opponents to pieces with rapid, rather than solid, punching, Carroll was called 'the red fox' because of his thinning red hair. He was a humble man, whose dislike of travel denied him greater opportunities overseas. Carroll fought 109 times: he won ninety, lost twelve, and drew seven fights. He was a prominent referee from his retirement in 1938 until the 1950s, when he became a successful trainer until his death in 1978.

HS

See **Boxing**.

CARROLL, TOM (1962–   ) won the world surfing crown in 1984–85 and remained one of the leading surfers during the 1980s. Curly-haired, freckle-faced Carroll took up surfing at an early age at Sydney's Newport Beach and became a member of the influential Newport Board-Riding Club. After winning the pro junior title in 1977 he won the State and national titles before opting for serious surfing in Hawaii. Carroll's victory in the 1982 World Cup at Sunset Beach was his first international triumph and marked the first success for a goofy-footer, who surfed the waves on the backhand rather than the forehand style of natural footers. Since this victory Carroll, who is noted for his flow-ing style, has achieved success around the world in the USA, Brazil, Japan, France, and South Africa. A former apprentice panel-beater, Carroll has proved to be a marketable and successful surfing symbol.
RC
See **Surfing**.

CARRUTHERS, JAMES (1929–   ), born Paddington, Sydney, was the first world cham-pion boxer in any division to retire without a loss or draw. A quick-moving left-hander, he represented Australia at the London Olympics. After turning professional in 1950, and with Bill McConnell as his trainer, Jimmy Carruthers won fourteen straight fights before defeat-ing Vic Toweel to claim the world title in Johannesburg. He was world bantamweight champion from November 1952 to May 1954. Carruthers first defended his title four months later, knocking out Toweel, and then defeated American Henry 'Pappy' Gault in November 1953 at the Sydney Sports Ground in front of 32 500 spectators, the largest crowd to watch an Australian boxing contest. After defending his title a third time, by defeating Chamren Songkitrat in Bangkok, Carruthers retired. He made a brief come-back in 1961 to lose his unbeaten record. He later became a leading boxing referee.
GC*
See **Boxing**.

CARRUTHERS, KEL (1938–   ), born Syd-ney, was the most technically astute of Australia's champion motorcyclists. He won the 1969 world 250 cc championship as a last-minute addition to the Italian Benelli team and went within an ace of defending the title on a privately entered Yamaha. His father Jack was an Australian cham-pion in speedway sidecar racing and owned a motorcycle business in Gladesville. From the age of 15 Kel worked in the family business but did not become a professional motorcycle rider until 23. From 1961 to 1965 he dominated Australian road racing, winning 115 races out of 161 starts. Carruthers had not raced in Europe until the age of 28 but made an immedi-ate impact there. Later he went to America, his racing ability, keen observations, profound knowledge of the sport, and friendly, dry, straightforward style making him a respected teacher. He became Yamaha's number one rac-ing technician and guided Americans Kenny Roberts and Eddie Lawson to world 500 cc titles.
DC

CARTER, DICK, a diminutive squash-player of the 1960s who was nicknamed 'the Ant' because of his size (166 centimetres), was a semifinalist in the British Amateur Squash Championship in 1962 and was twice runner-up for this title in 1966 and 1967. During 1962 and 1963 he was a member of an Australian team which achieved victories over some of the leading international squash teams including Pakistan and England. A hard trainer and a keen tactician, Carter exuded enthusiasm and enjoy-ment of the game.
KT
See **Squash Rackets**.

CASH, PAT (1965–   ), born Melbourne, has all the attributes of a great grasscourt player, including a powerful service, court speed, skil-ful undercut volleys, adequate ground strokes, and a fighting heart. All these strengths were evident when he won the 1987 Wimbledon singles title. At times, too, Cash has performed at his best in Davis Cup encounters. But his career has been plagued by injury and bouts of staleness which his long-standing coach, Ian Barclay, was not able to eliminate. Cash, who was an outstanding junior, became known for the specialist physiological and psychological assistance he sought in senior tournament play.
HCJP
See **Lawn Tennis**.

Casting
The first casting tournaments were held in 1939, and the Australian Casting Association was cre-ated in 1947; the first national championships were conducted in 1951. Both men and women contest a number of events, including plug accuracy, weight distance casting, fly casting, and plug distance casting. NSW hosted the first world surf casting championships in 1959, and at the 1974 world championships in Taree, Aus-tralians won five gold medals. Men and women at first competed against each other but now have separate sections.
KM

CATCHPOLE, KEN (1939–   ), set a stand-ard for rugby scrum-halfs which has rarely been emulated and is considered to be the best half-back Australia has produced. Possessed of an astute footballing brain, the slightly built Rand-wick half earned a reputation for his ability to instigate breaks and to back up, and for his unerring cover defence. He is also renowned for honing a long, accurate, bullet-like pass which allowed his five-eighth to stand deep and suited Australia's reputation for playing running football. His representative career, which began as a 19-year-old in 1959 playing for NSW against the British Isles, ended when he was seriously injured at the bottom of an All Black ruck at the SCG in 1968. During his seven overseas tours and twenty-seven Tests, including thirteen as captain, Catchpole won acclaim in the three rugby strongholds: Great Britain, NZ, and South Africa. After retiring from the playing field he could be heard for several years as an astute expert commentator on ABC radio.

GC†

CAVILL Family. The self-styled 'Professor', Fred Cavill (1839–1927), was one of Sydney's earliest swimming entrepreneurs. He arrived from England in 1879 and soon gained the lease of Lavender Bay baths. During the early 1880s he conducted popular 'learn to swim for a guinea' classes there for men, women, and children, later running them from his own floating baths moored in Port Jackson. Of his nine children— all of whom swam—several were to make their mark in world swimming. **Ernest Cavill**, the oldest (1868–1935), was 1000 yards champion of NSW at the age of 15. **Dick 'Splash' Cavill** (1884–1938), the first Australian to swim 100 yards in under 1 minute, held eighteen Australian and twenty-two NSW titles from 1900 to 1904, and was credited with introducing the crawl stroke to England. **Sydney Cavill** (1881–1945) won the Australian 220 yards championship at 16 years of age and claimed to have introduced the crawl to the USA. The world 5 mile championship was won by **Percy Cavill** (1875–1940) in 1897; **Charles Cavill** (1870–97), a professional swimmer, was the first to swim the entrance of San Francisco Harbour. **Arthur 'Tums' Cavill** (1877–1914)— an early exponent of the crawl stroke in Australia—held both Australian amateur and professional titles before becoming a coach and stunt swimmer. Both Charles and Arthur were killed while performing hazardous swimming feats in the USA.

VRW

See **EVE, RICHMOND**; **Swimming**.

Caving

The exploration of Australian caves began with the earliest explorers, who examined caves in the course of their land assessment activities. Sir Thomas Mitchell's work at Wellington in NSW is particularly worthy of note. Cave exploration for its own sake began with Jeremiah Wilson at Jenolan, NSW, in the 1860s. His work at Jenolan was followed by others, especially Wilburd and Edwards, and by would-be imitators in all other States of Australia. These early cavers were driven by the prospect of discovering caves suitable for tourism, and by the potential economic benefits from any discovery they might make. Although some bushwalkers occasionally entered caves as part of their recreational activity, caving as recreation did not begin until the late 1940s. A number of factors seem to have been responsible for this growing interest, including the training of commandos in caves during the Pacific War by Captain (later Professor) S. W. Carey, the translation into English of works by the great French caver Norbert Casteret, and the rise of living standards which led young people into more venturesome recreational activities. The first formal caving club was the Tasmanian Caverneering Club, formed in 1949 under the leadership of Professor Carey. Many others followed throughout Australia, and in 1956 these were linked together in the Australian Speleological Federation. The equipment used has advanced rapidly since the late 1960s, and Australians have played a leading role in both the improvement of techniques and in expedition caving in Mexico, Papua-New Guinea, and South-East Asia.

EH-S

See **BONWICK, JOHN**; **CAREY, SAMUEL**; **JAMES, JULIA**; **THOMPSON, JOHN**; **WARILD, ALAN**.

CAWLEY, EVONNE (née GOOLA-GONG), MBE (1951–), born Barellan, NSW, of a white father and an Aboriginal mother, moved to Sydney after her talent was spotted by Vic Edwards. Edwards became her coach and legal guardian and she lived with his family. Cawley won the Wimbledon singles in 1971, defeating Billie Jean King in the semi-finals and Margaret Court in the final when she was only 19. With her unspoilt charm and graceful court play, she was a popular champion. Before Wimbledon she had won the French Open. Cawley was runner-up in three subsequent Wimbledon finals, losing to King in 1972 and 1975 and to Chris Evert Lloyd in 1976, but she turned the tables on Lloyd when she won a memorable final in 1980. Evonne also won seventeen State titles, three Australian hard-court titles and four Australian Opens as well as the Italian and South African Opens. She was awarded the MBE in 1972. She married English tennis-player Roger Cawley in 1976 and they later settled in the USA.

KM-H

See **Aboriginal Sports Foundation**; **Aborigines in Sport**; **Lawn Tennis**.

CAZALY, ROY (1893–1963), born Melbourne, became a legendary Australian rules footballer. The phrase 'Up there Cazaly!' was a rallying cry for diggers during the Second World War. More recently Michael Brady's song 'Up there Cazaly' became an anthem of the AFL. The saying was first coined by Fred Fleiter, Cazaly's fellow South Melbourne ruckman, who would urge Roy to leap high to palm the ball to his rover. It was not long before the South Melbourne crowds took up the chant. Cazaly was the youngest of ten children. His father James was a great oarsman of his era. Roy Cazaly grew up with Walter Lindrum and was a close friend of Frank Beaurepaire at Albert Park School. After making a name for himself as a footballer at Middle Park Wesleys, Cazaly was invited to join St Kilda and became one of their star players from 1913 to 1920. He was named Champion of the State by 1920. He transferred to South Melbourne in 1921. In his later playing years he became a great wanderer. He played with Minyip in the Wimmera League (1925), South Melbourne (1926–27), Launceston City (1928–30), Preston in the VFA (1931), North Hobart (1932–33), Newtown (now Glenorchy) (1934–36), non-playing coach at South Melbourne (1937–38), Camberwell in the VFA (1941), Hawthorn (1942–43), assistant coach at South Melbourne (1947), and Newtown (1948–51). He also coached Tasmania. He played 422 senior games, including thirty-two for Victoria and Tasmania, and participated in more than a hundred mid-week games. Along with natural ability Cazaly, a self-taught physiotherapist, worked hard on his physical fitness. He died in Hobart on 10 October 1963.

EP

CERUTTI, WILLIAM HECTOR ('Wild Bill') (1909–65) played first-grade rugby for the YMCA club in Sydney at the age of 15 and did not retire from club rugby until his early forties. He also played for another five clubs and took part in 247 first-grade games. A front-row forward who played seventeen Tests and represented NSW forty-six times, he became a legendary figure in NZ and South Africa for his tough and uncompromising forward play—he is considered one of the hardest players ever to represent Australia—and for his larrikin image. Cerutti coached St George to their only first-grade premiership in 1957. He also encouraged junior rugby clubs and had some involvement in the tour of the Petersham Club in the 1960s.

TH

CERUTTY, PERCY (1895–1975) was one of Australia's greatest athletic coaches. While some of his critics labelled him as overpowering, bitter, abusive, and outrageous, he was also responsible for revolutionising running-training in Australia. Having become Victorian marathon champion at the age of 50, Cerutty set out to become a running coach. In the 1950s he coached Don MacMillan, Les Perry, and for a time John Landy, but Olympic 1500 metres champion Herb Elliott was his most famous protégé. Elliott had no hesitation in calling

Cerutty a genius. Cerutty believed in naturalistic training and the track was ignored in favour of the golf course, forest, and sand dune. He believed that success would come only to those who trained beyond the pain barrier, who strengthened their bodies, and who eschewed the dietary and recreational preferences of the sedentary, urbanised person. Cerutty's eccentric behaviour antagonised other athletes and generated constant media attention. He feuded frequently with other coaches, particularly Franz Stampfl. He also inspired many athletes to achieve sporting excellence.

RKS

See **STAMPFL, FRANZ**.

CHAPPELL Family is undoubtedly the most famous in the history of Australian cricket. Three brothers and a grandfather donned the green baggy cap. Victor York Richardson, OBE (1894–1969), born in Adelaide, was an aggressive batsman and brilliant fieldsman. It has been said that he only dropped one catch during his first-class career, and he still shares the world record of five catches in a Test innings. Between 1924 and 1936 he represented Australia in nineteen Tests, captaining the 1935–36 side to South Africa and winning the series 4–0. Vic's daughter Jeanne married Martin Chappell and they had three sons, all born in Adelaide: **Ian Michael** (1943–), **Gregory Stephen**, MBE (1948–), and **Trevor Martin** (1952–). Ian and Greg Chappell dominated Australian cricket in the 1970s and early 1980s, amassing huge scores and becoming the sixth- and second-highest run-makers respectively for Australia. All three brothers inherited their grandfather's fielding skills, and Ian and Greg emulated his feat of captaining Australia. Ian was one of Australia's greatest captains, whose leadership and tactical flair transformed the Australian side into world champions. Their records would be even more outstanding if their involvement with World Series Cricket between 1977 and 1979 were included. Ian represented Australia seventy-six times (thirty as captain) between 1964 and 1980, and Greg eighty-eight times (forty-eight as captain) between 1970 and 1984. Trevor played in three Tests in 1981. He will, unfortunately, be best remembered for the infamous underarm ball in the 1981 international limited-over final against NZ. Ian and Greg were champions of players' rights. At different times they were president of the Professional Cricketers Association of Australia, a players' association or union which operated between 1977 and 1982.

BD

See **Cricket; Underarm Bowling Incident**.

CHARLESWORTH, RICHARD IAN (1952–), born Subiaco, WA, had a remarkable career in hockey. He was selected in five Australian Olympic hockey teams between

1972 and 1988, retiring after the Seoul Games. Playing at inside right, the hallmark of his play was outstanding stick work and a mastery of individual skills: the body swerve, the dribble, the feint, and the ability to beat opponents on either side of his body. On field, the short, sturdily built Charlesworth was noted for his determination, aggression, and high work rate. He represented Australia 234 times in hockey, and appeared for WA in seventeen national championships between 1972 and 1989. As a left-hand batsman he also represented WA at cricket between 1972 and 1980, and since 1983 has been the Member of the House of Representatives for Perth.

MS

CHARLTON, ANDREW ('Boy') (1907–75) has been classified as one of Australia's sporting superheroes. He competed in three Olympic Games for Australia (1924, 1928, and 1932) and won five medals, one gold, three silver, and one bronze. He broke a total of eight Australian records and five world records, yet he never competed in an Australian championship. Charlton was one of the many Manly athletes who have successfully traversed the world's sporting stage. He captured the imagination of the Sydney public when, at the age of 14, he beat Hawaiian swimmer Bill Harris, going on at 15 to set a world record in the 880 yards freestyle, and later beating the veteran Frank Beaurepaire using a trudgen stroke which embodied characteristics of the crawl. He became a national hero at 16 when he defeated the great Swedish swimmer Arne Borg at the Sydney Domain Baths in the 440 yards freestyle in front of 6000 fans, establishing an Australian record and equalling Borg's world record in the process. He later beat Borg in the NSW 880 and 220 yards championships, securing a world record in the former and an Australian record in the latter. Charlton won a gold medal in the 1500 metres freestyle at the 1924 Paris Games, and a bronze in the 400 metres. He also achieved a silver medal in the 4 × 200 metres freestyle relay. Although a national hero, 'Boy' returned to his studies at Hawkesbury Agricultural College and went to work on the land at Gunnedah. Absent from swimming for two years, he returned in 1927 and defeated the Japanese swimmer Takaishi, setting a new world record in the 880 yards freestyle. He was selected for the 1928 Olympic Games in Amsterdam, and achieved silver medals in the 400 metres freestyle and the 1500 metres freestyle. He represented Australia in the 1932 Olympic Games, but the best he could manage was a sixth in the 400 metres freestyle. Charlton's performances were achieved with little training. He was popular with the Australian public because of his 'natural' ability together with a self-effacing nature. The Sydney Domain Baths were renamed the Andrew 'Boy' Charlton Baths in his honour.

RH and MH

See **Swimming**.

CHARLTON, EDDIE (1929–), known as 'Fast Eddie', learned to play billiards at his grandfather's club at the age of 9. He made his first 100 break in billiards at 15 and in snooker at 17. Charlton turned professional in 1960, and became a very consistent performer. In 1967 he created a world snooker record by making consecutive breaks of 135 and 137 without his opponent making a shot. The following year he won the world match-play and British Commonwealth titles. In 1972 Charlton won the international championship and in 1976 he won a three-way contest at eight Australian venues against pool champion Joe Balsis from America and billiards champion Rex Williams of the UK. He won the world match-play championship, defeating Ray Reardon, for a second time in 1977. Charlton has been Australian professional champion thirteen times and in 1969 held both the Australian and NSW professional titles along with the NSW Open and Australian match-play championship. Charlton became a household name through the BBC 'Pot Black' series which he won on three occasions. A great showman, he appeared in numerous exhibition matches where he played snooker with effortless skill, demonstrating a range of trick shots in the process. Charlton was a fine all-round sportsman who also played many other sports with skill, including boxing, cricket, surfing, and rugby league.

GC*

See **Billiards and Snooker**.

CHEESMAN, JENNIFER , AM (1957–), born Adelaide, was a basketballer for Glenelg and Canberra. She represented Australia as a point guard from 1975 to 1989, playing at the 1975, 1979, 1983, and 1987 world championships, as well as the 1984 and 1988 Olympic Games. She captained Australia between 1987 and 1989. Described as 'the epitome of a team player', Cheesman was a key part of Australia's rise in women's basketball in the 1980s. In the National Women's Basketball League she played for Canberra. Equipped with a degree in physical education, Cheesman was employed as an assistant coach at the AIS from 1983 to 1988, and as head women's coach from 1989. She was awarded an AM in 1989 for services to basketball. Between 1974 and 1979, Cheesman also represented Australia in softball, winning a bronze medal at the 1974 world championships.

SB

Chief Havoc, a greyhound, by *Trion* out of *Thelma's Mate*, was probably the greatest dog ever produced in Australia. His blood line included *White Hope*, *The Dickens*, *Micawber*,

Great Times, and *Cinders*, and his racing record was unequalled. From *Cinders* he acquired his track sense, an attribute shared by the all-time heroes of the track—*Muck the Miller* in the UK and *Real Huntsman* in the USA. Racing in the late 1940s, he won twenty-six of thirty-five starts. *Chief Havoc* was a highly successful sire, both in Australia and the USA. His son, *Rocker Mac*, also had a great influence on both continents.

TGP

Children

Children's sport has not been immune from wider social changes. Late in the 1960s, with a shift in emphasis in schools toward 'catering for individual differences' and 'variety of experiences', competition had fallen out of favour with many teachers. Sport was no exception. Yet at about the same time, when many schools were withdrawing teams from interschool sporting fixtures, there was a dramatic expansion in community, that is, club, sport for children, with regular weekend competitions being offered for children as young as 7 and 8 years. Before this, opportunities for youngsters under 15 or 16 to play in regular community-based sporting competitions had been rare; children's introduction to sporting competition had occurred at school, with regular intra- and interschool sport being an accepted and valued part of school life. It was not surprising that an outcry against certain aspects of children's club sport should occur early in the 1970s. Many volunteer coaches and officials who had had no formal training in sport or coaching, let alone studies in child development, were making demands of youngsters which were more in keeping with their own adult sports experiences and aspirations. Henry Pang's words at the XXth World Congress in Sports Medicine in Melbourne in 1974 were perhaps the first public utterance seriously questioning the appropriateness of sport for Australian children. Pang's statement focused on lack of basic skills, sense of failure, parental pressure, and a high drop-out rate of around 60 per cent. Others, however, contended that a retention rate as high as 25–30 per cent over a ten-year period was unusual and suggested that the sporting experience was unique in appealing to so many for so long. In 1976, as part of its 'Sportsnight' series, ABC Television showed a film entitled *The Ugly Parent*. The clear message from this film was that adult pressure was causing a good deal of stress for many participants in under-age sport. During the 1970s and 1980s the media provided a succession of stories focusing on the negative aspects of children's sport. Unfortunately, little attention was paid to the positive experiences enjoyed by many children or to the tireless efforts of a willing band of volunteer

coaches and officials, many of whom were making genuine attempts to improve their own performance by attending short courses in coaching and/or administration.

A number of conferences and seminars have been conducted in all States of Australia since the mid-1970s, addressing recurring themes such as childhood injuries, drop-out, rule modification and, more recently, girls' participation, in an attempt to come up with the right recipe. Several booklets outlining recommendations for the conduct of children's sport have been published by State Government departments of sport and recreation, and a national policy statement covering issues such as readiness, parent involvement, nutrition, stress, and frequency of training was prepared jointly in 1983 by three professional bodies, the Confederation of Australian Sport, the Australian Council for Health, Physical Education and Recreation, and the Australian Sports Medicine Federation. 'Fair play' codes, based on a 1970s Canadian model, have been distributed widely as part of Aussie Sports resource materials and, more recently, by the Australian Schools Sports Council. This plethora of publications and conferences was indicative of concern across the community about aspects of children's sport. In 1985 the Federal Government, through the ASC, launched its Aussie Sports Programme. The basic objective of the programme was to 'improve the quality, quantity and variety of sport available to Australian children'. Its rationale was expressed in the following words:

> Too many children enter high school deficient in the basic sports skills of running, striking, jumping, throwing, catching, balancing and kicking. They lack confidence, self-image, or even sport experience . . . Disturbing trends in both school and club sport have included over-intensive training, teaching of 'win-at-all-cost' attitudes, too early specialisation and over-high levels of representation.

Aussie Sports itself has not been without its critics. Physical educators have always regarded sport as being only part of a comprehensive physical education programme. They are concerned that the terms physical education, sport, sport education, and Aussie Sports are being used synonymously, and that the Aussie Sports Programme is little more than political expediency. The real need, according to physical educators, is for specialist teachers in sufficient numbers to mount broadly based physical education programmes, *including sport*, in all schools.

Some of the trends basic to the emergence of Aussie Sports were, of course, related to broader developments in Australian sport. It has been suggested that sports scientists and physical educators have become preoccupied with anatomical and technological factors

FOLLOW THE CRICKET WITH A

TASMA "TIGER"

The most remarkable A.C. operated MANTEL RADIO
of the year.

ELECTRIC MODELS ONLY,

PRICE £16/16/0
EASY TERMS ARRANGED.

GRICE'S

90-92 QUEEN ST., BRISBANE.

Branches at Toowoomba, Gympie, Rockhampton, Mackay, Townsville,
Cairns.

30 Broadcasting of ball-by-ball cricket descriptions in
Australia began in 1925. This advertisement in the *Courier-
Mail* in 1936 illustrates how sports broadcasting helped to
sell radios.

31 Broadcasting of rugby league began in Sydney in 1924.
Frank Hyde has continued this popular tradition.

32 In 1981–82 Beverley Buckingham, from Tasmania,
became the first woman to top the jockey's list in any
Australian State.

33 Evonne Cawley, regarded as one of the greatest
Aboriginal sports achievers, won the Wimbledon singles
title in 1971 and 1980.

34 Andrew 'Boy' Charlton and Johnny Weissmuller, from the USA, at the 1924 Olympic Games in Paris.

35 In the 1950s Percy Cerutty's 'sand–dune training' at Portsea, Victoria, attracted international attention.

maximising performance and have lost their holistic view. In a sense, then, it was inevitable that children's sport also would suffer from 'scientisation' in the form of intensive training, specialisation, and win-emphasis. Unfortunately, when children's sport becomes too serious, opportunities for fun and spontaneity tend to be limited and the social elements of play and games, so vitally important for rewarding junior sport experiences, are often replaced by adult direction and control. Another significant development has been in modification of rules, size of fields/courts and equipment, playing time, nature of fixtures, and length of season. Before the 1960s, when under-age community sport was available only to teenagers aged 15 and older, there was little need to modify the adult version of the game, but when sport was opened up to younger children it became obvious that the traditional game was not always the most appropriate. However, there has been opposition to modification by those who advocate a natural weeding-out process among the young as the means of identifying those individuals capable of measuring up in 'the real thing'. Proponents of modification advocated progressive elimination of special rules with increasing age so that the game would become more and more like the adult game. Interestingly, many sports have now embraced modified rules *and* a system of progressive elimination of those rules. Some critics of modification have questioned the blind faith of many proponents of modification and assert that the crucial factor in rewarding sports experiences revolves around the qualities of the coach or leader. They maintain that the important thing is how people relate to others within the structure, rather than whether the rules are modified or not. Since 1980 the National Coaching Accreditation Scheme has been a significant influence in the provision of quality coaches who are aware of the specific needs of different groups such as children. The scheme caters for a continuum from non-accredited 'Level 0' for teachers and parents who may have a short-term involvement in sport with their children to 'Master Coach' at the high-performance level.

Hand in hand with coaching are the contentious issues of talent identification and specialisation at an early age. Élitism does not sit comfortably with the notion of egalitarianism held by many Australians, especially when that élitism involves children. When young children were forced to leave home for extended periods to pursue sporting excellence at a central institution, the Australian Institute of Sport in Canberra, community concerns were heightened. Nevertheless, sports coaches and administrators are always keen to identify potential champions through their junior sports programmes, and many parents have been eager to support their children in sport from a very early age in the hope of eventual, possibly lucrative, success. Addressing the issue of talent identification and development, the director of the Australian Coaching Council, Lawrie Woodman, suggested that schools should play a key role, with fully qualified physical education teachers trained also as coaches. He saw schools as the ideal site for pursuing excellence in sport in a non-stressful environment. Over the years regional, State, and national championships have become an accepted part of children's sport in Australia in both school and community, but the practice has been criticised as being élitist and inappropriate for young children. The stormy response to the introduction of a new junior sport policy in SA late in 1990 was typical of opposition expressed when changes in junior sport have been proposed. One of the changes in this policy related to the abolition of interstate competitions and championships for children under 13. (WA and Tasmania, where modified approaches had enjoyed wide acceptance from the mid-1970s, had already withdrawn primary school teams from interstate sport.) Interestingly, the director of the SA Institute of Sport was quoted as saying 'it is adults, not children, who are having most trouble coming to terms with the changes'.

Apart from identifying talent, genuine encouragement of participation had been sadly lacking for the female half of the child population until discriminatory practices were seriously challenged in Australia in the 1970s. Policies for equal opportunity, sex discrimination, and affirmative action have signalled general acceptance of a new order for females in the community. This change has been reflected in stronger encouragement for girls to participate in a range of energetic physical activities and to fulfil their potential in sport. Initial reaction to the *Commonwealth Sex Discrimination Act* 1984 had given some cause for concern. For example, in response to a memorandum from the Victorian Director-General of Education early in 1985, the Victorian Primary Schools Sports Association decreed that '. . . access to any sporting activity [be] available to both boys and girls. No longer will separate events be conducted for boys and girls . . .'. In the short term at least, this policy would have resulted in the exclusion of all but a few girls from interschool sport. In fact a survey of NSW school sports associations found that if the NSW 1982–83 swimming teams had been picked on ability, regardless of sex, 92.8 per cent would have been boys. In the event, a one-year exemption from the provisions of the Act was granted to the Australian Primary Schools Sports Association for girls and boys under 12 years. The 'mixed or single-sex' debate continues, although a compromise appears to have evolved at the local level. Separate events are normally conducted for girls and boys, with opportunities also for interested girls to play in traditional boys' sports, and vice-versa.

In April 1991 the Australian Sports Commission released a summary of findings from market research into *youth* sports (13–18-year-olds). The research found strong approval for sport in this age group, but found also that the enthusiasm of teenagers for sport had not always been matched by pleasurable experiences—a reflection perhaps on their experiences in children's sport? The final page of the report included the recommendation that a range of opportunities in sport for this age group be provided through the Aussie Sports—Youth Programme.

The theme for a national conference held in Canberra in October 1991, 'Junior Sport—Time to Deliver', suggests that further changes in children's sport are warranted. Three issues appear to be high on the agenda. First, there is an urgent need for specialist physical education staff, especially in primary schools, to ensure that a broad range of basic movement experiences is provided for every Australian child. Further expansion of coach education will complement an enhanced schools physical education programme. Second, rationalisation of school and community programmes in children's sport must occur. A number of writers have commented on the unnecessary duplication resulting from parallel sporting programmes in school and community. Rationalisation would free resources and enable greater benefits for larger numbers of children. Finally, continued encouragement and support for participation by increased numbers of girls in physical activity and sport is required as well as more general acceptance that many boys may be interested in pursuing sports which do not fall within the traditional male domain.

DJ

See **Aussie Sports Programme**; **Australian Council for Health, Physical Education and Recreation**; **Australian Schools Sport Council**; **Crowd Disorder**; **Gender**.

CHURCHILL, CLIVE BERNARD (1927–85), born Merewether, Newcastle, NSW, was a rugby league full back who represented Australia in thirty-four tests. He captained Australia on a record twenty-four occasions. Leaving the Marist Brothers' College at Hamilton in 1944, he played for Newcastle Central in 1945–47. Dave Spring enlisted him in 1947 for South Sydney at £25 per match. He helped South Sydney to win five premierships out of six in 1950–55. He coached Souths in 1958 and Brisbane's Northern Suburbs in 1959, when he also coached and played for Queensland in a win over NSW. In 1960–61 he was player-coach at Moree; from 1966 to 1974 he coached South

Sydney to four premiership wins in 1967, 1968, 1970, and 1971. Churchill played in thirty-four Tests against Britain, France, and NZ. He toured England with the Australian Kangaroos in 1948, 1952, 1956, and, as coach, in 1959. He led Australia in 1950 to its first Ashes win since 1921, and became the first to captain Australia in three series against Britain. Churchill was a dominant force in rugby league in 1947–74. Only 170 centimetres tall and weighing 76 kilograms, he could demoralise opponents and electrify crowds with his skills and panache. His elusive running camouflaged his comparative slowness, and enabled him to set up three-quarter-line moves. His burying tackles intimidated forwards as well as backs, and complemented his provocative words and gestures, which only a knock-out could stop. He revolutionised full-back play, and evolved plans to co-ordinate all positions in brilliant teamwork. He was 'the Little Master'. He died in Sydney on 9 August 1985.

BN

See **Churchill Medal**; **Rugby League**.

Churchill Medal. The Clive Churchill Medal is awarded annually to perpetuate the memory of Australia's arguably greatest rugby league full back. After Churchill's death from cancer in 1985, the NSW Rugby League instituted the medal, to be awarded to the best player each year in the Sydney Premiership Grand Final. The inaugural winner was Parramatta half-back Peter Sterling, who dominated his team's narrow 4–2 victory over Canterbury in 1986. Subsequent Churchill medallists have been Manly five-eighth Cliff Lyons, Canterbury prop Paul Dunn, Canberra lock Bradley Clyde, and Canberra half-back Ricky Stuart.

PC

See **CHURCHILL, CLIVE**.

CLARK, ANNE, BEM (1903–83), was a distinguished netball administrator, serving the NSW Netball Association as vice-president for many years from 1929, as president from 1950 to 1978, and as patron until her death in 1983. She was also a State manager, selector, and coach. One of the inaugural All Australia Umpires Award Holders (1931), she umpired the first international match in Australia, against NZ in 1938. Clark also umpired the tours of NZ and England in 1948 and 1956 respectively. She was president of the All Australia Netball Association on numerous occasions; this association initiated an umpiring scholarship in her memory. The NSW Netball Association Headquarters was officially named in her honour in 1980.

DH and IJ

See **All Australia Netball Association**.

CLARK, CARNEGIE (1881–1959) was an influential figure in the promotion of golf in

Australia. Small in stature but extremely powerful, this likeable Scot was a leading professional for over forty years and helped establish the Professional Golfers' Association. While the professional at Royal Sydney, Clark also promoted the Vardon grip, the rubber-wound ball, and planned no less than sixteen links throughout the country. He had an excellent competitive record, winning the Australian Open Championship three times, the equivalent professional title on seven occasions, and the first well-sponsored tournament in the nation, the *Sun* £500 in 1924. He founded a successful club-manufacturing company whose equipment still bears his name.

MP

See **Golf**.

CLARK, DANNY, OAM (1951–), born George Town, Tasmania, is considered by many to be Australia's greatest track cyclist, winning four world professional championships, five silver and two bronze medals, and a silver medal in the 1000 metres time trial at the 1972 Munich Olympics. He announced his retirement in 1991 upon winning his fourth world title (equalling Sid Paterson's record) at the age of 40 after a career spanning more than twenty years. Clark dominated the Australian amateur track scene in the early 1970s, winning nine national titles between 1969 and 1973, before shifting his attention to the European professional circuit in 1975. In the same year he also won his first Australian professional titles over 10 000 and 15 000 metres. Clark won his first world title—the Kieren Sprint—in 1980 and his second in the following year. His third and fourth world titles were in motor-paced events in 1990 and 1991. A volatile figure, Clark has often been outspoken on the lack of recognition cyclists, including himself, have been accorded in Australia. His single-minded pursuit of victory has also had the effect of alienating him from his Australian peers. 'I'm not social,' he once said. 'I don't want to have beers. I come, I conquer, and I go and they're still in a daze.' Clark often returned to race in Australia while based in Europe, winning the celebrated Austral Wheelrace three times. His earnings in 1990 were estimated at $370 000. He subsequently settled in Launceston.

JS

See **Austral Wheelrace**; **Tasmanian International Velodrome**.

CLARKE, JUDITH ANNE (1954–), born Launceston, became a leading player of royal tennis. A teacher of physical education, she took up the game in 1973 and won the Tasmanian ladies' singles from 1974 to 1978 and the Victorian ladies' title from 1979 to 1981. She won the international ladies' title in 1975 and again in 1979 and 1982 before going on to take out the ladies' world championship in 1985 and

1987 and the world doubles championship (with Anne Link) in 1985. She remained world champion for virtually a decade and was never beaten in a singles match before her retirement in 1988. She played with great consistency and length in stroking, keeping the ball low over the net without excessive cutting, and had a keen competitive attitude.

GK-S

See **Royal Tennis**.

CLARKE, RON (1937–), born Melbourne, champion distance runner of the 1960s, at one stage held every world record from 2 miles to 20 kilometres. While often favourite, he failed to win an Olympic or Commonwealth gold medal—achieving one Olympic bronze and four Commonwealth silver medals. Clarke came from a sporting family and his brother Jack played football for Essendon. Ron was a brilliant young athlete, setting junior world records for the 1500 metres and 1 and 2 miles. He was selected to carry the torch into the stadium, and light the flame, at the Melbourne Olympics. He broke world records for the 6 miles and 10 kilometres in 1963 and was selected for the 1964 Olympics in the 5 and 10 kilometres and the marathon. He was placed ninth in the 5 kilometres and marathon but lost a tactical battle in the 10 kilometres to Billy Mills (USA) and Mohammed Gammoudi (Tunisia). He lost similar tactical races to the Kenyans Temu and Keino at the Kingston British Empire and Commonwealth Games in 1966. His defeat in the 1968 Olympics was due to high altitude; Clarke ran gallantly but collapsed, near death, after the 10 kilometres race. Clarke was a popular ambassador for Australia, shattering records wherever he went, setting eleven records in sixteen races in his 1965 European–American tour. He equalled Paavo Nurmi's record of seventeen world records in 1967–68 and later became a successful businessman and sports commentator operating from England.

JAD

See **STAMPFL, FRANZ**.

Claxton Shield was for many years the trophy for interstate baseball competition in Australia. It was donated in 1934 by Norrie Claxton, a former player and the Patron of the SA Baseball Association. The annual interstate carnival had been held for many years before this donation. The first such games were held in 1889 between Victoria and SA, regular Victoria v. NSW matches started in 1900, and in 1910 the first three-sided carnival was held when SA joined in. For two years Tasmania fielded a side but, with the exception of the war years, it was an annual carnival between Victoria, NSW, and SA. SA won the contest for the Claxton Shield for the first three years, a feat repeated immediately by NSW. WA first played for the shield in

1937 and Queensland in 1939, the last before the war. The annual carnival resumed in 1946 and attracted good publicity, culminating in its being televised for a few years in the 1980s. The Claxton Shield tradition was broken in 1989 when Queensland, the holders of the trophy, did not play in an interstate series as part of a national dispute over the Australian Baseball Federation.

BM

See **Baseball**.

Clayton Cup was donated in 1937 by Rueben Clayton, a member of the NSW Rugby League's Country Committee. It is awarded annually by the NSW Country Rugby League to the winner of a country group first-grade rugby league premiership which has the most outstanding record for the season. To 1990, inclusive, it has been won forty-nine times by forty-three clubs, with only Tweed Heads Seagulls winning it three times, while Cobar, Tumbarumba, and Young have each won it twice. When Narwan, from the New England zone, won in 1980, they were undefeated, as is often the case, and also the first all-Aboriginal team to gain the trophy.

TB

CLELAND, ALLAN (?1957–) until the age of 23 played a number of sports, including cricket, hockey, squash, badminton, and football, with moderate success before taking up croquet. The precision and pressure of the game appealed to him in that most shots 'you play are a bit like a three-foot putt in golf'. He won his first important tournament, the Victorian Gold Medal, in 1981 and after rising steadily through the rankings won the world singles championship in the USA in May 1989. For his victory he received a handsome gold watch from the tournament sponsor as this sport has limited sponsorship. Cleland conducts coaching classes in Victoria in an honorary capacity.

PD

CLEMENT, ELSPETH (1956–) first played hockey for WA in 1976 and made her Australian debut two years later. This was at a time when the Australian women's hockey team was beginning to tour overseas with increasing frequency, and Clement was to become the first Australian woman to play one hundred games for her country. She reached this milestone in the 1988 Olympic semifinal against Holland, and went on to play in the final against South Korea, retiring after winning a gold medal with the team. This fulfilled a long-held ambition, as she had been selected for both the 1980 and 1984 Games but missed both because of the 1980 boycott and injury in 1984. Clement was an unusual player, a full back who regularly scored goals from penalty corners. Her relatively small

stature belied an elusiveness, strong tackling, and a great sense of anticipation.

RQ

COCKBURN, BRUCE (1951–) won the World Trick Water Ski Championships at Copenhagen in 1969 and dominated Australian water skiing in the 1970s. In the 1973 world title in Bogota, he finished second in the 'tricks' and he was second in the 'jump' in 1975. Cockburn's family was very much involved in the sport. He was taught to ski by his father and a brother, Graeme, and sister, Lesley, who were both world-class skiers. He won his first major title when he was 12 and the State junior titles in 1966 and 1967. He won the NSW and Australian men's Opens from 1969 to 1976, with injury forcing him out of competition in 1977. Cockburn won the tricks eight times, the jump seven times, and the slalom four times in the Australian titles from 1967 to 1979. He was overall points-score champion eight times. He was inducted into the Sport Australia Hall of Fame in 1985.

RC

Coleman Medal. The John Coleman Medal is awarded by the AFL to the player who kicks most goals in the home-and-away series. The medal is named in honour of John Coleman, the legendary Essendon full forward. In a six-year career (1949-54), ended prematurely by injury, Coleman kicked 537 goals and led the VFL goal-kicking in four seasons. The medal was first awarded in 1981 to Michael Roach of Richmond. Bernie Quinlan of Fitzroy (1983–84) and Jason Dunstall of Hawthorn (1988–89) were the only multiple winners in the 1980s. In 1987 St Kilda's Tony Lockett became the first player to win both the John Coleman and Brownlow Medals.

DN

COLES, Dr ALLAN (1927–) returned to Sydney in 1966, after securing his doctorate at the University of California, Los Angeles, to become head of the Department of Physical Education at Alexander Mackie College. After a period as director of the School of Physical Education at Dalhousie University, Canada, Coles became head of the Department of Physical Education at the University of Queensland in 1972 where he established degree programmes in Human Movement Studies. He was appointed chairman of the Australian Sports Institute Study Group which tabled a report in Parliament in 1975. This formed the basis for the establishment of the Australian Institute of Sport in 1980. Coles was appointed director of the NSW Department of Recreation and Sport in 1978 and from 1983–87 was a consultant to the NSW Board of Education. He was also chairman of the Australian Fitness Accreditation Committee. His interests were wide-ranging and he was also a member of the Theatre Board of the Australia Council.

IJ

See **Australian Institute of Sport**.

'Colliwobbles' means the unique choking (or 'giving in') under pressure in football finals by Collingwood. The term was invented by Lou Richards in 1970 when the Magpies 'wobbled' (or collapsed) in the Grand Final and lost after leading by 44 points at half-time. Taken in conjunction with Collingwood's losses by 4 points and 1 point in the 1964 and 1966 Grand Finals respectively, the 'Colliwobbles' legend was gleefully disseminated and perpetuated by fans of all other clubs. Collingwood's thirty-one defeats in fifty finals between 1959 and 1989 furthered the myth, even though the team rarely 'choked' in the last quarter or second half. The concept was reinforced when Collingwood dissipated a 27-point lead at three-quarter-time and drew the 1977 Grand Final. The 'Colliwobbles' myth died on 6 October 1990 when Collingwood won its first premiership in thirty-two years; it was buried in a formal ceremony at Victoria Park presided over by Lou Richards on 18 November.

RS

Commonwealth Games
The fourteenth celebration of the Commonwealth Games opened in Auckland, NZ, in January 1990. When the Games concluded ten days later, Australia had achieved its finest performance ever, and dominated many events on the programme. Historically, Australia's commitment to these Games has been enthusiastic and successful, dating back to the late nineteenth century when the concept of multi-sport competition for the Empire was first advanced. That idea was the creation of John Astley Cooper, born in Adelaide to an immigrant Anglican cleric, but a long-time resident of England. During 1891, several articles appeared in the British press which put forward the idea of a 'Pan-Britannic Festival' to display the industrial, cultural, and athletic achievements of the Empire. By the next year Richard Coombes had become committed to the cause, and over subsequent years he energetically promoted Cooper's plan. Coombes had also emigrated from England, and was a reporter for Sydney's largest sporting newspaper, the *Referee*.

Although Cooper's suggestion should properly be seen in the context of the debate about the status and future of the British Empire, a topic of increasing concern as the nineteenth century drew to a close, it was the sporting section of his plan which captured and held the attention of the contemporary media. Empire-wide interest was evident throughout 1892 and 1893, and Coombes regularly editorialised about the value of the Pan-Britannic Festival to the Empire generally and to the still unfederated Australian States in particular. The discussion and debate which ensued enabled Coombes to promote Australian sport while at the same time pursuing Empire unity. While there was a great deal of theoretical support for Cooper's plan, a lack of concrete progress towards establishing the event eventually brought about a decline in interest, and by 1894 de Coubertin's highly visible efforts to 'revive' the Olympic Games had captured much of the world's attention. Nevertheless, there were sporadic reminders of the Pan-Britannic Festival in the Australian press, mostly contained in the *Referee*, and Coombes's loyalty to the idea was rewarded in 1911, when the coronation of the new king inspired the Festival of Empire, and he was named manager of the seven-man Australasian team which contested the modest sports programme staged in London during the festivities. Hampered by illness and injury, the Australasian team finished last overall behind Canada and the UK in the nine events held in athletics, boxing, wrestling, and swimming. Their only outright winner was Harold Hardwick of Sydney who gained a unique double victory in the 100 yards swim and the heavyweight boxing event. The sport administrators from the countries involved were most enthusiastic about the competition, and it was proposed by Coombes and James Merrick of Canada that the Empire countries should train together in London before departing for the 1912 Olympic Games in Stockholm. While this plan did not eventuate, the sentiment of Empire unity through sport took on increased power and significance from this time.

It would be incorrect to assume that sport had merely a symbolic importance for the Empire in the early years of the twentieth century: during and immediately after the Great War, sporting contests played an important part in maintaining the bonds of Empire. Britain had ceased to be the centre of world power, and this fact was magnified by the establishment of the League of Nations and the dominions' role in the Versailles peace treaty. There is clear evidence that during the 1920s formal political ties with the imperial power were in decline; informal cultural bonds like sport were, on the other hand, strengthened during the same decade. This trend was highly visible in the establishment of the British Empire Games in 1930, an event which followed a decade of fundamental political change within the Empire.

By the time of the 1928 Olympic Games in Amsterdam, Canadian officials were able to present concrete proposals for the initiation of a multi-sport festival confined to the Empire.

The increasing domination of the Americans in Olympic events, and a perception that the true spirit of amateur sport was not practised outside the Empire, made the notion of a private 'family' competition most attractive. On a more subtle level, this move provided the Empire with an alternative structure to replace its disintegrating political authority. Increasing demands for autonomy and equality within the Empire were being raised by politicians from South Africa, Canada, and the Irish Free State during the 1920s, and the 1931 Statute of Westminster gave full expression to this desire. Under its terms, individual countries could acquire legislative independence to the degree each deemed appropriate. Australia, generally ambivalent about major changes in the Empire, did not formally adopt the statute until 1942.

With the exception of England, the various members took up the cause of Empire Games quite zealously, none more so than the host city of Hamilton, Ontario. The local organising committee, under Bobby Robinson, secured extensive financial backing from the city council, and this support proved crucial when the funding of teams loomed as an insurmountable obstacle to establishing the Games. The timely offer of free food and accommodation, and a travel subsidy of Can$5000 reversed the Amateur Athletic Union of Australia's decision to decline its invitation to go to Hamilton; ultimately, all eleven competing countries except England received financial assistance from the organising committee. The Depression was taking on world-wide proportions by this time, and the expense of also sending teams to North America for the 1932 Summer Olympics made financial assistance from Hamilton all the more welcome—indeed, vital.

From their inception, the British Empire Games fostered a strong link with the monarchy, and a recognition of the Queen as the head of the Commonwealth is one of the few points in common today among the association's diffuse and disparate members. The political evolution of the British Empire into the modern Commonwealth, as well as the increasing cultural power of the Games, has been reflected in the name applied to the event since 1930: from British Empire Games (until 1954), to British Empire and Commonwealth Games (until 1970), to British Commonwealth Games (until 1978), and to today's Commonwealth Games. Australia has attended all fourteen celebrations, and has hosted the Games three times: in Sydney (1938), Perth (1962), and Brisbane (1982). The Australian British Empire Games Committee was established in October 1929 with E. S. Marks as chairman and James S. W. Eve as honorary secretary-treasurer, and this body has, with its name regularly updated, administered

Australia's affairs within the Commonwealth Games Federation ever since.

The 1934 Games were originally awarded to Johannesburg, but were moved to London when it became clear that the South African government would not admit non-white competitors. Even since its expulsion in 1961, South Africa has continued to affect the relationship in sport among Commonwealth countries. Its apartheid policies have influenced the Games, and on several occasions in the 1970s and 1980s have threatened their future existence. After a low point in Edinburgh in 1986, brought on by financial problems and a massive boycott by African, Asian, and Caribbean nations to protest against the British government's continuing refusal to apply economic sanctions to South Africa, the latest Games in NZ appear to have once again strengthened this bond through sport. However, the multi-racial Commonwealth must now deal with the fact that, with the single exception of Jamaica in 1966, the hosting of its Games has rotated among the old 'white dominions', a trend which clearly must change if the Games are to continue.

From the beginning, these self-styled 'Friendly Games' were meant to have a philosophy different from that expressed at the Olympic Games, but in the sixty years of their existence emphasis countries place on winning, not simply taking part, has revealed itself as an increasingly strong motivating factor. Australia's enhanced commitment to preparing its competitors for Auckland was reflected in the team's dominating performance. While the thinking underpinning the Commonwealth Games may have undergone some serious review in recent years, the Games still serve a central purpose in the cohesion of the modern Commonwealth and appear ready to carry on their important cultural role into the next century.

KM

See **British Empire and Commonwealth Games 1962 (Perth)**; **British Empire Games 1938 (Sydney)**; **Commonwealth Games 1982 (Brisbane)**; COOMBES, RICHARD.

Commonwealth Games 1982 (Brisbane). Local, State, and Federal governments combined to provide $37 million to construct badly needed sports facilities in Brisbane which served as the main venues for the Games, held from 30 September to 9 October. NZ's rugby ties with South Africa threatened to end in a boycott by the African and Caribbean nations, but ultimately a record forty-six countries sent 2150 team members to Brisbane. Australia's team of 209 competitors and fifty-four officials was the largest at the Games. Disqualifications abounded at the pool as Australia successfully re-established its dominance over Canada and England as the premier swimming nation in the Commonwealth. Tracey Wickham ended her international career with two more gold medals, while Lisa Curry won three events. Raelene Boyle also finished her career with a victory in the 400 metres, joining other athletics gold-medallists Garry Brown, Peter Bourke, Robert de Castella, Ray Boyd, Gary Honey, Debbie Flintoff, Glynis Nunn, and Sue Howland. As had been the case in Edmonton, the cultural Festival '82 attached to the Games provided a vivid demonstration of the Commonwealth's shared heritage and diverse cultures. Despite a suspension of many civil liberties in Queensland during the Games, and the attempts made to minimise the impact of the Aboriginal Land Rights movement, many Australians were content to cheer their country on its way to the top of the unofficial medal table.

KM

See **Commonwealth Games**.

Confederation of Australian Sport (CAS) is an independent industry grouping of national sporting organisations with a primary commitment to ensuring that the needs and aspirations of the Australian sports community are properly reflected in the deliberations and decisions of the Federal Government. CAS was formed in 1976 in response to the cutting of Federal funding to sport. From its inception CAS has embraced all sections of the sporting community: professional and amateur, male and female, disabled sport, sport science, and sports medicine. It has grown from an initial membership of forty-two national sporting organisations to 128 members representing almost seven million registered sports participants. One of the first actions of CAS was the preparation of a White Paper, *The Financial Plight of Sport in Australia*, which was an intensive lobbying campaign and resulted in the reinstatement of funding for sport in the 1977 Federal Budget. A national series of seminars throughout 1978–80 attracted local participation of almost 2500 and led to CAS's *Master Plan for Sport*, a blueprint for the development of sport in Australia. As CAS developed it was influential in identifying and addressing the needs of Australian sport.

It was responsible for the formation of the Confederation of Australian Sport Coaches Assembly (CASCA) which subsequently encouraged the formation of the Australian Coaching Council (ACC) and the administering of the National Coaching Accreditation Scheme (NCAS). It formed a Children in Sport policy committee after a campaign begun in 1978 to have sport and planned physical activity included as a key component of the core curriculum in schools; in 1991 CAS joined with the ASC to host a national conference on junior sport and formed a working committee to develop a national junior sport policy. CAS's Administrator's Education Committee was formed in 1979 and led to the establishment of the Australian Society of Sport Administrators (ASSA). In 1980 CAS introduced the annual Sport Australia Awards to recognise outstanding achievements in sport during the preceding twelve months. In 1981 the International Assembly of National Organizations of Sport (IANOS) was established with the CAS president, Wayne Reid, elected as president and the CAS executive director, Garry Daly, appointed as secretary-general; IANOS became the first major sports umbrella group outside Europe. APOSA (Asia Pacific and Oceania Sports Assembly), a regional equivalent of IANOS, was also an initiative of CAS. In 1984 CAS hosted a Women and Competitive Sport Conference and has continued to argue for the rights and appropriate acknowledgement of women in sport. CAS endorsed the establishment of multi-sport festivals for mature and aged adults in 1984 and gave approval for the Tasmanian Government to host the First Australian Masters Games; subsequent games have been held in Adelaide (1989) and Brisbane (1991). CAS established the Sport Australia Hall of Fame in 1985 to publicly acknowledge and perpetuate the contribution of sportspeople to Australia; by 1991 more than two hundred and fifty Australian athletes, coaches, and administrators had been inducted. Finally, *Sport Report* has been published quarterly by CAS since 1979.

By 1989 there was a feeling that CAS had strayed somewhat from its primary role as a lobby group for sport and its members elected to the board a so-called 'reform group'. Subsequently CAS appointed Dene Moore as executive director and moved its headquarters to the 'lobby belt' in Canberra. At a CAS seminar, 'Sport: A New Deal', in 1989, Federal Sport Minister Senator Graham Richardson praised the changes in CAS and stressed the need for an effective sports lobby. CAS completed a new headquarters building in Canberra in 1991.

DM*, TN, and IJ

CONNOR, DESMOND MICHAEL (1935–), born Brisbane, has the unique distinction of playing half-back for NZ and Australia, and in a nation-wide poll in 1990 was selected as the All Blacks greatest half since 1945. He played for Queensland from 1954 to 1959 and was in the 1957–58 Wallaby tour of the British Isles, France, and North America. He played for the All Blacks in 1961, and then toured Australia with them in 1962. He retired in 1965. He made a considerable contribution to rugby, by introducing the short line-out to the world and as Australian coach against NZ when he returned to Brisbane. He then took the Australian team to South Africa in 1969. He was an Australian selector from 1970 to 1971. His superb passing, kicking, and line-out innovation place him among the greats of the game.

RH and MH

COOKE, GRAHAM (1912–), born Toowoomba, Queensland, is acclaimed by many experts as the best rugby union second-rower Australia has ever produced. A tall, raw-boned man, he represented Australia from 1932 to 1948, the longest career of any international player. He toured South Africa in 1933 and was one of the successes of the tour. Considered too old to be selected for the 1939 Wallabies, he was Australia's toughest tour to 1946 tour to NZ and the 1947–48 tour of the British Isles, France, Canada, and the USA. He was the first Australian to play Tests against all the major rugby-playing countries.

RH and MH

COOMBES, RICHARD (1855–1935), an English immigrant, joined the Sydney *Referee* in 1890. An energetic journalist and sports administrator, Coombes was involved in athletics, walking, rowing, sculling, rifle-shooting, coursing, and cycling at State and national levels. His influence in athletics was most pronounced, founding the NSW Amateur Athletics Association in 1887 and serving as its president for forty-two years, while acting as inaugural and long-time president of the Australian Amateur Athletic Union from 1897. Coombes was a member of the International Olympic Committee for twenty-seven years, and one of the founders of the Australian Olympic Federation in 1895. A lifelong imperialist, Coombes faithfully supported any attempt to preserve the Empire through sport, and he managed the Australasian team to the Festival of Empire in London in 1911.

KM

See **Athletics**; **Athletics Australia**; **Australian Olympic Committee**; **Commonwealth Games**.

COOPER, ASHLEY (1936–), born Melbourne, was a solid tennis-player with excellent concentration. In 1958 he rose to be Australia's number one ranked player after winning the Wimbledon, US, and Australian Open crowns. Cooper's fine backhand return of service enabled him to effectively counter leading left-handers such as Mervyn Rose, Neale Fraser, and Rod Laver. After playing on the professional circuit Cooper settled in Brisbane to operate a large family tennis and squash complex. As a foundation member of the Queensland and National McDonald's Tennis Australia boards, Cooper was able to maintain his contribution to the game's development.

HCJP

COOPER, BRADFORD PAUL (1954–), was born in Singapore of working-class parents. The family moved to Rockhampton, Queensland, when he was 3. During his career Cooper won eighteen Australian Championships (thirteen individual and five team). He won gold (200 metres backstroke), silver (400 metres freestyle), and bronze (100 metres backstroke) medals at the 1974 British Commonwealth Games. At the 1972 Munich Games he achieved a gold medal in the 400 metres freestyle, and two seconds (4 × 200 metres freestyle relay and 400 metres freestyle) and a third (1500 metres freestyle) in the first world championships at Belgrade in 1973. He also set two world records, in the 800 and 400 metres freestyle. He was the first Australian, and the second in the world, to swim under 4 minutes for the 400 metres freestyle; the first Australian to break 16 minutes for the 1500 metres freestyle; and the first Australian to swim under 1 minute for the 100 metres backstroke. A remarkable athlete, he retired at 20 years of age.

RH and MH

Corbett Memorial Trophy was instituted in 1946 and is awarded to the captain of the winning team in the third Test in each England–Australia rugby league series played in Australia. Claude Corbett (1885–1944) was an Australian swimming champion in 1901 and later an accomplished rugby union player. He rose from copyboy to managing editor of the Hugh D. McIntosh publications, the *Sunday Times*, the *Referee*, and the *Arrow*, before spending twenty years as sporting editor of the Sydney *Sun*, for which he wrote extensively on many sports. Corbett accompanied and reported on three Kangaroo tours of Britain, the first in 1911–12. A widely respected journalist, he was the first pressman to become a life member of the NSW Rugby League. After Corbett's death, admirers subscribed to establish the trophy, which only one player has won twice—Clive Churchill, in 1950 and 1954.

TB

CORMIE, HEC, MBE (c. 1900–89), was introduced to hockey in 1921 when the Queensland Hockey Association was formed. He began a lifelong association with hockey as a player, administrator, and promoter of the game. One of the greatest exponents of left-wing play, Cormie represented Queensland on a number of occasions between 1922 and 1935 and was selected at national level in 1927 and 1929, and later as captain. On the administration side he was secretary of the Queensland Hockey Association (QHA) in 1924 and again from 1929 to 1939; he was also president of QHA from 1945 to 1950 and the national association president in 1949. As a promoter of the game, Cormie was founder of the journal

Hockey Circle, which he edited from 1933 until 1985. During this time he was one of the few voices promoting the sport. He was awarded life memberships of the Queensland and Australian Hockey Associations, as well as an MBE and an Award of Merit from the governing body, the Fédération Internationale de Hockey sur Gazon, for his services to the game.

BS†

CORRIGAN, THOMAS (1854–94), jockey, born Ireland, came with his family to Victoria in 1866, settling near Warrnambool. He began riding soon afterwards, at first on the flat, but it was over the jumps that he made his reputation. He won the first VRC Grand National Hurdle in 1881 on *Sir Peter*, as well as other major jumping races in Victoria, SA, and NSW. Dashing and sporting a huge moustache, Corrigan rode 239 winners in his career and had a large public following. There was enormous grief on his death in August 1894 when his mount *Waiter*, whom he owned, fell during the Caulfield Grand National Steeplechase.

AL
See **Corrigan's Funeral**.

Corrigan's Funeral. On 11 August 1894 the jockey Tommy Corrigan died as a result of injuries received when his horse fell in the Caulfield Grand National Steeplechase. The funeral, held four days later, was an event that confirmed Corrigan's place in Australian folklore. The long route from Corrigan's house in Caulfield to the Melbourne General Cemetery, a 1½ hour journey, was lined with people who wanted to pay their last respects to the popular rider. The cortège was an elaborate affair which took 30 minutes to cross Collins Street. It consisted of a representative assembly of jockeys on foot, numerous horse-drawn carriages, a large number of horsemen, and 240 vehicles. The carriages not only contained Corrigan's relatives but also leading dignitaries of Victorian and NSW clubs and representatives from the sporting community. At the service the vast crowd needed to be roped off and eventually dispersed by mounted troopers.

GC*
See **CORRIGAN, THOMAS**.

COTTEE, KAY, OAM (1954–), became the first woman to complete a solo, non-stop, and unassisted circumnavigation of the globe when she arrived at Sydney Harbour on 5 June 1988. The trip of 25 000 nautical miles in her 12 metre Cavalier 37 sloop *Blackmore's First Lady* had taken 189 days. It was a record in terms of the fastest time by a woman, the longest time at sea, and the greatest distance travelled without a break. Although she had suffered from a hole in the heart since birth which caused her to experience greater tiredness than other sailors, she averaged only six hours sleep per night during her epic voyage. At Cape Horn Cottee had battled huge seas and at the Cape of Good Hope narrowly missed being run down by a fishing vessel. For her efforts to raise money for the Life Education Centre, she received the OAM in 1989. She was also named Australian of the Year.

RC

COTTON, FRANK STANLEY (1880–1955), born Sydney, was a swimmer and physiologist. After graduating in science from Sydney University in 1915, he joined its department of physiology, later becoming professor. A university swimming 'blue' and NSW 440 and 880 yards champion in 1921, Cotton's lifelong interest was in the physiology of circulation and respiration. With the RAAF during the Second World War he helped invent the 'Cotton aerodynamic anti-G flying suit'. After the war he won international renown by testing the effects of strain on athletes in order to improve training and selection methods. Among those assisted by the congenial 'father of scientific training in Australia' were Jon Henricks and Judy Joy Davies (swimmers), Peter Evatt (sculler), and Edwin Carr (runner). Cotton died at Hornsby in Sydney, on 23 August 1955.

GW
See **Sports Science**; **Swimming**.

Country Show Sports
The agricultural show began as an annual display of farm stock and produce with the purpose of improving the quality of farming practice. However, as a major event in the annual calendar, a broader range of displays developed to provide for participation by women and children, and coupled with this widening focus, a variety of sporting and social events were also added. Travelling entertainers and showmen also moved from venue to venue to enhance the local events. Some activities were imported from European tradition. For instance, the now discredited event of chasing the greasy pig appears to have had its origins in the fairs of central Europe. Other pastimes evolved from the pastoral practices of the day: woodchopping, sheaf-tossing, and sheep-shearing all appeared. Still others became the province of the travelling showmen, and were often based upon an entrepreneurial assessment of what might be popular enough to make money. So the famous boxing tent gave young men the challenge and opportunity to prove their toughness. More importantly, it gave young boxers trying to make it in the professional arena a chance to gain both experience and income. Still other activities can only be described as idiosyncratic—events which arose in one specific district and which came to be seen as marking the distinctive identity of that district's own show. Examples include rolling-pin throws, rabbit-skinning contests, tractor ballet, and a number of others. These persist today,

often striving for inclusion in *The Guinness Book of Records*.

EH-S

See **Sheaf-tossing**; **Sheep-shearing**; **Wood-chopping**.

COUPER, GAIL (1947–   ) began surfing with school friends after her family moved to Lorne, Victoria, in the early 1960s. One year after she started surfing, she entered her first competition and won the Victorian State championships in 1964. She went on to represent Australia in the world titles the same year and finished among the top six. Since then, combining her surfing and teaching careers, she captured State and national titles until her retirement from the competitive scene in 1979–80. She held the Victorian women's title twelve times between 1964 and 1976, not competing in 1969 due to injury. The Australian women's title was hers in 1966, 1967, 1971, 1972, and 1975. Surfing for Australia in the world titles during her competitive years, she achieved consistently high placings and closer to home, but still on the international scene, Couper has won ten Bell's Beach Easter championships. She has combined her surfing with a variety of other interests including picture framing, photography, music, and skiing and now surfs the west coast on a 6 foot 4 inch Trigger Brothers thruster. She says about the sport in the 1990s, 'It's a sport you just keep doing because you enjoy the environment'.

MV

Coursing
One of the oldest of all sports, coursing is the competition between a pair of hunting dogs, usually greyhounds, in the pursuit of quarry, usually hares. In Britain greyhounds had once been the preserve of the aristocracy, and the sport was associated with the wealthy. In 1855 the National Coursing Club (NCC) was established to consolidate British practice, with the Waterloo Cup the premier event. In Australia greyhounds were included in the First Fleet, and took their place in kangaroo hunts, the local variant on fox-hunting. At Narracoorte in SA in 1868, local landowners organised Australia's first Waterloo Cup, which was repeated annually for several years, with wallabies as the quarry. A Victoria Coursing Club (VCC) was established in March 1873, adopting English NCC rules, and hosted what it described as 'the first public coursing meeting ever held in Australia in which hares were the game' over two days beginning on 29 May at W. J. Clarke's property at Sunbury. This, a comparative success, spawned a fashion for coursing and greyhound-breeding as an exclusive sport for the prosperous. English dogs were imported, and numerous country clubs formed. In Sydney the NSW Coursing Club (NSWCC) was created in February 1875, and in the same month Thomas Haydon (secretary of the VCC) and the NSWCC published the first *Australian Cours-*

ing Calendar, listing pedigrees and results of meetings. The NSW club most often coursed at Walter Lamb's Woodstock estate at Rooty Hill. By 1878 a National Coursing Club of Australasia (NCCA) had been formed, with delegates from coursing clubs including NZ and Tasmania.

Coursing was affected by the 1890s Depression, which diminished the fortunes of several of its supporters. The national Waterloo Cup was a matter of contention, with rival meetings held. In Melbourne the sport enjoyed a revival after the Cox family at Moonee Valley racecourse replicated the enclosed coursing meetings held in London at Plumpton. From 1901 the Australian Waterloo Cup alternated between Moonee Valley and Rooty Hill until 1912 when it went to Geelong. From 1919 it was run at various venues, including Rocklea in Brisbane, Warwick, Benalla, and NZ. At its peak, coursing attracted crowds of several thousands, and was followed in all States excepting WA, but it was rapidly eclipsed in popularity by 'speed coursing', introduced from the USA, where fields of eight or ten dogs pursued a mechanical hare over a small track. Speed-coursing clubs, emerging in 1927, came to dominate the NCC within a decade, although it was subject to government restriction in several States. The image of the sport was transformed as dog-racing was promoted as a recreation and gambling medium for the working classes. Speed coursing added a final blow to traditional coursing through press stories of cruelty to hares by dog-trainers. By 1947 the NSW RSPCA was urging a ban on live-hare coursing, and this was accomplished by 1953. Other States followed over the next three decades, SA being the last to outlaw the sport in 1986.

AL

See **Greyhound-racing**.

COURT, MARGARET (née SMITH) (1942–   ), born Albury, NSW, is regarded as the finest woman tennis-player produced in Australia. When only 15 the tall, athletic emerging champion moved from her birthplace to Melbourne under the guidance of coaches Keith Rogers and Frank Sedgman. When very young, it is said, she played as a left-hander. Eventually, after she had built up her strength, her right-handed first serve, strong forehand, and power net-rushing game made her a formidable player. In 1963, as Margaret Smith, she was the first Australian woman to win Wimbledon. The next year she lost the final to Maria Bueno but turned the tables in 1965. After briefly retiring at 24 she married and returned to the circuit as Mrs Court. She was to win the Grand Slam in her vintage year of 1970. Her victory over rival Billie Jean King at Wimbledon, with a score line of 14–12 11–9, was one of the tournament's longest and most tensely fought women's encounters. Her career record of sixty-two Grand Slam titles including eleven Australian, five French, three Wimbledon, and five US singles wins is the best recorded to date. Yet there were occasions when her weak second serve and centre-court nerves denied her expected victory. Early in her career she had disapproved of the Australian team management style of Nell Hopman, but her court demeanour was exemplary. Until her retirement in 1976 Court remained near the top, winning record prize-money which had not been possible in her earlier career.

HCJP

See **Lawn Tennis**.

Courtney International Goodwill Trophy. In 1936 NZ wool merchant Roy O. Courtney (1898–1961) donated this elaborate example of the silversmith's art. Intended to foster international goodwill and to honour the war dead, it cost £500, weighs 150 kilograms and is 1.25 metres high on a 1 square metre base. It features a Shrine of Remembrance, the emblems of the rugby league nations, and images of their pioneers. Above these, a silver globe, supported by silver dolphins, is surmounted by a gold figure representing 'Peace'. First won by England in the 1936 Tests against Australia, it was contested in Test series between all countries until, in 1955, it was decided to award it on a points-score basis over four-year periods, changed in 1960 to five-year terms. Too big and valuable to transport, the trophy is now on permanent display at the NSW Leagues Club in Sydney.

TB

COVENTRY, SIDNEY ALBERT (1899–1976), born Moonee Ponds, Victoria, was an Australian rules footballer. He played 227 games as a ruckman for Collingwood (1922–34), coached Footscray (1935–36) and was president of the Collingwood Football Club (1950–63). Coventry was the archetypal 'Collingwood six-footer', that is, 5 feet 11 inches. He captained Collingwood to four consecutive VFL premierships (1927–30), and unilaterally thwarted a threatened players' strike over a ten shilling pay cut in 1928. Coventry won the Brownlow Medal in 1927 and his club's best and fairest award twice (1927 and 1932). His brother Gordon played 306 games for Collingwood (1920–37), kicking a VFL record of 1299 goals.

RS

COX, LIONEL (1930–), born Brisbane, became best known as Russell Mockridge's tandem partner, but was a fast and aggressive sprint cyclist in his own right. An only child, he received great support from his mother Muriel, who acted as his timekeeper and helped raise money to enable him to attend the Olympics. After the family moved to Sydney, Cox built up his body strength by working at the Sydney fruit markets humping heavy bags of vegetables and fruit. After entering senior cycling ranks in

1948 he had his best season in 1951–52 when he was undefeated on the NSW track. With Mockridge, Cox won a remarkable victory in the 2000 metres tandem team event at the 1952 Olympics. Seven days before the event he had not ridden a tandem bicycle, concentrating his preparation on the sprint. Although given little hope in the 1000 metres sprint and with the final only one hour after the tandem victory, he secured a meritorious second in the event.

RH and MH

CRAMPTON, BRUCE SIDNEY (1935–), born Sydney, was the first Australian golfer to win more than $1 million in prize-money and became known as the ironman because of his long playing schedules. He became Australia's youngest-ever international, competing against NZ when only 17. In 1956, after winning the Australian Open, he joined the American circuit and grossed $1.4 million over the next twenty years. Although he won fifteen tournaments in America, the majors eluded him, but he was runner-up in the US PGA twice, as well as the US Masters and the US Open. Crampton's prickly manner won him few friends on tour, but he was a well-respected professional. After retiring in 1977 he later joined the US seniors tour and within a couple of years had won another million dollars. He became a big investor in the Texas oil industry.

GC*

See **Golf**.

CRAPP, LORRAINE (1938–) was the first woman to swim under 5 minutes for the 400 metres freestyle. A graceful, elegant freestyler, she won three gold, one silver, and two bronze British Empire and Commonwealth Games medals, and two gold and two silver Olympic medals. She was the first Australian swimmer, male or female, to hold world records in all freestyle distances at the same time. In all she broke—in individual and relay events—twenty-three world records and won nine Australian championships. Her greatest swims were achieved at the 1956 Melbourne Olympics, when she won the 400 metres freestyle and was a member of the victorious 4 × 100 metres freestyle relay, and was narrowly beaten by Dawn Fraser in the 100 metres freestyle. Crapp was awarded the city of Genoa Christopher Columbus Trophy as the outstanding athlete in the world in 1957. She came back to compete in the 1960 Rome Olympics and achieved a silver medal in the 400 metres freestyle relay, but her secret marriage, the night before she left for Rome, to Dr Bill Thurlow was treated as a scandal by the Australian press and officials and affected her morale. Crapp bowed out of swimming after the Rome Olympics, and worked as a receptionist for her physician-husband. A remarkable all-round swimmer, her world records ranged from the sprints to the middle- and long-distance events. Quiet and introspective, she often laboured in the shadow of sprinter Dawn Fraser. In 1956 she broke seventeen world records. She was a major cause of the resurgence of women's swimming in the 'golden age' of Australian swimming.

RH and MH

CRAWFORD, JACK (1908–91), born Albury, NSW, has been described as one of Australia's most stylish tennis-players. Crawford, tall and always impeccably attired in long cream trousers, was known for his flat-topped racquet which he used when he won Wimbledon in 1933. In that year 'Gentleman Jack' rose to be the number one player in the world when he also won the French and Australian Opens. However, the Grand Slam eluded him when Fred Perry was his conqueror in five sets at Forest Hills. Two years later Crawford turned the tables on Perry for his fourth Australian Open title.

HCJP

See **Lawn Tennis**; QUIST, ADRIAN.

CREMIN, ERIC JAMES (1914–73), born Sydney, was considered one of the best putters in Australian golf. After a stint as an assistant professional he won the first major championship he entered, the 1937 Australian PGA. He also won the NSW PGA in 1937 and 1938. After the Second World War he was runner-up in the 1946 Australian PGA, a position he secured another four times. His golden years were 1949 and 1950 when he captured twelve major tournaments including the Australian Open. Later he was club professional at Roseville, Sydney, before joining the Singapore Country Club where he died of a heart attack on the first tee.

GC*

Cricket

Cricket, the first team sport to be played in Australia, is the sport which comes closest to being the national game. Australia has developed its own traditions of play which include barracking, bush cricket, larger and better appointed ovals, bigger scoreboards, and the eight-ball over; it has also introduced distinctive cricketing terms such as 'guzunder', 'mully-grubber', and 'sundries'. Different conditions—brighter light and bouncier pitches—have encouraged pace and leg-spin bowling, for instance, and batsmen who play shots square of the wicket. Cricket was played in Sydney from 1803, but reports of the game were infrequent until 1826, when the Australian Cricket Club was formed. Many more clubs were formed in NSW and in other colonies in the 1830s. Most of them were organised around public houses, and gambling was a focal point. Many of these early clubs did not survive long, the most notable exception being the Melbourne Cricket Club, founded in 1838, which became the most powerful Australian club, even organising national tours in the late nineteenth century. Visiting regiments contributed to the growth of cricket and contests between civilian and military teams were frequent and popular. Intercolonial matches did much to enhance the popularity of cricket and to create a network of associations. The first match was between Tasmania and Victoria in Launceston in 1851, though it was not until 1856, when the NSW side defeated Victoria at the Melbourne Cricket Ground, that intercolonials became an annual event. They attracted large crowds and drew on the fierce rivalry which existed between one colony and another.

The visit of H. H. Stephenson's side of English professionals in 1861–62 followed by George Parr's team in 1863–64 provided a great stimulus to the development of Australian cricket, and the initial tour proved highly profitable for the promoters, the Melbourne catering firm of Spiers & Pond. The success of the visitors against local XVIIIs and XXIIs—Parr's side went through the tour undefeated—indicated the large gap between British and colonial cricket at the time. Aborigines from northern Victoria, organised by English professional Charles Lawrence, were the first Australians to tour England in 1868. Although there have been some fine Aboriginal cricketers, including Johnny Mullagh and Shield players Eddie Gilbert and Jack Marsh, none have represented Australia. By the time of the third English tour of Australia in 1873–74, domestic cricket had advanced enough for Victoria to play the tourists on even terms, though all other matches were against the odds. It was not until the visit of the professional team of James Lillywhite in 1876–77 that Australia won what was later defined as the first Test match, which featured a memorable 165 retired hurt by Charles Bannerman. The victory, which loomed large in colonial eyes, was not regarded so highly in England as the side did not include many of their star players.

It was not until the Australian tour of England in 1878 that English authorities took Australian cricket seriously. The improvement in Australian cricket was made clear when the tourists, spearheaded by Fred Spofforth and Harry Boyle, routed the powerful Marylebone Cricket Club side, defeating them by nine wickets in a day, in the second match of the tour. With the success of the tour Australian cricketers profited handsomely: their outlay of £50 returned a dividend of over £700. Tours to and from Australia occurred regularly from this point. The third Australian tour of England in 1882 proved the most memorable when the side captained by William Murdoch—the strongest Australian team in the nineteenth century—won its first Test in England in dramatic circumstances and helped create the Ashes mythology. The hero at the London Oval was Fred Spofforth, who cemented his reputation as the greatest bowler of his era by taking 14–90 and helping to dismiss England when the home side was coasting to victory. Other stars of the pre-

1900 era were fearless wicket-keeper Jack Blackham, who stood up to the pace attack, consummate all-rounder George Giffen, and pace bowler C. T. B. Turner.

The financial success of tours and the need for greater liaison between the organisers of tours and colonial cricket administration created the need for a national controlling body. The first authority, the Australasian Cricket Council, proved ineffectual and lasted only from 1892 to 1901. The Australian Board of Control (now the Australian Cricket Board), formed in 1905, had greater authority which was tested in 1912—over the question of whether the board or players should select the tour manager—when six of the leading players boycotted that year's tour. The board won this challenge to its authority. Domestic competition had been enhanced before this with the establishment of the Sheffield Shield, contested by NSW, SA, and Victoria in the 1892–93 season. The shield was named after its donor, the Earl of Sheffield, who financed and accompanied the 1891–92 English tour to Australia and presented £150, which paid for the shield. Australia played its first series against South Africa in that country in 1902–3 and at home in 1910–11.

The graceful style of the legendary Victor Trumper, the Australian batting star of the pre-war era, inspired his own and subsequent generations of cricket followers. M. A. Noble was an accomplished Australian all-rounder of this era and a successful Test captain as well, while off-break bowler Hugh Trumble was one of the leading bowlers who twice took Test hat-tricks at the MCG, in 1901 and 1904. Thomas Matthews achieved an even rarer feat, taking two hat-tricks in a 1912 Test against South Africa. First-class cricket was abandoned for three seasons during the First World War. Some notable cricketers, including 'Tibby' Cotter, died in action. Australian cricket was less depleted by war than English cricket and, captained by Warwick Armstrong, dominated the immediate post-war series.

The 1920s and 1930s represented the zenith of Australian cricket; the game was more popular than ever before, with ever-increasing crowds at Tests and at Shield games, and with even district games attracting thousands. Interest in cricket was heightened by the emergence of Donald Bradman in the late 1920s, the controversial bodyline series of 1932–33, and the beginning of national ball-by-ball broadcasting. The tactic of bodyline was designed to curb the phenomenal Bradman, who scored 974 in just seven Test innings in 1930 and became a sporting celebrity. Such was the interest in cricket in the 1930s that the ABC organised 'synthetic cricket' broadcasts during the 1938 series. Australian broadcasters, fed with scanty cable information at the end of each over, imaginatively recreated what might have occurred. This era produced many other stars including run-

accumulator Bill Ponsford, slow bowlers Bill O'Reilly and Clarrie Grimmett, and the barracker Yabba. Queensland joined the Sheffield Shield in 1926–27 but was still searching for its initial Shield win in 1992. The West Indies toured for the first time in 1930–31. After another lapse of three seasons during the Second World War the public was keen to watch cricket again. A powerful side beat England in Australia (1946–47) and in England (1948)—the latter side ranking as one of the great Australian sides along with the 1902 and 1921 teams. India toured for the first time in 1947–48. WA joined the Shield competition in the same season. After the retirement of Bradman in 1949 there was a decline in domestic crowds at all levels of cricket. With the loss of the Ashes in 1953 and the débâcle at Manchester in 1956 (when Laker dismissed all but one of the Australians), many Australians seemed to drift away from cricket to tennis, surfing, or more individualistic leisure activities. Australia played its first Tests on the Subcontinent in 1956, on the way home from England, suffering defeat at the hands of Pakistan, where they confronted Fazal Mahmood on matting at Karachi, but winning the three-Test series against India, 2–0. The cycle had turned by 1958–59 and Australia, captained by the youthful Richie Benaud, regained the Ashes in resounding fashion, 4–0. Benaud found a perfect foil for his attacking flair in West Indian skipper Frank Worrell, and they created an entertaining Test series in 1960–61 set up by the celebrated tie in the first Test at Brisbane. The series was saved (and later won) for Australia by a dramatic last-ditch stand between 'Slasher' Mackay and Lindsay Kline. When Benaud's side retained the Ashes in 1961 Australia recovered from a seemingly hopeless position at Old Trafford, with Benaud spinning the ball out of the rough to take 6–70. After 1961 cricket again seemed to slide in popularity. There was far less attacking cricket in the four subsequent series against England, with thirteen of the twenty Tests drawn.

Cricket's revival in the 1970s was related to television. The potential of television was first demonstrated during 1970–71 when there was national coverage of the entire Test series by the ABC, resulting in a huge television audience of more than a million per day. Although Australia lost this series 2–0, it was in the process of developing a youthful and very marketable side which held its own against the English team in 1972—a series which included Bob Massie's memorable sixteen wickets at Lord's. The 1974–75 and 1975–76 Australian team which triumphed over England and the West Indies was a well-balanced side, brimful of talent. Led by the shrewd and attacking captain Ian Chappell, the line-up included the feared Lillee-Thomson combination, backed up by the tireless Max Walker, the classical Greg Chappell, the laconic Doug Walters, and the acrobatic Rod Marsh. Chappell was able to get the very best out of his side, including the Houdini-like escape against Pakistan in 1973, and an unlikely eighth wicket stand of 83 between Johnny Watkins and Bob Massie rescuing the side in the West Indies later in the year when the home side was coasting to victory. Remarkably, NZ had to wait until 1973–74 to play its first Test on Australian soil: the three-Test series was won by Australia, 2–0. NZ had been no match for Australia in the previous encounter, when one Test was played on the 1945–46 tour to NZ and had to be satisfied with visits of Australian second teams in intervening years.

With the revival of public interest in cricket and an expanding viewing audience, cricket was ripe for the picking by television magnate Kerry Packer in 1977. Unable to gain a monopoly of cricket broadcasting, Packer signed up most of the leading international players to World Series Cricket (WSC) and for two seasons organised alternative international competition. The WSC 'takeover' split the Australian cricket world, outraged traditionalists, and generated heated public debate. The Australian media were at first hostile, accusing Packer of reducing cricket to 'circus' entertainment. However, WSC promotion of limited-overs or one-day cricket, and particularly night cricket, was popular. Forty-one-year-old Bob Simpson came out of retirement to lead a second- or third-string side against India and the West Indies, but after he retired Australia was no match for England in 1978–79 season. Cricket authorities were sufficiently worried about the future of cricket to agree to a truce with Kerry Packer by 1979. Although WSC lasted only two years as a separate competition challenging the 'official' game, it had a far-reaching impact. It introduced cricket under lights and coloured clothing and attempted, through aggressive promotion, to make cricket more accessible to the general public. It led to improved payment of players and provided better-quality television pictures. Programming changes, particularly the altered format of Test and one-day internationals, have been more controversial. With the greater amount of international competition the leading players are now full-time professionals.

There had been no tours of South Africa since 1969–70 when an Australian side lost all four Tests against a powerful home side. Kim Hughes was the captain of two rebel tours to South Africa in the period 1985–87. The tours deprived Australia of a few leading players for a time although Terry Alderman, Trevor Hohns, and Carl Rackemann subsequently made their way back into the national side. A team from Sri Lanka visited Australia for the first time in the 1982–83 season. The first Test between the two countries was played in Sri Lanka in 1983. Although they had some successes in the 1980s, such as the 2–1 defeat of England at home in 1982–83, Australian sides generally battled to compete with the West Indies and England. Allan Border, who became captain of the side in December 1984, played many gritty innings alongside the lower batting order to salvage respect. After some lean years Border reaped his reward when Australia won the 1987 World Cup in Calcutta. A year earlier Australia participated in only the second tied Test in history at Madras when the irrepressible Greg Matthews secured a wicket on the second last ball. Dean Jones played a heroic innings of 210. Australia consolidated its position in the Test arena when it won the Ashes 4–0 in 1989, with Terry Alderman securing his second English bag of over forty wickets and Mark Taylor, Dean Jones, and Steve Waugh playing some memorable innings. Although Australia was beaten 2–1 by the West Indies in 1991, it entered the 1990s as one of the three cricket powers along with Pakistan.

Australia has always had a strong tradition of country cricket and many of the greatest cricketers—Bradman, O'Reilly, McCabe, Walters, and Taylor—are from country backgrounds. Australia has a rich fund of bush legends, literature, and art, including the poem of McDougall's dog, who absconded with the ball to the advantage of McDougall, and the celebrated painting of Russell Drysdale. Australia has produced a number of prominent cricket journalists including J. C. Davis, Tom Horan, Jack Fingleton, and Philip Derriman, and commentators such as Alan McGilvray. It has had its share of writers, such as A. G. Moyes, Jack Pollard, and Ray Robinson; the cricket literature market, however, has never been as strong as in England. Australia has had a succession of annuals, none of which has lasted.

Women have taken a keen interest in the game from its first days in Australia, but their contribution for much of that time has been auxiliary—preparing afternoon tea for male players and watching the game. This role was recognised in the creation of separate ladies' stands at some of the major ovals in the nineteenth century. While they could attend cricket matches and were admitted to cricket clubs as associate members, they did not secure the right to full membership at the MCG and the SCG until recent times.

The first recorded women's match was played at Bendigo in 1874. Club cricket dates from 1886 when the Fernleas met the Siroccos at the SCG. Although there were good crowds at some of the first matches, women's cricket was not taken seriously as the sport was regarded as a 'manly' game, inappropriate and unhealthy for women since it involved competition and violence. Despite the persistence of prejudice, women's cricket associations were formed in Victoria in 1905 and in other States in the 1920s and 1930s. The Australian Women's Cricket Council, established in 1931, took the bold step of inviting an English team to visit in 1934–35.

The first ever women's Test at Brisbane was well supported and publicised. Following the success of this tour the Australian women visited England in 1937. Women's cricket looked set to have a promising future after the Second World War when an Australian team won the Ashes for the first time and produced a star in Betty Wilson. By the 1960s, however, the game was in decline and one of the State associations, Queensland, became defunct for more than a decade. Tours and Test matches became less frequent.

Women's cricket revived in the 1970s and 1980s. The Australian women won the second, third, and fourth World Cups and have dominated the world cricket scene since 1980. With more government and business support, greater co-operation between male and female cricket administrators, and an improving environment for women's sport, there is now more encouragement for girls and women to play cricket. There have been some fine achievements by Australian women in the past decade. Denise Annetts set a world Test record for women of 193 against England in 1987, Lindsay Reeler became a prolific scorer in one-day internationals (scoring 1034 runs in twenty-three innings) and Christina Matthews had achieved a world record forty-seven dismissals behind the stumps by 1991.

RC

See **Adelaide Oval**; ALDERMAN, TERRY; **Aluminium Cricket Bats**; ARMSTRONG, WARWICK; **Art**; **Australian Cricket Board**; **Australian Women's Cricket Council**; BANNERMAN **Brothers**; BARNES, SIDNEY; BENAUD, RICHIE; **Bodyline**; BORDER, ALLAN; BRADMAN, Sir DONALD; CHAPPELL **Family**; **Cricket: Sydney Club Competition**; **Cricket: Sydney GPS**; **Cricket Walk-offs**; **Crowd Disorder**; DAVIDSON, ALAN; DIVE, MOLLY; **Eighty-seven Myth**; FINGLETON, JOHN; **'Gabba'**; GASCOIGNE, STEPHEN; GILBERT, EDDIE; GIFFEN, GEORGE; GREGORY **Family**; GRIMMETT, CLARENCE; HARVEY, ROBERT; HILL, CLEMENT; HORAN, THOMAS; **Hordern Shield**; **International Cricketer of the Year Award**; LARSEN, LYN; **Law**; LILLEE, DENNIS; LINDWALL, RAYMOND; **Literature**; MACARTNEY, CHARLES; MAILEY, ARTHUR; MARSH, RODNEY; McCABE, STANLEY; McGILVRAY, ALAN; McKENZIE, GRAHAM; **Melbourne Cricket Ground**; MILLER, KEITH; MITCHELL, ANN; MORRIS, ARTHUR; MULLAGH, JOHNNY; MURDOCH, WILLIAM; NOBLE, MONTAGUE; OLDFIELD, WILLIAM; O'REILLY, WILLIAM; PONSFORD, WILLIAM; ROBINSON, RAYMOND; **Ryder Medal**; **Sheffield Shield**; SIMPSON, ROBERT; SPOFFORTH, FREDERICK; **Sponsorship**; **Strikes and Industrial Disputes**; **Sydney Cricket Ground**; TALLON, DON; THOMPSON, RAELEE; **Tied Cricket Tests**; TRUMBLE, HUGH; TRUMPER, VICTOR; TURNER, CHARLES; **Underarm Bowling Incident**; **Unionism**; WA **Cricket Association Ground**; WILSON, BETTY; **Women's Cricket: First Test**; WOODFULL, WILLIAM; **World Cup Cricket**; **World Series Cricket**.

Cricket: Sydney Club Competition. Organised cricket in Sydney dates from the foundation of the Australian Cricket Club in 1826. By the 1850s, club cricket, reinforced by intercolonial contests between NSW and Victoria (from 1856) and by the formation of the NSW Cricket Association (in 1859), had progressed from scratch combinations to organised groups. From 1893 to 1894 grade cricket was organised on an electoral or district basis. Of the clubs which originally formed the 1893–94 competition only Manly and Sydney University remain. In 1990–91 there were twenty clubs which each fielded five open teams and two under-age teams, and who played for the Sydney Smith Cup for club champions. The Sydney competitions have been dominated by first-class players, the best of whom graduate to the NSW and Australian teams. Victor Trumper is the only player to have scored three 200s (highest: 335); Bill O'Reilly took over one hundred wickets in a season three times; England captains Geoff Boycott, Tony Greig, and Mike Gatting played with outstanding personal success in the competition in more recent times. St George has won most (eleven) first-grade premierships (known as the Belvidere Cup since 1931–32) and has been runner-up on eight occasions.

JFR

Cricket: Sydney GPS. Although cricket was played informally in many of the NSW Greater Public Schools (GPS) almost from their foundation, coherent records date from the formation of the Athletic Association of the GPS (AAGPS) in 1892. The AAGPS has organised all official sporting contests, including cricket, among the schools from that time. From the beginnings, the first eleven competition was dominated by Sydney Grammar School (SGS) who were premiers twenty-one times in the first thirty years. Since then, the title has been more evenly shared, such that six different schools have been premiers in the six seasons before 1990–91. Until 1964, the games were played over two days, or one full and one half day. From 1965 until 1988, the competition was restricted to seven one-day, non-limited-overs matches, but from 1988–89 matches have been played during fourth and first terms, with a mixture of two-day and one-day games. The schools have produced many cricketers of quality. Jim Burke, who played his final Test in 1958–59, is the last former GPS cricketer to represent Australia, although the presence of GPS-educated players in recent NSW Sheffield Shield winning teams gives some hope for further higher representation. Possibly the most outstanding performance in one match belongs to Eric Barbour, scorer of 13 centuries for SGS's first eleven, who, in 1908–9 for SGS against Shore, scored 356 in 370 minutes and then took 11 wickets in Shore's two innings.

JFR

Cricket Walk-offs. Captains Ray Illingworth (England) and Sunil Gavaskar (India) both led walk-offs in Australian Test matches. In the seventh Test of the 1970–71 Ashes series, Illingworth's leading fast bowler, John Snow, struck Australian tail-end batsman Terry Jenner with a bouncer. After Snow's over, a section of the angry Sydney crowd greeted him at the boundary fence by throwing beer cans and one spectator grabbed Snow by his shirt. Illingworth led the Englishmen from the field to ensure their safety. Gavaskar's walk-off at the MCG ten years later was sparked by his own dismissal, leg before wicket. In protest, the Indian captain ordered partner Chetan Chauhan to leave the ground too.

DS

Cricko

Cricko was conceived by James Turner of Sydney and Peter Mullins of Kangaroo Point, Brisbane, who were brought together by their wives' mutual interest in vigoro. The game was first played in 1940. Mr Turner was the manager of the cricket department of Mick Simmons's sports store in Sydney and he developed the rules of the game by combining the laws of cricket and vigoro. They took the compulsory-run concept of vigoro, adapted it to be forward of the stumps, and combined it with the fundamentals of cricket where bowlers, using a vigoro throwing action, bowl eight-ball overs from both ends of the wicket in an attempt to get the person batting out in conventional cricketing ways. In this way cricko evolved as a fast, competitive game with the skills of cricket and the speed of vigoro. Through his involvement in sports equipment Turner successfully promoted this new sport for women, with fifty-three teams competing in Sydney and Newcastle by the late 1940s. The NSW Cricko Association was established in 1940. The Queensland Cricko Association was formed in 1941. Mr Mullins did not have the same promotional opportunities, and only eight teams competed. In 1990, however, Brisbane had five A Grade teams and four A Reserve Grade teams, while cricko has not been played in Sydney since 1966. The first interstate competition was held in Brisbane in 1941, with Sydney and Brisbane competing for a silver casket containing the ashes of the 1941 stumps and bails. The competition was the best of three games, and was held in the two cities in alternate years after 1945. The last interstate competition was held in 1966 in Brisbane; at that point Australian cricko became synonymous with Queensland cricko.

PH-S

See **Vigoro**.

CROLL, ROBERT HENDERSON (1869–1947), born Stawell, Victoria, was a bushwalker, writer, and much else; he was a committee member of the Melbourne Walking Club for fifty years. He published a weekly 'Column for Walkers' in the Melbourne *Herald* throughout the 1920s, as well as books including *The Open Road, Ways of Many Walkers*, and *Along the Track*. His writing about walking was probably one of the main factors underlying Melbourne's boom of interest in hiking during the 1930s. Croll had a multitude of interests, including natural history and anthropology, and Geoffrey Serle considered that 'few in his time made a more diverse contribution to cultural and intellectual life'.

EH-S

CRONIN, MICHAEL (1952–   ), born Gerringong, NSW, the son of a publican, was a rugby league centre three-quarter and goal-kicker. He was already recognised as a world-class player when he joined Parramatta in 1977 at the urging of coach Terry Fearnley, although he continued to live in his home town, travelling to Sydney for matches and training. Cronin first represented Australia in 1973. A surprise choice for the Kangaroo tour to England, he finished as the top scorer, with 77 points. In 1975 and 1977 his performances for his country were outstanding — he averaged over 10 points a match — and in 1982 he scored a record 108 points in the World Series. As well, in 1977 and 1978 he won successive Rothman's Medals as Sydney's best and fairest player; the latter year saw a massive tally of 547 points in a season (282 in premiership matches). A deceptively quick runner for a big man, Cronin was widely regarded as indestructible. He had surprising acceleration, great strength, and good hands. His defence was sound and he had the uncanny ability, possessed by all great ball-players, of being able to run to the open spaces. His goal-kicking was unsurpassed, although he occasionally had trouble in State of Origin games. With it all he was a man of great dignity, honesty and charm. Although now retired, Cronin has maintained his involvement in the game, coaching Parramatta.

TGP

Croquet

The game of croquet as played in Australia is known as Association Croquet, derived from the (English) Croquet Association. This form of croquet is played exclusively in the UK, Ireland, NZ, Australia and South Africa. Croquet was played in Australia only fifteen years after it was first introduced, in a very crude form, from Ireland into England. The first recorded Australian croquet club was formed at Kyneton, Victoria, in 1866 and the next club known to have been organised was at Kapunda in SA in 1868. As clubs formed a need for central direction began to be felt. The first State association

36 Betty Cuthbert, who became known as Australia's
'Golden Girl' when she won three gold medals at the
1956 Olympic Games in Melbourne, training with
Percy Cerutty.

37 Country Show Sports often included ploughing
matches, such as this intercolonial competition at Werribee
Plains, 1882.

38 The Springfield Coursing match, Finley, NSW, 1895:
at its peak coursing attracted large crowds.

39 Croquet being played at Angaston, SA, 1867.

40 Cricket in Australia received a boost with the arrival of
H. H. Stephenson's side of English professionals in 1861.

41 Henry Burn's watercolour, *The First International
Cricket; H. H. Stephenson's All England Eleven versus the
Victorian Eighteen, Melbourne Cricket Ground, 1 January
1862*, captures the significance of the occasion.

42 Cricket at Cooroy Showgrounds, Queensland, 1911.

43 Carlton Cricket Club players in front of their pavilion, 1895.

was founded in Tasmania in 1908. The other States followed: Victoria in 1914, SA in 1916, NSW in 1918, Queensland in 1922, and WA in 1928. State associations were, and in most ways still are, autonomous. The Victorian Croquet Association was the strongest of the State bodies and took a leading role. It was the initiative of that association which led to the first international teams event between Australia and England becoming established in 1925. A Melbourne industrialist, Sir MacPherson Robertson, presented a trophy for the event called the MacRobertson Shield. In 1930 NZ was admitted to the event, which is played every three to four years in each country in turn. Australia last won the trophy in 1937. The Australian Croquet Council (ACC) was formed and held its first meeting in Melbourne in October 1950. The ACC continued to conduct the affairs of Australian croquet up to 1987 when its name was changed to the Australian Croquet Association (ACA). Over the years Australia has become the largest croquet-playing country in the world in terms of registered players, who currently number more than six thousand.

CF

See **Australian Croquet Association**; CLELAND, ALLAN.

Crowd Disorder

While there is a long tradition of disorder in Australian sports crowds, such behaviour is not endemic, nor, with a few notable exceptions, has it been institutionalised. Nevertheless there are areas where repeated incidences of crowd violence or conflict have occurred and where authorities have had to take regulatory measures. First, from the 1960s to mid-1980, crowd disorder and riots occurred almost yearly at the Australian Grand Prix Motorcycle Races, formerly held at Bathurst, NSW. Races were held at the Mount Panorama circuit in Bathurst between 1931 and 1989, attracting crowds of up to 30 000 for the Easter weekend meeting. Early 1960s conflict between youth and police escalated during the 1970s and became institutionalised to become an almost annual riot in the 1980s, when 300–400 police were present each year. There were riots involving spectators and police in 1980, 1981, 1983, and 1985, each occurring on Easter Saturday, after sunset, outside the police compound on the circuit. Each year between 90 and 160 people were arrested and in the eight-hour riot of 1985 about ninety police and a similar number of civilians were treated for fractures, lacerations, bruising, burns, and other injuries. The numbers of spectators fell dramatically in the years after that riot and the races were abandoned after the 1989 event.

Researchers have examined 1500 records of people brought before the courts between 1960 and 1985 on charges relating to the Easter race meeting. These people were overwhelmingly male manual workers. They were essentially anti-police in attitude, with their hostility expressed in a ritual form that moved between play and seriousness. This anti-police sentiment had several sources: the motorcycle subculture from the 1930s onwards; the traditionally difficult relationship between working-class youth and police; and the resentment of some Bathurst racegoers to the construction in 1979 of a police compound on an area previously used for camping and informal games.

Various places in Australian cricket stadia have evolved a culture of licence in which crowd disorder has come to be expected. Until 1990 when it was demolished, Bay 13 at the MCG was one such site of rowdy behaviour and excessive drinking by mainly young working-class men. Arrests and ejections from the ground were common, but the disorder was never reported as violent. Sydney's main cricket ground, the SCG, has evolved a similar area in The Hill, a sloping grassy terrace which used to be without individual seating. This has always been the least expensive point of entry to the ground since its origins in the 1850s and because of this has attracted a working-class patronage and evolved a male-dominated culture to match. Rowdy behaviour rubbed shoulders with colourful barracking up to the 1960s, which saw an increase in drunkenness and abusive behaviour. The invention of the beer can and its companion, the portable cooler, added to the consumption of alcohol at Australia's cricket grounds at this time.

The commercial winds of change were directed upon cricket in 1977 as World Series Cricket, a new one-day game, was introduced to Australia. The game of cricket was transformed and so too was the cricket crowd as youth, women, and spectators lacking knowledge of the subtleties of cricket were drawn to the spectacle and excitement of the new cricket-as-entertainment. At this time disorder became much more frequent on The Hill: brawling and excessive drinking led to many arrests and more regulatory measures. The explanation for this worsening of behaviour probably lies in the convergence of the traditional rowdiness of working-class culture of The Hill and the emergence of international one-day cricket as a commercially packaged and aggressively promoted form of mass entertainment, with its new kind of spectator. Finally, it is possible that some spectators have reacted aggressively to the progressive whittling away of the area of the Hill and attempts to make it a place of individual seating. Throughout the 1980s and into the 1990s, crowd disorder has continued to be a problem at one-day cricket and various regulatory measures have been introduced to try to resolve the problem.

Although there was a period of crowd disorder at Australian soccer matches in the 1890s, such trouble has mainly occurred since the Second World War and has often been associated with immigrants from Europe. Many of them entered a relatively hostile Australian culture which was openly more sympathetic to an English-speaking, British presence than to one it saw as foreign. European immigrants had little power or position in Australia, but soccer gave them an opportunity to compete on equal terms and display their skills. Almost inevitably this freedom to release pent-up emotions—ambition, passion, frustration, or aggression—had consequences for crowd behaviour. Nationalistic loyalty also played a part: a club victory could take on the stature of a 'victory' for a homeland, just as a defeat was also somewhat about loss of national face. Different philosophies on how to play soccer also provoked some crowd disorder. The earlier British Australian approach was based on strength, stamina, and speed. In contrast to this robustness stood the style, elegance, balance, and precision of the Europeans. Grit and determination versus artistic expression often led to ill feeling and violence both on and off the field.

As junior sport, such as football, hockey, cricket, and tennis began to expand after the Second World War, the behaviour of players and spectators has become a continuing problem. Disorder here has been largely put down to an undue emphasis on competition and to zealous parents becoming too involved in the successes and failures of their children. As the problem grew, a council of all sport and recreation ministers in Australasia met in 1985 to declare that violence on and off the field was unacceptable. Part of the strategy to reduce off-field violence was the devising of codes of behaviour for administrators, officials, parents, spectators, coaches, teachers, media, and players. These codes, directed mainly at junior sport, have been accompanied by the modification of rules and entire games in an attempt to provide all children with an even chance to become involved. Such modified games also place a greater emphasis on enjoyment and skill development than on winning.

Historically, poor officiating has often contributed to crowd violence in cricket and soccer, especially the latter which, with its generally low scores, can often have the result influenced by one decision. Related to this is the violent nature of body-contact sport which is an obvious stimulus to certain kinds of spectator. A new element is commercialism and media hype. As sport in Australia evolved after the war, so too did commercialism further enter the playing fields to take sports like cricket, various football codes, and tennis into the realm of spectacular entertainment. New crowds, unknowledgeable in the finer and historical aspects of the games they were watching, were drawn to sport and, in the cases of cricket and tennis, contributed to a new wave of disorder in

the 1980s. Poor physical conditions such as substandard toilets, overcrowding, and inadequate seating have also been cited as factors contributing to frustration and violence among crowds.

Some commentators suggest that the media incite disorder by unnecessarily highlighting violent incidents; others cite historical evidence of crowd disorder being associated with gambling; and many argue that there is overwhelming evidence that alcohol is a major contributing factor to crowd disturbances. Several researchers, however, suggest that disorder in sports crowds results from deep-rooted social strains and structural tensions within society such as unemployment, economic deprivation, low status, and a decline in social standards and accepted conventions. In soccer, ethnic and nationalist rivalries have contributed as much to disorder as differing philosophies of sport. The researchers who examined riots at the Bathurst motorcycle races argued that a dynamic intersection of class, subcultural, youth, and masculine forces contributed to the disorder there. They also argued that policing strategies were both provocative and part of the process of institutionalising conflict between police and spectators.

Explanations of crowd disorder across various sports point to a variety of causes. What is clear is that sports-crowd disorder has resulted from a mixture of factors both *within* various sports and also *external* to them. As long as these external factors are seen as too deep-seated to be solved by specific measures, little can be done towards curbing the disorder.

RL

See **Ethnic Influences.**

CUMMINGS, JAMES BARTHOLOMEW

(1927–), born SA, achieved rapid fame by training the first two place-getters in the 1965 and 1966 Melbourne Cups, followed by the winner of the 1967 Cup. He consolidated his reputation by again training the winning quinella in 1974 and 1975, with *Think Big* triumphing twice. He also trained the winners in 1977 and 1979, bringing his tally to a record seven Melbourne Cups. Cummings was the son of a leading local trainer, Jim Cummings, whose horses included *Comic Court*, 1950 Melbourne Cup winner. Bart Cummings was based in Adelaide where he was the leading State trainer six times until 1985, but he also maintained a Melbourne stable and was the leading Victorian trainer for five seasons. His horses also raced successfully in Sydney. Cummings consistently won quality races including four Golden Slipper Stakes, six Caulfield Cups, six VRC Newmarket Handicaps and nine Australian Cups, five Victorian Derbies and three AJC Derbies, seven VRC Oaks, and six AJC Oaks. In 1985 Cummings moved his headquarters to Sydney and embarked on an ambitious plan for buying and syndicating yearlings. The collapse of the scheme led to protracted litigation between Cummings, yearling auctioneers, and accountancy firms. In the midst of these difficulties, Cummings won the NSW premiership (1989–90) for the first time and secured his eighth Melbourne Cup with *Kingston Rule*. In 1991 he brought this total to nine when *Let's Elope* and *Shiva's Revenge* finished first and second in the race.

AL

CUNEO, JOHN (c.1928–), born Sydney, came from a family with a yacht-racing tradition: his grandfather crewed on a boat which won two national 18-foot championships. He was brought up in Brisbane near the river at Hamilton and he and his brother 'used to hang around the boatsheds making a nuisance of ourselves until we got a ride' as crew members. With the support of George Lambert of the Royal Queensland Yacht Club (later Squadron), who financed and encouraged him throughout his career, Cuneo won his first Australian championship, in the Sharpie class, in 1956. In addition to winning another six championships in this class over the next decade, he also achieved success in the Australian championships in the 505 class in 1965 and the Dragon class in 1968 and 1969. With John Ferguson and Tom Anderson, Cuneo came fifth in the Dragon class in the 1968 Olympics. He went on to win the gold medal in the same class at the 1972 Olympics, this time with Tom Anderson and John Shaw. Sailing in *Wyuna*, they won the first three races and won the event by a substantial points margin. Cuneo was awarded the Ampol Australian Yachtsman of the Year Award in 1968.

RH and MH

CUTHBERT, BETTY (1938–), born Ermington, Sydney, is Australia's greatest woman sprinter. Successful in school sports, she came under the notice of sports mistress June Ferguson, who had won a silver medal in the 4 × 100 metres relay at the 1948 Olympics. Cuthbert then joined the Western Suburbs Athletic Club. Coached by Ferguson, she broke the national junior 100 yards in 1953 when she recorded 11.3 seconds. Before the 1956 Olympics Cuthbert had broken the world record for the 200 metres (23.2 seconds): rivalry with another Sydney sprinter, Marlene Matthews, extended both athletes before the Games. Cuthbert won both sprints and anchored the 4 × 100 metres relay to claim three gold medals at the Melbourne Olympics and the title of the 'Golden Girl'. Running with determination and mouth agape, she became an instant legend, admired for her spirit and unassuming nature. She was named ABC Sportstar of the year in 1956. The mantle of greatness rested uneasily on the shoulders of this shy and modest individual. Cuthbert was troubled by injury at the 1960 Rome Olympics and lost her sprint titles to American Wilma Rudolph. She retired to her father's nursery after 1960 but returned in 1964 to win the 400 metres at Tokyo in a record 52 seconds which she regarded as her greatest win. She was awarded the prestigious Helms Award in 1964. Since retirement Cuthbert has had to battle against the debilitating effects of multiple sclerosis.

JAD

See **Athletics**.

Cycling

The bicycle has had an important role in Australia since the 1890s, both for sport and recreation and as a means of transport. A velocipede (two wheels of equal size, with a crank and pedals attached to the front wheel) was built in Goulburn in 1867. The first ordinary ('penny-farthing' or 'high wheeler') bicycle was imported into Melbourne in 1875. The Melbourne Bicycle Club was formed in 1878, the Sydney Bicycle Club in 1879, a Tasmanian club in 1880, SA and Brisbane clubs in 1881, and the WA Cycling Club in 1891. Some rural towns also established clubs, such as Dubbo in 1886. During Australia's first cycling boom, in the 1880s, Melbourne was the centre. In 1884 Alf Edward became the first to cycle between Sydney and Melbourne, on an ordinary bicycle, in eight and a half days. In 1888 G. Burston and H. R. Stokes left on a round-the-world trip on a penny-farthing. The modern safety bicycle was developed in England in 1885, and was introduced to Australia about 1887; it was reported as being first commercially available in 1889. The pneumatic tyre was fitted to commercial machines by 1890, and manufactured locally by late 1892 by Dunlop.

In the late 1890s Australia had a cycling craze. About 200 000 bicycles had been sold by 1900; they were imported from Europe and the USA and, using foreign and local components, 'Australian' bicycles were produced as well. In 1897 over one hundred and fifty makes were available. The famous Malvern Star was founded by Bruce Small in the 1920s. During the 1890s the bicycle was adopted throughout the country by all classes. Its impact was enormous. Newspaper social columns described its use by doctors, lawyers, clergy, and women. Riding schools were founded. Thousands of cyclists commuted into central Melbourne. In 1898 the Post Office adopted bicycles to clear pillar boxes, each rider replacing a wagon, teamster, two horses, and postman. Numerous cycle clubs were formed, with their distinctive dress and rules. Eventually there was a major split in interests: organisations such as the League of Wheelmen focused on racing, others, like the NSW Cyclists' Touring Union, on touring and lobbying for better roads. By 1900 the novelty had worn off, but the use of the bicycle became more important than ever, both in cities and the country. In 1925 a two-day traffic count between Newcastle and Maitland recorded 5500 cyclists and only 2600 motor vehicles. Because of the economic circumstances of the Great Depression in the 1930s and the ensuing world war, the bicycle remained a major transport mode for Australians into the late 1940s.

The machine gave women a new mobility, and was an impetus for the rationalisation of their clothing. It also provided for vigorous social and sporting activities, though while many women attended the cycle races they were never readily accepted on the track. Women possessed enough economic influence to be specifically courted by the cycle and tyre companies. Australia's pioneer cyclist was Mrs E. A. Maddock of Sydney. In 1893 she made a 500 kilometre ride to Bega; in 1894 she pedalled to Melbourne in nine days; and in 1895 rode the 2600 kilometre return trip from Sydney to Brisbane, averaging 130 kilometres a day along the New England Highway.

Australian road maps and touring guides, designed to inform travellers of road conditions, directions, distances, and facilities, were developed by cycle touring organisations in the 1890s, before the advent of the motor car. Weekend pedallers travelled extensively about the countryside. In 1894 the Mount Hotham area had been ridden, and a cyclist reached the top of Mount Kosciusko in 1898. Intercapital tours were common. Major O'Farrell and George Broadbent were the principal map-makers in Victoria, and Joseph Pearson (with H. E. C. Robinson) in NSW. By 1910 Broadbent alone had sold 110 000 maps. The map-makers and cycle touring groups established the basic principles on which the later motoring organisations were founded; indeed, many cyclists were their initial members. In rural Australia the machine proved a remarkable device. Not needing food or water, being reliable, and capable of carrying heavy loads, it was widely adopted for several decades after 1895 by shearers, prospectors, the clergy, and various government workers and agencies. Its first important use was on the WA goldfields in the mid-1890s, for high-speed message delivery and general travel. The first transcontinental crossing was in 1893, from Croydon, Queensland, to Melbourne. In 1896 Arthur Richardson became the first to pedal the Nullarbor, and it was done in late 1898 at the rate of 166 kilometres a day by Pat O'Dea. In 1897 Jerome Murif made the first central Australian cycle crossing, through Alice Springs. The following year Albert MacDonald pedalled from Darwin to Adelaide in 29 days. These rides, through sparsely inhabited country, and along crude bush tracks and over extensive sand fields, were remarkable. The overland rides trod a fine line between 'sport' and 'travel'. All the early overlanders were travelling between destinations, but attempted to set records on the way. By 1899 the around-Australia effort was made by two competing groups, and was widely reported in newspapers throughout the country; Arthur Richardson rode clockwise around the continent in 1899–1900 in eight months, the first to do so.

Some Australians in the 1890s encouraged the bicycle's military adoption, citing overseas experience. However, the colonial (and later Commonwealth) military authorities resisted. Nonetheless, several private units were formed, and cyclists served in the Boer War, which saw the first significant wartime use of the machine.

In Australia, cycle dealers, tyre companies and cycling organisations combined to sponsor several races to demonstrate the machine's speed and utility. A relay ride was held in WA in 1899 from Albany to Perth. In 1909 Dunlop Tyres organised a dispatch relay ride from Adelaide to Sydney, via Melbourne. Sixty-four relay teams of cyclists covered the 1839 kilometres in 69 hours and 35 minutes, 10 hours faster than thought possible when organised. In 1912 a second relay ride was held between cyclists, motorcyclists, and car drivers, over the same route. It went through the sandy Coorong area of SA, and Dunlop's employment of George Broadbent to map it for the ride resulted in the first map made of the area, which was later made available to the military authorities. The cyclists covered the distance in virtually identical time as before (69 hours 32 minutes), while the motor cars won in 46 hours and 44 minutes.

In the 1890s bicycling, as a craze, and cycle racing were equally popular. Crowds of tens of thousands attended the major cycle races, and road races were popular. As the decade wore on, however, the craze subsided, cycle racing tended to become less popular, and was increasingly the sole province of racing cyclists. Early in the 1900s occasional international tours brought out large crowds. However, the advent of the faster, noisier, and more exciting motor cars and motorcycles displaced the bicycle as the main form of mechanised sport. Nevertheless road and track cycling has continued as a significant Australian sport which has produced world champions at both amateur and professional level.

JF

See **ANDERSON, PHILIP**; **Australian Cycling Federation**; **Australian Mountain Bike Association**; **Austral Wheelrace**; **BROWNE, IAN**; **CLARK, DANNY**; **COX, LIONEL**; **Ethnic Influences**; **GRAY, EDGAR**; **HOOBIN, JACK**; **Melbourne to Warrnambool Classic**; **MOCKRIDGE, RUSSELL**; **NICHOLS, KEVIN**; **OPPERMAN, Sir HUBERT**; **PATTERSON, SID**; **SPEARS, ROBERT**; **SPEIGHT, JULIE**; **SUTTON, GARY**; **Tasmanian International Velodrome**; **TAYLOR, MARSHALL**; **WALKER, DON**; **WOODS, DEAN**.

D

Dally M. Awards for rugby league in NSW were started in 1980, when the first Player of the Year was Rocky Laurie of Souths. The Dally M. Player of the Year is announced at a televised presentation, at which awards are given to the best player in each position, and to the captain, coach, rookie, and representative player of the year. Also recognised are the 'Players' Player of the Year', the leading try- and points-scorer, and a league figure deemed to have given outstanding service to the game. Only Peter Sterling (1986–87) and Gavin Miller (1988–89) have won the Player of the Year trophy twice. In 1988 Miller was also voted the Players' Player, the first man to win both awards in the one season. Terry Lamb, the 1983 Player of the Year, was the Players' Player in 1984 and 1986. Ray Price, judged best player in 1982, won the best lock-forward trophy five years in a row from 1982 to 1986, the most times a player has been rated the best in his position. The 1990 Player of the Year was Manly five-eighth Cliff Lyons.

KC

See **MESSENGER, HERBERT**.

DANSIE, SUE (1951–) was the first full-time female volleyball coach in Australia. A champion player in her own right, she was a gold-medallist at numerous international junior and senior championships. To promote volleyball in the community Sue Dansie founded the Volleyball School in Adelaide in 1980. As a coach at the SA Institute of Sport she was the only female coach of élite women's teams in this sport in 1991.

IF

DARCY, LES (1895–1917), born near Maitland, NSW, holds a secure place among the sporting legends of Australia. By mid-1914 he appeared on Stadiums Limited bills in Sydney, and defeated many famous imported boxers. Darcy was Australian middleweight champion in 1915 and heavyweight champion in 1916. Although only 170 centimetres in height he had extraordinary upper-body strength and an impressive reach. His success at boxing, with a religious devotion to his family, made Darcy the darling of fans. That attitude changed when he surreptitiously left Australia as a stowaway the day before the conscription referendum in 1916. Darcy went to America to gain the elu-

sive world middleweight crown and to secure his family financially, but bad advice, a degree of naivety, political point-scoring, and suspected sabotage from unnamed 'influential people' in Australia led to him having no contests during his five-month stay. Dental repairs caused an infection which poisoned his bloodstream, and Darcy died in Memphis, Tennessee, on 24 May 1917. His brief but hectic career (fifty bouts, forty-six wins) ended with exoneration, as thousands viewed his body in Sydney and attended the funeral in Maitland. In death, all seemed forgiven—Darcy's martyrdom was complete.

KM

Darts Federation of Australia. On 27 January 1927 darts-players from Queensland, SA, and NSW met at the Burwood RSL in Burwood, Sydney, and resolved that these States should form an Australasian Darts Council (ADC) with the aim of uniting the several State darts associations into one national body. Membership was to be open to any State controlling body in Australia and NZ. The first Australasian Darts Championship was held at the Burwood RSL in 1964 and they continued annually until 1979. The World Darts Federation (WDF) was formed in 1975. One of its conditions was that each member must represent one country only; since the ADC represented both Australia and NZ it was ineligible for membership. This was the catalyst for the formation of the Darts Federation of Australia (DFA) in Perth in 1975, with a constitutional meeting being held in Canberra in January 1976. The first Australian championship was held in the Newcastle Workers' Club in 1980. Australian championships, which include ladies' and men's teams of five, doubles, and singles, as well as mixed doubles, rotate among the States and Territories; junior championships are held in the same manner. Australia joined the WDF in 1976 and has competed in every world championship (held in odd-numbered years) and, since 1980, in the Pacific Cup (held in even-numbered years). Australia hosted the Pacific Cup in 1980 and 1992, and the World Cup in 1985. Australia has been successful in winning the Pacific Cup, which features a combined team of men and women, on four occasions. World Cup performances have been creditable, culminating in the 1991 World Cup in the Netherlands when Australia won a gold medal in the men's doubles, a silver in the ladies' singles, and came third overall in both the men's and ladies' competitions.

PMcM and IJ

DAVIDSON, ALAN KEITH, AM, MBE (1929–), born Lisarow, near Gosford, NSW, was a cricket all-rounder who in forty-four Tests scored 1328 runs at an average 24.59 and took 186 wickets at 20.53. Davidson was a fast-medium left-arm bowler who batted with verve and was an outstanding fielder, known as 'The Claw' for his uncanny ability to latch on to improbable catches. He was the first male cricketer to score 100 runs and take 10 wickets in a Test match. This all-round ability made him a captain's dream. Davidson has been president of the NSW Cricket Association since 1970.

SG

DAVIES, ATHOL BRYAN ('George'), BEM (1923–), born New Lambton, NSW, was the prime instigator, among a number of early enthusiasts, of spearfishing and skindiving in Australian waters. George Davies and his brother Trevor began to devise home-made spearguns and face-masks in 1939, and continued to experiment with underwater air-supply systems. They developed and patented what is claimed to be the world's first self-contained underwater weapon, which used compressed air as a propellant. It enabled the spearing of very large fish for the first time and went into 'commercial' production during the Second World War. Since its inception in 1953, George Davies has been active in the Newcastle Neptunes Spearfishing Club (NNSC), winning its spearfishing championship eight years in succession and serving as its secretary from 1957 till the present. He also secured for the NNSC the hosting of the first NSW Spearfishing Championships at Shoal Bay in 1957 and the Australian Pacific Coast Spearfishing Championships at Port Stephens in 1958. He has travelled widely as office-bearer and delegate for the Newcastle District Anglers Association and the NSW Amateur Fishing Clubs Association. In 1963 Davies became Federal Secretary of the Australian Underwater Federation and in that capacity served the sport of spearfishing from 1965 to 1990 as organiser, national selector, team member, national coach, and team manager at international competitions. He has also been active as a member of the NSW Recreational Advisory Council, the Australian Recreational and Sportfishing Confederation and the Pro-Am Committee of the Recreational and Commercial Fishermen's Association in northern NSW. He was awarded the BEM in 1979.

GK-S

DAVIES, BRIAN (1930–), born Brisbane, was a champion schoolboy swimmer who became a tall second-row rugby league forward with considerable pace and later developed into an accomplished scrummager as prop. He first played for Queensland in 1950, and between 1952 and 1958 played twenty-seven Tests, being second only to John Raper among Australian rugby league forwards at this time. In 1958 he was captain-coach of Australia. Davies captained Brothers club to Brisbane premierships in 1956 and 1958, and later played for Canterbury-Bankstown in Sydney.

SJR

See **RAPER, JOHN**.

DAVIES, JOHN G. (1929–) holds a record that will never be broken: he was the last Olympic swimming champion to use the butterfly arm action and the conventional frog kick. He was fourth at the 1948 London Games and won gold at the 1952 Helsinki Games in the 200 metres breaststroke. After the 1948 Games, Davies went to the University of Michigan to train with coach Matt Mann. He won the US Long Course Championships in 1951 and 1952 in his specialty. After the 1952 Olympics, Davies married an American and became an attorney and a top trial lawyer in the USA. He was appointed to the US District Court by President Reagan in 1986.

RH and MH

See **Swimming**.

DAVIES, WAYNE FOSTER (1955–), born Geelong, Victoria, became Australia's outstanding royal tennis player. A former squash and lawn tennis player, he played his first game of royal tennis in 1978 and perfected his game so rapidly that he soon became an international professional coach and manager in the sport. In 1982 Davies won the US Open singles and doubles as well as the Tiffany Cup doubles. After unsuccessful attempts to win the world championship in 1983 and 1985 he won the title in 1987 and has held it against all comers since. He has perfected the volleyed return of service and has converted the backhand from a defensive to an attacking shot. Davies has coached at some of the most prestigious international courts: Hampton Court near London, Bordeaux, and Manhattan.

GK-S

See **Royal Tennis**.

DAVIS, GREGORY VICTOR (1939–79), born NZ, came to Australia in 1963 and played rugby for the Drummoyne Club in Sydney. He represented NSW in his first year and was selected to tour South Africa with John Thornett's Australian team. A tough no-nonsense breakaway, he was renowned for his tackling. He toured NZ in 1964 and then played against South Africa in Australia. He was a member of the Wallaby tour of Great Britain and France 1966–67, played against NZ and France, and went on a short tour of Ireland and Scotland in 1968. He captained Australia from 1969 until his retirement in 1972, leading tours to South Africa, France, and NZ. He died of a brain tumour.

RH and MH

DAVIS, RODGER M. (1951–), a golfer who became known for his plus-twos and stockings and his penchant for record scores, had to overcome a disastrous investment in an unsuccessful Queensland motel project in 1984 which left him with barely enough money to continue his golf career. He won the Australian Open, the British match play and the Dunhill all-nations championships in 1986. Although his style may not please the purist, Davis has made his mark through sheer hard work. After a horrendous round in the 1988 Dunhill Cup at St Andrews, he bounced back a few weeks later to win the Bicentenary Australian Classic.

GC*

DAVISON, ALEXANDER NICHOLAS (1923–65), motorcyclist, was the only child of a wealthy Melbourne shoe manufacturer. He had the means to go racing and had ability to match. Lex Davison's feats are unique, having won four Australian Grands Prix (1954, 1957, 1958, and 1961) and three Australian Hillclimb Championships (1955–57) and he was greatly admired well beyond the small world of 1950s Australian motor racing. He enthusiastically combined family life, business, and racing and was within weeks of retirement when he was killed at Sandown track on 20 February 1965.

GH

DE CASTELLA, ROBERT ('Deek'), MBE (1957–), was the leading marathon runner of the 1980s. Since winning his first marathon at the Victorian championships in 1979, 'Deek' has contested eighteen other marathons, winning nine and finishing in the top ten in all but one. A graduate of Swinburne College of Technology, Melbourne, with a double major in biophysics and instrumental science, his marathon times have ranged from 2 hours 14 minutes 44 seconds to 2 hours 7 minutes 51 seconds, which stood as the world record from 1980 to 1984. De Castella's memorable world championship win at Helsinki in 1983 was interspersed with back-to-back Commonwealth Games gold medals in 1982 and 1986. His other major wins were at Fukuoka in 1981, Rotterdam in 1983 and 1991, and Boston in 1986. At the Olympics he finished tenth in 1980, fifth in 1984, and eighth in 1988. He was the Australian Marathon Champion in 1979 and Australian Cross-Country Champion in 1978, 1979, 1980, and 1988. Apart from the marathon he has had numerous wins over shorter races in Australia, Europe, England, and the USA, and

he set a world record for the 15 kilometres road run in 1983. De Castella was named Australian of the Year in 1983 and inducted into the Sport Australia Hall of Fame in 1986. He later became the director of the AIS in Canberra.

GC†

DE MESTRE, ÉTIENNE LIVINGSTONE (1832–1916), of French origin but born in Australia, was a racehorse-trainer who had his base at the property Terara near Nowra, NSW. He prepared five of the first eighteen winners of the Melbourne Cup, including dual winner *Archer*, setting a standard for professional training. He came to public attention in 1861 with the successes of horses bred by the partners Hassell and Roberts at Braidwood. In 1867 he trained *Tim Whiffler* to win the Melbourne Cup, in 1877 *Chester* (for James White), and in 1878 *Calamia*. From the 1880s, unsuccessful pastoral investments undermined de Mestre's career to the point where colleagues staged a benefit race meeting for him at Randwick in 1896. He retired to Moss Vale.

AL

See *Archer*.

DENNIS, CLARE (1916–71) learned to swim at Clovelly Beach in Sydney and by 14 years of age had won her first NSW and Australian championship in the 220 yards breast-stroke. When she broke the world record at 15 she was selected for the 1932 Los Angeles Games. Though the baby of the team she won a gold medal in her speciality. Dennis dominated breast-stroke swimming from 1931 to 1935, and in 1934 became the first Australian female to win a gold medal in the British Empire Games. Overlooked for the 1936 Berlin Olympics, she married George Golding, a fellow Olympic athlete at the 1932 Games, in 1941. She died of cancer at the age of 55.

RH and MH

See **Swimming**.

DEVITT, JOHN (1937–) had an outstanding swimming career that spanned thirteen years. In that time he won two gold, a silver, and a bronze medal in Olympic competition, three gold medals in the 1958 Cardiff British Empire and Commonwealth Games, broke fourteen world records (four individual and ten team) and won thirteen Australian championships (three individual and ten team). Devitt's first gold medal was in the 4 × 200 metres freestyle relay at the 1956 Games, where he also lost a close decision to Jon Henricks in the 100 metres. The highlight of his career was his victory in the 100 metres freestyle at the 1960 Rome Olympics. It was a controversial win over the US swimmer Lance Larson. Two of the three first-place judges adjudged Devitt as the winner, but two of the three second-place judges nominated him second. The timekeepers declared Larson faster than Devitt but the race was awarded to Devitt. This controversy was responsible for the introduction of electronic timing in international swimming competitions.

RH and MH

See **Swimming**.

DEVLIN, BRUCE WILLIAM, AO (1937–), born Armidale, NSW, was brought up in Goulburn where he took up golf at the age of 13 to help his father recover from a motor-accident injury. During the next eight years, while earning his qualifications as a plumber in his father's company, Devlin travelled around Australia achieving many golfing honours. He won his first important title, the NSW amateur championship, in 1958, became the first amateur in twenty-one years to win the Australian Open in 1960, and a year later turned professional. After three very lean years he won a number of tournaments including the NZ and Australian Opens. By 1966 Devlin had won a share of the prize-money in fifty-one successive tournaments including thirty-six American events—at the time a record sequence. Devlin's golden year was 1970 when he won $184,000 to be second on the world prize-money list. Although he has never won any of the world's four major tournaments, the smooth-swinging golfer is a millionaire.

GC*

DIBNAH, CORINNE (1962–), born Brisbane, was the first Australian golfer to win the British Women's Open Golf Championship. After being taught by veteran golfer George Tuxworth, as an 11-year-old, she spent five years developing her technique at her home town of Bowen. Like Greg Norman she was trained at Royal Brisbane by Charlie Earp. Winner of the Australian amateur title when only 19, she also won the NZ championship. She has represented Australia in the Commonwealth tournament, Australia v. Japan matches, the Queen Sirikit Cup, and the Tasman Cup. She joined the Women's Professional Golf Association tour in 1984 and became a success on the European circuit. She gradually worked her way up the order of merit, finishing third in 1986 with two wins, and winning again at La Manga, Spain, in 1987. Luck was on her side when she won the 1988 British Open: her wayward tee shot at the first play-off hole struck a spectator, breaking his nose and glasses but diverting the ball to safety.

GC*

See **Golf**.

DICK, HARRIETT ELPHINSTONE (1854–1902) was a distance swimmer and swimming instructor who emigrated from England, with her friend Alice Moon, in 1876 and began swimming classes for women at St Kilda. Dick, who was qualified to teach the Ling Swedish method of gymnastics, opened the Melbourne Ladies' Gymnasium in partnership with Moon in 1879. The gymnasium won the approval of educational and religious authorities, and classes were held there by several private schools. Women were taught various exercises: dumbbell, free, wand-jumping, club-swinging, and figure marching. Dick took over Miss Mary Foster's Ladies' Gymnasium in Sydney in 1888, and after she sold the Melbourne Gymnasium in 1899, opened a new School of Physical Culture in Collins Street, Melbourne. She died suddenly of a heart attack in 1902, but her Melbourne establishments continued well into the twentieth century. A feminist, she was a woman of great independence, athleticism and cultivation, and a great publicist. She introduced Swedish gymnastics to Melbourne before it gained firm recognition in England.

RO

See **Calisthenics and Physical Culture**.

DITTMAR, CHRIS (1964–), born SA, is a left-handed squash-player. He has been a regular on the international squash circuit for the last ten years, with the exception of 1985 when a knee injury, received while training with Australian rules footballers, forced him from the game for twelve months. He has been a member of two Australian teams which have won the world team championship (1989 and 1991) and he has also won the Australian Open twice (1988 and 1991). Dittmar has also reached the final of the World Open in 1983, 1987, 1989, and 1990 as well as being runner-up in the British Open in 1985. Although squash is Dittmar's first choice he is a keen follower of other sports, especially football, and rates Dennis Lillee and Muhammad Ali as his favourite sportsmen.

KT

See **Squash Rackets**.

DIVE, MOLLIE, OAM (1913–), born Sydney, was introduced to cricket by her brothers and by her father, who represented NSW. She played for Australia in seven Tests, all as captain, and scored two half-centuries with a highest score of 59. In 1948 she became the first Australian captain to win the Ashes and retained them during the 1951 Australian tour of England—an achievement she considered the highlight of her career. She was awarded the OAM for her services to cricket and hockey in 1986 and her contributions to sport were further acknowledged with the opening of the Mollie Dive Stand and Function Centre at North Sydney Oval.

LR

Diving

Diving was not an organised sport in Australia before the 1920s but was a common pastime whose popularity was increased in the early 1900s by performers such as Solomon Islander Alick Wickham, who, in 1918, accomplished a world-recognised high-dive record from a tower erected beside the Yarra River in Victoria. That dive of 62.7 metres still stands as a world record. The inaugural Australian diving championships for men were held in 1921, and for women in 1930. Although Snowy Baker competed in Olympic diving in 1908, finishing sixth in a heat of the fancy springboard, Australia has never been at the forefront of international competition. This has been due partly to historically poor training facilities, a fact which led to the development of innovative training techniques such as the use of harnesses on dry land. Nonetheless, many Australian divers have performed creditably over the years: Dick Eve received Australia's only gold medal to date in the 1924 Paris Olympics; Don Wagstaff won thirty Australian titles between 1966 and 1978 as well as four Commonwealth Games gold medals; and Valerie McFarlane in 1979 won the women's 3 metres springboard title at the Fédération Internationale de Natation Amateur World Cup in Texas.

JC*

See **BAKER, REGINALD**; **EVE, RICHMOND**.

DOBBIE, JOHN M., OAM (1914–), was the only lawn bowler to have represented Australia in five international bowls series. In 1964 he played singles in South Africa, then in 1966 at the first World Bowls in Sydney he won a gold medal for triples and a silver medal for fours. At the 1970 British Commonwealth Games he played in the fours, and in the World Bowls in Worthing, in 1972, he played in triples and pairs. He played in pairs again in 1974 in Christchurch. Dobbie also excelled at lacrosse. In 1947, at a time when he was reaching his peak in club bowls, he represented Victoria in lacrosse at the Australian carnival in Perth. In the same year he won the Glenferrie Hill Club Bowls Championship, defeating his father in the final. He went on to win this club title seventeen times. Dobbie first represented Victoria in 1948 and by 1980 had played 200 representative games for his State. He was Victorian Champion of Champions in 1950 and 1959. Later he became an active administrator in the sport. He received the OAM in 1977 and was inducted into the Sport Australia Hall of Fame in 1985.

RC

DONALDSON, JOHN ('The Blue Streak') (1886–1933), born Raywood, Victoria, was a professional athlete. Jack Donaldson came to public notice when he ran second in the prestigious Stawell Gift in 1906. Of medium stature but slight build—175 centimetres tall and 65 kilograms—he attracted notice with his sweeping stride and all-blue running costume. Because of his great confidence he was regarded as a 'cocky youngster'. Donaldson defeated the 1908 Olympic champion, South African Reg Walker, in 1910 and the two had many later tussles in Africa and England, with Donaldson usually the victor. He also had some memorable contests against Australian champion Arthur Postle who was five years his senior. While Postle was very quick over the short sprints, he could not match Donaldson over longer distances. Their contests became part of the folklore of Australian professional running. During his career Donaldson broke thirteen world records ranging from 60 to 600 metres. His 1910 record for the 100 yards—9.375 seconds—was not broken by any athlete, amateur or professional, until 1951. Donaldson was the epitome of the professional élite athlete, scorning the good life. In a time of charlatans he was a serious athlete who was respected for his dedication and talent. Between May 1909 and February 1910 he won twenty-five races, usually off the 'scratch mark' as he was not interested in 'running dead' to achieve a 'good mark'. A drinking fountain at Stawell and a memorial foot-race commemorate him. Donaldson and Postle were the greatest Australian professional athletes of their time.

JAD

See **Athletics**; **POSTLE, ARTHUR**.

DOOHAN, MICHAEL (1965–), born Brisbane, came from a motorcycling family. His father owned a motorcycle business; Michael, one of three brothers who all raced, displayed early talent in dirt-track racing. He was recruited for the Australian Yamaha team in 1988 and was an immediate success, securing a memorable victory on the rain-lashed Bathurst circuit. In 1989 he joined Honda as understudy to Wayne Gardner and Eddie Lawson. By 1990 Doohan had established himself as a force in the 500 cc class, finishing third in the world championship. Doohan had his best year in 1991 when he won three of the first seven Grands Prix and finished second in the world championship.

DC

DOUBELL, RALPH (1945–), only the third Australian male to win an Olympic track event, caused an upset by taking out the 800 metres event at the 1968 Games. His time of 1 minute 44.3 seconds equalled Peter Snell's world record. He trained under Franz Stampfl while a B.Sc. student in zoology and psychology at the University of Melbourne. At 180 centimetres and 64 kilograms he was ideally built for middle distance. Doubell won the national title in 1965 and 1966 and finished fourth at the Kingston British Empire and Commonwealth Games. After winning the national

title again in 1967 he set off for the US indoor-track circuit where he was unbeaten up to 1000 yards. A foot injury six months before the 1968 Olympics curtailed his preparation and he only just survived the first round of the 800 metres. However, he defeated the favourite, Kenyan Wilson Kiprugut, in the semifinal and once again outsprinted him in the final. Doubell competed on the US indoor circuit from 1969 to 1972, setting world records in the 880 and 1000 yards at Albuquerque. He regained his Australian title in 1969 and 1970 but was not selected for the 1970 British Commonwealth Games. He was accepted into the Harvard Business School when he retired from athletics in 1972.
GC†
See **STAMPFL, FRANZ**.

Drama
The many connections between sport and the stage in Australia can be summarised under four headings: language, industry, audiences, and narratives. The use of the term 'play' for both activities dates back to the classical Roman *ludus*; already in Roman times, however, there was a distinction between 'competitive' games and 'imitative' games. In medieval and renaissance England this dual meaning was preserved in the usages of both 'play' and 'game'; actors were often called 'gamesters'. Industrial connections began in the Elizabethan playhouse, with entrepreneurs such as Henslowe promoting fencing competitions as well as plays: their popularity with audiences led to actors training themselves in such skills and, by the early seventeenth century sword-fighting scenes were under attack by intellectual playwrights like Ben Jonson as being gratuitous populism which attracted the wrong kind of playgoer. The split in Anglo-Saxon culture between sport as body and drama as mind seems to date from this time; by the late nineteenth century 'Sport and Drama' was a phrase used (e.g. in many popular magazine titles) to encapsulate all leisure activities, but which could also indicate the varying interests of men and women, low-class and high, hedonist and intellectual.

During the first half-century of the European settlement of Australia the popular theatrical form of the hippodrome began to exploit sporting contests as spectacle, and to link these together by an episodic narrative involving well-bred young countrymen exploring the attractions of London. The seminal text was Pierce Egan's 1820–21 Regency bestseller *Tom and Jerry: Life in London*, which was dramatised by many playwrights, and staged with real horses enacting the Epsom Derby and real prize-fighters competing in the ring, among other sporting spectacles. When staged in Sydney in 1835, this representation of sporting and other city low life was extremely controversial, and at least one localised version was banned.

At the same time as these proto-sporting stories were appearing, the theatre industry in Australia was establishing itself on the lines of the British provinces, where the calendar of horse-racing carnivals in different towns and cities was used by theatre companies as the basis of performance circuits. Throughout nineteenth-century Australia actors followed the horses, with circuses, hippodromes, melodramas, and 'society' comedies all being presented in Melbourne at Cup time, in Sydney at the autumn carnival, and in smaller towns during Race Week. Theatres were initially built by publicans, who were also heavily involved in organising early sporting contests, and by the second half of the century leisure entrepreneurs were emerging whose interests embraced commercial theatre, professional sport, and catering. An early example was the actor-manager George Coppin, whose Theatre Royal caterers, Spiers & Pond, were the backers for the 1861–62 English cricket tour, and who in 1870 brought the 'world champion' sprinter, Frank Hewett, to Melbourne for a series of races against the colonial champion, John Harris. The most famous sport and drama businessman was Hugh D. McIntosh, whose many sporting and food-and-drink ventures were followed by control for a time of the Tivoli vaudeville circuit, and revue, musicals, ballet, and opera tours in the 1920s. The 1930s Depression and the collapse of commercial live theatre ended this conglomeration of leisure capital, although there are some signs (e.g. the circus and trotting investments of Michael Edgley) that it was being revived by the 1980s.

In the early nineteenth century too a genre of socially reactionary novels emerged which celebrated the traditional authority of the English landed gentry and their horse-riding and fox-hunting life-style. However, the sporting story as recognised today seems to date from Dion Boucicault's 1866 horse-racing melodrama *Flying Scud: or a Four-Legged Fortune*. Enormously successful, particularly in Australia and NZ where it was still being revived forty years later, this story features a young, penniless, upper-class country gentleman and his thoroughbred racehorse, his journey to the corrupt city, attempts to nobble the horse and its jockey, and the horse's victory in the Epsom Derby; many of its scenes would be familiar to readers of Dick Francis today. Until the 1930s, racecourse drama was a major genre of British, American, and Australian stages: the traditional landed classes always defeated the rising urban *nouveau riche*, and the eugenic argument about 'good blood' was symbolised by the aristocrat's horse (always the favourite) winning a major horse-race and helping to restore the family fortunes.

Localised versions of these plays such as *The Double Event* (1893) and *The Winning Ticket* (1910) substituted Australian races, mostly the Sydney AJC Derby and the Melbourne Cup. By the 1930s this drama of good breeding had begun to fail, although its influence can be seen in Australian racing films from *Silks and Saddles* (1921), through *Thoroughbred* (1936), to *Phar Lap* (1983). At least one long 'race call' speech was a highlight of every play, anticipating the modern race-caller by half a century.

Another major genre was boxing dramas. Since *Tom and Jerry* boxers had been appearing in plays and most famous boxers gave exhibition appearances in vaudeville houses to supplement their incomes. They quickly took on acting roles as well. In 1857 John 'Black' Perry was starring in a burlesque version of *Othello* in NSW; in the 1890s the West Indian-Australian boxer Peter Jackson played the name role in *Uncle Tom's Cabin* in New York, and in 1891 the world heavyweight champion John L. Sullivan toured Australia as the hero of *Honest Hearts and Willing Hands*, a homely melodrama which ended with a three-round contest against a villainous opponent (in fact Sullivan's sparring partner) whose below-the-belt tactics were unable to prevent the triumph of right. 'Gentleman Jim' Corbett was another American heavyweight pugilist-actor who toured Australia profitably during the First World War, while Australia's own Dave Smith and Snowy Baker became early silent film stars.

The great advantage of horse-racing stories however was their cross-class and cross-gender appeal, and the genre became a major weapon in the hands of turn-of-the-century managers trying to resist the breaking up of popular theatre into class- and gender-specific forms like vaudeville, drawing-room comedy, or operetta. 'Pit, box and gallery' all thrilled as the racecourse scene was staged: first with clockwork horses, then real horses in the 1880s, and between 1891 and 1910 with the horses on treadmills on stage in front of a moving back-scene to give the illusion of movement—the entire treadmill with the favoured horse on it being winched forwards just before the painted finishing line came rolling by. The 'on the lawn' scene before the race, and the equally obligatory race-ball scene afterwards, gave the actresses ample opportunity to display the latest gowns and hats, often imported from 'Worths of Paris' and other famous European fashion houses, thus ensuring 'something for the ladies'. The desertion of working-class audiences to film ended this kind of sporting story on the stage, although writers like the Australian Arthur Wright continued to produce racing novels, some of which were still being dramatised in the 1920s.

A brief but influential group of military chau-vinist plays and films in the period 1909–13 introduced into popular culture the alternative idea of sport as a trivial distraction from the serious business of war. The London success *An Englishman's Home* showed a representative family, 'the Browns', obsessed with football and cricket while 'Nearlanders' invaded their house; it was widely performed in Australia and imitated by the politician-playwright Randolph Bedford in his *White Australia: or, the Empty North*, where the overland telegraph line, choked with messages about cricket and racing results, failed to be used to warn of an imminent Japanese invasion. The onset of war led to consensual stories where the fitness and athletic skills of sportsmen anticipated their military heroism, and films like *Gallipoli* (1981) continue this ideology.

The idea of sport as the mindless obsession of trivial people was, however, enthusiastically embraced by the modern literary-intellectual theatre, with Australian men and women being attacked for their sporting interests. Some plays (e.g. *Image in the Clay* 1960) see sport as a meeting ground for Aboriginal or immigrant and Anglo-Australian society; others see this as the failed policy of assimilation. Exceptions to the sports-critical tendency are some recent plays, particularly about Australian rules (*And the Big Men Fly* [1963], *Goodbye Ted* [1975], *The Club* [1978], *Royboys* [1987]), which celebrate Melbourne tribalism. But sport as subject matter for story-telling has nearly always been a symbol of cultural totality, of an entire society as a singular functioning system. Consequently the concept of multiculturalism, and the exclusion of women from most representations of Australian sporting society, has led to a rejection of sporting stories by many writers from the 1980s onwards. Exceptions are school-based stories such as *The Heartbreak Kid* (1987), where sport continues to be both a meeting ground and a field of contest for different racial and class groups, and both genders.

RF*

See **Art**; **Film**; **Literature**.

Drugs

Although it seems likely that drugs in some form have been used to enhance athletic performance for as long as there has been organised athletics, it is only since the 1960s that international sporting agencies have begun to clarify their position on the matter, and to impose that position on participants. Given the nature of the competitive process and the increased application of science to the pursuit of optimum performance, in a context where victory often has political and financial significance, it is hardly surprising that competitors, in an effort to gain an advantage, would seek ergogenic aids. It is equally to be expected that among all the ergogenic aids, genuine and supposed, some will come to be regarded as undesirable in some way. A problem of enforcement then exists. If all the athletes in the world agreed that certain kinds of ergogenic aids were undesirable, if they trusted each other, and were justified in so doing, then the problem would not exist. It is when there is a breakdown in agreement and justified trust that rules, procedures, and penalties have to be devised and used to force people to do what is right, and to detect those who break the rules. The development and implementation of the rules, practices, and penalties always proves to be complex and expensive, and so it is with drugs in sport. What develops is an increasingly sophisticated contest between rule-enforcers and rule-breakers.

As an enthusiastic participant in international sport, and a strong advocate of the benefits of sport for all, in particular the young, Australia willingly followed the international trends in the banning of doping in sport. For example, all scholarship-holders at the Australian Institute of Sport have been required from the beginning to abide by a code of ethics which includes an agreement to undertake a random drug test if required and an agreement 'not to take or use drugs or stimulants nor participate in other practices prohibited by the Institute'. The international initiatives may be regarded as beginning formally in 1960 when the Council of Europe tabled a resolution against the use of doping substances in sport, based on medical, ethical, and moral principles. In 1964 cyclists at the Olympic Games were tested for stimulants; at the next Olympics routine testing for stimulants was extended to all sports. In 1971 the International Olympic Committee (IOC) published a list of banned drugs, to which were added later anabolic steroids (in 1974 when detection became possible) and diuretics. In 1985 blood-doping was banned. Rigorous testing came into existence at the Pan-American Games in 1983 when Professor Manfred Donike first made use of gas chromatography and mass spectrometry in the pre-games testing. The IOC list came generally to be taken as the basis for anti-drugs programmes, and is continually updated to include new discoveries such as human growth hormone and erythropoeitin.

In Australia the first significant local initiative, apart from implementation of the IOC regulations by the Australian Olympic Federation Medical Commission, formed in 1968, was the survey of drug use in Australian sport, begun in 1979 by the Australian Sports Medicine Federation (ASMF), and published in 1982. This was funded by the Federal Government and was the initiative of the ASMF Drugs Control Committee. The results of the survey, based on 4064 replies to 14 200 questionnaires, covered thirty-one sports, at all levels, and

sought information about the use of eight categories of substances: vitamins and food supplements; anti-inflammatory drugs for sporting injury; pain-relieving drugs; drugs for nasal congestion, asthma etc.; drugs to reduce weight; anabolic steroids; stimulants; and sedatives and tranquillisers.

A complicated picture of drug use in Australian sport was presented in the report. Drug use was not confined to a few competitors in a few easily identifiable sports: all sports and all age groups contained drug-users and about 5 per cent of the sample had used considerable numbers of drugs in connection with their sport. The authors concluded that there was a problem with drug use in Australian sport but that it was difficult to specify the exact nature and extent of the problem. They saw it as a cause for concern but noted that there was no clearly formulated set of guidelines, nor any generally accepted consensus of community attitudes towards, and expectations about, the use of drugs in sport. While there seemed to be general agreement that the use of drugs was wrong, there was no agreement about what constituted a drug, what constituted the use of 'drugs in sport' or what constituted the use of a drug to improve performance. In the absence of clearly defined answers to such questions it was impossible to say why vitamin supplements were acceptable but stimulants not, or whether drugs taken by an asthmatic athlete to ease his asthma were to be banned, or whether a pain-killing drug to help the athlete cope with injury was proscribed. In recognising the need for a national policy, so that the practice could be governed properly, they recommended that 'the policy to be formulated should consider the aims of sport, the relationship between the long-term interests of sports people and competitive success, the ethical issues involved in the use of drugs in sport, and the policy should reflect general community attitudes towards the issues involved'. This recommendation was an important one, theoretically, because it directed attention to the basic issues, thereby providing a sound basis for practice.

In 1985, in response to the ASMF report and the growing impression that not only was drug use common in sport but that sports authorities tended to be evasive and complacent about it, the Federal Government established the National Programme on Drugs in Sport (Anti-Drugs Campaign) under the Australian Sports Commission. The programme provided advice to government and help to athletes, introduced and conducted both random testing and testing at events, and produced educational materials. It also began the important process of establishing links with international agencies with similar concerns, for clearly a crucial part of any strategy had to be to ensure that all international competitors were subject to the same levels of scrutiny. Following a review in 1988, the government increased its commitment and the Australian Sports Drug Agency was established.

During the second half of the 1980s increasing publicity was given to incidents and allegations involving the use of drugs in sport. A significant event was the ABC 'Four Corners' programme of 30 November 1987 which not only suggested widespread use of drugs but made specific allegations about the AIS. There was considerable public interest and on 18 May 1988 the Senate resolved, without discussion, to refer to the Standing Committee on the Environment, Recreation, and the Arts the matter of 'the use by Australian sportsmen and sportswomen of performance-enhancing drugs' and the role played by Commonwealth agencies'. A long inquiry began which resulted in an interim report of over one thousand pages and a second report, following eighty-five submissions and twenty-nine days of public hearings as well as in camera hearings, all of which produced over six thousand pages of evidence. A large part of the two reports was devoted to investigating allegations of drug use, and the interim report was prepared 'to remove as soon as possible the uncertainties and difficulties being experienced by the AIS as a result of the inquiry'. Clearly, though, a most important purpose for the government had to be progress towards developing the policy called for by the ASMF report. In the words of the second report, the committee's central ambition was 'to ensure that Australian sport activities are as drug free as education programmes and contemporary detection technologies will permit, having regard to the civil rights of those athletes tested and the capacity of the Federal Government to meet costs'. The value of the inquiry therefore can be assessed in terms of the extent to which it showed a sound grasp of the complexity of the problems identified by the ASMF, and in terms of the mechanisms and strategies recommended to deal with those problems. Such an assessment would show that the recommendations address comprehensively all the relevant issues, once it is accepted that drug enhancement of performance is undesirable. In the matter of justification for the whole expensive paraphernalia, however, the Senate Committee tended to accept the usual rhetoric, and did not advance our thinking about this difficult issue. The ASMF report pointed to these matters, but they remain unilluminated. To some extent this is a consequence of the very necessary and desirable strategy of adopting the IOC list of prescribed drugs and procedures as the basis of the policy. This obviates the need to decide which drugs to ban and thereby avoids having to answer difficult questions about why any particular drug should be banned, and under what conditions it should be banned. Important questions are thus answered elsewhere, but the answers are hidden behind clichés about the ethics of sport and the notion of harm.

It is not always clear what people have in mind when they speak of the ethics of sport in this context. Sometimes there is a straightforward confusion of two questions: 'Should athletes take banned drugs?' and 'Should drugs be banned?' Clearly answering 'yes' to the first is to condone cheating and most people would regard that as unethical. To speak of ethics in regard to the second question is usually to focus on what the ASMF report referred to as 'the nature of sport'. If we ignore the problem of harm for the moment, the question arises whether a substance which enhances performance should be banned. Answering this calls upon the same kind of choice as is made in, say, cycling where it is decided on some grounds that there will not be standard bikes but that the development of new bikes is part of the contest. It could have been decided to limit the contest to cyclists, not to cyclists and bicycle technologists. What the grounds are for such a choice probably involves matters such as our reasons for valuing cycling contests. Similar choices are to be made about drugs, and they raise the same kind of questions. Should the benefits of harmless drugs be part of the contest just as the benefits of new technology are part of the contest? To answer this we must draw on our reasons for valuing sport. When we applaud the outstanding performance, what really are we applauding? The performance itself, the fact that it was done by an Australian, or what it took in the way of effort, training, and dedication to produce that performance? Would the same performance by a robot be equally applauded? If not, why not? American author and anti-drugs campaigner Bob Goldman gives an empirical answer to whether drug enhancement of performance is acceptable, and shows great faith in the spectator when he says that

> none are likely to admire, few will come to see, none will want to emulate those whose strength or skill is believed to come from a bottle of pills or a hypodermic needle. If athletes continue down this perilous path of natural destruction by synthetic chemicals, they will be denigrated, sneered at, diminished and viewed as curiosities like freaks in a side show.

The ASMF report and the Senate Committee reports likewise seem to attach importance to what the general view of the populace is. If the majority of Australians think drug enhancement of performance is right, does that make it right? Would that be the basis for allowing drugs to athletes, or for community education to change those views?

The Senate Committee attached much importance to the matter of harm to the health of athletes, although in accepting the IOC list the matter has already been decided. It is important to note, however, what is involved in deciding whether harm to the athlete is a compelling reason for banning drugs. First, does it mean that if there is no demonstrable harm then drugs should be allowed? Second, is it justifiable to prevent adults from knowingly risking their health in the pursuit of desirable goals? Ignorant risk-taking is of course to be avoided, but that can be dealt with. The argument regarding coercion is usually introduced here, because the drug-taking athletes force their opponents to join them if they wish to be competitive. They, of course, have a choice, and the coercion is only undesirable if it is believed that sport is good for people in some sense, and that dropping out is bad.

These, then, are some of the difficult fundamental questions which can remain unexplored when the IOC list is adopted. The Senate Committee expressed opinions concerning some of these matters but in general the supporting argument was weak. This was reflected in the vagueness concerning the matter of education about drugs in sport, because in specifying this, such basic questions need to be raised and answered. The Senate Committee was much more comprehensive and thorough in developing the plans for a good drug-testing programme which it defined as having the following features: a high, perceived risk of detection, appropriate penalties, education to alert people to risk of detection, clear and unambiguous results, and the support of reduced availability. To achieve the first purpose the committee recommended a combination of random, targeted, and event testing of such frequency as to make it unlikely that an athlete could make effective use of drugs. High risk of detection with severe penalties not only acts as a strong deterrent but also diminishes the coercion because athletes can feel more confident that their opponents do not have an unfair advantage. This diminishes a strong motivation to use drugs. The Committee recognised the importance of having uniform penalties among the different sports. Faced with evidence of various kinds of failure by sports administrators to act on positive test results in the past, the committee emphasised the importance of an independent testing authority, an independent commission to oversee all procedures, and an independent tribunal to consider appeals. All of this bureaucracy was seen to be necessary, on good grounds it seemed, to avoid the problem, as described by former US Olympic Sports Medicine official Robert Voy, of 'setting the fox to guard the henhouse'. Not only have athletes been under pressure to transgress, but likewise coaches and administrators, eager for success which leads not only to fame but to financial support for the sport. Much of the public discussion which led to the inquiry expressed a certain scepticism about sport handling its own drug-testing.

Clearly, if the testing programme is to act as a deterrent not only does it have to pose a high risk of detection but athletes have to know about it, and appreciate the risk. This then becomes an important part of an education programme which also deals with wider issues such as the dangers of drugs and the absurdity of their use in sport. The report suggests that drug use in sport can profitably be considered within the context of drug abuse generally in society. Hence the same strategies are appropriate. This seems to be a matter needing more thought and research, however. In the context of international testing, achieving clear and unambiguous results requires standard tests, strict procedures for handling, and the use of accredited laboratories to perform the tests. The committee was lucky to have, and wise to follow, in these matters, the IOC procedures. In the course of its investigations, the committee discovered widespread irregularities among doctors, pharmacists, and veterinarians in the prescribing and supply of banned drugs, particularly anabolic steroids. Wide-ranging recommendations to various agencies, changing the status of drugs, and increasing customs scrutiny, should serve, if implemented, to decrease availability of drugs. In conjunction with reduced pressure, increased chance of detection, and severe penalties, reduced availability should be effective.

It can be seen, therefore, that the Senate Committee has been thorough in its planning of a good testing programme. For those sports with funding from the government, participation in the programme is a condition of continued financial support. The committee also recognised the need to bring the professional sports into the testing programme and made recommendations designed to encourage this. Finally, recognising the futility of 'unilateral disarmament' in this matter, in that it would place Australian athletes at a disadvantage internationally, the committee urged that the relevant Australian authorities take a high profile in the international moves to secure world-wide implementation of comparable programmes. To that end Australian delegates have attended the two Permanent World Conferences on Anti-Doping in Sport, and, particularly at the second conference in 1989, took an active part in developing international agreement to combat doping. Meanwhile at home, in 1989, Australia's first national conference concerning drugs in sport was sponsored by the Department of Human Movement Science at the University of Wollongong, and supported by the Australian Sports Commission Anti-Drugs Campaign. Sports leaders such as Kevan Gosper, AOC president and IOC executive member, have taken a strong public stand against the use of drugs in sport. Thus in the last decade of the twentieth century, Australia is playing an active part in the world-wide thrust to combat the use of drugs in sport. At the moment there is consensus that drug enhancement of performance is wrong, and there is sufficient strength of feeling to support the considerable cost of acting on that belief. No doubt the costs will continue to rise, and given the absence of a carefully argued and widely understood justification for banning performance-enhancing drugs, and the continued pressure to achieve higher and higher standards one can only wonder how long the support will continue.

RJP

See **Australian Institute of Sport**; **Australian Sports Drug Agency**.

DUNK, WILLIAM EDGAR (1938–   ), one of the finest shot-makers in Australian golf, won more than one hundred tournaments and broke more than eighty records. The son of a greenkeeper, he learned his golf from Ryde-Parramatta professional Alex Wilson. After winning the Australian PGA in 1962, Dunk won twenty-five tournaments, including the NSW Open, two NSW PGA championships, and the NZ Spalding Masters, and set twenty-five records between 1967 and 1969. His ability to break records in tournaments which he did not win became one of the oddities of Australian golf. He represented Australia in three World Cups finishing third, partnered by Bruce Crampton, in his final appearance. A modest pessimist, he was his own most scathing critic.

GC*

See **Golf**.

DUNPHY, MYLES JOSEPH, OBE (1891–1985), born Melbourne, was a bushwalker and conservationist. He founded the Mountain Trails Club in 1914 as a private club, which survived until 1971, but gave rise to the Sydney Bushwalkers (1927), the National Parks and Primitive Areas Council (1932), and many others. He walked the most remote and rugged routes of the Blue Mountains, mapped the Blue Mountains, and encouraged hundreds of others to walk into primitive areas. Most importantly, Dunphy campaigned tirelessly throughout his life for the reservation and proper management of parks in areas such as the Blue Mountains and the Kosciusko region. He probably contributed more than any other single individual to the growth of the national park movement in Australia.

EH-S

See **Bushwalking**.

DURACK, SARAH ('Fanny') (1889–1956) was Australia's first female Olympic gold-medallist, winning the 100 metres freestyle at the 1912 Stockholm Games. The daughter of a Sydney publican, her career centred around Coogee Aquarium and Wylie's Baths. She broke at least eleven world records in a career that lasted from 1906 to 1921. Durack's date with destiny at Stockholm was fraught with problems. Control of women's swimming had been in the hands of the NSW Ladies' Amateur Swimming Association (NSWLASA) since 1906, under the presidency of a prominent public figure, Miss Rose Scott, who supported a rule of the association that women could not compete in front of male spectators. Despite Scott's objections and those of A. C. W. Hill, secretary of the Amateur (Men's) Swimming Association, the NSWLASA supported the selection of Fanny Durack and Mina Wylie for Stockholm. When the rule against allowing male spectators to watch female swimmers was later rescinded, Scott resigned her position. Mrs Hugh McIntosh started a fund to send the two women to the Games. Fanny Durack, with her sister Mary as chaperone, travelled on the French mail steamer *Armand Behic*, while Mina went with her father on the RMS *Malvia*. At the Games there was only one individual swimming event for women, the 100 metres freestyle, and a team relay event. In the 100 metres, Durack came first and Wylie second. In the first heat Durack bettered the world record. In 1918 and 1919 Durack and Wylie toured the USA but the visits were surrounded by controversy and both were suspended in the latter excursion for failing to keep an engagement. Durack would have defended her title in 1920 in Antwerp but she had an appendectomy a week before the departure of the team. She retired in 1921 and died of cancer on 20 March 1956. In 1967 she was posthumously elected to the International Swimming Hall of Fame. In December 1990 a headstone was unveiled at Durack's previously unmarked grave in Waverley Cemetery, Sydney.

RH and MH

See **Swimming**.

DURAS, FRITZ (1896–1964), 'the father of physical education' in Australia, established the first diploma course in the subject at a tertiary institution in this country. Following his medical degree he became director of the Sports Medicine Institute in Freiburg University from 1928 to 1933. Invited to establish a physical education course at the University of Melbourne, his initial appointment in 1937 was funded by the Carnegie Corporation, but in 1939 he was employed by the university as director of physical education, a position he held until he retired in 1962. Duras had a great

influence on the development of physical education as a profession: he conducted the first
World Congress on Physical Education in Australia which was held in Melbourne at the time
of the 1956 Olympics; he was the first president
of the Australian Physical Education Association
(now ACHPER) and a foundation member and
first vice-president of the Australian Sports Medicine Federation; and he was the first president of
the International Council for Physical Education and Sport. He was also very active in many
other spheres, being chairman of the Youth
Advisory Council and the Playgrounds and
Recreation Association of Victoria. Duras was a
kindly man who enjoyed challenges. The Fritz
Duras Memorial National Lecture is a feature of
ACHPER National Biennial Conferences.

IJ

See **Australian Council of Health, Physical Education and Recreation**.

DYER, JACK (1913–) was possibly the
most feared ruckman to play Australian rules
football, earning the title 'Captain Blood'. Tall
and immensely powerful, he would fearlessly
charge at the ball, scattering opponents in his
way. He was also a shrewd tactician who knew
the rules thoroughly. In his later playing days,
Dyer developed the drop-punt kick to great
effect, a development which led to the virtual
elimination of the drop-kick, stab-kick, and
torpedo-punt kicks from the game. After joining Richmond in 1931, he became a key member of the ruck trio of Bentley, Dyer, and
Martin and was a participant in the 1934 and
1943 premiership sides. Dyer was the club's
best and fairest twice (1940 and 1946), played a
record 312 games for the club and kicked 440
goals. He was captain-coach from 1941 to 1949
and after retirement coached for the next three
years. He represented Victoria sixteen times.
Later Dyer became a popular radio and television commentator who made good use of
humour and down-to-earth expressions.

EP

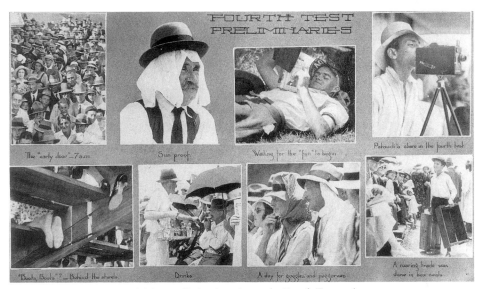

44 Cricket preliminaries prior to the Fourth Test against
England in Brisbane, 1933.

45 Cricket and politics are linked in this cartoon by Sam
Wells: Robert Menzies, Arthur Fadden and Ben Chifley
await the decision of the voters in the 1949 federal
election, at a time when Lindsay Hassett and Arthur
Morris awaited the Australian selectors' decision on
Bradman's successor as captain.

46 England versus the Bradman XI at the Bradman Oval,
Bowral, NSW, 11 December 1990.

47 The Bradman Exhibition, Bradman Museum,
Bowral, NSW.

48 Cyclist Ern Milliken with three sashes he received in 1931 for being the Amateur Road Champion of Victoria, the CACC 100 Mile Road Champion and the Victorian 20 Mile Senior Unpaced Road Champion.

49 Cyclist Alfred Twentyman rode professionally in Australia in the 1890s.

50 Les Darcy wrote this letter from St Louis, USA, outlining the obstacles he faced in obtaining a bout.

51 Although the sentimental explanation was that Les Darcy died of a 'broken heart', his death certificate indicates a more likely cause.

E

Eighty-seven Myth. This is a piece of cricketing superstition perpetuated by Australian commentators when they have no more illuminating comment to make on the state of play. The myth-makers would have us believe that 87 is a dread score, yet among the 348 cricketers who have represented Australia in 501 Test matches up to the end of the second Test against England in 1990, only eleven have had this number recorded against their name. Apart from individual superstition, the commentators have also attempted to convince us that Australian teams engage in collective paranoia whenever 87, 187, 287 etc. appears on the scoreboard. Again, however, the evidence is slim, as Australia has managed to avoid totals ending in 87 with amazing regularity. On only five occasions have the digits appeared in the total. The originator of the eighty-seven myth is sometimes said to have been the late Ken Mackay although fellow all-rounder Keith Miller has also claimed credit for the mischief.

BW

Electric Light Cricket

This game was invented in SA by Mr Alf Stone, a returned First World War serviceman, and is played outdoors under electric lights, almost exclusively within SA. It was introduced into sub-branches of the Returned Sailors and Soldiers Imperial League of Australia (RSSILA) in 1930 and the rules were vested in the RSSILA Electric Light Cricket Association. During 1936 this branch of the sport became firmly established and business houses, factories, workshops, and sporting clubs formed teams and associations. The rules governing electric light cricket were adopted at a meeting of the SA Electric Light Cricket Council on 6 December 1939. The game has many similarities to cricket but also a number of differences. Tennis balls are used and bowled underarm. Teams consist of a maximum of fifteen players and all players whose names appear on the team board must bowl and bat in the order they are listed. Each side has one innings of 36 overs or until the team has been dismissed. Only one batsman appears at the wicket at a time and is not required to run as a result of a stroke, scoring (4 runs or 2 runs) being calculated by the position in which the ball is fielded. A batsman who obtains 100 runs is required to retire. Matches usually last about three hours.

The playing arena is approximately the size of a tennis court. The game is vigorous but not excessively so and can be played from the age of 8 to an energetic 80. Three generations playing in a team is not uncommon. In its peak years up to the 1970s many RSL clubs had their own court; there were several city associations, and the game was also played in Broken Hill, Whyalla, and Murray Bridge. Notable cricketers like Sir Garfield Sobers, Ian Chappell, Gil Langley, and Barry Jarman have turned out in matches. The game has lost popularity in the last twenty years and Wayne Phillips has been one of the few international players to appear. Today there is one association, the SA Electric Light Cricket Association, with six courts in the South Parklands and about five hundred active participants. Women have played the sport since before the Second World War and at present field six teams in matches on Friday nights. An identical game, court cricket, was played during the day by schoolgirls for a number of seasons.

BW

ELLA Brothers. MARK, OAM, his twin **GLEN** (1959–), and **GARY** (1960–) were born in La Perouse, Sydney, to itinerant workers Gordon and May Ella. After they had played rugby league in primary school, Geoff Mould coached them as rugby union players at Matraville High. The Aboriginal brothers were an integral part of the unbeaten 1977–78 Australian schoolboys' side, when their attacking flair and fine understanding became legendary. The Ellas were ideally suited to the Randwick running style of play in the late 1970s and 1980s. Mark, a five-eighth who made his debut for Australia against NZ in 1980, was the most successful of the brothers, playing in twenty-six tests and captaining his country in nine of these. His career ended on a high note with his leadership of the 1984 'Grand Slam Wallabies' and his own success in scoring a try against each of the four home countries—the first player to achieve this. After retirement from international rugby he played club rugby for Randwick until 1990 and later coached in Italy. He was awarded the OAM in 1984 for his services to rugby union. Gary, a centre, played six Tests and Glen, a full back, four. The Ella brothers brought their unique skill and flair to rugby. Their high school coach, commented that 'people will watch the

Ellas play every day of the week ... They always play for the gods'. A sister, Marcia, OAM, played netball for Australia.

MC

See **Aborigines in Sport**.

ELLIOTT, HERBERT J., MBE (1938–), born Subiaco, WA, was educated at Aquinas College, Perth, and the universities of Melbourne and Cambridge. He ran his first mile race as a 14-year-old schoolboy. Some good judges predicted that with his build and natural flair he would become a world-class miler. He was inspired by the performance of the Russian Vladimir Kuts at the Melbourne Olympics. Coached by the famous Percy Cerutty, Herb Elliott improved: he built up his stamina and became a more determined competitor. The fruits of hard work were realised in 1957 when Elliott set world junior records for the 1, 2, and 3 mile events. The first of his sub-4-minute miles was on 28 January 1958 when he was clocked at 3 minutes 59.9 seconds. Elliott won both the half-mile and the mile at the Cardiff British Empire and Commonwealth Games that year and later, during the tour of the British Isles, ran the fastest mile of his career: in 3 minutes 54.5 seconds at Dublin. He set his sights on the 1500 metres in the 1960 Rome Games where he faced a top-class field. Fifth after two laps, he then blitzed the field, virtually sprinting to win by 20 metres in an Olympic- and world-record time of 3 minutes 35.6 seconds. This win was one of the most decisive in the 1500 metres in Olympic history. Elliott, who retired at his peak, recorded forty-four wins in his career and was never beaten over a mile or 1500 metres. Many honours later came his way including the 1958 Helms Award and the MBE.

WPR

See **Athletics**; CERUTTY, PERCY.

EMERSON, ROY (1936–), born Blackbutt, Queensland, was the son of a farmer and won more tennis titles, including twelve Grand Slam singles and sixteen Grand Slam doubles, than any previous player. A State champion schoolboy sprinter, who ran the 100 yards in 10.6 seconds at 14 years of age, he was known for his speed around the court as well as his strength and fitness. Emerson won the Australian men's singles in 1961 and from 1963 to 1967, and the doubles in 1962, 1966, and 1969. He won the Wimbledon singles two years in a row, in 1964 and 1965, and was denied a third title when injured in the quarterfinals in 1966. He won the title again in 1970 and was successful in the Wimbledon doubles in 1959, 1961, and 1971. He won the US title in the singles in 1961 and 1964 and the doubles in 1959–60 and 1965–66. He also achieved success in the French singles title in 1963 and 1967 and in the doubles from 1960 to 1965. He represented Australia in the Davis Cup from 1957 to 1967. He was ranked world number one in the mid-1960s. Emerson turned professional in 1968 but did not achieve as much success as he had as an amateur. It has been claimed that Emerson 'changed the pattern of the men's game' by 'maintaining a serve-volley technique through a long five-setter'.

VO'F

See **Lawn Tennis**.

EMMETT, EVELYN TEMPLE, OBE (1871–1970), born Launceston, became a prominent bushwalker. Director of the Tasmanian Tourist Department 1914–41, he was founder of the Hobart Walking Club in 1921 and author of *Tasmania by Road and Track*, a lyrical and amusing description of walking in Tasmania. He did a great deal to encourage walkers from other States to visit Tasmania, including his personal leadership of parties of walkers from the mainland along the Cradle Mountain–Lake St Clair track during the 1930s. He was later awarded the OBE.

EH-S

Equestrianism

Although various equestrian contests have been popular in Australia since the early nineteenth century, Australians have competed internationally only since the 1956 Olympic Games. The equestrian events for those games were transferred to Stockholm because Australia's strict quarantine regulations did not permit overseas horses to visit Melbourne. Nevertheless, Australian horses and riders have established a strong reputation in international competition over the past four decades. The controlling body of the sport is the Equestrian Federation of Australia which governs events such as dressage, show-jumping, harness driving, eventing, and hacking. Dressage is designed to test the horse's obedience and state of training. In an arena riders perform a series of movements, graded in difficulty, and are marked by a panel of judges. First included in the Olympic Games in 1912, it is the most graceful of all the equestrian events. In Australia, the horse was primarily regarded as a creature of utility and as such the finer points of training were felt unnecessary. Consequently when the first equitation tests were introduced into Australian gymkhanas, in the 1930s, they were not regarded as a serious event. This changed with the arrival of Franz Mallinger, Australia's first official instructor. As trainer of Australia's Olympic team, his common-sense approach to training both horse and rider helped to popularise dressage. Fostered by the Pony Club movement, which was established in the 1950s, dressage grew steadily until 1960 when the Dressage Association was formed. The discipline has prospered throughout Australia with dressage clubs now established in Tasmania, NSW, SA, and Victoria.

Show-jumping, under Fédération Équestre Internationale (FEI) rules, was introduced into Australia in 1951. Before this, show-jumping had been conducted at royal and agricultural shows under local rules where one of the most popular events was the high jump. The Australian record of 8 feet 6 inches, set in 1956, was not recognised by the FEI as it did not conform to international rules. In 1949 the Equestrian Federation of Australia (EFA) was formed and gained international recognition in 1950. Under the leadership of a Victorian, Sam Horden, the objects of the federation were to promote, encourage, and organise the entry of equestrian teams into the Olympic Games and other competitions. Progress was slow, and many show societies resisted putting on the new type of jumping. There was even talk of a (Sydney) Royal Easter Show boycott. One of the main problems concerned the building of the courses. So few horses completed perfect rounds that riders and owners considered the courses too difficult. This began to change in 1953 when Colonel Llewellyn was invited to build courses that suited the standard, as well as to lecture, and fully explain the new rules. In 1953 the NZ Horse Society decided to send a team to Australia. The tour was very successful and although the New Zealanders were far superior at this stage of the new sport, the competition provided a great incentive to local riders. Australia did not fare well in its first Olympic show-jumping event but the period after the Games became very important as riders and horses developed rapidly. This coincided with the growth and development of branches of the EFA in all Australian States. The first Australian to compete successfully on the international circuit was Kevin Bacon, who won more than $200 000 in prize-money.

Three-day eventing is still referred to as the 'Militaire' in Europe and evolved from an old cavalry exercise in which horses had to prove their obedience, boldness, and fitness over a three-day period. Starting with the dressage event, horses have to perform intricate movements in a confined arena before a panel of judges. This tests for obedience and training. The second day consists of a 27 kilometre endurance run that has to be completed within a given time; included in this run is a 6 kilometre obstacle course which contains obstructions such as drop-fences, water, hedges, and bridges. On the final day the horse is required to tackle a show-jumping course. Considered to be the most demanding of the events, show-jumping requires the horse to be extremely fit, bold, and well-schooled. The principal international three-day events, apart from the Olympic Games, are the World Championships and the European Championships. In Australia major three-day events are held in Melbourne, Adelaide, and Sydney.

Australia's first representation at the Olympics was at Stockholm in 1956. A team of six riders spent a year in Britain at the invitation of the British Horse Society. At the same time Laurie Morgan, at his own expense, took his horse *Gold Rose* to Britain and became the first Australian rider to have overseas success. He won the Windsor Three-Day Event at Badminton, the final international before the Games. Australia did not win a medal at the Games; its best effort came in the dressage where it took fourth place, demonstrating that Australia could compete at European standard in dressage. The most important aspect of the Stockholm Games was that it introduced three-day eventing to Australia. The first Olympic success came in 1960 with one of the most courageous acts of sporting heroics produced by an Australian. While riding in the three-day event, Bill Roycroft fell from his mount, and after finishing the course, was taken to hospital. He had sustained a broken collarbone and concussion. At the end of the second day Australia was ahead on points so, to ensure a strong finish in the team event, Roycroft rode in the final day's section. Needing to be lifted into the saddle, he rode a perfect round over twelve jumps and clinched the team gold for Australia. Roycroft also competed in the next two Olympics, showing similar grit to win a bronze medal, and teaming up with his son Wayne. Then as a 61-year-old he represented Australia with his two sons in the 1976 Montreal games.

GC*

See **LAVIS, NEALE**; **MORGAN, LAWRENCE**; **ROYCROFT, WILLIAM**.

Ethnic Influences

Many of the early immigrants to Australia retained an emotional attachment to the mother country, and British sports, as part of their cultural baggage, provided a link with home in an alien environment. In seeking to participate in their traditional sports the British were no different from later immigrants such as the Germans, who came to Australia in the wake of the European religious and political troubles of the late 1840s and brought with them skittles, crossbows, target rifle-shooting, and gymnastics. The British, however, were more numerous, and it was their activities that dominated the Australian sporting calendar.

Some immigrants wished to replicate more than British sporting activities. To the colonial élite certain sporting activities had implications for social status: they displayed themselves to the community at large by participating in field sports, by offering patronage to local race meetings, and by wearing the appropriate costume.

Indeed such was their determination to emulate their counterparts 'back home' that occasionally British practice was adopted even when it was unsuited to Australian conditions, such as the wearing of heavy morning suits to hot and dusty race meetings. The British influence was felt more indirectly, too, as the colonial élite sent its scions 'home' for an education that was cultural as much as anything and of which games were an important part. Perhaps the most outstanding, if exceptional, example is T. W. Wills who was educated at Rugby but modified his experiences to create Australian football upon his return to Melbourne. A less well known but typical example is H. M. Hamilton. Born to a Parramatta landowner in 1854, he went first to Britain to be educated, later to the Continent. At the University of Edinburgh he played rugby union for Scotland in 1874–75 and on his return to Sydney, where he eventually became a judge, he continued his interest in sport by membership of the Royal Sydney Golf Club.

The cultural continuity was reinforced by the continued flow of immigrants from Britain. Among them were the Muscular Christians, imported educators who transmitted to young Australians the games ethos and its emphasis on the character-building aspects of manly sports. Other immigrants brought with them the new sports of athletics, tennis, cycling, and golf, the last very much influenced by Scots such as Professor Horatio Carslaw who came to Australia in 1903 as professor of mathematics at Sydney University. As a Scot, he quickly became active in golf circles, one of the many whose presence helped establish not only the game itself but the cultural patterns of participation and behaviour surrounding it.

The most extensive non-British immigrant influence on Australian sport dates from the time of the mass European migration of the late 1940s into the early 1960s as refugees from war-torn Europe sought new lives, and later many thousands, often from Southern Europe, were brought in to man factories. As ethnic social clubs grew up, so did the traditional sports of these peoples, among them handball, bocce, volleyball, but above all soccer. It is to soccer that most people turn when the question of ethnic sports influence is raised, and it is fair to argue that the images of soccer have dictated the images of ethnicity in the minds of too many Anglo-Celtic Australians. While the sport reached Australia before the end of the nineteenth century, it was the 1950s before it attained significant status in numbers of participants and spectators. By the end of the 1950s the organisation of soccer was thoroughly grounded in an ethnic base of Italian, Greek, Spanish, French, Yugoslavian, Dutch, and other

nationalities. In some larger communities such divisions were extended by internal cultural separation, the most notorious being that between Serbian and Croatian interests. The 1990 Pratten Park disturbance, in which Serbian and Croatian supporters clashed in an extension of European political rivalries, was simply the latest in a series of such conflicts of cultural identity which have done so much to influence Australian attitudes about the different cultural attitudes in their midst. Soccer insiders argue that issues of ethnicity dictate organisational and political reform, selection procedures, and even the style of play. Leadership of clubs, associations, and the national body have swung as much upon creating cultural vote banks as upon a deep knowledge of and love for soccer. In short, the game has often been thought by outsiders to exhibit all the doubtful qualities of non-traditional Australian groups.

As a result, reform in soccer has often been primarily concerned with wider ethnic issues. Should ethnic team names like Olympic, Croatia, Windmills, and the rest be abandoned in the interests of assimilation, or should they be protected in the interests of multiculturalism? Because Australian attitudes towards ethnicity have shifted so constantly, so have attitudes towards the cultural role of soccer. And as Australia becomes increasingly multicultural as it approaches the twenty-first century, this is unlikely to change dramatically.

But soccer is not the only sport which raises the question of Australian cultural identity at the end of the twentieth century. Basketball is the country's fastest-growing sport and its foreign influence is unmistakable in its composition, organisational structure, and social penetration. All teams have some black American imports, a number of whom are now naturalised Australians. Basketball was the first sport in Australia to encourage wholesale private ownership of teams. And thanks to television and the National Basketball League, Australians are familiar with concepts such as 'dee-fense' and American basketball clothing (especially shoes and boots) becoming part of an Australian subculture. Australia's predominantly British cultural legacy is being challenged by this strong influence from America. On the Australia Day holiday of 1991 the ABC broadcast the Super Bowl final live, complete with a local American host. Meanwhile, the Australian Baseball League is under way, complete with substantial American backing in a bid to succeed where Albert Spalding largely failed a century earlier.

If Australian culture is becoming denationalised, as many critics argue, then sport must be seen as a major agency in that shift. In that sense there is an inherent logic to it, because Australian sport and its cultural position has always been calibrated by a foreign trend, an 'ethnicity' of some kind at every given point.

BS

See **Basketball**; **Bocce**; **Crowd Disorder**; **Golf**; **Gymnastics**; **Soccer**; **Volleyball**.

EVE, JAMES S. W., MBE (1899–1978), grandson of Fred Cavill, gave a lifetime of service to the administration of amateur sport in Australia. Eve was honorary secretary-treasurer of the Australian Olympic Federation from 1924 to 1947, and held the same office in the Australian British Commonwealth Games Association from its inception in 1929 until 1969. In 1938 he served as organising secretary for the British Empire Games held in Sydney, and was a member of the organising committee for the 1956 Olympic Games in Melbourne. Eve was a life member of the NSW Sports Club, the Australian Olympic Federation, and the British Commonwealth Games Association of Australia.

KM

See **British Empire Games 1938 (Sydney)**; CAVILL **Family**.

EVE, RICHMOND CAVILL (1901–69), born Parramatta, won the plain high dive at the 1924 Paris Olympics—the only Australian to win this event—with a perfect swallow dive. He also finished fifth in the springboard fancy diving. Dick Eve had a strong swimming background. His mother came from the famous Cavill family and his father was manager of the Manly Baths and later the Spit Baths. But Eve had little coaching and virtually taught himself to dive. He won Australia's first official diving championship in 1921 and was successful in the four following years. After accepting the job of managing the Manly Baths in 1925 Eve was stripped of his amateur status by the Australian Swimming Union. He was active in the lifesaving movement and figured in numerous rescues at Manly Beach. He was inducted into the Sport Australia Hall of Fame in 1985.

RC

See CAVILL **Family**; **Diving**; ROSE, IAIN MURRAY.

F

FAIRBAIRN, STEPHEN (1862–1938), rowing coach, was born in Melbourne but made his name in England. Educated at Cambridge, where he rowed four times in the Oxford–Cambridge race, Fairbairn worked in England from 1904, coaching Jesus College, Cambridge, with great success. Fairbairn rejected his contemporaries' belief in purity of style, pioneering a psychological approach to coaching: 'It has all got to come from inside you, laddies.' Despite his many detractors, his coaching and popularising of the sport made him one of rowing's greatest figures. He founded the head-of-the-river race on the Thames, an idea copied worldwide. His ashes rest near Jesus College.

SB

FAIRWEATHER, SIMON (1969–) won the Fédération International de Tir à L'Arc Target Archery Championship of the World in Poland in August 1991, breaking the Soviet and Korean dominance of this event. Later in the year he won the Seventh Asian Cup. Fairweather trained virtually on his own on a farm on the outskirts of a small country town, Strathalbyn, in SA until 1989 when he won a scholarship to the SA Sports Institute, enabling him to train full-time. He took up archery in 1984, won his first tournament in the same year, and by 1987 had won the Australian Open National Target Archery Championship. He competed in the 1988 Olympics when he was the youngest ever Australian Olympic archer. He was placed sixteenth, the best result for an Australian in Olympic archery.

DMcL

See **Archery**.

FAMECHON, JEAN PIERRE ('Johnny') (1945–) was the third Australian to win an undisputed world boxing championship. Born in France, Famechon emigrated to Australia with his family when he was 5. Both his father, André, and uncle, Ray, were professional boxers, the latter being a European featherweight champion. Famechon began his career as a professional in 1961 at the age of 16. Three years and twenty-two fights later, he beat Ollie Taylor to win the Australian featherweight title. His defeat of John O'Brien added the Commonwealth crown to his record and opened the way for a world-title fight against José Legra of Spain whom Famechon defeated narrowly on points in London in 1969. Famechon's defence

of his title six months later was a controversial one. After surviving three knock-downs Famechon won the fight by a mere point only because his Japanese opponent, Harada, demanded a recount after the American referee ruled a draw. He won by a knockout in a re-match in 1970. Two fights later he lost his title on points to former featherweight Vincenti Salvidar and retired a few weeks later. In 1991 Famechon spent several weeks in a coma after being knocked down by a motor vehicle and is currently fighting paralysis of the legs and left side.

GC*

See **Boxing**; PALMER, AMBROSE.

FARINA, FRANK (1964–), born of Italo-Australian parents, became Australia's most successful football export by signing for Bari in the Italian first division, the most demanding and highest-paying competition in world football. Farina owed much of his success to his appearances in Australia's colours, first as a young Socceroo and then in the senior team where, until 1991, he was selected for thirty-four full internationals and scored 9 goals. Well-built, brave, immensely quick, and opportunistic in front of goal, he was a hero in the domestic game before moving to Europe in 1988. His passport was two superb goals scored in Australia's 1988 Olympic campaign—the goal which ensured Australia's qualification against NZ and the winner in Australia's triumph over Yugoslavia in the finals. He was leading scorer in the Belgian league, with 24 goals in 1989–90 with Club Bruges.

LM

FARMER, GRAHAM ('Polly'), MBE (1935–), born Perth, was an Aboriginal footballer. Considered a half-caste, he was sent to Sister Kate's Orphanage to become 'assimilated'. Despite a shortened leg he was possibly the greatest of ruckmen, in a career which spanned 392 games in WA and Victoria. Farmer developed handball's offensive potential in masterly fashion; his recruitment by Geelong in 1962 was also an important early stimulus to the surge in expensive player transfers. An All-Australian on three occasions, Farmer won ten best and fairest awards at three clubs, two premierships as captain-coach of East Perth and Tassie, as well as the Sandover and Simpson (and nearly Brownlow) Medals. With Geelong rover Bill Goggin, 'Polly' forged a partnership as famous as his handball practice targets, which included rubbish bins and half-open car windows. Since his retirement he has been a strong supporter of Aboriginal participation in WA football.

DS

See **Aborigines in Sport**.

FARMER, KENNETH WILLIAM GEORGE (1910–82), born Adelaide, was known in the 1930s as 'Football's Bradman'. Like 'the Don' the Depression years were times of plenty for Farmer as the mercurial North Adelaide full forward notched up 100 goals in eleven successive years, from 1930 to 1940—a feat unparalleled in Australian rules football. Farmer's most remarkable effort was his personal tally of 23–6, from North Adelaide's 26–11, against West Torrens in 1940. In his career he kicked 1419 goals in thirteen league seasons and a further 71 goals in seventeen interstate matches. Farmer later became a successful league coach, leading North Adelaide to two premierships in 1949 and 1952.

BW

FARRELLY, BERNARD ('Midget') (1944–), born Paddington, Sydney, was the first Australian to win a major surfboard-riding title, the Tenth International Surfing Championships at Makaha, Hawaii, on New Year's Day 1963. This contest, organised by the prestigious Waikiki Surf Club, was considered the unofficial world championships. In May 1964 he won the first official World Championships at Manly, Sydney, in a contest organised by the newly formed Australian Surfriders' Association. He was placed second in two other world championships (1968 and 1970) and won two Australian national titles (1964 and 1965). Farrelly symbolised the Australian surfing movement in the early 1960s. As president of the NSW and the Australian Surfriders' Association he was a leading figure in the organisation of surfers and the sport. In the late 1950s and early 1960s, conservative Australia frowned upon surfers. The individuality of the sport and its close association with the new morality of pleasure and self-expression threatened established social values. This was particularly so when compared to the humanitarian and apparently structured and disciplined activities of the surf lifesaving clubs. Farrelly pressed surfers to mobilise and organise against the hostile Australian Surf Life Saving Association, municipal councils, and the press. His win at Makaha transformed local media opinion: national pride was focused on the Australian who defeated the Hawaiians at the sport they invented. Thus under Farrelly's leadership there was a positive reappraisal of surfing.

DB

See **Surfing**.

FARR-JONES, NICK (1962–) celebrated his fiftieth rugby union Test during the 1991 World Cup and has captained Australia with distinction. He made his reputation as a scrumhalf on the Grand Slam Wallaby tour to the British Isles in 1984, displacing Phillip Cox as the Australian Test player. A fierce cover defender and a noted passer of the ball, he ranks among the finest Australia has produced in his position, along with Syd Malcolm, Cyril Burke, Des Connor, Ken Catchpole, and John Hipwell. His career was enhanced by having five-eighths such as Mark Ella and Michael Lynagh. Perhaps his main features were his strength and robustness, which sometimes had him acting like a third breakaway, and his unyielding leadership qualities, which were vital in Australia's 1991 World Cup victory.

RH and MH

Federation Cup 1970 (Perth). The idea of a contest for women players akin to the Davis Cup had long been advocated by Australian Nell Hopman. The inaugural event was conducted in 1963. Australia's second victory on home soil came when the WA Lawn Tennis Association hosted the competition at the picturesque Royal King's Park Tennis Club in Perth in 1970. The world's leading tennis-players from twelve nations took part. The fine performance of the Australian team swelled the crowds to make it a profitable venture. In the final Evonne Goolagong and Margaret Court had singles wins over Britain's Virginia Wade and Ann Jones. Court and Lesley Hunt then combined to defeat Wade and Winnie Shaw in the doubles.

HCJP

FEIFER, KARL (1973–) was born in Subiaco, WA, with a deformed foot which was amputated at birth. With the aid of prosthesis, he played Australian rules football in the Little League, swam, and was a champion athlete by the age of 12. After a successful WA sports festival, Feifer was selected for the Pan Pacific School Games in 1988 where he won three gold and one bronze medal. An all-round athlete, Feifer's events included the 100, 200, and 400 metres, long jump, discus, javelin, shot putt, weightlifting, and pentathlon. He set a world record and four national records at the 1990 Australian Amputee Games. However, the highlight of his career to date was his winning of three gold and two silver medals, including the breaking of two world records, at the World Championships for the Disabled in Holland in 1990. In 1991 Feifer was voted Sportsman of the Year at the National Aboriginal Sports Awards.

CT and PT

See **Aborigines in Sport**.

FELTHAM, ENID (1922–) has given outstanding service to girls in the teaching of calisthenics in Victoria. She founded Regent Calisthenic College in 1939 and taught there for over fifty years. She began teaching in 1937, when she was herself a champion calisthenist. She was a foundation member of the Victorian Calisthenics Teachers Association in 1959, and became a life member. In striving to codify practice and to raise standards in calisthenics, she published a *Handbook of Basic Calisthenics*, and has contributed significantly over the years to the training of young teachers. Her club has made several overseas tours, and generated interest in calisthenics, particularly in the USA. She has insisted that calisthenics is for all, not just a talented élite, and has consistently produced teams which have dominated the competition circuit through the thoroughness of their preparation.

RO

Fencing

The first fencing club in Australia was formed in 1912 in Sydney. It disbanded the next year and Frank Stuart started the Sydney Swords, still the longest-running club in the country. The Australian Amateur Fencing Federation was established in 1948, and events at national open championships include women's foil and épée, and men's sabre, épée and foil. Age-group events for boys and girls are also held. Ivan Lund and Greg Benko have both represented Australia at four Olympic Games, with Benko's sixth place in 1976 the best performance by an Australian. Helen Smith has won nine individual Australian titles, and Alex Martonffy captured the national sabre championship nine times between 1952 and 1969. Nearly 300 competitors from thirty countries came to Melbourne in 1979 for the first world championships to be held in the southern hemisphere. The sport has been strengthened by immigrants, particularly Hungarians, who arrived after the Second World War.

KM

See **LUND, IVAN**.

FENECH, JEFF (1964–), the 'Marrickville Mauler', winner of three boxing world titles, was the sixth child of battling Maltese-born parents who emigrated to Australia in 1951. Born in Sydney, Fenech learned to scrap and survive on the streets of working-class Marrickville and St Peters. At 17 he found his way to the Newtown Police Citizens Youth Club run by Johnny Lewis, who became his mentor and manager, providing fatherly reassurance and shrewd tactical and business advice. Fenech suffered a major disappointment at the 1984 Olympics when the quarterfinal decision of the judges (3–2 in his favour) was overturned by the jury. After turning professional, he cap-

tured the Australian super-flyweight title and then the NSW bantamweight title. In 1985 Fenech defeated Satashi Shingaki to claim the International Boxing Federation bantamweight title and became world champion within six months of turning professional. After several impressive wins against highly rated boxers Fenech took nine months off from boxing because of injuries to his fists. He gained the World Boxing Council (WBC) super-bantamweight crown in 1987 after a fourth-round knock-out of Samart Payakarun. A year later he survived a bone-rattling uppercut from Puerto Rican Victor Callejas to score a tenth-round knock-out and take the WBC featherweight crown. After defending his title on three occasions, Fenech retired from boxing and played a few games for the second-grade Parramatta rugby league side. Returning to the ring he defeated Mexican Mario Martinez in November 1989. Many considered that Fenech was unlucky to only draw against Azumah Nelson when attempting to win a fourth world title in 1991, but he was soundly defeated by Nelson in a return bout in March 1992.

GC*

See **Boxing**.

FERGUSON, ADAIR JANELLE (1955–), born Brisbane, was a good all-round sportswoman who represented Queensland in cross-country running. Ferguson began rowing at 29 with immediate success, winning various Queensland titles in her first year and her first national title a year later. She was the Australian lightweight sculls champion in 1985 and 1989, the heavyweight sculls champion in 1986, and she shared the double sculls title in 1986 and 1988. She also won the Nell Slatter Trophy on three occasions (1985, 1988, and 1990). Internationally she was world lightweight sculling champion in 1985 and Commonwealth Games lightweight champion in the following year. For Ferguson, blessed with a perfect physique for the sport, rowing came easily.

SB

See **Rowing and Sculling**.

FERRIER, JIM (1915–), golfer, born Manly, Sydney, became an American citizen in 1944. In 1931 he played in the NSW amateur event at Royal Sydney: 'Young Jim Ferrier was quite equal to the occasion and justified his entry into State golf.' That masterly understatement in the press masked the incredible achievement of a 16-year-old beating veteran Eric Apperly for the title. He then went on to compile what may well be the best all-round amateur and professional record of any Australian golfer. Ferrier won four NSW amateurs, two Australian opens, four Australian amateurs, five NSW close championships, three Queensland opens, four Queensland amateurs, was runner-up in the

British amateur, won the Chicago amateur and three American opens as an amateur: St Paul, Milwaukee, and the Miami opens. As a professional from 1940, he won numerous tournaments, including one of the 'majors', the US PGA in 1947. From 1944 to 1953, he finished in the top twenty money-winners on the American circuit. Until his retirement from competition in 1953, he stood fourth on the PGA record of money-winners—behind Ben Hogan, Sam Snead, and Byron Nelson.

CT

See **Golf**.

Field Trophy. From 1961 until 1988 the VFA conducted a second division, and the J. Field Trophy was awarded annually to that division's best and fairest player. The trophy honours one of the VFA's most productive behind-the-scenes men. Jack Field, an officer of the Taxation Department and VFA treasurer for thirty-two years, was instrumental in forming an independent umpires' board. In the twenty-seven years the trophy was awarded, four clubs have won on three occasions: Sunshine, Mordialloc, Box Hill and Waverley. Only two players, G. Bryant (Box Hill) and D. Hall (Dandenong) have won the trophy twice.

GC*

FIFA Ban on Australian Soccer. Australia was suspended from world soccer from April 1960 to July 1963 by FIFA after Australian clubs, led by Prague in Sydney from 1958, had signed overseas players without obtaining either clearances or transfers from European clubs. Players involved included Austrian stars Leo Baumgartner, Karl Jaros, Walter Tamandl, Andy Sagi, and Herbert Ninaus. With fifteen others, from either Austrian or Dutch clubs, their combined transfer fees totalled £46 000, owed mostly to F. K. Austria and S. K. Grazer. The Australian Soccer Football Association had not been a member of FIFA in the late 1950s but the ban prevented Australian teams, at club or national level, from playing against any FIFA member teams. Australia was granted affiliation with FIFA in July 1963 after the Australian Soccer Federation (ASF), formed in 1961, had negotiated and paid a reduced transfer fee total of about £18 500. The chief ASF negotiator was Victorian Theo Marmaras.

PM

Figure Skating
The National Ice Skating Association of Australia conducts national championships in singles, pairs skating, and ice dancing, as well as junior events in the same disciplines. The governing body also awards gold, silver, and bronze medals for standards achieved by figure skaters. Australia's first international medal was a bronze in pairs skating won by Elizabeth and Peter Cain at the first International Skating Union junior championships in France in 1976. Robyn Burley of Melbourne claimed the 1979 women's world professional figure skating title in Spain. A few skaters, including Sharon Burley, Reg Park, Pat Gregory, and Robyn Burley, have gone on to success in overseas professional ice shows.

KM

Film
To talk about 'Australian sport on film' is to lump together many disparate sports, screen formats, and methods of narrative organisation. Six principal formats of Australian sport on film can be discerned: the instructional or celebratory documentary; the sporting biopic; the television mini-series; the videotape collection of sporting highlights; the fiction film; and the semi-incidental adjunct to more central narrative events in films crossing a number of genres. What is clear is that sport is a significant object for film-makers of all kinds, and not least for its capacity as a symbol of (a sometimes unattractive) nationalism and masculinity.

DOCUMENTARY
The first Australian film on record was an account of the 1896 Melbourne Cup, a sports spectacle which has been shot every year since then. It considered more than just the few minutes of the formal event, giving equal attention to arrivals and departures by transport, fashion sense, and general crowd conduct. The film was shown around the country and overseas, capturing a moment for those who could not be present in a way that has become a key event in Australian workplaces over the last eighty years, most notably since regular live television transmission began in the 1960s. Equivalent turn-of-the-century races were shot in other cities (e.g. the Perth and Brisbane Cups). Again, these were often the first films made in those places. Once more, sport became the vehicle for carrying information about classes of spectator. Of course, these films of record were being put together before the era of what we now call the 'documentary', or information text, which dates formally from just half a century ago. By the time of the First World War, the Federal Government had established a film unit (now known as Film Australia) which has continued to make factual movies, often of an instructional nature. Many of them cover sports such as surf lifesaving, cricket, tennis, and so on. By the 1980s, Film Australia was well and truly influenced by the social-realist tradition of documentary film-making, and subjects such as the oft-neglected history of women's cricket came to be treated alongside 'how to' productions. Of course, it would be absurd to imply an absolute split between coaching-film texts and films of celebratory

record; both have an educational function and both tend to use role models deemed worthy of emulation. Some are of great archival significance, such as material showing Bradman at bat.

The euphoric tones of a film such as *Aussie Assault* (1984), an account of the 1983 *America*'s Cup yachting, are far from mellifluous in their sanctimonious self-congratulation. Most of this is verbal, and much of it metaphorical: boats stand for business; for commercial, personal and, ultimately, national success. Because film needs action, there is no pretence at exhaustive coverage of any particular race. Rather, shots of crew-work and the overall complexion of the contest are intercut with moral homilies and scene-setting. This, in turn, is some distance from the Australian surf movie, which continues to thrive, via its own special exhibition circuit, up and down the east coast. It is an amalgam of spectacular shots, individualised travelogues, and rock music. While films such as *Morning of the Earth* (1972) and *Crystal Voyager* (1974) have achieved very wide recognition, this genre is basically designed for a specialised, participatory audience.

Somewhere in between live television, teaching films, and movies like *Aussie Assault* comes the newsreel. Over about forty years, it preceded the main feature at Australian cinemas. Before the advent of the domestic screen this was the key mode of distributing moving images of cricket, football, athletics, tennis, swimming, and other 'national' (mostly white male) sporting concerns. Sound was usually through a voice-over recorded in the studio, rather than actuality commentary and effects. The focus was principally on élite sports. Minority or women's sports tended to be covered only for novelty value.

THE SPORTING BIOPIC

The individual screen biography has rarely been used in Australian cinema, the two significant exceptions being the feature films *Dawn!* (Fraser) from 1979 and *Phar Lap* (1983). *Dawn!* won a Writers' Guild award for Joy Cavill's screenplay, but it failed commercially and ultimately attracted Fraser's disapproval for its account of her sexuality. Conversely, *Phar Lap* is one of the highest grossing local films ever made, taking its keynote from a treatment of tensions in the Australia–US relationship and a racehorse's epic status as a symbol of the difficulties faced by a small nation trying to export its culture to a great power. The tale of *Phar Lap*'s destruction stood for much more than sport. Helen Townshend has recently co-authored a script with Evonne Cawley about the tennis-player's life. It is yet to be produced but provides ample space for a consideration of an important figure in black women's sport.

THE TELEVISION MINI-SERIES

The Kennedy-Miller organisation has been responsible for some of the most critically and commercially successful screen output in Australia. Its retelling of the famous cricket controversy, *Bodyline* (1984), covering the 1932–33 tour of Australia by the MCC, is probably the most significant 'fictional' (docu-drama) screen text in the world on cricket. Despite quibbles from those who were there and historical obsessives ('Larwood bowled faster than that') it is remarkable for its capacity to draw on a multitude of perspectives on a complex set of events. For all the temptation to turn the story into a criticism of Douglas Jardine, it typically refrains from so doing, humanising him through the character of a fictive girlfriend. This exemplifies the series' attempt to eschew easy stereotypes or parochial conclusions.

In 1987 the telemovie *The First Kangaroos* appeared. The first such co-production between Australia and the UK, it told the story of the 1908 tour of England by an Australian rugby league team. (There was some controversy in this country because the writer, lead actor, and director were not Australian.) The precedent for co-productions having been set, the following year saw *The Four-Minute Mile*, an account of the Landy–Bannister challenges of the 1950s that was reputed to be shooting on a budget in excess of $1.5 million per hour of screen time. With production under way on a mini-series covering the life of black boxer Lionel Rose, the genre was clearly strong at the end of the 1980s. Taking fact and fictionalising it had become a style for a sector of Australian screen drama that was rapidly achieving the best budgets, and highest production values, in the industry.

THE VIDEO TAPE COLLECTION OF HIGHLIGHTS

Australia has one of the highest rates of domestic video access in the world, and sporting videos have proven popular for both hire and purchase. They fall into two basic categories. First, stars take the viewer through the basics of their game, rather as they have traditionally done in books. Greg Norman on golf and Wally Lewis on rugby league offer what amount to personalised, 'live', illustrated primers. Second, videos concentrate on the particular feats of such stars, perhaps showing a selection from their finest moments. There might be 'Great Marks of Australian Rules' or, for instance, a record of the country's performance at an international event. It was only a matter of weeks after the 1990 Commonwealth Games, for example, that video highlights of Australian achievements were on sale. The marketing of that tape on TV sports shows seemed to argue that purchasing it was akin to an act of patriotism.

FICTION FILM

Racing, surfing, and Australian rules have provided the richest lode for sporting features. In the earlier decades trackside narratives were the setting for a host of thrillers and comedy thrillers such as *The Double Event* and *The Cup Winner* (both 1911), *Silks and Saddles* (1921), *Gone to the Dogs* (1939), and *Thoroughbred* (1936). *Palm Beach* (1979) and *Puberty Blues* (1982) provide the most interesting and important treatments of sport in Australian film. *Palm Beach* is Albie Thoms's critical investigation of surfing subcultures. Sydney's northern beaches are the site of misogyny, crime, recreational drug use, and a special record of a particular group's own systems of making meaning. It is given poignancy and legitimacy by the presence of former world surfing champion Nat Young in a leading role. Thoms's background as an avant-garde film-maker informs his innovative use of sound–image track relations, which see much of the dialogue semi-submerged beneath the noise of a seemingly ever-present, but seldom directly relevant, commercial radio. It is a small masterwork of social realism. Bruce Beresford's *Puberty Blues*, adapted from the reminiscences of Kathy Lette and Gabrielle Carey, two lapsed Cronulla 'surfie chicks', traces the girls' struggle for affirmation in the eyes of their parents, the boy surfers whom they adore, and themselves. Realising that they are never going to be recognised by others on acceptable terms, the girls eventually take to the surf themselves. A film that has traced the descent of a subculture into drug-induced semi-ruin concludes with one of them doing the unthinkable: riding a board in front of the boys. *Coolangatta Gold* (1984), although much criticised, is important too. It blends the relatively complex threads of an Oedipal crisis around training for an ironman race, a narrative given realistic contour by the inclusion of Grant Kenny as himself. The treatment of Australian sport and masculinity is as far-reaching as anything else achieved on screen. For all its patchiness, the film has a great deal to offer. Finally, Australian rules has been the backdrop to two significant comedies, *Salute The Great McCarthy* (1975) and *The Club* (1980). Both based on stage successes, by Barry Oakley and David Williamson respectively, they are as much about class and organisational politics as anything else, deploying sport as a metaphor to go elsewhere.

THE SEMI-INCIDENTAL REFERENCE
It is important to conclude with some reference to the many other films that use sport as a component, perhaps to build up the profile of a character, but which traverse a lot of other terrain besides, films which may only touch on sport, but use it quite critically. One thinks here of John Duigan's *The Year My Voice Broke* (1987). It establishes a young man's violence and sexuality by showing him driving a stolen car around a racecourse, dunking a girl at the local swimming hole, and playing football well. More than half a century earlier, *Kid Stakes* (1927) had underscored its point about cheerful

young urban urchins by having them play street cricket. And it is hard to conceive of *Gallipoli* (1981) without the running competition between the two men, a skill that is enshrined in Peter Weir's final telling shots of slow-motion death and synthesised music. One can also discern a genre of Australian road movies, where racing and stealing cars become signs of restless, angry youth. Examples include *The FJ Holden* (1977), *Running on Empty* (1982), *Freedom* (1982), and *Backroads* (1977).

TM*

See **Art**; **Drama**; **Literature**.

Fine Cotton Affair. Backed in a $2 million nationwide plunge, the racehorse *Fine Cotton* won the Second Commerce Novice Handicap over 1500 metres at Eagle Farm, Brisbane, on Saturday, 18 August 1984 but was disqualified when identified after the race as the much better performed *Bold Personality*, purchased just two days earlier. Five men were charged with the ring-in. The charges against John Fraser Dixon were withdrawn; Tommaso Di Luzio was found not guilty, but Robert Ray North and *Fine Cotton*'s trainer, Hayden Haitana, were sentenced to twelve months' hard labour and John Patrick Gillespie to four years' hard labour. The five, along with John Mort Green, were warned off by the Queensland Turf Club on 21 March 1986. The Australian Jockey Club inquired into betting on *Fine Cotton* in NSW and in November 1984 warned off and revoked the licences of bookmakers Bill Waterhouse, Robbie Waterhouse, Peter McCoy, and clerk Robert Hines. Warned off also were Gary and Glenis Clarke, John Gough, Ian Murray, and Father Edward Brian O'Dwyer. All were alleged to have had prior knowledge. Gough appealed successfully. Hines and Murray turned Crown witnesses. Criminal charges laid in November 1986 against McCoy and Glenis Clarke were dropped in April 1987 and those against Robbie Waterhouse, Gary Clarke, and O'Dwyer were quashed and permanently stayed on 20 May 1988.

WAE

FINGLETON, JOHN HENRY WEBB, OBE (1908–81), born Waverley, Sydney, was a cricketer who scored 1189 runs at 42.46 during eighteen Tests, once scoring 4 Test centuries in a row. He was a right-hand opening batsman, solid rather than fluent but capable of attractive aggression. Superb in the field, he often fielded close on the leg side. Commentator and author of ten cricket books, he was also a noted political journalist. Fingleton had a keen sense of humour and easy public manner which led to television exposure late in his life, much to his surprise and delight.

SG

See **Cricket**.

FISCHER, SYD was a dominant and fiercely competitive figure in Australian ocean racing who came into prominence from 1970 to the mid-1980s. He was best known as the owner-skipper of six boats, all known as *Ragamuffin*, which won every major race offshore except handicap honours in the Sydney to Hobart race—though *Ragamuffin* twice secured second place. Fischer has produced a number of *America's* Cup contenders including *Advance* (1983), *Steak'n Kidney* (1987), and *Challenge Australia* (1992). A former Sydney surfboat-rower and house carpenter, Fischer built himself an empire of development companies through effort and enterprise. He became world champion in the One Ton Cup Class which was sailed off Auckland in 1971 and participated in a number of Admiral's Cup events including the 1979 Cup which was won by Australia. Fischer won the Ampol-Australian Yachtsman of the Year Award in 1971.

RC#

FITZGERALD, LEONARD CHARLES (1929–), born Melbourne, made his league debut with Collingwood at the age of 15. A beautifully balanced footballer and champion sprinter in his youth, Fitzgerald left Collingwood in 1950, after ninety-five games, when the club failed to assist him to transfer his indentures as an apprentice plumber to another employer. Fitzgerald went on to spectacular sporting success in SA where he was appointed captain of Sturt after three games. Fitzgerald's graceful movement, powerful kicking, fine marking, and versatility enabled him to win three Magarey Medals in 1952, 1954, and 1959—the first at centre half-back, second as a ruck-rover, and third as a centre half-forward.

BW

FLACK, EDWIN (1873–1935), born England, emigrated to Australia with his family in 1878. At Melbourne Church of England Grammar School—where, appropriately for his later Olympic wins, he studied classics—'Teddy' Flack never became the school athletics champion, but in 1893, after joining the Old Melburnians, he won the Victorian and Australasian mile championships. He repeated this success a year later. After qualifying as an accountant Flack joined his father's Melbourne firm. Seeking more experience, he travelled to England in 1895 to work for the accountancy firm Price Waterhouse. Flack joined the London Athletics Club and performed well as a middle-distance and cross-country runner. When athletes from his club decided to contest the first Olympic Games in Athens, he was encouraged to join them. He won the 800 metres comfortably and was also successful in the 1500 metres. His victories were popular—he was lauded as 'the lion of Athens'—as US athletes were dominating the competition. As an Australian flag could not be found an Austrian flag was used to salute

his wins. Flack was favoured in the marathon, although he had never run further than 10 miles. He ran a fine tactical race and led at the 30 kilometre mark but had to retire with 6 kilometres to run. He was unsuccessful in his other event, tennis. Flack competed in England in 1896 and 1897 before returning to Melbourne to join the family firm. Before his trip to Athens, the English *Sporting Life* had written of Flack: 'Though hardly up to the best English form, Flack has, however, shown sufficient pace and stamina to earn for himself a distinct and meritorious place as a crosscountry runner at home.'

JAD

See **Athletics; Olympic Games**.

FLEGG, HENRY ('Jersey') (1878–1960) was rugby league's longest-serving administrator. A State representative rugby union forward in 1902, he switched to league in 1908, captaining Easts that year and in 1909. From 1910 to 1929 he was a State selector, from 1925 vice-president of the NSW Rugby League, and from 1929 to his death was its active, forthright president. From 1941 to 1960 he was chairman of the league's Australian Board of Control.

CC

See **Rugby League**.

Fleming Medal. The Bill Fleming Medal is awarded annually to the player of the year in the Victorian State (soccer) League. From its introduction in 1971 until 1989 only Tommy Cumming (Essendon-Croatia) had been a dual winner of the award. On eight occasions between 1971 and 1989 the same player won the Bill Fleming Medal and the State League's Gold Medal.

MH*

Flemington Racecourse
Flemington Racecourse in Epsom Road, Flemington, Melbourne, is one of the great racecourses in Australia. It has played a very important role in the development of Australian horse-racing, most notably as the venue for the Melbourne Cup. Originally run over 2 miles and now over 3200 metres under handicap conditions, the Melbourne Cup has become, in the course of its 130-year history, the centrepiece of Australian racing. When *Carbine* won the Cup in 1890 and £10 230 for his connections, the race was the richest handicap in the world. Cup Day has become a national festival and a peculiarly Australian celebration of national identity. Flemington on the first Tuesday in November attracts today around 96 000 people to the course and millions of viewers on television and listeners on radio. The record crowd was 120 000 in 1926.

Flemington Racecourse is run by the Victoria Racing Club (VRC) but the history of Flemington is older than that of the VRC by almost a quarter of a century. The first race meeting at Flemington was on 3–5 March 1840, just two years after the first races in Melbourne were conducted by the Melbourne Racing Club at what is now Spencer Street Railway Station. The name Flemington reputedly derived from a butcher of the area, Tom Fleming, around whose shop a small village had clustered. It might, however, have been named after Flemington Estate in Lanarkshire, Scotland, by Tom Watson, pastoralist and sportsman, in honour of his wife's father who managed the Flemington Estate. The Saltwater (now Maribyrnong) River flats provided excellent conditions and have been used ever since for racing. By December 1840 the Port Phillip Turf Club had formed and held its annual races at Flemington. In 1848 the government leased Flemington to the trustees of the Victoria Turf Club but in 1857 a rival club, the Victoria Jockey Club (VJC), was founded. Tensions and rivalry between the two clubs resulted in the demise of both, but not before the Victoria Turf Club had started the Melbourne Cup in 1861, won by *Archer*. The two clubs were replaced by the VRC, which assumed their assets and liabilities, on 9 March 1864.

On 18 March 1864, the VRC appointed R. C. Bagot as its secretary, in which position he served until his death in 1881. Bagot, an Irish immigrant in the mid-1840s who was an engineer and architect, and H. Byron Moore, his successor as VRC secretary, who served from 1881 to 1925, transformed Flemington into a first-class racecourse. Numerous improvements were begun to the racetrack itself and to the facilities for patrons and those conducting and promoting racing. For the Spring Meeting of 1865, at which the Melbourne Cup was worth 100 sovereigns, the lawns were repaired, facilities improved, and complimentary ladies' tickets were given to each club member. These moves had the intended consequences. Attendances increased dramatically and fashion has remained a part of the spring racing season. The attendance for Cup Day 1865 was 13 000, an increase of 7000 over the year before. The railway was extended as far as the course in September 1866, adding rail to road and river as ways of getting to the venue. Flemington continued to develop as a racing centre and by 1880 the Melbourne Cup was clearly established as the most important race in Australia, and Flemington as a course equalled by few and bettered by none. Over £10 000 was spent by the VRC between 1864 and 1871 in developing Flemington. This sum does not include the cost of Bagot's new grandstand, finished for the 1873 meeting. The grandstand, designed to accommodate 4000 people, was a long stand with thirteen bays and a low roof so as not to interfere with the view of patrons on the popu-

lar hill behind it. The natural setting of Flemington, with its hill sloping down to the river flats, was complemented by the planning and improvements of Bagot and Moore. They wanted every racegoer to have a good view of the whole track, a feature which has remained an important element in the continuing popularity of Flemington among racegoers.

Along with the development of Flemington went the promotion of handicap racing. Bagot and the VRC did not see horse-racing with the English perspective of the primacy of breeding and its emphasis on the classics. Racing was entertainment and handicaps provided thrilling finishes. It was no coincidence that the Cup became, under Bagot's stewardship, the greatest of Australian races. The Irish-born Bagot proved closer to the values and directions of his adopted homeland than did those who wished to emulate British models in society and racing. The ideal of the handicapper to produce a race in which all contestants have an equal chance of winning, and in which those advantaged by breeding, environment, or natural ability carry heavier burdens than those less successful became a metaphor for the egalitarian values and mythology of Australian society. The 63 000 people who attended Cup Day in 1873 reflected the attraction of Flemington and its racing. Moore continued the priorities established by the VRC in developing Flemington as a racetrack and as a venue at which spectators could enjoy good racing in very comfortable surroundings. The American writer Nat Gould described Flemington in the 1890s as 'the most complete racecourse I have seen', because of the quality and scope of its appointments. Gould marvelled at the provision of facilities for spectators and for those involved in racing: the stewards, the members' stands, the spacious Maribyrnong Stand, the extensive telegraph offices, easily visible scratching board, saddling paddock, and the flat with its free entrance (a charge of one shilling was introduced in 1913).

Flemington was not owned by the VRC when that club was formed. The land was at first in private hands and later leased to the Victoria Turf Club (VTC). In recognition of the development of Flemington by the VRC, the land (then 297 acres) was demised to the VRC under the Victoria Racing Club Act of 1871 to be maintained as a racecourse for ninety-nine years from 8 January 1872 at an annual rental of 'two peppercorns'. A further ninety-nine-year lease was granted as from August 1958 at a rental of one shilling if required. Flemington at present covers 312 acres. The course circuit is 2300 metres with a home straight of 453 metres. The steeplechase track is 2029 metres and includes a variable number of fences. The 'straight six' chute joins the home straight, making, as its name suggests, a straight-sprint course of 1200 metres. Modern developments have included the new Members' Grandstand in 1925, the multiple training tracks, totalisator betting, the photo finish and steward's films since 1946, the swabbing of racehorses, and the continued upgrading of the track and facilities. Notable among the latter were the Lawn Stand built in 1960, the modern Hill Stand in 1979, and the Prince of Wales Stand erected in 1985.

Flemington is famous for its great tradition of staging races. In addition to the Melbourne Cup (established 1861), it is the venue for the Victoria Derby (1855), the Grand National Hurdle (1881), the Grand National Steeplechase (1866), the VRC St Leger (first series began in 1850, second in 1857), the VRC Oaks (1861), and the Australian Cup (1863). Flemington is celebrated for its sprinting races such as the Newmarket Handicap. The Newmarket, first held in 1874, is run down the famous 'straight six' furlong course and is one of the most prestigious sprint races in the country. A testing course and a superior wet weather track, Flemington is widely recognised as providing an equal chance to horses leading or coming from behind, over all ranges of distance. The design and spaciousness of the racetrack have long been among the important factors in the popularity of racing at Flemington.

WAE

See **Melbourne Cup**.

FLETCHER, JOHN WALTER (1847–1918), born England, was the 'father of soccer'. The son of a barrister, educated at Cheltham College and at Pembroke College, Oxford, Fletcher was a keen sportsman, acquiring an Oxford 'blue' in athletics. He emigrated to Australia in late 1875 and established Coreen College in Sydney in 1876. Under the press pseudonym 'CC' he advocated soccer's establishment in 1877 but the Wanderers, Australia's first club, was not formed until 1880. Fletcher was the club's first secretary. He then began a club with his Coreen College students in 1881 and established the (NSW) English Football Association in 1882. Fletcher moved to the Blue Mountains in 1884 and established Katoomba College, teams from which played from 1885 to 1889. Besides soccer, Fletcher was also a pioneer of lawn tennis, playing the game in 1875 while assistant master at H. E. Southey's Mittagong school, Oaklands. Friendship with fellow members of the exclusive Union Club in Sydney led to his involvement in the foundation of the Australian Golf Club, the nation's oldest, in 1882. It was Fletcher's wife, formerly Ann Marian Clarke, who presented the embroidered velvet bag in which cricket's famed Ashes were taken to England in 1883. Fletcher joined the Bar in 1893, became a police magistrate in 1899, retired in 1914, and died in Sydney.

PM

See **Soccer**.

FLINTOFF-KING, DEBBIE (1960–   ), born Kew, Melbourne, is a hard-working athlete who, after early interests in netball and the heptathlon, steadily developed supremacy in the demanding 400 metres hurdles event. After Commonwealth gold medals in 1982 and 1986, Flintoff-King competed in Europe in 1987 where her powerful and determined running matured as a result of her intense dedication and the careful coaching of her husband, Phil King. Her desire for gold at Seoul in 1988 was jeopardised by physical and personal setbacks which were overcome in a gritty last-stride victory in Olympic record time.

AB

See **Athletics**.

FOLEY, LARRY (1851–1917) was Australia's first great boxer, never losing a fight, and becoming known as the 'Father of Australian Boxing'. Born into an Irish Catholic family near Bathurst, he developed into a brawling larrikin, a member of a gang which terrorised sailors in Sydney's Rocks area. Foley had some celebrated bouts with Sandy Ross, Protestant heavyweight champion. The first clash between the two lasted 2 hours and 40 minutes before the referee declared a draw after seventy-one rounds. Foley knocked out Ross in a re-match later in the year. Foley's 1879 contest against tough-talking Englishman Abe Hicken attracted wide interest. As prize-fighting was outlawed in Victoria, the bout was staged in southern NSW. Special trains and coaches brought fans from Sydney and Melbourne to see Foley win a torrid affair. Between 1866 and 1879 Foley won twenty-two bare-knuckle fights and claimed to be Australia's first heavyweight champion of the gloved era—all except two of his fights were bare-knuckle events. Foley established a boxing academy in Sydney known as the Iron Pot, where he trained boxers including 'Young Griffo' and Bob Fitzsimmons.

GC*

See **Boxing**.

FOOT, ROBERT F. (1932–   ), volleyball referee, administrator, and coach, was the longest-serving president of the Australian Volleyball Federation (AVF) from 1966 to 1975. A foundation member of the AVF Referees' Commission in 1969, his duties as a referee extended from national to international competitions including the role of head of the Australian Referee Delegation at international championships. Bob Foot was appointed president of the Oceania Volleyball Federation from 1972 to 1974. He also trained the Australian national youth teams for championships in NZ (1976) and Hawaii (1978). He was awarded life membership of the AVF in recognition of his services to the sport.

IF

Football

Football takes several major forms in Australia. **Australian rules football** (often referred to as Australian rules or, in many quarters, simply as football) is a game invented in Australia in which the ball can be kicked and punched but not passed by hand as in either of the rugby codes. It originated in the late 1850s and established itself as a major sport in Victoria, SA, and WA during the third quarter of the nineteenth century. **Rugby union** football (generally known as rugby union or simply union) was imported from Britain in the 1860s and became the main code for a while in both Queensland and NSW. In 1907, however, **rugby league** emerged as a breakaway sport and soon became the main football code in NSW and also in Queensland, though much later. Although the methods of scoring are the same, league has two less players per team and the rules have been formulated to promote a different style of play from union. **Association football** (always now referred to as **soccer** in Australia) was also imported from Britain. It became formalised in the 1880s in NSW and spread to the other colonies over the next two decades. Fuller histories of each code can be found elsewhere in this volume.

WV

See **Australian Rules Football**; **Rugby League**; **Rugby Union**; **Soccer**.

Footscray Football Club Community Fights Back. Footscray had not performed particularly well, on or off the field, during the 1970s and 1980s. Its season-ticket sales had declined, its local football arena had not been significantly upgraded, and the threat of insolvency had accompanied a growing indebtedness. Thus, as part of a rationalisation programme, the VFL announced in September 1989 that Footscray would be merged with another local league club. The response of the Footscray community defied all expectations. Local supporters organised rallies at which thousands of fans voiced indignation against bureaucratic administrators who were consigning their club to oblivion. Enthusiastic fund-raising efforts saw the modest financial contributions of working-class supporters swelled by those of local businessmen, and the Footscray City Council committed substantial expenditure to improving the facilities at the Footscray football ground. Consequently, the VFL capitulated and agreed that the merger would be called off. What saved the Footscray Football Club from extinction was the realisation that it was vital to a sense of community in the western suburbs. The football team was seen as providing role models for youth in a depressed social and economic environment as well as being a source of pride, entertainment, and identification for local residents. In addition, a revolt against the in-creasing commercialisation of sports generated support from fans of other football clubs and in the media.

RS

FORBES, DAVID (1934–) was involved in top-level yachting competition for over twenty years. He was ten times an Australian champion (in the Star, 5.5 metre, Soling, and Etchell classes), an Olympic gold-medallist in 1972 in the Star class, a world champion in the 5.5 metre class, three times an Olympian, and twice a member of an *America*'s Cup challenge. With a family waterfront home at Sydney's Pittwater, Forbes gravitated towards sailing and other water sports. He met his future wife, June, also a sailing enthusiast, at the Palm Beach Sailing Club. She crewed for him as well as sailing in her own right and won the National Open Star Class Championship in 1973–74 with her husband as a crew member. Forbes dominated the Star class, winning five successive national championships from 1964 to 1969, and competed in this event in the 1968 Olympics, finishing sixth. With John Anderson, Forbes raced consistently in the seven heats of the event in the 1972 Olympics to win the gold medal. He also competed in the 1976 Olympics in the Soling class, finishing eleventh. Earlier, in 1970, Forbes won the world championships in the 5.5 metre class. A company director of Shelleys Soft Drinks, Forbes has been captain of the Royal Prince Alfred Yacht Club. In 1986 he became a director of the Ocean Racing Club of Australia and was inducted into the NSW Hall of Fame.

RH and MH

FORD, MICHELLE JAN (1962–), born Sans Souci, Sydney, showed early promise, swimming the fastest-ever 100 yards freestyle in the world for a 12-year-old. During her career Ford won six Australian individual championships (200 metres butterfly, 200, 800, and 1500 metres freestyle) and one relay championship, and competed in two Commonwealth Games in 1978 in Edmonton (one gold, two silver, and two bronze medals) and 1982 in Brisbane (one gold and one silver medal). She swam in two Olympic Games, in 1976 at Montreal and 1980 at Moscow. It was at the Moscow Games that she reached her peak, winning a gold medal in the 800 metres freestyle and a bronze in the 200 metres butterfly. Ford did not compete in her third Olympic Games because of a clash with officialdom.

RH and MH

See **Sport Australia Awards**; **Swimming**.

FOSTER, DAVID (c.1957–), a Tasmanian woodchopper, stands about 196 centimetres tall and weighs around 150 kilograms but has the agility of a cat—an essential ingredient in this sport which requires hitting a log two times per second. His father, George, was also a champion axeman. David Foster, who was given a tomahawk to play with as soon as he could lift it, began competing in 1976. He is as far ahead of the world as any champion might be, finishing first 840 times, and has won 670 championships. Since 1979, when he won the first world championship, he has collected 105 world titles—yet he believes that he is six or seven years from his peak. Foster has achieved little recognition outside Tasmania—Australia's top woodchopping State—and little money. His success helped him to become public relations officer with Associated Pulp and Paper Mills.

PD

FRANCIS, BEV (1960–), a body-builder and powerlifter, began her sporting career at college. Attracted to weights, she excelled at shot put and represented Oceania in the 1979 World Cup. Later she began competitive powerlifting, using her own training style and focusing on bench presses and squats. By 1985 she had won six successive world powerlifting championships. She then concentrated on body-building, largely teaching herself from magazines, to build up a powerful physique and became a symbol of the muscular female. After moving to New York she published a guide to body-building.

SW

FRANCOU, JULIE (1957–) played with the Kiwi Netball Club in Whyalla, SA, at the age of 9. An extremely versatile netballer, Francou played as centre, wing attack, and wing defence for SA and Australia in open competition for over ten years. Although selected for the World Netball Tournament in 1975, she did not tour; but she did play in the next series in the West Indies and captained the Australian team to become undefeated world champions in 1983. This year was a great one for Francou: teams in which she played did not lose a game at club, national, or international level. She was the Australian vice-captain for the World Games in 1985.

PB and IJ

See **ROBRAN, BARRIE**.

FRASER, DAWN LORRAINE (1937–), born Balmain, Sydney, was selected in 1988 as Australia's greatest female athlete. She was the first swimmer to win the same event in three consecutive Olympic Games and the first female to swim the 100 metres freestyle in under 1 minute. She held thirty-nine world records (twenty-seven individual and twelve team); she was also the 100 metres freestyle record-holder for sixteen years, from December 1956 until January 1972. She amassed thirty Australian championships (twenty-three individual and seven team), eight Olympic medals

(four gold and four silver), and eight British Empire and Commonwealth Games medals (six gold and two silver), as well as winning the highest number of Olympic medals of any Australian athlete, male or female, in any sport. Born into a poor family, the youngest of eight children, Fraser captured the imagination of the Australian public because of her resistance to authority, her affable roguishness, and sometimes larrikin behaviour. Her career was dogged by controversy, culminating in her ten-year ban after the Tokyo Olympics of 1964 when, along with others, she attempted to 'souvenir' a flag from the Emperor's Palace. Despite clashes with officialdom, Fraser always had more supporters than critics. A daffodil, a rose, and an orchid were named after her, and the Elkington Park Baths were renamed the Dawn Fraser Pool. More books have been written about her than any other female swimmer, and a movie was made of her life. With her working-class background, she offered proof to many of the egalitarian nature of Australian sport. In recent years she has competed in masters competitions around the world. In 1988 she was elected to the NSW Parliament, where she represented the seat of Balmain until 1991.

RH and MH

See **GALLAGHER, HARRY**; **Sport Australia Hall of Fame**; **Swimming**.

FRASER, NEALE (1933–), born Melbourne, won his first Grand Slam singles in 1959 with a victory in the US Open. The following year he took the Wimbledon crown from compatriot Rod Laver and then successfully defended his US title, again against Laver. In 1960, however, after holding several advantages Fraser lost the Australian Open final in a five-set battle with Laver. Some observers claim that Fraser, who ranked number one in Australia between 1959 and 1961, had been the best-credentialled player never to win his own nation's open. A tall left-hander with a powerful serve, he believed that it was imperative to get a high percentage of first serves into play. His attacking game, aided by a strong forehand, enabled Fraser to cloak his much weaker backhand. By the time Fraser made his last Davis Cup appearance for Australia in 1963 he had already forsaken several lucrative offers to turn professional. He was destined in 1970 to become the non-playing captain of Australia's Davis Cup team. The success of the Australian team in 1973, 1977, 1983, 1986, and 1988 ensured that Fraser retained a high profile in Australian tennis. In concert with his brother John, who also held a national ranking, Neale was prominent as a tennis administrator as well as being highly regarded as a coach.

HCJP

See **Lawn Tennis**.

52 Drama and sport in Australia have had a long and
interesting association. David Williamson's play, *The
Club*, celebrated Australian Rules and Melbourne
football 'tribalism'.

53 Ethnic influences have partly shaped the patterns of
Australian sport, as can be seen in Cuthbert Charles
Clarke's drawing in 1861 of *The Caledonian Games* at
Castlemaine, Victoria.

54 Mark Ella played in twenty-five tests and captained
Australia in ten of these.

55 Graham 'Polly' Farmer is regarded as having
introduced the attacking potential of handball into the VFL
when he was recruited by the Geelong club in 1962.

56 Karl Feifer, born with a deformed foot that was amputated at birth, won numerous gold and silver medals in track and field events at the World Disabled Championships in The Netherlands in 1990.

57 An athlete with paraplegia competing in the 800m track event at the Paralympic Games, the Olympic equivalent for athletes with disabilities, which have been held each Olympic year since 1960.

When you support Special Olympics, we all win.

58 Special Olympics is a sports training programme, created by the Joseph P. Kennedy Foundation in the USA, which provides sports competition for those with an intellectual disability.

VICTORY CEREMONY
====================

400M HURDLES (WOMEN)

1 FLINTOFF-KING   AUS 53.17

2 LEDOVSKAIA T.   URS 53.18

3 FIEDLER ELLEN   GDR 53.63

59 Debbie Flintoff-King and the scoreboard at the 1988 Seoul Olympics highlighting her win.

FROST, VIC (1941–), born Wollongong, NSW, lived at nearby Dapto for much of his youth. His introduction to horses came at the age of 12 when his father, who supplied pit ponies to the nearby mines, gave a pony to Vic, who later rode in local show events. Frost's successful harness-racing career soon followed. His first Harold Park win came with *Galway Boy* in 1957 when he was still only 16. In later decades he became one of Sydney's most successful trainer-drivers. In one of the highlights of his career he finished fourth when representing Australia in the World Drivers' Championship conducted over a series of races held in 1972 in the USA and Canada.

    JO'H

FULTON, BOB ('Bozo') (1947–), a rugby league player, was born in Warrington, Lancashire, his family emigrating to Unanderra, NSW, when he was still young. An unpredictable and skilful three-quarter and five-eighth, Fulton played 213 games for Manly-Warringah between 1965 and 1976 before ending his career with Easts. His brilliance and two tries secured Manly a win in a torrid 1973 Grand Final against Cronulla. Fulton toured Great Britain twice and NZ once as a Kangaroo and played in four World Cups. He captained the 1978 Kangaroos, securing a 2–1 series win. Since retiring as a player in 1979, Fulton has been a successful coach for Easts, Manly, and Australia.

    BC*

G

'Gabba'. The Woolloongabba ground in Brisbane, affectionately known as the 'Gabba', is Queensland's equivalent of the Melbourne and Sydney Cricket Grounds. Although the Queensland Cricket Association (QCA) was formally organised in 1876 and Queensland had played its first intercolonial cricket match as early as 1869, it was not until 1889 that the QCA had secured a ground, the Albert Sports Ground. In 1895 twelve hectares of land at Woolloongabba were formally dedicated as the Brisbane Cricket Ground, and the first ground management committee were Messrs W. H. Hastead, Pring Roberts, J. V. Francis, and John A. Clark. The first cricket match played at the 'Gabba' was on 19 December 1896, between teams representing Parliament, captained by the Hon. T. J. Byrnes, and the Press, captained by F. W. Ward. The match, twelve-a-side, was a draw, with each team getting 61 runs. The first international match played at the 'Gabba' was in 1897 against A. E. Stoddart's English team, while the inaugural match against another State was later in that year against a combined Queensland-NSW team. The first recognised international match was played there in 1899, while the ground's initial Test match was held in 1931, against South Africa. Some particularly historic events at the 'Gabba' include Bradman bowled for a duck by Eddie Gilbert; Englishman Eddie Paynter coming out of hospital to score a crucial 83 to win a Test for his country; the end of Ian Meckiff's career after the umpire called him four times for 'chucking'; and the famous 'tied' Test in 1960 against the West Indies. The 'Gabba' has been used for other sports as well. In the late 1890s cycling and tennis were held there and pony-racing in 1900. Over the years, rugby union, rugby league, lacrosse, soccer, Australian rules, and greyhound-racing have used the venue. One of the most memorable occasions was in 1932, when the rugby league Test between Australia and England attracted a record 76 204 spectators and was termed the 'Battle of Brisbane' because of its ferocious nature. Australia won 15–6. The Sir Leslie Wilson Stand and the Clem Jones Stand were built in 1975, and the Sir Gordon Chalk and Arthur Dibden buildings later provided a wider range of facilities for the ground.

RH and MH

Gaelic Athletic Association of Australasia. In the early 1840s there was a newspaper report of a form of Gaelic football in SA, and it is acknowledged that similar games were played on the goldfields of Victoria in the 1850s. However there is a lack of evidence for many organised games of hurling or football at the interstate level until challenge matches between the Irish of Melbourne and Sydney in the 1920s and 1930s. Associations were formed in Victoria and NSW to control and organise local competitions. In 1963 an association was formed in Adelaide, and in Perth and Brisbane soon after. A tri-State carnival was held in Melbourne between NSW, Victoria, and SA in 1971. At a meeting convened in Sydney in June 1974, representatives from NSW, SA, Victoria, and WA formed the Gaelic Athletic Association of Australia to promote, control, and organise games on a national basis. Despite the fact that fewer people were emigrating from Ireland, the standard and general conduct of games improved, especially in football. Australians of Irish and non-Irish parentage have been encouraged to play the game and, with the affiliation of the Auckland Gaelic Association, the name of the association changed to its present title of the Gaelic Athletic Association of Australasia. There have been several tours of Australasia by teams from Ireland since 1968.

GR and IJ

GALLAGHER, HARRY, OAM (1924–), born Sydney, was one of a group of swimming coaches who played a role in Australia's swimming success at the 1956 Melbourne Olympics. While he trained swimmers such as Michael Wenden and Jon Henricks, his name will forever be linked to that of Dawn Fraser. It was Gallagher's perception that first recognised Fraser's potential, and his coaching and guidance that moulded her into one of the world's greatest swimmers. He was inducted into the World Swimming Hall of Fame in 1984, and was awarded the OAM in 1986.

PH

See **Swimming**.

Gardiner Medal. Awarded annually to the best and fairest player in the reserve grade of the National Football League, the medal was inaugurated in 1926. It was named after one of the Reserve Grade League's former presidents, Frank Gardiner. A. Jacobson (South Melbourne) and R. James (Essendon) tied for the first medal, a feat that was repeated twice in the following four years. T. Liberatore of Footscray, later to win the Brownlow Medal, has the distinction of being the only player to win the Gardiner Medal on two occasions. Footscray is the best represented club, with ten winners.

GC*

GARDNER, WAYNE (1959–), born Wollongong, was the first Australian to win the world 500 cc road-racing crown and to become a millionaire from motorcycle-racing. His first motor sport was go-karting. He switched to motorcycles after he discovered a broken-down minibike. Gardner first participated in dirt-track minibike-racing then switched to tarmac (road racing) in 1977. In his first European season in 1981 he secured a contract to join Honda's British team for 1982. By 1986 Gardner was team leader for Honda world-wide and won three Grands Prix that year, finishing second overall to American Eddie Lawson. After Honda redesigned its 500 cc racer for 1987 Gardner was unstoppable. He won seven Grands Prix in a fifteen-race season to clinch the world championship and returned a national hero. Machine problems blunted his hopes of a second world title in 1988 and he finished second to Lawson, while a broken leg in the US Grand Prix ruined his 1989 season. A series of crashes, injuries, and mechanical failures spoilt a promising 1990 season but he did win a further two Grands Prix to take his tally to seventeen— the most by an Australian in any Grand Prix class—at the end of 1990. Gardner was a 'big moment' performer with great determination. In his Phillip Island victories he had to overcome deficiencies in his machine and, in 1990, won despite the pain of a broken wrist. Gardner's successes lifted the profile of the sport in Australia.

DC

GARRARD, DICK, OBE (1909–), amateur wrestler, represented Australia at four British Empire and Commonwealth Games from 1934 to 1954 and at four Olympics between 1936 and 1956. He won three gold and a bronze medal in the lightweight freestyle division in British Empire and Commonwealth Games competition, winning the event in 1934, 1938, and 1950. He lost it on a split-point decision in 1954. He achieved a silver medal in welterweight class at the 1948 Olympics and was selected for the 1956 Olympics but did not compete because of injury; he was 45 at the time and president of the Australian Wrestling Union, and had not been beaten in a match in Australia for twenty-five years, having won his first Australian title in 1930 and his last in 1956. Garrard was Australia's flag-bearer at the 1954 British Empire and Commonwealth Games. He officiated at five Olympics and in 1976 the International Wrestling Association awarded him a gold

medal for his services to the sport. He was also awarded the Order of Sikatuna-Rank by President Marcos of the Philippines. Awarded the OBE in 1977, he was inducted into the Sport Australia Hall of Fame in 1985.

RC

GASCOIGNE, STEPHEN HAROLD ('Yabba') (1878–1942), a Balmain 'rabbito', was a celebrated cricket barracker of the 1920s and 1930s. He was nicknamed 'Yabba' because he was a 'bit of a talker'. Possessing a gravel-like stentorian voice, an acute sense of timing, and keen understanding of the game, Yabba's comments from the Sydney Hill became legendary. They included: 'Your length is lousy, but you bowl a good width' to a wayward bowler, and 'Whoa there! He's bolted' to a slow batsman who finally secured a run. Players and spectators enjoyed Yabba's barracking. Englishman Jack Hobbs acknowledged Yabba at the time of his last Test in 1929 and Yabba appeared on radio and was the subject of a Cinesound newsreel report.

RC

GASNIER, REG (1939–), a rugby league centre, was a champion schoolboy sportsman at Kogarah Intermediate High School and later at Sydney Technical High School, where he excelled in rugby union, cricket, baseball, and athletics. In 1957–58 Gasnier was forced to choose between cricket and rugby league when he was tipped for State honours in both sports. Rugby league won and Gasnier joined St George in 1958. By the end of 1959 Gasnier was an established member of the State and national teams. He toured England in 1959–60 and after an early hamstring injury displayed brilliant football, including scoring three tries in his Test debut at Swinton. This Test was symbolic of his career which included triumphal tours of England in 1963 and 1967, the latter as captain. Gasnier was Australia's youngest-ever captain when he led his country against England in 1962, aged 23 years and 28 days. Unfortunately in 1967 a cruciate injury in a minor match in Avignon, France, ended his career. Gasnier was an important member of the all-conquering St George side in the 1950s and 1960s and after his retirement he wrote and broadcast widely on rugby league, displaying conciseness, lucidity, and considerable analytical ability. Australia has produced few footballers as good as Gasnier. He was a beautiful runner, with sure hands, and a superb change of pace; he also possessed great anticipation, tackled strongly and well, and was always looking for support. He was the all-round footballer, matched only by Dally Messenger, Dave Brown, and Frank Burge.

TGP

See **Rugby League**.

GATEHOUSE, ELEANOR WRIGHT (1886–1973), born near Geelong, Victoria, was the winner of three Australian golfing championships, five Victorian titles, and was the first Royal Melbourne Women's Champion in 1906, an event which she won ten times over a period of thirty years. She was a grand-daughter of Thomas Austin, a Geelong pioneer. She played golf at the Geelong club from her school-days and won her first national title in 1909, the same year in which she married James Gatehouse. As well as being an accomplished golfer, Eleanor Gatehouse was a skilled administrator, serving as president of the Australian Women's Golf Union and of the Royal Melbourne Associates. She also completed seven terms as president of the Royal Society for the Prevention of Cruelty to Children. The Nellie Gatehouse azalea was named in her honour.

GC*

GATH, GEORGE (1908–), born Victoria, was one of Australia's best harness-racing trainer-drivers. He drove his first winner at the age of 19 in 1927. For the next fifty-two years he drove regularly at all of Melbourne's main trotting and pacing tracks before retiring at the age of 71. Gath was recognised late in his career as probably the most prolific driver of harness-race winners in Australia. He was particularly successful with trotters, with which he won fourteen of his seventeen Derbies. Nevertheless Gath did not taste success in the Interdominion pacing final or the Miracle Mile, although his son Brian won the 1978 Interdominion in Melbourne, with *Markovina*. Brian and his brother Neville were both successful reinsmen who have also won the Melbourne Drivers Premiership.

JO'H

GAZE, ANDREW BARRY CASSON (1965–), born Melbourne, the son of Lindsay Gaze, is a basketballer with Melbourne Tigers, Seton Hall (USA), and Australia. A small forward-guard, Gaze first played in the National Basketball League at 18, quickly becoming one of the most prolific scorers in the league. Between 1984 and 1990 he represented Australia in two world championships and two Olympics, and in 1988–89 was a leading member of the Seton Hall college team which was the losing National Collegiate Athletic Association finalist. By the 1990s the exposure from these successes had made Gaze one of the most well-known basketballers in Australia.

SB

See **Basketball**; GAZE, LINDSAY.

GAZE, LINDSAY JOHN CASSON (1936–), born Adelaide, made his sporting name in Melbourne. He was a basketballer with Melbourne Church and Melbourne Tigers and basketball coach with Melbourne Tigers and Australia. Gaze first played basketball in 1954 when the sport was in its infancy in Australia, and his talent was obvious enough for him to be selected for Victoria in 1957. Gaze went on to international honours, representing Australia as a guard at three Olympics and two world championships. Gaze's impact was greatest in administration and coaching. A major figure in Victorian basketball for many years, he held various positions with the Victorian Basketball Association, including that of General Manager. Soon after the 1970 World Championships he became coach of the Melbourne Tigers senior men's team, a position he continued to hold after the club's entry into the National Basketball League in 1984. In 1972 Gaze became Australian men's coach. He took the team to four Olympics and three world championships, a period which saw Australia move up steadily in the rankings until it was firmly placed in the top ten nations, a development which owed much to Gaze's efforts. He left the national position in 1985, but continued coaching his club team. The Gaze family produced a number of first-class players, most notably Lindsay's son Andrew.

SB

See **GAZE, ANDREW**.

Gender

Australian sport has a gendered history: clearly it has affected the sexes in different ways. Even today, despite some specific efforts to create equal opportunities for women, sport remains stamped by its early development as essentially a male activity and continues to play a key role in the production and reproduction of masculinity and male dominance.

Very early, white Australia became renowned for its commitment to sport, that is, to men's sport. Indeed some commentators saw sport as an obsession. Horse-racing and professional running, with gambling an integral element, were popular with the colonists from the very first days. But the development of cricket and the football codes have had the greatest import for gender relations because they involved, and continue to involve, such a large proportion of the population. The effects of these sports have been magnified by the constant publicity they received since their early days. A survey undertaken in the mid-1980s found that 81 per cent of men over 16 years expressed interest in football and 73 per cent in men's cricket. The respective figures for women were 61 and 59 per cent.

From the beginning, men's sport incorporated beliefs about toughness, competitiveness, self-reliance, independence, and character development. Press coverage of the early development in Victoria of Australian rules football expressed views similar to those popularly referred to as Muscular Christianity in Britain in the mid- to late nineteenth century. Sport was lauded for its capacity to develop attributes such as manliness, leadership skills, and gracious acceptance of defeat. The adage that the Battle of Waterloo was won on the playing fields of Eton was argued with as much conviction in Australia as it was in Britain. The fact that Eton's involvement in organised sport post-dated the battle of Waterloo did not dampen the conviction. The key values promoted by men's sport are the notions of leadership, male solidarity, power, and control. The early football games were unruly and often violent affairs, with umpires particularly at risk. A system of protection was gradually developed, for example, through the institution of separate dressing rooms for match officials. While the codification of football progressively attempted to contain the more dangerous direct aggression of both players and crowds, force and power remained features of the game. As one founding player of Australian football claimed in 1870, 'football is essentially a rough game all the world over, and ... not suitable for men poodles and milksops'.

The explicit maleness of these sports is high-lighted by what was being constructed for girls. The restrictive life-style which Victorian society allowed women did not encompass an interest in vigorous sport. Whereas for boys most sport was competitive and involved teams, for girls mild exercise to promote good health was all that was encouraged. A legitimating principle for directing girls to a modicum of healthy exercise was to counteract the negative effect which it was feared education would have on their capacity to bear children. A leader in girls' education was Presbyterian Ladies' College, Melbourne, which in 1875 advertised that

> Great attention is paid to the health of the boarders. The hours of work are strictly limited; and the garden and grounds, nearly two acres in extent, afford ample opportunity for out-doors exercise and amusement. A large room is fitted up with all the newest and most approved apparatus for gymnastic exercise.

Girls and women were given licence to in-dulge in diversionary sporting activities, pro-viding these did not jeopardise their ladylike demeanour. Indeed the clothes they wore pre-cluded strenuous activity. Women were not meant to raise a sweat and were expected to remain graceful and modest at all times. How-ever a gradual relaxation in the restrictive nature of clothes was achieved and this helped lead to greater physical liberation. During the latter half of the nineteenth century, an increasing range of activities gained approval, though most could be indulged in only by the better-off. Archery, croquet, golf, fencing, lawn tennis, cycling, and swimming became accept-able. Some team sports for young women,

hockey, cricket, and basketball, had their be-ginnings and became popular. The first women's cricket match is reported to have been played in Bendigo in 1874 and in 1890 there was a match between Victoria and NSW.

Tennis was one of the few mixed sports to develop. It gained popularity more as a family than a competitive activity, though the first recorded female competition occurred in 1884. Most upper-class and many middle-class homes had their own courts. The heritage of this is seen in the interest that women maintain in tennis today. In the mid-1980s tennis was rated by one survey as the top sporting interest for women, with 68 per cent expressing an interest; it rated third for men (60 per cent), behind football and cricket.

Over more than a century of women's sport in Australia, women have increased the areas in which they participate. Their involvement has often been started by the determination of indi-vidual women, or groups of women, and the struggle must be seen as part of the more gener-al struggle for liberation. Women's sport still reflects the legacy of these beginnings. Sport remains largely in the control of men and it is men's sport which dominates the popular cul-ture. Even in the Olympic and Commonwealth Games, where nationalism would seem to dic-tate even-handedness, men's sport remains in the ascendance. In the Commonwealth Games women still do not compete in as many sports or events as men. In the inaugural Games in 1930 (then the British Empire Games), women participated in only one of the six sports, swim-ming and diving. In 1982 women participated in only five of the ten sports represented in the Games, with the number of women taking part very little more than the number of men in 1938. By 1990, with the inclusion of women's cycling, women were excluded from only two of the ten sports, boxing and weightlifting. The 1994 programme will once again include wres-tling and women will be excluded from three of the ten scheduled sports. Even when women are 'allowed' to compete in a sport they are likely to have fewer events than men. In 1990 when women's cycling was included there were only three events for women compared with eight for men.

The Olympics present a similar picture. Although a few women had competed in the second modern Olympics in 1900, the first Australian women to compete did so in 1912. These were two swimmers, Fanny Durack and Mina Wylie, who respectively won gold and silver medals in the 100 metres. In 1928 women were first allowed to compete in athletics. The number of women's athletics events has in-creased gradually since then, but even in 1988 women could compete in only eighteen events, compared with the men's twenty-four. On top of this, control of the Olympics is very much in male hands. Until 1981, when three women were elected out of eighty-nine members, there had never been a woman on the International Olympic Committee. Nonetheless, Australian women have performed well in the Olympics and many of the best known sportswomen have followed the Durack tradition. Proportional to their involvement, Australian women's performance in the Olympics has been better than that of Australian men. Names like Marjorie Jackson, Shirley Strickland, Dawn Fraser, Betty Cuthbert, and Shane Gould are just a few of Australia's Olympic heroines.

Despite these and some other well-known individual sportswomen, and some few women's sports teams, it is apparent that gender bias in sport remains. Media coverage demonstrates this with great clarity. The situation is not improving, despite some explicit government policies. A study of the coverage of sport by the capital city daily newspapers carried out by Helen Menzies in 1980 showed that 96.2 per cent of reportage was devoted to men's sport. The study was repeated in 1988, and the figure was virtually the same: 95.8 per cent. The position on the employment of women sports journalists has improved. In 1980 only three newspapers had a female sports journalist. By 1988 the number was seventeen, on thirteen newspapers. This lack of media recognition reflects a very general tendency to ignore women's achievements, and an associated tendency to trivialise these when women's sport is reported. Such gender bias was given clear recognition by the establishment of a Federal Government cross-party Working Group on Women in Sport. In 1985 this group produced its report, *Women, Sport and the Media*, which ultimately led to the establishment of the Women's Sport Promotion Unit in 1988. Anti-discrimination legislation has made it increasingly difficult for sporting clubs to exclude or in other ways treat women differently, though old attitudes die hard. The AIS is also helping to promote female athletes, though its support for men has been stronger than for women. In 1988 there were 211 male scholarship-holders but only 114 female.

While sport is not monolithic, and different sports embody different values, the main organised sports have been, and remain, masculine events. This is important because sport is one of the most significant areas for forming and maintaining masculine and feminine identity, and this in turn underpins the reproduction of male dominance. The major sports are competitive and they systematically celebrate physical difference, with the most valued elements being those at which men, because of certain male physical characteristics, are likely to excel. Thus strength has been generally valued over

grace, co-ordination, rhythm, and control. Also the dominant sports in which Australian men have historically participated, notably football and cricket, are team sports and this embodies an additional element—that of a gender solidarity which of its nature excludes women. The effects of these sports on masculine identity are magnified by the prominent place they occupy in the public culture. Women as well as men accept their centrality in public life, and mass spectating turns these events into a ritual, which *inter alia* supports and promotes male dominance.

Sport occupies a central place in the lives and in the social development of boys, promoting in them a sense of power, forcefulness, mastery, and skill. These are part of a constellation of qualities which Australian sociologist Bob Connell has identified as hegemonic masculinity. Today boys are still taught in a quite straightforward way that sport is a significant part of manliness. The achievement of basic skills of ball-throwing, kicking, and batting, is a project to which boys are introduced at a young age by proud, committed fathers and mothers. Girls are introduced to the same skills, but in a negative manner as something which they cannot do well. Female sport does not have a similar significance for girls. Male sport, however, through its contribution to the construction of hegemonic masculinity, actually reinforces traditional notions of femininity in which women are cast as passive, physically unskilful, and not forceful. Femininity is defined largely in the negative by male sport, as involving lack of skill and an inability to play valued games. A process of disparagement of that which is feminine is implicit in the celebration of masculinity. This is expressed in the abuse traditionally meted out by coaches and fans who, when irritated by poor play, complain that their hero is 'playing like a girl'. Dominant male sport also proscribes non-hegemonic forms of masculinity, such as homosexual masculinity. This is clearly expressed in another routine chastisement of poor players as playing like a fairy, sissy, or poofter.

When we consider the history of women's sport in isolation, we can readily identify a consistent and unproblematic process of development. In a little over one century, opportunities to participate have grown from a narrow range of ladylike activities, with very restricted competition, to a wide range of sports, an extensive network of competition at local, national and international levels, and a range of official encouragement not only for an élite but for more general participation. While such a detailed history has yet to be written, we can piece together information which shows that women's endeavours to participate in sport form part of the general struggle for liberation.

The picture, however, looks less rosy when we compare men's and women's sport. In Australia as elsewhere, women's sport still takes a secondary position to men's. The most intractable issue of all is that sport acts as a crucial element in the development of masculinity and femininity. Though there has been and continues to be challenge, sport still reinforces notions of men as more skilful and powerful and this in turn underpins male domination. Women's achievements remain underreported and undervalued.

LB

See **Children**; DURACK, SARAH.

GEOGHEGAN Brothers, IAN ('Pete') (1939–) and **LEO** (1936–), sons of Edna and Tom Geoghegan, a garage and taxi proprietor in Liverpool, NSW, achieved great distinction in motor sport. Their 1960s racing team at one stage embraced six motor vehicles in three different categories. Dressed in matching black uniforms, theirs was probably the first professional Australian motor-racing team. Sports-car racing saw the brothers compete against each other but more commonly Leo chose open-wheeler racing while Ian drove a variety of touring cars. The most successful of these were two Ford Mustangs with which he won the Australian Touring Car Championship in successive years between 1966 and 1969. Driving a Lotus, Leo was Gold Star Champion in 1970. In 1970–71 Leo masterminded Chrysler Australia's motor-racing programme, leading to the development of the Valiant Charger for touring-car racing.

AM

See **Motor Racing**.

GEORGE, Sir ARTHUR THOMAS, AO (1915–), is a solicitor, successful businessman, and soccer administrator. Honours bestowed have included a knighthood in 1972 and the Order of Australia in 1987. George's involvement in soccer progressed from Sydney club Pan Hellenic and the NSW Soccer Federation to president of the Australian Soccer Federation 1969–88. George has served on FIFA's executive since 1981. Under him Australia qualified for the 1974 World Cup. A National Soccer League was formed in 1977 and Australia hosted the World Youth Championship in 1983. Highlights of his career were matched however by controversy involving coach selection for the national team in 1974–86.

PM

GIFFEN, GEORGE (1859–1927), born Adelaide, was Australia's premier cricket all-rounder of the late nineteenth century. A fine forcing bat and quality bowler of medium-paced off-breaks and cutters, Giffen recorded the greatest performance of first-class cricket when he scored 271 in one innings and took 16 wickets for 166 runs for SA against Victoria in 1891. He is the only Australian to make 10 000 runs and take 1000 wickets in first-class cricket. Yet Giffen was criticised for engineering a place for his less talented brother, Walter, in Australian sides and of overbowling himself when captain for his State and country. Giffen scored the first goal for Norwood in the SA Football Association, played in the 1878 and 1879 Norwood premiership teams, and represented SA in 1879. A grandstand at Adelaide Oval bears his name.

BW

See **Cricket**.

GILBERT, EDDIE (1908–78), born Baramba Settlement (Cherbourg), Queensland, was a dynamic fast bowler, achieving exceptional pace from a very short run-up. Despite being plagued by accusations of throwing and by injuries, he played twenty-three first-class matches for Queensland between 1930 and 1935, claiming 87 wickets at the cost of only 28.97 runs apiece. His pace was such that after bowling at Bradman 'the Don' was moved to write that 'he sent down in that period the fastest bowling I can remember . . . I unhesitatingly class that short burst faster than anything seen from Larwood or anyone else.' Gilbert was one of only fifteen bowlers ever to dismiss Bradman without scoring. Against Leary Constantine's powerful West Indian side, he took 5–65 and 2–26. Gilbert died in 1978 in a state mental institution, having spent the last twenty-three years of his life there, totally incapable of speech.

CT and PT

See **Aborigines in Sport**; **Cricket**.

GILL, EUNICE, MBE (1918–90) received her Diploma of Physical Education from the University of Melbourne in 1944, taught in schools and returned to that university as a lecturer until her retirement. In addition to her contribution to physical education, especially the Australian Physical Education Association, Gill had a great impact on sport in Australia generally and netball specifically. She was president of the All Australia Netball Association (AANA) in 1954, manager-coach of the Australian team which won two of three Tests against NZ in 1960, a delegate to the third world tournament in Jamaica (1970–71), and a senior official and delegate to the fourth world tournament in NZ in 1975. Her contribution to AANA also included being honorary secretary-treasurer (1958–60 and 1966–68). Gill was senior vice-president of the International Federation of Netball Associations (IFNA) from 1975 to 1987. She also served on the board of directors of the Confederation of Australian Sport (CAS) for nine years from its inception in 1976 and chaired both the CAS Sport Coaches Assembly and the Australian Coaches Assembly. She was elected vice-president of

CAS in 1983. Eunice Gill was awarded the AANA service award in 1966, received an MBE in 1975, life membership of the Australian Council for Health, Physical Education and Recreation in 1979, an IFNA Service Award in 1983, and was elected a Fellow of CAS in 1986.

DH and IJ

See **Netball**.

GILTINAN, JAMES JOSEPH (1866–1950) was a Sydney businessman and sometime cricket umpire who, as founder and secretary of the NSW Rugby Football League, organised a rugby union team to play against visiting NZ professionals in August 1907. In 1907 also he financed the three matches played in Sydney by A. H. Baskerville's All Golds. In the following winter of 1908 his committee established a local rugby league club competition and in 1908–9 Giltinan managed the first Kangaroo tour of Britain, but was bankrupted by the venture. Also a yachting enthusiast, in December 1934 he founded the NSW Eighteen-Footers Sailing League. Sydney's premiership competition trophy was named after him until the NSW Rugby League changed the competition's name to the Winfield Cup.

CC

See **All Golds**; **Giltinan Shield**; **Rugby League**.

Giltinan Shield. When the first Sydney Rugby League Premiership began in 1908, clubs competed for the Royal Agricultural Shield, named after the society which, despite bitter opposition, leased its Sydney Showground to the league. In 1913, it was won permanently by Eastern Suburbs. In 1950, it was decided to reintroduce a trophy and commemorate entrepreneur James Joseph Giltinan, regarded as the founder of the game in Australia. South Sydney were the first winners of the Giltinan Shield, in 1951. It is still awarded to the premiers although now overshadowed by the current sponsor's Winfield Trophy.

TB

See **GILTINAN, JAMES**.

GLENCROSS, BRIAN (1941–), born Narrogin, WA, was a hockey-player with a fine understanding of tight defence, which made him a valuable member of Australian hockey sides from 1964 to 1973. At full back he played a role that kept mistakes to a minimum and evolved a defensive pattern in Australia's play that opponents found difficult to penetrate. A good striker of the ball who read the game well, this thinking defender captained the WA senior team for several seasons and Australia from 1968 to 1973. A triple Olympian (in 1964, 1968, and 1972), he played in ninety-three Tests and since 1980 has been the coach of the national

women's hockey team which won the gold medal at the 1988 Olympics.

MS

Gloaming (1915–39), a thoroughbred racehorse by *The Welkin* out of *Eager*, was the most prolific winner of top-class races in Australia and NZ racing history. Bred by Ernest Clarke at Melton in Victoria, the bay gelding was sold to G. D. Mason of NZ and recorded fifty-seven wins and nine placings from sixty-seven starts including a winning sequence of nineteen. He won the AJC Derby at only his second start in race-record time, the NZ Derby, and the Great Northern Derby, and continued to win until the age of 9. His much-publicised clashes with Sydney champion *Beauford* (each winning two of the four races) drew large crowds to Randwick in 1922.

AL

Gold Racket. In November each year royal tennis players compete at the Royal Melbourne Tennis Club for the Gold and Silver Rackets. A complex set of rules governs the competition which culminates with a series of challenges. The competition was first held in 1882 when Thomas Stone, the club's first professional, presented the miniature (nine-inch) solid-gold racket and Roderick Travers presented a silver racket. There is no record of the winners of these trophies for some years in the 1940s and 1950s. However, club records list the winners of both trophies for eighty-six of the one hundred and nine years of the club's existence. J. B. Box, one of the founders of the club, won the Gold Racket fourteen times between 1882 and 1899 and Dr C. H. Mollison won it fifteen times between 1903 and 1923. In more recent times, Geoff Hiller won it seven times between 1968 and 1975.

FM

See **Royal Tennis**.

'Gold Star' Championship. The Australian 'Gold Star' Drivers' Championship is an annual motor-racing event conducted by the Confederation of Australian Motor Sport. Run over a series of races held throughout the country, drivers receive points for finishing in the top six positions until, at the completion of the last race, the leading Australian driver is presented with a 9-carat gold star. Inaugurated in 1957, the championship has always used the open-wheeler vehicle but has been conducted over six, eight, and even twelve races. Today the series is run over four races, mainly because of the expense of modern motor racing. The first championship was won by the popular Lex Davison. Both Bib Stilwell and Alfredo Costanzo have won on four consecutive occasions.

GC*

Golf

Golf's introduction into Australia was widespread but spasmodic, and invariably associated with a Scot. As early as the 1820s a Scotsman, Alexander Reid, played with wooden clubs and the 'feathery' ball on farmland just outside Hobart, but interest in the game was short-lived. Similarly, the game was introduced by individuals of Caledonian heritage into other parts of the country: in Melbourne, it was played by the Honorable James Graham; in Sydney by solicitor John Dunsmore; in Adelaide by the Governor of the colony, Sir James Fergusson; and in Queensland it was the Ivory family who laid out a few holes at their Eidsvold cattle station. Influence from the Scots also extended to the foundation of clubs. When the first permanent club, the Australian (1882), was established it had a distinct Caledonian flavour. The Australian's genesis is attributed to the officers of a Scottish regiment who, after displaying their golfing talents, bequeathed their clubs and gutta-percha balls to the bemused onlookers. Likewise, it was a member of a famous Scottish golfing family, R. A. A. Balfour-Melville, a man noted for his St Andrews' style, who was a foundation member and the first captain of Geelong Golf Club in 1892. Melbourne Golf Club (later Royal Melbourne) was formed by men of the same ilk. Both J. M. Bruce, who was educated at St Andrews, and Thomas Brentnall, a member of Royal Musselburgh Golf Club (one of the oldest clubs in Scotland), were instrumental in the club's genesis in 1891.

There was also the contribution from the Scottish professional golfers. Even though the first professional in Australia, Richard Taylor, was an Englishman, the majority were Scots who emigrated at the turn of the twentieth century. These men serviced the needs of the clubs and also led the way in new techniques and technology. Carnegie Clark, who emigrated from Carnoustie, pioneered the manufacturing of clubs and was the first to introduce the now universal Vardon grip and the revolutionary Haskell ball. His enterprise was matched by his golfing prowess—he dominated the game by winning three Australian Opens and six Professional Championships. An equally talented player was a fellow Scot and Clark's good friend, Daniel Soutar. He won several major titles but, more importantly, wrote the first treatise about golf in the Antipodes, *The Australian Golfer* (1906).

These men also lent their expertise to course design: many established links throughout Australia owe their present layouts to these Scottish imports. Soutar and Clark, for example, designed at least fifteen courses, and no less than nine other courses are credited to James Herd Scott, originally from Carnoustie, who was the professional at Royal Adelaide Golf Club for twenty years. In fact, Melbourne's famous courses in the sand-belt area as well as the Australian Golf Club, the NSW Golf Club, the Royal Adelaide Golf Club, and the Royal Queensland Golf Club owe their magnificent designs to the internationally renowned golfing architect of Scottish heritage, Dr Alister Mackenzie. Australian golf owes a sizeable debt to the men from Scotland.

Another characteristic of early golf in Australia was the servile nature of the employment of professionals. They suffered from the division, evident in many other sports, between the amateur (who played for the sport's intrinsic rewards) and the professional (who received remuneration for his skills). On the one hand, the golf professionals taught and played with the members, they supplied and repaired golfing equipment, and their opinions on golfing matters were canvassed and respected. On the other, they had restricted use of the clubhouse and facilities, and only on the course did they approach familiarity with the members. More talented professionals supplemented their earnings from the clubs by designing courses as well as playing occasional challenge matches and by competing in a small number of paid competitions.

The amateur/professional distinction was less important during the 1920s. By this time, the club professional could make a decent living and was well respected if his teaching and service were adequate. For example, the NSW professional J. Victor East used his pedagogical skills to make a name as a teacher in America. In addition, the promotion of well-sponsored tournaments was gaining popularity. The *Sun* £500 match-play event in 1924 marked the beginning of present-day golfing tournaments and circuits in Australia and elsewhere which are so potentially lucrative through television coverage, sponsorships, endorsements, and prize-money that modern professionals have the options of remaining with their clubs, becoming touring players, or doing both. Tournaments that originated at the turn of the century—the Australian Open Championship (1904), the Australian Amateur Championship (1894), and the Australian Professional Championship (1904)—have produced household names in Australian golf such as the legendary Peter Thomson and Greg Norman, and other stars like Joe Kirkwood, Jim Ferrier, Norm Von Nida, Henry (Ossie) Pickworth, Kel Nagle, Bruce Crampton, David Graham, Billy Dunk, Graham Marsh, and Wayne Grady.

The distinction between the early professionals and club members indicates another salient aspect of golf: its association with certain classes in society. The formation of the early clubs typified this. The Australian Golf Club, for instance, drew its patronage from the socially prominent Union Club. Likewise the Sydney Golf Club, situated at Rose Bay overlooking Sydney Harbour, attracted membership from the upper echelons and was granted the Royal Charter in 1897. When Royal Melbourne was established, its first president was Sir James McBain while the remaining members were leading men from commercial, pastoral, and public spheres of life. Similarly at the Brisbane Golf Club, the only golfing institution in that city for over two decades, membership was dominated by the established professions: banking, law, medicine, and politics. Regular players included Sir William Forgan Smith, a former premier of Queensland, Sir Samuel Griffith, a lawyer and politician who was renowned for his contribution to the Australian constitution, and Lord Lamington, the former governor of the State, who donated the club's oldest trophy, which he won in 1900. The élite clientele of the Brisbane Golf Club was epitomised by the high percentage of members who also belonged to the aristocratic and exclusive Queensland Club.

Groups who could not gain access to these institutions, because of restrictive membership procedures that excluded people on both social and financial criteria, established their own clubs all over Australia. Moreover, the democratisation of the game was assisted by the establishment of public courses, and more recently by the boom of resort venues found on the east coast of Australia that allows ordinary golfers to enjoy magnificent courses for fee costs only. Similarly, there are the championship links of the Murray River basin which, fuelled by poker-machine money, provide excellent conditions very cheaply. The only limiting factors facing modern golfers, unlike their compatriots at the turn of the century, are the expenses associated with equipment and green fees.

For many years technological changes, originating in other parts of the world, have had a direct effect on golf in Australia. The development of the revolutionary Haskell ball (1899), for example, radically changed the game by enabling golfers to hit further. Made of elastic rubber wound at tension around a rubber core, the Haskell spawned a proliferation of similarly constructed balls: technology had given the golfer the ascendancy. The effect was immediate. Many existing courses were found to be too short and had to be extended. Three decades later, the approval of tubular-steel shafts, which eliminated the difficulties associated with torsion and allowed the benefits of whip to be built into the shaft, contributed to improved skills on the links. More recently, advantages gained from experimentation with new materials such as carbon fibre and alterations to club faces have been negated by meticulously planned courses with strategically placed hazards.

While many innovations have been of international origin, Australians have made contributions in manufacturing and design. For many years, golfers were supplied with equipment that was made in Australia and firms such as Precision Golf Forgings and Dunlop had reputations nation-wide for their merchandise, but regrettably the present trend is for products to be manufactured in Asia and assembled locally. Several individuals, however, have given an Australian flavour to golfing equipment. David Graham, for example, has designed and marketed much golfing apparel, and Tom Crow, an Australian amateur champion who left his native land for America, established the well-respected Cobra Company that is about to 'buy' one of the leading world players, Greg Norman.

Golf has always been a popular sport for women. Even though golfing institutions were usually founded by men, McLeod Country Club (Queensland) and the Birchmore Ladies' Golf Club (SA) being the exceptions, female participation was always present. The story of women at the Australian Golf Club is typical of many other clubs. When the links of the club were established at Queens Park, Waverley, in 1895, women, even though denied any form of membership, were permitted to play on Mondays and Thursdays. These golfers fought hard for time on the links; they were initially made honorary members and eventually, after alterations in the rules at the turn of the century, women joined as associate or lady members. It is only as recently as 1984 that women, through the Sex Discrimination Act, have had the right to full membership.

As well as club involvement, women golfers from the earliest days have conducted State and interstate competitions and have the distinction of staging the first national golfing championship (1894) a few months before the men. For several reasons the game was popular at all levels of participation. First, female golf was non-threatening to male players. Initially limited to putting contests, then playing over nine holes on restricted days, and in clothes that inhibited rather than enhanced performance—the early attire consisted of hats, stiff collars and ties, long-sleeved jackets and blouses, and skirts to the ankles—women could not challenge their male counterparts. Second, golf complemented the cultural image of women because the actions of the game were essentially pacific and non-aggressive. For this reason, golfers did not experience the resistance that characterised women's forays into the more robust and stressful sports. Third, it provided the opportunity for women to mingle with males and females of the same social standing, and mixed golf, particularly the foursomes events, enabled single golfers to meet potential spouses. Last, golf was popularised in the belief that it was a healthy form of moderate exercise and therefore suitable for ladies.

Women's zest for golf has produced many great Australian players. The best known are Leonora Wray, who amassed seven State and national titles, Mona McLeod, the winner of four Australian championships, Dame Joan Hammond, the national representative and world-famous soprano, Jan Stephenson, Women's World Champion, and Corinne Dibnah, the first Australian to capture the British Women's Open. In fact, the story of golf in Australia is special because it is one of the few sports that women have been involved in since its early days. The early prominence of Scottish influence has dwindled with the development of local expertise and the emergence of other golfing nations to rival the traditional sole ruling authority, the Royal and Ancient Golf Club in Scotland. As the role of the Scots has changed, so has the life of the professional. The stigma of the early years has been discarded and many young golfers aspire to professional status for the apparent glamour, prestige, and wealth associated with the touring life. Technological innovations still alter the game. New substances are frequently trialled for added advantages for club or ball, but, unlike at other stages in the game's development, there is now a fine balance between technology and the challenge provided by the courses. One thing that has not changed is the association of golf with certain sections of society, but this exclusiveness is tempered by the establishment of a variety of different courses that has opened the game to a wider cross-section of the Australian community.
MP

See **Australian Ladies' Golf Union**; BACHLI, DOUGLAS; BORTHWICK, PATRICIA; CLARK, CARNEGIE; CRAMPTON, BRUCE; CREMIN, ERIC; DAVIS, RODGER; DEVLIN, BRUCE; DIBNAH, CORINNE; DUNK, WILLIAM; FERRIER, JIM; GATEHOUSE, ELEANOR; GRAHAM, DAVID; HAMMOND, JOAN; HATTERSLEY, HARRY; KENNEDY, EDWINA; KIRKWOOD, JOSEPH; LOCK, JANE; MARSH, GRAHAM; NAGLE, KELVIN; NETTLEFORD, LEN; NEWTON, JACK; NORMAN, GREGORY; PICKWORTH, HORACE; POPPLEWELL, FRED; SCOTT, Hon. MICHAEL; SOUTAR, DANIEL; STEPHENSON, JAN; Technology; THOMSON, PETER; VON NIDA, NORMAN; WHITTON, IVO; WILLIAMS, HARRY; WRAY, LEONORA.

GORDON, ADAM LINDSAY (1833–70), horseman and poet, rode three steeplechase winners at Flemington in a day, a unique feat, on 10 October 1868. Of wealthy English parentage, Gordon was considered a wild youth and was sent to SA in 1853. Inheriting a large

sum in 1864, he was able to indulge his passion for steeplechasing. He began publishing romantic sporting verse which gained immediate popularity. A decline in fortune saw him move to Ballarat in 1866 to run livery stables, with little success. The death of his baby daughter added to his chronic melancholia. He had several successes in the saddle in 1868–69 but suffered injuries from race falls in 1870. In debt again, he shot himself at Brighton in Melbourne on 24 June 1870.
AL
See **Literature**.

GORMAN, DIANNE (1952–), born Wellington, NSW, a brilliant attacking hockey centre-half, represented Australia seventy-two times between 1972 and 1981 and was a member of every NSW and Australian team during that period. Strong and fast, with outstanding ball control, she was always up with the play, whether in attack or defence, and earned a reputation of leadership by example. She captained Australia on four occasions and was twice vice-captain. Recognition of her standing in world women's hockey was Gorman's selection as captain of the International Federation of Women's Hockey Associations World Team that competed at a golden jubilee tournament in Scotland in 1980. She represented Illawarra from 1970 to 1980 and NSW at every national title from 1970 until her retirement in 1981.
MS

GORMAN, TOM (1901–78), born Mackay, Queensland, began playing representative rugby league football for Toowoomba and Queensland in 1920. The Toowoomba team, 'the Galloping Clydesdales', were pre-eminent in Queensland football, even defeating England in 1924, until Gorman transferred to Brisbane in 1926. He represented Australia from 1924 to 1930, and was the first Queenslander to captain an Australian Kangaroos tour of England, in 1929–30. For some of this time, 1922 to 1926, Queensland became the dominant rugby league State. A very unselfish centre three-quarter, Gorman was fast, elusive, and a fine handler in attack; he was sure, though not punishing, in defence, and had a great sense of positional play.
SJR
See **Rugby League**.

GOULD, SHANE ELIZABETH (1956–) was born on 23 November, the day after the opening ceremonies of the 1956 Melbourne Olympics. She created Olympic history by becoming the first and only female to win three individual swimming gold medals in world-record time. Gould astonished the swimming world by holding every swimming record from 100 to 1500 metres. She either broke or equalled eleven world records (100, 200, 400, 800, and

1500 metres freestyle, and 200 metres individual medley), and won fourteen Australian individual championships (100, 200, 400, 800, and 1500 metres freestyle, 200 and 400 metres individual medley and 100 metres butterfly) and three relay championships (4 × 100 metres medley relay and 4 × 100 metres freestyle relay—twice). This was all done by the age of 16, when she retired. Coached by Forbes Carlile, Gould set herself a near impossible task in the 1972 Munich Games by entering five individual events and one relay event. Her gold medals came in the 200 and 400 metres freestyle and the 200 metres individual medley. She earned a silver medal in the 800 metres freestyle, Keena Rothhammer of the USA winning in world-record time. In the 100 metres freestyle, her first final, she achieved a bronze medal. Her other event was the 4 × 100 metres freestyle relay, in which the Australian team were placed eighth in the final. It was the greatest performance by any Australian at a single Olympics. After the Games Shane Gould turned professional, married Neil Innes whom she had met at House of the New World, and moved to the Margaret River area in WA, where she and her family live a simple Christian existence.

RH and MH
See **Swimming**.

Government Policy

Contact between organised sport and the Australian Government is almost as old as the Australian Federation itself. In 1908 and 1912 representatives of organised sport asked for financial assistance in preparing and transporting teams to Olympic competition. Despite the notion that Australia would field its first national team, the government showed little enthusiasm for a direct financial commitment. It was only from 1924 that the Federal Government contributed to Australian Olympic crusades. Apart from this *ad hoc* commitment the only other government sports policy was the utilitarian National Fitness Act, passed during the Second World War in response to defence needs. The government's apparent lack of interest in sport remained the norm until 1956 when an eleventh-hour intervention by the Menzies Government ended years of procrastination and bickering among parochial Federal, State, and local government politicians. Menzies' action averted the ultimate sporting disgrace—the execution of Avery Brundage's threat to take the Games of the XVIth Olympiad away from Melbourne.

Deliberate non-involvement in a policy area constitutes a policy in its own right. The 1950s saw the Commonwealth approach sport with the same philosophy that they applied to the economy: the industrious, talented, and resourceful would be rewarded, irrespective of the level of aspiration. As for the role of local government in the provision of infrastructure such as swimming pools, ovals, and other public facilities, this was a matter for negotiation between the States and local authorities, the Federal Government having no role to play.

The government knew that problems were developing. As early as 1956 there were many on both sides of the House who unsuccessfully argued that the Commonwealth should maintain its interest in sport beyond that year's Olympic Games. The experience of élite sport in the 1960s and 1970s showed little change from the previous decade, with declining performances relative to traditional rivals and to newly emerged nations of the post-war period. An examination of Australian politics explains why public policy did not respond. Robert Gordon Menzies, Prime Minister of Australia for a record sixteen years, seemed to believe that sport was an area of free choice for the individual, being ideologically and financially beyond the realm of Federal responsibility. State and local authorities were on their own where sport was concerned. His successors maintained the philosophy until the Coalition lost office in 1972. By this time sport had joined a range of other urban and social issues which illustrated a clear need for Federal planning.

The philosophy of Australia's economy carrying all before it could not solve the various demographic problems caused by rapid urbanisation. This was manifest in sprawling, low-density suburbs which had roads, water, and power, but little else in the way of services. It was the promise to transform Australia's urban environment by linking the fate of the cities to the Federal Government's financial power that swept the Australian Labor Party, under Gough Whitlam, to office in 1972. Whitlam became the first Australian prime minister formally to acknowledge the link between politics and the public administration of this complicated policy area. His government placed sports policy firmly on the planning agenda, recognising that Australia's mortgage-belt suburbs lacked a range of quality-of-life resources—libraries, child-care centres, and facilities for sport and recreation. Labor broke with the conventional practice of relegating planning to the States and local government authorities. The new order for urban problems involved the Federal Government as never before.

The Commonwealth Area Improvement Programmes, and Capital Assistance for Leisure Facilities, translated political hopes and aspirations into realisable administrative outcomes. Projects were funded in association with local authorities grouped into regional associations. The strategy emphasised a large number of smaller projects, improving or upgrading existing facilities. The benefits were immediately accessible to all. Projects included floodlighting or resurfacing playing areas, replacing obsolete mechanical plant, or making minor structural improvements. Several larger community leisure facilities in SA and NSW were built in co-operation with an unemployment relief scheme. The administrative mechanism to effect the link between local authorities and the Federal Government involved the use of specific-purpose grants, made under Section 96 of the Constitution. Funds were transferred to a State on the condition that the money be spent in a specific way. The technique is generally resented by the Australian States—especially by those governed by Liberal and National parties—being interpreted as a derogation of their sovereignty. There was also direct contact with sporting associations, building on an existing volunteer framework. The government made direct cash grants for specific projects such as hosting or travelling to world championships, administration, or coaching development. Government assistance met training and travel costs. A task force, chaired by Dr Allan Coles of the Department of Human Movement Studies at the University of Queensland, investigated the need for an Australian Institute of Sport. Nevertheless, the government never altered its fundamental goal: to develop a national system of mass-participation sport based on facilities located in Australia's suburbs. The policy process followed identifiable steps: information-gathering, consultation, and experimentation. Whitlam was particularly fond of involving expertise from outside the public service. Committees of inquiry comprised of sportsmen, physical educators, and public servants provided advice in a completely new policy area.

Labor lost office in November 1975—the same month in which the Task Force Inquiry recommended the establishment of an Australian Institute of Sport. Nonetheless, the Whitlam Government can reasonably claim to have seriously addressed the question of access to sport and recreation within Australia's urban environment. The period remains a mark against which policies of successive governments can be measured. The importance placed on the role of local government, the gradual progression through a series of initiatives, and the willingness to experiment and learn from mistakes, make it unique, not only in the history of Australian sport, but Australian politics in general.

The Fraser Government promised to reverse what it believed were centralist tendencies, and the expansion this brought to the size of the public sector. The mechanism was a revised system of Federal financial relations: the States and local government would resume primary responsibility for a variety of social and urban matters, including sport and recreation. The States would receive a block share of internal revenue. Funding local government would re-main exclusively a State responsibility. But the States appeared reluctant to accept Fraser's 'New Federalism', and to instigate new forms of taxation to make up any revenue shortfall. There was little incentive to maintain the urban emphasis of Whitlam's sport and recreation policy. The same was initially true for Australia's élite representatives, but, after 1980, policy in this area changed. Fraser's apparent reluctance to help Olympic athletes, evident in 1976, underwent a change, at least for the nation's star performers. While the public outcry over the relatively poor performance at Montreal was most likely not the sole motive for the establishment of state sponsorship, it helped to justify its maintenance. This was the case with the Australian Institute of Sport (AIS), which developed rapidly. Nonetheless, the Fraser Government had waited until 1980 before implementing the 1975 Task Force recommendation to establish the AIS.

Sport, it appeared, brought practical solutions to political problems. It breathed new life into a ministerial career cut short in Cabinet. The Institute—and sport generally—allowed a man gifted in politics, the law, and administration to leave his mark, not only on Australia's political, but also on its sporting history. Bob Ellicott, Minister for Home Affairs, had resigned his portfolio as Attorney-General after a disagreement with the Prime Minister. A determined and talented man, Ellicott had the Institute operational one year after the announcement that the government would proceed with the idea.

It would appear that the government became only too willing to consider requests from the AIS for assistance. The Coalition's gratification of Australia's lust for Olympic gold, it can be argued, was generally well received. Sport also helped the Coalition to pursue its foreign policy. The Gleneagles Agreement and scholarships for athletes from the Commonwealth helped to publicise government policy on apartheid. But one area remained the same. The Fraser Government did not revive the Whitlam initiatives to develop sport in the suburbs of Australia's cities. The Coalition, it would appear, regarded the AIS as the primary responsibility of its sports policy.

The Hawke Government was elected to office in 1983 promising an even better deal for sport. It was aware of the political and administrative history of this area of public policy. Funding doubled to $50 million, but the election promise of seventy-five community leisure centres, made while Bill Hayden led the party, was quietly abandoned. An interim committee established under the Minister for Sport, Recreation, and Tourism, John Brown, recommended the establishment of the Australian Sports Commission (ASC). It told the government that sport needed more than money, that there was a need to understand its social significance. Sport and recreation reflect other areas of social policy in that identifiable groups such as women, the old, the young, the unemployed and those of non-English-speaking background may find access difficult. At first, however, the ASC's task, among others, was to tap private financial sources to supplement budget outlays. Even the Confederation of Australian Sport, the peak national body, observed that the beneficiaries were unmistakably the nation's élite performers. There appeared little immediate progress undertaken to address the developmental issues raised in the interim committee's report. Initiatives such as Aussie Sports for children, and public awareness campaigns on the personal and national importance of women's sport, have begun to redress an area of policy amnesia.

Politically, the ASC and the AIS give the government the economic and political room to manoeuvre, elements essential to the firm control of policy. Whitlam's emphasis on sport within an urban context is not as evident after 1983. Sport acquired a more symbolic quality as entertainment, distraction, and as an icon of political soundness: it helped to symbolise a Labor Party of stability and fiscal restraint. The Hawke Government firmly believed in sport's contribution to the economy, generating employment, sales tax, and tourism. Support for the *America*'s Cup, the Adelaide Grand Prix, as well as the athletics World Cup, exemplify the view that public investment in sport brings political and economic returns. Sport plays its part in the emphasis the Hawke Government placed on visibly sound economic management. Politically, it helped Bob Hawke cultivate contact with the electorate, something his successor, Paul Keating, has yet to emulate.

While acknowledging government recognition that problems confronted identifiable disadvantaged groups, the allocation of resources suggested that increased participation was a policy goal aspired to rather than actively sought. An examination of public policy since 1975 shows that there was apparently an unwillingness to address both policy goals with equal fervour—fostering high-performance athletes, and mass participation. The public funds spent on state-sponsored athletes remained unavailable for projects designed to overcome barriers to participation. Yet this was justified on the assumption that a few winners would inspire Australians to eschew a sedentary life-style, finding the resources to involve themselves in sport and physical recreation. Research by the Australian Council for Health, Physical Education and Recreation indicates that Australia's children are among the least aerobically active in the western industrialised world. The strategy of helping local authorities to situate facilities close to centres of population growth was one the Federal Government appeared reluctant to explore.

Unlike its counterparts in Western Europe, Australian sports policy has a short history. While Europeans throughout the post-war period pursued dual policies intended to foster mass participation as well as the identification and fostering of élite performers, Australian governments left both areas almost exclusively to volunteers. The results can be summarised as follows: an apparent need for more trained coaches and well-maintained suburban facilities; occasional concern that levels of performance by élite representatives have remained static; and difficulty in overcoming sedentary and other life-style behaviour patterns in the population at large. The problem is one of planning within a federal system.

TA

See **Amateurism**; **Australian Institute of Sport**; **Australian Sports Commission**; **Betting on Sport**; **Springbok Tour 1971**.

GPS Head of the River. In all States the major school rowing event has long been the annual Head of the River regatta, with Victoria's being the oldest, dating from 1868. The annual regattas began as races for fours, but today all are for eight-oared boats, with Queensland (1955) and Tasmania (1959) the last to switch to the larger boat. At each regatta, minor events are held before the climax of the Head of the River—the race between first eights. These regattas, which provide a major social event for their followers, rival the annual Greater Public School athletic carnival as the major occasions when GPS students display their collective fervour as they support their school's endeavours. During the 1980s the most successful school in any State was Hutchins School (Hobart) with eight titles won in the decade.

SB

GRAHAM, DAVID ANTHONY (1946–   ), born Melbourne, was the first Australian to win the US Open Golf Championship. At the age of 14 he became an assistant professional to George Naismith at Riversdale Golf Club, who changed him from a left- to a right-handed golfer. Graham was spotted playing in the Australian Schoolboys Golf Championship by Billy McWilliam, who recommended him to a Sydney golf club firm. Graham justified McWilliam's support when he won the Queensland PGA in 1967. After a succession of high placings in tournaments, Graham obtained a five-year contract with noted manager Bucky Woy. Graham won a string of tournaments in the early 1970s including the Japanese Airlines, the NSW, Victorian, and Tasmanian. He achieved his first American win in 1972 when he won a play-off with fellow countryman Bruce Devlin in the Cleveland Open. Graham then won big tournaments in Japan and Great Britain along with the Australian Open and the World Match Play Championship. He also represented Australia successfully in the Dunhill and World Cups. His prestige as a golfer was enhanced when he won the US PGA in 1979, beating Ben Crenshaw on the third hole of a play-off. His success in the US Open in 1981, where he played faultless golf to win by three strokes, was his greatest win. Graham has won eight US tournaments and twenty other events around the world and attained millionaire status in the 1980s. He has written an excellent instructional book and another on golf psychology.

GC*

See **Golf**.

Grant Memorial Trophy. The Joe Grant Memorial Trophy is awarded to the best player on the ground in the Queensland Australian Football League (QAFL) Grand Final. The trophy was first presented in 1981 to honour the memory of Joe Grant, secretary of the QAFL from 1960 to 1980. The inaugural winner of the trophy was Kevan Sparks, who played for Windsor Zillmere. While playing for Southport, Gary Dempsey, the VFL Brownlow medallist in 1975, won the award in 1987. The only dual winner of the trophy is Zane Taylor (Southport).

MH*

GRAY, EDGAR LAURENCE ('Dunc') (1906–), Australia's first Olympic cycling champion, was born the son of a lime merchant at Kingsdale, near Goulburn in NSW. As his family lived three miles from the nearest school, Edgar learned to ride a bike at an early age. After joining the Goulburn Amateur Bicycle Club, Gray went on to become Australia's dominant cyclist, winning twenty-five State and twenty national titles between 1925 and 1943. He was an extremely versatile rider, his victories ranging from sprints to long-distance events up to 10 miles. Snowy Baker referred to this country rider as a paragon who was a teetotaller, non-smoker, and a good churchman. Although Gray had no coach and limited international experience he came third in the 1000 metres time trial at the 1928 Olympics. Despite suffering from illness when the 1932 Olympics began, Gray won the 1000 metres time trial in 1 minute 13 seconds, a world-record time. He repeated this success at the 1934 British Empire Games. Gray had the honour of being Australia's flag-bearer at the 1936 Olympics but was unable to defend his title as another Australian was selected for this event. He won the 1000 metres sprint at the 1938 British Empire Games where he led the teams on to the Sydney Cricket Ground. His achievements were acknowledged by the Helms Award for the outstanding Australian athlete in 1932.

RH and MH

Great Australian Camel Race. One of the most colourful events of the Australian Bicentennial was a camel race from Ayers Rock to the Gold Coast. On 10 April 1988 sixty-nine camels and their riders began a 3000 kilometre trek across outback Australia for total prize-money of $104 000. The heavily sponsored three-and-a-half-month endurance event was for the benefit of the Royal Flying Doctor Service. Despite setbacks and discomforts, the eventual winner of the thirty-nine finishers was Gordon O'Connell who completed the trek in 480 hours.

GC*

GREEN, DENNIS, BEM (1931–), born Epping, Sydney, was Australia's most successful paddler (kayak and surf ski). He was a member of five Australian Olympic kayak teams between 1956, when he achieved a bronze medal, and 1972, and coached the Australian kayak team at Montreal. He won sixty-five Australian Open kayak titles (singles, pairs and fours) between 1953 and 1974. As a surf lifesaver, Green won the single and double ski events in the official world championship titles in 1956. Between 1954 and 1967 he won nine Australian championships including one single-ski and eight double-ski titles. Green regards carrying the Australian flag at the 1972 Munich Olympics as his most memorable sporting achievement. He competed in the kayak at the World Masters Games (eight gold medals in Toronto, 1985; nine gold medals in Copenhagen, 1989) which he stated gave 'a tremendous sense of satisfaction'.

DB

See **Canoeing**.

GREGORY Family was an Australian cricketing dynasty. Edward William Gregory (born 1805) emigrated to Sydney from England in 1814, and had joined the Australian Cricket Club, the first in Australia, by 1832. Edward was the father of thirteen children, four of whom—**Edward James** (1839–99), **David William** (1845–1919), **Charles Smith** (1847–1935), and **Arthur Herbert** (1861–1929)—played cricket for NSW. Two of the brothers went on to play Test cricket. Tall, heavily bearded, and single-minded, 'Handsome Dave' Gregory was an all-rounder considered more an astute leader than a skilful player. He was Australia's first cricket captain, leading his side to victory over England at Melbourne in 1877. His most enduring contribution to the game, however, was his skilful leadership of the first Australian tour to England in 1878. Despite rivalries between some players and opposition towards the tour from cricket administrators, he led a highly successful tour which established the pattern for future visits abroad. Edward 'Ned' Gregory's single Test appearance was in the first Test in 1877 in which he scored Test cricket's first duck. Ned Gregory was a professional cricketer and the curator of the SCG for over three decades. He greatly improved facilities for NSW players and spectators by advancing methods of wicket construction and by designing and building the first comprehensive scoreboard at the SCG. The family's third generation was perhaps the most gifted. Ned was the father of **Charles William Gregory** (1878–1910), who was the first Australian player to score a triple century in a day in first-class cricket, and **Sydney Edward Gregory** (1870–1929), who played fifty-two Tests for Australia including six as captain in 1912 at the age of 42. Charles (senior) was the father of **Jack Morrison Gregory** (1895–1973), who played twenty-four Tests for Australia, scored the fastest-ever Test century and is remembered as possibly Australia's greatest all-rounder.

DM

Greyhound-racing

Greyhounds have been on Australian soil since the First Fleet arrived. They were originally used to catch game which helped supplement the diet of the early settlers. The first sporting use of greyhounds can be traced back to live-hare coursing in the 1860s in SA and the 1870s in Victoria and NSW. In the mid-1920s, Jack Munro, manager of the Sydney Stadium, attempted to attract financial backing to introduce a new American version of the sport into Australia. He had secured the rights to the 'mechanical hare' but could not sell the idea to local coursing enthusiasts. Two years later, an American, Frederik Swindell, launched the sport at Epping Racecourse (later to be known as Harold Park). Initially called 'Electric Hare Racing', the first meeting was held, under lights, on 28 May 1927. Swindell's success convinced Munro that he should build a centre at Mascot. Shortly after its opening, under pressure from local church groups, the NSW Government banned night greyhound-racing and betting on the mechanical-hare races. Both tracks then substituted live-hare racing and this seemed to satisfy both the church and the government, but by 1931 the Depression and a change of government had ensured that the sport had reverted back to mechanical hares and night racing.

In 1933 private promoters such as Swindell and Munro were forced out of the sport when Harold Park came under the control of the NSW Trotting Club and the supervision of greyhound-racing was transferred to the Greyhound Racing Control Board. During the 1930s greyhound-racing began to rise in popularity. Simultaneously animal welfare groups such as the RSPCA pressured the State governments to prohibit coursing. Night racing remained popular in the major population centres but the real growth areas of greyhound-racing became provincial areas, where horse-racing was less

frequent. By the mid-1950s, the Victorian Government had legalised the sport in Melbourne, and the various greyhound associations began to formulate a promotional pattern. Before this era Australian attendance records were established at Harold Park in 1944 when 17 000 people watched the champion dog *Chief Havoc* attempt a series of time–distance records, and in 1949 when 18 600 people attended the reopening of the newly remodelled Wentworth Park.

Although there is no national controlling body all the State associations work in harmony, as demonstrated by the National Championships. These were first staged in 1965, at Harold Park, as the National Sprint Championships and, since the introduction of the TAB, have become the biggest greyhound-races in Australia. They were transferred to Olympic Park, Melbourne, in 1966 and have since rotated annually around the various main venues.

Greyhounds are graded on the basis of age, past performance, and times. Races are conducted over a number of distances, which vary according to the individual tracks, but most Australian classics are under 550 metres, with the main exceptions being the marathons run over 950 metres.

GC*

See *Chief Havoc*; **Coursing**; *White Hope*.

Gridiron

American servicemen introduced gridiron to Australia during the Second World War but the players were virtually all US personnel based in Australia, who tended to stick to their own sports, baseball and gridiron. Games occurred in such Queensland towns as Charters Towers and Cloncurry. In August 1943 a crowd of 8000 in Cairns witnessed the Base 2 All Stars lose, 12–6, to a group of US army engineers. In October 1943 two American teams, the Northwest Cougars and the Texas Terrors, played a scoreless tie in a game in Rockhampton which was complete with bands and cheerleaders. The largest wartime American football crowd numbered 30 000; these fans saw the army defeat the navy in Sydney. Gridiron largely disappeared with American servicemen at the end of the war. It reappeared only when visiting American warships personnel played occasional matches against local Melbourne and Sydney teams during the 1960s and 1970s. The game regained popularity in the 1980s with the telecasting of professional football games from the USA. This resulted in the formation of various amateur gridiron competitions in Sydney and Melbourne. Often these players did not possess proper equipment, playing without helmets, and using pillows instead of pads.

The Australian American Football Association was formed in 1985 in an attempt to establish a national league. It did not succeed due to

60 Rosey Boehm's photograph of lacrosse-player, Vicki
Ingham, won a national photographic competition
designed to raise the profile of women's sport in Australia.

61 Eddie Gilbert was a dynamic fast bowler of the 1930s
who achieved sizzling pace from a short approach.

62 *Adam Lindsay Gordon Steeplechasing at Flemington, 7 November 1868.* An oil on board painting by T. H. Lyttleton.

63 Golf is played in many parts of Australia where the lack of water prevents the construction of 'greens', such as Blinman in the Flinders Ranges, SA.

64 Gymnastics enthusiasts from Germany had established their 'turnverein' in Australia by 1878.

65 Gymnastics for women sometimes included the use of Indian clubs, such as at this Ladies' Gymnasium in Collins Street West, Melbourne, 1881.

66 A handball match between Victoria and NSW at the Victoria Barracks ball-alley, 27 February 1875.

67 Hockey is supposedly depicted in this 1842 sketch by John Rae entitled *A Game like Hockey in Hyde Park, Sydney*.

68 As a non-contact outdoor team game, hockey was regarded as suitable for women although, as can be seen from this photograph of a hockey team in 1904, long skirts had to be worn.

lack of interest, possibly because of competition from the increasingly commercial promotion of other football codes. In the mid-1980s there was an attempt to promote games between touring American university teams. The most successful event took place at VFL Park where a crowd of 15 000 turned up for a 'Bowl' Game.

At present, delayed telecasts of professional games from America continue, but actual participation in Australia has not taken off. The game is played in the six States but not in the ACT and NT. Grand Finals are held in Victoria, Queensland, and NSW at the end of the winter season; leagues in WA, Tasmania, and SA play during the summer so as not to clash with the more established winter football codes. There is concern among gridiron players that the expansion of rugby league will adversely affect the number of participants. There is also evidence that the increasing popularity of basketball has hurt attendance at games. Nevertheless there are more than fifty teams competing within Australia, and there has even been an overseas tour of an unofficial national Australian gridiron team, the Kookaburras. Any future tours would now come under the aegis of the National Gridiron League of Australia, formed in early 1991.

TD

GRIFFITHS, ALBERT ('Young Griffo') (1871–1927), born Sydney, was a stocky featherweight and a fine defensive boxer. In a ring career spanning twenty-five years he fought 166 bouts, losing only nine. A newspaper boy who grew up in Sydney's Rocks area, Griffiths began as a bare-knuckle fighter. With immense natural talent, 'Young Griffo' rarely bothered to train. After winning the Australian featherweight championship in 1889, he outpointed New Zealander Billy Murphy in Sydney in 1890, claiming the world title. Although he had previously been to America defeating Ike Weir, their leading featherweight, Americans refused to acknowledge Griffiths as world champion. After defeating Murphy again in 1891 Griffiths returned to America, losing unluckily to Jack McAuliffe and drawing with the great Joe Gans and George Dixon. He retired in 1904, though he later made a brief come-back in 1911. Griffiths remained in America where he became a celebrity recounting stories of his career. He spent the rest of his life in the saloons of New York, ending his days in an asylum. Money was raised in Australia in the 1920s to bring him home but he died in New York and was buried in Woodlawn Cemetery.

GC*

See **Boxing**; FOLEY, LARRY.

GRIMMETT, CLARENCE VICTOR (1891–1980), born NZ, represented Wellington in the NZ Plunket Shield. He emigrated to Australia at the age of 23 and played cricket in Sydney and Melbourne (representing Victoria) before settling in SA. Picked in the Test side at the age of 34, Grimmett took 11–82 on debut. He took 216 wickets in thirty-seven Tests—being the first to reach 200 wickets—at a cost of 24.21 and took a further 668 wickets for SA. Small-statured and stooped, wearing a cap because of premature baldness, Grimmett bowled his leg-spinners with a round-arm action and pinpoint accuracy. He and Bill O'Reilly formed a potent spin combination in the 1930s. He spent hours perfecting his craft by developing variations, including a 'flipper'. He even trained his fox terrier to retrieve balls bowled on a backyard pitch. Grimmett, who represented SA until 1941, was disappointed to be overlooked for the 1936–37 and 1938 Test series.

RC

See **Cricket**.

Grogan Medal. Awarded by the Queensland Australian Football League (QAFL), the J. A. Grogan medal is presented to the season's best and fairest player. The medal was named after Joe Grogan who was secretary of the long-standing QAFL club Mayne. The first two medals (1946–47) were won by Doug Pittard of Western Districts. In 1954 21-year-old Noel McGuinness won his second Grogan Medal and in doing so became the youngest player to achieve this honour. More than half the medals presented since 1946 have been won by three clubs, Morningside, Western Districts, and Coorparoo.

GC*

Gunsynd (1967–83), a thoroughbred racehorse by *Sunset Hue* out of *Woodie Wonder*, was foaled in NSW and sold as a yearling to a syndicate from Goondiwindi, Queensland. Initially trained in Brisbane by Bill Whelow, the grey colt won his first four races, and performed well as a 3-year-old in Sydney. Transferred to trainer Tommy Smith, *Gunsynd* won most of the major mile races and many other contests in Sydney and Melbourne. Idolised by the public, *Gunsynd*'s finest performance was perhaps his brave third to *Piping Lane* in the 1972 Melbourne Cup when unsuited to the distance. He retired to stud in that year.

AL

Gymnastics
Modern Olympic gymnastics has its origins in systems of physical training developed in Europe in the early nineteenth century. Its proponents looked back to regimens of the ancient Greeks for inspiration and argued moral, military, and patriotic benefits for their theories. The systems of the Swede Pehr Ling were brought to Australia by Gustave Techow, a former officer in the Prussian army who had trained at Ling's

gymnastic institute in Stockholm in 1845. By 1864 Techow had persuaded the Victorian Government to establish a National Gymnasium to train volunteer soldiers and teachers in physical education. The British army had adopted a similar programme in 1860. In 1866 Techow published his *Manual of Gymnastic Exercises for the Use of Schools and At Home*, which asserted that gymnastic exercise was also beneficial for women and invalids as well as for men. His apparatus included most of those used in modern gymnastics (rings, vault, pommel horse, parallel and horizontal bar) as well as balancing and escalading, climbing, pole-vaulting, and the use of the trapeze, though little was said of tumbling. In 1868 he was employed by the Board of Education as Lecturer of Gymnastics for trainee teachers.

Private gymnasia predated Techow's arrival, but the emphasis of these had been on exercise and physical culture rather than gymnastics. Other German immigrants had established a *turnverein*, or gymnastics club, in Melbourne by 1878. Affected by anti-German sentiment, gymnastics suffered a decline during and after the First World War, although it still played a part in military physical training. It was promoted in the 1920s by the YMCA which in Melbourne staged an annual 'gymnastic circus' from 1923. In 1937 a gymnastics association was founded in Victoria, leading to the formation of the Australian Gymnastics Union (later Federation) in 1948.

Gymnastic events for men were included at the first modern Olympics in 1896 (and women's events from 1928), and evolved gradually to their modern form, but Australia did not compete at this level until the Melbourne Olympics in 1956 when the best result was Graham Bond's fifty-fourth place in individual exercises. These games brought international champion gymnasts such as Larissa Latynina and Boris Shaklin to Australia for the first time. This and television coverage of later Olympics helped to broaden greatly the appeal of the sport in this country. Australia sent gymnasts to all subsequent Olympics, and to world gymnastic championships since 1966, with a gradual improvement in performance. Lindsay Nyland and Marina Sulicich finished thirty-fourth and thirty-second in the men's and women's events respectively at Moscow in 1980. Nyland was the first Australian to win a medal in international competition, with a silver and bronze at the 1978 Commonwealth Games. Inclusion of gymnastics at the AIS from 1987 has done even more to raise standards, with Monique Allen, Kylie Shadbolt, and Joanna Hughes approaching the top world-class level.

AL

See **ALLEN, MONIQUE**; **Australian Gymnastics Federation**; **MEREDITH, KEN**.

H

HAFEY, TOM (1931–) achieved notable early success by coaching VFL team Richmond to four premierships between 1967 and 1974. He was unable to win another premiership with Geelong, Sydney, or Collingwood—he was the first outsider to coach Collingwood. Only Jock McHale and Allan Jeans exceeded Hafey's 522 matches as coach. Hafey's coaching, especially at Richmond, was marked by a direct, long-kicking, physical style of play. Hafey, who was famous as a tea-drinker, defied winters with only a well-known t-shirt over the impressive chest, which illustrated his personal dedication to physical fitness. Hafey's unyielding approach wore thin with some players, however, and possibly contributed towards his sackings.

DS

HALES, THOMAS (1847–1901) was the most successful jockey in major horse-races in Australia in the 1870s and 1880s. By the standards of modern champions his tally of 495 winners was modest, but by any standards seven Victoria Derbies, seven AJC St Legers, ten VRC St Legers, eight Australian Cups and victories in many other major races was remarkable, and his success rate was very high. Acknowledged as a beautifully balanced rider and an expert judge of pace, the dapper Hales with his flourishing moustache was immensely popular. Towards the end of his riding career he set up a stud farm near Wodonga, Victoria.

AL

HALL, DUNCAN (1925–), born Home Hill, Queensland, played junior rugby league football in Rockhampton before joining Valleys in Brisbane in 1948. He made an immediate impact and was selected for Queensland and the 1948 Kangaroo tour. He made his Test debut in the second row but afterwards moved to the front row. The highlights of a career encompassing twenty-two Tests were his role in the winning sides of the 1950 and 1954 series. After retiring in 1956, Hall became one of Brisbane's leading bookmakers. His son Duncan Junior played fifteen Tests for the Australian rugby union team in the early 1980s.

MC

HALL, P. J. (1911–), born Leichhardt, Sydney, is one of harness racing's most revered characters and one of the reinsmen who dominated the sport at Sydney's Harold Park for three decades. He was born into a trotting family and from the age of 8 worked a horse or two for his father Clyde on the Epping (later Harold Park) track each day before school. Later he graduated to share in the full range of family businesses, including managing one of the family butcher shops at Penrith. He also dabbled in greyhound-training, winning enough cash to fund his first ventures into harness-racing ownership. Perc Hall drove his first winner at Richmond, NSW, in April 1929, but it was not until night trotting began at Harold Park twenty years later that he made harness racing his main occupation. In the twenty-eight years of night trotting before his compulsory retirement in 1977 Perc was the leading driver at Harold Park on five occasions and the leading trainer four times. He almost always figured in the top four placings in each category. When he drove *Ronrobin* to victory in 1977 he became the first person to drive 500 night-time winners at the track. Perc won two Interdominion finals and almost every feature race in NSW as well as a handful of interstate feature events. Although the Miracle Mile escaped him, he was privileged to train and drive one of our greatest pacers, *Ribands*.

JO'H

See **Harold Park Racecourse**.

Halwes (1952–?) became Australia's fastest pacer with a 1968 record of 1 minute 57.3 seconds at Harold Park, although WA pacer *Classic Garry* lowered it soon after by 2.4 seconds. *Halwes* also won the 1968 Craven Filter Miracle Mile by 20 yards in an Australian record time of 1 minute 58.6 seconds. At the end of the 1967–68 season, when he earned $43 850, *Halwes* was voted NSW Harness Horse of the Year. He also had a world-record run in NZ when he won the 11-furlong Interdominion heat from a standing start in 2 minutes 50.8 seconds. His record in this year was thirteen wins, a second, and two thirds in seventeen starts. Since his retirement *Halwes* has sired some classic feature-race winners such as *Cheeky Chick*, *Agnate*, and *Green Lea*.

GC*

HAMMOND, JOAN, OBE, CBE, CMG, DBE (1912–), born NZ, a world-renowned and revered soprano, was also a phenomenal golfer. A childhood accident left her with a two-inch difference in arm lengths. In the tension between a musical or sporting career, both won out. In 1929 and 1930 she won the NSW junior championship. She was NSW Champion of Champions twice, represented Australia abroad against NZ and Britain in 1934, was runner-up in the Australian amateur in 1933, and won the NSW ladies' championship in 1932, 1934, and 1935. Funds were collected by women golfers to send her to Italy for singing studies. In 1947, then world-celebrated, she reciprocated by giving concerts in Sydney to raise funds to send a womens' golf team to England in 1950.

CT

See **Golf**.

Handball

Handball is not standardised world-wide and versions can be played indoors or out of doors by teams of up to eleven a side. Australian handball derived from the indoor singles or doubles game imported by early Irish immigrants. The sport is similar to English fives or Spanish pelota and is normally played on a three-wall court with no back wall. A court built by a publican in Little Bourke Street in Melbourne is believed to have been the first in Australia. Unofficial competitions between NSW and Victoria began in the 1870s, and the first Australian championship was held in 1920. At present men compete for national three-wall championships (singles and doubles), Australian masters doubles championships, and the Australian four-wall open title. Since 1952 the States have attempted to gain the O'Connor Cup at the national carnival. Paul Fallon of NSW won the Australian singles title eleven times in the 1950s and 1960s as well as eight doubles titles between 1956 and 1973. The game is controlled by the Australian Handball Council.

JC

Hang-gliding

This is a fast-growing sport in Australia with an estimated 5000 pilots nation-wide in 1988. Lawrence Hargraves was the earliest Australian to fly in box kites at Stanwell Park, NSW. Flights using the familiar Rogollo wings date from 1968, but in the early years an inability to control its participants and the spiralling accident statistics resulting from a trial-and-error approach to both design and training led to its decline. During the mid-1970s, however, the Australian Self Soar Association (ASSA) began to gain more control over hang-gliding operations and the sport was instructed to develop a pilot-grading programme for the then aviation authority, the Department of Transport. By the end of the 1970s ASSA had become the Australian Hang Gliding Association; membership was compulsory and representatives in competition were performing well in overseas cross-country-style events. The association in its present form, the Hang Gliding Federation of Australia (HGFA), influenced further the improvement in training systems, membership control, and general pilot responsibility toward other airspace-users. Australian hang-gliders dominated world championships throughout the 1980s, with Steve Moyes of NSW winning the individual title at the world championships in West Germany in 1983. Moyes's three team-mates all finished in the top ten, giving Australia the team title as well. The national team's success at the world championships continued when they gained gold medals in 1983 and 1987, and silver medals in 1985 and 1989.

IJ* and IJ

HANSFORD, GREGG (1952–), born Brisbane, won more motorcycling Grands Prix than any Australian except Wayne Gardner. He was second in the world 250 cc championship and third in the world 350 cc title in 1978 and 1979. He won ten Grands Prix, including 'double victories' in the 1978 French, Swedish, and Yugoslav Grands Prix—a feat which can never be repeated because rules now restrict riders to one class. Hansford cut his teeth in motocross and dirt-cycle racing. A naturally gifted rider, he won six Australian titles from 1973 to 1977. He joined Team Kawasaki Australia in 1975 and remained with them during his career. After a serious crash in 1981, Hansford retired from motorcycle racing, switching successfully to touring-car racing. He was unfortunate not to win a world championship. Too heavy and broad-shouldered for the 250 cc and 350 cc classes, he would have been more suited to the 500 cc class, but loyalty to Kawasaki prevented him from riding the more competitive 500s.

DC

HARDMAN, DAMIEN (1965–), of North Narrabeen, became World Professional Surfing Champion in 1987 and 1991. He started his march to the champion's throne after winning the 1984 Australian junior amateur championships. As a professional surfer he won the XXXX Stubbies class in 1986, and since then he has consistently finished in the top four, with fifteen major career victories. His training programme for each season includes weights, swimming, cycling, and boxing and his interests are tennis, golf, fishing, rugby, and reading. He was inducted into the Surfing Hall of Fame in 1992.

MV

HARDWICK, HAROLD HAMPTON (1888–1959) was an outstanding versatile athlete from Sydney. Double champion in swimming and boxing at the 1911 Festival of Empire, Hardwick was also a winner of one gold and two bronze medals in swimming at the 1912 Olympic Games. He was both amateur and professional heavyweight boxing champion of

Australia. During his brief professional career (four wins and four losses) Hardwick knocked out Les Darcy's teeth in 1916. After serving in the First World War Hardwick was voted Ideal Sportsman in the British Forces. Denied reinstatement as an amateur in 1921, the unassuming Hardwick devoted himself to his job in the NSW Education Department, eventually rising to the post of deputy director of physical education before retiring in 1953.

KM

See **Swimming**.

HARDY, Sir JAMES, OBE (1932–   ), who came from a leading SA wine-producing family, skippered Australia in a number of prestigious international yachting events including two *America*'s Cup challenges, in *Gretel II* and *Southern Cross*. A handsome and urbane man—he was known as 'Gentleman Jim'—he proved a fine ambassador for Australia, dealing skilfully with a series of controversies surrounding the *America*'s Cup. Hardy was the sailing master of the Australian Admiral's Cup team in 1973 when *Apollo II* finished second. He was also the owner-skipper of *Runaway*, which competed in the 1977 series. He has won Australian championships in a number of classes—Sharpie, Flying Dutchman, Tempest, and Soling—and has sailed in numerous Sydney to Hobart races. He won the world championship in the 505 Dinghy Class in 1966 and competed in the 1964 and 1968 Olympics. Hardy played a role in *Australia II*'s 1983 victory in the *America*'s Cup: he was a syndicate director, sailing adviser, and deputy helmsman. He received the OBE and was knighted for his services to sport and the community.

RC#

See *America*'s **Cup**; *Australia II*.

Harness Racing
The standard-bred horse, derived chiefly from thoroughbred stock, has been bred to excel at fast pacing and trotting. The trotter's gait is diagonal, the pacer's lateral, and both race at about three-quarters of the speed of the galloping thoroughbred. The breed developed from road horses used for pulling light carts, but trotters were often ridden in the saddle. Informal contests on the road were reported in Sydney in the first decade of the nineteenth century, and a match race between trotters was included in a holiday sports programme at Parramatta in April 1810. As thoroughbred racing developed, trotting events were occasionally included at race meetings, but no meeting exclusively for trotters was held in Australia until January 1860 when 'American Trotting Races' were held at Flemington Racecourse. A few descendants of the foundation American trotting stallion *Messenger* were brought to Australia, notably *Vermont Boy* in 1863, but there

were too few trotters to sustain the sport as a distinct code.

Prejudice by some thoroughbred enthusiasts also discouraged the sport, but it was a thoroughbred breeder, J. J. Miller, who formed a syndicate and persuaded the American breeder Dr John Weir to bring trotters to Melbourne and Sydney in 1881, including the influential sire *Childe Harold*. The group established the Victorian Trotting Club (VTC) and opened a special track at Elsternwick on 1 April 1882. Once again, the small number of trotters restricted the sport and the VTC was forced to programme gallops to attract custom. A Sydney driving-park club staged meetings at the showgrounds at Moore Park from October 1885, and from 1890 private promoters staged trotting races at Lillie Bridge (later Harold Park) racecourse. Competing interests squabbled over the control of trotting in NSW until 1911 when the government recognised the non-proprietary NSW Trotting Club as the principal body. One Brisbane driving-park club had introduced the sport at Eagle Farm in 1888, and the Norman Driving Park club was the first to experiment with night trotting under electric lights at the Brisbane showgrounds in 1889, but the sport failed to gain a following in Queensland at this time. In Adelaide several trotting meetings were fostered at the Old Course (Victoria Park) from as early as 1880, but were hampered because betting was illegal. Technical developments in the 1890s, notably the lightweight bicycle sulky using ball-bearings, improved the speed of trotters and helped popularise trotting. Several private racecourses in Sydney, Melbourne, Brisbane, and Tasmania catered for growing public interest, though there were conflicts with those who wanted control of the sport to rest with genuine sporting clubs. Trotting was also frequently tarnished by allegations of malpractice.

The number of standard-bred horses increased steadily in the following decade. At Mentone the Tye brothers, Melbourne retailers, established a large stud and training stable, Allandale Farm, which was managed by the NZ horseman Lou Robertson. Allandale imported extensively from the USA and established yearling sales. Percy Miller at Kia-Ora, one of the largest stud farms in NSW, also turned his attention to breeding trotters, while Robert Simpson became another prominent breeder in that State. Horses were traded with NZ where trotting was flourishing. In 1910 the sport was started in Perth, largely through the efforts of James Brennan and William Foy, and was an instant success. In Melbourne John Wren established a monopoly on trotting by gaining control of Richmond and Ascot racecourses in 1907; he promoted the sport's first big purse, the Melbourne Thousand, in 1911. A dispute between Wren and

Hugh Coulter, an owner and trainer, prompted Coulter to move to SA and develop a trotting stud there. Coulter promoted night trotting at the Jubilee Oval in 1920. Between the wars trotting developed unevenly in the different States according to the local legislation on race dates and betting facilities. In Adelaide trotting began at the Wayville Showgrounds in 1925 but did not progress further until betting was legalised in 1933. Night trotting with full betting was permitted at Perth's new trotting track, Brennan Park (later Gloucester Park), from 1929 and the sport soon rivalled racing as the dominant code. The first Interdominion Championship was staged in Perth in 1936. In Tasmania, too, trotting rivalled the gallops, and several turf clubs programmed harness races as part of their meetings until after the war.

After Wren's Victorian Trotting and Racing Association lost its Ascot course for army purposes in the Second World War, a nonproprietary body, the Trotting Control Board, headed by A. G. Hunter won government approval to establish night trotting at the Melbourne Showgrounds. The first meeting was on 15 November 1947. In NSW night trotting was approved in 1949. In Queensland trotting continued to have only a small following until a new track with full betting facilities was opened at Albion Park in 1969. Interdominion Championships and the televising of trotting races in the 1970s contributed greatly to the progress of the sport, as did the development of off-course totalisator betting from the 1960s. This also gave a boost to country trotting clubs in all States. Mobile starts improved standards, and new facilities and courses attracted larger crowds. In Melbourne, trotting moved to Moonee Valley in 1976, and in Adelaide to Globe Derby in 1974.

Australian-bred trotters and pacers, overseas in origin, have proven themselves at international standard. Pacing has virtually eclipsed trotting as the preferred gait for races, and the term 'harness racing' has generally superseded 'trotting' as the name of the sport in Australia.

AL

See *Cardigan Bay*; HALL, P. J.; *Halwes*; **Harold Park Racecourse**; *Hondo Grattan*; *Paleface Adios*; WREN, JOHN; *Walla Walla*.

Harold Park Racecourse. Sydney's leading harness-racing venue is located about four kilometres west of the city and acts as the headquarters of the NSW Harness Racing Club. It covers approximately nine hectares and can comfortably accommodate 25 000 spectators. The venue began operations in 1890, about twenty years after Australia's first trotting meeting was conducted in Melbourne. It was originally called Lillie Bridge, but before the name Harold Park was given in 1929 it was variously known as Forest Lodge and Epping. The present name was derived from the pioneer trotting stallion *Childe Harold*. The erratic development of Harold Park from 1890s swamp land reflects the poor regard in which the sport was held for many years. Support for the code was consolidated in 1902 when the NSW Trotting Club was formed, although its emergence as a controlling body was unable to offset periodic downturns in support for the sport. Legislation passed in 1927 provided for an increase in the number of trotting clubs and meetings per year. This, along with the introduction of greyhound-racing at the course, helped to boost Harold Park's revenue and enabled the Trotting Club to increase prize-money. Harness racing at Harold Park blossomed in the late 1940s when night racing replaced daytime meetings. Crowds which had averaged only 2500 during the late 1930s leapt to 17 300 twenty years later, and a world-record attendance of 50 341 for this sport was recorded at the 1961 Interdominion final. The novelty of a new form of evening entertainment was partly responsible, as was the rising disposable income of Australians.

TR

See **Harness Racing**.

HARRISON, HENRY COLDEN ANTILL (1836–1929), born Molonglo Plains, NSW, was a legendary figure in Victorian sport during the latter half of the nineteenth century and the early part of the twentieth. He was an outstanding runner and footballer, and after retirement became a leading administrator, fostering the development of athletics and Australian football in the best traditions of Muscular Christianity. His first claim to fame was as Victorian champion sprinter, middle-distance runner, and hurdler from 1859 to 1867 during which time he claimed the world record over 440 yards (50.25 seconds). His contests with L. L. Mount of Ballarat were feature events of the period. At football Harrison followed the lead of his cousin, T. W. Wills, as an early champion at Australian rules, being captain of Richmond, Geelong, and Melbourne (nine years), and playing a leading role in developing the rules. He was vice-president of the VFA from its inception in 1877, was first chairman of the Australian Football Conference (from 1905), and served the MCC on its committees for record terms: full committee member for fifty-eight years, vice-president for thirty-seven years, and a member of the Melbourne Amateur Athletic Sports Committee from its inception in 1864. He was registrar-general of titles in Victoria.

RH*

See **Australian Rules Football**.

HARVEY, ROBERT NEIL, MBE (1928–), born Fitzroy, Melbourne, was one of four brothers and played first-class cricket for Victoria and NSW. Neil Harvey played in seventy-nine Tests as a dashing left-hand batsman, scoring 6149 runs at 48.42 with twenty-one centuries. One of the best Australian batsmen of all time, noted for his nimble footwork and attractive strokeplay, he was also an unsurpassed fieldsman. During a tour to South Africa, his eyesight was professionally diagnosed as deficient. He was modest and undemonstrative and served as a Test selector after retiring. His three brothers—Mervyn (1918–), Clarence Edgar ('Mick') (1921–), and Ray (1926–)—also played first-class cricket. In addition, Mick was an international umpire and Queensland selector. His daughter, Pauline Harvey-Short (1954–), represented Australia in softball. Robert (1972–), a grandson of Mervyn, plays football for St Kilda in the AFL.

SG

HATTERSLEY, HARRY WILLIAM (1908–66), born Sydney, was a champion golfer over a long period: he won his first NSW foursome's title in 1931 and the last of his seven wins in that event was in 1949. He won his first national foursome in 1930 and his last in 1955. In between he was Victorian amateur champion three times and NSW amateur title-holder three times. He won the national amateur event in 1930, and again in 1947. This immensely long hitter reached the quarterfinals of the British amateur competition in 1938 and captained the Australian team in 1948. In the 1930s the critics were in constant debate as to who was the better golfer, Hattersley or Jim Ferrier. One paper summed him up: 'we have come to regard him as a golfing Bradman—minus the commercial inclinations.' In 1966 he died of a heart attack while playing in the NSW Open.

CT

HAWKES, JOHN BAILEY (1899–1990), born Geelong, Victoria, was a leading tennis-player of the 1920s. Brought to tennis through his family's involvement with the Geelong Easter tournament, Jack Hawkes from the age of 15 had the distinction of winning the under-19 Victorian schoolboys singles five times without conceding a set. He went on to play interstate matches and then competed in the 1921, 1923, and 1925 Davis Cup teams. In 1926 Hawkes became Australian singles, doubles, and mixed doubles champion. In 1928 he made a successful private overseas tour, having been passed over in Davis Cup selection, becoming runner-up with Gerald Patterson in the Wimbledon and US doubles, and winner, with Helen Wills, of the US mixed doubles. Hawkes was a tenacious left-handed singles player, but was more renowned as a controlled and intelligent left-court doubles player, using great touch and spin.

Later he became a successful businessman, managing the Hawkes Brothers wholesale hardware firm in Geelong. Like his father he had a long stint as secretary (1923–35) and president (1936–42) of the Geelong Lawn Tennis Club.

GK-S

See **Lawn Tennis**.

HAYES, COLIN SYDNEY (1924–), born Adelaide, was the outstanding horseman of the 1980s. He was the leading trainer in Victoria for a record thirteen successive seasons, 1977 to 1990, and in SA for twenty-seven seasons, the last seventeen in succession. Hayes began training modestly, his first success coming with *Surefoot* who was placed in the 1948 Great Eastern Steeplechase at Oakbank. Based at his Surefoot Lodge stables at Semaphore, Hayes had won his first Adelaide training premiership by 1956. In 1970 he formed a syndicate to purchase the historic Barossa Valley property Lindsay Park, which he transformed into a breeding and training complex. This was an immediate success through the stallion *Without Fear* who produced a record thirty individual winners in his first crop to race in 1975–76. In that season Hayes trained 112 winners in Adelaide, many of them bred at Lindsay Park. He exceeded this mark with an astounding 136 wins in 1985–86. His best two horses were *Dulcify*, winner of the AJC Derby and Cox Plate, who broke down in the 1979 Melbourne Cup and was destroyed, and *Better Loosen Up*. He won the Melbourne Cup with *Beldale Ball* (1980) and *At Talaq* (1986) and enjoyed success in most other major Australian races. Hayes retired in 1990 at the peak of his form. His son David took over the running of Lindsay Park, with success in the Cox Plate, five Group One winners on the VRC's Derby Day, the Japan Cup, the Golden Slipper, and many other races, in his first year.

AL

HAYMAN, ERIC, OAM (1917–), was an Australian champion wrestler before becoming a volleyball administrator. He was elected president of the Victorian Amateur Volleyball Association in 1973 and two years later became president of the Australian Volleyball Federation. He was also organising chairman of the first Asian Championships held in Melbourne in 1975 and two years later was appointed vice-president of the Asian Volleyball Confederation. Hayman guided Volleyball Victoria Inc. through its vital years of growth and development. He was a member of the Organising Committee for the Melbourne Olympic Games and was an Australian official at the 1976, 1980, and 1984 Games.

IF

See **Volleyball**.

HENDY, TREVOR (1968–), Ironman, of Surfer's Paradise Surf Lifesaving Club, has been World Ironman Champion in 1988, 1990, and 1991. He was also World Malibu Champion in 1991.

RC

See **Ironman**.

HENRICKS, JON MALCOLM (1935–) became the first Australian to win the prestigious Olympic 100 metres freestyle at the 1956 Games since Fanny Durack won the inaugural women's event in 1912. Harry Gallagher, Forbes Carlile, and physiology professor Frank Cotton encouraged Henricks to concentrate on the shorter distances, which he did with great success, winning three gold medals at the 1954 Vancouver British Empire and Commonwealth Games (the 110 yards freestyle, the 4 × 220 yards freestyle relay and the 4 × 110 yards medley relay) and two gold medals at the Melbourne Games (the 100 metres freestyle and the 4 × 200 metres freestyle relay). After the Games he took up a sports scholarship at the University of Southern California. Though selected for the 1960 Olympics, he contracted severe gastroenteritis and had to withdraw from competition. He married an American and settled near Chicago.

RH and MH

See **COTTON, FRANK**.

HENSELL, WILLIAM DAVID (1882–1959), born Richmond, Melbourne, learnt the art of turning billiard and bowling balls after joining Alcock & Co. He became so proficient at his trade that he became official bowls tester for the WA Bowling Association. Hensell later improved the quality of bowling balls by using vulcanite and by 1918 these balls were successfully introduced to Victorian greens. An even more important innovation was the creation of the all-plastic 'Henselite' bowl in 1937. By 1972 more than three million 'Henselite' bowls had been produced. W. D. Hensell and his son Ray helped to produce the most accurate bowls in the world.

RC

HICKEY, REGINALD (1906–73) gave unmatched service to the Geelong Football Club, both as its longest-serving coach and captain. Hickey's 245 games as a tough, dashing centre half-back included a famous triumph as captain-coach in 1937, when he masterminded Geelong's triumph over Collingwood in a spectacular win. Skilful, lightning-fast Geelong teams coached by Hickey won two further premierships (1951 and 1952) and won twenty-three consecutive games to set an unbroken VFL record. Appropriately, one of the Kardinia Park grandstands is named after this pillar of Geelong.

DS

HIGGINS, ROY (1938–), jockey, was born in northern Victoria. After a successful apprenticeship at Deniliquin, Higgins moved to Melbourne and by 1964–65 had won the first of his eleven jockey's premierships, equalling the record set by Billy Duncan. He rode extensively for Bart Cummings, and won two Melbourne Cups for him with *Light Fingers* (1965) and *Red Handed* (1967). Riding a total of 2300 winners in all Australian States, Higgins created several records including twelve winners over three successive race days at the VRC autumn carnival at Flemington in 1972, and eight successive winners over three meetings starting in December 1976. He retired in 1984.

AL

HILL, CLEMENT (1877–1945), was born in Adelaide into a cricketing family. His father John made the first century on the Adelaide Oval, playing for North Adelaide; five of his seven brothers also played for SA. Clem Hill was a schoolboy star at St Peter's College and in one match retired at 360. He toured England four times between 1896 and 1905 and captained Australia in ten Tests from 1910 to 1912. Possibly his finest innings was his 188 against England at Melbourne in 1898, when he was still 20; Hill and Trumble added a match-winning 165 after Australia was 6–58. Hill, a fine left-handed bat, secured successive Test scores of 99, 98, and 97 in 1902. While he scored seven Test centuries, he was dismissed five times in the 90s. Hill also achieved notoriety for his role in a celebrated brawl—which lasted twenty minutes—with fellow selector Peter McAlister over the selection of an Australian team in 1911. He was one of six players who withdrew from the 1912 tour. Hill was square and sturdy, 175 centimetres tall and weighing 76 kilograms, with a crouched stance and a bottom-hand grip. He was a nimble-footed attacking batsman, merciless on anything short, a good hooker and cutter, and was also a fine driver. He was a brilliant outfielder and made a celebrated catch at Old Trafford in 1902 when he sprinted round the boundary to take a catch which helped Australia win the match by three runs.

RC

HILL, JOHN SINCLAIR LESLIE, OBE (1934–), born Moree, NSW, is the outstanding figure of Australian polo. He began playing in 1953 and, after two years in England, returned on four goals. Soon after, his masterly stroke-play, vigorous horsemanship, and natural flamboyance established him as the most dynamic player of his time. Bold, innovative, and a radical tactician, he was uncompromising in his quest to become the world's best, culminating in his 10-goal rating—he is one of only two Australians to have achieved this ultimate ranking—in 1972. Despite his genius he remained an unselfish team-player, contributing to tactical development and coaching. Retiring prematurely in 1974 after injury, he had captained both Australia and England, won many interstate series, and eight NSW championships with his Quirindi Club. He received the OBE in 1980. A strident and forthright patriot, he was involved with the formation of the Workers' Party in 1975 and, later, a campaign to restructure the beef industry. He has extensive pastoral interests.

GL*

Hill-climb Championship

Hill-climbing has been a popular motor sport in Australia since the turn of the century but the inaugural event in the Australian Championship was not staged until 1947 when it was held at Rob Roy, Victoria. It was won by A. Wylie in a Ford A Special. In 1954 the event was transferred to Collingrove, SA, and has now been contested in all Australian States except WA. Although many of Australia's finest circuit racers have won the championship, the most successful competitor is Victorian Bruce Walton who won six successive titles from 1958 to 1963.

GC*

See **DAVISON, ALEXANDER**.

HINTON Family was famous in motorcycle-racing, with three generations winning twenty-five Grand Prix events at Bathurst between 1937 and 1985. Three Hintons also won Australian championships. The founder of the 'dynasty', **Harry** (1911–78) was born in Birmingham, England, but grew up in Sydney. His career, lasting from 1928 to 1955, spanned beach racing, dirt track, road trials, and road racing. From 1931 he raced without the use of his left eye after a road accident. He scored the first of his seventeen Bathurst victories on a self-tuned BSA and his last in 1955 on an ex-factory Norton. Hinton was selected as an Australian representative in the 1949 Isle of Man Tourist Trophy and raced in the 1949 and 1950 European seasons. He was the first Australian rider to record a top-three finish in a world 500 cc championship Grand Prix. Three sons of Harry Hinton all raced successfully. **Harry Junior** (1932–59) won two Australian titles in 1957 but, after heading overseas, died of pneumonia following a crash in Italy. **Eric** (1934–) raced in Europe from 1956 to 1959 and 1965 to 1969. He won the 1959 Czech 500 Grand Prix. He also won six Australian titles and three Grand Prix events at Bathurst. **Rob** (1944–), who showed talent as a tennis-player, was forbidden to race after the death of his elder brother. He overcame the parental ban by going to Europe as a mechanic for brother Eric. He later took up racing, winning three Australian Grand Prix

events at Bathurst in 1975–76 before injury forced him to retire. Eric's sons, **Peter** (1959–) and **Tony** (1961–), both raced. Tony won Australian Grand Prix events at Bathurst in 1984 and 1985, giving the family three generations of success at Mount Panorama. Peter narrowly lost a national title in 1983.

DC

HISCOE, KEN ('The Bear') (1938–) was responsible for introducing the 'nick' shot to Australia and was Australia's first squash-player to achieve international success. An all-round sportsman, he took up squash at the relatively late age of 18 after representing NSW in lifesaving and playing football and tennis with success. He had great natural ability and was runner-up in the Australian junior championship in his first competitive season. Hiscoe won the Australian title seven times between 1960 and 1967. His most successful season was in 1963 when he won the Grand Slam of squash—the Australian, British, Scottish, and South African titles. He was the first Australian to win the British Open championship, regarded as the unofficial world title. Although a back injury restricted Hiscoe after 1963, he was ranked among the world's top ten players for another decade. From 1965 to 1971 he captained an undefeated Australian team. Hiscoe turned professional in 1971. He was still, at the age of 38, able to make the quarterfinal of the first World Open in 1976. Hiscoe must take some credit for the staging of this event and in 1973 he was elected president of the International Squash Players' Association. Hiscoe contributed to squash both as a player, paving the way for future Australian dominance of the international circuit, and as a leader of these professionals.

KT

See **Squash Rackets**.

HOAD, LEW (1934–), born Glebe, Sydney, won the Wimbledon singles title in 1956 and 1957. In 1956 he missed winning the Grand Slam when he was defeated by Ken Rosewall in the US Open final. Both Hoad and Rosewall were labelled whiz-kids and were the mainstays of the Australian Davis Cup teams in the mid-1950s. Hoad's serve-and-volley game, using only one grip, could overpower the world's best. Unfortunately his career was restricted by a recurring back injury. He turned professional in 1957 and later established a tennis-coaching school in Spain.

HCJP

See **Hopman–Hoad Towel Incident**; **Lawn Tennis**; ROSEWALL, KEN.

Hockey

Hockey was introduced to Australia near the end of Queen Victoria's reign. English schoolmistresses fostered and promoted it as a winter sport in private girls schools in 1900, and about the same time members of the Royal Navy visiting Adelaide took part in exhibition games. In the early years of Federation, girls at the Methodist Ladies' College, Launceston, were playing the game with imported English cherry-wood sticks, and the Friends School in Hobart also took up the game. By 1903 the sport began to flourish in private girls' schools. In Melbourne, both Lauriston and Ruyton engaged in regular competition and in the same year the Cambridge school in Sydney included hockey in its curriculum.

Though aggression, strength, and competitiveness were much admired in men's sports, any woman displaying these traits in a sporting contest was considered unladylike. As a non-contact outdoor team-game, hockey was seen as suitable for women. For decades, however, women's hockey continued to struggle for support and recognition in a society that placed a higher premium on men's competition and achievement.

The first men's association, the SA Hockey Association, was created in 1903; Forestville (1905) in SA is the oldest existing club in the country. Initially perceived as a women's sport, the popularity of hockey as a winter game for men spread steadily. There were 130 Victorian men playing the game in 1907 when the State Amateur Hockey Association was founded. By 1914 there were twenty-two teams in the VAHA with 350 registered players. Their great sporting rival, NSW, also formed an association controlling men's hockey in 1907. Interstate rivalry helped promote the game. A 1908 tour of NSW by the Victorian club Brighton, the first interstate match between NSW and Victoria in the same year, and the inaugural intervarsity competition between Sydney and Melbourne undergraduates in 1909 brought hockey increasingly before the public. Matches were being played in WA as early as 1903, and five years later its own association was formed.

The first women's association, the NSW Ladies' Hockey Association, was established by six Sydney-based clubs on 26 March 1908, and by 1910, when NSW, Tasmania, Victoria, and SA participated in the first interstate tournament at Rushcutter's Bay, these four States had women's associations. The women's game took a recognisably modern shape in July 1910 with the formation of a national association, the All Australian Women's Hockey Association, to control hockey. Four years later an All Australian team played its first international match against an English eleven on its way to NZ. Between 1910 and 1914 NSW won the interstate series three times and Tasmania and SA once each. The dress and behaviour of women playing the game were strictly controlled. They were required to wear long skirts, starched

blouses, ties, and stockings, and no player was to be seen on the street in her uniform unless covered by a long buttoned overcoat.

The steady growth of men's hockey was reflected in the formation in 1925 of a national body, the Melbourne-based Australian Hockey Association (AHA), to govern the men's game. In Queensland after the war, army cadets formed three clubs, and together with the oldest club, City, established the Queensland Hockey Association in March 1921. It was estimated in 1925, when the Australian Men's Championship was started, that there were about one thousand male players in the country. WA joined NSW, Victoria, SA and Queensland in the Australian championships for the first time in 1928, and won the carnival in the following year. The championships acquired a more representative character in 1935 when Tasmania first took part, having established its State association the year before. No one State dominated the men's titles between 1925 and 1939; Queensland was the most successful, winning on five occasions, Victoria and WA three times each, and NSW twice. International competition for men in the inter-war period was confined to annual contests with NZ, begun in 1922, for the Manning Memorial Cup.

From the beginning, administration of men's and women's hockey was divided, and they continued on their separate ways. Women had formed a national association and conducted a regular interstate series fifteen years before the men, and Australia was one of the eight founding members of the International Federation of Women's Hockey Associations (IFWHA) in 1927. Domestically, Tasmania and NSW emerged as the major forces in women's hockey between 1920 and 1939, winning or sharing the Australian Women's Championship on six occasions each; Victoria were four times winners, SA three times, and WA twice. Interstate tournaments were rotated annually among the main capital cities. WA joined the other four States in this competition in 1921, and four years later Queensland made its initial appearance in the interstate series at Launceston.

An English women's team which travelled to Australia in 1927 was far too skilful for its opponents in matches in Adelaide, Melbourne, and Sydney. At the end of the tour an Australian team was invited to visit England, which it did, as well as playing in South Africa, Rhodesia, Belgium, Germany, Holland, and France. In its matches with Australia in 1936 and 1941 England remained in a class of their own. The first World Women's Hockey Tournament, organised by IFWHA, was held in 1933, but it was not until 1936 that Australia sent a national team to participate in the Third International Tournament in Philadelphia. Throughout the inter-war period Mrs F. J.

Davy remained the most influential figure in Australian women's hockey, secretary of both the NSW State body and the All Australian Association, and manager of all touring teams until 1939.

The AHA introduced an Australian Colts Championship (under-21) in 1946, and an Australian Junior Championship (under-17) began four years later. Only 407 teams were registered with the AHA in 1947 when NSW left the association, but by 1954 the national body was again in control throughout Australia with an affiliation of about one thousand teams; in 1978 1400 senior clubs were registered with the AHA.

The striking feature of post-war Australian hockey has been the dominance of WA. The rapid rise of men's hockey in that State owed much to a strong Anglo-Indian influence, especially to Kevin Carton, Merv Adams and the five Pearce brothers. Five times champions between 1946 and 1959, WA men won a further twenty-one national titles between 1960 and 1990. In the Australian Women's Championships, WA has been even more formidable than in the men's, having won the national title on thirty-eight occasions between 1946 and 1990. In recent decades WA has invariably produced more Australian representatives than any other State; for example, eight of the members of the 1984 men's Olympic team, and half of the women's team at the 1988 Olympic Games, were from WA.

In terms of administration, hockey clubs in metropolitan or country areas belong to a local district association which in turn is affiliated with the State association. Each State association is affiliated with the national men's or women's body. The growth of hockey in Australia has been difficult to quantify because of the lack of statistics on the number of players and clubs, but since the 1960s success in the international arena has given hockey an increased status and popularity. A game of precision, speed, and fine timing, the advent of synthetic surfaces, regular television coverage, and the introduction of indoor hockey have added to the sport's appeal. After a team was entered in the Olympics for the first time in 1956, Australian men's hockey quickly grew in stature, winning a bronze medal at Tokyo in 1964 and silver medals at the 1968 and 1976 Olympics, to be ranked among the leading hockey nations. Notable successes in the last decade include the 1983 Pentangular tournament in Kuala Lumpur, the Hong Kong Ten Nation tournament and Champions trophy in Karachi in both 1983 and 1984, the Champions trophy in 1985, and the World Cup in England in 1986.

Australian women were represented at the IFWHA conference tournaments, the premier international women's competition, staged every four years between 1953 and 1979. The other controlling world hockey body, Fédération Internationale de Hockey, organised the first Women's World Cup in 1974, and was successful in having women's hockey admitted to the Olympic programme in 1980. The Australian women's team came fourth at Los Angeles in 1984, and at the 1988 Games defeated South Korea 2–1 in the final to win the gold medal. In the 1990 World Cup in Sydney, Australia lost to the Netherlands in the final.

It is estimated that there are 200 000 women and girls playing hockey in Australia. There are almost 21 000 senior women players registered with the AWHA and 11 000 juniors. NSW has the largest number of registered players, followed by Queensland, Victoria, and WA. Victoria had 253 senior metropolitan teams registered with the AHA in 1989, followed by WA (236) and NSW (125). NSW, with many strong regional centres, has by far the largest number of senior country teams registered, with 348; Victoria has 180, and WA 168.

MS

See **Australian Hockey Association**; **CHARLESWORTH, RICHARD**; **CORMIE, HEC**; **GLENCROSS, BRIAN**; **GORMAN, DIANNE**; **IRVINE, JIM**; **McNAB, FINLAY**; **MORLEY, CHARLIE**; **NILAN, PATRICK**; **PEARCE Brothers**; **PEARCE Sisters**; **PISANI, SANDRA**; **PIPER, DES**; **RILEY, RON**; **SMITH, TREVOR**; **Women's World Cup Hockey**.

HOGAN, HECTOR (1931–60) was the leading post-war amateur male sprinter. 'Hustling Hec' ran some of the fastest times in the world in this era, including a world record for the 100 yards of 9.3 seconds, which he held for six years, and an unrecognised time—because it was a handicap for men and women—of 10.2 seconds for the 100 metres. Hogan won ten straight individual Australian titles from 1952. At the Melbourne Olympics he made a quick start in the 100 metres and led his fancied opposition at the halfway mark but finished third—the first Australian male to secure a medal in the sprint since Stan Rowley in the 1900 Olympics. While still at his peak he was struck with leukaemia. Never disclosing the nature of his illness, he retired in 1959 and died the following year.

GC*

See **ROWLEY, STANLEY**.

HOLMAN, KEITH VICTOR, MBE (1927–   ), born Ballarat, Victoria, changed the nature of rugby league scrum-half play, adding rugged defence to the expected brilliant attack. Holman was raised by foster parents at Yarra Bay, a southern Sydney suburb. There he became a schoolboy supporter of the All Blacks, a local Aboriginal team in the South Sydney junior competition. Educated at St Peter's School, Surry Hills, where his constant chatter earned him the nickname 'Yappy', he was rejected by South Sydney as being too small. Instead he added two years to his age and joined the RAAF in 1944. While serving, he built up his strength and fitness and played football at Ipswich and Dubbo, before becoming scrum-half for Western Suburbs in 1948. In partnership with his club five-eighth, Frank Stanmore, Holman starred for Australia in its 1950 Ashes victory over England. He went on to play in fourteen Tests against England and thirty-two against all countries. For Wests, he had 203 first-grade games, including a premiership win in 1952, before he retired in 1961. Holman later took up refereeing and controlled the 1971 Grand Final and two Tests in 1972. He later coached Wests, winning the Amco Cup knock-out competition in 1977. More recently, he has become a representative-team selector and member of the NSW coaching panel. He was awarded the MBE in 1977. Now retired, Holman, a teetotaller, was for twenty-five years a sales representative for John Cawsey & Co., liquor merchants.

TB

HOLT, MICHAEL ('Jack') (1879–1951), born Berwick, Victoria, was the leading racehorse trainer in Victoria for much of the two decades following the First World War. He trained horses in Gippsland before establishing stables in the Melbourne suburb of Mordialloc. Holt's name was associated with many champions of the 1920s in particular, including the Caulfield Cup winners *Eurythmic*, *Maple*, and *High Syce*, as well as *Easingwold*, *Heroic*, and *Second Wind*, and he was known as 'the Wizard of Mordialloc'. Holt also trained *Heroic*'s son *Hall Mark* to win the 1933 Melbourne Cup. On his death Holt left a substantial fortune to charity.

AL

Hondo Grattan (1968–?) was the only pacer to win consecutive Interdominion finals. He began racing as a 2-year-old but made his name as a 3-year-old when he was successful in seventeen of twenty-one starts. In the 1973 Interdominion *Hondo Grattan* joined an élite group of pacers who went through the competition undefeated. He then won the final by a head. Starting from the 15 metre mark he won the next series at Perth in 1974. Some other notable wins included the 1974 Craven Filter Miracle Mile run in 1 minute 59 seconds, and the 1973 and 1975 NSW Lord Mayor's Cups. During the 1974–75 seasons his total racing earnings passed $200 000—he was the first pacer to achieve that standard. He also eclipsed *Bay Foyle*'s record of twenty-one wins at Harold Park.

GC*

HOOBIN, JACK (1922–   ), born Victoria, in 1950 became the first Australian to win the World Amateur Road-Cycling Championship. Hoobin gained a place in the Australian team for the 1948 Olympics in London on the strength of his wins in the Victorian championship and the 125-mile Sun Classic. He was also placed second over 10 miles in the 1948 Australian Amateur Track Championships and third in the 5 mile event. After finishing seventh at the Olympics, Hoobin returned to Europe in 1949 to try his luck at the World Amateur Road Championships. He finished seventh. Hoobin returned to Europe the next year, and overcame tough opposition from experienced French and Italian riders to win the world title.

JS

Hopman Cup. The inaugural Hopman Cup, an international mixed doubles tennis competition, was conducted at the Burswood Resort Casino in Perth between 28 December 1988 and 1 January 1989. Named after the legendary Harry Hopman, the event was said to be 'the culmination of a dream come true' for tennis-circuit friends Charlie Fancutt, Paul McNamee, and Pat Cash. Fancutt believed there was potential for a mixed doubles tournament combining aspects of the Davis Cup and Federation Cup. McNamee, a Wimbledon doubles champion, was emerging as an entrepreneur in tennis. Cash, soon to win Wimbledon, expressed a desire to play in the event, if it came to fruition. Four years later, Cash was to partner Hana Mandlikova in reaching the final which was won by the Czechoslovakian pair of Miloslav Mecir and Helena Sukova. The quality field of eight teams attracted over forty thousand spectators, Perth's largest tennis spectacle.

HCJP

See **HOPMAN, HARRY; McNAMEE, PAUL.**

HOPMAN, HARRY ('The Fox') (1906–85), born Sydney, was captain of the Australian Davis Cup team in 1938 and 1939 and later became non-playing captain from 1950 to 1969. On three consecutive occasions from 1930 to 1932 he was runner-up to either Edgar Moon or Jack Crawford in Australian Open singles finals. During these years he captured State Open titles in SA and WA. With his first wife, Nell Hall, he reached the final of the mixed doubles at Wimbledon in 1935 and won the Australian mixed doubles championship on four occasions. For more than a decade he was nationally ranked in the top ten and regularly represented Australia in the Davis Cup. Although a competent player in his own right, Hopman is better known for his long tenure as the non-playing captain of the Australian Davis Cup team. During this time Australia won the Davis Cup on twenty-one occasions. Hopman was known as 'The Fox' but it was his strict discipline and inspiration in difficult situations rather than mastery of tactics which earned him that tag. Given his role in discovering and training so many great players, he left an indelible mark on Australian tennis. In 1969 Hopman moved to Florida, USA, to establish a junior development coaching school. Early in his career he had clashed with officialdom in his determination to wear shorts rather than trousers in tournaments. Soon after his death his name was perpetuated with the establishment of the Hopman Cup competition.

HCJP

See **Hopman Cup**; **Hopman–Hoad Towel Incident**; **Lawn Tennis**; **Squash Rackets**.

Hopman–Hoad Towel Incident. One of the most memorable moments in the annals of Australian tennis took place when captain Harry Hopman, 'The Fox', threw a towel at Lew Hoad during a crucial stage of the 1953 Davis Cup challenge round in Melbourne. With the tie standing at two rubbers to one in favour of the Americans, Lew Hoad was Australia's hope against Tony Trabert. The latter had easily defeated Ken Rosewall on the first day. Hoad won the first two sets but Trabert fought back on the rain-drenched turf to level the match. In the second game of the fifth set Hoad dramatically tripped and fell headlong near Hopman's chair. Before 'The Fox' helped the 19-year-old star to his feet he threw a towel at Hoad and gave him an encouraging push, but could not refrain from reportedly saying 'you clumsy oaf'. Hoad recognised the symbolism in Hopman's action which echoed the act of a boxer's seconds in 'throwing in the towel' to stop the fight and save their man from further punishment. Hoad responded brilliantly by winning a string of games to win the match. Rosewall, controversially replaced in the doubles by Rex Hartwig, then maintained his mastery of Seixas to clinch the Cup. It seemed, however, that the towel incident was the turning point of the tie.

HCJP

See **HOAD, LEW**; **HOPMAN, HARRY**.

HOPTON, VERA (1900–) was a key figure in Victorian calisthenics. She first learnt calisthenics at Alfred Crescent State School and then at Bosworth College, a specialist training institution for the discipline. As a young primary school teacher she introduced Saturday outdoor classes at Merri State School, North Fitzroy, and later became a teacher at Bosworth College, a specialist institution training calisthenics teachers, and ultimately principal of Bosworth for twenty-five years. She founded her own phenomenally successful Clifton Calisthenic College in 1925 and the college dominated competition until it closed in 1977. Hopton was a foundation

member of the Physical Culturalists' Association of Victoria which established a chair in physical education at the University of Melbourne. Her work at Bosworth and Clifton mark her as one of the greatest Victorian physical educators of the twentieth century.

RO

HORAN, THOMAS PATRICK (1854–1916), born Middleton, County Cork, Ireland, came to the Australian colonies as a young boy. The stockily built, heavily whiskered Horan was an aggressive right-hand batsman and occasional round-arm bowler for Victoria, and played in fifteen Tests including the first in Melbourne in 1877. He captained Australia twice during the 1884–85 season. Concurrent with his playing career Horan contributed a column on cricket to the *Australasian*, the weekly supplement to Melbourne's *Argus*. Under the pseudonym 'Felix', Horan's erudite journalism revealed both a deep understanding of the game and a critical eye over its development in Australia. His observations over four decades enjoyed a vast following and have become a standard resource for historians of the game. He died in Melbourne.

DM

See **Cricket**.

HORDER, HAROLD NORMAN (1894–1978) was known as Australian rugby league's 'wonder winger'. Playing first grade for South Sydney from 1912, in 1921 he switched to North Sydney, which won the premiership that year and the next. Horder toured England with the third Kangaroos in 1921–22 and was the leading scorer. He moved to Queensland in 1924 and played for Coorparoo. A good goal-kicker, he was a great attacking winger, whose speed off the mark, side-step from either foot, and hare-like swerves were spectacular.

CC

Hordern Shield. Donated by Samuel Hordern, a leading Sydney retailer, the Hordern Shield was presented to the annual winner of the Sydney Electorate or District Cricket Competition which began in 1893–94. The inaugural winner was the East Sydney club. The Paddington club finally took possession of the shield after winning the competition for the fourth time during 1902–3. Made by Blashki & Sons of Melbourne, the shield contained about 150 ounces of sterling silver and was valued at one hundred guineas. It featured the SCG with a match in progress and was surmounted by a batsman at the wicket.

SG

Horse-racing
There is hardly a town or settlement in Australia which has not at some time in its past conducted a race meeting. Even today, after

several decades of rationalisation and greatly improved transport, there are more than four hundred registered racecourses throughout Australia which in the 1989–90 season staged 3700 meetings involving more than twenty-five thousand races. The 37 265 individual starters in these races were competing for a total of $190 million in prize-money. They were just part of a thoroughbred population which included 39 000 broodmares and a crop of 21 000 foals. This equine population explosion dates from 1788 when the First Fleet unloaded at Sydney Cove seven horses from the Cape Colony in South Africa. The stock was chiefly Arab: the first thoroughbred to arrive in Australia is believed to be *Rockingham* (probably a son of the English *Rockingham*, by *Highflyer*) in 1799. There were 200 horses in the colony by 1800, and 1100 ten years later.

In a primarily penal colony the military authorities did not care to authorise horse-races, but there is evidence of a 'race ground' in use on the Hawkesbury River near Richmond as early as 1806. Press mention of match races at a holiday gathering at Parramatta was made in April 1810. The first official race meeting, chiefly organised by officers of the 73rd Regiment, took place over three days (15, 17 and 19 October 1810) at Hyde Park in Sydney. In common with most meetings in Australia in the next half-century, the Sydney races used heats, longer rather than shorter distances, older rather than younger horses, set weights according to the age and sex of the horse, frequent match races between two horses, and sweepstake prizes. Owners most often rode their own horses; stewards and judges were appointed by the organising committees and the course was marked out with flags and posts. Novelty events such as hack races, ridden trotters, and hurry-scurries were often included to widen the appeal. The sport made an appearance at Hobart with a meeting on a course near Cornelian Bay on 10 July 1813. The horses came from stock sent from NSW. Private matches were regularly contested between horses of the wealthy residents and officers of the colony until Governor William Sorell suppressed horse racing from 1817 to 1824. At the new colony of Swan River in WA, James Henty arrived in 1829 with four well-bred thoroughbreds from the Earl of Egremont's stud in Sussex. Two of these died; he soon afterwards took the survivors to Van Diemen's Land. Meanwhile the Governor, Captain Stirling, imported further Egremont stock to Perth in 1834. A race meeting involving Timor ponies had been run at Fremantle in October 1833, but the first race in the West for thoroughbred stock was not held until 1836 at a meeting at Guildford.

Racing committees began to give way to racing clubs. The Sydney Turf Club (STC) (the first of three bodies to carry this title) formed itself in March 1825 as the first racing club in Australia; it was under the leadership of Sir John Jamison. It held spring and autumn meetings at various Sydney venues including 'Bellvue', Parramatta, Hyde Park, and Camperdown. Progress was marred by rivalries during the regime of Governor Ralph Darling, who encouraged the formation of the Australian Racing and Jockey Club in 1828. By 1831 both clubs had lapsed. In 1833 Darling's successor, Richard Bourke, reserved a racecourse site beyond the outskirts of the town. Later known as Randwick, the course was first descriptively called the 'Sandy Race Course'; its inaugural meeting, organised by a subscription committee, was held on 19 April 1833. The unstable surface was too difficult to maintain and the course was virtually abandoned. The absence of major meetings in Sydney in 1839 or 1840 prompted the formation of the Australian Race Committee in 1840 which established a good racecourse at Homebush, nine miles from the city. With the success of the first meeting in 1841, the committee reconstituted itself into the Australian Jockey Club (AJC), in January 1842.

Pastoral expansion led to settlement in the regions that later became the colonies of Victoria and Queensland, and colonies under separate administration were formed in SA and NZ. Thoroughbreds were brought to the new settlements, both from NSW and from England. The first race meeting in Adelaide was held on open land west of the town on New Year's Day 1838, less than two years after its foundation. Melbourne, first settled in 1835, staged its first race meeting in March 1838 on a plain west of Spencer Street. In March 1840 a permanent racecourse was established on the Saltwater River further from the town; originally called the Melbourne Racecourse, it later took the locality name of Flemington. Although Brisbane had been settled as a penal town in the 1820s, it was not opened to free settlement until 1841. A race meeting was held on scrubby ground at nearby Cooper's Plains in July 1843. Annual meetings moved to New Farm, closer to the town, in 1846, but depended on the reluctant support of squatters from the Darling Downs. These pastoralists preferred their own meetings closer to home: races were first held at Drayton (Toowoomba) in 1848 and Warwick in 1850 but were weakened by local rivalries. The riverport town of Ipswich emerged as a compromise location, and for the next decade it hosted Queensland's most important race meetings.

With forty-five districts in NSW reporting new race meetings in the 1840s, and dozens more in the other colonies over the next two decades, meetings became more elaborate and there emerged a demand for professional horse trainers and jockeys. Racing clubs formed, and built grandstands. The AJC began modelling classic races such as the St Leger and Derby on English example, but it was the gold-rich colony of Victoria that rapidly became the centre of Australian racing, including steeplechasing. Rival clubs, the Victoria Turf Club (1852) and the Victoria Jockey Club (1856), staged increasingly lavish meetings at Flemington. An intercolonial match race between Victoria's *Alice Hawthorn* and the Sydney champion *Veno* drew a crowd of 40 000 to Flemington in 1857. It inspired the running of an Australian Champion Sweepstake at the same course in 1859. This race, won by the local outsider *Flying Buck*, provoked enormous intercolonial interest. It was imitated in several centres in Australia in the next decade. In 1861 the Victoria Turf Club introduced a rich 2 mile handicap, the Melbourne Cup. This again drew intercolonial attention and large betting interest. Success went to the NSW horse, *Archer*. Though not always the richest race in Australia, the Melbourne Cup has been unrivalled in fame and prestige.

Economic reversal in the early 1860s forced the two Victorian clubs to disband and re-form in 1864 as the Victoria Racing Club (VRC). Meanwhile in Sydney the AJC obtained a lease at Randwick, laid down a good grass track and built grandstands. Its first meeting at the revived course was in May 1860. The club's main race was its Derby, but it successfully introduced major handicap events in 1865–66, including the Sydney Cup. Similarly the SA Jockey Club established a rich Adelaide Cup in 1864 at its racecourse at Thebarton, while in Brisbane the Queensland Turf Club was formed in 1863, a racecourse was opened at Eagle Farm (1865), and the inaugural Brisbane Cup was run there in 1866. Eagle Farm soon overcame the supremacy of Ipswich.

The flourishing racing scene in all colonies saw many new racecourses during the 1870s. In Adelaide the SAJC abandoned Thebarton in favour of a new course at Morphettville (1875), while private entrepreneurs continued racing at the 'Old Course' in the parklands (Victoria Park from 1898). In Hobart the Tasmanian Racing Club was formed in 1874 and opened its beautiful Elwick racecourse in 1875, while in Launceston the Tasmanian Turf Club (1871) remodelled the Mowbray course in 1877. In Melbourne the Victoria Amateur Turf Club (VATC) was formed in 1876, initially to provide competition for amateur riders, and took a lease on the primitive suburban racecourse at Caulfield (first used in 1859). With the rapid success of its Caulfield Cup (first run in 1879) it became a strong rival to the VRC. Another older suburban club, Williamstown, also improved its standard. The racing boom encouraged several private racecourses into the game, including Croxton Park

at Northcote (1869), W. S. Cox's Kensington Park (1874), Elsternwick (1882, initially as a trotting course), Brighton Park, and Cox's new course Moonee Valley, first used on 15 September 1883. In Sydney a similar expansion occurred, with the Sydney Hunt Club (1873–75) becoming the Sydney Amateur Turf Club in 1877 and then the Sydney Turf Club in 1880. Unlike the VATC, it did not have its own course; racing at Randwick, it became an adjunct of the AJC before being dissolved in 1905. Private courses at Canterbury Park (1884), Rosehill (1885), Moorefield (1888), and Warwick Farm (1889) together provided weekly race meetings in Sydney. Except in Adelaide, the profits generated by racecourses encouraged many more ventures in the latter part of the boom of the 1880s. In other capitals, courses were expressly designed for pony-racing, a development resented by the older clubs. Several of these succeeded in banning pony-owners, trainers, and jockeys from participating in the traditional meetings.

In Melbourne the new courses included Mentone (1888), Oakleigh Park (1888, renamed Sandown Park in 1892), Epsom (1889), Maribyrnong and Aspendale (1891), and pony tracks at a second Oakleigh course (1891), and Ascot (1893). An automatic starting barrier at the Oakleigh pony track was used experimentally in 1893; within two years versions developed by various inventors were in use at all metropolitan tracks. Sydney's new pony tracks included Botany (1891), Lillie Bridge (1893 later renamed Forest Lodge, then Epping, and finally Harold Park), Kensington (1892), and Rosebery Park (1895). In Brisbane the ponies were catered for at Kedron Park (by 1889) and Breakfast Creek (1893, later called Albion Park).

Australian racing prosperity had peaked by 1890 when the NZ-bred *Carbine* earned an unprecedented £10 000 in winning the Melbourne Cup. Economic depression soon reduced prizemoney, and contributed to a large fall in the market for horses. WA, with a mining boom in the 1890s, escaped the Depression: wealthy racing clubs were established at the arid goldtowns of Coolgardie, Boulder, and Kalgoorlie; private courses opened in the Perth region at Canning, Helena Vale, and Burswood (later Belmont); while the Ascot racecourse at Perth was completely rebuilt in 1902–3. In all States in the new Commonwealth of Australia in the first decade of the twentieth century there was a backlash against the unrestricted growth in race meetings and betting activity, and strict legislation diminished illegal off-course betting. This increased attendances at races and made private racecourses more profitable. New pony tracks were opened in Sydney at Ascot (1906) and Victoria Park (1908). When the NSW Government legislated to restrict the number of race meetings within forty miles of the capital, entrepreneurs responded by opening courses, accessible by railway, just beyond the limits, including Gosford, Kembla Grange, Wyong, and Menangle. John Wren, forced from his profitable totalisator in Collingwood by Victoria's 1906 Gaming Act, bought into private pony and trotting tracks in Melbourne, Perth, and Brisbane. In 1910, with partner Ben Nathan, he purchased the tiny Brisbane sand track of Albion Park which he instantly made popular through clever promotion and large stake-money for feature races. Keeping most of their moves masked from the public, Wren and Nathan controlled every course in Brisbane by 1922 except the QTC's Eagle Farm.

The principal clubs in all States, particularly the AJC and the VRC, campaigned against pony-racing and unregistered racing, and strengthened their own control of the sport through initiatives such as allocating race dates to clubs, placing control of all registered meetings into the hands of paid stewards, creating a compulsory and uniform system of horse registration (1910), purchasing the Australian Stud Book (1910), and adopting the Australian Rules of Racing (1912). Governments also extended their control over racing during the First World War when the sport was restricted. In WA the government terminated unregistered pony-racing in 1917. The post-war decade saw racing enjoy an enormous boom. The most potent factor in this growth was the promotion of racing in the developing mass media, including pictorial newspapers and magazines, and cinema newsreels. Most influential of all were radio broadcasts of racing which had begun by the mid-1920s. Crowds exceeded ninety thousand at Randwick for *Heroic*'s Derby victory in 1922; more than one hundred and twenty-six thousand patrons attended Flemington when *Spearfelt* won the 1926 Melbourne Cup. The Easter meeting at Oakbank in the Adelaide Hills was by this time attracting more than forty thousand visitors, many of them coming by motor car. Courses everywhere undertook lavish improvements in stands, tracks, and amenities. In 1922 the AJC purchased Warwick Farm and virtually rebuilt it for its reopening in 1925. The most significant effect of the boom was the upsurge in well-organised, illegal off-course betting, with SP (starting price) bookmakers making extensive use of telephone and radio. The racing boom made top jockeys, trainers, and horses into national celebrities—none more so than the NZ gelding *Phar Lap*, whose versatility and virtual invincibility on Australian tracks between 1929 and 1931, together with the melodramatic and sensational events surrounding his career, ensured his place in turf legend.

After the boom of the 1920s, thoroughbred racing faced many challenges during the Depression. There was severe competition from night trotting in Adelaide and Perth, and from pony- and dog-racing in Sydney. In Brisbane a royal commission recommended the abolition of private racecourses, and revealed that the formation of the Brisbane Amateur Turf Club (BATC) in 1923 (which took over Albion Park and a projected new racecourse at Doomben) was a device of Wren and Nathan's to retain a financial interest in the courses. After recasting its finances, the BATC was permitted to open Doomben in 1933. The creation of the Doomben Newmarket (later the Ten Thousand) and Doomben Cup gave Brisbane racing a national focus. In Victoria the government ordered the closure of several courses in 1931, notably Sandown Park, Fitzroy, Aspendale, and Richmond. The remaining proprietary courses converted themselves into 'clubs', as Moonee Valley had done in 1917. Under financial pressure, the government also legalised the on-course totalisator. The NSW Government also came under pressure to end proprietary racing and reduce the number of courses and meetings in Sydney. Events of the Second World War overtook plans, and in 1943 the government legislated to form a new Sydney Turf Club to take over existing private tracks. The STC retained Rosehill and Canterbury and became an innovative rival to the AJC. It pioneered the Australian use of photo-finish equipment and mobile starting stalls at Canterbury in 1946. Government controls were even more intrusive during this war than during the previous one, with many racecourses occupied for long periods by the military. Some, such as Williamstown, never reopened. There were severe cuts in race days, and restrictions on transport and fodder. Racing clubs devoted most of their profits to patriotic funds.

Post-war prosperity saw racing boom once more. The Queensland champion *Bernborough* attracted a record crowd exceeding one hundred thousand to Caulfield in 1946, but the favourite was defeated by *Royal Gem*. City racing clubs reaped the benefits from the reduction in courses and the ending of unregistered racing. Transport of horses by air allowed for far greater mobility of racing, and in time saw an influx of NZ horses which achieved an impressive record in top races, particularly *Rising Fast* who, with the Sydney horse *Tulloch*, was the equine hero of the 1950s. The introduction in 1957 by the STC of the Golden Slipper Stakes for 2-year-olds, which soon came to rival the Melbourne Cup in prize-money, signalled a continuing shift towards shorter races and events for younger horses. Prize-money and racecourse amenities improved dramatically. A benchmark for modern facilities was the new Sandown Park racecourse opened by the VATC in 1966, with a track layout designed for ease of viewing, and closed-circuit television

69 Lacrosse, an adaptation of a game played by North American Indian tribes, was introduced into Victoria in 1874 and quickly spread to other colonies.

70 John Landy's and Roger Bannister's struggle in the final stages of the 'Miracle Mile' at the V British Empire and Commonwealth Games in 1954 is immortalised in this bronze statue erected outside the stadium in Vancouver.

71 Lawn bowls was initially played on public 'greens' beside hotels and inns, but clubs soon became established in more 'respectable' locations such as the MCG.

72 Lawn bowls was dominated by males until the 1890s, but the formation after 1900 of exclusively women's clubs and associations did much to increase women's participation.

for patrons. Attendances at city courses were high through the late 1960s and early 1970s.

Racing became a vehicle for the introduction of metric weights and measures in Australia, with a changeover from miles and furlongs, stones and pounds to metres and kilograms from 1 August 1972. In 1979, after a long campaign, women were given the right to be registered as jockeys to ride in open company against men. New Zealander Linda Jones scored the first win at Doomben on 7 May 1979.

The development of legal off-course totalisator betting from 1959 and its subsequent computerisation allowed for a dramatic increase in the scale and scope of betting in the 1980s, with television coverage of local and interstate races and updated, approximate odds becoming common in TAB agencies. Although betting volumes continued to grow, the off-course service was such that, except at carnivals such as Oakbank and the Melbourne Cup, racecourse attendances diminished. Economic extravagance in the 1980s saw the creation of lavish incentive schemes for yearling buyers such as the Magic Million races inaugurated at Southport on Queensland's Gold Coast in 1987. There were also tax-minimisation schemes for yearling buyers and the floating of public companies on the stock exchange devoted to breeding and racing horses. The collapse of several such schemes at the end of the decade saw a sudden decline in the price of horses at yearling sales.

Rapidly rising revenues from racing encouraged State governments to play an increasingly direct part in the conduct of the sport. All States now have ministers in charge of racing with legislative powers over aspects of the sport but, under these limitations, the principal clubs continue to control racing in their respective States or regions.

Australia's isolation and quarantine regulations have restricted, though not prevented, participation in the international racing scene. The greatest international successes have been Australian jockeys, particularly Frank Wootton, Frank Bullock, Rae Johnstone, Edgar Britt, and Scobie Breasley. From a small number of Australian horses sent overseas to race, the wins of *Merman* in the nineteenth century, *Sailor's Guide* (Washington International 1957), *Crisp's* gallant second to *Red Rum* in the Grand National Steeplechase at Aintree in 1973, and most recently the win of *Better Loosen Up* (Japan Cup 1990), to name a few, have shown the high standard of our racing. A handful of Australian-bred stallions have also been successful internationally, notably *Bernborough*, *Shannon*, and *Royal Gem* in the USA. *Carbine*, who sired a dynasty of English Derby winners, must be conceded as a New Zealander, but his locally born son, *Wallace*, was not only a champion Australian racehorse but was also among the greatest Australian stallions of all time. In short, Australian racing must be viewed as part of the international racing scene.

AL

See **Adelaide Cup Run at Flemington**; *Ajax*; **Ansett Awards**; *Archer*; *The Barb*; *Bernborough*; **Betting on Sport**; BREASLEY, ARTHUR; BUCKINGHAM, BEVERLEY; *Carbine*; CORRIGAN, THOMAS; **Corrigan's Funeral**; CUMMINGS, JAMES; DE MESTRE, ÉTIENNE; **Drama**; *Fine Cotton* **Affair**; **Flemington Racecourse**; *Gloaming*; GORDON, ADAM LINDSAY; *Gunsynd*; HALES, THOMAS; HAYES, COLIN; HIGGINS, ROY; HOLT, MICHAEL; HOYSTED, FREDERICK; JOHNSTONE, WILLIAM; *Jorrocks*; *Kingston Town*; LEWIS, ROBERT; *Malua*; *Manikato*; McCARTEN, MAURICE; McCARTHY, RICHARD; **Melbourne Cup**; MOORE, GEORGE; *Mosstrooper*; MUNRO, DAVID; **Literature**; **Oakbank**; PAYTEN, BAYLY; *Peter Pan*; *Phar Lap*; **Randwick Racecourse**; *Rising Fast*; ROBERTSON, LOU; SCOBIE, JAMES; SELLWOOD, NEVILLE; *Shannon*; SMITH, THOMAS; SMITH, Sir JAMES; *Tulloch*; *Wakeful*; **Warrnambool Grand Annual Steeplechase**; WOOTTON, FRANK; WREN, JOHN.

HOWARD, ARTHUR (1919–), born Fairfield, Victoria, began canoeing on the Yarra River in 1936. He designed and manufactured canoes (with Carl Sierak) from 1945 to 1964. He was president of the Victorian Amateur Canoe Association from the 1940s to the 1960s, from which position his enthusiasm and helpfulness did a great deal to encourage and promote canoeing in Australia. He later became a life member of both the Victorian Association and the Australian Canoeing Federation.

EH-S

HOYSTED, FREDERICK WILLIAM (1883–1967) was the most successful member of an outstanding racing family, being leading trainer in Victoria in fourteen seasons between 1932 and 1960. His grandfather and namesake (1818–1901) who established himself as a trainer at Benalla, had a large family: many of the sons and grandsons made their mark as jockeys, trainers, bookmakers, and race-callers. Fred Hoysted showed early brilliance as a boy jockey in the Wangaratta district but like many, weight halted his riding career. He moved to Melbourne in 1927 and by 1932–33 had won his first trainers' premiership, aided by his champion steeplechaser, *Redditch*. Hoysted took over the training of *Rising Fast* in the horse's last two seasons on the turf. Fred Hoysted's sons included N. D. ('Bon') and Robert Edward Hoysted, trainers of champion sprinter *Manikato*.

AL

HUNT, GEOFF, MBE (1947–), Australia's most successful male squash-player, began playing at the age of 12 when his English-born father, Vic, took up the game for health reasons. Vic became known as an accomplished player and administrator for the Squash Rackets Association of Victoria in his own right but was also influential as a coach and mentor for Geoff. Geoff won his first championship, the Victorian junior title, in 1962, at the age of 15. In 1963 he won the Australian junior championship and his first senior event, the Victorian State championship. At the age of 18 he became the youngest player to win an Australian title—his first of seven—in 1965. Hunt went on to win every major squash tournament in the world. Possibly his greatest achievement was to win eight British Opens, six of them consecutively, a record not broken until 1990 by Pakistani Jahangir Khan. Hunt was ranked world number one from 1975 to 1980. During this period he won the inaugural World Open Championship in 1976. His defeat of Pakistani Mohibullah Khan in a 2-hour 2-minute final is considered one of his finest performances. Hunt has been described as a perfectionist or a technologist. His style may reflect his quiet manner and academic background—he has a Bachelor of Science degree from Monash University. When the AIS opened its squash unit at Brisbane in January 1985 Geoff Hunt was appointed head coach.

KT

See **Squash Rackets**.

Hunting

Fox-hunting was an activity by which genteel Englishmen and women could be recognised as such. Indeed, Anthony Trollope declared hunting 'the great national pastime' which defined Englishmen of class. He himself rode to hounds regularly in England and even did so in Australia when he visited his son Frederick in 1871. Those who aspired to upper-class status in the Australian colonies thus used fox-hunting to define their place in the new society; to pronounce both their 'Englishness' and their upper-class status as Trollope suggested. Officers of the 73rd Regiment in Sydney brought with them their own packs of hounds and the earliest account of a hunt with hounds was January 1811 when a kangaroo was killed 'after an exciting run of two hours'. Hunt clubs were established in Bathurst (1826), Parramatta (1833), and Cumberland (1838). Francis Dutton announced in 1846 that in the new colony of SA, the new Britannia in the Antipodes, '. . . all the purely English sports are kept up with much spirit . . . hunting, racing and . . . cricket are, in the proper seasons much patronized.'

Bell's Life (3 June 1865) congratulated those settlers who sought to bring 'proper' English game to Australia—foxes, rabbits, hares, pheasants, and deer—and called for the propagation of the fox as a 'legitimate object of the chase' instead of kangaroo and wild dogs. Thomas Chirnside of Werribee Park (Victoria) and Thomas Austin of Barwon Park (Victoria) were two notable lovers of English field sports who imported game into Australia. Thomas Pyke, 'gentleman farmer' from Wiltshire, who regularly hunted the Port Phillip area in Victoria, is credited with (or blamed for) the first importation of foxes to Australia. Thomas George Gregson hunted in the Jericho area of Tasmania in the late 1820s. A Northumberland man, it was said of him that he was 'reared in the tradition of the hunting squire'. The *South Australian Magazine* in 1842 assured each reader in England that 'go to what colony he may, he will find a pack of hounds in full work'. The author of the article ('Jager' = German for 'huntsman') mentioned the presence of four imported packs in SA including the Adelaide Hounds under the direction of George Hamilton as master. This was a subscription pack, like so many others in colonial Australia. Its frequent financial difficulty reflected the current economic condition of the colony and its aspirant gentry membership. Eventually the Adelaide Hounds were sold at auction, but in 1869 the Adelaide Hunt Club (AHC) was formed by William Blacker, 'squire of Fulham'. This club still hunts the Adelaide Hills. The Melbourne Hunt, also still in existence today, predates the Adelaide Hunt, having been formed in 1839. The MHC thrived under the direction of one of Ireland's best known hunting families, the Watsons, and like the AHC attracted the colonial gentry to display their community status through membership.

The hunting season in Australia extended from the middle of May (Queen Victoria's birthday) until the end of September. Midweek hunts declared the activity to be reserved for the leisure class and fees, dress, and sponsored membership ensured this. Riding to hounds in Australia in the nineteenth century was a means of displaying one's status as a member of the colonial gentry. The annual hunt club ball, hunt races, and steeplechases, all attended by the Governor, further confirmed this order in society, and the media always accorded the local hunt club enough space and many photographs to attest this.

Mechanisation in the early twentieth century meant an inevitable reduction in the number of horses and reduced interest in hunting. Horse-riding gave way to car-driving as a skill. Hunt runs were cut by railway lines, asphalt roads, and suburban development. The hunt clubs moved out of the cities and established their kennels in the nearby countryside. Significant social institutions as they were, the major hunt clubs like the Melbourne and the Adelaide not only were now 'out of sight', they became 'out of mind' anachronisms of a bygone era. There were some compensations. As young men discovered the motorcar, young women realised their ambition to be allowed to ride at the head of the chase and increasingly hunt club lists included more women than men.

The form of the hunt also changed. In the past, landowners accepted the time-honoured principle of allowing huntsmen to ride across their property in pursuit of the fox. Now the hunt had to gain approval and that was not always forthcoming. Some considered the sport barbaric—a 'blood sport'. Both issues were resolved by designing runs over capped fences and pre-ordained courses and following an aniseed trail (a 'drag') instead of a fox.

Membership of Australian hunt clubs is no longer an indicator of social status: lists include riders from all walks of life. Indeed the lack of exclusivity has deterred many of the upper class from remaining as members. At present there are fifteen registered hunt clubs in Australia. The hunts continue as riding clubs, as social events, and as colourful reminders of a British colonial past.

JAD

Hyde Park was the first sportsground in Sydney and in Australia. A proclamation on 13 October 1810 by Governor Lachlan Macquarie dedicated the area for the 'Recreation and Amusement of the Inhabitants of the Town, and a Field of Exercise for the Troops'. Situated to the west of the town, Hyde Park had already become the popular venue for sport and recreation as reflected in its previous names: 'The Common', 'Exercising Ground', 'Cricket Ground', and 'Race Course'. Hyde Park was the first home of Sydney horse-racing. The first official meeting on 15, 17, and 19 October 1810 was held on a course which had been laid out by the officers of the 73rd Regiment. Hyde Park remained the focal point for Sydney horse-racing until 1825 when it was transferred to the Bellevue course. The park was also the early home of Sydney cricket, and a cricket ground was laid out on its north-western section. Most of the important club cricket matches were played there from the 1830s to 1856. Many other sports were played on Hyde Park including hurling, quoits, and rugby. Although Hyde Park was a convenient ground for sport, there was always the problem that it was both a sportsground and a park; in effect, something of a town common. Cricketers, for instance, complained regularly that they did not have exclusive right to their particular ground. They had to share the park with the military, who drilled there; the general public, who cut paths across the cricket ground; other sports, which did not respect the sacred turf; and with stray cattle, sheep, and goats. The quoits players, who practised close to the cricket pitch and sometimes damaged it, were a particular nemesis of the cricketers. Meanwhile the authorities were keen to improve the park by creating walkways and planting ornamental trees and shrubs. With the growth of organised sport by the 1850s it was recognised that Hyde Park could no longer serve the dual purpose of park and sportsground and the major sport still played there, cricket, was moved to the Outer Domain. Sport returned to Hyde Park briefly in 1865 when the first known rugby club games were played there between the Sydney and Australian clubs in July.

RC

HYLAND, DEIRDRE, OAM (1936–), has been president of the Queensland Netball Association (1974–80), the All Australia Netball Association (1978–88), and the International Federation of Netball Associations (1987–91). She has managed Australian teams on overseas tours and been official delegate at world tournaments on numerous occasions. Hyland has also been a board member of the AIS (1981–83) and the Confederation of Australian Sport (1987–88), and chair of the Organising Committee of the Eighth World Netball Championships held in Sydney in 1991. She was admitted as an associate member of the Sport Australia Hall of Fame in 1989 and was awarded the OAM in 1990.

PB and IJ

See **All Australia Netball Association**.

I

Ice Hockey

A form of ice hockey has been played in Australia since 1904 when a notice appeared at Adelaide's ice-rink convening a meeting of skaters interested in creating a new form of amusement on ice, similar to ice hockey. The first official game was played in 1908 in Melbourne between sailors from the visiting US warship *Baltimore* and a Victorian representative team; the Australians lost. Sydney formed its first team in 1908 and the first interstate series between Victoria and NSW was held in Melbourne in 1909; this championship became known from 1921 as the Goodall Cup and is now Australia's premier championship.

Sticks began to be imported from Canada, so Australian players no longer had to use field hockey sticks; the first pucks arrived at about this time also and they replaced the tennis balls. New rules were required to go with the new equipment and these were based on a combination of English 'bandy' and Canadian ice hockey with seven in a team. Ice hockey competition ceased during the First World War and began again in Sydney and Melbourne in 1920. Protective equipment in the form of gloves, pads, and elbow guards started to arrive from Canada from 1921. The Australian Ice Hockey Federation was formed in 1923. There was a break in competition during the Second World War and matches recommenced in Sydney, Melbourne, and Adelaide in 1946.

Australia was invited to participate in the Winter Olympics at Cortina, Italy, in 1956 but did not attend because of a lack of funds. Australia competed at the next Olympics in Squaw Valley, California, and defeated Denmark to record their first international victory. Since then Australia has participated in Olympic qualifying and world championships at the junior, youth, and open level and has hosted both Asian–Oceania and world championships. In 1987 Australia hosted the World D Pool Ice Hockey Championship in Perth and won its first gold medal. Australia set a world record at these championships when it beat NZ 58–0. The goal-a-minute result eclipsed Canada's 47–1 record win over Denmark in 1953.

Ice hockey is now played in all States in approximately fifteen ice-rinks scattered from Cairns to Hobart and from Sydney to Perth. There are at present approximately fifteen hundred ice hockey players, male and female, aged between 8 and 60 years. Most teams have twenty players and play one match a week during a season that runs from April to September.

IC and IJ

ILLINGWORTH, Captain JOHN, RN, a

British Royal Navy captain on duty in Sydney as an engineer, was instrumental in establishing the Sydney to Hobart Yacht Race in 1945. He also skippered the winning yacht, *Rani*, in the first race. It was Illingworth's idea that a planned 630 nautical mile cruise from Sydney to Hobart should be turned into a race. He also showed how to handicap boats according to the British Royal Ocean Racing Club's formula. Beginning on Boxing Day and capturing media and public attention, the race was an immediate success. Illingworth's boat, *Rani*, which 'disappeared' at sea, turned up in dramatic circumstances 50 nautical miles from the finishing line to win the event in 6 days 14 hours and 22 minutes — 17 hours before the next boat. Illingworth, who had a long career as a British yacht-racer, was the author of several books on yacht-racing.

RC

See **Sydney to Hobart Yacht Race**.

Indoor Cricket

Indoor cricket in Australia originated in 1978 in WA as a practice programme for outdoor cricket. Since its inception the rules and playing facilities have been developed and refined to the point where it is a most popular sport in its own right and is played by nearly three hundred and fifty thousand participants in about three hundred specialised venues around Australia. Originally the control of the sport was shared by two organisations, Indoor Cricket Arena—a franchised company which developed a national chain of arenas—and the Australian Indoor Cricket Federation, an association of independent clubs throughout Australia which was formed in 1983. Early in 1990 all indoor cricket clubs within each State amalgamated into one national body, the Australian Indoor Cricket Federation (AICF). In 1990 the AICF was recognised by the ASC and received funding for the establishment of a national office. The AICF is totally integrated at all levels and represents and conducts competitions for men and women of all ages. All States conduct interclub competitions, with regional and State championships culminating in national championships, the first of which was held in Perth in 1985. At international level the first competition was a men's Test series in NZ in 1985; in November 1991 a meeting was held to form a world body and plan the first World Cup for men, to be held in Australia in 1992. An Australian women's team toured NZ in 1990. Indoor cricket has developed rapidly since 1978 and is one of the top four team-participation sports in Australia.

KW and IJ

INGATE, GORDON (1926–) was the skipper of *Caprice of Huon* which was successful in three of the four races to win the Admiral's Cup in 1964. He was already well known for his successes in the 5.5 metre and Dragon classes. He won the Australian 5.5 metre championships five times in the 1960s and was Australian Tempest-class champion three times in the 1970s. He took *Caprice of Huon* to second place in the 1972 Sydney to Hobart race and to victory in the 1969 Sydney to Montagu Island race. He skippered *Gretel II* in the 1977 elimination series, for the right to challenge for the *America*'s Cup, but lost to the Swedish boat *Sverige* in a tie-breaking seventh race.

RC

International Cricketer of the Year Award was started in 1979 by Benson & Hedges, the cigarette manufacturers, who have sponsored Test and one-day cricket since that date. The company has provided a car each year for the winner, who is chosen by a panel of umpires, commentators, and cricketing officials. It is based on the performance of players in both Test cricket and one-day international matches played during the Australian season. Up to 1991, the award has been won by the following players: V. Richards (three times), D. Lillee, B. Yardley, D. Gower, D. Boon, C. Broad, R. Hadlee, D. Haynes, Imran Khan, and S. O'Donnell. The choice of the adjudicators has not always been free from controversy. In 1985–86 Richard Hadlee refused to comply with the tradition whereby the car is sold and the proceeds of sale distributed among teammates, taking the not unreasonable view that he had won the Test series for NZ single-handed. In 1990–91 the award was made to Simon O'Donnell who had not played in even one Test match. It was reported that O'Donnell was embarrassed to receive it.

JNT

Ironman, the Surf Life Saving Association's (SLSA) most glamorous sporting event, is a multi-disciplined race involving a 500 metre surf-ski paddle, a 400 metre board paddle, and a 300 metre swim, with a 40 metre sprint between each section. A ballot is conducted before the event to determine the order of the three water disciplines. Australian lifesavers were introduced to the Ironman during their tour of the USA in 1965. The event was subsequently incorporated into the Australian championships in 1966. Two lifesavers have won four Australian titles: Grant Kenny (1980–83) and Trevor Hendy (1987–88 and 1990–91). The commercial potential of the Ironman was recognised in the early 1980s after the success of *Coolangatta Gold*, a film based on a 42 kilometre Ironman race and starring Grant Kenny. The event, which was staged for the film and featured lifesavers, drew excited media and public attention. Confronted by entrepreneurs organising events outside its control, the SLSA and its sponsor Kellogg introduced a Grand Prix circuit in 1986 comprising six endurance events varying between 15 and 19 kilometres, and an 'Ironman Gold' over 42 kilometres. Darren Mercer won the first five Ironman circuits. Dissatisfied with the management and administration of the circuit, several lifesavers formed an alternative competition in 1989, the Ironman Super Series, and secured sponsorship from Uncle Tobys. The Ironman thus became a site of competition between professional sportspersons and the National SLSA Council, the latter unable to reconcile professional sport with a humanitarian and voluntary organisation, and between two food corporations trying to increase their market share of breakfast cereals. The struggle is between the SLSA and the Ironman Super Series to produce and market the most credible event, one which encapsulates excitement, professionalism, and integrity.

DB

See **HENDY, TREVOR**; **KENNY, GRANT**; **LEECH, GUY**; **Surf Lifesaving**.

IRVINE, JIM (1948–), born Paddington, Sydney, began a representative career in hockey at the age of 15. He played in Victorian teams from juniors to seniors (under-16 in 1963, and 1964; under-21 in 1965 and 1966; and seniors from 1964 to 1984). At the national level he was originally selected as a forward before moving to the back line. With 188 games for Australia between 1969 and 1984, and vice-captain 1977–84, Irvine was known for his strong defence as well as his strong hitting ability, which led to many goals from penalty corners. During this period he represented his country at three Olympics, four World Cups, and five champions trophies, accumulating a gold, three silver, and four bronze medals. In recent times Irvine has devoted his time to coaching. He was appointed Victorian coach in 1988, assistant Australian coach in 1989, and men's hockey coach at the Victorian Institute of Sport in 1990.

BS†

IRVINE, KEN ('Mongo') (1940–90) was an outstanding rugby league winger of the modern era and the North Sydney Club's most illustrious son. After joining the club in 1958, Irvine soon established his credentials as a prolific try-scorer and was selected to play with the 1959 Kangaroo tourists. For the next fourteen years he used his blistering speed and uncanny positional sense in establishing try-scoring records, which remain unsurpassed at club and international level. At Dubbo in 1963 he ran 100 yards in 9.3 seconds, setting a world professional sprint record. After retiring from football in 1973, Irvine worked as a journalist and salesperson. He died of leukaemia in December 1990. A fitting testimonial, the scoreboard at North Sydney Oval, is dedicated to his memory.

AM

J

Jack Affair. The Interstate Single Sculls Championship of 9 May 1908, hosted by the Victorian Rowing Association (VRA), provided an example of the controversy over amateurism. Before the event concern was expressed as to the eligibility of the Tasmanian Rowing Association's (TRA) nominee, E. Jack. The TRA was requested to confirm Jack's eligibility under the 1896 interstate amateur agreement. Although this was not forthcoming, Jack rowed in and won the sculling championships. The VRA decided to investigate Jack's amateur status before awarding him the winner's certificate and requested a statutory declaration from him that he had not been employed 'in or about boats for money or wages'. When he responded that he was involved in building boats of various types with his father, Jack was disqualified from the race by the VRA at a meeting in August 1908. The race was awarded to the runner-up, H. Brasch (Victoria).

DL
See **Amateurism**.

JACKSON, MARJORIE (later NELSON), MBE (1931–), sprinter, was born in Coffs Harbour, NSW, but was brought up in Lithgow. She attracted attention when she defeated Olympic champion Fanny Blankers-Koen over 100 yards in Sydney in 1949. She won the first of six sprint titles in world-record time, 10.8 seconds, in 1950. She set four world records in that year. At the Auckland British Empire Games she won both sprints and was a member of successful sprint relay teams: she was dubbed 'the Lithgow Flash' soon after. By 1952 she had reduced the record for 100 yards to 10.4 seconds and went on to dominate the sprints at the Helsinki Olympics winning the 100 metres by 3 metres and the 200 metres by 5, becoming the first Australian female to win an Olympic gold medal in athletics. In the process she equalled the world record of 11.5 seconds for the 100 metres. Her only disappointment was dropping the baton in the women's sprint relay. Jackson was an unassuming and candid champion. Australians identified with 'Our Marjorie', who had to prepare for Helsinki in the Lithgow fog, the track lit up by motor-car lights. After repeating her successes at the 1954 Vancouver British Empire and Commonwealth Games, Jackson retired when only 22; she had married Olympic cyclist Peter Nelson in 1953. Jackson was ABC Sportsman (*sic*) of the Year and was elected to the Helms Hall of Fame (USA) in 1952. She was awarded the MBE in 1953. After her husband died in 1977 she raised money for leukaemia research. She also became involved in sports administration.

JAD
See **Athletics**.

JACKSON, PETER (1861–1901), born Christiansted, West Indies, arrived in Australia, his adopted home, in 1880. He won the Australian heavyweight title in 1886, before boxing twenty-eight top fighters overseas (1888–92), losing to none. His 187 centimetre, 86 kilogram frame gave him speed, strength, strong jabs, and clever feints. Sadly, the 'colour line' was drawn against him by the white champions. His sportsmanship and deference to white power made him universally popular. Unable to obtain fights after 1892, he declined, his health affected by tuberculosis and fast living. Jackson boxed circus exhibitions in Australia from 1898 almost to his death in 1901. He rests in Toowong cemetery, Brisbane.

RB
See **Boxing**.

JAMES, JULIE MARY (1938–), speleologist, was born at Ledbury, Herefordshire. She started exploring caves while in the UK but emigrated to Australia in 1967. She has since explored and researched caves throughout the world. James is particularly noted for her leadership of expeditions to Atea Kanada and other giant caves of the Papua New Guinea highlands, and her involvement in exploration of the most challenging caves elsewhere. She became vice-president of the International Union of Speleology.

EH-S

JANE, BOB (1929–), born Melbourne, turned to motor racing in the late 1950s with the same determination he applied to his business activities. He won four Australian Touring Car Championships (1962 and 1963 in a Jaguar, 1971 and 1972 in a Chevrolet Camaro) while building an Australia-wide tyre-service franchise. As a race promoter from 1974 he has used his highly developed Calder venue on the northern fringe of Melbourne as a potent (if not always successful) tool for change in the power structure of Australian motor racing.

GH

JEROME, JERRY (1874–1950), boxer, was born at Jimbour Station, Dalby, in Queensland. In 1913 he became the first Aboriginal title-holder when he won the Australian middle-weight boxing championship. A left-hander, he had his first fight at the age of 33. With the help of an exemption certificate from his employer, Jerome was free from the special and restrictive laws then applying to Aborigines. He was able to pursue his interests in horse-riding, shoot-ing, and boxing. His aversion to training often caused him to fight in poor condition. Popular with the crowds, he earned large purses, which he quickly lost. Boxing writers rate several of his fights as some of the most memorable in Sydney Stadium history. Although he never drank, he was considered a 'pernicious influ-ence' by the authorities because he 'incited' fellow Aborigines to refuse to work unless they were paid for it. He died, penniless, at Cher-bourg settlement in 1950. Jerome had fifty-six professional bouts, winning thirty-seven of them, thirty-one by knock-out.

CT and PT
See **Aborigines in Sport**.

JESAULENKO, ALEX ('Jezza') (1945–), born Salzburg, Germany, at first played soccer and rugby union, but became a highly skilled and exciting Australian rules footballer. In 256 games for Carlton, he featured in four premier-ships, one as captain-coach in 1979, before transferring to St Kilda. He moved interstate, returning to coach Carlton in 1989–90. Whether in defence or attack, Jesaulenko was scrupu-lously fair, possessing amazing speed, anticipa-tion, and reflexes. His genius produced many match-winning performances, none more memorable than his soaring, perfectly balanced high mark in the 1970 Grand Final.

AB

JOHNS, LESLIE (1942–) was a brilliant rugby league full back from Souths, in Newcas-tle, NSW, whose performance helped that city to defeat the touring Englishmen in 1962. From 1963 he played for Canterbury-Bankstown in Sydney. He toured with the Kangaroos in 1963 and 1967, playing in all three Tests in the latter series. He retired in 1971, having played twelve Tests for Australia. A fine athlete with flair in attack and courage in defence, he was also an accurate goal-kicker. Johns was, in addition, a first-rate cricketer.

CC

JOHNSON, PETER (1937–) was a durable and long-serving hooker who played in forty-two Tests, including three as captain. A member of the Randwick club in the Sydney competi-tion, Johnson made his Test debut against the British Lions at Brisbane in 1959 after playing in NSW's 18–14 win over the tourists. His

courage and toughness were unquestioned when confronting the huge Springbok pack in 1961, and after the South African tour he com-bined with John Thornett and Jon White to form one of Australia's great front rows. A fine player in the loose as well as the tight, Johnson made an indelible contribution to scrummaging techniques and will also be remembered for his astute football judgements and his humorous writing on the game.

GC

JOHNSTON, CRAIG (1960–), Australia's best known soccer player, was born in Johan-nesburg, South Africa, but was raised in the Lake Macquarie area in NSW. Beating child-hood bouts of the potentially crippling bone-marrow disease osteomyelitis, he progressed through school and junior representative ranks until he went to England at the age of 15 to play soccer professionally. Despite some problems of homesickness and adjusting to the British game, he secured an apprenticeship with Mid-dlesborough. At 17 he was the youngest player to represent Middlesborough in an FA Cup Tie when he made his first appearance in January 1978 against Everton. His debut was a suc-cessful one and set him on the road to stardom. Later his relationship with the club soured and he was transferred to Liverpool for a fee of more than $1 million in 1981. Johnston collect-ed a league championship medal in his first full season followed by another championship and League Cup win the following year. He was a member of the treble-winning 1983–84 side which won the League Championship and Cup and the European Cup. In the following season, he played in the tragic game at Brussels when thirty-nine fans died. The 1985–86 season was the peak of Johnston's career when the League Championship was regained, with him scoring an all-important goal in his team's FA Cup Final win over Everton. After playing two more seasons, Johnston surprised the soccer world by retiring at 27 and returning to Aus-tralia. He has focused his attention on his own marketing company. He currently holds the title of Australian Soccer Federation 'Ambassa-dor to Youth' and is charged with popularising the modified soccer game, Rooball, with the young.

GC

JOHNSTONE, WILLIAM RAPHAEL ('Rae') (1905–64), born NSW, was a jockey who achieved the bulk of his considerable rid-ing success overseas. He was apprenticed at 13 and won his first city race in Sydney in 1920. An instant success, he had several disagree-ments with stewards and in 1927 was suspended for two years for pulling a mount. Resuming in 1930, he rode in India until 1932 when he made his base in Paris. Here, his expert timing, whereby he devoured opponents in the final stages of a race, earned him the name of 'Le Crocodile'. His best years came after the war: he won the English Derby three times, in 1948, 1950, and 1956, the French Derby twice, and the Irish Derby once, and in all rode more than two thousand winners. He retired in 1957, and trained horses in France until his death.

AL

See **Horse-racing**.

JONES, ALAN (1946–), born Melbourne, was the 1980 world Formula One (motor-racing) champion. He was the only son of Stan Jones, one of Australia's fastest drivers of the 1950s, and he inherited his father's stocky build, direct manner, and will to win. After a few Australian races in the late 1960s he started his real career in 1970 in the crucible of Formula One, the British minor formulas. Obvious speed and refusal to quit gradually brought him recognition (in England if not in Australia) and he had his first Formula One drives in 1975. His first Formula One victory came in 1977, in an Arrow. From 1978 until his retirement at the end of 1981 he raced for Williams.

GH

See **Sport Australia Awards**.

Jorrocks (1833–61), a thoroughbred and part-Arab racehorse, was accorded by contemporaries an 'undisputed claim to the first niche in the Gallery of Australia's Winning Horses': bred at Mudgee, his sire *Whisker* and dam *Matilda* were winners on the Sydney turf. A bright bay with black points, *Jorrocks* was short but compact. Used as a stock horse, he did not begin racing until 5 years old. He had various owners but was most often trained, raced, and ridden by John Higgerson. Although few race meetings were available, *Jorrocks* amassed at least sixty wins (including several walk-overs). Many of these were at Homebush in Sydney, where he had his last start (unplaced) in October 1852, aged 19.

AL

Judo

The sport of judo can be traced to the Japanese Samurai warriors of many thousands of years

ago. If confronted with an unarmed combat situation the Samurai would resort to a style of fighting which later became refined into ju-jitsu, which is designed to injure or kill an opponent. Ju-jitsu flourished until Japan opened its doors during the Meiji era in the mid-nineteenth century, and these fighting skills became less popular and unnecessary in modern warfare. Judo was established as a modern sport by Jigoro Kano (1860–1938) and is the only Olympic sport to have originated in Asia. The first ju-jitsu demonstration to be held in Australia was in Sydney in 1906 for Police Commissioner MacKay. One of the demonstrators was English-born Cecil Elliott who had been graded a First Dan in Yokohama, Japan, in 1904 and began teaching ju-jitsu in Sydney in 1905. The first Australian judo book was written by Dr A. Ross in 1949; Ross had studied at the Kan School, Tokyo, and had become honorary chief instructor at the Brisbane Judo Club, founded in 1928. The inaugural meeting of the Judo Federation of Australia (JFA) was held in Sydney in 1952 with delegates from Queensland, NSW, Victoria, WA, and SA in attendance. Australian Judo Championships conducted by the JFA began in 1950 for men and in 1956 for women. Australia's first entry into international events was in the 1961 world championships in Paris, when Andrew Wake competed. Australia has been represented at every world championship since and at every Olympic Games where judo has been included. Ted Boranovski won a bronze medal at the 1964 Olympics. Women's international competition began with the 1975 Oceania championships. Participation in many European events followed, as well as representation at the inaugural women's world championships in 1980. The sport has developed steadily, especially since the introduction of the National Judo Coaching Scheme which commenced in 1980. Outstanding performances at the 1988 Olympics in Seoul, with Suzanne Williams and Julie Reardon receiving a gold and bronze medal respectively, have ensured the continued development of this sport.

MB and KS

K

KABBAS, ROBERT (1955–   ), born Cairo, Egypt, arrived in Australia at an early age when his family emigrated to Melbourne. Representing Australia in weightlifting at three Olympics, from 1976 to 1984, he won a silver medal in the 82.5 kilogram class at the 1984 Games. His Commonwealth Games performances were also notable. He won a gold medal at Edmonton in 1978 in the 82.5 kilogram class and at Brisbane in 1982 in the 90 kilogram class. He rounded out his career at the Edinburgh Games in 1986 with a silver medal in the 82.5 kilogram class. His performances were always identified by an aggressive and determined style.

MN

Kangaroo Tours. There have been seventeen 'Kangaroo' tours of Britain by Australian rugby league teams, from the pioneers of 1908–9 to Mal Meninga's successful 1990 side. Since 1933, Kangaroo tours have included matches in France. The sixth Kangaroos were the first to play a Test in France, on 2 January 1938. The original Kangaroo tour was an arduous and unprofitable 45-match venture. The first Australia v. Great Britain Test was drawn 22–22 in London, on 12 December 1908. Two later Tests were lost. The second Kangaroos of 1911–12 were captained by Chris McKivat and lost only five of thirty-five matches on tour. The Test series was won 2–0, with the second Test drawn. Between 1912 and 1963 eight Kangaroo teams returned without the Ashes. The fourth Kangaroos went close in 1929–30, losing a fourth Test 3–0 after the third ended scoreless. The 1933–34 and 1948–49 sides failed to win a Test in Britain. In 1963 the eleventh Kangaroos thrashed Britain 28–2 and 50–12 in the first two Tests to become the first team since McKivat's to win an Ashes series in England. No Kangaroo side has lost a series since. The unbeaten Test record of the second Kangaroos remained unmatched until 1982, when the fifteenth Kangaroos, the 'Invincibles', won every game on tour. That feat was matched in 1986 by Wally Lewis's side. The 2–1 series win by Meninga's Kangaroos left Australia with twenty-four Ashes Test victories in Britain, one less than Great Britain. Three Tests have been drawn.

PC

KEARNEY, KEN ('Killer') (1924–   ), a rugby league and union hooker, was a powerfully built slow-moving man, once described as a tank built close to the ground. He began his career playing rugby union and represented Australia in seven internationals before he joined English rugby league team Leeds following the 1948 Wallaby tour. Kearney played in England until 1952 when he returned to Australia to join the powerful St George team. He led the club to the first six of its eleven consecutive premierships, being captain in 1956 and captain-coach from 1957 to 1961. During these years he also represented Australia in twenty-two consecutive Test matches and played in two World Cup series (1954 and 1957) until injuries forced him to retire in 1962. He later coached Parramatta and Cronulla-Sutherland. A surprisingly quick striker of the ball, Kearney was a superb scrummager when scrums really mattered. His defence was punishing, especially when he was called on to tackle head-on, and he had brilliant ball skills, which had been perfected at Leeds. Kearney took heavy punishment throughout his career but never flinched: he once moved the bandages to his good leg to fool opponents and was regarded as a hard man in a game famous for enforcers. Possessed of a quick wit, he was friendly, intelligent, and a born leader who received spontaneous support from colleagues and younger players.

TGP

KELLERMAN, ANNETTE (1886–1975), born Marrickville, Sydney, was introduced to swimming as a means of strengthening her legs, weakened by a childhood illness. After learning to swim at Cavill's Baths in Sydney, she rapidly became proficient at all strokes and by the age of 16 had won two State titles, the 100 yards and the mile. During the next two years, she gave demonstrations of swimming and diving, performed in a stage play and swam the Yarra in record time. In 1905 her father decided they should go to Europe to promote her professional career. After several hair-raising distance swims—including three unsuccessful though highly publicised attempts to swim the English Channel—and a season at the London Hippodrome, Kellerman went to the USA in 1906. Almost immediately she gained fame and notoriety and, following a profitable year in vaudeville, she was arrested on a Boston beach for wearing a brief one-piece bathing costume. Throughout her career in entertainment she continued her spectacular swimming feats, including all her own movie stunts. Kellerman believed that her great achievement was in helping to dispense with the neck-to-knee swimming costumes. But she did more than that: she helped to popularise women's swimming and to make it socially acceptable. After a varied career in America, Annette Kellerman finally resettled in Australia in 1970. She was inducted into the Swimming Hall of Fame in 1974. She died in hospital at Southport, Queensland, on 6 November 1975.

PH

See **Swimming**; **Synchronised Swimming**.

KELLY, PEARL (née O'BRIEN) (1894–1983) was born at Koo-wee-rup, Victoria, but it was in Perth at the age of 16 that she began to drive and ride harness horses. After her marriage to Charlie Kelly during the First World War she moved to Melbourne and continued her career. In addition to her own horses she drove for leading trainer Percy Shipp, finishing third on the Melbourne Drivers' Premiership in the early 1920s. Despite her success the Victorian Trotting and Racing Association was unconvinced that the sport was safe enough for women. In the late 1920s they banned the issue of driving permits to women, although Kelly continued to train horses until 1961. By the time of her death in 1983 a new generation of women had taken her place and reversed the attitudes of the late 1920s.

JO'H

KENNEDY, EDWINA (1959–) was the first Australian to win the British Women's Amateur Golf Championship, a feat which she accomplished on her nineteenth birthday. Receiving a cut-down set of golf clubs when 2 years old she was enrolled at the Wentworth Falls Golf Club at 7 and carded under 100 one year later. At 16 she won the Australian foursomes with Sue Goldsmith and then went on to win the Australian junior championship in four consecutive years. In 1979 Kennedy became the first woman to play in the Australian universities team championship, winning all her matches from the men's tee. She has represented Australia in four world amateur team championships and has been a member of successful Australian teams in the Espirito Santo world championship, the Commonwealth series, Australia v. Japan, and the Asia Cup. In 1986 she eventually captured the Australian Women's Amateur Golf Championship.

GC*

KENNEDY, JOHN ('Kanga') (1928–) coached Hawthorn Football Club from 1960 to 1976, achieving three premierships. His 'Commandos' pioneered high levels of fitness and a fierce approach at the ball, sometimes to the detriment of other skills. The introduction in the early 1970s of a square to prevent central crowding was partly a response to Kennedy's strategies. Kanga's famous drab overcoat matched his taciturn manner. In a distinguished playing career as a tough ruckman he captained Victoria and his club, and won Hawthorn's best and fairest four times. He surprised the football world by later coaching North Melbourne. Kennedy's son, John, was a valuable Hawthorn premiership player.

DS

KENNY, GRANT (1963–), Ironman, surfer, and kayak exponent, was born at Maryborough in Queensland. He came from a sporting family; his father, Hayden, was Australia's first Ironman Champion and operated a surfboard and surfcraft business. His grandfather and grandmother were both prominent in sport in the Maryborough district. Learning to swim at an early age, Kenny was Australian Cadet Malibu Champion at 14 and before he was 20 had won four Senior and two Junior Ironman Championships of Australia and had received twelve Australian surf gold medals. He was a versatile athlete: by 1983 he had represented Australia in surf, starred at two world titles in kayaks, and won the Molokai to Oahu (Hawaii) Marathon Ski Race four times. He also represented Australia as a kayak-paddler in the 1984 and 1988 Olympics. Appearing on television, in a movie, and endorsing Kellogg's Nutrigrain, Kenny, with his movie-star looks, became a surfing superstar who did much to popularise the Ironman contest. He later married Olympic swimmer Lisa Curry.

RC

See **Ironman**.

KERLEY, DONALD NEIL (1934–), born Adelaide, was known as the 'Iron Man' and 'King of South Australian Football'. From the 1950s to the 1990s he was a rugged ruck-rover and an inspirational captain and coach of West Adelaide, South Adelaide, Glenelg, West Torrens, Central District, and the SA State team. Like his equivalent Ron Barassi, Kerley established a record for lifting mediocre sides to premiership contenders although he won only four premierships. His most remarkable effort was taking South Adelaide from bottom to top of the ladder in 1964 and his personal magnetism has caused fans to follow him from club to club. Kerley became team manager of the Adelaide Crows in 1991, but later resigned to coach West Adelaide once again.

BW

KIERAN, BERNARD BEDE (1886–1905) was born in Sydney of Irish Catholic parents. A delinquent at 13, he was committed to the nautical-school ship *Sobraon* and became interested in swimming. By April 1905, using the 'amble crawl', Barney Kieran had won six State and six Australasian freestyle titles and set 'world' marks for every distance from 200 yards to 1 mile—the last record of 23 minutes 16.8 seconds stood until 1924. In England, Scotland, Ireland, and Sweden the '*Sobraon* Boy' won every race but two, setting world records including 6 minutes 7.2 seconds for 500 yards, recognised by the Fédération Internationale de Natation Amateur in 1908. Unspoiled by success, Kieran was the greatest swimmer the world had seen. After winning three more Australasian titles in Brisbane, he died after an appendectomy on 22 December 1905. He is commemorated by a monument at Gore Hill cemetery, Sydney, the B. B. Kieran Memorial Shield, and at the International Swimming Hall of Fame, Florida, USA.

GW
See **Swimming**.

KILBORN, PAM, MBE (1939–), born Melbourne, started hurdling at the age of 16 and was unfortunate to miss selection for the 1960 Olympics. She won the 80 metres hurdles at the 1962 British Empire and Commonwealth Games by an impressive 4 metres and later in the afternoon won the long jump with 6.268 metres, the best in her career. After finishing third in the 80 metres hurdles at the 1964 Olympics, Kilborn equalled the world record for this event a few days later. She retained her hurdles crown at the 1966 British Empire and Commonwealth Games and was a member of a successful sprint relay. She won a silver medal in the 80 metres hurdles at the 1968 Olympics and another two gold medals, in the 100 metres hurdles and relay event, at the 1970 British Commonwealth Games, just a few weeks before her thirty-first birthday. Kilborn, who was ranked first in her event in 1966 and 1967, was the first woman selected to carry the Australian flag at an opening ceremony in the 1970 Games.

GC*

KING, WILLIAM FRANCIS (1807–73), better known as 'The Flying Pieman', was born in London and arrived in Sydney in 1829, probably as a remittance man. Between 1842 and 1851 he specialised in bizarre walking, running, and jumping feats around Sydney, the Hunter Valley, and Moreton Bay. His feats included 1634 miles in 39 days, 1000 quarter-miles in 1000 quarter-hours, 192 miles in 46½ hours, 6 miles in 1 hour 4 minutes 4 seconds, 1½ miles in 12 minutes carrying an 80-pound goat, and twice beating the mail coach from Sydney to Windsor. On retirement he became one of Sydney's famous street characters, selling pies and haranguing passers-by. He died a pauper at the Liverpool asylum on 10 August 1873.

GW
See **Athletics**.

King's Cup. The men's eight-oared interstate rowing championship was first held in 1878 and continued until the years 1915–19, when, like many other sporting events, it was postponed for the duration of the war. King George V presented a cup for an eights event at the Henley Royal Peace Regatta, which was won by an AIF crew. By permission of the King, the cup became the trophy for the interstate championship, known from 1920 as the King's Cup race. The race has been held annually except in the years 1931, 1940–45 and, as a consequence of an extraordinarily fierce storm, 1989. Victoria (twenty-five) and NSW (twenty) dominated the sixty-three races held between 1920 and 1990. In 1960 the distance was altered from 3 miles to 2000 metres.

SB

Kingston Town (1976–90), a thoroughbred racehorse, by *Bletchingly* out of *Ada Hunter*, was bred in Victoria by his owner, David Hains. Offered unsuccessfully for sale as a yearling, *Kingston Town* was sent to Sydney trainer Tommy Smith. After failing at his first start he was gelded; thereafter he won thirty of his forty starts, including eleven in succession, and was unplaced on only three further occasions. The first Australian horse to win $1 million in prizemoney, *Kingston Town*'s victories included the AJC Derby, the Sydney Cup, and a record three Cox Plates. He was beaten by a short half-head by *Gurners Lane* in the 1982 Melbourne Cup.

AL

KIRKWOOD, JOSEPH H. (1897–1970), born Sydney, began playing golf at the age of 8. His skill as an exponent of trick shots overshadowed his ability as a golf professional. By the time he was 21 he held records on several Australian courses. In 1920 he won the Australian PGA and Open championships—carding an Australian record of 290—and the NZ Open. He settled in America in 1921 and won a number of tournaments but earned more money from his exhibitions of trick shots. Teaming up with the American Walter Hagen, Kirkwood's dexterity enthralled audiences. One of his favourite stunts was to arrange three balls on top of each other on a tee and to drive the middle ball down the fairway without touching the other two balls. He could also play equally well with left- and right-handed clubs. Kirkwood was a golfing entertainer and entrepreneur with a lively mind and a sense of humour: he nicknamed his twin sons 'Pitch' and 'Putt'. During the 1930s he was attracted back to the legitimate circuit and won the Canadian and North and South Opens.

GC*
See **Golf**.

KONRADS, JOHN (1942–), born Riga, Latvia, came to Australia at the age of 7. After a mild attack of poliomyelitis, swimming was prescribed, and he took his first lessons from his father at a migrants' camp near Wagga Wagga. He and his sister Ilsa, born in 1944, attended Revesby Primary School, where Don Talbot (who assisted Frank Guthrie at the Bankstown Club) was a teacher. Konrads joined the Bankstown Club in the 1953–54 season and by 1956 won the national junior 440 yards freestyle. At the age of 14 he was named as a reserve for the 1956 Olympic squad. From 1958 onwards Konrads broke fourteen individual world records and he became the first individual to hold every record from 200 metres to 1650 yards at the one time. He broke six world records within eight days: 200, 400, and 800 metres and the 220, 440, and 880 yards. In the 1958 British Empire and Commonwealth Games he was victorious in the 440 yards, the 1650 yards, and the 4 × 220 yards relay. At the 1959 Australian Championships he became only the sixth person to take every men's freestyle title in one year. In the 1960 Australian Championships he set world records in the 400 and 1500 metres, as well as the 440 and 1650 yards. The highlight of his swimming career was his gold medal at the 1960 Rome Olympics in the 1500 metres, beating Rose, Breen, and Yamanaka. He also swam to a bronze medal in the 400 metres, behind Rose and Yamanaka, and won a silver in the 4 × 200 metres relay. The Konrads story is not complete without reference to his younger sister Ilsa, whose swimming peak was in non-Olympic years. She set six world records from 1958 to 1960, but her best Olympic performance was a silver medal in 1960 in Rome in the 4 × 100 metres freestyle relay.

RH and MH
See **Swimming**.

Kooyong. The name of an inner Eastern suburb of Melbourne has been popularly appropriated to refer in tennis circles to the internationally famous tennis centre and private members' club located there. Kooyong was developed from the purchase for £3080 of 17½ acres of freehold land in 1919, an investment made by the Lawn Tennis Association of Victoria (LTAV) in response to the need to promote the further expansion and development of tennis, earlier locations having proved cramped or unsatisfactory. The first clubhouse was opened in 1923 at a cost of £7783 and the first stadium in 1927, but continuing drainage problems and flooding were not overcome until major expenditure in the 1930s. Further stands were built over the next thirty years to increase gate takings and thereby reduce the heavy financial burden of maintaining such a venue. For example, in 1934, the northern stand, with a seating capacity of 1633, was completed in time for the Victorian Centenary Championships. Further expansions were made, culminating in the erection of the Norman Brookes stand in 1956 at a cost of £53 456. The overall seating capacity was 11 700 but was supplemented at various times to allow seating for several thousand more spectators. From the 1922–23 summer season, Kooyong has been the central headquarters of the Lawn Tennis Association of Australia and the LTAV, as well as the venue for many international, national, State, and local tennis events. The stadium was also used to boost the LTAV's revenue through rock concerts, boxing title fights, basketball, and professional tennis matches. The venue at Kooyong was long regarded as the greatest tennis centre in the southern hemisphere and by the 1950s was attracting crowds of over twenty thousand. Just as the LTAV had recognised the need for the new venue of Kooyong in the 1920s, so tennis administrators recognised the need to establish a new national tennis centre at Flinders' Park, Melbourne, in the 1980s. This new centre, which has replaced Kooyong as the home of the Australian Open since 1988, has a hi-tech all-weather court surface, sliding roof, and modern facilities and is able to attract players of international calibre, but it has not replaced the tradition, charm, and memories which are synonymous with Kooyong.

VO'F
See **Lawn Tennis**.

Korfball
Korfball is a mixed-gender team-sport which originated in Holland early this century. It is similar to basketball and netball but with emphasis placed on sportsmanship. Points in fact can be earned for team skills and behaviour as well as goals scored. It was first established in Australia in 1977 by Roy Kirkby of Scotch College in Adelaide. From there it was introduced into the local community at Blackwood Recreation Centre where, for the first couple of years, it was played socially by a small but growing group of young adults. In 1978 the Australian Korfball Association was formed and interest in the sport began to be shown by other States, particularly in schools. It was in the school system that Kirkby and the early pioneers saw the sport's best chance for development since it tied in well with the increasing interest in providing more opportunities for girls to be involved in sport, as well as more mixed-team sport. Schools in all States now play it. The development of Aussie Sports and Youth Sports by the ASC saw korfball administrators taking a leading role in the production of resources and programmes, and these initiatives have supported the base for the sport. In the community, leagues have been established

mainly in SA and Victoria, but all States are expected to have them by 1993. At the highest level, Australian teams have done very well despite few opportunities for international competition. In 1983, in the first world championships which the country contested, Australia finished seventh; in 1987 its final placing was sixth. Élite-level national squads are maintained at under-17, under-19, and open levels. In 1999 Australia will be hosting the Korfball World Championships.

RK

KOSMINA, JOHN (1956–   ), born Adelaide, captained the Socceroos in their first appearance in the Olympic Games soccer tournament at Seoul in 1988. He is considered one of Australia's greatest strikers. Encouraged to take up the game by his Polish father, Kosmina was one of the first Australians in the modern era to play professionally in England, making several appearances with Arsenal Football Club. His performance, with 102 Socceroo appearances from 1976 to 1988, during which time he scored 43 goals, will be used as a yardstick when measuring future Australian soccer success.

Kosmina equalled Atti Abonyi's record of 25 Socceroo goals at full international level and is the National Soccer League's highest goalscorer, with 133 goals.

PK

KRNCEVIC, EDDIE (1960–   ) was the first Australian soccer-player to have significant success in continental Europe. A tall, lanky striker with dominant heading skills and superb positional sense in scoring situations, he reached his peak in 1989 when he became Belgium's leading scorer, with 23 goals. Ambitious to crack full-time professionalism in his youth, he bought out his contract from Sydney club Marconi in 1981 to join Dinamo Zagreb. His career later took him to MSV Duisburg (Germany), Cercle Bruges (Belgium), Anderlecht (Belgium), Mulhouse (France), and FC Liège (Belgium). Despite being unavailable to play for Australia between 1981 and 1988, he represented his country in twenty full internationals, scoring 4 goals. He returned to Socceroo duty after a seven-year break for Australia's two World Cup qualifiers against Israel in 1988.

LM

L

LACIS, GUIDO (1925–) was an outstanding volleyball player and coach. At the second Australian Cup in 1965 Lacis occupied three important positions: captain-coach of the NSW men's team and president of the NSW Volleyball Association. He was vice-captain of the NSW men's team and coach of the NSW women's team in 1972 when both teams won the premiership without losing a set, a performance never repeated by any other State teams.

IF

See **Volleyball**.

Lacrosse

Indian tribes of North America played a game called 'baggataway' for its intrinsic enjoyment but also as training to quicken and strengthen the bodies of young warriors. Modern lacrosse is based on baggataway but bears little resemblance to it. From rules which were formalised by the Montreal Lacrosse Club in 1856 the game spread internationally and was introduced in Melbourne in 1874 by the Canadian athlete L. L. Mount. Originally seen as an alternative to Australian football, it was played as an amateur winter sport by predominantly middle-class enthusiasts. After gaining a foothold in Melbourne, the game spread during the 1880s to Victorian regional centres such as Sandhurst, Ballarat, and Kyneton. Five hundred men and 1000 women at present compete regularly throughout Australia.

After clubs were formed in Sydney (1884), Adelaide (1885), and Brisbane (1887), each colony followed Victoria's lead and quickly formed an association. Despite the problems faced by the various associations in defining common rules, intercolonial contests began in 1888 with a match between Victoria and SA. In the mid-1890s the game spread to Tasmania and also to the towns and goldfields of WA. After Federation, regular intervarsity matches began and a visit by a Canadian team in 1907 led to the introduction of improved equipment and new tactics. It also provided the stimulus for a national championship, first held in Adelaide in 1910. A trophy presented by Messrs Garland of Canada and McHarg of Australia during the first visit has remained the coveted prize in these championships.

Following a decline during and after the First World War, the game revived in the 1930s when Victoria could boast twenty-eight clubs and over eleven hundred players. The Australian Lacrosse Council for men's lacrosse was formed in 1931 and the game was further enhanced when Victorian women began playing a non-contact version of lacrosse which led to two teams, Williamstown and YMCA/University, forming the Victorian Women's Lacrosse Association (VWLA) in Melbourne in 1936. The VWLA affiliated with the All England Ladies' Lacrosse Association in 1938 and the US Women's Lacrosse Association and the Women's Amateur Sports Association in 1940. An international match was played at the University of Melbourne in 1938 against visiting American hockey-players who also played lacrosse. The Second World War caused another serious decline. Equipment was scarce and most matches were between composite teams. Postwar import restrictions on hickory led to a shortage of crosses (lacrosse sticks) and almost caused the demise of the game in NSW and Queensland. The game revived again in the early 1960s and Australia moved on to the world scene. The men's team began touring and finished second at the world titles in 1967, while teams from Britain and North America became regular visitors. A definite move to re-establish the women's game was made after an advertisement was placed in an Adelaide newspaper by a Mrs Shaw, who had played for Wales. The prospect of interstate competition was the impetus needed and the SA association was formed, along with the re-establishment of the Victorian association in 1962. It was following the first interstate match of that year that the Australian Women's Lacrosse Council (AWLC) was formed. The AWLC were invited to play the interstate match between Victoria and SA at the men's lacrosse carnival in Perth in 1965; the West Australians were persuaded to form an association and enter a team and the competition became the first women's lacrosse championship. The International Lacrosse Federation was established in 1974 at the World Lacrosse Championships which were played in Melbourne.

Annual national women's championships are held for senior and junior competition, and every two years for under-19 teams. The first under-16 championships were held in 1970 and in 1982 the first under-19 interstate match was played between Victoria and SA. International teams from the USA and UK first visited Australia in 1969 and in 1972 an Australian women's team toured these two countries and played an exhibition match in Hong Kong. The first World Cup of Women's Lacrosse was played in Nottingham, England, in September 1982; Australia defeated every team during the preliminary matches and played in the final against the USA, whose only loss had been to Australia. Australia, however, lost the match in extra time. At the second World Cup, in Philadelphia in 1986, Australia again defeated all countries in the preliminary rounds, met the USA in the final, and won. The third World Cup was held in Perth in 1989 and Australia was placed third. In the National Senior Women's Lacrosse Championships of Australia, SA have won on nine occasions during the period 1965–91.

In 1984 the Australian Lacrosse Council (ALC) developed the game of 'sof-crosse' which was endorsed as an 'Aussie Sport' and it has been reported by the ASC that sof-crosse was one of the fastest-growing modified sports throughout Australia. 'mod-crosse', a transitional game between sof-crosse and lacrosse, has also been endorsed by the ALC. Lacrosse is played in regular competition in SA, WA, Victoria and Tasmania and is being introduced into NSW. It is expected that it will soon be played regularly in Queensland and the NT following the success of the modified versions of the sport.

RG, RR, and GFT

See **Lacrosse Helmet Controversy**.

Lacrosse Helmet Controversy. In 1983 the optional use of protective headgear was trialled by the SA Women's Lacrosse Association, a move opposed not only by some of its own members but made in defiance of threats of disaffiliation from the national body. Some feared that helmets would encourage rough play and that they were potentially damaging to the image of women's lacrosse as a non-contact sport. Despite initial set-backs, the optional use of helmets was approved in SA in 1984 and they have been permitted in each subsequent season except 1989. This issue continues to divide women's lacrosse and while other State associations have followed the SA lead in trialling helmets, the national body remains firmly opposed to their use.

LR

LAIDLAW, AUB, BEM (1909–92), born Balmain, Sydney, was a controversial beach inspector at Bondi Beach from 1929 to 1969 who became famous in the 1960s for his enforcement of dress codes, which included ordering women in bikinis off the beach. He was a champion swimmer as a schoolboy and later won the NSW 100 yards event. Laidlaw was selected for the 1928 Olympics but did not attend through lack of funds. He joined the North Bondi Life-

saving Club at 15, becoming its youngest-ever life member at 25. He was present at Bondi on 'Black Sunday' 1938, helping to rescue about three hundred people from the surf. Laidlaw was awarded the BEM in 1972 for his community services through lifesaving.

RC

See **Black Sunday**.

LANDY, JOHN (1930–), born Melbourne, dominated Australian middle-distance running from 1952 to 1956 and was a central figure in the much-publicised quest to break the 4-minute mile along with Englishman Roger Bannister and American Wes Santee. Landy was expected to be first, given his consistently fast runs, but Bannister ran 3 minutes 59.4 seconds at Oxford in May 1954. Landy shattered this record a few weeks later in Turku, Finland, running 3 minutes 57.9 seconds. The clash between Bannister and Landy at the 1954 Vancouver British Empire and Commonwealth Games was billed as 'the race of the century'. Landy led from the start but lost as he turned into the final straight and looked back over his shoulder. Bannister took that moment to pass on the right and won a narrow victory in 3 minutes 58.8 seconds. It was discovered later that Landy ran with four stitches in his foot, but after the race he made no excuses. A fine sportsman, Landy came to be regarded as a symbol of all that was good in sport. When Ron Clarke fell in a 1956 Melbourne mile race, Landy, considering himself to be at fault, stopped to check Clarke's condition and apologise. He then chased the field to win the race, but the delay probably cost him a world record. Landy finished a courageous third in the 1500 metres at the Melbourne Olympics, having overdone his pre-Games racing. He was a popular choice to read the oath of competition at the opening ceremony.

JAD

See **CERUTTY, PERCY**; **Olympic Games 1956 (Melbourne)**.

LANE, FREDERICK C. V. (1880–1969), born Sydney, was the first Australian Olympic swimming champion. He was the sole Australian swimming representative at the 1900 Paris Games, winning two gold medals in the 200 metres freestyle and the 200 metres obstacle race. The 200 metres freestyle was included at the 1904 Games, but was not swum again until 1968, when Michael Wenden won. The 200 metres obstacle race made its first and last appearance in the 1900 Olympics. It was a novelty event consisting of going over and under rowing boats alternately. Lane learned to swim at Ive's Baths, Lavender Bay. When he was 14 the family went to England to collect an inheritance, and Lane saw the trudgen stroke being used, and thereafter perfected it. In the trudgen, both arms are recovered over the water

73 An intercolonial lawn tennis tournament at Moore
Park, Sydney, 1887.

74 Australians dominated international tennis in the 1950s
and 1960s, and 'clinics' for children, such as this one in
Brisbane, were popular.

75 Sam Wells's cartoon of Norman Brookes exhorting Frank Sedgman, Bill Sidwell and John Bromwich of the 1949 Davis Cup team to return victorious from Forest Hills, USA.

in an alternate action as the legs execute a frog-like kick. His adaptation was a narrowed scissor kick with a whipping arm action. At 19 Lane won his first Australasian championship, the 100 yards, at Christchurch in NZ. In 1899 he travelled to England where he won the national 220 yards and 440 yards championships, the former in world-record time. Overall he won five English and three Australasian championships, and set seven world records, though only one was officially recognised. He returned to Australia in 1902 and became a successful master printer.

RH and MH

See **Swimming**.

Lang Park. Brisbane's Lang Park, possibly one of the world's finest rugby league grounds, stands on the site of the former Paddington cemeteries. From the early 1840s there were seven separate denominational cemeteries which served as the general burial grounds for the town of Brisbane until the population growth in the Paddington area forced their closure in 1875. The cemeteries fell into disrepair; they became littered with broken headstones and dilapidated fences overgrown with lantana, and neighbourhood goats roamed freely. The area became such an eyesore that in 1911 the Paddington Cemeteries Act was passed authorising the Queensland Government to resume this property. The land was cleared and levelled and in 1914 became a public park known as Lang Park, in memory of the colonist John Dunmore Lang, who was a Presbyterian clergyman and politician. In 1934 the Queensland Amateur Athletic Association leased Lang Park from the Brisbane City Council; events such as horse shows, circuses, and carnivals were also held there. In the early 1950s the Queensland and Brisbane Rugby Football Leagues, keen to find a new venue after their disagreements with the Brisbane Cricket Ground Trust at Woolloongabba, began negotiating with the Council for the use of Lang Park. In 1957 a lease was finally given to the leagues with a sublease to the Athletic Association. An Act of 1962 awarded the land to the Lang Park Trust in perpetuity for use as a sport and recreation ground, but after the Athletic Association moved in the mid-1970s, rugby league became the sole tenant. The five-member trust had included three rugby league representatives, but in 1988 it was increased to six members and restructured to give the State Government control of half the membership. Lang Park has hosted international rugby league, rugby union, and soccer events. John Landy completed a mile race on the cinder track, while recently a local baseball competition was conducted there. In 1990 the trust deemed that Lang Park should become a multi-purpose sport and recreation facility with a stadium capacity of 45 000, and launched an architectural competition seeking designs to upgrade the existing venue to cater for the next century.

ES

LANGLANDS, GRAEME ('Changa') (1941–), a rugby league full back and centre, began his career on the south coast of NSW, representing his State in 1962. The next year he joined St George as full back, but representative selectors switched him to the centre where he scored 20 points in Australia's 50–12 rout of Britain in the second Test in 1963–64. Langlands played thirty-four Tests and he also represented Australia in two World Cup series (1968 and 1972), as well as in the 1975 world championship. He was Australian captain-coach in the successful 1973 and 1975 sides, and was regarded as an astute, if somewhat unorthodox, tactician and an inspiring coach who led by example. An excellent club man, Langlands excelled for St George. He was a clever runner with great anticipation, a superb step, and good hands. His defence was exceptional and his positional play faultless, although at times he was accused of being a 'lair' and of being over-confident of his ability to beat opposing players. Unfortunately he is remembered by many for wearing white boots when St George was humbled by Easts 38–0 in the 1975 Grand Final. Langlands was a complete footballer—a larrikin who played like an angel—and his partnership with Gasnier in 1963–64, captured on film, is a highlight of Australian rugby league.

TGP

See **Rugby League**.

LARSEN, LYN ('Whisper') (1963–), born Tuntable Creek, Lismore, NSW, graduated with a B.Ed. from Northern Rivers College of Advanced Education. She was born into a cricketing family, with her brother, father, and grandfather all keen on the game. An all-rounder, at 22 she became, in 1986, the youngest woman ever to be captain of the Australian women's cricket team. She has been the most successful Australian captain ever—never losing a Test series and leading Australia to victory in the 1988 World Cup. Quietly spoken and even shy, she is a keen tactician and respected by her team.

AW

LAVER, ROD (1938–), born Rockhampton, Queensland, became the first Australian in 1962 to win the tennis Grand Slam. He repeated this feat in 1969 after he had won the first open Wimbledon in the previous year. A left-hander with extraordinary natural ability, Laver possessed powerful wrists, speed, and could play virtually every tennis shot. He had the ability, using a continental-type grip, to come over the ball on both the backhand and forehand side.

Although Laver was only 174 centimetres tall and weighed just 68 kilograms, his swinging service was most effective. When these attributes were coupled with an instinct for tennis it is understandable that many judges ranked him as one of the legends of the game. For a time he was virtually unbeatable as an amateur, and then as a professional had the distinction in 1974 of being the first player to pass $1 million in prize-money in career earnings. In Davis Cup Laver won twenty of his twenty-four singles matches for Australia and was a member of five winning teams from 1959 to 1962 and in 1973. By the time of his last Davis Cup tie Laver was 35 and beginning to reduce his Australian visits and tournament commitments. After marrying an American he eventually settled in the USA. Laver, the 'Rockhampton Rocket', had a humble beginning and never lost either his freckles or his poker-faced appearance in tournament play.

HCJP

See **Lawn Tennis**.

LAVIS, NEALE (1930–) was an equestrian who came from a rural working-class family; at 172 centimetres and 71.7 kilograms he had an ideal build for the sport. From 1950 to 1954 Lavis was a regular and successful competitor in the Sydney and Melbourne Shows and was also a competent rodeo rider. He won the inaugural Australian Three-Day Event at Centennial Park, Sydney, in 1957. He acquired a tractable and understanding horse, *Mirrabooka*, in Cooma for just £100 and rode it in the 1960 Olympics. With Laurie Morgan and Bill Roycroft, Lavis won the gold medal at Rome in the three-day team event and achieved an individual silver medal in the same event. He also won the Great Auckland One-Day Event in the same year.

RH and MH

Law

Sporting activity has never been immune from the law. Even a cursory look at the sporting pages of any newspaper, in any period of Australian history, would readily demonstrate that legal issues and disputes have featured prominently in the social history of sport.

LIABILITY FOR INJURIES

An area of increasing importance is the liability of sporting organisers for injuries to spectators. The common law has tended to draw artificial distinctions between different categories of 'visitors'. Thus an 'invitee' was one who came on to premises in some kind of 'business capacity'. In a 1938 case in SA it was held that an injured trotting driver was to be classified as an invitee, and thus entitled to a higher standard of care than if he had been there simply by permission. An even higher duty is owed to a person who comes to premises in pursuance of a contract. This is the usual position of a specta-

tor at an organised sporting event. A contract need not be in writing. It may be established simply by virtue of the payment of the entrance fee. A thorny question is the extent to which a sporting promoter or the owner of premises used for a sporting encounter can avoid liability by expressly stating that the spectator 'enters at his own risk'. In a 1961 case concerning a spectator at Bathurst, who was watching car-racing for the first time in his life and was seriously injured by a car that ran out of control, the organisers were held liable, even though it was argued that this was a common risk associated with attendance at motor-car races. But the law does not provide a remedy for every spectator who is injured. Organisers are not required to ensure the safety of all spectators. The law has been moving gradually to a position where only those dangers that were reasonably foreseeable, and should have been guarded against, give rise to legal liability to spectators, regardless of their category. Indeed, in 1983, Victoria abolished the categories of visitor, and enacted a system of liability based on a 'common duty of care'. Likewise, the courts have been concerned with cases involving injuries to players in the course of a game or sport. Spectacular and controversial cases in recent years have concerned the potential for criminal charges to be laid against players. In 1985, a case in Victoria involving the famous Hawthorn Australian rules footballer Leigh Matthews brought to the attention of the public the possibility of police action. Mr Matthews was charged with criminal assault for an attack 'off-the-ball' on another professional Australian rules player. He was fined $1000, but on appeal the fine was substantially reduced. As was predictable, the case raised an outburst of fury from sportsmen and administrators. It was argued that this law should have nothing to do with sport, and that the problem of violence on the sporting field could and should be left to sporting tribunals. However criminal prosecutions had taken place for over a hundred years and several English decisions, including an 1878 soccer case where a player was charged with manslaughter after killing his opponent by a foul tackle, provided precedents.

A less controversial, indeed incontrovertible, incursion by the law into the world of sport has been the increase of *civil* actions for injuries sustained in sport. An assault can be both a crime and a civil wrong. It would surely be a monstrous lacuna in the law if it failed to provide a remedy to a sportsman who lost his livelihood as a result of blatantly foul play by an opponent. Nevertheless it was not until 1967 that a decision finally laid to rest false notions that participation in a game or sport amounts *per se* to running the risk of being injured, or that the sporting arena is somehow exempt from the ordinary legal processes. The case involved a water-skier, who was injured while being towed by a driver. The latter failed to warn the skier of the presence of a boat in the direct route of the skier, who collided with the boat. He successfully sued the driver. It was held that the driver owed a duty of care to the skier. He had breached that duty of care by failing to give a warning signal to the skier. The High Court made short shrift of the argument that the plaintiff had assumed the risk of injury by participation. There have been many subsequent cases where a participant has sued another, either for negligence or for the tort of assault. One such instance was the Australian rules football case, in which the defendant had injured the plaintiff by a foul tackle after the plaintiff had released the ball. The judge found, on this evidence, that the blow was intentional, and was contrary to the rules of the game. Although the rules of the game are not determinative of liability, in this case the judge readily found that the plaintiff could not have been considered to consent to the infliction of injury in this manner. These cases establish precedents for the liability of a participant who flagrantly breaks the rules of a game. The extent to which a breach of the rules will be actionable, however, remains problematical. Not every inadvertent breach will give rise to action: it may be that some element of intention or recklessness is necessary. Each case depends on its own facts.

The potential for liability, however, extends beyond the participant personally. For it is well-established law that an employer is vicariously liable for the torts of his/her employee. On this basis, a club would be liable for the wrong-doings of its professional players. Likewise, a school would be liable for the torts of its teacher-coaches. And, similarly, if the school is a state one, the education department would be liable. It was on this basis that in 1987 a schoolboy in NSW was able to sue the Department of Education when he was paralysed as a result of an injury received when playing school rugby. The teacher-coach had placed him in the scrum despite the fact that he had a long neck. The NSW Education Department had failed to circulate a medical report which had unequivocally pointed to the danger to long-necked players of playing in the scrum. It was held that the boy, who was rendered a paraplegic, was entitled to $2 million damages from this department.

There is a general responsibility on all those who play a part in the organisation and over-sight of a sport or game to act in accordance with ordinary prudence. They are seen to owe a duty of care to those who they can reasonably foresee would be damaged by their failure to act reasonably. And so it may be possible for a player to sue a referee or umpire who wrongly allows play to take place when the pitch is unfit,

or to sue a groundskeeper for inadequately preparing the surface. Sporting activity sometimes takes place—indeed, may well be encouraged—at work, during a lunch-break for instance. Some firms and companies may even provide sporting and recreational facilities, and exhort their employees to use them so as to maintain maximum health and fitness. In some cases employees have suffered injury during these exertions and there have been several actions brought for workers' compensation in these circumstances. In 1962 it was held that an employee injured while playing cricket on the premises of his employers, during the lunch-break, was acting in the course of his employment. And in 1979 it was determined that a customs officer playing football for his department was injured in the course of his employment, even though the game did not take place on the department premises.

DEFAMATION

Another tort in which sporting personalities have occasionally featured is that of defamation—divisible into libel, if in permanent form, and slander, if temporary or transient. In 1980, a well-known rugby league player, Les Boyd, sued the Sydney newspaper the *Daily Mirror*, which published an article accusing Mr Boyd of being 'slow, fat and unpredictable'. This case was heard in the NSW Supreme Court, before a judge and jury. The jury decided that those words did lower the reputation of Mr Boyd, and awarded him substantial damages. Not all adverse comment on a sportsperson, however, is actionable. There are several defences to an action in defamation: 'truth' may be a defence, in some States; 'fair comment' on a matter of public interest also operates as a defence. And there are some occasions where the situation demands absolute frankness, and communications are 'privileged'—that is to say, the contents are confidential and not amenable to an action in defamation unless made maliciously.

DISCIPLINE AND NATURAL JUSTICE

A branch of law which has assumed great importance in sporting circles is that known as 'administrative law'. Actually, this broad concept covers a multitude of issues but it impinges on sport wherever a non-judicial body, that is, not a court of law, is called upon to make a decision affecting a sportsperson. The number of formal tribunals which may adjudicate upon a sportsperson's conduct or performance is quite large, but in addition, sporting clubs themselves may establish informal tribunals that have considerable adjudicatory powers. For instance, a golf club may appoint a committee to oversee applications for membership or a disciplinary committee of a club may decide to fine, suspend, or otherwise punish a player. The general principle pertaining is that it behoves any adjudicatory body sitting in judgment to act in accordance with the principles of natural justice. This concept, however, is flexible and may vary according to the exigency of the particular circumstances, and the need for an urgent resolution. It is thus clear that not all tribunals are required to provide all the procedural safeguards that would be appropriate to a court of law. As early as 1880, however, when a member of the SA Jockey Club was expelled without having full opportunity to state his case, it was held that a court of law may review the decisions of committees of sporting associations. It was maintained that this decision, which had grave social consequence for the member, was challengeable in the courts. A decision by a sporting tribunal may also be challenged on the basis that its own rules were not followed. Even if the rules of the club purport to exclude the jurisdiction of courts, such exclusion would be void.

Several Australian cases have sought to determine what are the constituents of natural justice, as applied to sporting tribunals. Certainly it is necessary that an alleged offender should be notified clearly, and thus have the opportunity to refute the charge. It has been argued that natural justice requires that legal representation should be, if not provided, certainly permitted. But in a 1975 case involving a NSW soccer club it was held that there was no such right. Nevertheless, the position may be different where the charge is very serious, or where the accused's livelihood is at stake. A case in point is a 1981 Victorian decision where a young, inarticulate jockey appearing before the Racing Control Board of Victoria had been denied representation. The judge found that this was a denial of natural justice. Moreover, it has been held in a 1977 case in NSW that even on an admission of guilt, natural justice requires that the accused person be permitted to make representations in mitigation of the offence.

CONTRACTS

A great deal of sporting law has been made in recent years in the area of contract law. Sporting bodies must necessarily enter into many commercial contracts of an ordinary business nature. Some considerable difficulties arise if there is a breach of contract and the sporting body is not an incorporated association. It may be difficult to know who is liable to be sued. Such a case in 1970 involved the Carlton and Fitzroy Australian Rules Football Clubs where, when a Fitzroy Football Club negotiation with the St Kilda Club to use the Junction Oval was in breach of an agreement made with the Carlton Club, Carlton was left without a remedy because of its inability to find someone to sue. In other cases, however, the committee members or sometimes the whole membership of the club has been held liable. It is hoped that such difficulties will be minimised by the increasing tendency of sporting clubs to incorporate. A cheap and simple machinery under the Associations Incorporation Acts of every State is now available and is being increasingly used by sporting clubs.

Much litigation has been engendered in recent years by contracts which are *sui generis* to sport. The rapid increase in sponsorship contracts is a good example. The jurisdiction of the *Trade Practices Act 1974* may well be involved as such a contract may be adjudged void as not being in the public interest. Particularly vulnerable to challenge have been sponsorship contracts with cigarette and liquor companies. The moral issues involved in using sport to advertise a product that has been officially condemned as damaging to health are manifest. But even when such a contract is validly formed, it may be the subject of challenge and investigation under some statutory provision. Thus a complex case initially decided before the Australian Broadcasting Tribunal, involving cigarette advertisements on football grounds where matches were being televised, reached the Federal Court of Australia in 1985. It was decided that signs on the grounds did not constitute direct advertisements, and therefore did not constitute a breach of the Act. Several cases have come before the courts involving employment contracts between clubs and professional players. Tension necessarily exists between the two. A club will rush to hold on to the exclusive services of a good player whereas the player may wish to pursue to his or her own best financial advantage, which may well mean transferring to a wealthier or more prestigious club. Contracts used to be regarded as sancrosanct and inviolable. Hardly ever were they the subject of scrutiny. The nineteenth-century prevailing philosophy of *laissez-faire* suggested that a contract freely entered into could not be broken with impunity. But this pure doctrine has been totally exploded in this century, with the rise of standard form contracts between parties of completely unequal bargaining power. Today, both legislation and court decisions give a lie to the notion that unfair contracts are nevertheless always binding on their parties if entered into without duress.

In one area of contract law, indeed, sporting cases led to new appraisals. That is the law relating to contracts in restraint of trade. Since the seventeenth century, it has been accepted that courts do have power to declare a restraint void, if it is unreasonable. Until recently, most restraints had involved either a vendor and purchaser of a business, or an employer and employee, and had usually been declared void if they were too wide, in scope, in time or in place, to be reasonable. But in a landmark case in 1971 the High Court of Australia found that the NSW Rugby League's retain and transfer system constituted an unreasonable restraint on players. While some restraint would be reasonable, the system was unduly restrictive on the player, and thus prevented him from being purchased by another club. In 1978 an English case actually involved a private Australian promoter of cricket, Kerry Packer. He sought to break the monopoly on English cricketers' services enjoyed by the English County Cricket Clubs. By inducing Tony Greig and other English cricketers to break those contracts, he forced the Test and County Cricket Board (TCCB) to take the players to court, so as to test the validity of those contracts. It was held that the clauses in the contracts preventing the players from playing cricket otherwise than as authorised by the TCCB were unreasonable restraints. A similar decision was reached in a comparable Australian case involving World Series Cricket.

These cases had the effect of permitting a private promoter to 'poach' a large number of players, and thus devalue first-class cricket in Australia. The Australian Cricket Board was forced to reach a compromise with Packer's organisation, and to redraft contracts more in favour of the players. Nevertheless, the validity of those more liberal contracts was challenged in 1985, when a group of players led by former Australian cricket captain Kim Hughes signed contracts to play in South Africa. These contracts were clearly in breach of the players' existing contracts with the Australian Cricket Board, and the board had no option but to sue the players for an injunction restraining them from playing in South Africa. It should be noted that it is well-established law that the board had no power to seek an order of specific performance of their contracts, so as to *require* the players to observe them: this would amount to an acquiescence in a system of slave labour. The board settled the case, probably to avoid ruinous litigation costs, and the players went to South Africa. Although one of the terms of the settlement was that all players consented to a declaration that the Australian Cricket Board's contracts with the players were valid and enforceable, it is difficult to avoid the suspicion that the board was apprehensive that certain clauses of the contract would be declared by the court to be unreasonable restraints.

In Australian rules, too, there have been further developments. In 1983, the footballer Sylvio Foschini won an important case in the Victorian Supreme Court when he was required to move from his home town of Melbourne to Sydney, his club, South Melbourne, having been transmogrified into the Sydney Swans. Another Melbourne Club, St Kilda, offered Foschini a position, but the Sydney Swans would not release him. It was found that the Victorian Football League procedures and practices which did not allow the player a right of appeal from the club's decision to the Appeal Board were unsatisfactory and constituted a restraint.

The success of the players in these and other cases may have encouraged other players to view contracts as documents not worth the paper on which they were written, and able to be broken with impunity. But two 1987 cases in the Victorian Supreme Court, both involving Hawthorn Australian Rules Football Club, disabused them of that notion. Both Gary Buckenara and his colleague, Harding, failed in their attempts to break their existing contracts with Hawthorn and, no doubt, accept higher terms from other clubs. The Victorian Supreme Court found that the contracts were reasonable. Although, for the reason given above, the court could not specifically enforce the contracts, it did order an injunction, in effect restraining the players from pursuing their careers as footballers in the Victorian Football League with any club other than Hawthorn. These 'negative orders' had the effect of persuading the players to turn out for Hawthorn, after all.

JNT
See **Restraint of Trade**.

Lawn Bowls

The local lawn bowls club is a feature of almost every Australian community. In 1990 the Australian Bowls Council, the national administrative body for the men's sport in the country, claimed the affiliation of 2225 clubs with 274 943 members. The Australian Women's Bowling Council had comparable figures of 2185 clubs and 148 547 members. In fact, Australia boasts 43 per cent of the world's bowling population, and the successful performance of Australian representatives at world championships and Commonwealth Games is well known. Besides having such a wide following, Australian lawn bowls is distinguished by the number and predominance of its organised clubs and by the fact that the majority of club members are also players. The history of the game in Australia also helps to explain its mass appeal. Following to some extent the example of early nineteenth-century Britain, lawn bowls was largely encouraged and developed in Australia by and for male members of the colonial élite: businessmen, politicians, civil servants, and other community leaders. As in Britain, 'public' greens in Australia were initially formed beside hotels and inns. Since such venues meant proximity to such 'unruly' activities as bare-knuckle pugilism, cock-fights, greyhound-coursing, pigeon-shooting, and foot-races, early Australian bowls organisers consciously emphasised the respectability of bowls. In the colonies lawn bowls was advertised as an opportunity for men of business to find some gentle relaxation and 'civilised' company among their own kind—as well as augmenting the publican's takings. One early advertisement read:

Thomas Shaw, of the Woolpack Inn, Parramatta Road, has much pleasure in announcing to his numerous patrons, Friends and the Sporting Gentlemen of Sydney and its environs that he has just completed . . . a full-sized, beautifully-turfed bowling green . . . [He] confidently looks forward to being honoured by a large meeting of gentlemen, especially amateurs in the true old English game.

Taverns in two localities vie for the honour of the site of the first public green in Australia in 1845. One is at Sandy Bay in Tasmania; the other is the Woolpack Inn, Petersham, NSW. A third and lesser known contender is Norfolk Island, where a rink is believed to have been established in 1834. Without seeking to resolve the competing claims for precedence, it is enough to note that these 'public' greens, unlike their British counterparts, never really developed into a public green movement. The successful greens originally established on Australian hotel sites, which subsequently flourished, were those which eventually instituted membership fees to keep out the 'riff-raff'.

Meanwhile, drawing on the habits of their class in Britain, the early creators of private greens in this country provided another feature of early Australian lawn bowls. Perhaps the most celebrated of these private greens was established in 1878 by Sir John Young at Kentville, his property in Annandale, Sydney, where Sir John's friends and associates were transported to the rinks by ferry. Young's example indicates the typical origins of many clubs, which began through the provision of a private green of this kind, or through the largesse of a wealthy patron. The enduring influence of the private green-owners was also apparent in the enthusiasm with which prominent men, who had previously patronised their friends' or colleagues' greens, saw the merit in establishing greens on public land.

It was not until 1864 that the first club was formalised—separate from both private homes and hotels—with the Melbourne Bowling Club (Chapel Street). The membership dues were one guinea (twenty-one shilllings) a year, a considerable sum in a period when male earnings ranged between five and ten shillings a week. Membership of an Australian club demanded that players equip themselves at their own expense, which could, again, be considerable—the bowls in this period were made of expensive imported wood. Until about 1900, however, bowlers did not always use a mat, and no special clothing was required, though players commonly turned out in slippers to go with their top hats and frock-coats. The increasingly organised nature of the sport in the twentieth century, however, did make participation in lawn bowls an expensive recreational activity, especially in times of economic distress.

This nineteenth-century model for the origins of lawn bowls clubs was generally the basis on which the game subsequently developed in Australia. Notable exceptions occurred, however, in this white, male-dominated club scene in lawn bowls. At Stawell (Victoria), women, who had been taking part in bowls matches since October 1881, organised an early ladies' tournament in 1896. Similarly, the Colac Club (Victoria) was established by eight women in June 1899, and only later became a men's club. Another exception to the European domination of early bowling was the 1866 Invitation Match when the Fitzroy Club (Victoria) invited the Aboriginal cricket team to play. Several rinks were also created in the late nineteenth century by businesses, industries, and public enterprises (such as the NSW Railways at Fraser Park, Marrickville) in response to the 'open-air' movement, when it was believed that a healthy employee was a better worker. Nonetheless, white, male, and middle-class tended to be the predominant characteristics of lawn bowlers until after 1900.

Though a comparatively slow process, it may be supposed that women's entry into Australian lawn bowls was merely a part of the more liberal attitudes towards women which characterised the twentieth century. But this explanation neglects the strenuous efforts by women bowlers themselves. The late nineteenth century had seen many attempts to begin women's clubs, not all of which were successful. In many parts of Australia, women seem to have begun playing bowls alongside or alternating with men, as the Victorian examples suggest. The formation after 1900 of exclusively women's clubs and associations did much to increase women's participation. In the twentieth century, moreover, many men's clubs opened their doors to associate membership for wives and friends. Eventually, the Australian Women's Bowling Council was formed in 1947 and held their first carnival in Sydney in 1949.

A major role in encouraging the development and organisation of the sport in Australia is often attributed to Sir John Young, donor of the Annandale green and leading light in the formation of the NSW Bowling Association (1880) and the Imperial (later the English) Bowling Association. In the promotion of the first international men's competition between British bowlers and those in the Australian colonies (1901), Young's efforts were matched by those of Charles Wood, president of the Victorian Bowls Association. Sir John is also commonly credited with arranging the first intercolonial match in Australia (between Victoria and NSW, and won by the southerners) held at Annandale in April 1880. This event was a spur to the establishment of the associations in NSW and Victoria later the same year, and the other colonies followed in the subsequent decades: WA (1898), SA (1902), Tasmania-North (1901), Queensland (1903), and Tasmania-South (1905). After ten years of negotiation, it was agreed to found the Australian Bowls Council in 1911.

The main difficulty in organising these inter-colonial and international competitions lay in the need to reach agreement on standardised playing conditions. In 1880 the first intercolonial match between NSW and Victoria, for instance, had involved players who adhered to different rules. But this was not a peculiarly Australian prob-lem: for much of the nineteenth century, the rules of the game in England were quite differ-ent from those in Scotland. The formation of the regional associations and the Australian Bowls Council, however, led in the first dec-ades of the twentieth century to standardised rules for such contentious issues as the length of greens, size of mats, ditches, and 'touchers'. This Australian initiative towards regularisation also had an influence on the formation of the Imperial (English) Association, and greatly assisted the world-wide development of lawn bowls.

Developments in twentieth-century lawn bowling have been dramatic and were closely aligned with changes in Australian society and culture. In the two States with the largest bowl-ing populations, NSW and Victoria, the prolif-eration of clubs shows interesting parallels with other social developments. The period 1900–20 saw a steady increase in the number of clubs, apart from an unsurprising levelling off during the First World War: in NSW there were about twenty clubs in 1900, and about seventy in 1920. In Victoria, the comparable period saw an in-crease from sixty-two clubs to one hundred and forty-four. With the Depression of the 1930s followed by war, the rate of growth in the number of clubs increased, though only slightly, and mostly in country districts. From 1946–55 however, the growth of lawn bowls was dra-matic: in NSW, for instance, the number of clubs increased from 220 to 740, and a similar rate of growth was evident in Victoria. In part this trend may be related to the returning ser-vice personnel and to Australia's massive post-war immigration. It may also be significant that the 1950s and 1960s in Australia were the dec-ades of the family, where the often displacing effects of rapid 'suburbanisation' were met by attempts to foster community ties. The rela-tively prosperous years of full employment and the prevalence of the male-dominated, single-income household in this period may also have contributed to the increasing involvement of women in lawn bowls, both as players and administrators. Since 1965, however, the re-markable expansion of bowls clubs has slowed.

Despite this general trend, the active involve-ment of visually impaired bowlers is one less publicised direction in which Australian bowls is presently being extended. Lawn bowls for the visually impaired began towards the end of the First World War through the collaboration of returned services organisations and repatriation hospitals, such as that at Caulfield (Victoria) in 1917. Clubs have been started in various States within the past two decades (the Victorian Blind Lawn Bowls Club, for example, was founded in 1975), and visually impaired bowlers now organ-ise a regular series of national and international events. Unfortunately, no significant sponsor-ship is so far available for such players, whose competition costs include the travel and accom-modation expenses of their sighted assistants.

The growth of the post-war period was not, of course, confined to the establishment of new clubs. Many were renovating and enlarging established premises to cater for extra members; there were more and better rinks, extended clubhouses, and additional facilities for mem-bers and their guests. Active involvement in bowling is still a distinctive aspect of Australian club members, but for many suburban localities and indeed outback communities in the 1990s, the bowls club is also an important social and cultural meeting place. A major influence on the bowls clubs' social role has been the liquor laws. Compared with NSW, for instance, Queensland has had more restrictive licensing laws. Until recently, Queensland bowling clubs could not serve take-away alcohol, they could not serve alcohol in-house if no game had been played that day, and even if a game had been played, the licence was only until 8 p.m. This helps to explain why Queensland's experience (such as the smaller number of clubs) has been rather different from that of other States, where the licensing regulations have allowed the bowls club to take on other functions than merely providing the venue for a game.

Another great change of the last decade has been the emergence of a new brand of profes-sionalism. For some time there had been calls to recompense players who played 'away', or had other expenses involved in championship or pennant competitions. But the emergence of corporate sponsorship for major events, and the mass exposure allowed by television, have con-tributed to the separation of full-time profes-sional players from the majority of weekend and mid-week amateurs. In addition, and mir-roring similar changes in other sports, profes-sional attitudes are moving the game away from its traditional turf towards synthetic surfaces, where the run of the green is more exact and the weather has less influence.

Change is still occurring. The view that lawn bowls is a game for the elderly (or even more specifically, a game for retirees) has probably never been very accurate, but it is a persistent myth which recent initiatives are trying to dispel. In Queensland, for example, clubs hold 'youth days' to encourage younger people to try their hand. This is proving a successful and popular method of introducing new members, while a programme is under way in SA to promote lawn bowls as a school sport. Perhaps it is precisely because lawn bowls is not a contact sport—because it is a game suited to the elderly as well as the young, to people with disabilities as well as the able-bodied—that the game will survive and thrive as we move into a more 'leisured' historical period in the twenty-first century.

LMcC

See **Australian Bowls Council**; **Australian Women's Bowling Council**; BOSISTO, GLYN; DOBBIE, JOHN; HENSELL, WILLIAM; PARRELLA, ROB; RICHARDSON, MERLE; ROCHE, DOROTHY; YOUNG, Sir JOHN.

Lawn Tennis

Lawn Tennis in Australia, when it began in the 1870s and 1880s, had its origins in at least two forms of game-playing skill and codification. The more distant was the parent game of royal or real tennis, by then played in an enclosed court, but dating from the ball games of the early Greeks and Romans and refined in European royal courts, monasteries, and streets over the centuries. Then, closer in time, came the variants of lawn tennis that began with experimental games held at places such as Edgbaston and in the grounds of the mansion of the Marquis of Landsdowne in Berkeley Square, London, in the late 1860s and the patenting of the game by Major Walter Clopton Wingfield in 1874. Wingfield produced tennis kits for sale, consisting of 'a bat, or racquet for each player, six or nine India-rubber balls, several plain balls, polished ash poles, a strong tanned cord net, lines, rubbers, malet, drill and racquet-press'. These implements cost from £1 5s to six guineas. The game was thus exportable, and the first Wimbledon championship made it even more so. In 1875 the Marylebone Cricket Club revised Wingfield's rules of the game and his suggested court shape and dimensions, as well as lowering the height of the net. The rules of the game, as we know it, were complete when in 1877 the All-England Croquet Club further refined them and, adding lawn tennis to its title, staged its inaugural Gentlemen's Singles Championship, the first 'Wimbledon'.

In the years between the dissemination of Wingfield's tennis kits and the establishment of the first lawn tennis club in the Australian colonies, games of lawn tennis in Australia were as varied as the situations in which they were played, the sophistication of the rackets and balls used, the experience and skill of the players, and what they wanted of the game. In 1878 the Melbourne Cricket Club (MCC) put down the first asphalt court in the colonies (repeating the pattern in Britain and America where tennis often began as an adjunct to cricket and as a gentle game suitable for ladies) and founded the first Australian lawn tennis club. In 1880 the MCC Lawn Tennis Club laid a grass court and held the first tournament in the colonies, the precursor to the Victorian Tennis Championships. Sydney Lawn Tennis Club was founded in 1880, again as an adjunct to cricket, at the Sydney Cricket Club, and the first NSW championships were held in 1885. Championships were first held in Queensland in 1889, in Tasmania in 1893, and in WA in 1895. The first intercolonial championships were held between Victoria and NSW at the Sydney Cricket Ground in 1885.

Lawn tennis in Australia in the years from 1878 until the turn of the century was by and large male-dominated and experimental, although obviously vital and growing steadily in attraction beside traditional sports such as cricket and football that were popular across the range of social class. During the 1880s, for instance, the uncovered indiarubber ball was in common use, its advantage being that it was easily dried by a towel during rain. Play in tournaments did not commonly stop for rain, unless it was very heavy or until 'it had done enough damage to rackets and play'. The introduction of women's events in tournaments and championships lagged several years behind that of men's events, but ladies of a certain social class in the cities or on country properties played social tennis to a considerable extent. Many competitive events were handicaps rather than championships in the 1880s and 1890s. In the early 1880s, coming so soon after Wingfield's initiation of the game, the volley was considered not to be *de rigueur* in social tennis because it curtailed rallies, but it had become a major weapon in competitive tennis by the 1890s. Male tennis attire among club players in the 1870s and 1880s consisted of long trousers or knickerbockers with flamboyantly striped wide elastic belts or cummerbunds, stiff-collared white shirts with ties, black stockings, skull caps, and flannel blazers. The ladies wore their hair upswept and gathered in a bunch, with a straw 'gem' hat pinned to its top. White blouses and long skirts, reaching some three inches short of the ground, commonly completed the outfit. By the time of Australasia's ascendency in world tennis in the early 1900s, men's attire as club players had settled on long white trousers, a white open-neck shirt, and a tennis blazer.

As a result of the rationalisation and standardisation of the various balls available, which was begun in the early 1880s by the Staten Island Cricket Club, the 'covered' ball came into common use in the early 1890s. The first covered balls were indiarubber ones bandaged with two strips of cloth, the uncovered ball being considered too light for competitive play. At first unpopular, the covered ball gained greater and greater acceptance as methods of attaching a 'nap' to the ball became more sophisticated.

A number of players distinguished themselves in pre-Federation competition and in the first ten years or so of the new century, but primarily within the ambit of colonial tennis, rather than overseas. Among the men were A. H. Colquhoun, the country's leading player in the late 1880s; Gus Kearney, the Geelong player who figured prominently in intercolonial matches, becoming Victorian singles champion four times and NSW champion twice; and others like Horrie Rice, L. O. Poidevin, W. H. Eaves, H. E. Webb, A. D. Webb, Alfred Dunlop, Harry Parker, Ben Green, J. Cramond, Barney Murphy, and Norman 'Smasher' Bayles. The most notable lady players were Miss P. Howitt (Cater), Miss Lily Addison, Miss McKenzie, Miss Gyton, Miss E. Raleigh, Miss Simson, Miss Marsh, Miss Shaw, and Miss Payten.

The climate in which Australian players could begin to figure on the stage of world tennis was established in the 1890s and the early years of the twentieth century. In 1904 a national body for Australian and NZ tennis, the Australasian Lawn Tennis Association, was formed in order that Australasia might enter a team in the new international event, the Davis Cup. The Cup was donated by the American Dwight Filley Davis in 1900 and was open for competition among countries with recognised national tennis associations. New Zealanders Alfred Dunlop and Anthony Wilding and Australian Norman Brookes constituted Australasia's talented first Davis Cup team which was defeated in 1905 by the USA in the tie to decide the challenger to play Great Britain, the holder of the Cup. In Brookes Australia had a player who would dominate men's tennis for some time to come and who would go on to become Australian Davis Cup selector and captain, tennis administrator and entrepreneur, and president of the Lawn Tennis Association of Australia (LTAA) from 1926 until his retirement from that position in 1955, after which he continued as an influential figure in Australian tennis. Brookes died in his ninetieth year in 1968.

Norman Brookes and other male and female players after him—Alfred Dunlop, Rodney Heath, Gerald Patterson, Jack Hawkes, Pat O'Hara Wood, Bob Schlesinger, Jack Clemenger, 'Sos' Wertheim, Lily Addison, Esna Boyd, and others—typified one career path in Australian tennis: they were people of private means, who could afford time to practise and to make tours of Australian and overseas tournaments. A second path was provided to players of talent who were employed by sporting-goods firms as sales and public relations representatives. Yet another was via success in Australian country tennis tournaments and in the annual Country Week championships held in the capitals, particularly in NSW, Victoria and Queensland.

Brookes was outstanding at ball games from football to billiards. Like a number of the country's most accomplished players, both men and women, he could turn the advantages of private wealth and the ability to practise and fraternise with other strong players to effect by several means: representing Victoria as a 19-year-old in 1896; participating in the 1905 Davis Cup competition; winning the Wimbledon Men's Singles in 1907; and combining with Wilding to win Australia's first Davis Cup in the same year. Students of Australian tennis are by and large united in regarding the 1908 Davis Cup challenge round, the first to be held in Australia, as an event which forced the general public, as distinct from existing devotees and players of the game, to alter its image of tennis as essentially a ladies' game. The torrid, five-set struggles of Brookes and Wilding in defeating the American team in heatwave conditions made it apparent to the followers of cricket and football that mental toughness, strategy, and great physical endurance were essential to the making of national and international tennis-players. Australasia again won the Davis Cup in 1909, 1914 and 1919, while Brookes won the Wimbledon Singles once more in 1914, participated in the Australasian Davis Cup team from 1911 until 1920, and then captained the teams from 1927 until 1935, as well as several in later years. Australia had established a place in world tennis.

The 1920s saw many well-to-do Australian players compete in the international tournaments circuit, which included the Wimbledon Championships, the French and Italian Championships, and the US Championships. Among those who travelled to contest these tournaments were Gerald Patterson, a protégé of Brookes and winner of Wimbledon in 1919 and 1922, and those who shared Davis Cup play with him in Australasian teams: Pat O'Hara Wood, Jack Hawkes, Bob Schlesinger, J. O. Anderson, 'Sos' Wertheim, Norman Peach, and Clarrie Todd, as well as others who toured privately. The foremost lady players were Mall Molesworth, Esna Boyd, and Daphne Akhurst, followed by Sylvia Lance (Harper), Louie Bickerton, Lily Addison, Meryl O'Hara Wood, and Gladys Toyne. Ladies' participation in the overseas circuit largely awaited the establishment of the Wightman Cup competition in 1923. In 1927 the LTAA shed its Australasian connotations and the first true Australian Championships were held at the newly developed courts of the Lawn Tennis Association of Victoria at Kooyong, Melbourne. In 1924 the International

Lawn Tennis Federation had set its imprimatur on Australian tennis and the standard of its players by ranking the Australasian championships with the French, American and Wimbledon titles.

In the 1930s another path to the international circuit, particularly for men, was via the assistance to, or provision of suitable employment for, players of undoubted talent. J. O. Anderson was a player with great talent who depended on his small business for support of his tennis forays. Jack Crawford—participant in nine Davis Cup campaigns, first Australian to win the Australian, French and Wimbledon titles in one year, four times winner of the Australian Men's Singles Championship—was country-born, but from his teenage years was employed by sporting-goods manufacturers in Sydney. Fred Kalms, a member of the 1924 Davis Cup team, rose to national prominence through Country Week tennis and the State championships in NSW. Kalms of West Wyalong and others like Clarrie Todd of Trundle and Marjorie Cox (Crawford) of Narrandera were precursors of a string of Australian players, extending to the present, nurtured by country tennis: Gar Moon, Adrian Quist, Rex Hartwig, Margaret Smith, Evonne Goolagong, Jan Lehane, Roy Emerson, Tony Roche, Chris Kachel, Mal Anderson, Bob Mark, Dianne Fromholtz, Mark Edmonson, Rod Laver, and many others.

The pattern of dominance in Australian men's tennis—which received the far greater share of publicity before the Second World War—follows roughly the demarcation of the decades of this century, and so too do influential elements in the game, such as style of play, the position of women in the sport, and the advent of professionalism. Crawford and his smooth stroking style were paramount from the beginning of the 1930s, while Joan Hartigan emerged from the ruck of fine players in the early years of the decade to hold a less certain ascendance among female players in the mid-1930s. Like Daphne Akhurst before her, who had toured abroad in 1928 and reached the semifinals of the ladies' singles and doubles and the final of the mixed doubles with Jack Crawford at Wimbledon, Joan Hartigan was able to travel abroad and became the second Australian woman player to figure prominently in overseas tournaments. Tennis at the State and national level, as well as at club level, was still primarily a male preserve. Tennis clubs in general, however, were by now much more pluralist, although some of the more exclusive grass court clubs in the capitals might still place some emphasis on the social acceptability of applicants for membership. The ruling bodies of tennis at State and national level were generally conservative in adherence to rules of dress. It was largely through influential players flouting the accepted norms

that change occurred. In 1933 both Wimbledon and the Lawn Tennis Association of Victoria were forced to accede to the acceptance of shorts as suitable wear for men players—Adrian Quist and Harry Hopman both persisted in wearing shorts against official sanctions, as did Nancye Wynne (Bolton) in 1935. In 1933, in a concession to women's status in the game, females were allowed to call the lines for the first time at the final of the Australian Ladies' Singles Championship at Kooyong.

By the late 1930s the names of players who had struggled in the shadow of Jack Crawford—Hopman, and even more importantly, Quist and Bromwich—began to gain prominence. In 1939 Bromwich and Quist won the Davis Cup from the USA for the first time as an Australian team, as distinct from an Australasian team, and established themselves as one of the greatest doubles pairs in Australian tennis. From 1937 Nancye Wynne (Bolton) began a career in women's tennis in Australia that can only be compared to the earlier Brookes in the male ranks, or to Margaret Smith (Court) who was to come to prominence in the 1960s. Wynne (Bolton) was six times winner of the Australian Women's Singles Championship from 1937 to 1951, although she was unable to tour abroad regularly. She turned professional in 1952. Nell Hopman who, among others, had played in Nancye Bolton's shadow, was to become playing captain and later coach of Australian Wightman Cup teams. She established the Federation Cup for women's international competition in 1963, the first matches being played at Kooyong.

Much of the change in Australian tennis occurred about the time of the advent of Frank Sedgman. When he came to prominence in Melbourne at the end of the 1940s he ushered in a style among men players, modelled on the style of play and the strategy employed by the American Jack Kramer from the mid-1940s, in which power in service and speed to a killing volley or smash replaced the patience, placement, and tactics of the 1940s as exemplified by Crawford, Bromwich, and Quist. Sedgman was also of the post-war era, when Australia's Davis Cup battles were played in the American zone and overwhelmingly against the USA. Australia, a nation whose population rose from a mere eleven million to thirteen million people in the period, played in the challenge round each year from 1946 until 1968, winning fifteen of those twenty-three encounters. Sedgman's career coincided with the beginnings of that tennis ascendancy, and with the advent of Harry Hopman as non-playing captain and coach of the Australian Davis Cup teams from 1950 to 1969, during which time Australia won the Cup on sixteen occasions. Sedgman was Hopman's first protégé. He was followed by Ken McGregor, Lew Hoad, Ken Rosewall, Mal

Anderson, Ashley Cooper, Neale Fraser, Rod Laver, Roy Emerson, Fred Stolle, John Newcombe, Tony Roche, Bill Bowrey, Ray Ruffels, and John Alexander.

Sedgman also was the person who ushered professionalism into the thinking of Australian players and the spectator public. Sir Norman Brookes, aware of the inducements likely to be made to Australian players, organised the setting up of Sedgman and McGregor in business as a financial encouragement to remain 'amateur'. In 1952 Sedgman won the singles, doubles, and mixed doubles at both Wimbledon and the USA national championships before returning to Australia to win all his matches in the Davis Cup challenge round. Within two days, with Ken McGregor, he was signed as a professional with Jack Kramer's tennis troupe. He was to be followed by his successors Ken Rosewall in 1956, Lew Hoad in 1957, Rod Laver in 1963, and Roy Emerson, John Newcombe, and Tony Roche in 1966–67.

In this golden period of Australian men's tennis, from 1950 to 1968, an Australian won the Wimbledon men's singles eleven times, the French singles championship nine times, and the American championship twelve times. Australians also won the Wimbledon men's doubles thirteen times and the Davis Cup fifteen times, finishing as runners-up four times. Of the players involved, Rod Laver was perhaps the most accomplished, winning Wimbledon four times and becoming the first player in the world to win the Grand Slam (i.e. win the French, Wimbledon, American, and Australian championships in one year) not once but twice. The feat has not yet been equalled, and may never be, given the multitude of talented players brought on by computer-ranked professionalism.

It was in the period 1960 to 1973 that Australian women's tennis produced its greatest player thus far—Margaret Smith (Court). She won the Australian women's singles championship eleven times and Wimbledon three times, as well as the Grand Slam, and represented Australia in many Federation Cup matches. Court's career was partly shared with her successor, Evonne Goolagong (Cawley), winner of the Australian women's singles four times and Wimbledon twice.

Within two years of the opening of Wimbledon to professionals in 1968 there were major changes not only in the nature of world tennis, but in the administration of Australian tennis in particular. In that year Sir Norman Brookes died. He had been replaced on his retirement as president of the Lawn Tennis Association of Australia by Don M. Ferguson (1955–60). Then followed Norman Strange (1960–65), C. A. Edwards (1965–69), Wayne Reid (1969–77), Brian Tobin (1977–88), and Geoff Pollard from 1988 to the time of writing.

Since 1984 the Federal body in Australian tennis has been incorporated and since 1986 has traded under the name Tennis Australia. In 1969 Harry Hopman retired as Australia's Davis Cup captain, to be replaced by one of his protégés of the 1950s, Neale Fraser.

In the years since the opening of Wimbledon and other Grand Slam tournaments and the advent of computer ranking there has been a proliferation of very good players on the world circuit, a development that has seen the traditional ascendance of Australia and the USA in tennis eroded, to be replaced by a new pluralism. Thus, while Australia in the period from 1950 to 1968 won the Davis Cup fifteen times, drawing on its seven winners of the Wimbledon men's singles in that period, in the years since 1970 the only Australian to win Wimbledon has been Pat Cash. Australia also lost its fifth Davis Cup challenge round in that period in 1990, having won the Cup only four times but having reached the semifinals or better on fourteen occasions.

Australian women players in the same period have been perhaps more thoroughly eclipsed by the ascendancy of increasingly younger players coming from several nations. Since the 1960s Australian women players have fought several battles against the male-dominated administration of Australian and overseas tournaments. In 1961, with women's tennis vitalised by the appearance of Margaret Court, women players staged a self-imposed lock-in in the Kooyong dressing rooms during the Australian championships until they were accorded a more reasonable allocation of the centre court for women's matches. In 1970 two Australian women players sharing the forefront of world women's tennis—Kerry Melville (Reid) and Judy Tegart (Dalton), runner-up in the Wimbledon ladies' singles in 1968—joined six others centred about Billie Jean King and Julie Heldman to boycott the Pacific Southwest tournament promoted by Jack Kramer, for which women's prize-money was little more than half that for the men. Thus, with the aid of Gladys Heldman, editor of *World Tennis*, was born the first tournament of the women's professional circuit—the Virginia Slims. The SA championships in Adelaide in 1973 were the first Australian tournament to offer equal prize-money to women players. In 1974 the Australian Women's Tennis Association (AWTA) was founded and conducted its first sponsored tournament in Sydney at which Wendy Turnbull's national and international career began. In 1990 the AWTA became the Australian Federation Cup Tennis Foundation.

In 1982, with the venue of the Australian Open championships firmly established at Kooyong, the Australian women's championships were reintegrated with those of the men to ensure that the tournament met the standards of the International Tennis Federation as a Grand Slam event. In that year Jim Entinck, the long-standing referee of the Australian Open championships, retired. In 1983 the total prize-money for the Australian Open Championships exceeded $1 million, and work began towards the planning of a new National Tennis Centre in Melbourne. It was opened five years later as the venue for the 1988 Australian Open, an event which draws the best women and men players in the world.

GK-S

See **AKHURST, DAPHNE**; **ANDERSON, JAMES**; **BOYD, ESNA**; **BROOKES, Sir NOR-MAN**; **BROMWICH, JOHN**; **CASH, PAT**; **CAWLEY, EVONNE**; **COURT, MARGARET**; **CRAWFORD, JACK**; **EMERSON, ROY**; **Federation Cup 1970 (Perth)**; **FRASER, NEALE**; **HAWKES, JOHN**; **HOAD, LEW**; **Hopman Cup**; **HOPMAN, HARRY**; **Hopman–Hoad Towel Incident**; **Kooyong**; **LAVER, ROD**; **LEHANE, JAN**; **McNAMARA, PETER**; **McNAMEE, PAUL**; **Memorial Drive Tennis Club**; **MOLESWORTH, MARGARET**; **NEWCOMBE, JOHN**; **O'HARA WOOD, JOHN**; **PATTERSON, GERALD**; **QUIST, ADRIAN**; **ROCHE, TONY**; **ROSEWALL, KEN**; **Royal Tennis**; **SEDGMAN, FRANK**; **Tennis Australia**; **Tennis: Élite Players since 1930**; **Tennis: Open Champions before 1930**; **Tennis: Championship**; **TURNER, LESLEY**; **WYNNE, NANCYE**.

LAWRENCE, LAURIE (1941–), born Townsville, lived and worked in Queensland. After a successful career in rugby union football he began coaching swimmers in 1966 and became one of the most prominent Australian swimming coaches. He has been widely involved in community-service activities, including learn-to-swim classes for physically handicapped children. His inspirational coaching of such swimmers as Steven Holland, Tracey Wickham, John Sieben, and Duncan Armstrong brought them Olympic and Commonwealth gold medals and numerous world records. His competitiveness and patriotism has endeared him to many Australians.

PH

See **Swimming**.

LAWSON, AUB (1916–77), born Warialda, NSW, was one of Australia's greatest speedway stars, the best rider never to win the world championship. While he rode in nine world finals, more than any other Australian, his best result was a third at Wembley in 1958 when he was 42. Lawson scored more world-final points (73), rode in more Tests (84), and scored more points in Test matches (680) than any other Australian. He also shares the record for Australian Championship wins (five) with Billy Sanders and for NSW Championship wins with Jim Airey (five). Lawson began as a leg trailer

before adapting to the foot-forward riding style. He signed for Wembley, London, in 1937 and in a long racing career rode with Middlesborough, West Ham, and Norwich. After retirement he promoted speedway at Westmead in the 1960s and then at Claremont after settling in Perth in 1968. He died there on 20 January 1977.

PW*

LEBEDEW, WALKIRI VALERY WALTER, OAM (1933–), was the co-founder in 1963 of the Australian Volleyball Federation (AVF) and was its longest-serving secretary (1963–75). Wally Lebedew introduced the first official volleyball rule book into Australia and was founder and editor of the *Australian Volleyball Journal*. He was general manager of Australian international teams, delegate to various international volleyball conferences, and chairman of the Oceania Volleyball Council (1979–83). He was made the first life member of the AVF in recognition of his deep commitment to the growth of the sport.

IF

See **Volleyball**.

LEE, STEVEN JOHN (1962–), a NSW skier, spent his early life in the Falls Creek ski fields in Victoria. He represented Australia at the 1984 (Sarajevo), 1988 (Calgary), and 1992 (Albertville) Winter Olympics. A win in a super giant slalom World Cup race in Japan in 1985 boosted his world ranking that year to seventeenth. In 1986 he won a World Cup combined event at Vail, USA.

KR

LEE, WALTER HENRY ('Dick') (1889–1968), born Collingwood, Melbourne, was an Australian rules footballer. He was called Dick to distinguish him from his father, Walter Henry Lee (head trainer at Collingwood, 1892–1942), and most people were unaware that Richard was not his Christian name. Lee played 230 games for Collingwood (1906–22), kicking 713 goals in a low-scoring era; he headed the VFL goal-kicking ladder ten times. Lee's career was riddled with injury; he underwent the first successful cartilage removal operation for a footballer in 1911. Lee was 'Champion of the Colony' twice (1910 and 1915), captained Collingwood twice (1920 and 1921), and served sixteen years as the club's vice-president (1923–34 and 1950–53). Photographs of his freakish high marking have appeared in print more often than those of any other footballer.

RS

LEECH, GUY (1964–), Ironman, from the Manly Surf Lifesaving Club, has won the world Ironman championship in Vancouver, Canada. Leech is a versatile athlete who has been Australian marathon swimming champion, a gold-medallist in the Australian Surf Lifesaving Championship, and a member of the Australian champion dragon-boat team.

RC

LEHANE, JAN (later O'NEILL) (1941–), born Grenfell, NSW, was an outstanding junior who temporarily, in 1960, rose to be the number one ranked senior in Australian tennis. She won several State championships and the 1959 Australian hardcourt title. The emergence of Margaret Court confined Lehane to runner-up status and this was her fate from 1960 in four consecutive Australian Opens. With Court she was runner-up in the 1961 women's doubles at Wimbledon. In 1963 she was a member of Australia's inaugural Federation Cup team. She was Australia's first prominent woman double-handed backhand player.

HCJP

LEMAISTRE, Dr E. H. (1908–89), a physical education pioneer, managed, with the assistance of Professor Frank Cotton, to have a Board of Studies established at the University of Sydney in 1940. The degree plans were well under way, including a proposed School of Physical Education, when war halted progress. Financial problems after 1945 delayed the programme, so it was not until the early 1950s that LeMaistre was appointed in charge of physical education at the University of Sydney. With lecturer Marjorie Swain he was seconded to Sydney Teachers' College until 1959 when the first degree students were admitted. His drive and dedication resulted in a strong and professional degree in physical education, with an emphasis on health education. Having completed a M.Ed. in 1957 from the University of California, Los Angeles, Hal LeMaistre was also responsible for much of the early interest and developments in NSW school health education programmes.

MK

LESTER, JOYCE (1958–), born Brisbane, was an outstanding softballer; a powerful long hitter and a strong aggressive catcher with a lethal throw to second. Lester began her softball career at the age of 10 and in 1974 was selected as the under-16 Queensland softball captain and entered the open Queensland team the following year. This began a long senior representative career for her State and country during which she has captained her State continuously since 1983, and her country since 1985. In 1977 she was selected to play for Australia in the Test series against NZ. She led Australia in the world series in NZ in 1986, and was named in the World All-Star Softball Team and in the World Series Top-Ten Batters List. Lester maintained this high standard and in 1989 was named in the All-Star Team after the Intercontinental Cup in

Italy. Lester has played continuously for Australia since 1977, during which time she has played in four world series, received the Advance Australia Award in 1991, captained Queensland to three national titles, and coached her club team to a national club championship in 1987 and to second place in 1990. As a primary-school teacher and softball sportswriter, Lester has great influence on the development of softball. Her sister Leigh also played representative softball for Queensland during the late 1970s and early 1980s.

PH-S

LEWIS, HAYLEY JANE (1974–), born Brisbane, taught herself to swim. She was later coached by Roy Holland (father of Stephen), John Wright, and then Joe King. Her first major success, at the age of 10, was when she swam the 100 metres in 1 minute 4 seconds—the fastest junior time ever recorded. She won the 200 and 400 metres at the 1985 Australian junior championships. Although she qualified for the Seoul Olympics, at 14 she was considered too young. She was a popular and modest champion of the 1990 Commonwealth Games, winning five gold medals in the 200 and 400 metres, 400 metres individual medley, 200 metres butterfly, and the 4 × 200 metres relay. She won the 200 metres freestyle at the 1991 world championships, and came second in the 400 metres freestyle and 400 metres individual medley, and third in the 200 metres butterfly.

RH and MH

See **Swimming**.

LEWIS, ROBERT (1878–1947) began his riding career at the age of 10. His first city win was in 1894, and he rode the first of four Melbourne Cup winners in 1902. Lewis owed much of his success to his association with the leading trainer James Scobie. His record included eight Victoria Derbies, four AJC Derbies, three Adelaide Cups, and three Hobart Cups, as well as many other important races. Bobbie Lewis continued riding, with diminishing success, until he retired in July 1938, aged 60. During his long career he was suspended only once.

AL

LEWIS, WALLY (1959–), born Brisbane, one of the dominant figures in Australian Rugby League since the Second World War, was the first Queensland player to captain an Australian rugby league tour of Britain since Tom Gorman in 1929–30. He toured Britain in the 1977 Australian schoolboys rugby union team. He then played for the Brisbane Valleys club (as lock), and, from 1984, Wynnum-Manly. He first played for Queensland as a reserve in 1979, and from the first State of Origin match in 1980, began an almost uninterrupted sequence of State and, from 1981, Australian representation, until his arm was broken in 1990. From 1981 Lewis has normally played as a five-eighth. Whatever his position, he is inventive and extraordinarily gifted in reading a game. He captained Queensland from 1981, Australia from 1984, and has played in more winning Australian Test teams than any other rugby league footballer (twenty-eight). His 1986 Australian team was unbeaten throughout its British tour. Lewis has remarkable ball skills, both in tactical kicking and long, accurate passing. He has great strength and determination, and his anticipation and positional sense more than compensate for a comparative lack of top sprinting speed. In 1989 he won his seventh award as man of the match in State of Origin games. Lewis's stature as Queensland and Australian captain was important in the very successful introduction of the Brisbane Broncos into a widened Sydney Rugby League competition in 1988. He captained the teams until late 1989. In 1991 be began to play for the Gold Coast Seagulls. For most of his career Wally Lewis has excited overwhelming media attention and intensely partisan response: his picture topped the sales of cartoon posters of State and national celebrities at Brisbane's Expo in 1988.

SJR

See **Rugby League**.

LEXCEN, BEN (1936–88), originally Bob Miller, was a former sailmaker who became an acclaimed designer of yachts and achieved international fame for his revolutionary winged keel which enabled *Australia II* to win the *America's* Cup in 1983. The wings were devised after years of study and four months of experiments in 1982 in the Dutch Wageningen tank. He won the 1983 Award for Design Excellence for *Australia II* and also won the Ted Kenyon Memorial Trophy for the person who had done most for boating in 1983. After a tough childhood—some of it spent in a home, Boys' Town—Lexcen virtually educated himself in higher mathematics and hydrodynamics to become a brilliant designer of all manner of craft including dinghies, 18-footers, and ocean racers. He designed the heavyweight *America's* Cup 12 metre *Southern Cross* in 1974 and co-designed *Australia* in 1977. He designed *Australia III* and *Australia IV*, defence contenders for 1987. Lexcen was also a fine sailor and was many times Australian champion in the Soling Class, the Flying Dutchman class, and the 18-foot class. He was also successful in the VJ, 16-foot, VS, and Star classes. He represented Australia in the 1968 and 1972 Olympics and in the 1972 Admiral's Cup. The Ben Lexcen Sports Scholarships, at the University of NSW, were created to honour his name.

RC

See *Australia II*.

LILLEE, DENNIS KEITH, MBE (1949–   ), born Subiaco, Perth, was a fast and fearsome right-arm bowler with a classical action. Lillee is Australia's highest Test wicket-taker, with 355 at 23.92. He began Test cricket as a tear-away express bowler in 1971, but a severe injury in 1973 saw him withdraw from Test cricket, returning as the supreme pace bowler in the 1974–75 season, combining a demoralising short ball with expert control of cut and swing. He was a focal point of success for World Series Cricket during 1977–79 and returned again to Test cricket to harry batsmen all over the world. Lillee became an entertainer, enjoying the stage that modern Test cricket had become, but supported this with a fitness regimen, courage, determination, and a smouldering belligerence that could transform any match. His partnership with Test wicket-keeper Rodney Marsh was productive: Marsh contributed to 95 of Lillee's Test wickets. Lillee was often the centre of controversy—the aluminium bat incident, the fracas with Javed Miandad, and the 1981 bet against his own side—but always remained popular with the Australian public because of his whole-hearted effort. After retiring from Test cricket in 1984, he coached in many countries. Lillee made a short come-back to Sheffield Shield cricket in 1987, playing for Tasmania and taking a wicket with his first ball. He is rated as one of the greatest fast bowlers of all time not only because of the number of wickets he gained but also because of his impact upon the Tests in which he played.

SG

See **Aluminium Cricket Bats**; **Cricket**.

LINDRUM, HORACE (1912–74), a nephew of Walter Lindrum, became, in 1970, the first player to compile 1000 snooker centuries. Lindrum showed talent as a youth, making his first snooker century at 16. After turning professional he won the Australian Professional Snooker championship when just 19. Three years later he won the Professional Billiards Championship. He then played in Britain, South Africa, NZ, India, and Rhodesia. He scored the highest possible snooker break (147 points) at Penrith in 1941 and became World Snooker Champion in 1952, defeating Clark McConachy 94 frames to 49. After retiring in 1957 he made a come-back, winning the Australian Open snooker title in 1963.

GC*

See **Billiards and Snooker**.

LINDRUM, WALTER ALBERT, MBE, OBE (1898–1960), born Kalgoorlie, WA, was the greatest billiards-player the world has known. He was official world champion from 1933 to 1950, and established over fifty world records, many of which are never likely to be broken. His dominance was such that several times the rules of billiards were altered to curb his prolific scoring, and to even the contests he gave all his nearest rivals the benefit of substantial handicaps. His records include over 800 breaks of more than 1000, more than 30 of over 2000, at least 6 of over 3000, a world record 4137, and a record match aggregate of 36356. He holds the record break for every country in which he played, and a string of record cannon sequences. Many of these records were made under the pressure of competition, some after prolonged periods of sustained concentration, and all at amazing speed—some of his best times being 1101 in 30 minutes, 663 in 15 minutes, and 100 in 27.5 seconds. Lindrum came from a line of billiards and snooker champions. His father, a strict disciplinarian, coached him from an early age. At 16 he had established his first world record, after which he was never beaten in an even contest. Lindrum's feats were in world prominence during the 1930s Depression and did much to boost Australian morale. His name was often linked with Don Bradman's. Early in Bradman's career, Neville Cardus described him as 'the Lindrum of cricket'; after Lindrum's death, newspaper headlines referred to him as 'the Bradman of billiards'. Lindrum was a tireless worker for charities, especially in wartime. He raised over $1 million, mainly through staging nearly four thousand exhibition matches throughout Australia. His memory is perpetuated in the 'Lindy' award to the outstanding sportsperson of the year, and the Walter Lindrum Memorial Scholarship in technical education. He was awarded the MBE in 1951 and the OBE in 1958.

RH*

See **Billiards and Snooker**.

LINDWALL, RAYMOND RUSSELL, MBE (1921–), born Mascot, Sydney, played cricket for NSW and Queensland. In sixty-one Tests he took 228 wickets at 23.03 and collected two centuries among 1502 runs scored at 21.15. Lindwall, 180 centimetres tall, bowled right-arm fast, with a perfect action which allowed him to generate intimidating pace and a lethal bouncer. A disciplined player who could bowl an eight-ball over in 4 minutes, his control of the ball has rarely been equalled by fast bowlers. Lindwall was also a fine rugby league full back and experts judged him good enough to have played for Australia. He worked at his fitness which allowed him to play Tests until he was 38 then retired to a prosperous florist business.

SG

Liston Trophy. Named after a leading Williamstown (Victoria) identity and former VFA president (1929–43), the J. J. Liston Trophy is presented annually to the VFA's best and fairest player. Inaugurated in 1945, the trophy predates

the Brownlow Medal by twelve months. The first winner was B. Beard from the Oakleigh club. Preston is the best-represented club with nine winners. Although no player has won the trophy on three occasions, 1990 proved to be a remarkable year as four players tied on the same votes and shared it.

GC*

Literature

Under a reliable and congenial sun, white Australians embraced sport—and its by-products—so enthusiastically that from the earliest colonial decades it fostered a strong sense of community (for better or sometimes worse) and became one of the most powerful influences on social development. Aspiring Australian writers could not ignore it, even if they had a mind to. A long line of commentators and creative writers has utilised or speculated upon this seminal area of Australian behaviour. From John Dunmore Lang in the 1830s to Mark Twain in the 1890s, Nettie Palmer in the 1930s to Patrick White, Olga Masters, and Roger McDonald in the 1980s, Australian and overseas writers have either cast a critical eye on the Australian sporting passion or they have made clever artistic use of it.

First, the critics and their social context: John Dunmore Lang was arguably the first important writer to weigh in on the subject. Singling out horse-racing in his *An Historical and Statistical Account of New South Wales* (1834), and never one to resist the possibility of a pun, Lang maintained that '. . . *the march of improvement* is too weak a phrase for the meridian of New South Wales: we must there speak of the *race of improvement*; for the three appropriate and never failing accompaniments of advancing civilization in that colony are a race-course, a public house, and a gaol.' A race meeting for Lang was not an assemblage of wealth and beauty, as government propagandists claimed; rather, it concentrated all the colony's 'vice and villany [sic] . . . gambling, and drunkenness, and dissipation . . .'. Lang also claimed that if 'gentlemen of the first rank' were 'busily employed in training up race-horses and betting lustily on their performances, perspiring at a cricket-match or huzzaing at a regatta, what can [native youth] possibly suppose but that such puerile and contemptible employments are fit for men?' Alas for Lang, sport under the Australian sun held firmly captive gentlemen of the first, middle, and lower ranks.

After the discovery of gold in 1851, visitors to the Australian colonies increased dramatically; so, too, did the number of self-appointed social commentators keen to pass judgement on local idiosyncrasies. Many of the transient endorsed Lang's bleak Presbyterian point of view on sport. The young English writer Frank Fowler, for example, labelled Australia 'a depot for the scum and scoundrelism of the old world'. While he considered horse-racing 'comparatively harmless', the fact that 'Every little Australian settlement has its race-course' undoubtedly contributed to the colony's 'gambling mania' and 'every-day debauchery'. Richard Henry Horne, a resident in Australia from 1852 until 1869, approached the issue with more tact, yet he could not hide his puzzlement with certain native enthusiasms, especially the 'fashionable patronage' of racing and cricket: 'The mania for bats and balls in the broiling sun during the last summer [1858] exceeded all rational excitements.'

James F. Hogan, historian of the Irish in Australia and eventually a member of the British House of Commons, also contributed to what was fast becoming a tradition of damning analyses of sporting Australia in an article for the *Victorian Review* in 1880. Anticipating the 'new type of humanity' in Australia in the new century, Hogan predicted that the three principal characteristics of the future citizenry would be an inordinate love of field sports; a very decided disinclination to recognise the authority of parents and superiors; and a grievous dislike to mental effort. For Hogan, too many young men (he would not be the first nor the last to ignore women completely), in the 'spring-time' of life indulged in 'physical pleasures at the expense of mental cultivation'; they looked only to the 'arena of muscle'. Hogan felt the Australian national character itself was at issue and late in the century his arguments received support from an unlikely source: Henry Lawson. In an article, 'Our Countrymen', published in the *Worker* (1893), Lawson struck out at the mediocrity surrounding him. He labelled the average Australian boy 'a cheeky brat with . . . no ambition beyond the cricket and football field'; the average Australian youth a 'weedy individual . . . [with] a cramped mind devoted to sport'; and he suggested that the average Australian 'thinks more about *Carbine* than one-man-one-vote'. Others, however, argued in defence of the Australian propensity for sport. The case mounted by the *Australian Observer*, on 5 January 1856, is typical: 'Laws are frequently arbitrary enactments, passed, repealed, and forgotten; but the amusements of the people are of national growth and of universal influence . . . [Since] recreation is a necessity of our existence, the man who devises a means of healthful, rational, moral amusement is a benefactor of society.' In *The Future Australian Race* (1877), Marcus Clarke—like many of his contemporaries a more aggressive patriot once he had decided to reside permanently in Australia— challenged those who continued to judge with jaundiced Anglocentric eyes: 'Read the accounts of the boat races, the cricket matches, and say if our youth are not manly . . . deny, if you can, that there is here the making of a great nation.'

And so were the battle-lines drawn in the nineteenth century. Australia: a mighty nation in the making, a nation athletic, healthy, and moral; or a population besotted with sport, uncivilised, and given to the huzzaing of madmen? In the twentieth century the arguments have become more complex, occasionally sophisticated, but they have only confirmed the framework of the old dichotomy. When Patrick White determined to play a more assertive role in Australian public life after the election of the Whitlam Government in 1972 he made a number of assertions about our social and cultural milieu, immediately locating himself within the tradition working back through Lawson to Lang. On Australia Day 1984, White wrote that it 'seems as though life itself now depends on sport'; a few years later he elaborated in characteristic style, a mixture of bombast, wit, and insight:

> . . . today, the sight of thugs writhing in the mud and bashing the hell out of one another in the name of sport has perhaps become part of our national 'coltcher' . . . A great number of Australians always seem to be running to or from somewhere—city-to-surf in my native city—capital-to-capital . . . This passion for perpetual motion: is it perhaps for fear that we may have to sit down and face reality if we don't keep going?

Whether one approves of Australia's extravagant sporting life or deplores it, one cannot avoid it. Australia's creative writers, or more precisely those with an egalitarian or larrikin streak, have traditionally reflected that significance in their work. Barry Andrews detailed the extent of the relationship in his monumental article 'The Willow Tree and the Laurel: Australian Sport and Australian Literature' (1977). Rather than venture over the same ground trailblazed by Andrews, and as a homage to and extension of his pioneering work, this essay concentrates on Australian literature's three most celebrated sports down through the years: horse-racing (the most popular by a country mile), cricket, and football (rules, rugby, and rugby league).

HORSE-RACING

In its April issue, 1899, *The Bookfellow* offered 10s 6d for the 'best Quatrain' on the subject of Australia. According to A. G. Stephens' conditions, the verse must '"*breathe*" Australia, as a gum-tree breathes. Marry Australia to Poetry . . .' Dowell O'Reilly won the competition and the coin but R. H. Croll tickled everyone's fancy with his quatrain about Australia 'In Contemporary Literature'.

> Whalers, damper, swag and nosebag, Johnny-
>   cakes and billy tea,
> Murrumburrah, Meremendicoowoke,
>   Yoularbudgeree,

76 Media coverage of sport in Australia was enhanced with the introduction of live telecasts, the first being the Melbourne Olympics in 1956, and the 'OB' van soon became a familiar sight at many venues.

77 Mal Meninga began his rugby league career with Souths in Brisbane, and then joined the Canberra Raiders.

78 Netballers from Australia playing in Lincoln's Inn,
1956, after an invitation from the All England Netball
Association.

79 Australian teams have won six of the eight
international netball tournaments that have been held
every four years since Australia won the first in 1963.

Cattle-duffers, bold bushrangers, diggers,
drovers, bush race-courses,
And on all the other pages, horses, horses,
horses, horses.

Three novels published in the last few years—
Peter Carey's *Oscar and Lucinda* (1988), Roger
McDonald's *Rough Wallaby* (1989), and Tim
Winton's *Cloudstreet* (1991)—have all reaffirmed
a long-standing relationship between Australian
writers and horse-racing, a relationship which
on occasion has bordered on an obsession, as
Croll's quirky quatrain testifies. In *The Unlucky
Australians* (1968), Frank Hardy maintained that
if '...a small fraction of the cunnings, guiles,
mathematical skills, thoughts, studies, obsessions, horses for courses cogitations, state of the
track transactions, that go into horse racing
went into science and culture, we would have
bred a race of geniuses instead of idiots'. He
misses the point. Horse-racing in Australia is
more than a 'track transaction', more even than
a national sport; it is folklore, legend, a cherished part of our cultural heritage.

In his book on A. B. Paterson, *The Banjo of
the Bush* (1966), Clement Semmler writes that
'Paterson alone of any Australian writer has
made it [horse-racing] a considerable and enduring subject of his attention'. Perusing the
form on the board of the very smart field of this
country's finest writers, it is impossible to dis-
agree with him. It was Paterson, after all, who
in his extremely entertaining and informative
manuscript *Racehorses and Racing* (1914) began
chapter one with an epigraph entitled 'The Australian Declaration of Independence': 'All men
are born free and equal; and each man is entitled
to life, liberty and the pursuit of horse racing.'
And it was Paterson who, in a script for the
ABC in 1935, captured the Australian love for
horse-racing with dry bushie humour: 'Before
the North Pole was discovered, some cynic said
that it would be discovered easily enough by
advertising a race meeting there, when a couple
of dozen Australians would infallibly turn up
with their horses . . .'

Banjo Paterson is unquestionably the doyen
of Australian punter-writers but there have
been many others who have shown more than a
passing interest in equine pursuits. Semmler
lists only Adam Lindsay Gordon, Frank Hardy,
Cecil Mann, and Nat Gould (hardly an Australian writer, since only eleven of his sixty-two
years were spent in this country) as showing
any worthwhile commitment, which leads him
to the assertion that horse-racing has made only
'a slight impact on our literature'. In fact, racing
has had a suitably colourful, distinctive role in
the work of major writers as diverse as Marcus
Clarke, Rolf Boldrewood, Xavier Herbert and,
more recently, Vincent Buckley and Gerald
Murnane, in company with McDonald, Carey,
and Winton.

Adam Lindsay Gordon arrived from England
as a 20-year-old in 1853 and Marcus Clarke
disembarked on southern shores a decade later,
aged 27. Both men were destined to spend the
remainder of their relatively short lives in Australia. Gordon loved horses and horse-racing,
especially steeplechasing; Clarke, in his capacity
as a journalist, covered all aspects of the sport
for the *Argus* and the *Melbourne Herald*. When
committing their responses to print—Gordon
as the vigorous balladeer, Clarke as the sometimes cynical reporter—both writers established
the basic patterns of response of all Australian
writers to follow. They focus on the positive
aspects: the beauty, dignity, and courage of
thoroughbred racehorses; the excitement and
spectacle of Australia's most famous, mythologised race, the Melbourne Cup; the wry
humour and individual style surrounding aspects of the turf, particularly the subcultures of
race-tipping and race-fixing; and the art, for
some the science, of punting successfully. Gordon and Clarke also canvas, and far more descriptively, the seedier aspects of racing, Clarke
in particular revealing what punters, punting,
and bookmaking are often really like.

Inevitably, Australia's greatest horse-race
figures prominently in the sport writing of both
men, just as it dominates racing literature in
Australia generally. In *Hippodromania*, for example, Gordon writes of the fervour of the
fifth Melbourne Cup (1865), with its 'gloss and
polish and lustre'. Marcus Clarke covered the
Cup two years later for the *Argus* newspaper
and it is obvious in his article that the passion
and devotion of the entire Australian community were already at an intense level. If, as
Clarke says, 'Anglo Saxons are proverbially
partial to racing', their Australian descendants
were seriously smitten. Of the 1867 Cup, he
observed that: 'To each and all, bookmaker and
spectator, to the rich squatter from the country,
clerk from his bank or warehouse, or labourer
from the field, the race for the Melbourne Cup
was the central point of interest of the day.'
When Mark Twain visited Australia in the later
1890s, most of the peculiarities surrounding the
Melbourne Cup—the myths and the madness
—had become institutionalised. In the Australian section of *Following the Equator* (1897), Twain
felt bound to comment on this unique southern
phenomenon. Melbourne, he remarked, 'is the
mitred Metropolitan of the Horse-Racing Cult.
Its raceground is the Mecca of Australasia.' He
went on: 'The Melbourne Cup is the Australasian National Day . . . I can call to mind no
specialized annual day, in any country, whose
approach fires the whole land with a conflagration of conversation and preparation and anticipation and jubilation. No day save this one; but
this one does it.' Little has changed in the many
decades since.

If Twain was astounded and not a little impressed by the conflagration of the racing South, Xavier Herbert in his fiction expresses his disgust with the inebriation and community flagellation in the racing North. His prototypical NT Cup meeting in *Poor Fellow My Country* (1975), the annual Beatrice River races, while unashamedly egalitarian, is also crude, chaotic, and at times violent. Pouring themselves out of the trains, 'the mob' celebrates its survival of twelve months in the Never-Never with 'riotous excess', a '*bonhomie*' of booze'. Horse-owners are not toffs. They can be, like the 1936 Cup-winner Piggy Trotters, obese, unsophisticated 'gin-jockeys'; they're sometimes miners in town for a once-a-year binge, like the Knowles boys, Nobby and Nugget; they might be silvertails, like Lord Alfred Vaisey; indeed, they might even be of much-maligned 'Celestial persuasion'. On these few days each year, black, white, tawny, rich, and poor meet as near-equals. The Beatrice River races in the 1930s and 1940s accurately represent their non-fiction counterparts in Darwin, Pine Creek, Katherine, the Alice, and Borroloola, from the 1870s onwards.

Curiously, both Mark Twain and Herbert—harsh observers of human foibles—concentrate on the spectacle of Cup celebrations. Neither writer pays any attention to, nor displays any knowledge of, betting. Herbert can't even discriminate between odds-on and odds-against. Adam Lindsay Gordon, horseman par excellence, could. Indeed, his skills of poesy and punting were such that he was asked by the editors of *Bell's Life in Victoria* to contribute to their pages in the fashion of the day: a Melbourne Cup tip in verse. The numerous stanzas of '*Hippodromania*' finally sling *Tim Whiffler*, who would finish fourth in the Cup of 1865.

As Gordon well knew, tipping winners is never easy—and it is this difficulty which, more often than not, leads to the other side of racing, its seedier aspect. As the world-wise Billy Borker tells young Jerome Smith in Frank Hardy's *The Yarns of Billy Borker* (1965) 'there's no certainties in racing . . . Only two kinds of people punt the horses, the needy and the greedy . . . It's not a sport mate, it's a lottery with four-legged tickets.' Race-fixing, in particular, is as old as the first betting on a horse-race and it has been the source of much of the humour, especially of the tall-tale variety, in Australian racing literature. One of the best scenes in Rolf Boldrewood's classic *Robbery Under Arms* (1882–83) occurs in chapter XLII, when Starlight, the Marstons, and Old Jacob Benton successfully ring-in Starlight's fleet-footed horse *Rainbow* into the Turon Grand Handicap, of 2 miles, in front of 20 000 wildly enthusiastic miners desperately trying to lose their dough.

Frank Hardy and Banjo Paterson produced some of the more memorable accounts of race-

fixing; Hardy in stories such as 'The Greatest Slanter in the History of the Game' and 'The Smart Bookmaker from the South Who Took His Horse to the Darwin Races', and Paterson in a series of poems, best known of which is his 'How the Favourite Beat Us' (no doubt written in response to Gordon's wishful 'How We Beat the Favourite'). Printed, appropriately, in the Rosehill racebook of 9 November 1894, the opening stanza has established an honoured place in punting—and literary—folklore:

'Aye', said the boozer, 'I tell you it's true, sir,
I once was a punter with plenty of pelf,
But gone is my glory, I'll tell you my story
How I stiffened my horse and got stiffened
    myself.

Roger McDonald's energetic contemporary yarn, 'Rough Wallaby' (based on the *Fine Cotton/Bold Personality* ring-in scandal at Eagle Farm on 18 August 1984), provides a clever reworking of a time-honoured theme.

Recent novels have reinforced the sleazier aspects of racing. Augustine Killeaton, the thwarted and obsessive father in Gerald Murnane's *Tamarisk Row* (1974) wonders, towards the end of the novel, whether 'he can live with himself for the rest of the night' after another desperately unlucky interface with the pitfalls of punting; Frank Hardy graphically portrays the increasingly tortured, aberrant acts, and eventual tragedy, of his three principal characters in *The Four-Legged Lottery* (1958); while Peter Carey's two protagonists, Oscar Hopkins and Lucinda Leplaistrier, the obsessive and compulsive punters respectively in *Oscar and Lucinda* (1988), wrestle with their passion throughout the book. Oscar, born into a strict Plymouth Brethren family, decides through a strange game—a glorified toss of the coin—that he will walk the spiritual path of an Anglican. Ultimately, he heads to Oxford and he is exposed, not to the more elaborate and sustaining of High Church comforts, but to a Mr Wardley-Fish, a student betting man. Shortly after they meet, Wardley-Fish enquires of Oscar whether he would 'like a flutter'. Oscar agrees, and when his first horse wins, the case history of a pathological gambler begins. Later in the novel, when Lucinda asks Oscar for absolution for her gambling, he refuses, replying: 'Where is the sin . . . Our whole faith is a wager, Miss Leplaistrier. We bet . . . we bet there is a God. We bet our life on it. We calculate the odds, the return, that we shall sit with the saints in paradise.'

Would that God were the only variable involved in betting. Unfortunately, this is not the case. Marcus Clarke's novel *Long Odds* (1869) addresses the hard-earned racecourse lesson that horses are pulled and nobbled, while Banjo Paterson lists the types encountered at the course in the jargon of his time: 'knowledge boxes', 'hard-heads', 'whisperers', 'battlers', 'runners', and good old 'urgers' and 'hangers on', like Dear Boy Dickson and Spider Ryan in the novel *The Shearer's Colt* (1936). While it is true that Sam Pickles and Lester Lamb get themselves on to a winning roll in Tim Winton's *Cloudstreet* (1991) with a horse called Blackbutt (Sam regards it as the 'Hairy Hand of God' or 'Lady Luck'; Lester's more tactile personality feels it 'was like sex'), their success provides the exception to the rule. And what are the rules? For these, there is only one impeccable source: The Banjo. In *Racehorses and Racing*, and a 'wireless talk' he once gave, Paterson provides a wealth of maxims. Punters take note:

> An ounce of luck is worth a ton of judgement.
>
> Racing is, on the average, a losing business.
>
> If you back favourites, you'll have no laces in your boots.
>   English bookmaker, Joe Thompson.
> If you back outsiders you'll have no boots.
>   Same source.
> I don't know which is the hardest, the human race or the horse race.

For every one escaped into the romance and humour of the turf, Paterson includes numerous caveats. Horse-racing in Australian literature is a grand, but ultimately cautionary, tale.

FOOTBALL

When Rugby-educated Thomas Wentworth Wills returned to Melbourne in 1856 he sought a code which would eliminate the worst of English rugby practices. Rugby was perceived as too rough for the hard Australian playing fields. So the Melbourne Football Club began in 1858 and by 1860 the fundamentals of Australian rules football had been established. Allies of the code quickly jumped to its defence. Tom Jones in *The Footballer* (1875) called the rugby scrum 'the last relic of barbarism'; Richard Twopeny in *Town Life in Australia* (1883) designated 'the Victorian game' as 'by far the most scientific . . . altogether the best . . .'. It would not be long before the Australian States split on football lines: NSW and Queensland would remain firmly rugby (and, later, rugby league); the rest of the states accepted rules, with the bi-partisan NT parading its climate with its insistence on playing all codes. In his last Barassi Memorial Lecture (1978), Ian Turner clarified the geography of this footballing Maginot line: '. . . Australia is divided by a deep cultural rift between the north and the south known as the Barassi line. It runs between Canberra, Broken Hill, Birdsville and Manangrita and it divides Australia between Rugby and Rules.'

Australia's creative writers have inevitably divided according to the social strictures of the Barassi line. Those from the Aussie rules regions are known for their passion and parochialism. Anne Summers in *Damned Whores and God's Police* (1975) maintains that the 'disdain many intellectuals feel for the activities of the masses does not so often extend to [Australian rules] football, which secures often fanatical support . . .'. Ian Turner might have been stretching it a little when he referred to the body of theses available in 'serious academic discourse'—such as Professor Bradley's 'penetrating analysis', *Barassi and Hamlet—a Comparative Study in the Tragic Hero* and Professor Andrew's 'piledriving paper' on *Minor Surgery of the Back Pocket*—but the appeal of Aussie rules to a range of (male) writers is undeniable. Playwright Louis Esson in a letter to his mate, Vance Palmer, (1927) designated rules 'the most serious matter in the State'. Manning Clark, a devoted Carlton man, went on record in the *Age* one Grand Final day as saying that a win for his team would be 'to see my love come to me'. Mark O'Connor celebrated Collingwood's 1990 pennant with his poem 'The 1990 AFL Grand-final in Beijing', a clever synthesis of Magpie lore and Beijing vistas, dedicated to Manning Clark, who had asked: 'Why not a quatrain for Mick McGuane? Or a threnody for that great half-back line of Lucas, Kingston, Tuck.' Other more elaborate expressions of love for the game include the Leonie Sandercock and Ian Turner volume *Up Where Cazaly? The Great Australian Game* (1981) and Garrie Hutchinson's *From the Outer: Watching Football in the 80s* (1984).

Australian football appeals to its more creative devotees in three distinct ways: its egalitarianism, its aesthetic qualities, and the incontrovertible social implications of the game (that is, those zones south and west of the Barassi line). As early as the 1870s, 'The Vagabond' remarked that Aussie rules in Victoria was 'followed by all—larrikins, mechanics, clerks and (self-esteemed) young aristocrats'. A century later, poet and academic Chris Wallace-Crabbe described the democracy of the modern rapture: 'Footy is, after the weather, the universal subject for small talk and every little girl or boy that's born into this world alive becomes a supporter . . .' Bruce Dawe's 'Life Cycle', arguably the best-known contemporary sporting poem, builds on the idea. Dedicated to Big Jim Phelan, it begins:

> When children are born in Victoria
> they are wrapped in the club-colours, laid in beribboned cots,
> having already begun a lifetime's barracking.

Only commitment of this kind—a 'collective madness' according to Barry Oakley—could explain the actions of some fans. One notable effort caught the attention of Hal Colebatch, who responded with a poem entitled 'Lines written upon learning that a man had had his ashes buried between the goal-posts of a football ground', while John Morrison graphically portrays the sad and sombre Saturday evening of a loving Magpie supporter in his short story 'Black Night in Collingwood'.

For many Australian rules fans the wait between winter Saturdays is difficult; between seasons it is almost impossible to endure. George Johnston, in *The Australians* (1966), quotes the remark of a Sydney acquaintance that 'Melbourne has no summer, only a period of hibernation between football seasons'. Johnston then remembers his own return to the mecca of football, the Melbourne Cricket Ground: '. . . that unbelievable roar of over 100 000 screaming zealots . . . No other sporting event in Australia draws a crowd as big or committed as this. For a time men become gods and heroes.'

Curiously, the three most significant longer works about Australian football—Alan Hopgood's *And the Big Men Fly* (1969), Barry Oakley's *A Salute to the Great McCarthy* (1970), and David Williamson's popular play *The Club* (1978)—concentrate, not on the game or the players, the 'guernseyed Icaruses' as Bruce Dawe has termed them, but on the unsavoury aspects of the sport off the field, the men and manipulation behind the scenes. Achilles Jones, Jack McCarthy, and Geoff Hayward are forced to move in a world of hypocritical officials and a media given to clichés and character assassination. Achilles and Jack go back to the bush— Jack heading for his home town of Warwick 'for therapy' because he 'went too close to the bright lights and copped a fast burn on the behind', Achilles retreating to the security of his farm 'Cause it ain't been real fun. Too many bad things have happened since I started.' David Williamson has Geoff Hayward vent his feelings about 'The Club' scene: 'If you really want to know, what's going on is that I'm sick to death of football . . . It's all a lot of macho-competitive Bullshit.'

Welcome recent additions to his broad category of literary works are the stories of Aboriginal writer Archie Weller, especially 'Going Home' and 'Cooley' in the *Going Home* (1986) collection. Weller's stories generally depict young Aboriginal men desperately trying to decipher the conflicting codes of an oppressive white society. Football represents opportunity; however, in 'Going Home' Billy Woodward learns the hard way that his footballing notoriety counts for nothing back in his racist WA home town, and the tragic Reg Cooley—aspiring to the life of his celebrated footballing brother, Ben, and role models like 'Stephen Michael or Maurice Rioli or the Krakouer brothers'—is killed at the end of the story by a policeman's errant bullet. Caught up in the pathos of the story, the narrator sums up:

Here lies not a Polly Farmer, Lionel Rose or Namatjira; only a small-town halfcaste who tried to raise himself out of the dirt and was kicked back down again . . . He had leaped high for the mark on cold grey days, sent long, graceful kicks up high in the air . . . Only a halfcaste who had lived in a world of football and dreams.

When rugby union and rugby league have received literary attention, the results have usually confirmed the very physical nature of both codes. True, last century Edward Kinglake labelled Australian rules football a game for 'semi-barbarian races' and popular *Bulletin* short-story writer and balladist Edward Dyson did depict a rules clash in his poem 'A Friendly Game of Football' (between The Dingos of Squatter's Gap and the likely lads of Gyp's Diggings) that degenerated into a mêlée. Nonetheless, historically, union and league have been the codes persistently portrayed as the more violent. One of the earliest rugby stories, John Arthur Barry's *Far Inland Football*, pits the men of the little township of Crupperton against the 'Thicklegs' of nearby Saddlestrap. The rules of both clubs are 'simplicity itself': the solitary axiom, 'Kick whatever or whenever you can, only kick.' From the opening 'hot scrimmage', the game develops largely as a series of boots-and-all brawls. Crupperton, claiming victory after the Saddlestraps break and flee, feels emboldened to challenge the more distant and genteel 'City' of Cantleville. Asked by Cantleville officials if he and his team-mates play rugby rules, the Crupperton blacksmith replies, 'No, we don't . . . We plays Crupperton.' After the inevitable fracas ensues, and the 'City' calls in its constabulary, the Crupperton blacksmith dismisses the opposition as 'a lot o' tiddleywinkers'.

Stereotyped ocker Norm, in Alex Buzo's controversial play *Norm and Ahmed* (1969), is struck from the Crupperton mould. When the Pakistani, Ahmed, mentions having no time for sport, Norm nostalgically recalls his pre-war rugby league playing days as a lock:

I was always a clean player, Ahmed, I never put the boot in. I remember one bloke. A real coot. Played prop for Balmain juniors. Tall bloke, he was. A long thin streak of pelican shit. He tried to lay one on me at Leichhardt Oval once, so I administered a knuckle sandwich to him.

At play's end, Norm does the same to Ahmed—a 'Fuckin' boong'—for failing to adhere to his particular masculine code. Paul Sherman's recent poem 'Broncos v Balmain', with its references to rugby league as 'more than Thuggery Legal' and Queensland's Lang Park as a 'Colosseum', reinforces this common portrayal of the code.

There have been several notable and varied exceptions to this image of aggression, however. First, the superb 'sermon' of J. M. Davis, published in the *Bulletin* (1899), which elaborately describes the fundamentals of rugby in terms of an assortment of biblical texts and concludes with the exhortation of I Corinthians 9:6: 'eat, or drink, or whatsoever ye do, do all for the glory of God'. Second, the splendid writer David Campbell, one of Australia's finest poets, who also happened to captain the King's School rugby First XV and later played for Cambridge and, ultimately, England. Third, a delightful article, 'My Boy Roy' by the highly praised Olga Masters, published in Sydney's *Manly Daily* and written in response to her editor's suggestion to cover the Manly Penrith league match (in June 1974) because her 'boy Roy' was coach of the Penrith side. Fourth, the dazzling verbal skills of Alex Buzo's play *The Roy Murphy Show* (1970), a thinly disguised satire about Sydney's rugby league commentary teams in the 1960s. Buzo mercilessly exposes all the inadequacies of host Roy Murphy's on-camera verbal idiosyncrasies, replete with clichés ('the game's not over till . . .'), alliteration, Australian pronunciations ('restaurong') and confused mixed metaphors ('go through 'em like a packet of chalk and cheese'). Fifth, and finally, mention must be made of Ironbark Press's most recent publication *The Greatest Game—a Celebration of Rugby League* (1991), the first meaningful attempt to gather the best writing on rugby league since its inception early this century. Contributors include A. B. Paterson, Hugh Lunn, Kenneth Slessor, Ian Moffit, and Tom Keneally.

CRICKET

In 1877 an Australian eleven won what most regard as the first cricket Test against England. The Melbourne *Punch* could not contain its excitement:

> There came a tale to England,
> 'Twas of a contest done:
> Australian youths in cricket fields
> Had met the cracks and won . . .

Australian cricket had come of age; in the ensuing decades its appeal would increase accordingly. Twopeny in *Town Life in Australia* (1883) asserted the pre-eminence of the sport in all southern colonies—indeed, as he pointed out, 'not to be interested in it amounts almost to a social crime':

> Every little Australian that is 'born alive' is a little cricketer, a bat, or bowler, or field. Cricket is the colonial *carrière ouverte aux talents*. As Napoleon's soldiers remembered that they carried a marshal's *baton* in their knapsacks, so the young Australians all remember that they have a chance of becoming successors of that illustrious band of heroes who have recently conquered the mother-country and looted her into the bargain . . .

Such intense popularity had to exert some effect on Australia's writing community, though contemporary poet Jamie Grant is correct when he states that cricket 'does not appear in Australian creative writing as often as you might expect . . .'.

As with horse-racing and football, the links that do exist between cricket and literature have a distinctive and often humorous quality. In the decade following the 1877 Test, a few writers puzzled over this sporting euphoria. Creve Roe (Victor Daley), for example, contemplated Victor Trumper's mesmeric batting and its debilitating effect on other areas of the national consciousness:

> Ho Statesman, Patriots, Bards make way!
> Your fame has sunk to zero:
> For Victor Trumper is today
> Our one Australian hero . . . .
> Evoe Trumper! As for me
> It all ends with the moral
> That fame goes on the Willow Tree
> And no more on the laurel.

Decades later, Nettie Palmer did not feel nearly as threatened. Rather, she wrestled with the philosophical implications of the 'art' and social profile of arguably the three most popular Australian sportsmen before Bradman: Victor Trumper, Walter Lindrum, and Norman Brookes. For Palmer (1932) they were 'inferior artists', yet their creation of 'images of swiftness, precision and perfect rhythmic movement . . . undoubtedly created what can only be called beauty'.

High art, low art, or not art at all—many of Palmer's literary peers didn't seem to care. They simply loved their cricket. The only two things that could get Australia's first playwright, Louis Esson, out of his study were the footie and the cricket. He thought Warwick Armstrong's conquering side in England in 1921 had 'a touch of genius' about it and he considered W. H. Ponsford—'Ponnie'—to be (in 1926) 'the greatest bat in the world'. Henry Handel Richardson, a most unlikely fan, was at one with her compatriots in doting on 'the Don'— Donald George Bradman. Apparently when novelist Vance Palmer paid Richardson a call in 1930 she could talk of nothing else. The Don, of course, crossed all social, artistic, and intellectual barriers. In the second volume of his autobiography, *The Quest for Grace* (1990), Manning Clark recalls the frustration of a visiting scholar in Australia in the 1930s who had come to discuss the country's economic problems. He soon discovered that the only thing professors down under wanted to discuss was the incomparable Don Bradman.

It is appropriate that when Dal Stivens— easily our best cricketing creative writer— collected ten of his finest yarns in *The Demon Bowler and Other Cricket Stories* (1970), he should dedicate the volume to Bradman 'as a modest tribute to the pleasure he has given me and others'. Most of Stivens's stories maintain the tradition of T. E. Spencer's classic poem 'How McDougall Topped the Score' (1906)—known verbatim by generations of Australian school-children—demonstrating his love of the tall tale. Stivens always gives his stories a completely plausible setting. An excellent example is 'When Trumper Went to Billabong'. The great Victor Trumper takes a team of internationals, as part of a goodwill tour, to the small country town of Billabong. The locals are ecstatic and prepare for weeks, but when the big day arrives Trumper catches a spike in the netting pitch and Alf Tonks—incredibly—bowls him with one of his 'donkey drops'. Worse still, local skipper Mallee Mick appeals and, of course, Trumper walks. The town is paralysed with disappointment and anger. Stivens ends his story with a dry, Lawsonian touch: 'A couple of kids had heaved gibbers and a dead cat at [Mallee Mick] as he made off in Swampy Joe's buggy.' This is vintage Stivens, certainly one of the highlights of Australian sporting literature, and perhaps matched only by Stivens's other classic story 'The Batting Wizard from the City'. All his yarns have that laconic, identifiably Australian flavour.

Playwright Alex Buzo's preoccupation with language—and cricket—led to his several memorable contributions to *The Longest Game* (1990) including articles on the unmitigated boredom of the 1962–63 Australia–England Test series; the austerity and recession cricket of the 1982–83 Sheffield Shield season, especially the symbolic closing of the SCG Hill; the excitement of the 1989 Sydney Test between Australia and the West Indies; and, lastly yet perhaps most elegantly, his article on the Don at 80. Two wonderful sentences demonstrate Buzo's deft literary and sporting touch. First, on a typical Bradman innings: 'There was none of the intriguing struggle against doubt that characterised an innings by Cowdrey or O'Neill, just a whole lot of glorious certainty.' Second, on the Don's Test performance: 'His average finished up at 99.94, with its tasteful gesture towards fallibility.' Buzo's most humorous responses to cricket come in four sections late in the book when, with Jamie Grant, he selects three 'First Elevens'—of tautology, clichés and 'mixoes' or mixed metaphors—along with an 'Invitation Eleven' of 'Great Quotations'. *The Longest Game*, a 'collection of the best cricket writing from Alexander to Zavos, from the Gabba to the Yabba', also includes a large section on the creative responses of writers as diverse as Kenneth 'Seaforth' McKenzie, Kate Jennings, Louis Nowra, Jean Bedford, Laurie Clancy, Jamie Grant, C. J. Dennis, Ray Mathew, Nicholas

Hasluck, Robert Gray, Peter Kocan, Clive James, and John Romeril.

DH†

See **Art**; **Drama**; **Film**; GORDON, ADAM LINDSAY.

Little America's Cup. The International Catamaran Challenge Trophy is a seven-race series first held by the Seacliff Yacht Club in Long Island, USA, in 1961 for developmental catamarans with two crew. Open to all 'C' class catamarans of no more than 25 feet in length, 14 feet in width and 300 square feet of sail, the Cup is an international club-to-club challenge, one of only two in the world. The right to challenge is restricted to amateur clubs. The Little America's Cup was held throughout most of the 1960s by the UK, then by Denmark in 1969. Yachtsmen Bruce Proctor and Graham Candy became the first Australians to win the Cup with *Quest III* in 1970. They brought the trophy to Victoria's Sorrento Yacht Club. Six years and three defences later the Cup was regained by the USA. In 1985, McCrae Yacht Club on Victoria's Mornington Peninsula ended a nine-year American domination when the trophy was won by the catamaran *Victoria 150*, sailed by Olympic bronze-medallists Chris Cairns and Scott Anderson. Since then Australia has successfully defended the Cup on several occasions.

TM

LOCK, JANE MELINDA, MBE (1954–   ), born Sydney, grew up in Melbourne where she learned to play golf at the age of 16 and achieved a single-figure handicap within a year. At 17 she won the first of her three successive Australian junior championships and in 1975 completed the double, winning both the Australian junior and senior championships. She won three Australian championships, represented Australia more than thirty times, set course records in six countries, and sank the winning putt to secure the Espirito Santo World Amateur Golf Championship for Australia for the first time in 1978. She received the MBE when only 20, and while completing her Bachelor of Applied Science degree. Lock turned professional in 1980, playing on the American circuit. After fracturing her arm at the Glendale Open in 1986, she returned to play golf in Australia.

GC*

LUKE, KENNETH GEORGE, CMG (1898–1971), steered the VFL to becoming a commercial enterprise in his energetic term as president from 1956 to 1971. He was also the driving force behind the VFL building its own stadium, VFL Park, a decision fundamental to that approach. Something of a self-made man, Luke's engraving and engineering business established him as a giant of industry. His involvement in Victorian sport also extended to the Carlton Football Club as a long-serving president, the Olympics Construction Committee, and the Olympic Park board of trustees.

DS

LUKIN, DEAN (1960–), Australia's first Olympic weightlifting gold-medallist, was born into a hardworking Yugoslavian fishing family. In 1964 the family moved to Port Lincoln in order to establish what was soon to become a multi-million-dollar fishing business. As the business expanded so did the young Dean Lukin, who became known at school as 'Dino the Dinosaur'. Poling tuna, which requires great strength, proved an ideal preparation for sport. Lukin was gifted at many sports, excelling at Australian football, basketball, and soccer. After joining the Lincoln Lifters, Lukin entered the State junior titles and won the national schoolboys' championship in 1975. He won many subsequent schoolboy competitions, creating records along the way. Lukin entered his first national senior championship in 1980, breaking the 200 kilogram barrier in the clean and jerk. He was successful at the 1982 Commonwealth Games, lifting 221 kilograms and setting three records in the super-heavyweight class. At the 1984 Olympics he lifted 240 kilograms in the clean and jerk, for a total lift of 412.5 kilograms to win a gold medal. In recognition of his achievement he carried the Australian flag at the closing ceremony of the Games. After the Games Lukin returned to the family tuna-fishing empire, preferring the solitude of the sea to his new-found celebrity status. He returned to the spotlight once more when he won another gold medal at the 1986 Commonwealth Games.

CH

See **Weightlifting**.

LUND, IVAN (1929–) fenced at four British Empire and Commonwealth Games, from 1950 to 1962, where he won a total of thirteen medals; he also took part in four Olympics from 1952 to 1964. He was a member of the successful épée team in 1950; both of his individual best results were in the épée individual which he won in 1954 and 1962. Lund dominated Australian fencing in this era, winning eleven Australian and fourteen NSW foil and épée championships. He was Australian flag-bearer at the 1958 British Empire and Commonwealth Games and took the Games Oath at the 1962 Perth Games. Later he was active in the administration of the sport.

RC

See **Fencing**.

LYNAGH, MICHAEL (1963–), a product of Gregory Terrace and the University of Queensland, became the world's leading rugby points-scorer with over 700 points in 1992. His unerring place-kicking made a significant difference in Queensland and Australian teams, helping them to be competitive on the world scene. Surprisingly he rarely captained Australia, appearing at a time of long-serving Australian captains. A fine all-round athlete, he has no weaknesses, having good hands, a safe frontal defence, and a brilliant cover-defence. He is an accurate punter of the ball, possesses rare football instincts, and has an analytical approach to the game. He scored a vital match-winning try against Ireland in Australia's successful 1991 World Cup campaign.

RH and MH

M

MACARTNEY, CHARLES GEORGE (1886–1958), born Maitland, NSW, was a devastating right-hand batsman who displayed such authority that Kent cricketer Kenneth Hutchings nicknamed him the 'Governor-General'. His grandfather, George Moore, a leading NSW slow bowler, taught him to bat using apples from his orchard. Macartney was first noticed, playing school cricket, by M. A. Noble, who urged him to join North Sydney in 1902 and Gordon in 1905. Macartney's rapid rise to the NSW team led to his selection in all five Tests against England in the summer of 1907–8. Macartney toured England with the 1909, 1912, 1921 and 1926 Australian teams. In 1921 he hit an astonishing 335 runs before tea on the first day of the match against Nottinghamshire. At the age of 40 he became the second batsman to score a century before lunch on the first day of a Test match (Headingly, 1926). Neville Cardus wrote, 'there was always chivalry in his cricket, a prancing sort of heroism ... The dauntlessness of his play, the manliness, the brave beauty and original skill, bring tears to my eyes yet.'

PS

MACARTNEY-SNAPE, TIM (1956–), born Tanzania, came to Australia at the age of 11. Gangly, freckle-faced and with the looks of a boy scout, he became one of the world's great mountaineers. He developed an early passion for climbing mountains and demonstrated courage, determination, and skill by climbing Mount Dunagiri and the south face of Annapurna II in 1978. He led the first Australian team to conquer Mount Everest by climbing the northern face—without supplementary oxygen—in 1984. Two years later he climbed Gasherbrum IV, a beautiful but treacherous mountain. His sea-to-summit ascent of Everest in 1990 was his greatest achievement to date. When he travelled from the Bay of Bengal to the top of the world—solo and without oxygen—he became the first person to climb the full height (8874 metres) of this famous mountain.

RP

See **Mountaineering**.

MACHIN, CHARLENE became world karate champion in July 1991, the first occasion that she represented her country. The Newcastle-based martial arts instructor took up karate seven years before and later achieved her black belt. She rose to the top of her sport not long after winning the open division in the Australian Cup in Sydney in 1990.

RC

MACKENZIE, STUART ALEXANDER (1936–) is the only sculler to have won Henley's Diamond Sculls on six occasions (1957–62). He also won two European championships in 1957 and 1958 and a British Empire and Commonwealth Games title in 1958, and came second in the Olympic sculls in 1956. Late in his career he rowed for England in eights. A controversial character, forever offending officialdom, particularly in England where he refused to accept rowing's 'establishment' ethos, Mackenzie's view of sport was simple: 'Sport is about winning.'

SB

See **Rowing and Sculling**.

MACKINTOSH, DONALD (1866–1951) was Australia's forgotten gold-medallist. One of the world's finest shooters, he competed in the Paris Olympics of 1900. Because the Games were chaotic and disorganised they were referred to as 'Concours Internationaux d'Exercises et du Sports'. Mackintosh entered three pigeon-shooting competitions, winning one from 166 competitors and coming second in another. During his lifetime Mackintosh was never listed as an Olympic medallist but on 14 September 1987 the International Olympic Committee declared that Mackintosh had won gold and silver medals at the 1900 Olympics.

RH and MH

Magarey Medal is awarded to the player adjudged by field umpires 'fairest and most brilliant' in the SA National Football League. The criterion of 'fairest' differentiates the award from the otherwise comparable Victorian Brownlow Medal and also indicates certain moral and stylistic connotations. The medal was inaugurated in 1898 at the behest of, and personally designed by, W. H. Magarey, a person of judicial and social distinction who, in the same year, resigned his position as chairman of the (then) SA Football Association. The first recipient of the award was A. Green of the Norwood Football Club. It was not bestowed during the war years of 1916–18 and 1942–44.

PW

Maher Cup was donated in 1919 to Tumut Rugby Union Club by local publican E. J.

Maher, but by 1921 had become a rugby league trophy for challenge competition between NSW Riverina towns. It was contested on the holder's home ground and the challenger, if victorious, took the Cup home to await the next contender. Fierce intertown rivalry, with imported players (including 'ring-ins'), brawls, protests, and writs, resulted in 'The Old Pot' or 'The Win, Tie or Wrangle Cup' becoming part of the folklore of rural NSW sport. At times kept in gaol cells for safety, chained up in shop windows, and thrown into the Murrumbidgee River, it attained a sentimental value far exceeding the £13 5s it originally cost. The Cup was contested 718 times among twenty-five towns until Tumut, who had lost it in the first challenge in 1921, won it back in the last, in 1971. With challenge competitions no longer popular, the battered old trophy has since been on honoured display at Tumut Soldiers' Club.

TB

MAHER, ROBYN (née GULL) (1959–   ), basketballer for Exies, Dandenong, Telstars, Nunawading, Hobart, and Australia, learned her basketball in Ballarat but made her name in Melbourne. A guard forward, she was a key player in Nunawading's unparalleled run of National Women's Basketball League (NWBL) titles (1983–84 and 1986–89), winning the Most-Valued Player award in 1985 and 1987, and a place in the All-Star teams of 1983–84 and 1986–88. An Australian representative at two Olympics and four world championships, Maher's outstanding career-figures for points scored, rebounds, steals, and assists indicate the consummate all-rounder, described as 'one of Australian basketball's truly complete champions'. She married Tom Maher, coach with Nunawading (NWBL) and Hobart (National Basketball League).

SB

MAILEY, ARTHUR ALFRED (1886–1967), cricketer, born Sydney, played for Redfern, Balmain, Waverley, Manly, and Middle Harbour clubs. One of the greatest right-arm spinners, Mailey in twenty-one Tests (1921–26) took 99 wickets at 33.9 apiece. On two English tours he took 287 wickets for less than 20 runs each. In 1920–21 in only four Tests he took 36 at 26.27 each, an English–Australian series record for fifty-seven years. Between 1912–13 and 1930–31 in all first-class matches he captured 779 wickets at 24.1. A talented cartoonist and journalist he published *And Then Came Larwood* (1933), his delightful autobiography *10 for 66 and All That* (1958), and several booklets of anecdotes and cartoons. One of cricket's most unassuming and lovable characters, he died at Kirrawee on 31 December 1967.

GW

Malua (1879–96) was a thoroughbred racehorse, noted for his versatility. He was bred in Tasmania at Calstock stud farm, sold as a yearling, and raced at first under the name *Bagot*. After a win at Flemington in spring 1882 his owner, Thomas Reibey, sold him to John Inglis who changed the horse's name. Notable victories followed, ranging from sprints such as the Newmarket Handicap to staying events including the Adelaide, Australian, and Melbourne Cups. Retired to stud in 1886 (where he sired the 1891 Melbourne Cup winner *Malvolio*), *Malua* was later put back into training and won the 1888 Grand National Hurdle, ridden by his owner, and the 1889 Geelong Cup.

AL

Manikato (1975–84), a thoroughbred racehorse, recorded an unprecedented four successive wins in the VATC Futurity Stakes and five wins in the weight-for-age Moonee Valley William Reid Stakes. He won the premier 2-year-old VATC Blue Diamond Stakes and the STC Golden Slipper in 1978, and at 3 years won eight of his twelve starts. After four more wins, a bleeding attack interrupted his progress and a leg problem thereafter made him difficult to train, but he won twelve and was placed in nine of his remaining twenty-two starts. By *Manihi* out of *Markarto*, he was bred in SA and bought as a yearling by Mal Secull for $3500. After the death of his trainer N. D. Hoysted in 1978, he was transferred to Hoysted's brother Bob. *Manikato* was ridden in all but two of his races by Gary Willetts.

AL

See **HOYSTED, FREDERICK**.

Marching

Marching as a sport was introduced into Australia from NZ in the late 1940s. The first teams were formed in the Hunter Valley about 1952, and under the sponsorship of returned soldiers it has grown into a new form of recreation and competitive sport. Freestyle phases have developed the sport into a creative form of artistic expression as well as a rigid discipline. The routines which are performed have an emphasis on military-style marching involving precision, uniformity, complex turns, wheels, and echelons; the freestyle march has recently been expanded and now permits rhythmic, thematic, or theatrical exhibitions within the parameters of set rules. Teams compete at all levels from club to international standard, and the sport is conducted by the Australian Marching Association, which is an affiliated member of the Confederation of Australian Sport and receives funding through the ASC.

RS*

MARKS, ERNEST SAMUEL, OBE (1871–1947), born West Maitland, NSW, was a prominent sporting administrator, politician, and woolbuyer. He won over forty trophies as an athlete from 1888 to 1890 and was founder and executive member of the NSW Amateur Athletic Association, the Athletic Union of Australasia, and the International Amateur Athletic Federation. He was also involved in Olympic and British Empire Games organisation and, as touring manager, attended the 1908 and 1912 Olympics. He was associated with many other sports including swimming, rugby union, boxing, wrestling, billiards, and coursing and founded a number of clubs including Manly Surf Club. An alderman of the Sydney City Council, Lord Mayor in 1930, and for some years Member of the Legislative Assembly, Marks was largely responsible for the construction of the Sydney Athletic Field, which came to bear his name. He donated his large collection of sporting documents to the Mitchell Library and a bequest from his estate to the Amateur Athletic Association finances the annual E. S. Marks Memorial Award. Marks was an active member of the Sydney Jewish community.

RC

See **Athletics**; **Athletics Australia**; **British Empire Games 1938 (Sydney)**.

MARONEY, SUSAN JEAN (1974–), a twin, was born prematurely in Sydney and competed in swimming carnivals from the age of 7. She proved successful in endurance events and at 14 came second in the first Australian marathon (16 kilometres) championship for women in 1989. Three months later she won the US championships at Long Beach (25 kilometres) before coming second in the 48 kilometres Manhattan Island swim. She swam the English Channel in record time at the age of 15 and then won the Australian marathon championship in Tasmania in 1991. In July 1991 she became the first Australian to complete a double crossing of the English Channel in the world-record time of 17 hours 14 minutes. Her older sister Lindy made her inaugural Channel swim in the same month.

RH and MH

MARSH, GRAHAM (1944–), born Kalgoorlie, WA, was a promising cricketer (like his brother Rod) but preferred golf, which he first took up to strengthen his arms. By the age of 18 he was a scratch player and a regular member of WA golf teams. After reaching the final of the Australian amateur title in 1967 he turned professional. He won the Swiss Open in 1970 but his most important win was the World Match Play Championship in England in 1977 followed by success in the Heritage Classic in the USA. Marsh has played more golf in Japan than anywhere else. He has in recent years become involved in designing golf courses, and has played a part in the establishment of a golf

foundation to coach WA junior players. He has also served as president of the Australian PGA.

WPR

See **Golf**; MARSH, RODNEY.

MARSH, RODNEY WILLIAM ('Bacchus') MBE (1947–), born Armadale, WA, had an inauspicious Test cricket debut as wicket-keeper, earning himself the nickname of 'Iron Gloves'. Marsh worked hard on his game, and reduced his weight, to become the most successful Australian wicket-keeper ever—achieving a world record 355 dismissals—and was famous for his acrobatic work against the fast bowlers. Marsh was the keeper for almost every Test ball bowled by Dennis Lillee, and 'caught Marsh, bowled Lillee' became a familiar form of dismissal, occurring ninety-five times in Tests. The naming of a stand at the WA Cricket Association the Lillee-Marsh stand perpetuated the combination. Marsh was a powerful left-handed bat who scored three Test centuries. A shrewd cricketer, he led WA with success.

KM-H

See **Cricket**; MARSH, GRAHAM.

MARSHALL, BOB (1900–?), born WA, is considered to be one of the best Australian billiards players produced after Walter Lindrum. Marshall created two world records in the 1959 Australian amateur title by making 1876, to better his own one-session aggregate set in 1938, and with a combined total of 3391 bettered both his own and Tom Cleary's records. Marshall held the record for the most world-title wins (four); he succeeded in winning the Empire title in 1936, regained it in 1938, and won it once again in 1951, when play was started again after the war. In 1938 he displayed seven century breaks, another world record. His highest break in official competition was an impressive 702, achieved in 1953.

CJF

MARSTON, JAMES EDWARD ('Joe'), MBE (1926–), born Leichhardt, Sydney, was probably Australia's best locally born soccer-player. He played professionally for Preston North End from 1950 to 1955 and in the 1954 FA Cup Final when Preston North End lost 3–2 to West Bromwich Albion. In 1955 he represented the English League v. Scotland at Hampden Park, Glasgow. In his teens Marston was coached by Jack 'Digger' Evans, an Australian representative in the 1930s. In 1942, aged 16, he joined Leichhardt-Annandale Football Club, making the first team in 1943. As a right full back he progressively represented Sydney, NSW, and Australia between 1944 and 1949. He worked in a paint-brush factory, but through the recommendation of an old Preston North End supporter Marston became a full-time professional footballer in 1950. Fashioned by Preston into a centre-half, his team-mates included Tom Finney and Tommy Docherty. Marston returned to Australia in 1955, rejoining Leichhardt-Annandale. His return brought more representative honours, leading to a career total of thirty-five national appearances. He captained Australia twenty-four times. A year after the establishment of the NSW Soccer Federation, Marston joined the Italian-backed club Apia-Leichhardt in 1958. He retired in 1964. Marston's playing days were complemented by coaching stints with Apia, Western Suburbs, Auburn, and (in the Philip's [national] Soccer League for part of 1978 and 1979) Sydney Olympia. He was national coach versus the visiting Italian team AS Roma in 1966. Marston was awarded the MBE in 1981 and was inducted into the Sport Australia Hall of Fame in 1988. The Joe Marston award is given to the outstanding player in the National Soccer League Grand Final. The award was instituted in 1990 to honour the contribution made by Marston to Australian soccer.

PM and MH*

MARTIN, RODNEY CRAIG (1965–), originally from Sydney but later a resident of Queensland, was the top-ranked Australian squash-player in 1991. He won the first of his three Australian titles in 1985, the same year as he was awarded an AIS squash scholarship. The following year he joined the Australian team and won two titles, the Hong Kong Open and the British under-23, as a member of the touring squad. Other titles and achievements have quickly followed: for example Martin was the first man to defeat both Jahangir Khan and Janser Khan, although Jahangir has since extracted his revenge, beating Martin three times in the final of the British Open. Martin's biggest victory to date has been his 1991 World Open Championship, defeating Jahangir Khan in the final and enabling him to achieve his 1991 world ranking of number three.

KT

See **Squash Rackets**.

Masters Games

The successful staging of the first World Masters Games (for mature athletes) in Toronto, Canada, in 1985, to which Australia sent 302 competitors, led to a sports festival for the mature-aged held in Alice Springs in October 1986. The games attracted 992 participants in twenty-one sports. Subsequent festivals in Alice Springs have attracted 1901 participants in 1988 and 3089 in 1991. The status of these games is disputed, with the NT Government promoting them as national events and the Confederation of Australian Sport viewing them as regional festivals. Before the first Central Australian Games were held, the Tasmanian Government and the Confederation of Australian Sport had

agreed to hold the first Australian Masters Games in Tasmania in 1987. These were staged throughout Tasmania's three main regions in November and December 1987 and catered for 3695 competitors in thirty-five sports. The average ages of participants was 50 (male) and 49 (female). The ages of the competitors, their preference for motel-style accommodation rather than athletes' villages, and their tendency to tour the State before or after their competition led to the festival being dubbed the 'Credit Card Games' by the local media. Nevertheless these games stimulated masters sport in Tasmania to the extent that the State has conducted two subsequent State Masters Games carnivals, attracting 2000 competitors in 1989 (Launceston) and 2500 in 1991 (Hobart). The second Australian Masters Games, held in Adelaide in October 1989, rivalled the first world games in size. Forty-two sports attracted 8045 participants whose average ages were 46 (male) and 45 (female). The third games held in Brisbane in October 1991 were marginally smaller but large enough to ensure that the biennial national games will continue. The ready acceptance of the masters games has led to a willingness of governments and other promoters to stage various multi-sports festivals for mature sportspeople. State masters games were also held in 1990 in Victoria and WA. Regional games have been held in Wagga Wagga and Maryborough. State and local governments have supported the various games with major financial assistance but for the Australian Masters Games the most significant sponsorship has been provided by the ASC, with a contribution of $400000 to the first three games.

RKB

See **Veterans**.

MASTERS, JAMES WILLIAM ('Judy') (1892–1955), born Balgownie, NSW, was a scheming soccer centre-forward who played for Australia from 1919 to 1925 and was captain 1923–25. He was the best Australian-born player before and during his time. He entered senior ranks at 15½ years of age and played for Balgownie, Newtown, Granville, and Woonona. In more than four hundred club and representative games he was never cautioned. His efforts against an English professional eleven in 1925 marked the height of his career. He retired in 1929. Masters served with the Australian Imperial Force from 1915 to 1919 at Gallipoli as well as in Egypt, France, and Belgium. A coalminer for forty years, he was also long-serving bandmaster of the Balgownie Citizens' Brass Band.

PM

MATICH, FRANK (1935–), born Sydney, was one of the first truly professional Australian racing drivers, and one of the most successful. He combined great natural ability with progressively acquired skills in car development and in the commercial world. Matich dominated Australian sports-car racing between 1960 and 1970, from 1967 driving self-built cars of his own design. In 1970 he moved effortlessly into Formula 5000 single-seaters and won the 1970 and 1971 Grands Prix, the 1971 race in another self-designed car. In a long and very active career Matich seemed to drive the best cars; it was often because he had made them that way.

GH
See **Motor Racing**.

MATTHEWS, LEIGH ('Lethal') (1952–) was a destructive rover who played 340 games, captained Hawthorn and Victoria, and played in four premierships. He may be best remembered, however, as the coach who in 1990 broke Collingwood's 32-year-old premiership drought. The reputation that won the burly Matthews the name 'Lethal' endured from the time he collided with West Australian Barry Cable in an interstate match to his final season (1985) when Matthews faced unprecedented assault charges in the Victorian courts after Geelong's Neville Bruns suffered a broken jaw. Dangerous near goal, Matthews headed the VFL goal-kicking in 1975, and only three players have exceeded his career total of 915.

DS

MATTHEWS, MARLENE (later WILLARD) (1934–) was one of Australia's unluckiest athletes. She missed selection, when 18, for the 1952 Olympics due to a leg injury when many believed she was on the verge of becoming world champion. Injury again forced her out of the 100 yards at the 1954 British Empire and Commonwealth Games. Expected to win at the 1956 Olympics she achieved bronze medals in both sprints and surprisingly was not picked in the winning 4 × 100 metres relay team. She defeated Betty Cuthbert, the 1956 gold-medallist, at the Australian titles in a wind-assisted 10.1 seconds. Eventually several world records came her way.

CJF

McAULIFFE, RON (1918–88), born Brisbane, was a rugby league administrator. An Australian Labor Party senator in the Federal Parliament 1971–81, he was joint secretary of the Queensland Rugby League (QRL) and Brisbane Rugby League 1953–59, and president of the QRL 1970–85. McAuliffe is best known for his transformation of the traditional Queensland–NSW matches to a State of Origin series, beginning in 1980, but his energetic and imaginative leadership also saw the extensive development of the Lang Park ground in Brisbane and the restructuring of rugby league administration in Queensland.

SJR
See **Rugby League**.

McCABE, STANLEY JOSEPH (1910–68), cricketer, was born at Grenfell, NSW. A graceful, aggressive right-hand batsman who was a notable hooker and thrived on crises, McCabe averaged 48.21 in Tests and 49.38 overall. He is best remembered for three epic Test innings: 187 not out in 240 minutes at Sydney in the bodyline series; 189 not out in 195 minutes in a dust-storm at Johannesburg in 1935; and 232 in 235 minutes at Nottingham in 1938. McCabe, who was Australian vice-captain in three Test series and NSW captain 1936–42, was admired for his ability and character. A sports-shop proprietor, he died as a result of an accident at his Mosman home.

JMcH
See **Cricket**.

McCARTEN, MAURICE (1902–71), a jockey and trainer, was born in NZ where he was leading jockey in 1922 and 1923. He visited Australia in 1923 to ride *Ballymena* to win the AJC Derby. He settled in Australia in 1926. McCarten was at his best in weight-for-age races and classics, winning six AJC St Legers, six AJC Sires' Produce Stakes, four AJC Derbies, and two Victoria Derbies; but he also won four Brisbane Cups (including two on *Spear Chief*) and two Sydney Cups, two Epsoms, and two Doncasters. Turning to training in 1942, he was four times leading Sydney trainer. He trained several of the best horses in Australia including *Delta*, *Columnist*, *Noholme*, *Prince Cortauld*, and *Todman*.

AL

McCARTHY, RICHARD LAWRENCE ('Darby') (1944–) was the son of a Cunnamulla stockman. Leaving school at 8, he worked on a property in south-west Queensland and began his riding career at 10. He moved to Brisbane as an apprentice jockey and rode his first winner in 1957. His illustrious career included winning the Newcastle Gold Cup in 1962; three Stradbroke Handicaps in 1963, 1964, and 1966; the Brisbane Cup in 1966; the Doomben One Hundred Thousand in 1968; and the incredible feat of riding successive winners in the AJC Derby and the AJC Epsom at Randwick in 1969. Regarded by critics as 'one of the finest jockeys ever seen', 'a genius rider', and 'a freak', Darby's later career was beset by personal problems and disqualification. Despite these set-backs, he made come-backs in 1978 and 1990. In a sport that offered so little access for Aborigines, McCarthy managed to achieve both recognition and praise, and used his vast experience to put something back into coaching young riders.

CT and PT
See **Aboriginal Sports Foundation**; **Aborigines in Sport**.

McCLEMENTS, LYN (1951–), swimmer, was born in Nedlands, WA, into a working-class family. From 1967 on she came under the influence of coach Kevin Duff and concentrated on the butterfly stroke. Within a year she had won the State senior butterfly title in record time in both the 100 and 200 metres. In her first senior national championships she won the 100 metres butterfly and was selected at 16 for the 1968 Olympic team. At the Mexico Olympics she achieved a silver medal in the 4 × 100 metres medley relay and a gold medal in the 100 metres butterfly. At the 1970 Australian championships she was disqualified and retired from competitive swimming, though she has in recent years performed well in seniors competition.
RH and MH

McCONCHIE, LORNA represented Australia in netball as a player and coach. Coach of the first Australian netball team to visit England in 1956, she returned the next year to represent Australia at a meeting to discuss rules for international play. She coached Australia to victory in the first World Netball Championships in 1963. As convenor of the initial International Federation of Netball Associations (IFNA) Rules Subcommittee from 1963 to 1967, and as a member for twenty-five years, she did much to establish the rules of netball. She was awarded the IFNA Service Award in 1991.
DH and IJ

McCRACKEN, ALEXANDER CHARLES (1856–1915) was a notable Australian rules football administrator from the age of 15 until his death. He was the first secretary of the Essendon Football Club (1871–84) during which period his father Robert was president. He was club delegate to the VFA from its inception in 1877 and was president of Essendon Football Club from 1887 to 1903. He played a leading role in the formation of the VFL and was its first president from 1897 until his death in 1915. He became a life member of both the VFL and Essendon Football Club. McCracken was also a leading member of the VRC, the Oaklands Hunt Club, and the Royal Agricultural Society of Victoria. McCracken Avenue, at the Melbourne Show Grounds, honours him.
CH

McGILVRAY, ALAN DAVID, AM, MBE (1910–), born Paddington, Sydney, was a NSW cricket captain in the 1930s but became a respected cricket commentator when his broadcasting and playing were declared incompatible by cricket authorities. He developed a style which was instantly recognisable and his traditional values and mellow delivery provided a balance to the post-Packer atmosphere of controversy and contrived drama. McGilvray was sought out for advice by modern captains but did not allow this contact to undermine his critical objectivity. He left cricket commentary in 1985 after fifty years of informed contribution.
SG
See **Cricket**.

McHALE, JAMES FRANCIS ('Jock') (1881–1953), born Botany, Sydney, was an Australian rules footballer and coach. His ironic nickname was derived from a cartoon by Wells during the 1920s depicting this staunch Catholic in a kilt. The three obsessions of his life were the Catholic Church, the Collingwood Football Club, and the Carlton brewery (where he worked for fifty years until 1947). McHale played 262 games in the centre for Collingwood (1903–18), including a club-record 191 consecutive games. He captained the team twice (1912 and 1913) and served as vice-president of the club from 1939 to 1953. McHale coached the Magpies for a VFL record thirty-seven years (1913–50), winning eight premierships and guiding the team into eighteen Grand Finals. His coaching method emphasised team-work, discipline, and fitness, qualities that led to Collingwood's play being described as machine-like. McHale was not an exceptional teaching coach, but his intolerance of individualism and of losing became part of the Collingwood spirit and attitude. His unabashed love for the club was evidenced in emotional half-time addresses where he exhorted players to win for the guernsey.
RS

McHUGH, DOROTHY, OAM (1923–), has contributed greatly to netball development and management at State, national, and international levels. In addition to holding numerous positions in netball in NSW, where she has served on the State council for thirty-six years, she has been a member of the All Australia Netball Association Council for thirty years. As an influential member of the International Federation of Netball Association Umpires, McHugh has made a major contribution. National liaison officer from 1979 to 1989, she represented Australia at international conferences from 1979 to 1987. She played an important role in the expanded membership of the International Federation and was appointed general secretary in 1987. A life member of the NSW Netball Association, she was also the recipient of the All Australia Netball Association Service Award, and the OAM in January 1992.
PB and IJ
See **All Australia Netball Association**.

McINTOSH, HUGH DONALD ('Huge Deal') (1876–1942) was a Sydney sporting and theatrical entrepreneur and newspaper proprietor. After selling pies at racetracks and prize-fights, he staged and refereed the world heavyweight championship bout at Rushcutters Bay, Sydney, on Boxing Day 1908 at which Jack Johnson defeated Tommy Burns. 'Huge Deal' McIntosh bought the Tivoli circuit of vaudeville theatres as well as the *Sunday Times* Sydney newspaper and opened a chain of milk bars in England, but died penniless in London.

CC

See **Boxing**; **Burns–Johnson Fight**; **Drama**; **Stadiums Limited**.

McINTOSH, JILL (1955–) played her early games of netball in WA and was chosen in the All Australia Schoolgirl Netball Team in 1970. She was a member of the WA Open team from 1973 to 1986, and at various times was vice-captain, captain, and captain-coach. McIntosh was a member of the All Australia Netball Team in 1974 and 1980–86, won the New Idea Australian Netballer of the Year award in 1981, and was WA Sportswoman of the Year in 1983. She began her career playing goal defence but played mostly in the centre-court area at international level. McIntosh has become particularly active in administration and coaching since her retirement as a player: she was head coach of netball at the WA Institute of Sport from 1984 to 1989 and Australian under-21 coach from 1990 to 1992. She became the All Australia Netball Association's national coaching director in 1991.

PB and IJ

McKAY, HEATHER (née BLUNDELL), MBE (1941–), was Australia's most successful squash-player and is one of the nation's outstanding sportspersons because of her unparalleled dominance. She began playing squash in Queanbeyan, NSW, initially to improve her fitness for hockey—a sport in which she represented both NSW and Australia. Her greater success, however, was on the squash court. During her amateur career she lost only two matches—to Yvonne West in 1960 and Fran Marshall in 1962—and was undefeated over the next eighteen years. She won the Australian Amateur Championship in fourteen successive years (1960–73) and the British Amateur, later Open, Championship sixteen straight times (1962–77). She won the ABC Sportsman (*sic*) of the Year award in 1967. Due to a lack of financial support and public acclaim McKay turned professional in January 1976. She won the inaugural Women's World Open Squash Championship in 1976 after which she moved to Toronto, Canada, to coach professionally. While the move barred her from defending her British Open title, she managed to win the Women's World Open Squash Championship and the US Amateur Women's Racquetball titles in 1979. McKay returned to Australia in 1985 and became coach at the AIS's squash unit in Brisbane.

KT

See **Squash Rackets**.

McKENZIE, GRAHAM DOUGLAS ('Garth') (1941–), born Cottesloe, WA, was a schoolboy prodigy. His father and uncle both played first-class cricket and hockey for WA. After securing 5–37 in his first Test at Lord's in 1961, he became a permanent fixture in the Australian cricket side until 1971, often being used as both strike and stock bowler. His best series were against England in 1964 (29 wickets) and the West Indies in 1968–69 (30 wickets). With his broad shoulders and muscular build McKenzie was nicknamed 'Garth' after a comic-strip character. He bowled from a ten-stride run-up, gaining pace from an explosive body action which meant that he was deceptively fast. McKenzie remains the youngest bowler to take 200 Test wickets and his total of 246 wickets is the third highest in Australian Test cricket. As WA's first regular Test player he was an inspiration to Dennis Lillee and others.

EJ

McKIVAT, CHRISTOPHER HOBART (1879–1941), was the captain of victorious rugby union and rugby league international football teams. Born at Burrawang in NSW, he played union at Orange, then joined Glebe in Sydney in 1905. He did not switch to league in its first season, but toured with the first Wallaby team to England. A sturdy half-back of equable temperament, he captained the gold-medal-winning Australian team at the 1908 London Olympics. Expelled from rugby union for playing for the Wallabies against the Kangaroos in 1909, McKivat played league for Glebe until 1914 and captained the second Kangaroo team to England in 1911–12 when the Australasians won all three Tests. In 1921 and 1922 he coached North Sydney to premiership wins.

CC

See **Rugby League**.

McLEAN Family was an outstanding rugby-playing family. **Douglas James McLean** (1880–1947) played three Tests for Australia on the wing in 1904–5 and later appeared in the first Australian rugby league team against the NZ 'All Golds'. **Alexander Douglas McLean** (1912–61), his son and also a winger, toured South Africa in 1933 and played against NZ in 1934 and 1936. He was selected for the Kangaroo rugby league tour to England in 1937–38 and later managed a Kangaroo team. His younger brother, **William Malcolm McLean** (1918–), was a tough breakaway who was selected on the 1939 Wallaby tour which played no games because of the war. He captained the 1946 Australian team to NZ and the 1947–48 team to the British Isles, France, and North America. A broken leg in the sixth match of that tour ended his Test career. Another brother, **John ('Jack') Reginald McLean** (1923–74), was a member of the 1946 Australian tour of NZ but played no Tests. Bill's son, **Peter McLean**

(1954–), known as 'Spider' because of his rangy build, was an outstanding line-out jumper who played in fifteen Tests. Bill's brother **Bob** was also a fine player but injuries restricted his career. Bob's two sons, **Paul Edward McLean** (1953–) and **Jeffrey James McLean** (1947–), both represented Australia. Jeff, a winger, played thirteen Tests, but Paul was an outstanding family member, who played thirty-one Tests and became Australia's leading points-scorer. A five-eighth of rare ability and good hands, he had a raking kick and unusual footballing instincts. While he became a legend in Queensland, acceptance in NSW was more difficult. The McLean Stand at Ballymore honours this family.

RH and MH

McNAB, FINLAY, OBE (1914–), who began his hockey-playing career in the mid-1930s, represented Victoria before and after the Second World War. But it is in the administrative arena that McNab has had a significant impact on the game in Australia. He has held a number of positions with both the Victorian and Australian associations, including that of president of the Australian Hockey Association from 1964 to 1975. It was during this period that Australian hockey came of age in international competition. It was due in part to McNab's vision and drive that Australia emerged from the middle levels of international hockey to be rated among the world's top three nations. McNab has also distinguished himself at the international level by holding a number of positions with the Fédération Internationale de Hockey sur Gazon. His dedication to the sport has been recognised with the OBE and life memberships of the Victorian and Australian Associations.

BS†

McNABB, JAMES (1910–), born Weston, NSW, made seventeen appearances as Australia's soccer goalkeeper. Overseas touring sides rated him highly. His career spanned 1926 to 1940, all at Weston Football Club. Initially a full back who represented NSW in 1930, ankle injuries caused McNabb to switch to goalkeeper in 1931. As keeper he represented NSW from 1932 and Australia from 1933 to 1939. At 173 centimetres tall, McNabb was small for his position, but a solid build protected him from physical challenges. Excellent reflexes complemented immaculate positioning. McNabb's penalty save against England Amateurs in the deciding match in 1937 gave Australia a historic series win.

PM

McNAMARA, DAVID JAMES (1887–1967) became legendary as a prodigious kicker in Australian rules football. Some of his place-kicks travelled more than a hundred yards. A tall, powerful follower and forward, he first played with St Kilda Football Club in 1905, was appointed captain at 21, was 'Champion of the Colony' in 1907 and 1914 and represented his State in 1908 and 1914. After a dispute with the St Kilda Club he played three seasons with Essendon in the VFA where in 1912 he became the first player in senior Victorian football to score 100 goals in a season. He kicked 18 goals in one match against Melbourne. After returning to St Kilda in 1913, he became captain in 1922–23. He played 122 games for St Kilda, kicking 187 goals.

CH*

McNAMARA, PETER (1955–), born Melbourne, rose to be Australia's number one ranked tennis-player in 1981 and 1982. Although briefly ranked in the world's top ten in singles, it was as a doubles player, in partnership with Paul McNamee, that he left his main mark. The 'Supermacs' won the Australian Open doubles in 1979 and then claimed the prestigious Wimbledon doubles crowns of 1980 and 1982. McNamara was a tall, solid right-hander whose career was curtailed by injury. To cover a knee brace he gained some notoriety by wearing long cream trousers in tournament play. Upon retirement McNamara became a prominent coach in Victoria.

HCJP

See **McNAMEE, PAUL**.

McNAMEE, PAUL (1954–), born Melbourne, was in the Australian tennis spotlight variously as the nation's number one ranked player (in 1985), a Davis Cup performer, doubles champion, commentator, and entrepreneur. With Peter McNamara he won many prestigious doubles titles including the 1980 and 1982 Wimbledon crowns. During 1979 he had taken time away from the circuit to develop a two-handed backhand. NcNamee was always a crowd favourite because of his non-stop action. When he retired from the circuit he played a vital role in establishing the Hopman Cup in Perth.

HCJP

See **Hopman Cup**; **McNAMARA, PETER**.

Media

Proliferating forms of media and communication have been major contributors to both the expansion and meaning of Australian sport since the onset of its modern growth in the later nineteenth century, indeed since the arrival of European settlers in 1788. Our knowledge of sport, along with our attitudes about and concern for it, has been derived largely from newspapers and magazines, radio, and television.

From the earliest days until the end of the First World War, newspapers were the principal public source of knowledge about sport. The *Town and Country Journal*, the editions of *Bell's Life* and the *Referee* had all flourished by the turn of this century, while specialist journals for cricket and other sports sprang up and died all over the country. Major daily papers like the *Sydney Morning Herald* and the *Sun*, the *Age* and the *Argus*, the *Adelaide Advertiser* and the *West Australian* all devoted considerable space to sport, indicating the significance afforded the activity by the Australian public. Innovations such as the telegraph, cheaper printing processes, specialist writers, illustrators, and (later) photographers all added to the wealth of sporting information from which Australians could select and at the same time have their views shaped. During the inter-war period this was supplemented and extended by the arrival of radio, which quickened media immediacy. Before the telegraph, sporting news from overseas came by ship; in the 1920s it became almost instantaneous. Sporting events were among the first to be broadcast live in Australia, and by 1939 sports commentators were among the greatest of media stars. While the newspaper writers were still important, their roles were changing perceptibly. Whereas in the early days a newspaper 'team' might cover a match to gain comment from all sections of the ground, the players, and officials, by the eve of the Second World War the writers were beginning to become more interpreters than reporters, with the latter role increasingly going to the radio men (women did not feature until much later).

By the early 1950s the race-callers, cricket and football commentators, and the rest were celebrities, highly paid and among the most skilled in the world. They took sport to every community in Australia, and many of them broadcast to and from the world as the image of Australian sport became increasingly burnished. But in 1956 television took over, its importance encapsulated in the prominence given to telecasting the Olympic Games of that year. By the 1960s the telecasting of live sports events and the beginnings of magazine sports shows were well entrenched. With the advent of colour television in 1975, sport became a staple item in television diets on commercial and non-commercial networks alike.

In this evolution from print-only to multi-electronic forms of sportscasting, several trends important for sport should be noted. The first is that the explanatory ability of the media has been almost completely blunted. As newspapers then radio became superseded, the coverage of sport became increasingly superficial. In part this was because of the availability of space: column inches gave way to radio minutes then television seconds; in part it stemmed from the dilution of professionalism in sports coverage as trained writers and broadcasters yielded their positions to former sports stars who talked mainly of their own experiences and prejudices. The second trend concerned the commercial

aspects of sport. In the initial stages newspapers advertised the existence of sport and so attracted spectators to subsequent events. While associated advertising sometimes drew attention to the sporting connection, grounds themselves were largely unadorned with commercial propositions. Radio began to change that because sportscasts by definition contained opportunities to link listeners to advertising during the course of the action. Sport, for example, encouraged consumers to buy the radio sets in the first place. When television arrived, the process accelerated. In the early radio days, for example, sports organisations commonly paid for their events to be put to air. By the 1970s with television that process was reversed, and by the 1980s sports in media demand were earning millions of dollars annually by selling broadcast rights to media organisations keen to make their own profits by way of advertisers who, in turn, took their cut from the consumers. Via the media, then, an increasing number of intermediaries came between the event itself and the consumer. By the last decade of the twentieth century, sports venues and participants alike had become saturated billboards.

The third trend was for the very playing conditions and practices of sport to become calibrated by the media. This has been the case especially in the television age where game times and playing circumstances have been altered to suit television and associated advertising schedules. In some cases alterations allegedly dictated by 'the interests of the game' have in fact been indirectly brought about by the exigencies of television. Then some sports like tennis and golf have witnessed the rise of the 'for television' exhibitions and special events which really are advertising showcases built around personalities who just happen to be active in sport.

This gives rise to the fourth trend, the creation and remuneration of sports stars. Prominent players have long been lionised by the various media forms, with the drive inexorably towards the construction of the personality cult. While newspapers made the public aware of sports stars, radio turned them into personalities, and television transformed them into celebrities. In golf, for example, Peter Thomson (five British Open victories) and Greg Norman (one) are separated by just twenty years and television—the latter alone has turned Norman into a multi-millionaire as his image and imprimatur are lent to airlines, hire cars, computers, fast food outlets, and numerous other products ostensibly unconnected with his sports expertise. Newspapers, radio, and newsreels did not offer Thomson the impact which the immediacy of television created instantaneously between Norman and his audience.

80 Winners at the 1896 Olympic Games in Athens
received medals of silver; this is one of two won by
the sole Australian competitor, Edwin Flack.

81 The London Olympics of 1908 included rugby union
and members of the Australian 'Wallabies' received a gold
medal and a certificate when they defeated Cornwall, the
only other team in the competition.

82 The Australasian team, without uniforms, at the
opening ceremony of the 1908 Olympic Games.

In the fifth trend, television has internationalised Australian sports tastes and, possibly, undercut national identities. Newspapers and radio reported within the groove of traditionally determined sports affinities: cricket, tennis, golf, football, and other sports were viewed mainly as a cultural representation of British imperial identity. Television has brought baseball, basketball, and American football to the point in the late twentieth century where their clothing (marketed through television) is as evident in daily life as the traditional games' gear was in the past. Television exposure certainly has made basketball among the fastest growing of Australian sports.

Finally, it is important to recognise the media role in the preservation of sport's social status quo. Newspapers reported in bulk only those sports in which the readership was already interested; there was little in the way of an educational role, and that continued into radio and television. The importance of this is that, as social changes gradually impinged on the sportsworld, few if any of those changes were immediately visible in the media outlets. While soccer, for example, became highly significant in Australia as part of the immigrant diversification process in the 1950s and 1960s, one of its major obstacles in seeking widespread acceptance was the difficulty it faced getting media exposure. Similarly, the women's movement's impact on sports participation in the 1970s and 1980s is still largely unreflected in media structures towards the turn of the twenty-first century: there are a handful of women writers, fewer radio sports presenters, and a number of television sports hostesses but few who actually report or call games themselves. The sports media world has been and remains solidly a male one: even in sports like gymnastics male sports presenters with no knowledge are always preferred to knowledgeable female ones. This emphasis remains largely because of the perceived construction of the sports media audience as a largely male one, despite surveys which suggest variations in the pattern.

Nevertheless, new emphases are emerging, ironically as a result of the changes wrought upon sport by the media in the first place. As the economic, political, ethical, and social complexity of sport increases, in part due to media influences, so sections of the media begin to turn a more analytical eye towards it. The major newspapers now employ feature writers to investigate the great sports issues like drugs and financial transactions; even television shows now devote some time to the less attractive aspects of modern sport. Sports matters are now as likely to be found in the political and business areas of the media as in the traditional sports ones. And newer media forms have

changed or promise to change matters further: SBS (Special Broadcasting Service) has done this in soccer promotion and sports investigation, while the arrival of pay TV should cause further relocation.

BS

See **Amateurism**; *Bell's Life*; **Boxing**; **Broadcasting**; **Cricket**; **Film**; **Gender**; *Referee*; **Technology**.

Melbourne Cricket Ground (MCG) sits within Yarra Park, only a ten-minute stroll from the central business district. Over seven thousand cars are accommodated at the MCG on big match days; two train stations, trams, and buses also help to move approximately one hundred thousand spectators efficiently to or from the ground. Ever since the 1853–54 season, when the Melbourne Cricket Club (MCC) lost its second oval to Australia's first steam-train line, this site has been available for 'the playing at cricket'. It was originally known as 'The Police Paddock', being a horse-agistment area for colonial troopers after it was claimed from local Aborigines in 1835. Near the MCG a few eucalypts still bear 'canoe' scars cut into their bark by stone axes, and Aboriginal middens may be found thirty centimetres below Yarra Park's green turf.

The MCG 1927 Members' Pavilion reminds visitors about history made at the world's largest cricket ground: the first international cricket tours of the 1860s, as well as the 1877 Test, and 'Ashes' match origins. Long corridors and the MCC museum and library are filled with paintings, books, photographs, and memorabilia. The Australian Gallery of Sport and Olympic Museum in an adjacent building commemorates twenty sports as well as the 1956 'Friendly' Olympics. Australian rules was devised by the MCC and played in Yarra Park's 'Richmond Paddock'. The first rules match was allowed on to the MCG oval in 1869, but it took many more years before regular football fixtures appeared there each winter. Australian rules became so popular with spectators at Victorian cricket ovals that financial gains by cricket clubs led to conflicts with some football clubs over ground control. Eventually, in the MCG's case, the AFL agreed to move its headquarters into a giant new $160 million stand in 1992. Financed by AFL rentals, annual subscriptions from 50 000 MCC members, sponsor-box leasing, and catering rights, the Great Southern Stand will be even more attractive to over one million spectators who watch football at the MCG each year. Cricket followers at the MCG number a little under half a million per annum. Victoria's love of sport is celebrated and amplified at the MCG. Well patronised summer and winter, the ground receives no government subsidies to help the MCC maintain and develop its world-class facilities which have so influenced sporting activities in Australia for over a hundred years.

TMcC

See **Cricket; Olympic Games 1956 (Melbourne)**.

Melbourne Cup

The Cup is Australia's most important horse-race and the nation's premier gambling event, but it has not always been so. When it began in 1861 it was a pale imitation of the Australian Champion Sweepstakes, a competition between the country's best horses, which had rotated among Sydney, Melbourne, Hobart, Ipswich, and Geelong. The champion race attracted the best horses from each colony and gained status from intercolonial rivalry. The Cup, however, had a different attraction. As a handicap event it drew larger fields and became, almost from the beginning, a gambling spectacle. In its second year the Cup had twenty starters, a rare sight on colonial racecourses. The fact that in 1862 the NSW horse *Archer* trounced the large field by ten lengths in repeating his victory of the previous year helped to engender a soft spot for the Cup in the affections of NSW racing followers.

The real importance of the Melbourne Cup is to be found in what it symbolises. The inherent uncertainty of the race and its promotion of the concept of equality of opportunity symbolised colonial Australia. In other racing countries the great race of the year is a Derby or some other set-weights race run over 10 or 12 furlongs (2000–2400 metres). The weights ensure that the horse of greatest ability should win. As a result, the winners of races such as the English Derby or the Kentucky Derby are recognised as the champion horse of their year. Their value for both racing and breeding purposes skyrockets, as does the value of their near relations. In Australia the Melbourne Cup winner is idolised but strangely, in most cases, its value as a racehorse does not increase to the same degree, and studmasters have become wary of Cup winners as prospective sires. Of 131 Melbourne Cups only eight have been won by sons or daughters of previous Cup winners and only three of these have occurred this century, the most recent in 1984 when *Black Knight* emulated the performance of his sire *Silver Knight* in 1971. As a general rule Melbourne Cup winners do not become great sires or dams and only a minority continue as successful racehorses. Most are handicapped out of racing because of undue emphasis given to their Cup successes. Some seldom find races over a suitable distance and for others the effort of winning the Cup proves too much for them. They fail to recapture their peak strength and fitness. In the twelve months after his win in the 1974 Cup *Think Big* won only one race, the 1975 Melbourne Cup.

This state of affairs would seem strange to American or European racing followers, who expect that the nation's greatest race should be won by the best horses or at least by horses with the best bloodlines; but the explanation is simple: the Melbourne Cup winner is seldom the best horse in the race because the race is designed to reward mediocrity. The fact that the Cup is a handicap race means that the handicapper must attempt to provide 'equality of opportunity' for all the entrants, regardless of their ability. In theory, if the handicapper does the job perfectly all horses should cross the finish line together in a multiple dead heat. If a horse displays good form in the lead-up races, suggesting that it has beaten the handicapper, then that person is invited to reconsider the weight allotted and imposes penalties. Seldom is there a 'handicapping certainty' in the Melbourne Cup. When *Just a Dash* won the 1981 Cup the champion in the field, *Kingston Town*, ran last. The following year *Kingston Town* appeared to have the race won until his handicap took its toll and he was run down by the less brilliant *Gurner's Lane*. Two years earlier the champion horse *Dulcify* appeared to have the race at his mercy, until he broke down in the straight, ending an illustrious career.

The other major factor contributing to the Cup's uncertainty is its length—3200 metres—a distance raced over only infrequently in this country. In most years the majority of the contenders have never run over that distance. Accordingly their handicaps and their reputations are based on their previous performances over shorter distances. These are the factors which make the race such a great gambling contest. The uncertainty turns the race into a virtual lottery. The student of form revels in the apparently generous odds offered on the top-class horses. The once-a-year punters know that their favoured 'long-shots' really have as great a chance as any other — well, almost.

Of 131 Cups nineteen have been won by outright favourites, but eight Cups have been won by horses starting at odds of 40 to 1 or more. Not all Melbourne Cup winners deserve the title 'champion'. Most would be described more accurately as good solid stayers. The true champions of the Australian turf are those few who won the Melbourne Cup despite the best efforts of the race itself to prevent them. *Carbine* carried 66 kilograms to victory in 1890 and *Phar Lap* carried 62.5 kilograms in 1930. A few others like *Galilee*, the 1966 winner, and *Rain Lover*, who won in 1968 and again in 1969, proved themselves by continuing to race successfully after their Cup victories. More often the Melbourne Cup is won by a 'battling' horse. The race usually cuts the 'tall poppies' down to size, giving ordinary horses the opportunity to become equine millionaires. It is a symbol and an expression of Australian egalitarianism.

JO'H

See *Archer*; *Carbine*; **Flemington Race-course**; *Phar Lap*.

Melbourne to Warrnambool Cycling Classic is the most arduous one-day professional road race in Australia. The handicap event originated in 1895 when limit riders started at 2 a.m. on their 260 kilometres trek from Warrnambool to Melbourne. The winner was awarded a Raleigh bicycle for his ride of 11 hours 44 minutes 30 seconds, having received a two-hour start on the scratchmen who clocked 10 hours 52 minutes. Between 1895 and 1958 the annual race travelled from either Melbourne to Warrnambool or from Warrnambool to Melbourne. Since 1959 the direction has remained as Melbourne to Warrnambool. The race record, established in 1980, now stands at 5 hours 37 minutes 10 seconds, and limit riders set out at 7.15 a.m. The 1990 winner received $6500 plus trophies, while the holder of the fastest time received $2000 plus trophies. Former winners and fastest-time riders include many internationally successful Australian cyclists, such as Hubert Opperman, Russell Mockridge, Barry Waddell, Hilton Clarke, Dave Allan, and Peter Besanko.
DRS

Memorial Drive Tennis Club and its courts have an important place in the history of Australian tennis. As early as 1889 the SA Tennis Association was established at Memorial Drive in Adelaide. A separate Memorial Drive Tennis Club was formed in 1929. This picturesque location, now with over thirty courts and a seating capacity of 6000, has been the venue for some of the nation's major events. Between 1910 and 1967 a total of fourteen Australian Open Championships were staged at Memorial Drive. When the 1952 Davis Cup challenge round was held at Memorial Drive it was the first occasion on which the event had been conducted on Australian soil outside Melbourne or Sydney. Further challenge rounds were held there in 1956, 1963, and 1968.
HCJP

MENINGA, MAL (1960–), born Bundaberg, Queensland, is a member of Australia's now indigenous South Sea Island community. He began his rugby league career with Souths in Brisbane, then joined Canberra Raiders. A giant of a man, he has played in the second row but his successful career has been as a centre. By the end of the 1991 season, he had appeared in three Grand Finals for Canberra. He has played twenty-nine State of Origin games for Queensland. His Test tally is remarkable: including three tours to England and other internationals abroad, he has played in thirty-four Tests, twelve as captain of the Kangaroos. A successful goal-kicker, he kicked 48 points against Britain in the 1982 Tests, and 166 points on that tour. Immensely popular with players and the crowds, Meninga has done much to encourage young Aborigines in this sport. With an end to special racial laws and a lessening of discriminatory

attitudes, black Australians came to the fore in the 1980s: Meninga as captain of the national league side, Ella the captain of the rugby union side, and Steve Tutton as captain of the national volleyball team.
SJR and CT
See **Aboriginal Rugby League Test Players**; **Aborigines in Sport**; **Rugby League**.

MEREDITH, KEN (1963–) joined the AIS gymnastics programme after working with the Brisbane YMCA programme. From 1984 to 1989 he attained medals in every national championship. In 1987, his best year, he won the all-around, floor exercise, pommel horse, and rings, and achieved a silver medal in vault and high bar. Meredith represented Australia in five world championships between 1981 and 1989 and was a member of the bronze-medal team at the 1986 Commonwealth Games. He achieved Australia's first gymnastics gold medal at the 1988 Liberation Cup in Czechoslovakia, winning the all-around as well as the floor event. He achieved a personal best score—112.10 out of 120—at the Seoul Olympics.
KO'B

MESSENGER, HERBERT HENRY ('Dally') (1883–1959), born Balmain, Sydney, is acknowledged as rugby league's greatest player, and is known simply as 'The Master'. He worked in his family's boatshed and played football at Double Bay Public School. A good cricketer and sailor, from about 1900 he played rugby union football with Warrigals and in 1905 joined Easts. The next year he played first grade and won a following for his great ball skills, cheeky tricks, and accurate, long-range kicking with either foot. A centre-three-quarter, his running with the ball was spectacular and inventive. In August 1907 his decision to play against the visiting professional NZ rugby union team was a key element in the founding of the rugby league code, and Messenger went on to tour England with the New Zealanders. Returning to the first Sydney rugby league season in 1908 he played for Easts and then again toured England, this time with the first Kangaroos in 1908–9. Again he was the star player. He did not tour with the second Kangaroos and his 1911 season tally of 270 points was a record until it was passed by Dave Brown in 1935. Dally Messenger retired from football in 1913. A typical working-class Australian who became famous through sporting prowess and saw the world, but kept little of the money he made, he was rugby league's first and greatest hero.
CC
See **Dally M. Awards**; **Rugby League**.

METCALFE, JACK (1912–) was a triple jumper, who set a world record of 15.78 metres in 1935. Coming third in this event at the 1936 Olympics, he was the only Australian to secure a medal at the Games. Ironically he was beaten by two Japanese competitors whom he had advised in pre-Games training. Metcalfe won the triple jump at the 1934 and 1938 British Empire Games. He was a versatile athlete who also held the Australian record in the high and long jumps and won the NSW javelin, decathlon, and pentathlon titles. Later he had a long career in sport administration and became a leading coach. He was honoured with two Helms awards: in 1934 for athletics and in 1955 for services to athletics.

RC

See **Athletics**.

MILLER, KEITH ROSS ('Nugget'), MBE (1919–), was a cavalier and charismatic cricket all-rounder who was a dashing batsman and a fine exponent of the drive. He scored seven Test centuries. Starting as a reluctant fast bowler, due to wartime back problems, Miller formed a formidable pace partnership with Ray Lindwall. Bowling off a relatively short run, Miller surprised many batsmen with his pace, bounce, and unpredictability. He secured 170 wickets in Tests. Miller had broad interests from classical music to swift horses. He was a controversial character who clashed with authorities. As an intuitive and aggressive captain for NSW he secured some remarkable victories for his State. C. B. Fry noted that Miller played with generous abandon. Tall, good-looking, and with a flowing mane, he was one of the most popular cricketers of his time.

KM-H

MILLER, TONY ('Slaggy') (1929–88) was one of Australia's toughest, longest-serving, and most versatile rugby league forwards. Miller's forty-one Tests included two as a lock-forward, twenty-five as a second-rower, and a further fourteen in the front row. Although he was unavailable to tour because of work commitments for almost a decade during his sixteen-year Test career, which began against Fiji in 1952, he missed few matches in his twenty-three seasons with the Manly club in the Sydney competition where he played 345 first-grade games. Few adversaries enjoyed packing down against the fit and uncompromising Miller whose involvement with the game continued as coach, initially with Manly and later with the fledgling Warringah club.

GC†

MILLER, WILLIAM ('Professor') (1846–1939), an all-round athlete, born England, came to Victoria as a boy. Australian broadsword champion in 1872, between 1874 and 1880 in the USA he won fifty-five of seventy-two boxing and wrestling matches (eleven were drawn), walked 102 miles in 24 hours, and lifted 703 kilograms of iron. In the 1880s he opened gymnasiums in Sydney and Melbourne and fought

Larry Foley to a draw over forty rounds. The only holder of Australian championships in each of boxing, wrestling, fencing, and gymnastics, 'Professor' Miller weighed 89 kilograms, stood 177 centimetres, and had 43 centimetre biceps and calves and a 117 centimetre chest. In 1895 he published *Health, Exercise and Amusement*. He returned to the USA in 1903 and became an athletic instructor to the New York Police. When he died in Baltimore on 11 March 1939 he was described as 'one of the greatest all-round athletes in the world'.

GW

MILNE, MALCOLM (1948–), skier, born Myrtleford, Victoria, was the brother of **Ross**, who was killed while training for the 1964 Olympics. Malcolm learned skiing at Falls Creek and became a member of the Australian Junior Ski Team at 14. He was asked to join the French B team to train in France in 1964 and first represented Australia at the 1968 Grenoble Winter Olympics. His best results in international ski-racing were in the 1969–70 seasons when he became the first Australian to win a downhill race in a World Cup event, at Val d'Isère, was first in the combined at Bear Valley, and third in the downhill at Val Gardena. In the lead-up to the 1972 Sapporo Olympics, Milne was one of ten skiers Avery Brundage wanted to ban for alleged professionalism. Milne, who retired after 1972 because of injuries, became a hops-grower at Myrtleford.

KR

See **Skiing**.

MINOGUE, DANIEL THOMAS (1891–1961), Australian rules footballer, was recruited by Collingwood from California Gully, Bendigo, at 17. He captained the club from 1914 to 1916 before joining the first AIF. After the war he transferred to Richmond as captain-coach assisting the club to win its first VFL premierships in 1920–21. He then coached at another four clubs: Hawthorn (1926–27), Carlton (1929–34), St Kilda (1935–37), and Fitzroy (1940–42). In all he coached in 363 matches. He was the only footballer to have a playing or coaching involvement with six VFL clubs. He was also the first of only three players to captain three VFL teams. Overall he played 180 VFL matches, kicking 77 goals. He also served as Players' Advocate at the VFL Tribunal.

CH*

MITCHELL, ANN, OAM (1945–), born Sydney, first played cricket with Sydney University Club in 1962. Since then her involvement has extended to all facets of the game: manager, coach, selector, journalist, commentator, and administrator. Initially manager of the NSW junior and senior sides, 1977 marked the beginning of her long and successful term as manager of the Australian team. She has held positions at all administrative levels, including president of the International Women's Cricket Council for six years, and president of the Australian Women's Cricket Council since 1988. A regular contributor to cricket journals, a Sydney radio presenter and ABC television cricket commentator, she was also involved with the production of *Fair Play*, a documentary on women's sport. She was awarded the OAM in 1990.

LR

MOCKRIDGE, RUSSELL (1928–58), was a multi-talented road and track cyclist, who exploded on to the Australian scene with a win in his first competitive event in Geelong. With the physical handicap of an inherited eye weakness which made him near-sighted, he was an unlikely champion. He competed at the 1948 Olympics without great success but in the 1950 British Empire Games he won two gold medals and stamped himself as a world-class cyclist. The 1952 Helsinki Games confirmed him as a genuine cycling talent—he won a gold medal in the 1000 metres time trial and then, later in the day, teamed with Lionel Cox to win a second gold medal in the 2000 metres tandem. During 1955 he won the Paris Six Day and had a creditable ride in the Tour De France. Mockridge then returned to Australia and dominated cycling for three years. In 1958, during the Tour of Gippsland, Mockridge was killed when he smashed into a bus.

CS

Modern Pentathlon
In a sport which incorporates competition in horse-riding, pistol-shooting, fencing, swimming, and running, Forbes Carlile (1948 Olympic team swim coach) was the first Australian to enter the Olympic modern pentathlon in 1952. The Amateur Modern Pentathlon Union of Australia was organised in 1954, State titles began in 1955, and the next year Neville Sayers became the first national champion. Peter Macken appeared at his fifth successive Olympic Games in the sport in 1976 and was seven times Australian champion between 1961 and 1976. The fourteenth world championships were held in Melbourne in 1966, and Australia finished ninth overall.

KM

MOLESWORTH, MARGARET ('Mall') (née MUTCH) (?1895–?), born Brisbane, was the daughter of Alexander Mutch, a Scottish-born interstate cricketer and footballer. She won the first Australian women's singles tennis title when this event was introduced in 1922 along with women's and mixed doubles. Her range of shots, particularly her powerful backhand drive and her volley were considered unusual in that era. Some have claimed that she had the widest range of shots of any player, male or female, in the early 1920s. She won eight Queensland and many other State singles and mixed doubles titles before turning professional in 1939. Her career as a tennis coach was highly successful. She married B. H. Molesworth, professor of history at the University of Queensland, and later became a prominent ABC administrator.

VO'F

See **Lawn Tennis**.

MONEGHETTI, STEPHEN JAMES (1962–) was awarded the title 'world's top road runner 1990' by British magazine *Athletics Today*, won Britain's Great Northern half-marathon in unofficial world-record time (60 minutes 34 seconds), and the Berlin marathon in 2 hours 8 minutes 16 seconds to become the world's thirteenth-fastest marathoner. He first came to prominence when he won a bronze medal in the Edinburgh Commonwealth Games marathon in the fastest time by an Australian on debut. Since then he has won the Zatopek 10 000 metres twice, Sydney's City to Surf three times in succession, fifth place in the Seoul Olympic Games marathon (equalling Robert de Castella's best placing by an Australian in an Olympic marathon), a silver medal in Auckland's Commonwealth Games marathon, and second place in the Chiba international cross-country race in Japan. Moneghetti was Australian Junior cross-country champion in 1982. He is a civil engineer working as an educational consultant.

RH*

MOORE, GEORGE THOMAS DONALD (1923–), a jockey and trainer, born Queensland, holds a record of ten jockeys' premierships in NSW. He rode as an apprentice at Mackay, moving to Brisbane in 1939. During the war he moved to Sydney where in 1943–44 he was leading apprentice. In 1954 he lost his licence for two years but returned in top style to win the 1956–57 and 1957–58 premierships. He then made the first of several visits to Europe, where he rode the winners of many classic races including the English Derby on *Royal Palace*. In Sydney he was the leading jockey throughout the 1960s, in close association with trainer Tommy Smith. Retiring in 1971, he spent thirteen years in Hong Kong where he was leading trainer in eleven seasons.

AL

MORAN, HERBERT MICHAEL ('Paddy') (1885–1945), born Sydney, was a rugby footballer. Educated at St Joseph's College and at St Aloysius' College, he graduated in medicine from Sydney University in 1906. He played first for Rose Bay club, then University, and in 1906 represented NSW against Queensland.

A vigorous forward and deadly tackler, he captained the first Wallaby tour to Britain in 1908. Dogged by injury, he played in only one Test when Australia lost 9–6 to Wales. On retirement he qualified as a surgeon and after war service devoted his life to cancer research. In addition to medical papers, Moran wrote feelingly about the enjoyment of rugby, especially in the first of his three largely autobiographical books, *Viewless Winds* (1939). He died of cancer in Cambridge, England, on 20 November 1945.

GW

MORGAN, LAWRENCE ROBERT (1915–), equestrian, born Janefield, Victoria, came from an established family of graziers. A rugged and tough man, he excelled at many sports. He was Victorian heavyweight champion at 19, was selected for the King's Cup in rowing (but did not race because of appendicitis) and played thirty-three games as a ruckman for Australian rules football club Fitzroy. He also represented his State at football in 1938. After moving back to the land, when he acquired a sheep and cattle property, in 1939 he represented Australasia in polo and took up steeplechasing and horse-racing. He was also a successful horse-breeder. Morgan had an unlikely build for an equestrian: he was 82.6 kilograms in his prime and 180 centimetres tall; he also averaged about four pots of beer a day, smoked, and ate generously. Considered a certainty for the 1956 Olympics, he was not selected. In order to prove everyone wrong and to gain valuable international experience he financed himself on a trip to England where he outshone the Australian team and became the first Australian to be placed in the Windsor three-day event at Badminton. At the age of 45 he won two gold medals at the Rome Olympics in the team and individual three-day event. He became the first rider in Olympic history to receive maximum points for cross-country and endurance and was the first individual competitor to receive a plus score. He won the Badminton Horse Trials in 1961.

RH and MH
See **Equestrianism**.

MORLEY, CHARLIE (c.1910–88) began his hockey career with the Camberwell club in Melbourne in the early 1930s. He had an immediate impact on the game as a tenacious player and coach and as a thoughtful and innovative administrator. Morley held many posts at both State and national level including secretary of the Australian Hockey Association in 1956. He represented Victoria as a player between 1937 and 1962, and was also manager and coach of the Victorian team over many years, variously as player-coach and coach-manager. At the national level Morley represented Australia as a player, manager, and coach on many occasions

between 1948 and 1967. Morley was also a State and national selector over a number of years.

BS†

MORRIS, ARTHUR ROBERT, MBE (1922–), a left-hand batsman, became the first player in the world to score a century in each innings of his initial first-class match, for NSW against Queensland in 1940. Born in Dungog, he learned the rudiments of the game from his father, a schoolmaster, who played for Sydney's Waverley club. Arthur Morris joined the St George club as a bowler but soon established himself as a batsman. His promising career was interrupted during the war when he served in New Guinea. In his first Test series in 1946–47 he made three centuries including a century in each innings in the fourth Test. Morris scored another three centuries in the 1948 series, including 196 at the Oval in London and a match-winning 182 at Leeds when Australia reached 3–404 in the fourth innings. Morris, who made twelve centuries in forty-six Tests, retired because of his wife's illness in 1955. An aggressive bat, noted for his hooking, Morris was an unruffled batsman respected for his high standard of sportsmanship.

RC

Morrish Medal, inaugurated in 1947, is awarded annually to the National Football League's under-19 best and fairest player. Established to perpetuate the memory of the former treasurer of the Reserve Grade's League, Tom Morrish, the medal's inaugural winner was A. Dale from the Essendon club. North Melbourne are the most represented club with ten winners, while R. Bruerton of South Melbourne is the only player to win the medal twice.

GC*

MORRISON, DONALD PETER (1928–) was a belt swimmer who proved his superiority in a variety of surf conditions. A member of the Cottesloe Surf Lifesaving Club, Morrison was short and muscular with immense body strength. He was no stylist, relying upon superb fitness and surf skills. Between 1948 and 1959 he won four Australian Senior Belt-Race Championships and was placed on another six occasions. He was also Interstate Belt-Race Champion twice (1951 and 1958) and was three times a place-getter in Australian Surf-Race Championships. While at his peak Morrison represented Australia in four national teams. He also won eight consecutive belt-race championships, from 1948 to 1955, in WA and had further victories in 1958 and 1959. His tally of national wins and placings as a belt swimmer has never been surpassed.

EJ

Mosstrooper (1921–?), a thoroughbred steeplechaser, has the best record of any Australian jumper, with five wins in major events (two VATC Australian Hurdles, one Australian Steeple, one VRC Grand National Hurdle, and one VRC Grand National Steeple), three wins at Moonee Valley, and four placings in major events. This puts even the achievements of *Redleap*, *Roisel*, and *Redditch* in the shade. A chestnut by *Kenilworth* out of *Keego*, *Mosstrooper* was placed in only one of his eighteen starts on the flat, and fell at his first start over jumps before finding success. He was trained throughout his jumping career by Gus Powell.

AL

Motocross

Previously known as scrambling, motocross is similar to speedway racing except that the large fields of riders compete over a dirt-surfaced, twisty, undulating circuit. The sport has flourished since the 1970s in NSW, Victoria, and SA. The Willoughby Motorcycle Club was the first club to stage a point-score championship at Amaroo Park. Trevor Flood (Victoria), Jim Seaysbrook (NSW), and Laurie Alderton (NSW) were early champions. By 1975 the success of the sport ensured that promoters could afford to invite top-class riders from the UK, USA, Japan, and Italy to compete in local events. In 1980 the Sydney Showground became the first arena used for stadium motocross, racing conducted on a specially constructed track which closely resembles a motocross circuit. Promoter Blair Shepherd invited riders from America to compete against Australian champions and attracted an estimated 30 000 spectators. In 1992 a three-round series for 125 cc and 500 cc bikes will replace the single event.

GC*

See **Motorcycling**.

Motor Racing

Especially after 1945, comparatively high levels of motor vehicle ownership, coupled with the popularity of many forms of racing, meant that motor racing was quickly accepted as a prominent part of Australian sporting culture. The first car-race staged in Australia was reputedly at Maribyrnong Gymkhana, Victoria, in 1903. The winner is not known. Grand Prix racing was first conducted at Phillip Island in 1928. At this time the British Grand Prix was only two years old and even the prestigious Monaco Grand Prix had not yet started. Australian motor-car racing was therefore a precocious infant, but slow to mature. It could not be said that it fully came of age until November 1985 in Adelaide with the staging of a round of the Formula One World Drivers' Championship.

Between 1903 and 1985 motor sport's crude origins were gradually supplanted by technical and commercial sophistication. Early on, motor-car racing was linked with speedway. In 1925 Maroubra Speedway opened. For eighteen months large crowds thrilled to the antics of the likes of Phil Garlick and Hope Bartlett driving road-racing cars on a steeply banked concrete saucer not unlike Brooklands. The track was corrugated and extremely dangerous; the driving style harum-scarum, with little attention paid to either personal safety or mechanical sympathy. After several fatalities Maroubra Speedway was closed and the distinction between motor racing and speedway became more clear when the latter transferred to the Sydney Showground Royale using midget speedway cars. Motor-car racing became focused on the annual Grand Prix event, the inaugural winner at Phillip Island on handicap being Captain A. C. Waite in an Austin Seven. The track was unsurfaced, potholed, and dusty; similar conditions applied at the picturesque Mount Panorama circuit at Bathurst which opened in 1938. By this time most motor-racing vehicles tended to be front-engined, home-made 'specials', epitomised by Stan Jones's famous series of Maybach specials, one of which used parts from thirty different vehicles.

The 1955 Australian Grand Prix at Southport was a major turning point. For one thing it was the last time a home-made 'special' had any chance of winning—importing racing machines from Europe became the dominant practice; for another, the race was won by the 29-year-old Jack Brabham, whose victory *Wheels* magazine saluted as 'Rising Star takes Grand Prix'. In 1956 the brilliant Stirling Moss, driving a Maserati, won the event at Albert Park. The supremacy of overseas drivers was unchallenged until 1964 when Sydney driver Frank Matich demonstrated that he could lap as fast as Europe's finest.

The years from the Albert Park Grand Prix until the early 1970s were the champagne years of Australian motor racing. Energetic promoters like Geoff Sykes of the Australian Automobile Racing Club organised memorable race meetings at Warwick Farm; the Tasman Cup series brought international stars such as Jim Clark, Graham Hill, and Jackie Stewart to Australia. Despite inferior machinery, local drivers like Matich and Leo Geoghegan were surprisingly competitive. Spectator attendance figures were vast. More recently, environmental and ecological considerations have conspired to ensure that these days of glory are unlikely to be repeated. Thus, paradoxically, when the Adelaide Grand Prix finally established Australia on the international motor-racing map, its domestic roots were less strong than twenty years earlier.

Motor racing's growing sophistication was shown in a number of ways. In common with other sports, there has been a general shift from amateurism to professionalism. For much of its history those involved in the upper echelons of this strongly masculine sport tended to be wealthy men whose business interests were related to the motor industry, usually as car- or tyre-dealers such as Bob Jane. Growing levels of corporate investment created a small number of full-time professional motor-racing drivers such as Allan Moffatt and Peter Brock. The sport, however, has never been egalitarian or democratic. The Victorian open-wheeler driver Alfredo Constanzo is a rare example of someone from a non-Anglo-Saxon background rising to prominence. Motor racing, nevertheless, has a plebeian base among its spectators and participants at the car-club level. In comparison with the UK, 'car culture' in Australia has been a working-class phenomenon. Speed shops in Sydney, for instance, are largely concentrated in working-class suburbs in the west and south-west.

Professionalism and sophistication have brought both advantages and disadvantages. Motor racing has been increasingly codified and regulated. The Confederation of Australian Motor Sports (CAMS) was established in 1953. Some competitors have found CAMS to be intrusive and bureaucratic, but the implementation of increasingly stringent safety regulations and licensing requirements has made the sport safer for competitors and spectators alike. Rising levels of commercial investment, however, have tended to diminish its sporting status such that its critics allege that it is no more than an extension of the advertising budget of large automobile, tyre, cigarette, or alcohol companies. The turning point here was perhaps in 1968, when advertising decals were first allowed on motor-racing vehicles.

Since 1960 a distinctive feature of Australian motor racing has been its preoccupation with touring-car racing. This contrasts strongly with Europe, where most attention focuses on Formula One or the 24-hour sports-car event at Le Mans. The major race on the Australian motor sport calendar has become the long-distance sedan car event at Mount Panorama. Initially known as the Armstrong 500, most recently as the Tooheys 1000, this race dominates motor-racing budgets and media attention. What began, however, as a race designed to display the capabilities of sedans 'off the showroom floor' has become progressively diluted. Extensive modifications are now permissible and sometimes competing vehicles are not even available for purchase in Australia. Nevertheless, the annual 'Ford v. Holden' aspect of the race, especially in the late 1960s and early 1970s, made the race an inspiring spectacle and encouraged the production of classic motor cars like the Falcon GTHO and Holden Torana GTR UI. Running a close second in terms of public interest are the rounds of the Australian Touring Car Championship. Sedan car drivers like Norm Beechey in the

1960s and Dick Johnson in the 1980s achieved almost folk hero status.

AM

See **BEECHEY, NORM; BRABHAM, Sir JACK; BROCK, PETER; DAVISON, ALEXANDER; GEOGHEGAN, IAN; Gold Star Championship; Hill-climb Championship; JANE, BOB; JONES, ALAN; MATICH, FRANK; Motor-racing Grand Prix; Mount Panorama Racing Circuit, Bathurst; THOMPSON, W. B.; Touring Car Championship; WHITEFORD, DOUG.**

Motor-racing Grand Prix. The first Grand Prix was held in March 1928, over the dusty circuit at Phillip Island in Victoria. Run over 161 kilometres around a 10.5 kilometre track, it was won by the British driver Captain A. C. Waite driving a 747 cc Austin Seven. He was to be the last non-Australian to win the event until 1956 when Stirling Moss coasted to an easy win at Albert Park. The Grand Prix continued at Phillip Island until 1935, during which period it was won three times by Melbourne driver Bill Thompson. It was then conducted on various courses around Australia. In 1969, after establishing a measure of international fame, the Grand Prix was included in the annual Tasman Series and began to attract world-class drivers during the northern hemisphere off-season. The Grand Prix was originally a free-formula affair, with no restrictions on engine capacity until the 1960s when a 2.5 litre formula prevailed. In the 1970s it was governed by Formula 5000 regulations and was dominated by resident Australian drivers. Now that the race has world championship status the chance of even an occasional Australian win in our own Grand Prix seems remote.

GC*

Motorcycling

Although motorcycle-racing is recorded as having taken place around SCG's concrete cycling track on New Year's Day 1901 when Jack Green averaged 37.7 kilometres an hour on his motorised tricycle, before the First World War competitive motorcycling concentrated on reliability trials and hill-climbs. The first Australian club to be formed was the Pioneer Motor Cycle Club, established in Sydney in 1904, but this was followed soon afterwards by the Victorian and Perth Motor Cycle Clubs. Perhaps the most significant development in Australian motorcycling history was the Easter 1938 opening of the Mount Panorama Circuit at Bathurst which was to be a major venue for fifty years to come. Road racing has been the basis of motorcycling in Australia but from time to time other forms have gained popularity. In the late 1920s attention focused on speed-bowl racing around banked concrete tracks at the Melbourne Motordrome and the Olympic Speedway in Maroubra

(NSW). Speedway developed at the same time but retained spectator appeal for a longer period. In the past decade stadium motocrosse has come to the fore as a crowd-pleaser.

JC*

See **CAMPBELL, KEITH; CARRUTHERS, KEL; Crowd Disorder; DOOHAN, MICHAEL; GARDNER, WAYNE; HANSFORD, GREG; HINTON Family; Motocross; Mount Panorama Racing Circuit, Bathurst; PHILIS, TOM; Speedway**.

Mount Panorama Racing Circuit, Bathurst, 210 kilometres inland from Sydney, has been in almost continuous use for car and motorcycle racing since 1938. It is Australia's oldest surviving road course, and one of the fastest and most difficult. Its prime distinguishing feature, and its greatest natural asset, is its hillside location which provides steep climbs (maximum gradient 1 in 6.3, height gained 170 metres), a twisting precipitous descent, a great variety of corners, and excellent close-up and long-distance viewing. The outright record for the 6.17 kilometres lap was set in 1970 by Niel Allen (M10b McLaren F5000, 2 minutes 09.7 seconds, 171.31 km/h), and the motorcycle record in 1983 by Andrew Johnson (Honda 500, 2 minutes 13.1 seconds). Slightly lengthened to 6.21 kilometres in 1987, with a chicane on the main straight, the circuit's record is now held by Mark Skaife (Nissan GTR, 2 minutes 15.46 seconds), set in 1990.

In 1936 Bathurst City Council obtained unemployment relief funds for a 'tourist and scenic road' built to full public road construction standards but with a view to occasional use as a race circuit. The city's continuing involvement with maintenance, upgrading, and preservation of the circuit during various disputes over safety, promotion, or crowd behaviour has given Mount Panorama a durability and continuity unique among Australian motor sport venues upon which an unrivalled tradition has been built.

The Easter motorcycle meetings have been compared with the Isle of Man Touring Trophy events, and attracted crowds of far-travelled spectators and riders for magnificent racing until 1988, when they were suspended after confrontations between police and 'bikies'. The equally long history of four-wheeled racing includes four Australian Grand Prix events (1938, 1947, 1952, and 1958) and an October endurance race for touring cars introduced in 1963. Since 1974, when race length was increased from 500 miles to 1000 kilometres, the latter has been the sole race meeting for cars each year. Intensive television coverage, complemented by the superb location, has made the race very much a part of the broader Australian sporting calendar. Nonetheless, Mount Panorama is highly capitalised considering its present use, and its 1930s layout is often difficult to adapt to modern safety requirements. The circuit, and its once-a-year race, must soon expect some challenges.

GH

See **Crowd Disorder; HINTON Family**.

Mountaineering
Although Australian mountains lack the degree of difficulty necessary for serious climbing, snow- and ice-climbing techniques have been carried out in the Australian Alps and on Tasmanian mountains. Beginning in the late 1940s in Victoria and NSW, the sport soon matured so that by the 1960s most of the country's major climbing areas had been discovered. The motivation for this can be attributed to Sydney climbers John Ewbank and Bryden Allen who uncovered major routes such as Lieben on Crater Bluff and Elijah on Bluff Mountain, both cliffs in the Warrumbungles in NSW. Ewbank developed the open-ended numerical system of climb-grading which is used in various forms around the world. Recent Australian mountaineering achievements have included several new ascents on Mount Everest by Greg Mortimer and Tim Macartney-Snape.

GC*

See **MACARTNEY-SNAPE, TIM**.

MULLAGH, JOHNNY (c.1841–91), born near Harrow, Victoria, was the first Aborigine to excel at British sports. As well as being a fine athlete he was the leading player in the Aboriginal cricket team which toured England in 1868. He played forty-five matches on tour and scored most runs (1698), achieved the highest average (23.65), highest score (94), bowled the most overs (1877) and took 245 wickets at an average of 10.00 (second-best). His performance was better than Charles Lawrence, a leading international all-rounder, who captained the team. Mullagh also served as reserve wicket-keeper. During that tour, the greatest English fast bowler, George Tarrant, believed Mullagh to be one of the finest batsmen he had ever bowled against. After 1869 Mullagh went into obscurity, but from time to time returned to play outstanding innings against some of the world's best bowlers. In 1878–79 he top-scored in the second innings for Victoria against the visiting English team under Lord Harris; in 1884–85 he carried his bat during a match in Adelaide against George Giffen at his best.

RH*

See **Aborigines in Sport; Cricket**.

Mulrooney Medal. The John Mulrooney Medal was instituted in 1936 in recognition of the services to the ACT (Australian) Football League of John Mulrooney. Between 1928 and 1946 Mulrooney served as president of the ACTFL with only one break in 1935. In recognition of his services, he was awarded the MBE.

He was also made a life member of the ACTFL. The Mulrooney Medal is awarded to the best and fairest player in the ACTFL on the basis of votes awarded by the umpires after each game. Dual winners of the Mulrooney Medal are R. Watterson (Queanbeyan-Acton) and J. Moody (Royal Military College).

MH*

MUNRO, DAVID HUGH ('Darby') (1913–66), born Sydney, was the son of a trainer, Hugh Munro. His brother **Jim** (1905–74) was one of the leading jockeys in the 1920s and twice won the Melbourne Cup, but the more flamboyant Darby had a longer career in the saddle. His first big win was the 1930 AJC Doncaster Handicap; he went on to win five Victoria Derbies, five AJC Derbies, and three Melbourne Cups. Popular with racegoers, but frequently in trouble with the stewards, Munro served several suspensions but continued to ride until 1955.

AL

MURDOCH, WILLIAM LLOYD (1854–1911) was a fine all-round sportsman, excelling at golf, pigeon-shooting, and rugby, and was the most successful nineteenth-century Australian cricket captain. He was born at Sandhurst in Victoria. He led his team to victory in the 1882 Ashes Test and also captained the 1880 and 1884 touring sides. A popular captain, with a fine sense of humour, he withdrew from first-class cricket after 1884 because of a dispute over player payment, but returned to captain the 1890 touring side. He was one of the leading batsmen of his era, the first to score a Test double century (211 in 1884) and a triple century (311 for NSW in 1882) in intercolonial competition. A solicitor by profession and an Anglo-Australian at heart, he settled in England after 1890. He toured South Africa with the 1891–92 English side and captained Sussex from 1893 to 1899. Murdoch died while watching a Test match at Melbourne in 1911. His body was embalmed, returned to England and buried at Kensal Green cemetery in London.

RC

See **Cricket**.

MURRAY, IAIN (1959–) began competitive sailing when he was only 12 and at 13 became the youngest person ever to win the Australian Cherub Championship, in a boat which he designed himself. Murray next took up sailing 18-footers, winning the world title when only 18, the youngest yachtsman ever to do so. He accepted an offer to skipper the 12 metre yacht *Advance* in the 1983 *America*'s Cup Challenge but was unsuccessful in the races to choose the challenger. He was more successful in 1987 in Fremantle when *Kookaburra III* defeated the other Australian contenders but lost the Cup in four straight races to Dennis Conner's *Stars and Stripes*. Murray won the 1984 world championships in the Etchell 22 Class and earned the Australian Yachtsman of the Year Award in that year.

RC

See **Sailing and Yachting**.

MURRAY, JACK ('Gelignite') (1910–83) was an all-round sportsman who became a household name in motor sport when he was one of the stars of the Redex Round-Australia Reliability Trials in the early 1950s. He earned his nickname from his liberal use of explosives to remove fallen trees and other obstacles in his path. Murray won five straight amateur wrestling titles, between 1930 and 1934, and several water-ski championships.

RC

See **Redex Trials**.

MURRAY, KEVIN, MBE (1938–), delighted the football community in 1969 by winning the Brownlow Medal at 31, an age greater than that of any other winner. As persistent as the back injury for which he wore a brace, he endured to set the then VFL record of 333 games. While Fitzroy often struggled, Murray's determination as a half-back and ruck-rover made him the obvious choice as captain from 1963 to 1972, apart from two years with East Perth. A regular State representative, Murray captained Victoria and also served as captain-coach of WA.

DS

Muscular Christianity was part of a complex ideology which also embraced imperial duty, nationalistic pride, and moral character. The term originated in Britain and was made popular through the works of Charles Kingsley and Thomas Hughes, in particular in their *Westward Ho!* (1855) and *Tom Brown's Schooldays* (1857) respectively. In effect it added a physical dimension to the moral endeavour by which Christian men should develop their character. It attracted many adherents who subsequently lauded many British sports, especially cricket and football (soccer and especially rugby), for their perceived ability to contribute to a player's moral character through sportsmanship, team spirit and obeying a captain's orders. It was this association with organised sport which was primarily responsible for the introduction of the concept of Muscular Christianity to Australia where early expressions of its philosophy appeared in *Bell's Life in Victoria* and *Sporting Chronicle* in the late 1850s. Within a decade Muscular Christianity was embedded in Australian social thought, though increasingly there was often only token recognition of its religious element.

WV

See **ARNOLD, RICHARD**; **Australian Rules Football**.

N

NAGLE, KELVIN DAVID GEORGE, OAM (1921–), born Sydney, a former carpenter, won the Centenary British Open Golf Championship in 1960 and another thirty tournaments at an age when most might consider retirement. At a young age he became an assistant professional at Pymble Golf Course, working sixteen hours a day to absorb golf knowledge. After enlisting in the army in 1939 he gained membership of the PGA. Nagle was runner-up in the 1948 Ampol tournament and in 1949 he won the first of his six Australian PGA championships. When his selection in Australia's 1954 World Cup team was criticised, he silenced his critics by helping Peter Thomson to win the cup. In 1959 Nagle again was part of a cup-winning team. In addition he became only the third player to win the Australian Open and PGA in the one year. Nagle created an Australian record in 1961 when he shot 260 in the Irish Hospitals Tournament—the lowest score in a 72-hole event. He continued to win tournaments regularly in the 1960s and 1970s before retiring in 1977.

GC*

See **Golf**.

NANCARROW, CAMERON JOHN (1946–), born Sydney, took up squash at an early age after his father won a squash racket and a set of shoes in a club raffle. A rawboned and rather ungainly 6-foot left-hander, Nancarrow became an unorthodox and unpredictable squash-player with an effective forehand kill to the front left of the court. He twice reached the final of the world amateur championships, in Melbourne in 1967 and New Zealand in 1971. Having won the Australian, British, Canadian, and South African titles, he finally won the world title in 1973.

KT†

See **Squash Rackets**.

National Australian Football Council (NAFC), formed in 1906 as the Australasian Football Council, has passed through several name changes and has seen several decades of development, both on and off the field. The NAFC comprises the Australian Football League (AFL), the Australian Amateur Football Council, and State controlling bodies. Its main functions are to co-ordinate the development of Australian football and to standardise the laws and player registrations. This involves four major concerns: the laws of the game, national championships, interstate player transfers, and national development. The AFL is responsible for administering and promoting the national professional competition, with teams in Victoria, NSW, SA, WA, and Queensland; the NAFC co-ordinates development and provides a vital forum for discussion on all areas affecting Australian football. Since the mid-1970s the NAFC has instituted a most extensive development programme which has included national coaching accreditation schemes, the Aussie Footy programme for children of primary-school age, and production of high-quality resources. With the coming of the AFL's National Draft Recruiting Scheme, the NAFC's National Development Plan has been critical in ensuring the nurturing and development of players from the grass roots through a player pathway to senior level. The National Development Plan is one of the major initiatives in the promotion and future planning of Australian football and through the AFL–NAFC agreement will be the vehicle for substantial AFL funding support for junior football.

EB and IJ

National Ice Skating Association of Australia (NISAA). The Glaciarium in Melbourne was the first rink for figure skating in Australia and it was at this location that the NISAA was formed in 1911. One of its objectives was 'the furtherance of the art of skating with the view of attaining the highest proficiency amongst the skaters at the Glaciariums in Australia'. The Sydney 'Glaciarium' was the home of the Sydney Ice Club, which was the main figure-skating organisation in NSW. The two bodies operated within their own States but in June 1931 a formal agreement was signed between the State organisations of NSW and Victoria to form the Council of NISAA with objectives which included holding Australian championships in figure skating, which began in the same year. NISAA became a member of the International Skating Union in 1932 but it was not until 1948 that the first Australian competitor took part in a world figure-skating championship. Skating rinks were established in Queensland and SA in the 1960s and both States joined NISAA in the 1970s. The WA Association was founded in 1977, that of the ACT in 1982, and the Tasmanian in 1988. NISAA is concerned

primarily with the establishment of rules, technical matters, and national and international issues.
GM and IJ

Nationalism

Any attempt to nominate the most important constituents of Australian identity must give sport a prominent place. Sport is commonly associated with egalitarianism and fair-mindedness, with glorification of mateship and the 'common man' (invested with their principally masculine meanings). Linking these elements is the assertion of Australian nationhood, to which international sporting competition gives popular expression. The idea of nationalism rests on the identification and celebration of geographically bounded social characteristics which are perceived by citizens to be desirable and virtuous. This positive self-perception is reinforced when people from other nations are regarded as lacking those qualities. Nationalism is an ideology which advances universal national ideals, images, and sentiments while ignoring or dismissing as unimportant the ethnic, racial, gender, class, regional, and other divisions within a nation. Rather than seeking to identify the positive and negative features of nationalism, it is more productive to view it as an inherently contradictory ideology whose meaning and application is contested by different social groups seeking to align their own and the nation's interests. Nationalism's main use has been to persuade young men to go to war, to have consumers buy patriotically packaged commodities, and to canvass support for political parties and their platforms.

Sporting success has been one of the most enduring symbols of Australian progress and in this way has contributed directly to the creation and maintenance of nationalist sentiment. In the early days of the colony, when the social activities of the white settlers were firmly rooted in English and Irish culture and where there was a strong desire to 'protect' white society from an alien land and its indigenous people, sports from the home countries were emulated rather than challenged. Boxing, horse-racing, and cock-fighting, in which gambling played a central role, were the most popular sporting activities. The infusion of Victorian-era bourgeois values such as loyalty, 'duty', and Christian manhood into the colonial culture, together with the upper middle-class view that sport was a good training ground for 'higher' causes such as business and warfare, had a significant impact on the development of amateur sports like rugby union. In contrast, the emerging working classes, many of whom were resentful of Britain's paternalistic rule, brought to sport elements of anti-authoritarianism, parochialism, and anti-imperialism. Such groups celebrated Australia's 'difference' and sought to develop

sports which might reflect that difference. The underlying concern throughout the century was that Australia's difference from Britain was based not on simple variety but on colonial inferiority. The sporting victories of Australia's cricket teams in the 1880s—in particular, the defeat of England at the Oval in 1882—were important in fostering a sense of shared 'Australianness'.

The national self-image of Australians at the turn of the century was one of an egalitarian, self-confident, 'manly', iconoclastic yet practical people who had showed great pride in their capacity to win at sport. It is perhaps no coincidence that this period was also one in which the Australian worker enjoyed one of the highest living standards in the world. This self-confident national character was tested in another arena. During the Boer War some 16 000 Australian men fought on behalf of England, with imperial cricket playing a not insignificant role in producing the necessary 'climate of sentiment'.

This dedication both to cricket and to war was heralded as a feature of Australian life. However, in sport, as in wider Australian life, there was an emerging split between those (mainly Anglophile and bourgeois) Australians who cherished Victorian values of imperial sporting amateurism and those (mainly Irish Catholic and working-class) people who believed in political independence. The latter group supported the professionalisation of sport, seeing it as a legitimate form of escape from the drudgery of work for players and spectators alike. During the First World War, as battalions of young middle-class Protestant men abandoned their amateur rugby union duties to fight for the Empire, many of the working-class, often semi-professional, rugby league players refused to swap their footballs for guns.

This tension over sporting philosophy seemed to have disappeared during the 1930s Depression. Sport symbolically helped to unify a people whose material class divisions were becoming increasingly apparent. During the infamous 'bodyline' cricket series of 1932–33, the somewhat aloof English captain, Douglas Jardine, became a focus for nationalist antagonism. Don Bradman, in contrast, was reconfirmed as a fair-minded Australian sporting hero who mirrored the nation's best attributes. Within a few years, however, anti-British sentiment was submerged again in wartime. The national character, comprising democratic spirit, egalitarian nature, and commitment to social justice, was tested once more, but now on the side of the sporting enemy. Australia was not as severely ravaged by war as many other countries and emerged after 1945 with the image of a young, productive nation whose people were willing to accept the dispossessed and disillusioned of Europe. The national identity in its most respectable form was encapsulated in the surf lifesaving movement, which linked sport, nationalism, masculinity, and militarism. It was the lifesavers who had taken pride of place in the famous March to Nationhood pageant in 1938 and were again on duty for the visit of Queen Elizabeth II in 1954. The movement was widely seen as truly Australian in spirit, with an apparently democratic function realised in an idyllic context of sun, sea, and sand.

If Australian sportswomen have not yet been mentioned it is because they were largely excluded from a male-constructed and male-focused national identity. The national stereotype was, as we have seen, of a practical, no-nonsense male who loved sport. Women were regarded predominantly as the nurturers who supported male success. It was ironic, therefore, that so many sporting heroes of the 1950s—Ilsa Konrads, Lorraine Crapp, Shirley Strickland, Marjorie Jackson, Dawn Fraser, and Betty Cuthbert—were women. The extent to which their success altered or modified the Australian national self-image is yet to be systematically addressed by sports historians. What can be said is that individual athletic and swimming performances did little to enhance the status of women's team-sports such as cricket, netball, and hockey; the success of individual sportswomen did little to shake the entrenched male domination of sport, which was reinforced as Australian men began to make their mark in world tennis. Australia won the Davis Cup eight times during the 1950s and great national pride was taken in its success over their American 'colonial' rivals.

Sporting victories, however, masked a much wider and deeper shift in the relationship between the two countries. At the very time when Australia was basking in its sporting superiority, the Americans were busily 'winning' significant sections of the Australian economy. Sport was a continuing focus for Australian nationalism during the turbulent 1960s and 1970s, when ambivalent relations with superpowers and ethnocentric responses to immigration prompted widespread debate about the distinctiveness of Australian culture.

The sporting image of Australia was greatly tarnished when Australian competitors failed to win a gold medal at the 1976 Montreal Olympics. The opening in 1981 of the lavishly funded Australian Institute of Sport, with the express purpose of intensively training élite athletes to be successful in international sporting competition, marks a crisis in the belief that Australia produces a 'natural' bounty of sporting champions.

At the end of the twentieth century Australia has emerged as a mainly suburban yet cosmopolitan nation. While much of its colonial past is romanticised as an exciting world of convicts, bushrangers, and explorers, and its more recent history represented as stable and culturally uni-

form, other voices have sought a hearing for their concerns and a recognition of their separate identities. The Aboriginal, feminist, and immigrant movements now forcefully express the experiences of subjugation, in sport and other social spheres, which have long been camouflaged by myths of a happy and egalitarian nation. In such uncertain times sport is called on to secure national cohesion in areas ranging from politics to advertising.

Nationalist hysteria over Australia's winning in 1983 of the America's Cup was successfully instigated by the media, by entrepreneur-led corporations, and by political parties, each of which had clear vested interests in drawing lessons for the nation from its sporting triumph. The idea that success in this domain can be readily transferred to other areas of society and also that it symbolises the nation's general health has considerable appeal for those organisations which claim credit for winning and which are in search of audiences, positive public relations, investors, and voters.

The sport–nationalism nexus has often been of considerable importance in recent attempts by commercial corporations to mould their public profile. Overseas-owned companies like McDonalds and Ricoh are particularly eager to demonstrate their national credentials by financially supporting Australian sports in international competition, while colourless and bureaucratic organisations like banks and accountancy firms (for example, Westpac, National Australia, and Coopers & Lybrand) seek to popularise their image by likening their structure and operations to those of sports teams. Sport is also used by politicians to display patriotism and the common touch. Bob Hawke, the Australian prime minister whose tenure bridged the 1980s and early 1990s, assumed the media-bestowed title of 'Australia's Number One Sports Fan' and relentlessly pursued the positive association of sport with national politics. The all-party support for Melbourne's unsuccessful bid to host the 1996 Olympic Games reveals the perceived electoral potency of sporting nationalism.

In an economy increasingly dominated by foreign capital and a society fragmented by structural inequality and cultural pluralism, sport is mobilised as a link between an idealised, unified past and a mythologised, cohesive present. Contemporary Australian sports stars may live abroad, may have lost their local accents, and may be contracted to endorse goods and services from overseas, but they will be called upon to affirm their national affiliation. There are few signs of any attenuation of sport's reciprocal importance for nationalism. In 1990 the *Sydney Morning Herald*'s Commonwealth Games (a legacy of the colonial past) feature opened with a full-page colour photograph of

Olympic gold-medal winner Debbie Flintoff-King raising her arms in salute with the Australian flag as a backdrop beneath the headline THIS SPORTING NATION. Later in the same year the Australian Rules Football Grand Final had as its half-time entertainment a joint 'salute' to its former players and to returned soldiers with, again, a huge Australian flag featured.

While such nationalist sentiment is obviously orchestrated, it would be a mistake to believe that it is the sole product of marketing exercises. The nation-state remains an important means of collective identification in a world where there has been a marked decline in national sovereignty. Australia, with its colonial heritage and its constitutional, economic, and cultural legacies, is historically sensitised to issues of national independence and character. Sport's ready capacity to provide symbols of unity, progress, and decline fits it well for the function of bearer of meanings for the nation. In consequence, the meanings of, and claims to, 'this sporting nation' will continue to be contested by those who wish to use it for their own ends, as well as by those who resist its oppressive applications. The historical ties between sport and Australian nationalism, however reformulated, will be carried strongly into the twenty-first century.

GL† and DR*

See **America's Cup**; **Australian Institute of Sport**; **Bodyline**; **Ethnic Influences**; **Gender**; **Sponsorship**; **Surf Lifesaving**; **War**.

NEALL, GAIL (1955–) reached her swimming peak at the 1972 Olympic Games. Though she had won three Australian championships before the Games (the 400 metres individual medley, twice, and the 200 metres butterfly), and a silver medal in the 400 metres individual relay in the 1970 Edinburgh British Commonwealth Games, she was not the favourite in 1972. Known as the 'Mighty Mite', however, she had great determination and courage. Swimming in lane 7 in the 400 metres individual medley because of her qualifying time, she came from behind to win, in world-record time. One of the pools at the Ryde swimming complex is named in her honour. She and Shane Gould went to the same school, Turramurra High in Sydney.

RH and MH

NELSON, MARJORIE ('Midge'), BEM (1937–), Australia's greatest softball player, competed in four World Series (1965, 1970, 1974, and 1978)—an International Softball Federation record yet to be equalled. She also represented Australia in hockey and Victoria in basketball. Nelson's softball career spanned eighteen years, from 1960 to 1978. She played in a record twenty-three consecutive national titles, playing four times for WA and nineteen

for Victoria. She played fifty games for Australia (twenty-five as captain) and had a career batting average of .205 and a fielding average of .944. When Australia won the World Series in 1965 Nelson played a key role in that event. She captained Australia in the 1974 and 1978 series. She received the BEM in 1978 for her services to softball, was inducted into the International Hall of Fame in 1983 and the Sport Australia Hall of Fame in 1985. A special medal was struck in the same year, the Midge Nelson Medal, for the most valuable player in the national championships.

RC

See **Softball**.

Netball

It was not until 1970 that the game known in Australia as 'women's basket ball' officially became 'netball'. A comparatively modern sport, netball is a derivation of the 'basketball' game devised by James Naismith in America in 1891. In his game, a goal was scored when a player threw a soccer-type ball into a basket. The umpire then had to climb a ladder to retrieve the ball. The bottom of the basket was removed a few years later but the name of the game was retained. The conversion of the game to netball played by females began with the introduction of basketball to the students of the Bergmann-Osterberg College of Physical Education, Hampstead Heath, England, in 1895 by the visiting American Dr Toll. The college was moved to Dartford and it was there that metal rings with nets were used for goals instead of baskets and the game was played outdoors on grass, with the court divided into three sections. The restricted areas and the type of clothing worn by women at this time did not allow much speed and the game was more one of co-operation than competition. In 1906 a book entitled *The Game of Netball and How to Play It* was first published by the Ling Association (now known as the Physical Education Association of Great Britain and Northern Ireland). One of the key statements in that book was: 'Teams may number either five, seven, or nine-a-side; for the first two a piece of ground 100 feet long by 75 feet wide is sufficient; for the latter, 150 feet by 75 feet wide; but the seven-a-side with the shorter ground is the game usually played.' Curiously, it was this statement which caused considerable difficulty in the spread of this sport of netball/basketball both nationally and internationally because of the flexibility in the number of players in a team.

The early history of netball in Australia is not well documented. It was played in primary and secondary schools around the turn of the century and was probably introduced by teachers from England. In Victoria an interschool seven-a-side competition was conducted in primary schools by 1913 and in secondary schools by 1915. At the YWCA hostel in Church Street, Richmond, the sportsgrounds included netball courts, which attacted other girls' clubs to play there, leading to the formation of the Melbourne Girls' Basket Ball Association. Since the 1920s the game has spread through both schools and community clubs.

During the years preceding the formation of the All Australian Women's Basket Ball Association (AAWBBA) there were active city, regional, and State associations throughout Australia, but some played the seven-a-side and some the nine-a-side rules. It was in 1926 that a team representing the Melbourne Girls' Basket Ball Association travelled to Sydney. This is the first recorded interstate match and it led, in 1927, to the formation of the AAWBBA which promoted seven-a-side netball. However, a synopsis of the 1932 annual reports from each State provides evidence that nine-a-side was still being played in Queensland and five-a-side in WA in addition to the seven-a-side game.

In the constitution of the AAWBBA, accepted in the minutes of 1927, are its stated 'objects' which were 'to promote friendly relationships between the Basket Ball Associations of the various States, to develop through contests a high standard of team play, to organise interstate and inter-national matches, and to control the seven a side Basket Ball code for women in Australia'. There were five foundation members of the AAWBBA: NSW—City Girls' Amateur Sports Association (changed to NSWWBBA in 1929); Queensland—Australian Ladies' Basket Ball Association (changed to QWBBA in 1931); SA—SAWBBA; Victoria—Melbourne Girls' Basket Ball Association (changed to VWBBA in 1928); and WA—Basket Ball Association of Perth (changed to WAWBBA). The first AAWBBA tournament was held in Melbourne in September 1928, with representative teams from NSW, Queensland, SA, and Victoria. Matches were played under the rules as stipulated in the AAWBBA minutes of 22 May 1928, some of which included the following:

> the ground shall be 90 feet long and 45 feet wide; the goal shall consist of one iron ring, 15 inches in diameter, placed horizontally 10 feet above the ground, projecting 6 inches from the supporting surface, and with or without a net; the ball shall be an ordinary sized Association [soccer] football, between twenty-seven and twenty-eight inches in circumference.

Tasmania has been represented at interstate carnivals since 1933; the ACT and NT have been represented since 1976 and 1977 respectively. From 1927 to 1938 interstate teams competed for the Prouds Challenge Cup; since 1939 the winners of the interstate tournament have received the Elix Shield, presented by Mrs M. Elix (née Hargrave).

Australia's earliest international matches were played against NZ, but initial negotiations were difficult because New Zealanders played nine-a-side netball. An important step was made in 1937 when Miss Edith Hull visited NZ as a representative of the AAWBBA. The opportunity for Hull's visit arose because of the cancellation of the annual interstate carnival in 1937 due to the outbreak of infantile paralysis (polio) in the host city of Melbourne. During the visit Hull, who was president of the AAWBBA, extolled the virtues of the seven-a-side game and invited a team from NZ to take part in the interstate tournament the following year. As well as playing against the States, the team also played an all-Australian team in a seven-a-side match: Australia won its first game under 'international rules'. The final score of the match, 40–11, was apparently not indicative of the closeness of the play—it transpired that the NZ game used a larger goal-ring which was placed directly adjacent to the pole rather than six inches from it as in Australia. The international rules drawn up were a mixture of the NZ, Australian, and English codes of play. These 'new rules' were accepted by the AAWBBA and they urged the various State associations to adopt them.

The tour by NZ generated much enthusiasm in Australia for further international competition, and a reciprocal tour of NZ by Australia in 1940 was proposed. An Australian team was selected after the 1939 interstate carnival, but war intervened and it was not until 1948 that an Australian team first played netball abroad. The Australians won the three 'test' matches against a representative NZ team under seven-a-side rules, as well as all other matches played either under seven-a-side or nine-a-side rules. The players themselves financed most of the tour, bearing much of the cost of the playing and street uniforms, insurance coverage, and medical examination. The NZBBA arranged billeting, while the AAWBBA purchased the team ball and a minor part of the playing uniform!

Australia's first encounter against an England team did not occur until 1956 and followed correspondence between the AAWBBA and All England Netball Association (AENA), which included this note from AENA's president in April 1955:

> ... if some of your players could come here we will do our best to give them some matches, and entertain them in various parts of England. As you say, the rules of netball are not too much different from your B.B. rules and we probably could have a little time training your players so that matches could be played under AEA rules.

The Australian team spent many hours on board ship learning the 'new' game and after winning their first match in England a columnist in the *Evening News* wrote: 'Netball possesses no Ashes—yet! But I can't help remembering that we once taught the Australians how to play another ball game. And look what they did with it.' The outcome of matches on the tour was sixty-four wins and only three losses. The possibility of a 'conference to discuss a possible standardization of playing rules' arose from this tour and took place in England in 1957, resulting in the formation of the International Federation of Basketball and Netball Federations (now known as IFNA). This body met in Ceylon in 1960 and proposed that international netball tournaments would be held every four years, with the first to be in 1963. The standard of play of All Australia Netball teams has been such that Australia has secured the title of World Champions for six of the eight tournaments including the 1991 World Netball Championship held in Sydney.

Since its early beginnings at the turn of the century, netball has become the largest participant sport for girls and women in Australia. Netball is popular because it is simple to play; it can be played on any even surface (grass, bitumen, concrete, or wood) and at any age or skill level; it has a low fee structure and is organised by women for girls and women. Approximately four hundred thousand players are currently registered with AANA; when one includes school, church, tertiary, social, business institutions, and Combined Australian Netball Association (CANA) the number swells to more than seven hundred and fifty thousand. It has been estimated that seven out of fifteen females between the ages of 8 and 40 play netball.

Netball was a foundation sport of the AIS in Canberra in 1981 and is included in all State institutes of sport. A modified game for young players—Netta Netball—operates within the Aussie Sports Programme and is a popular activity which prepares players for school and club fixtures. The All Australia Netball Association has talent squad selection for under-17 and under-19 players as well as international opportunities for élite State players in various age groups. Netball was a demonstration sport at the XIVth Commonwealth Games in Auckland in 1990, where Australia won the competition, and has been approved as an optional sport for future Games. The Australian team was also victorious in the eighth World Netball Championship held in Sydney in 1991, beating NZ 53–52 in the final. Outstanding personalities in Australian netball have been Gwen Benzie, Eunice Gill, Joyce Brown, Wilma Shakespear, and Anne Sargeant.

IJ and PB

See **All Australia Netball Association**; **BARHAM, PAMELA; BENZIE, GWEN; BROWN, JOYCE; CALDOW, MARGARET; CLARK, ANN; FRANCOU, JULIE; GILL, EUNICE; HYLAND, DEIRDRE; McCONCHIE, LORNA; McHUGH, DOROTHY; McINTOSH, JILL; SARGEANT, ANNE; SHAKESPEAR, WILMA; SMITH, KAREN.**

NETTLEFOLD, LEN (1905–), born Hobart, was with the tragic genius Harry Williams one of Australia's two greatest left-handed golfers. Nettlefold established an amazing record. He was twice Australian amateur champion, in 1926 and 1928. He won the Tasmanian State title eight times, was runner-up in the Swiss Amateur event in 1927, and in that same year reached the quarterfinals of the prestigious British Amateur competition. He also won innumerable State and national men's and mixed foursomes titles. Later he was much involved in golf administration and captained the Australian team that went to Britain in 1938.

CT

NEWBIGGIN, BOB ('Newbo') (1921–), a noted surf swimmer, was also a fine still-water swimmer and when 15 was touted as a successor to 'Boy' Charlton. 'Newbo' grew up not far from the big and often unmanageable Newcastle surf. After winning the Australian junior 110 yards freestyle championship in 1937 he competed in the 1938 British Empire Games. From then on he concentrated almost entirely on surf swimming. As a member of Cooks Hill (Newcastle) Surf Lifesaving Club, he won the Australian junior belt and surf double in 1937 and 1938, repeating the feat in the seniors in 1940 and 1941. Newbiggin won a record five consecutive Australian senior surf race championships from 1939 to 1948. A noted big-surf swimmer, Newbiggin was a member of another four clubs: Manly, Nobbys, Ballina, and Tasmanian club Hobart-Carlton where he was the first captain and chief instructor. He was inducted into the Sport Australia Hall of Fame in 1985.

RC

NEWCOMBE, JOHN ('Newk') (1944–), tennis-player, born Sydney, won the last of the all-amateur Wimbledons. He proved his greatness with further Wimbledon titles in 1970 and 1971. In Australia one of his most courageous performances was his defeat of Jimmy Connors in the 1975 Australian Open final. 'Newk', with his Zapata moustache and broad mischievous grin, was a popular champion. He played a straight-ahead game with a powerful service and forehand. These strengths enabled Newcombe, with regular partner Tony Roche, to be one of the world's best doubles players. Upon retirement, with twenty-five Grand Slam titles, Newcombe gained a high profile in the media.

HCJP

See **Lawn Tennis**.

83 Track and field events for women were introduced at
the 1928 Olympic Games in Amsterdam. Edith Robinson
of NSW was the sole Australian female entrant in the
track events.

84 At the opening ceremony of the 1912 Olympic Games
in Stockholm the Australasian team included women for
the first time: swimmers Sarah 'Fanny' Durack and
Wilhelmina 'Mina' Wylie.

85 The Australian team for the 1920 Olympic Games at Antwerp. Back row: W. S. Herald, H. M. Hay, K. Kirkland, J. Stedman, R. V. Thomas, S. R. Parker, W. W. Hunt, F. Beaurepaire. Front row: J. King, G. Halpin, H. A. Bennett (Manager), L. Beaurepaire, T. S. Hewitt.

86 Members of Australia's water polo team at the London Olympic Games, 1948. Left to right: Colin French, Roger Cornforth, Arthur Burge, Les McKay, Jack Ferguson, Eric Johnston, Ben Dalley.

87 Competitors in the 1956 Olympic Games resided at the Athletes Village, which was built by the Victorian Housing Commission as part of its West Heidelberg Housing Estate.

88 The Olympic Organizing Committee for the 1956 Olympic Games vacillated over the site for the main stadium.

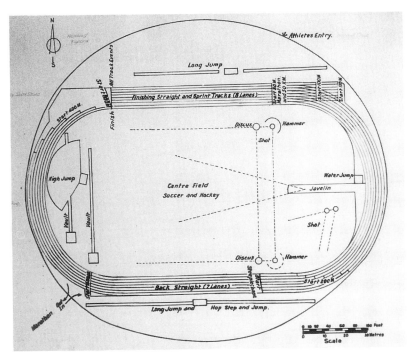

89 It was decided that the MCG would be the main stadium for the 1956 Olympic Games and plans were prepared for its renovation.

90 All was in readiness for the Opening Ceremony of the Games of the XVI Olympiad on 22 November 1956.

NEWMAN, KEVIN (1934–), born WA, began working in harness-racing stables at the age of 13. After three years he travelled to Sydney with trainer Stan Woodworth and a team of horses. The next year he joined Bill Picken's stable in Sydney's outer west and soon began to dabble in training horses for himself. Newman has been a force in Sydney harness racing ever since. He has been the leading driver at Harold Park on eight occasions and has won the trainer's premiership ten times. He has been associated with many top horses, the best being *Halwes*, the champion from Tasmania. Newman is a favourite with the Harold Park crowd, who cheer his victories and boo his failures in a manner which suggests that not only are they 'talking through their pockets' but also that they believe he is such a master horseman that any loss or any win is determined more by his driving than by the ability of the horse.

JO'H

NEWTON, JACK (1950–), born Cessnock, NSW, had his golf career cut short by an accident when he stepped into an aircraft propeller. Excelling in many sports, he played his first round of golf at 11 and won the NSW schoolboys' championship in three consecutive years. After winning thirty amateur tournaments and the Australian amateur foursomes with Barry Burgess he turned professional. Returning to golf after two years of national service, Newton shot a 65 to lead the 1975 British Open but was beaten in a play-off by Tom Watson. He had five birdies in his first six holes of the 1980 US Open but finished second to Seve Ballesteros. His more notable successes include the 1972 Dutch Open, the 1974 Nigerian Open and British match-play championship, and the 1978 Buick Open. Later Newton became an outstanding golf commentator.

GC*

NICHOLLS, Sir DOUGLAS, KCVO, OBE, KSEJ (1906–88), an Australian rules footballer and sprinter, was born at the Cumeroogunga Aboriginal Mission Station in NSW. After playing country football for Tongala he joined the Carlton pre-season training in 1927. Rejected by this VFL club, possibly because of racial hostility, he joined Northcote in the VFA, becoming a star wingman. During five years at Northcote he played in two premiership sides and represented the VFA against the VFL. At this time he had a stint of boxing in Jimmy Sharman's tents. Nicholls played for Fitzroy from 1932 to 1937, receiving various club awards. He represented Victoria against WA at Perth in 1935, returning to Northcote for the final years of his football career. Nicholls was also a professional runner, winning the Nyah Gift and the Warracknabeal Gift in 1929. He later became a pastor of the Churches of Christ

Aborigines Mission and co-director of the Aborigines' Advancement League of Victoria. He was knighted in 1972 and became Governor of SA in 1976, resigning the following year because of ill-health.

DN

See **Aboriginal Sports Foundation**; **Aborigines in Sport**; SHARMAN, JIMMY.

NICHOLS, KEVIN (1956–) represented Australia as an amateur track cyclist at three Olympic and three Commonwealth Games between 1974 and 1984, winning four gold medals and one silver. He was a gold-medallist in the 4000 metres pursuit team at Los Angeles in 1984, along with Michael Grenda, Michael Turtur, and Dean Woods. He also won a gold medal in the teams pursuit at the 1978 Commonwealth Games in Edmonton, Canada, and in the teams pursuit and 10 miles track events at the 1982 Brisbane Commonwealth Games. After early successes, including Australian titles over 8 kilometres as a junior in 1973 and 20 kilometres as a senior rider in 1975 and 1976, Nichols abandoned an economics degree at Sydney University to concentrate on cycling. A member of the St George club in Sydney, the affable Nichols supported himself by working as a computer systems analyst and adopted an unorthodox training regimen which included riding 60 kilometres a day to work and training on an ordinary exercise bike. After returning from Los Angeles, Nichols briefly tried road racing before retiring from competitive cycling in 1988.

JS

NILAN, PATRICK JOSEPH (1941–), hockey-player, was born at Darlington, Sydney. Playing at inside left, his exceptionally high work rate and brilliant passes in mid-field created countless goal-scoring opportunities and made him an indispensable member of Australian hockey teams. Between 1964 and 1972 he played sixty-four Tests and twenty-two first-class games for Australia (including three Olympics). At the 1964 and 1968 Olympics, Nilan played a prominent role in his country's bronze and silver medal successes. He appeared sixty-five times for NSW seniors, twenty-nine of these as captain, and in the Sydney competition he was a vital cog in the Glebe first-grade side between 1959 and 1978, playing 391 first-grade games for the club and captaining it for twelve seasons.

MS

NOBLE, MONTAGUE ALFRED (1873–1940) was a consummate cricket all-rounder who scored 1997 runs and took 121 wickets in forty-two Tests, reaching the double of 1000 runs and 100 wickets in only twenty-seven Tests. Born in Dixon Street, now Sydney's

Chinatown, Monty Noble learned to play cricket in the streets of Paddington with his seven older brothers. A large man, 185 centimetres tall and weighing 83 kilograms, he had sizeable feet and his specially made boots attracted the notice of cartoonists. He was a very useful cricketer who could bowl a mixture of spin and swerve and medium pace, securing 32 wickets in the 1901–2 series against England including 7–17 and 6–60 in a Melbourne Test. Noble was a hard-hitting bat who could also stonewall when required. He toured England on four occasions between 1899 and 1909 and also visited NZ twice and South Africa once. He was a shrewd captain and firm disciplinarian who led Australia in fifteen Tests, winning eight. After retirement he contributed to cricket off the field; his prestige was such that at one time he was sole selector for NSW. He wrote a number of highly regarded books and also was involved in the synthetic cricket broadcasts. He was the driving force behind the erection of a new stand at the SCG which was later named after him.

RC

See **Cricket; Sydney Cricket Ground**.

NORMAN, DECIMA, MBE (1909–83), born West Perth and small in stature, won the WA sprint title in 1925. She was overlooked for the 1936 Olympics, despite times superior to most other athletes, because her State did not have an official athletics association. After a WA body was formed in 1937, she was selected for the 1938 British Empire Games in Sydney where she won a record five events: the 100 and 220 yards, the long jump, and as a member of the 440 and 660 yards relays. Such was her success in 1938 that Norman moved to Sydney to prepare for the 1940 Olympics, which were never held. After retirement she actively campaigned for sport in WA and was awarded the MBE for her services to sport.

JAD

NORMAN, GREGORY (1955–), born Mount Isa, Queensland, did not take up golf until the age of 15. After a brief stint at Beverley Park, Sydney, he joined the Royal Brisbane Golf Club and was coached by Charlie Earp. He finished third in his first PGA tournament and then beat a strong field in the 1976 West Lakes Classic which earned him selection in Australia's World Cup team at Palm Springs. Norman embarked on the world circuit, playing his first US Open in 1979. Victory in the 1980 Australian Open earned him an invitation to the US Masters. In his first full season on the American circuit in 1984 he pocketed $300,000, with two victories. Norman won the 1986 British Open, dispelling stories about his big-match temperament. Although he has won more than fifty victories world-wide and is a millionaire many times over, Norman still has his critics.

He is, however, one of the most sought-after professionals, often commanding an appearance fee of $250,000. A personable and popular champion, the 'Great White Shark', with his white mane and ready smile, offered his services free of charge to promote Australian tourism.

GC*

See **Golf**.

NORMAN, PETER (1942–), a Melbourne schoolteacher and Salvation Army officer, was a runner who won a silver medal at the 1968 Mexico Olympics in the 200 metres, equalling the world record of 20 seconds flat. His picture on the victory dais gained maximum publicity because the two Americans, Tommy Smith and John Carlos, gave the Black Power salute. Norman, who wore a peace and unity badge on his tracksuit top, appeared to support the protest. Although he was an asthmatic and a slow starter, he won the Australian 200 metres title in 1966, the first of five successive titles. Neville Sillitoe, his coach and mentor, played an important role in his success.

RC

NORTHAM, Sir WILLIAM, CBE (1905–), born Torquay, England, was an Olympic yachtsman. He came to Australia when he was 7. A resourceful and hard-working man, he rose from humble beginnings as an apprentice engineer with Sydney Ferries to become managing director of Johnson & Johnson, and he was a Sydney City Council alderman for nine years. During this time he dabbled in many sports including football, gymnastics, golf, motorcycle-racing, and car-racing, and he competed in three Grand Prix races at Phillip Island. He took up sailing at the late age of 46, bought the 8 metre yacht *Saskia* in England and won the prestigious Sayonara Cup in 1955 and 1956. He then had many successes in *Caprice of Huon* and the Sabre-class *Jazzer*. He competed in two Sydney to Hobart races, his boat finishing third in 1958. In 1963 he commissioned *Barrenjoey* to be built in a bid to win at Tokyo and won the Australian championship the same year. With his crew of Dick Sargeant and Peter O'Donnell, Northam won the first heat of the 5.5 metre class at the 1964 Olympics and retained the lead to secure a gold medal at the age of 59. He was a grandfather of five and the oldest Australian to win an Olympic event. The CBE was awarded to him in 1966 and he was knighted in 1976. He was inducted into the Sport Australia Hall of Fame in 1985.

RC

NUNN, GLYNIS (née SAUNDERS) (1960–), born Toowoomba, Queensland, began competing as a heptathlete at the age of 9. She was successful in a wide range of events by her early teens. Her parents drove her regularly 130 kilometres to train and compete. When she was 15 she won six events in the State championships, setting records in five. While still a junior, Nunn was selected for the 1977 Dusseldorf World Cup and the 1978 Commonwealth Games. After missing the 1980 Moscow Olympic Games she transferred to Adelaide where she developed a close working relationship with the national athletic coach, John Daly. Nunn won the gold medal for heptathlon at the 1982 Commonwealth Games and the 1984 Los Angeles Olympic Games. After watching her battle for Olympic success over two tense days of competition, Australians had a greater appreciation of this event. A year or two earlier Nunn had fun with a raw journalist, informing him that the heptathlon was a seven-sided implement which she threw.

JAD

See **Athletics.**

O

Oakbank. The premier picnic race meeting in Australia is held every Easter at Oakbank in the Adelaide Hills. It centres around the Great Eastern Steeplechase, first run in 1877, the year following the inauguration of the Oakbank event. The establishment of the meeting as part of both the SA social and racing calendars owes much to the entrepreneurial vigour of Alfred von Doussa, foundation secretary of the Onkaparinga Racing Club.

WV

O'BRIEN, IAN LOVETT (1947–) came from Wellington, NSW, and learned to swim in the local non-filtered pool. The turning point in his career occurred when he came under the tutelage of former breast-stroke champion Terry Gathercole. O'Brien's career spanned two Olympic Games: he won a gold medal at Tokyo in 1964 in the 200 metres breast-stroke and a bronze medal in the 4 × 100 metres medley relay. At the Perth British Empire and Commonwealth Games in 1962, when only 15, he won three gold medals (110 and 220 yards breast-stroke and 4 × 100 yards medley relay), and four years later, at the Kingston Games, he swam to two more victories (110 and 220 yards breast-stroke). After winning fifteen Australian championships he retired when only 21 years of age.

RH and MH

O'DONNELL, PETER JOSEPH PATRICK ('Pod') (1939–), a remarkably versatile yachtsman, was successful in many events. He won the world championships in the Etchell (1980) and 5.5 metre (1970) classes, the Sydney to Hobart ocean race twice, the Australian Staff Class Championship, and an Olympic gold medal in the 1964 Games in the 5.5 metre class with William Northam and James Sargeant. He has also sailed in an *America*'s Cup Challenge and a US Admiral's Cup team. O'Donnell joined the Middle Harbour Yacht Club at the age of 16 and competed regularly on Saturday afternoons. At 19 he was a crew member on *Siandra* which won the Sydney to Hobart race and he was a forward hand on *Gretel* in her challenge for the *America*'s Cup. Selected for the 1964 Olympics, O'Donnell played an important role in the victory of *Barrenjoey*. While Northam was the helmsman and Sargeant the forward hand, O'Donnell was the tactician who drew on his wide experience of ocean racing.

RH and MH

O'DONNELL, PHYLLIS (1937–), born NSW, began surfing with friends on the weekends while living in Sydney. On moving to the Gold Coast she developed her surfing ability and won the women's title at the Australian invitational competition held at Bondi in 1963. She won the 1964 Australian Championships and went on to win the first Women's World Championship held at Manly Beach in the same year. In 1965 she again won the Australian women's title. Between 1964 and 1973 she was the Queensland women's champion eight times. She represented Australia and defended her world title at competitions in California and Hawaii. She has written a surfing column for newspapers and has contributed sponsorship and trophies to encourage surfing in the 1990s.

MV

O'HARA WOOD, JOHN JAMES, born Melbourne, was an Australian tennis enthusiast and barrister. Early twentieth-century tennis writers nominated O'Hara Wood as the founder of the game in Australia though his son Pat has questioned this. O'Hara Wood Senior was undoubtedly a keen player and was reported to have made use of the 'first batch of tennis implements'. He also encouraged his sons to take up the game. Arthur, his eldest, became a prominent club and university player and won the 1914 Australasian men's singles title. Pat (Hector), his younger son, became an international tennis champion in the 1920s, winning many titles in Davis Cup, Wimbledon, and Australian tennis.

VO'F

See **Lawn Tennis**.

OLDFIELD, WILLIAM ALBERT STANLEY, MBE (1894–1976), born Alexandria, Sydney, played in every cricket Test series from 1920–21 to 1936–37. A short, dapper man who was punctilious in his preparation, he was known as the 'gentleman in gloves' because his appeals were modest and were made only when he believed a batsman was out. He stumped fifty-two of the one hundred and thirty batsmen he dismissed in fifty-four Tests, an international record for the number of stumpings and their proportion to catches. His most celebrated stumping was achieved off fast-medium bowler Jack Ryder in 1925 when he brilliantly dismissed Hobbs down the leg-side. Oldfield was later a successful businessman; his sports store, W. A. Oldfield Pty Ltd, was opened in

1922. He served in both World Wars and played with the AIF cricket team in 1919. He was awarded the MBE in 1970.

RC

Olympic Bids by Australian Cities

The city of Sydney is bidding for the summer Olympic Games of the year 2000, following Melbourne, which was one of six cities contending for the privilege of hosting the 1996 Olympics, and Brisbane, which was third in its quest to host the largest and most significant multi-nation, multi-sport festival in the world—the 1992 Summer Olympic Games, held in Barcelona.

It is not only in recent years that Australian cities have put forward a proposal or bid. It was mooted in 1912 that Perth should host the 1916 Olympic Games. This celebration would have coincided with the opening of the transcontinental railway. When the advocates for Perth were reminded that Berlin had already been allocated the Olympics for 1916, there was a suggestion that Perth should transfer its efforts to the VIIth Olympiad of 1920. The expected completion date for the erection of the Sydney Harbour Bridge was to have been 1930 which, it was suggested, would provide an excellent opportunity to invite the world to that city for the Olympics. Of course, the celebration of the Olympiad did not fall in that year. It is a pity that it could not have been foreseen that the completion of the bridge was to be delayed until 1932, but by then the idea had been forgotten and the Olympics were granted to Los Angeles.

Arguments in support of Melbourne's bid to host the 1956 Olympic Games included the following: that Australia was one of only four nations to be at every summer Olympics and because of that it was far more senior in the Olympic movement than any other competitor in the southern hemisphere; that there was a concept of the Olympics being a 'world' games and that with the development of pressurised aircraft it would take at most thirty hours to reach Melbourne, a time lag comparable to any of the potential venues, which included Buenos Aires, Detroit, Los Angeles, Mexico City, and London. The decision in April 1954 was reached after the fourth ballot in which Melbourne received 21 votes to Buenos Aires' 20.

The bid for the 1972 Olympic Games was an interesting one because, even by May 1965, it seems that no other nation had indicated a desire to stage the Games. International politics was important at the time because at a meeting of international sports federations it was decided that the country staging the 1972 Olympic Games must issue visas to all athletes entitled to compete; it was felt that this ruling automatically eliminated NATO countries as possible contenders because they would not issue visas

to East Germans. Sydney mounted a campaign and even Avery Brundage, president of the International Olympic Committee, was receptive to the idea, telling the press 'Sydney can do it', but financial support was not forthcoming.

Sydney started as early as 1971 in its proposal to host the 1988 Olympics, but the movement lost momentum. A proposal for Melbourne to host the 1988 Games was endorsed by the Australian Olympic Federation; an Australian delegation presented Melbourne's case to the General Association of International Sports Federations in Monaco in October 1980, but the next stage, the trip to Lausanne, was thwarted because the Federal Treasurer, John Howard, announced in February that the necessary funds would not be forthcoming.

Reference has already been made to the Brisbane bid for the 1992 Olympic Games. The euphoria of the 1982 Commonwealth Games was the catalyst for this proposal. The bid was unsuccessful, but Brisbane's efforts rekindled the interest in the bigger southern cities of Melbourne and Sydney and stimulated them into action. The Melbourne bid for 1996 was regarded as being outstanding; Sydney should benefit from the bids for 1992 and 1996 and the harbour city will be a worthy contender for the year 2000.

IJ

See **Olympic Games 1956 (Melbourne)**; **Olympic Games**.

Olympic Games

In the many writings on Baron Pierre de Coubertin and the modern Olympic Games there have been various interpretations of the historical beginnings of what has become the world's foremost multi-sport, multi-nation event. De Coubertin, a French nobleman, was concerned about the level of fitness and health of the youth of France in the late nineteenth century. Following several visits to England, de Coubertin's opinion of 'sport education' which he had seen at British public schools became evident when he wrote an article in 1887 entitled 'L'Éducation Anglaise'. He stated that sport was the inner engine of the system because 'it reacts upon the whole . . . [Its role] is at once physical, moral and social.' With the publishing of this article de Coubertin began his campaign to bring to France what he took to be the legacy of Thomas Arnold, the headmaster of Rugby School—'la pédagogie sportive' or athletic education.

The argument about the extent of Arnold's influence on the relationship between sport and character development through the British public school system will not be pursued here. It is necessary only to establish that de Coubertin, less than a decade before the revival of the Olympic Games, was most impressed by a system of education in which he perceived that competitive sport was paramount in influencing positive character traits and physical prowess in youth. Although impressed by British 'sport education', de Coubertin was also sensitive to the fact that it would be difficult to persuade French educational authorities to whole-heartedly and dispassionately accept a system of education which came from across a channel of water which had divided the two countries physically and culturally for centuries. Fortunately, since the middle of the nineteenth century much of the Western world had been stimulated to excitement about the way of life in ancient Greece. There was particular interest in Olympia, the site of the ancient Olympic Games, following archaeological discoveries in the mid-1870s. De Coubertin was fascinated and impassioned by these recent discoveries because he was able to interpret the ideals and objectives of the ancient Olympic Games so as to inculcate the values of 'athleticism' which he had perceived in British education. He formulated and utilised these notions in his scheme to establish the modern Olympic Games.

De Coubertin valued sport and in particular the 'love of sport'. Of course, in his day the true lover of sport was the 'amateur', a term which is no longer in the Olympic charter but which was significantly a class-based issue in the late nineteenth and early twentieth centuries. Artisans and manual labourers were ineligible to compete as amateurs, and indeed some of the rules of amateur sports associations were devised to preserve upper-class traditions. Interestingly the International Athletic Congress at the Sorbonne in Paris in 1894 was called ostensibly to discuss matters of amateurism and professionalism, but de Coubertin arranged the agenda so that the Congress broke into two sections, one of which discussed the revival of the Olympic Games within the framework of 'advantages from the athletic, moral and international standpoints'. The International Olympic Committee (IOC) was established at that Congress and it was decided that the Olympic Games would be revived as an international amateur sports festival. Although it was originally felt that the inaugural Games would be held in Paris in 1900, the enthusiasm was such that Athens hosted them four years earlier in 1896. Over three hundred athletes from thirteen nations assembled in the renovated marble stadium in central Athens to take part in a great sports festival.

The International Congress in Paris in 1894 entrusted the IOC with the task of developing the Olympic Games and it had three responsibilities, as expressed in the prose of the era: the regular celebration of the Games; making the Games increasingly perfect, more and more worthy of their glorious past and in keeping with the high ideals that inspired those who revived them; and encouragement of the organisation of all events and, in general, the taking of all steps likely to lead to modern athletics along the right lines. One may ask whether these aims are being fulfilled as we approach the centenary of their revival. The Summer Games of the XXVIth Olympiad in Barcelona in 1992 provide a reference point for reflection. It has always been the hope and desire that both the Summer and Winter Olympic Games, which are the primary and paramount festivals of the Olympic Movement (as distinct from World Olympic Day, the IOC Congress, the IOC-sponsored regional games, etc.), would influence the values of modern society. Certainly, the reverse has occurred and the Olympic Games have come to reflect our society. But this merely provides the challenge for those who would preserve sport and its Olympic ideals.

In the early 1890s, many sport administrators in Australia were more interested in the proposals for a Pan-Britannic sports festival which preceded the notion of Pierre de Coubertin to revive the Olympic Games. However, the success of a sole Melbourne athlete, Edwin Flack, at these first Olympic Games in 1896 established the history and tradition of Australia and the Olympic movement. For his wins he received laurel wreaths, the tradition of the Olympic Games of ancient Greece, and silver medals, because the tradition of gold medals had not been established.

The Olympic Games of 1900 and 1904 were held in association with world expositions in Paris and St Louis respectively. Much of the significance of the Olympic Games was lost and some events were little more than sideshows, but Australians were there, including swimming champion Freddie Lane who won a gold medal in the 200 metres freestyle, swum in the River Seine. Australia and NZ competed as 'Australasia' in 1908 and 1912 and a strong team gathered in London for the Games of the IVth Olympiad, which were again held in conjunction with a world exhibition. The successful Australian touring rugby union team defeated the only other entrant in this event to win a gold medal and it was at these Olympics that a young 17-year-old lad from Melbourne, Frank Beaurepaire, won a silver medal in swimming. Beaurepaire also won medals at the 1920 and 1924 Olympic Games and later, as a city councillor and knight of the realm, he was instrumental in Melbourne gaining the right to host the Olympic Games in 1956. Swimming events for women were introduced at the Stockholm Olympics of 1912 and Australia's first female Olympic competitors, Fanny Durack and Mina Wylie, won gold and silver respectively in the 100 metres freestyle. This helped resolve the contentious issue of mixed bathing in Australia.

War intervened and the next Games were held in 1920 in Antwerp. Australia's strength in aquatic sports was most evident during the next few Olympic Games, with gold medals being won by Dick Eve for diving and Andrew 'Boy' Charlton in swimming in 1924, Bobby Pearce in rowing in 1928 and 1932, and Claire Dennis in swimming in 1932. The first Australian gold-medallist in a field event was Anthony Winter who won the hop, step, and jump (now known as the triple jump) in Paris in 1924. It was in Amsterdam in 1928 that Duncan Gray became the first of many Australian gold-medal-winning cyclists. Track and field events for women were introduced at these Olympics; Australia's sole competitor was Edith Robinson, a sprinter who also ran in the infamous 800 metres event which led to such distance events being regarded as unsuitable for women.

The post–Second World War period was the beginning of the golden age of Australian sport culminating in the glorious decade of the 1950s, in the middle of which were the magnificent Melbourne Olympic Games. Olympic gold-medallists over these years became household names and included Marjorie Jackson, Russell Mockridge, Lorraine Crapp, Jon Henricks, Betty Cuthbert, Murray Rose, David Theile, Shirley Strickland, Herb Elliott, John Devitt, Dawn Fraser, and John Konrads.

The kindling of the Olympic flame at the Melbourne Cricket Ground on 22 November 1956 signalled the opening of the first Olympic Games in the southern hemisphere, the right to host the games having been won by only one vote. Like Flack sixty years previously, distance runners were evident on that opening day of the Games: the young Ron Clarke, later to become holder of several world records over distances from 1500 metres to 6 miles, carried the Olympic torch into the stadium and lit the Olympic flame. The then world-record holder for the mile, John Landy, regarded by many as the epitome of sportsmanship, delivered the Olympic oath on behalf of the athletes, and the Games began. The two weeks from 22 November until 8 December resulted in the Melbourne Olympics being revered and remembered as the 'Friendly Games'. One of the reasons was because of the implementation of the idea of John Ian Wing, an apprentice carpenter from Melbourne. This teenager wrote a letter to the Games organisers suggesting that on the final day the Olympic competitors should enter the stadium, not as nations, but mingled together in a bond of Olympic harmony. Wing wrote, '. . . no team is to keep together . . . they must be spread out evenly, and THEY MUST NOT MARCH but walk freely and wave to the public'. This emotional closing ceremony is now an Olympic tradition.

Since those halcyon days of 1956 Australia has maintained a successful Olympic involvement and profile. Australia was there when Herb Elliot dominated the 1500 metres in Rome in 1960; when Ron Clarke collapsed after his courageous effort in the rarefied atmosphere of Mexico City in 1968; when John Carlos and Tommie Smith of the US Olympic team gave the black power salute while standing on the dais with Australian silver-medallist Peter Norman; when Shane Gould won five medals in 1972 in Munich; and in Seoul in 1988 when, although canoeist Grant Davies' name flashed up on the scoreboard as the winner, he was later told there had been a timing error and he won the silver medal by the shortest official margin and said 'if that's the biggest disappointment in life, then I have no problems . . . the other bloke won it fair and square, so what can you say?'

Australia has also been there with its contribution to the Olympic Movement. Richard Coombes was the first Australian to be a member of the IOC; current members are Phil Coles and Kevan Gosper, the latter being the first Australian to be appointed to the position of vice-president. The 'People of Australia' were awarded the 1988 Olympic Cup by IOC president Juan Antonio Samaranch, who said that the award marked the importance of sport in the Australian lifestyle and the country's strong commitment to the Olympic movement since its participation in the first Olympic Games of 1896. Indeed, Australia is one of only three countries to have competed at all Summer Olympic Games. The Winter Olympics commenced in 1924; Australians have competed since 1936. It is a great history and tradition of involvement.

IJ

See **Australian Olympic Committee**; FLACK, EDWIN; **Olympic Bids by Australian Cities**; **Olympic Games 1956 (Melbourne)**.

Olympic Games 1956 (Melbourne)
It was only one year after the cessation of Second World War hostilities that a group of Victorians banded together to attract the 1956 Olympic Games to Melbourne. Sir Frank Beaurepaire, the great swimmer of the 1908, 1920, and 1924 Olympic Games, was reported as stating that Melbourne should have a sporting stadium with 'all facilities for holding the Olympic Games in Australia'. One would have thought that the magnificent Melbourne Cricket Ground (MCG) would have been a singular choice for the main venue, but this was not an automatic selection. In fact, the Olympic Organizing Committee vacillated over the site for the main stadium (Olympic Park, Princes Park, the Showgrounds, and the MCG) and even the president of the International Olympic Committee expressed concern over the lack of progress.

At 3.30 p.m. on 22 November 1956, however, athletes from Greece entered the stadium to the cheers of over a hundred thousand spectators. They were the first of sixty-seven nations; the Australian team, as hosts, entered last behind the flag-bearer, rower Mervyn Wood. Junior mile record-holder Ron Clarke was the final torch-bearer of the Olympic Flame, which had been lit 13 000 miles away in Olympia, Greece. The first relay runner on the host nation's soil was an Australian-born Greek, who passed it on to an Australian Aborigine. The Gas and Fuel Corporation of Victoria had built the giant cauldron which kindled the flame for the duration of the Games. Following the rendition of the Hallelujah Chorus by the choir to the accompaniment of the RAAF band, the flag-bearers of all the nations formed a semicircle on either side of the rostrum and John Landy pronounced the Olympic Oath. Many thousands who had purchased the *Official Programme of the Opening Ceremony* for two shillings had difficulty following the great miler's version because he had been supplied with a different one from that printed in the programme.

Athletes had travelled to the stadium from the athletes' village which comprised 365 houses built by the Victorian Housing Commission at West Heidelberg. There was no way the hotels and boarding houses could accommodate the visiting spectators from interstate and overseas, so Melburnians responded to the plea by the Civic Committee to open their homes and the billeting scheme became a popular and memorable part of the Games. For those who could not be there, live and recorded coverage was available on radio and the newly installed television. One disappointment was that the Organizing Committee defined the Games as entertainment rather than news. This set a precedent of 'ownership' of broadcasts and the committee refused to provide free television coverage, thereby limiting the extent of world-wide viewing.

The venues and sports were: Main Stadium (MCG)—Opening Ceremony, athletics, football (soccer), hockey (finals), demonstration sport (Australian rules football), and Closing Ceremony; Olympic Park—cycling, football, hockey, and swimming; Exhibition Building—wrestling, weightlifting, modern pentathlon, fencing, and basketball; West Melbourne Stadium—boxing and gymnastics; St Kilda Town Hall—fencing; Williamstown—shooting; RAAF Station, Laverton—clay pigeon-shooting; Port Phillip Bay—yachting; Broadmeadows—cycling road race; Oaklands—modern pentathlon (riding); Lake Wendouree, Ballarat—rowing and canoeing.

Australian athletes won a total of thirteen gold medals, their best-ever performance; swimmers Lorraine Crapp, John Devitt, Dawn Fraser, Jon Henricks, Faith Leech, Murray Rose, Sandra Morgan, Kevin O'Halloran, and David Theile won eight of them. Track stars Norma Croker, Betty Cuthbert, Fleur Mellor, and Shirley Strickland and the 2000 metres tandem cyclists, Ian Browne and Tony Marchant, gained the rest. For many Australians, however, the 1956 Olympic Games was an opportunity to really comprehend the dictum, 'It's not the winning but the taking part'; it was great to have 'been there' and it is hoped that there will not be too many more Olympiads before an Australian city hosts another 'Friendly Games'.

IJ

See **BEAUREPAIRE, FRANK**; **Melbourne Cricket Ground**; **Olympic Games**; **Olympic Bids by Australian Cities**.

Olympic Handball

Also known as team or European handball, this game, played on an indoor court, calls for one goalkeeper and six field players per team who attempt to score by throwing the ball into the opponent's goal. The NSW Handball Association was formed in 1979, and governing bodies followed in Queensland (1982), Victoria (1984), and SA (1986). The Australian Handball Federation was created in 1985, the year national championships for senior State men's teams were inaugurated. Olympic handball remains a minority sport in Australia.

KM

ONDIEKI, LISA (formerly MARTIN, née O'DEA) (1960–), born Gawler, SA, started her athletics career as a hurdler before switching to cross-country and marathons. The winner of back-to-back Commonwealth Games gold medals in 1986 and 1990, Ondieki began her marathon career with a win at Huntsville, Alabama, in 1983; she won at Canberra in 1984 before finishing seventh at the 1984 Olympic Games. She ran second to her arch-rival, Greta Waitz, in the prestigious 1985 and 1986 New York marathons but won at Pittsburgh in 1985, Edinburgh in 1986, and Osaka in 1987. After failing to finish in the World Cup at Seoul in 1987, the year she suffered from glandular fever, Ondieki defended her Osaka title in 1988 with a run of 2 hours 23 minutes 51 seconds, a time which still heads the Australian all-time list. She finished second behind Rosa Mota at the 1988 Olympic Games. After winning seven and coming second four times in thirteen marathons from 1983 to 1988, she was ranked second in the world by *Track and Field News*. She took time out in 1990 to marry Kenyan runner Yobes Ondieki and started a family before resuming training and winning the 1991 Australian 15 kilometres road-running championship. A hip injury forced her to withdraw from the 1991 World Championships in Japan.

GC†

OPPERMAN, Sir HUBERT FERDINAND (1904–　) was born in Rochester, Victoria. His seemingly endless stamina and thirst for fitness reaped early rewards when, by 20 years of age, he was Australian road-cycling champion. He retained the title in 1924, 1926, 1927 and 1929 and created many world records ranging from 849 to 1000 miles. By 1928 he had won the French Bol d'Or, a tandem paced event. In 1931 he captained Australia's Tour de France team for the fourth time, won the world's longest non-stop road race, and was crowned sportsman of the year by the French newspaper *Auto*. Opperman served in the RAAF in the Second World War. He was a member of Federal Parliament from 1949 to 1967, becoming Minister of Shipping and Transport (1960–63) and of Immigration (1963–66) in the Menzies Government. He was High Commissioner to Malta from 1967 to 1972 and was knighted in 1968.

CJF

O'REILLY, WILLIAM JOSEPH ('Tiger'), OBE (1905–　) was a 190 centimetre-tall loose-limbed cricketer of Irish descent who was the finest exponent of right-arm leg-spin bowling in cricket history. His antipathy towards batsmen earned him the nickname 'Tiger'. O'Reilly bowled at a speed approaching medium and presented many problems, with subtle variations in pace and length and a virtually undetectable sharply bouncing 'bosie'. Off a 13-pace run he lumbered in, right arm swinging through a wide arc, left hand clawing at the air, face distorted equally with strain and venom. Many regard him among the best three bowlers of all time. Country-born, O'Reilly's early cricketing career was interrupted by teaching duties away from Sydney. Returning to the city, he was selected for the last two Tests against the 1931–32 visiting South Africans. In nineteen Tests over four series against England he secured 102 wickets, exceeding 20 wickets in each series. He took 144 wickets in twenty-seven Tests at 22.95 and 774 wickets in all first-class games at a cost of 16.60. Despite heavy workloads, he was remarkably free from injury and his stamina and nagging accuracy kept his per-over cost in Test runs at just above 2. Batsmen who survived for significant periods felt drained from the concentration required. Aggressive, forthright, erudite, gregarious, and perceptive, he contributed further as a journalist and writer and had a successful commercial career.

JMcH
See **Cricket**.

Orienteering
The first formal Australian orienteering event was held in 1969 at Beaconsfield near Melbourne. Before this, mountaineering and bush-walking clubs had organised orienteering events in Australia as early as 1955. SA orienteers formed an association in 1957 but it was soon abandoned. In 1965, Paddy Pallin started an annual competition in NSW which was a long trek through the bush in search of control points, often located under old buckets. This contest lasted much longer than the orienteering event, the course taking several hours to complete. The competitors dressed in bush-walking gear and did not run between control points. These contests were important precursors to the permanent establishment of pure orienteering in Australia.

The man principally responsible for the beginning of true orienteering on a permanent, continuing basis was Tom Andrews. In June 1969, during a trip to Scandinavia, he was taken to the Swedish orienteering championships by Alvar Kjellstrom, the owner of Silva Compasses, who had helped to develop the sport there forty years earlier. Upon his return to Melbourne, he decided to hold an orienteering meeting at Beaconsfield and to encourage both bushwalkers and cross-country runners to participate.

Before 1970 Victoria was the only State conducting orienteering competitions in Australia. On 21 April 1970, at the same meeting which constituted the Victorian Orienteering Association, the Orientation Federation of Australia (OFA) was formed. The growth of the OFA generally followed the spread of orienteering throughout Australia and the establishment of State associations, which were formed as follows: the ACT in 1971; NSW in 1972; Tasmania in 1973; WA and Queensland in 1974; and SA in 1975. Early in 1972 the OFA joined the International Orienteering Federation, its initial membership fee being paid by Bjorn Kjellstrom. The first international competition was against NZ in 1971 and the inaugural interstate competition was held in 1972. By 1985, Australia staged the world championships at Bendigo, followed by the Asia-Pacific championships at St Helens, Tasmania, in 1988.

Orienteering has proved to be not merely a temporary diversion from track running or bushwalking but has developed into a skilled sport with a devoted core of élite enthusiasts and a large group of casual but continuing participants. Orienteering map-making has evolved into a skilled art form and for some a source of livelihood. Course-setting and event organisation has developed to a high level with the increased number of top-class competitions in Australia.

TD, DH*, and IJ
See **PALLIN, FRANK**.

P

PAGE, PERCY PEMBROKE (1889–1986) was an innovative sport administrator in Australian rules football. Page was secretary first of Richmond Football Club (1924–32) when that club played in five final series, winning the VFL premiership in 1932; then at Melbourne Football Club during its years of revival which culminated in a hat-trick of premierships (1939–41). A delegate to the VFL, he helped introduce the McIntyre-Page system of playing finals matches. He also helped persuade the VFL to publish its own *Football Record*. In addition he made outstanding contributions to St Vincent's Hospital and the Olympic Park Trust.

CH*

Paleface Adios (1969–?) captured the imagination of the Australian trotting public with his distinctive straight-legged action and harness-racing records. In 1973 he became the first 3-year-old in Australasia to run under 2 minutes in winning the Simpson Sprint at Harold Park in 1 minute 59 seconds. Two years later *Paleface Adios* ran a time trial in 1 minute 57.6 seconds, creating a Queensland mile record. He won the inaugural Grand Circuit Champion award which was decided on a points system over eight major races across Australia. *Paleface Adios* won eight out of ten Interdominion heats but was unable to win any of the four finals contested. In achieving his one hundredth win in 1980 he set a record both for thoroughbred and standard-bred horses. By the time he retired, in his eleventh year, he had secured one hundred and eight wins, forty-three seconds, and twenty-five thirds from two hundred and thirty-nine starts for total prize-money of $535 640.

GC*

PALLIN, FRANK AUSTIN ('Paddy') (1900–91), born England, emigrated to Australia in 1927. By 1930 he had opened the first of his outdoor shops in Australia selling imported camping and hiking equipment. He also began publishing a series of books on bushwalking. By the mid-1930s he had begun to manufacture bushwalking gear in Australia because of the unavailability of quality products. During the Second World War, he manufactured army clothing and camping material. Pallin's business interests evolved from his lifelong involvement in outdoor recreation. He initiated, in 1956, the Paddy Pallin Classic cross-country ski race. He himself learned to ski competitively in 1957 at the age of 57, only ceasing to ski at 88. In the mid-1960s he played a key role in establishing orienteering in Australia. Pallin celebrated his ninetieth birthday in 1990. His sixty years of promotion of outdoor activities is without parallel.

TD

See **Bushwalking**; **Orienteering**.

PALMER, AMBROSE (1910–), born Footscray, Melbourne, was an Australian amateur boxing welterweight title-holder. In 1927 he turned professional, winning the Australian middleweight title in 1930, and the light-heavyweight and heavyweight titles in 1932. He retired in 1936 but made come-backs until 1938. Palmer was a conventional fighter but had a solid punch and fast reflexes. He fought sixty-seven times, winning fifty-eight, losing seven, and drawing two. Palmer cut a fine-looking, well-dressed figure and had the added glory of playing sixty matches for Footscray in the VFL. He later trained more than twenty Australian and Commonwealth champions, as well as Johnny Famechon, World Featherweight Boxing Champion in 1969.

HS

PALUBINSKAS, EDDIE (1950–) was a basketballer, in both Australia and the USA, with St Kilda, Ricks College and Louisiana State University (LSU). A forward, he was Australia's first internationally recognised basketball champion, being the second-highest points-scorer at the 1972 Olympics and the highest four years later; he also played in the 1974 world championships. After a successful college career at LSU, Palubinskas was drafted by both Atlanta (National Basketball Association) and Utah (American Basketball Association), but was never contracted. An exceptionally fit and speedy player, Palubinskas was renowned for his shooting, being described as 'one of the purest shooters the game has ever seen'. He lived in the USA after his retirement.

SB

Parachuting

The sport has a long history in Australia, where early enthusiasts jumped from balloons in the late nineteenth century; today, competitors leap from planes. The establishment of sport parachuting as a continuing activity and distinct from display jumping by professionals did not occur, however, until mid-1958. In June of that year, a former RAF parachute instructor announced that he would be forming a parachute club in Sydney. The first training day was held on 26 July at Bankstown airport and the first descents were at Camden airport on 2 August. Sport parachuting was introduced into Victoria with the formation of the McKenzie Flying School's Parachute Wing, with the first jump being held on 6 July 1958 at Lord Casey's airfield at Berwick. As a result of the publicity from these jumps, sixty-five people applied to join the McKenzie school. The Queensland Parachute Club was also formed in July 1958 and by November of that year the idea of creating a national parachute association was conceived. A meeting was held at Camden of representatives of NSW and Victoria parachute clubs as well as officials from the NZ Parachute Federation; the Federation of Parachute Clubs and Centres was established. The first official meeting of that organisation took place at the Camden Inn Hotel on 23 October 1960. In October 1961 the name was changed to the Australian Parachute Federation (APF) and in 1962 a system of State parachute councils was adopted to administer the sport. Since those beginnings in 1958 the sport of parachuting has grown in various directions including classical style and accuracy, relative work, canopy relative work, and freestyle. Student training via the static-line-based course has been largely replaced by the accelerated free-fall course, and tandem jumping has shown its potential as an instrument of training. Round canopies have been replaced by ram-air canopies, even for students on their initial jump. For the average jumper, non-competitive free-fall formation remains the staple activity—jumping just for the fun of it. The Civil Aviation Authority has devolved much of the administration of the sport to the APF. This has had the advantage of placing the direction of the sport in the hands of those who understand it but has also added the burden of meeting the expenses of administration.

FM* and IJ

Parramatta's First Rugby League Premiership in 1981 did as much for the people of Sydney's western suburbs as it did for rugby league. Joining the Sydney premiership in 1947, Parramatta had suffered consecutive Grand Final defeats to Manly (1976) and St George (1977). Their supporters had begun to wonder if their club was destined ever to win a premiership. However, in 1981, before a crowd of 57 333, Parramatta scored four tries to Newtown's three, with the goal-kicking of Michael Cronin inflating the score line to 20–11. The 1981 team was inspired by the forward play of Ray Price, with the back line sparked by Peter Sterling and Brett Kenny. Their talents were complemented by the class of Michael Cronin,

Steve Ella, and the awesome strength and speed of Eric Grothe.

RA

PARRELLA, ROB (1944–), born Italy, played bocce in the backstreets of Naples as a youngster. Coming to Brisbane at the age of 10, he became the first Australian to achieve an individual gold medal in bowls at the Commonwealth Games when he won in Auckland in 1990. He had previously finished second in the 1982 Games. An exuberant and occasionally controversial character, the Brisbane taxi-driver loves to entertain and to express his personality on the green. Parrella is one of the more charismatic figures to emerge in the previously staid sport. Favouring the cradle grip, he is an accurate and fast driver who has almost perfect natural balance.

RC

PATCHING, JULIUS LOCKINGTON ('Judy'), OBE, OAM (1917–), is a person synonymous with service to sport in general and to the Olympic Movement in particular. His early love of sport came through athletics and he became captain and life member of the Geelong Guild, a coach of Old Melburnians, and a coach at Melbourne University. He was chief starter and member of the technical committee at the 1956 Olympic Games in Melbourne and was delegate to the International Amateur Athletic Federation from 1960 to 1970. His service to the Olympic Movement has been outstanding. He is a life member of the Victorian Olympic Council, having served for forty years as a representative of athletics and judo, as a member of the fund-raising committee since 1947, and currently as president. He is a life member of the Australian Olympic Federation, his service having included honorary secretary-general 1973–85; athletics manager, Rome 1960; assistant general manager, Tokyo 1964; and general manager, Mexico City 1968 and Munich 1972. His service to the Olympic movement on the international scene included being secretary-general of the Oceania National Olympic Committee 1981–89, and being a member of the Executive Board of the Association of National Olympic Committees from 1981–89. There was even time for Judy to have a full-time job: he was superintendent of recreation for the City of Melbourne from 1966 to 1983. This modest, unassuming, genial, and fun-loving man has received numerous awards for his service to sport and the Olympic Movement, including the OBE, the OAM, the International Olympic Committee's Olympic Order Silver Medal, the Association of National Olympic Committees' Award of Merit, and an Advance Australia Award.

IJ

See **Australian Olympic Committee**.

PATRICK, VIC, OAM (1920–), the son of an oyster farmer, was born Patrick Lucca in Woolloomooloo, Sydney; he later changed his name by deed poll. Patrick did not take up boxing until he was nearly 20, at which time he came under the guidance of the legendary Ern McQuillan. Patrick's boxing career was a remarkable fifty victories—with forty-four by knock-out—as against four losses and one draw. Patrick took part in some memorable fights. He beat Tommy Burns with a ninth-round knock-out and was himself knocked out by Freddie Dawson—then the world number-one contender—in the very last round when Patrick was regarded as ahead on points. Later Patrick became a respected fight referee and a successful publican. He was inducted into the Sports Australia Hall of Fame and also received the OAM.

GP

See **Boxing**.

PATTERSON, GERALD LEIGHTON (1895–1965), born Melbourne, was prominent in international tennis from 1919 to 1930. He won the Wimbledon men's singles from Norman Brookes—his mentor and doubles partner—at his first attempt in 1919, repeating the feat in 1922. He was a member of the successful Australasian Davis Cup team of 1919 and played in five more teams in the 1920s. A powerful service, volley, and smash were the touchstones of his game. The French player Jean Borotra was knocked unconscious in 1927 by one of his fierce high volleys. Patterson won the Australian men's singles championship in 1927, the Australian men's doubles five times, and the US doubles with Brookes in 1919. The grass court and gardens of the Patterson home at Kooyong were often the scene of tennis parties. A nephew of Dame Nellie Melba, Patterson later devoted himself to business, becoming chairman of the Mitchell Estate founded by his grandfather. He stood unsuccessfully for the United Australia Party in the Federal seat of Corio in 1940. In 1946 he served as non-playing captain of the touring Australian Davis Cup team.

GK-S

See **Lawn Tennis**.

PATTERSON, SID (1927–) cycled with success on all types of surfaces and won events, including four world titles, ranging from sprints to six-day marathons. A strapping 14-stone 6-footer, Patterson began competitive cycling at 14 years of age and while still in his teens carried off the Victorian and Australian amateur titles over almost every distance from 1000 metres to 10 miles. In 1949 Patterson became the first man to win every Australian championship—the sprint, time trial, 1 mile, and 5 miles. Later that year he won the first of his world titles at Copenhagen when he won the sprint final. He

was the first to go through a World Series without losing a heat as well as notching up Australia's first world cycling title. A year later at Liège he lost his world sprint crown but won the pursuit. Patterson had to settle for two silver medals in the sprint and time trial at the 1950 British Empire Games due to the brilliance of Russell Mockridge. Turning professional in 1951 he won the world pursuit title in 1952 and 1953. Patterson won numerous other events in the 1950s and 1960s, taking the Victorian professional title for the seventh time in 1964 and the Australian title in 1967 for the twelfth time. He retired from competitive cycling in 1968. He was inducted into the Sport Australia Hall of Fame in 1985.

RC

See **Austral Wheelrace**.

Pattison's Trophy. Presented to the cricketer making the most runs during the season of 1898–99 in all intercolonial matches, including those against NZ, this trophy was donated by Pattison's Ltd of O'Connell Street, Sydney. Victor Trumper, the Paddington Club cricketer playing for NSW, received the trophy after scoring 674 runs, including a score of 253 in the last of six qualifying matches in which he played. It is an ornate work of silver and gold and was valued at £100 at the time of presentation.

SG

PAVEY, PERCY (1902–), a rifleman, was the winner of fifteen King's and Queen's prizes including the King's prize at Bisley, England, in 1948. In 1952 he became the first man to win a King's or Queen's prize and the Jamieson Aggregate in the same year. He represented Australia at Bisley six times and won the Bisley Grand Aggregate in 1956. A marksman of rare quality, he won the first King's prize in 1930 when he took the Victorian and Queensland prizes. His career as a top-level marksman spanned more than thirty years. He won the Canadian Grand Aggregate in 1928 and the Scottish championship and Scottish Grand Aggregate in 1956. He is regarded as the finest Australian competitive rifleman and the best to compete in full-bore rifle-shooting. He was inducted into the Sport Australia Hall of Fame in 1985.

RC

PAYTEN, BAYLY (1896–1948) was the leading racehorse-trainer in Sydney for seven of eight seasons from 1940 to 1948. He was the third of eight children of Tom Payten (1855–1920), and inherited his father's training stables at Randwick. These were built in 1918, replacing the historic Newmarket stables which Tom Payten sold to auctioneer William Inglis. Newmarket had been owned by the Hon. James White, the most successful racehorse-owner in

Australia in the 1870s and 1880s. Tom Payten, second in command, took over as White's trainer on the death of Martin Fennelly in 1887 and continued the stable's phenomenal run. When White died in 1890, Tom Payten bought Newmarket and continued as a public trainer with outstanding results. Bayly Payten trained fewer champions than his father but consistently produced winners and won many top races including three AJC Oaks. His best performer was the brilliant filly *Valicare*. He was only 52 when he died, at the top of his profession.

AL

PEARCE Brothers are a famous hockey family. English-born public servant Cecil Henry Pearce and his Irish wife Gladys Mary raised their five children at Jubbalpore in India before emigrating to Perth in the late 1940s. Two sons played hockey for the Cricketers Club and the younger three sons joined the Trinity Club. The brothers also honed their skills in vigorous backyard games. **Cecil Francis** (1923–) was a tireless worker and fine tactician and represented Australia at inside left from 1950 to 1958. **Melville George** (1928–) was a prolific goalscorer at centre-forward who first represented Australia in 1952. A leg injury ended his career prematurely. **Eric Robert** (1931–) initially played for Australia in 1955. He was an uncanny, free-scoring centre-forward who represented his country for thirteen years. He took part in four Olympics (1956 to 1968), carrying the Australian flag at the closing ceremony in Mexico. **Gordon Charles** (1934–) was a tough and rugged defender (at inside right and right half) who never gave an inch. A triple Olympian (1956, 1960, and 1968), he played his last game for Australia in 1969. The youngest brother **Julian Brian** (1937–) was a very cool, constructive centre-half whose passes demolished the opposition. Another triple Olympian (1960 to 1968), he retired in 1970. The skills of the Pearce brothers played a big part in WA winning fourteen national hockey championships from 1949 to 1970. Eric's daughter **Colleen** (1961–) carried on the family tradition when she was a member of the Australian women's hockey team at the 1984 Olympics.

MS

See **Hockey**.

PEARCE, HENRY ROBERT (1905–76), born Sydney, an amateur and professional sculler, was the son of Henry Pearce, a former Australian sculling champion, who was his first coach. Bobby Pearce won his first open race at 14, his first major event at 21, and the first of three successive NSW sculling titles at 22. Despite accusations of professionalism, Pearce competed at the 1928 Olympics and won the single sculls in world-record time, but, as an

artisan, he was barred from the 1928 Henley-on-Thames regatta. Despite his success, Pearce had trouble finding work, and after winning the 1930 British Empire Games single sculls at Hamilton, Ontario, he accepted an offer of employment in Canada, where he lived for the rest of his life. In 1931 he was permitted to compete at Henley, winning the diamond sculls. Despite his Canadian residency, Pearce completed the Olympic sculls double for Australia by winning at Los Angeles in 1932. After turning professional, he won the world title in 1933, but such was the decline in professional rowing that when he relinquished the title after the Second World War he had defended it only twice. Standing 188 centimetres tall and racing at 92 kilograms, Pearce was an impressive figure when seated in a flimsy outrigger, and observers agreed that the power of his sculling overwhelmed opponents, particularly in rough water. His claim to be the best sculler yet produced by Australia is justifiable. He was to have been a rowing commentator at the Montreal Olympics, but died shortly before the Games began.

SB

See **Rowing and Sculling**.

PEARCE Sisters played an important role in WA's dominance of women's hockey from 1936 to 1956. Emanating from the tiny farming settlement of Moulyinning, the four Pearce sisters were unrelated to the legendary five Pearce brothers. **May** (Campbell, 1915–81), **Jean** (Wynne, 1921–), and **Morna** (Hyde, 1932–) all captained both their State and country. The fourth sister, **Caroline** (Ash, 1925–), also represented her State and country though not as captain. May is regarded by many as one of the greatest players produced in her State. Playing at left-inner, she was a goal-scoring phenomenon: she scored 100 goals in interclub, interstate, and international hockey in 1936 and netted 20 out of WA's total of 30 goals in the 1938 interstate carnival. After representing Australia from 1936 to 1948 she later contributed as a coach and administrator. Jean, a centre-halfback, was a past master at reading the play who liked nothing better than moving up in support of the forwards at deceptive pace with her long, loping strides. She represented WA from 1939 to 1953 and made the Australian team in 1946. She retired after leading Australia to a famous first victory over England in 1953. Caroline, known as 'Tib', had a shorter career from 1946 to 1950 but played alongside May and Jean in the 1948 unbeaten Australian team which toured NZ. Morna, like her sisters, had adroit stick work and was deadly in the circle. She played for Australia under Jean's captaincy in 1953 and was Australian captain herself by the time of the next international tournament at Sydney in 1956. She won WA's inaugural Sportsman (sic) of the Year award in 1956.

AN

PERKINS, CHARLES (1934–) was born at the Old Telegraph Station in Alice Springs. As a teenager he moved to Adelaide and there played junior soccer with the Port Thistle Club, a place 'where he could be somebody'. At 21 he was playing for Budapest where he won their best and fairest award and became one of their highest-paid players. After a disastrous attempt to join Everton Football Club, he became a member of the renowned amateur side Bishop Auckland. In a match against Oxford, the seeds of a university career were sown. Returning to SA, he captained Croatia, then moved to Sydney's Pan-Hellenic. Soccer paid for his Sydney University arts degree. He began a career of campaigning for black rights: as leader of the famous Freedom Ride in NSW in the 1960s; an executive member of the Federal Council for the Advancement of Aborigines and Torres Strait Islanders; chairman of the Aboriginal Development Commission; and secretary of the Department of Aboriginal Affairs, the first and only Aborigine to head a Federal Government department. In 1987 Perkins was appointed vice-president of the Australian Soccer Federation. He was responsible for founding the Australian Aboriginal Cricket Association and for their subsequent tour of England in 1988.

CT and PT

See **Aboriginal Sports Foundation**; **Aborigines in Sport**.

Peter Pan (1929–41), a thoroughbred racehorse, by *Pantheon* out of *Alwina*, was foaled in NSW. He was bred and raced by R. R. Dangar and trained by Frank McGrath. He won nine of his eleven starts as a 3-year-old including the AJC Derby and, after nearly falling during the race, the 1932 Melbourne Cup. In claiming the 1934 Cup on a shockingly heavy track, *Peter Pan* became the first horse since *Archer* to win the race twice. The same season he set an Australian record for 1 mile in the AJC All-Aged Stakes. Carrying 10 stone 6 pounds he was unplaced in the 1935 Cup. In all he won twenty-eight races. He retired to stud in 1936.

AL

Phar Lap (1926–32), a champion thoroughbred racehorse, was foaled at Timaru in NZ, a son of a failed race mare, *Entreaty*, and an imported English sire, *Night Raid*, who raced in England and Australia with little success. The breeder, A. F. Roberts, sold the colt to trainer Harry Telford who bought on behalf of David Davis, a Sydney businessman. Unimpressed on seeing the horse after its arrival in Sydney, Davis gave Telford a three-year lease. *Phar Lap*, by now gelded, won only one of his first nine races but began to show promise as a 3-year-old and, after winning the Rosehill Guineas, established race records in winning the Victorian and the Australian Jockey Club Derbies. From the time of his Rosehill Guineas victory he won thirty-six of his remaining forty-one starts, including fourteen in succession, and was unplaced only once. A large, striking chestnut, *Phar Lap* became a national celebrity, the legend fuelled by public disagreements between Davis and Telford and by the devotion of his attendant, Tommy Woodcock. A short-priced favourite for the 1930 Melbourne Cup, which he won, *Phar Lap* was shot at from a moving car a few days before the race but was unharmed. After more success as a 5-year-old, *Phar Lap* was beaten into eighth place in the 1931 Melbourne Cup carrying 10 stone 10 pounds. Davis now sent the horse to the USA against Telford's wishes, with Woodcock in charge, and in March he won a rich race at Agua Caliente racecourse in New Mexico. Two weeks later the horse died at its stables near San Francisco. Tests detected traces of arsenic in his body, but there was no agreement on whether these were at a fatal level or how the substance was ingested. *Phar Lap*'s hide, mounted by an American taxidermist, remains the most popular exhibit at the National Museum in Melbourne.

AL

See **Horse-racing**.

Phelan Medal is awarded each season to the best and fairest Sydney first-grade Australian rules player. It was first presented in 1926 but remained unnamed until 1932 when it became known as the Provan Medal after the donor, Aub D. S. Provan, then president of the NSW AFL. The name was changed to the Phelan Medal in 1937 in recognition of J. E. Phelan's lifetime contribution to Australian football in Sydney. A former player, Phelan founded the Newtown Club and became league secretary after the First World War. The inaugural winner of the medal was R. H. Powers from the Sydney club, which has had more medal winners (eight) than any other club. J. Williamson of the East Sydney Club is the only player to have won the medal on four occasions.

GC and MH*

PHILLIS, TOM (1934–62), born Marrickville, Sydney, was the first westerner to win a world championship Grand Prix on a Japanese motorcycle. Contracted to Honda, he won four 125 cc Grands Prix and two 250 cc Grands Prix in 1961. He was the first Australian to win two Grand Prix classes—the French 125 and 250—in a day. He became the world 125 cc road-racing champion and was runner-up in the 1961 world 250 title. Phillis was relatively tall (178 centimetres) for a rider. He took up motorcycle racing as a result of a chance meeting during national service. Four years later, in 1958, he and wife Betty were travelling to race meetings in Europe in a converted furniture van. Phillis was a quiet, devoted family man with a ready grin and a wry smile. Racing at the Isle of Man on 6 June 1962 he crashed into a wall and died soon after.

DC

PICKWORTH, HORACE HENRY AL-FRED ('Ossie') (1917–69), born Manly, Sydney, developed very powerful hands and dominated Australian golf for a decade. Looking anything but a top-class athlete, the large, chain-smoking Pickworth won four Australian Opens, three Australian PGA championships, and five of the first seven Ampol tournaments. He toured Britain in 1950, finishing runner-up in the Daily Mail Open Golf Championship and winning the Irish Open before homesickness and the weather dampened his enthusiasm. Pickworth represented Australia in the inaugural Canada Cup where he and Peter Thomson finished third. Pickworth played golf in a hurry and often looked casual on the course but was rarely far off the tournament lead. He survived several heart attacks and a thrombosis operation before he died at the age of 52.

GC*
See **Golf**.

Pigeon-racing
Organised by the Melbourne Pigeon and Canary Society, the first pigeon-race in Australia was flown over 90 kilometres from Kyneton to Port Melbourne on 22 July 1875. At present two series of races are organised each year, with one series, January to March, being for young birds and the second series, from August to November, for older birds. The races are flown over distances which vary from 50 to 960 kilometres. Long-distance races of between 1336 and 1600 kilometres are flown in SA and WA annually. During the Second World War, Australian pigeon-fanciers donated 20000 birds to the AIF Pigeon Service where two pigeons received the Dicken Medal—the animal version of the Victoria Cross. Although there is no central controlling body the Pigeon Fanciers' Protection Union acts in an advisory capacity to the numerous clubs and federations.

GC*

PIPER, DES (1941–) was introduced to hockey in the early 1950s, and developed into one of Victoria's and Australia's best known forwards—a fierce and firm competitor, with exceptional skills. Representing Victoria from 1954 at under-16 and under-21 levels, he was always promoted before his age limit was reached. His senior career started in 1958 and extended to 1972 when injury prevented him from playing at the top levels. Piper's leader-

ship abilities were recognised when he was selected as Victorian captain at the age of 21. At the national level Piper missed only one game between 1961 and 1972. During this time he played in two Olympic Games (1964 and 1968) and in the inaugural World Cup competition. Since 1980 Piper has been an Australian selector.

BS†

PISANI, SANDRA, OAM (1959–), made her debut for SA in 1979 and first played hockey for Australia two years later at the World Cup in Argentina. Her usual position as centre-half best suited her forceful and aggressive style. Always a strong competitor, with exceptional speed and ball sense, Sandy Pisani represented her country eighty-five times, participating in three World Cups, two Olympic Games (winning a gold medal at Seoul in 1988), and numerous other tournaments and Test series in Australia, Europe, Asia, and the USA between 1981 and 1988. She was Australian captain in 1985 and 1986. Pisani was awarded the OAM in 1989 and works at the SA Sports Institute.

RQ

POIDEVIN, SIMON (1958–) played fifty-nine rugby union international matches for Australia, including three as captain. His career as a mobile and tenacious breakaway spanned the 1980s and early 1990s. A product of St Patrick's College, Goulburn, Poidevin was selected in the non-touring Australian schoolboys' team of 1976 and made his Test debut against Fiji in Suva in 1980. A hard training regimen, a fierce determination to succeed, and strength and skill in rucking and mauling have made Poidevin a very tough adversary, but one with a reputation for good sportsmanship. His career highlights include the 1984 Grand Slam tour of the British Isles, Bledisloe Cup wins over NZ in 1980 and 1986, and especially the Wallabies World Cup victory in 1991. Poidevin and David Campese share the world record for the most appearances against one country. Both have played twenty-one Tests against the All Blacks. Poidevin was inducted into the Sport Australia Hall of Fame in 1991.

GC†

POLLOCK, JUDITH FLORENCE (née AMOR) (1940–), born Macedon, Victoria, was world-record holder in the 400 metres, 440 yards, and 800 metres in the 1960s. Pollock, who became a physical education teacher, ran as Judith Amor before her marriage in 1964. After winning her first State titles in 1963 she came third in the 400 metres at the 1964 Olympics, an event won by Betty Cuthbert. On her return to Australia she ran a world-record time of 52.4 seconds in the 440 yards. In March 1965 she became the first woman ever to win all five flat races in the Victorian championships: 100 metres and 100, 220, 440, and 880 yards. Later that year she set a world indoor record for the 400 metres of 55.6 seconds. She then won gold in the 440 yards and silver in the 880 yards at the 1966 British Empire and Commonwealth Games. After becoming pregnant she missed the 1968 Olympics and was unable to compete at the 1972 Games due to injury. She participated in the 1976 Games but was eliminated in the heats.

RC

Polo

Polo is played on the largest playing field of any sport, with areas of up to 275 metres long and 180 metres wide. Players are rated according to their ability in terms of goals, with the maximum of ten indicating a world-class performer: a 20-goal tournament is thus limited to teams whose players do not exceed an aggregate 20-goal rating. Polo probably came to Australia from India by word of mouth of cavalry remount buyers. It was first played in Australia at Warrnambool in Victoria in 1874 though the first recorded public match was played on 10 December 1875 at Albert Park in Melbourne. The first intercolonial competition was played in Adelaide in 1883 between Adelaide and Warrnambool. For many years Australian polo was mainly played in paddocks at weekends using horses which during the week were also used for mustering sheep and cattle. In the past few decades, however, much greater attention has been directed to lifting the standards of playing surfaces and Australia now has two world-class grounds at Ellerston and Warwick Farm, both in NSW.

Polo in Australia is organised on a State basis with each State polo association conducting its own championships. Principal tournaments have been the Australasian Gold Cup, established in 1925 for competition between the States and NZ; the Countess of Dudley Cup established in 1910 in Sydney; the Royal Easter Show three-a-side at the Sydney Showgrounds under lights; the 23-goal Easter International held in Sydney, the 16-goal Melbourne Cup Polo Tournament held during the VRC's Spring Carnival; and the recently established 40–40 Challenge Cup and 26-goal Ellerston Open.

CY and IJ

See ASHTON Family; HALL, JOHN; SKENE, ROBERT.

Polocrosse

The sport of polocrosse originated in Australia in 1939 and was developed by Marjory and Edward Hirst of Ingleburn near Sydney. During a visit to England in 1938 the Hirsts had witnessed a new indoor horse-riding exercise played by teams of two players using modified polo sticks, a rubber ball, and elongated basket-ball nets as goals. On their return to Australia, the Hirsts enlisted the assistance of Alf Pitty to help them convert this exercise into an outdoor sport which they called 'Polocrosse' (the word is a blend of 'polo' and 'lacrosse'). They believed that polocrosse was ideally suited to Australian conditions: it was played outdoors, could by played by both sexes and all ages, and required only one horse per player. In 1939 the first polocrosse demonstration was conducted at the Ingleburn Horse and Pony Club grounds and that same year the first club was formed at Ingleburn with Marjory Hirst as president. The Second World War slowed the progress of the sport and it was not until 1945 that the second polocrosse club, Bundaroo, was formed near Bowral. The following year the first official polocrosse match was held between the Ingleburn and Bundaroo clubs at Ingleburn. On 17 October 1946 the Polocrosse Association of Australia was formed. Since then the sport has grown rapidly, spreading to Queensland and Victoria in the late 1940s, to SA and WA in the early 1950s, and to Tasmania and the NT in the 1970s. The first interstate championships were held at Ballarat in 1953 between NSW, Victoria, and SA with the first Australian National Polocrosse Championships conducted in 1968 at Dubbo. These national championships are held every second year. By 1990 there were almost three hundred polocrosse clubs in Australia with about five thousand registered players and 177 accredited coaches. There are now competitions against teams in NZ, Papua New Guinea, Zimbabwe, Canada, and Vanuatu. An International Polocrosse Council was formed in June 1976 with an Australian, Max Walters, as its founding president.

JC and MW*

PONSFORD, WILLIAM HAROLD MBE (1900–91) was one of Australia's greatest cricketers and probably the best-ever batsman against spin bowling. Immediately before the impact of Bradman, he was the heaviest scorer the game had known. In December 1927 he scored 1146 runs in five innings. He is the only batsman to score more than 400 on two occasions in first-class cricket (429 v. Tasmania in 1923 and 437 against Queensland in 1927) and one of two Australians to score over 300 in a day in Australia (445 against NSW in 1926). His record partnerships are legendary: first wicket 456 with E. Mayne against Queensland in 1923–24; second 451 with Bradman (v. England 1934); third 389 with McCabe (v. England 1934); 388 with Bradman (v. England 1934); as well as twenty first-class century partnerships with Woodfull, five of them over 200. Ponsford retired prematurely at the height of his prowess, finishing in much the same way as he had started his career: he scored centuries in his first

91 The final torch-bearer in the relay which had brought the Olympic Flame to Melbourne from Olympia, Greece, was Ron Clarke, then the world junior mile record-holder.

92 Although the 1956 Olympics have become known as the 'Friendly Games', political turmoil in the Middle East and Hungary resulted in strained relations between some competing nations.

93 World record breakers in the 4 × 100m relay, Sandra
Morgan, Faith Leech, Dawn Fraser and Lorraine Crapp,
at the 1956 Olympic Games.

94 Julius 'Judy' Patching was a member of the Technical
Committee and chief starter for track and field events at
the Melbourne Olympic Games.

95 Douglas Nicholls, born at the Cumerrgunga
Aboriginal Mission Station in NSW, played Victorian
League football for Fitzroy.

96 *Phar Lap* became a national celebrity during the
depression of the 1930s. His hide, mounted by an
American taxidermist, is the most popular exhibit at the
Museum of Victoria, Melbourne.

97 An intercolonial polo tournament at Albert Park, Melbourne, 1880.

98 Bill Roycroft, riding *Our Solo*, despite a broken collar-bone from a heavy fall, won Australia's first equestrian gold medal for the three-day event at the 1960 Olympic Games.

two Tests (110 and 128) and in his last two (181 and 266), the only batsman ever to do so; in his first ten matches for Victoria he amassed 1580 at an average of 121.54 and in his last four Tests scored 569 runs at an average of 94.83, marginally ahead of Bradman (94.75). In all first-class matches he scored 13 819 runs (at an average of 65.18), and scored forty-seven centuries, thirteen of which were 200 or more. In forty-eight Tests he scored 2122 runs (at an average of 48.22) including seven centuries. Ponsford was also a first-class baseballer, was a member of the only Australian team to beat an American team, and was once invited to play with the Brooklyn Dodgers. He died at North Fitzroy.

RH*

See **Cricket**.

Pony Club began as a junior rider organisation within the British Hunt Society and is now a world-wide youth organisation in its own right. The Australian Pony Club Council (APCC) is the co-ordinating body of all State and Territory Pony Club associations in Australia and as such represents the largest Pony Club group in the world. Pony Club members are taught horsemanship and horsemastership, learning not only how to ride but also how to care for horses. Progress can be assessed by sitting for certificates which have a high practical content. Anyone up to the age of 21 (26 in some States) may join Pony Club but most have to have their own horse, saddle, bridle, and sundry tackle. Included in the many activities of Pony Club are the Olympic disciplines of dressage, cross-country jumping, and show-jumping as well as other activities such as trail-riding, endurance riding, polocrosse, polo, sporting events, Prince Philip mounted games, tetrathlon, campdrafting, and harness. A balance is achieved between riding for fun and leisure and the more serious competition events. International exchange competitions are held regularly.

RB† and IJ

POPPLEWELL, FRED ('Popp') (1887–?), born Double Bay, Sydney, as a young boy joined Carnegie Clark and Dan Soutar as a professional at Royal Sydney Golf Club where he served for twenty-one years. He won two NSW professional titles and two Australian Opens, in 1925 and again in 1928. In the latter year he was up against the 'Titans': Michael Scott, who had won the event twice, Clark, with three wins, Whitton with (then) three wins, and the legendary Joe Kirkwood. At Royal Sydney's third hole, 'Popp' holed out, eventually winning by one shot. 'Surely was Popplewell the Darling of the Gods,' wrote the journalists, 'for he is deservedly a favourite with all.'

CT

POSTLE, ARTHUR (the 'Crimson Flash') (1881–1965), born Pittsworth near Toowoomba, Queensland, was a sprinter with a crouching yet graceful style who was virtually unbeatable up to 75 yards; he held world professional records from 50 to 200 yards. Known as the 'Crimson Flash', because of the colour of his running singlet, he turned professional in 1902. In 1906 before a crowd of 20 000 at Kalgoorlie he beat Irishman Bernard Day and set a world record for 75 yards of 7.2 seconds. On the same occasion he defeated his opponent at 300 and 130 yards. Many of Postle's most outstanding performances were abroad in Britain and South Africa. He was acclaimed as World Sprint Champion in 1910 when he won a 130 yards match race against a class field which included his Australian rival, Jack Donaldson, American C. E. Holway, and South Africa's Olympic gold-medallist Reginald Walker. He was inducted into the Sport Australia Hall of Fame in 1985.

RC

See **Athletics**; DONALDSON, JOHN.

Powerboating

With convenient access to numerous waterways, powerboating has long been popular in Australia. Competition started with the founding of the Motor Boat Club in Sydney in 1905. The Australasian unlimited open championship competition for the Griffiths Cup dates from 1910, the inaugural race being won by A. Davies in *Fairbanks*. In order to co-ordinate activities and standardise rules the Australian Power Boat Association was formed in 1927, and by 1955 all States had governing councils for the sport. In 1978 Ken Warby, aboard *Spirit of Australia*, broke his own world water speed record, averaging 511.11 km/h; the boat, which he built in his backyard, was subsequently housed in the National Maritime Museum at Darling Harbour, Sydney.

KM

See **WARBY, KEN**.

Powerlifting

In Australia, State bodies started forming in the early 1970s, most being breakaways from weightlifting bodies reluctant to continue an involvement in powerlifting after the inaugural Australian Powerlifting Championships in Adelaide in 1971. At that event, a decision was made to establish a separate Federal body for powerlifting, and consequently the Australian Amateur Powerlifting Federation (a forerunner of today's Australian Powerlifting Federation Inc.) was formed in 1972. Powerlifting comprises three exercises: squat, bench press, and dead lift. Powerlifters compete in eleven weight classes for men ranging from 52 kg to over 125 kg, and in ten classes for women, from 48 kg to over 90 kg. Women succeeded in being accepted in the sport during the 1970s, and in Australia they now comprise nearly 25 per cent of all members. Apart from open competition, there are junior divisions at under-18 and under-23, as well as masters events for lifters over 40 and over 50.

BK

PRATT, BOB (1912–), born Mitcham, Victoria, became, in 158 games for South Melbourne, one of the greatest forwards in Australian football, kicking 680 goals. Three times he was top VFL goal-kicker, with over 100 goals on each occasion—a unique feat. While Pratt was a key force in South's 1933 Premiership, the 1934 season was his epic year, with 150 goals in twenty-one matches. Like all champions, Pratt laboured at developing the basic skills of his craft, but the many high marks which made him a legend in the 1930s were the product of genius.

AB

PRICE, RAYMOND ALAN (1953–), born Sydney, was a dual rugby union and rugby league international footballer. He played for Parramatta in both football codes, as a breakaway forward in union and as a lock forward in league. After touring with the Wallabies in 1975 he switched to league and was a member of the successful Kangaroo teams of 1978 and 1982. He was a crucial part of the Parramatta team which took the Sydney first-grade premierships of 1981, 1982, 1983, and 1986. The winner of the Rothmans medal for best and fairest player in 1979, Price was an ungainly but courageous and indefatigable athlete.

CC

PRIGG, WALTER JOSEPH (1908–), played first-grade rugby league football for Central in Newcastle from 1927. He was selected for the State side in 1929 and toured England with the Kangaroos in 1929 and 1933, and as captain in 1937, his third successive tour of England, which created a record. An alert and efficient lock forward, with speed, sure handling, and sound defence, he was able in emergency to play in practically every position in the backs. He played in seventeen Tests for Australia.

CC

PROVAN, NORM ('Sticks') (1931–), a rugby league second-row forward, joined the Sydney club St George in 1951 and soon displayed a mixture of toughness and intelligence. In 1953 he represented his State, and a year later played his first Test against England, retaining his position for five years and featuring in the World Cup series in 1954 and 1957 and the Kangaroos' tour of 1956. A formidable defender, Provan was also an excellent ball distributor who pioneered a new style of play by a second-row forward. His strengths were seen at St George where he played in ten consecutive premiership teams, being captain-coach between 1962 and 1965. Later he was a successful coach of Parramatta and Cronulla. Despite some business setbacks Provan achieved considerable success in the retailing of white goods. A gentle, generous man, he will be remembered for his ability, sportsmanship, and love of playing the game. His photograph, taken with Arthur Summons after the 1963 Sydney Grand Final, is seen by many as representative of the spirit of Australian sport.

TGP

Public-house Sports
In nineteenth-century Australia, public houses were prominent and important community centres which served a variety of official functions, while also providing food, drink and shelter, entertainment, and recreation. It is in the context of public houses as community centres that tavern sports were significant forms of social interaction. Tavern sports emerged from British cultural traditions, and a variety of games and contests familiar to British immigrants appeared in Australian public houses. In an entrepreneurial capacity, publicans generally organised and sponsored such events. They were primarily seeking to attract male patrons who ate and drank heartily. Skittle alleys and quoit grounds were common in public houses, being especially popular among working-class males. Billiards was a more prestigious and expensive pastime. Proud publicans boldly advertised slate surfaces and English cloth, some even offering special billiard rooms and tuition in the finer points of the game.

Public houses were also venues for blood sports involving animals: cock-fighting, dog-fighting, and bull-baiting. However, during the nineteenth century these contests were progressively outlawed by legislators who viewed them as barbaric. Nevertheless, the status of rats as vermin gave them no legal protection. Ratting pits remained in some nineteenth-century public houses, with prize-money offered for dogs who captured the most prey.

Boxing and wrestling saloons were provided in some public houses, particularly those that predominantly attracted male working-class labourers. In this environment the capacity of a man to fight was highly prized. Moreover, it was good entertainment for spectators, and thus a boon for public-house trade. However, the police and legislators feared problems of public disorder arising from such arrangements, and pugilistic contests were ultimately driven from public houses to more clandestine surroundings. Sports were also evident on grounds adjacent to public houses. Pigeon-shooting was a prestigious event, held at the 'better' class of establishment. Boxed birds were released systematically, enabling shooters to engage in a contest. Ploughing matches were family affairs in which the men and boys demonstrated their skills, while the ladies gave moral support from the sidelines. Inevitably, a dinner at the nearest public house was held afterwards, at which prizes were presented.

Some sporting events were more impromptu affairs, such as single-wicket cricket and pedestrianism. These types of contests could be either light-hearted or earnest. Pedestrianism sometimes involved large stake-money and wagering as 'backers' of runners ostentatiously declared their support. Gambling was also evident in the match-racing of horses and low-grade trotters, often held on the roads in front of public houses. Entrepreneurial publicans acted as stewards, and their patronage continued in the form of the 'publican's purse' at organised race meetings.

Public houses were essentially male-dominated social venues. In this context, women were generally excluded from participation in public-house sports. Women and children were, however, sometimes present as spectators. They watched men who sought status and identity from contests of chance, strength, endurance, and skill, held in familiar and convivial surroundings. The role of public houses as community and cultural centres became less important during the twentieth century. This was reflected in the decline of traditional tavern sports. New games such as darts and eight-ball became popular, especially in the front bar of working-class hotels. The recent introduction of cable television and TAB betting facilities in hotels has added a vicarious dimension to sport and gambling in public houses.

DA

See **Animal Baiting**; **Lawn Bowls**.

Q

QUILL, ALFRED LOUIS (1910–), born Ultimo, Sydney, was a prolific goal-scorer and soccer centre-forward, whose career spanned 1927 to 1949. His 868 goals in senior games is an Australian record. Prodigious speed made up for a lack of height though Australian selectors often preferred burlier rivals. Quill made seven national appearances and scored 8 goals. Principally a Wallsend player, he also played for Pyrmont, Annandale-Leichhardt, Goodyear, and Lake Macquarie. A part-time professional, he played for Goodyear Tyre and Rubber Pty Ltd from 1934 to 1936 because Goodyear offered him employment. Quill coached the Australian national team against Yugoslavia's Hadjuk Split Football Club in 1949.

PM

QUIST, ADRIAN (1913–91), born Medindie, SA, was the son of Karl Quist, an interstate cricketer. He was known for his outstanding doubles play in tennis, his left-hand court play, his overhead shots, and placement. He won the Australian singles in 1936, 1940, and 1948, and was ranked number one in Australia in 1936 and 1937, but achieved even greater success as a doubles-player. Partnered by Jack Crawford he won the French and Wimbledon doubles in 1935. He formed an even more potent partnership with John Bromwich, who dominated the Australian doubles championships from 1936 to 1940 and 1946 to 1950. The pair won the 1939 US doubles and the 1950 Wimbledon doubles. Quist represented Australia in the Davis Cup from 1933 to 1939 and in 1946 and 1948. He worked for the Dunlop company from 1932, becoming general manager of its sportsgoods division by 1963. He became a radio and television tennis commentator and wrote candid but perceptive articles for newspapers on tennis controversies including open tennis. Quist contributed to tennis administration, managing the Australian team of 1963, and participated in international senior competitions in the 1960s. He was inducted into the International Hall of Fame in 1984.

VO'F

See **BROMWICH, JOHN; CRAWFORD, JACK**.

R

Rallying

Motor-car rallying was a natural extension of both the intercapital-city speed dashes that had aroused much public interest since before the Great War and the famous Redex reliability trials of the 1950s. Increasingly regulated and supervised after 1962, the sport was also 'Australianised', tempering the European focus on speed with additional motor vehicle ruggedness. Cars like the Peugeot and the Volkswagen first gained credibility in the Australian marketplace after a string of successes in round–Australia rallies. While the Europeans increasingly used pace notes for 'special stages', Australian rallying at its peak level emphasised navigation. Conducted on rough country or forestry roads, success was a complex equation of navigational and driving skill, coupled with vehicle strength and mechanical aptitude. The balance of these has now changed. The advent of professional support teams diminished the need for the last, though the best Australian rallyists like Colin Bond are both skilled mechanics and drivers.

With the exception of particular events like the 1968 London to Sydney marathon, Australian rallying has rarely enjoyed a high public profile. Even in its heyday of the 1970s, the premier Australian event, the Southern Cross rally, attracted more interest overseas than at home. In 1976 factory teams were entered by Mitsubishi, Datsun and Ford (UK) yet the winner of that event, Scotsman Andrew Cowan, driving a works Mitsubishi Lancer, is one of the few foreign drivers to enjoy success in Australia. 'Australian' manufacturers have seen more advertising potential in circuit racing. Nevertheless, semi-official enterprises such as the Holden Dealer Team of the 1960s and 1970s were very successful.

Rallying enjoys a strong amateur following at the car club level, though it has become increasingly expensive and the type of vehicle entered tends less and less to be the family car. Australian rallying has produced no equivalent of circuit racing's Jack Brabham, though in recent years the Canberra-based Greg Carr, driving various Datsuns, Fords and Lancias, has demonstrated that he can match the best from overseas. In 1990 a round of the World Rally Championship was conducted for the first time in Australia.

AM

See **Redex Trials**.

Randwick Racecourse.

Situated five kilometres from Sydney's post office, Randwick Racecourse has held regular meetings since a crowd of 8000 turned out to watch the first race meeting on the course in May 1860. It is NSW's premier track and ranks second to Victoria's Flemington in national prestige. Randwick is the home of the Australian Jockey Club which conducts races run over distances from 1000 to 3200 metres. It has a circumference of 2213 metres and uses shutes in clear view of the grandstands for the start of the 1600, 1400, and 1200 metres races. It is considered that most horses have an equal chance of winning at all barriers except in the 1000 metres where only a short run to the home turn frequently drives the younger, inexperienced horses wide. Timing a finishing run is vitally important as the straight is 410 metres long and there is a steep rise to the 200 metres mark. The racecourse's first grandstand, which could accommodate 1500 spectators, was built by M. W. Stone for £2500. This provided the AJC members with a better place to view races than the racecourse used previously at Homebush. In 1914 the Paddock Stand had seats for 14 300 while the rebuilt St Leger stand seated 11 000. New offices, semaphores, and tea rooms were also added on the flat. George Julius's automatic totalisator was introduced on 22 December 1917 and by 1921 prize-money at Randwick reached $250 000. Decorated with wrought-iron latticework, the racecourse had a unique old-world charm which was not destroyed completely with the building of the luxurious multi-storied Queen Elizabeth Stand, which continues the traditional practice of segregating members from non-members and trainers. The record crowd for the course was set on Doncaster Day 1948 when 93 746 spectators watched the day's racing. Although it races all year round, Randwick holds two major carnivals each year — the Spring and Autumn Carnivals. The major races conducted include the AJC Breeders' Plate, the Metropolitan, Doncaster, and Epsom Handicaps, the AJC St Leger, the Sydney Cup, the AJC Queen Elizabeth Stakes, the AJC Derby, and the Oaks. Although Randwick is primarily a racecourse it has been used for a number of other public gatherings. In 1970 250 000 people attended Mass celebrated by Pope Paul. In March 1992 the racecourse was officially given the royal title by the Queen.

GC*

RAPER, JOHNNY (1939–), a rugby league lock forward, began his first-grade career with Newtown in 1957, aged 17. In 1958 he played for Sydney against the touring Englishmen and joined the crack St George club. He was a member of the Australian team between 1959 and 1968, playing in thirty-three Tests and in the World Cup series of 1960 and 1968. Raper was a key part of the all-conquering St George teams of the 1950s and 1960s, developing a style of lock-forward play which combined brilliant cover defence—including ball-and-all tackles—with intelligent and aggressive attack, often linking up with half Bill Smith and five-eighth 'Poppa' Clay. Somewhat of a larrikin, Raper has had a stormy retirement punctuated by unsuccessful coaching terms with Newtown and Cronulla-Sutherland. The man who captained Australia in 1968 was charged with receiving stolen goods in the 1970s but was acquitted. Later he became a national selector and deeply involved in his old club, St George. A brilliant, somewhat ingenuous footballer, Raper revolutionised the play of the lock forward.

TGP
See **Rugby League**.

RASIC, RALE (1935–), born Yugoslavia, is the first coach to take the Socceroos to a World Cup final series. Their 1974 appearances in West Germany remain the furthest Australia has progressed in this tournament. Orphaned during the Second World War, Rasic developed his love of sport in the orphanage playgrounds of Vojvodina where he excelled at soccer. He represented Yugoslavia at under-21 level and played professionally in Europe before settling in Australia to coach. Rasic coached Australia in fifty-eight international matches from 1970 to 1974 and was later inducted into the Sport Australia Hall of Fame.

PK

RAUDONIKIS, TOM (1950–), a rugby league half-back, began his career in Wagga Wagga, NSW, but was signed by Sydney club Western Suburbs on the advice of former national captain Arthur Summons. He first played for Australia in 1971 against NZ, thus beginning a career which comprised twenty-three Test appearances, one World Cup series (1972) and two world championship series (1975 and 1977), and which was highlighted when the half led his country to a 15–5 win over Great Britain in the last international of the 1973 tour. A clever, scheming half-back, who was a great leader, Raudonikis is remembered for his toughness. He asked for no quarter, and certainly never gave any. His defence was ferocious, his authority undoubted: he was once referred to as 'the brick outhouse with fists'. A loyal, dedicated club man, he served Western Suburbs well during a time when he virtually

carried the team and he was later with Newtown during its brief burst of glory in the 1980s. He subsequently became a highly successful coach in Queensland where he instilled toughness and discipline into young enthusiastic sides such as Ipswich.

TGP

Redex Trials. In 1953, 187 cars left the Sydney Showground to compete in the first of three Redex around-Australia trials. Run in 1953, 1954, and 1955, they captivated the Australian public. Organised by the Australian Sporting Car Club and Redex (Australia) Ltd, an arm of the British oil-additive company, the trials amounted to demolition derbies, run over some of the worst roads in Australia. The 1953 trial was driven over 10 460 kilometres and was won eventually by a Maitland chemist, Ken Tubman, and his co-driver, John Marshall, in a Peugeot 203. The success of the 1954 event was such that the following year the Redex Trial, over a distance of 17 000 kilometres, was included in the Fédération Internationale de l'Automobile (FIA) calendar. Unfortunately this trial was surrounded by controversial decisions to such an extent that Redex withdrew their sponsorship.

GC*
See **MURRAY, JACK**; **Rallying**.

Referee (1886–1939) was a Sydney weekly newspaper launched in 1886 to compete with the Melbourne *Sportsman* and later the *Arrow* and the *Sydney Sportsman* for the attention of the growing sporting public. During its existence it was dominated by W. F. Corbett and his son Claude, but in its earlier days Nat Gould and 'Smiler' Hailes were prominent contributors. Its demise in 1939 was caused less by competition from local sporting journals than by the increasing popularity of evening newspapers such as the *Sun*.

GC *

RENFORD, DES, MBE, IHC (1927–), born Sydney, did not take up marathon swimming until aged 39 although he had swum competitively from the age of 10. From 1970 to 1980 he swam the English Channel nineteen times and was proclaimed 'King of the Channel' for swimming it more than anyone else. He also became, in 1980, the first person to swim the Channel three times in a season. He swam 50 laps of Bondi Beach in 1970 and was selected as one of the top ten marathon swimmers in the world in the same year. He won the 37 kilometres Shorncliffe to Tangalooma race in 1973 and the Watsons Bay to Wollongong Harbour race in 1975. Renford produced five movies including the sports documentary *King of the Channel* (1976), which won a Logie award. He received the MBE in 1976 and a papal knighthood in 1990.

RH and MH

Restraint of Trade is based on the common-law principle that individuals should not have impediments placed on their employment against their wishes. A restraint can be defended if it passes a test of reasonableness, which is usually defined in terms of furthering the legitimate interests of all parties and the public interest. The leagues of a variety of sports have instituted various labour-market controls—such as zoning, retain and transfer systems, drafting, controls on income, and other restrictions—claiming that they help achieve sporting equality and maintain the integrity of their sport.

Following the 1961 Eastham case, where the English courts struck down soccer's retain and transfer system, Australian courts have tended to look unfavourably on controls which restrict the employment rights of players. The most famous of these have been the 1971 Tutty case which ruled against the NSW Rugby League's transfer system, the 1977 Hall, 1978 Adamson, and 1983 Foschini cases which found against zoning and transfer systems in Australian football, and cricket's 1978 Greig and 1986 Hughes cases which ruled against prohibitions placed on players associated with World Series Cricket and tours to South Africa respectively. In 1991, against this trend, the Federal Court of Australia ruled that a drafting system introduced by the NSW Rugby League was a reasonable restraint of trade; however that decision has been overturned on appeal.

BD

See **Law**.

REYNOLDS, RICHARD (1915–) was a champion Australian rules football wingman then rover. Dick Reynolds won three Brownlow Medals and polled well on other occasions while playing 320 games for Essendon and nineteen for Victoria. Reynolds spent twenty-eight years with Essendon, eighteen as player and ten as coach, in which time the club won four premierships. He was captain-coach for a record twelve seasons, was the club's best and fairest seven times, and kicked 441 goals. A thorough gentleman on and off the field, Reynolds was known as 'King Richard' to Essendon supporters. He later coached West Torrens in SA.

EP

RICHARDS, LOUIS CHARLES, OBE (1925–), born Collingwood, Melbourne, into 'a Magpie family', was a celebrated Australian rules footballer and sports commentator. He, his brother Ron, his uncles Alby Pannam and Charles Pannam Junior, his grandfather Charlie Pannam Senior and his great-uncle Albert Pannam collectively played more than nine hundred senior games for the Collingwood Football Club; Alby Pannam and Charlie Pannam Senior were Collingwood captains. Lou Richards also captained Collingwood (1952–55) and led it to a VFL Premiership in 1953. He played 250 games as a rover between 1941 and 1955, kicking 425 goals. Immediately upon retiring from football, Richards became a radio commentator and a sports columnist for the Melbourne *Sun* and has remained in both capacities for thirty-five years. He was the first ex-footballer to become a television personality, starting 'World of Sport' with Ron Casey in 1958 and co-starring in 'League Teams', which developed a small cult following. In 1981 Richards was King of Moomba, and he was awarded the OBE in 1984. Richards's quick wit, jovial sarcasm, and bantering exchanges have made him the best-known ex-footballer in Australia. He has written four best-selling books, *Boots and All*, *The Footballer Who Laughed*, *The Footballer Who Laughed Again*, and *The Kiss of Death*. The latter title reflects his uncanny ability to pre-ordain football teams to defeat by tipping them to win, often accompanied by outrageous statements about what he will do if he is wrong.

RS

See **Colliwobbles**.

RICHARDS, MARK (1957–), a tall, gangly Newcastle athlete who learnt to ride the waves at Merewether Beach, became world surfing champion four years in succession from 1979 to 1982. Before that time no one had won back-to-back titles. He was encouraged by his father Ray, a champion sprint swimmer, who operated the largest surf shop in Newcastle. Australian junior champion in 1973, Richards won numerous major tournaments including three successive Bell's Beach championships (1978 to 1980). He also won World Cups in 1975 and 1979; World Pro-Am in 1975; the Duke Kahanamoku Classic in 1979; the Pipeline Masters in 1980; the Stubbies in 1979 and 1981; and the NSW Surfabout in 1976. In all he won twenty-one major professional and sixteen Grand Prix titles. Known as the 'Wounded Seagull' because of his highly individual style, he was a versatile surfer who could perform in both big and small surfs. Richards made many of his own surfboards in a worked at the rear of his father's shop. After his 1982 world championship he virtually went into retirement though he continued to participate on the Australian circuit. He was inducted into the Sport Australia Hall of Fame in 1985.

RC

See **Surfing**.

RICHARDS, RANDELL WILLIAM ('Ron') (1910–67), born Ipswich, Queensland, was the son of an Aboriginal timber-cutter. He began fighting in Smally Higgins's boxing tent at Boonah when he was 15. Together with Dave Sands and Les Darcy, many pundits regard him as one of the greatest fighters ever produced in Australia. He was a tough fighter and expert counter-puncher who had the looks and attire of a matinee idol. He was Australian middleweight champion in 1933 and again 1936–42; light heavyweight champion, 1937–41; and heavyweight champion, 1936–38 and 1940–41. He beat Gus Lesnevich, later world light heavyweight champion for eight years, and lost twice to the 'immortal' Archie Moore, incontestably the greatest light heavyweight of the century. Mismanaged, he fought too often, including no less than ten fights against Fred Hennebury. He developed an alcohol problem and was sent to the Aboriginal settlement at Palm Island where he tended gardens and refused to talk about boxing. He died of a heart condition at Dulwich Hill, Sydney, in 1967. Richards had one hundred and forty-six fights: he won a hundred and six, drew eleven, lost twenty-eight and one was a no-contest.

RB

See **Aborigines in Sport**; **Boxing**.

RICHARDSON, MERLE, OAM (1930–   ), began playing lawn bowls in 1959 after her husband invited her to roll the first bowl under the newly installed lights at the Bulli Club on the NSW south coast. Her first win was recorded within the next twelve months when, playing against the club champion, Richardson took out the president's singles competition. Over the next thirty years she won over two hundred and fifty different games at all levels of competition. In 1970 Richardson was the NSW Champion of Champions and has represented Australia in international competitions three times. At the 1985 Melbourne women's international competition she won both the world singles and pairs competitions. In the wake of these successes she was made the Illawarra Sportsman (*sic*) of the Year, the first time this award was made to a woman and the first time to a lawn bowler. In 1986 she was awarded the OAM for services to lawn bowls. Notwithstanding her outstanding achievements in lawn bowls, Richardson is perhaps most famous for her participation in what was dubbed 'the Battle of the Sexes'. This competition, between the two world champions—Peter Belliss (NZ) and Merle Richardson—was held in 1986 in Doncaster, Victoria, and was won by Richardson. The score card used during the game is displayed in the Hall of Champions in Melbourne. In 1988 Richardson published her book, *Bowls for Everyone*, under the ABC imprint, and although she plays for the enjoyment of the game, believes that 'winning is the most important thing'.

LMcC

RILEY, RON (1947–   ), born Arncliffe, NSW, was a brilliant hockey centre-forward who possessed blistering acceleration, great anticipation, and the ability to score spectacular goals. He played seventy-two internationals for Australia between 1967 and 1980, including competing at three Olympic Games. He was recognised as the world's finest centre-forward in 1971 when he scored sixteen goals in six international matches in Australia. At the Montreal Olympics he scored three goals in Australia's 6–1 defeat of India. Riley played 295 first-grade games for the Sydney club St George and was the captain-coach for twelve seasons. He came from a strong hockey background: his father played hockey for NSW seniors and his grandfather was an Australian hockey representative.

MS

Rising Fast (1949–?), a thoroughbred racehorse, was a NZ-bred stayer, by *Alonzo* out of *Faster*, who dominated Australian racing from 1954 to 1956. Bought as a yearling for 325 guineas by Leicester Spring, *Rising Fast* was initially trained by Ivan Tucker. Not finding form until 3 years old, the bay gelding then won seven of fifteen races. Taken to Melbourne for the spring of 1954, he won nine of his eleven starts including the Caulfield Cup, Cox Plate, Mackinnon Stakes, and Melbourne Cup. As his usual rider, Bill Williamson, was injured, Jack Purtell rode him in the Cup. Four days later, *Rising Fast* won the C. B. Fisher Plate. The horse returned to NZ, but Tucker lost his licence when another of his horses proved positive to a drug test. Spring sent *Rising Fast* to the leading Melbourne trainer F. W. Hoysted, but the two voyages had undermined the horse's health. He managed only one win in the autumn and failed in the Sydney Cup. In the spring of 1955 he was back to his best, winning his second Caulfield Cup. He ran poorly in the Cox Plate but won the Mackinnon Stakes, and started favourite to win his second Melbourne Cup under 10 stone. The dream was shattered by another NZ-bred horse: while *Rising Fast* had a difficult passage, the lightly weighted *Toporoa* gained a winning break in the straight and beat the champion by just under a length. Once again, *Rising Fast* went on to win the C. B. Fisher Plate. He recorded three more wins in his final year on the turf, and lost to *Ray Ribbon* by a short half-head in the 1956 Cox Plate. He bravely carried 10 stone 2 pounds to fifth place behind *Evening Peal* in the Melbourne Cup. At Moonee Valley on 24 November 1956, *Rising Fast* gave a farewell gallop and was festooned with flowers in front of an emotional crowd before being retired to NZ.

AL

See **HOYSTED, FREDERICK**.

ROBERTSON, LOU (1881–1953), a trotting and thoroughbred racehorse trainer, was born in NZ where he excelled as a driver of trotters. In 1900 he was invited by the brothers A. and G. Tye to establish the largest trotting stud and training complex of its time in Australia, Allendale Farm at Melbourne. This was a great success, but by the First World War they had come into conflict with John Wren who was tightening his grip on the sport in Victoria. They sold their trotting interests and turned to thoroughbreds. Here they were just as successful, combining to win the 1915 Caulfield Cup with *Lavendo*. Robertson gained wealthy owners including the former bookmaker Sol Green, for whom he trained the sprinter *Gothic* and the 1927 Victoria Derby winner *Strephon*. Robertson's best year was 1935 when his horses won the Melbourne Cup, Cox Plate, Victoria Derby, VRC Oaks, Williamstown Cup, and Newmarket Handicap, and he continued to train top-class winners through to the 1949 Caulfield Cup winner *Lincoln*.

AL

ROBINSON, RAYMOND JOHN (1905–82) was a prolific and widely read cricket writer. A trained journalist, who began as a cadet reporter for the Melbourne *Herald* in 1922, Ray Robinson contributed to many Australian and international newspapers and magazines over the next five decades. His first cricket book, *Between Wickets*, was published in 1946 and he published another three cricket books before his last, and possibly his best book, *On Top Down Under* (1975). Robinson was a meticulous researcher—he even measured the precise distance of six hits with a tape—who was widely respected for his tact in deciding what to print. He wrote in a lively style, had an apt turn of phrase, and a nice sense of irony. He was one of the pioneers of Australian cricket literature.

RC

See **CRICKET**.

ROBRAN, BARRIE CHARLES (1947–), born Whyalla, SA, is possibly the best Australian footballer not to play in the VFL. Robran won three Magarey Medals (1968, 1970, and 1973) but could have won double that number had he not suffered a severe knee injury in an interstate match against Victoria in 1974. A wiry 185 centimetres, Robran played centre half-forward, centre and as a follower with distinction. Thousands of South Australians remember his opponent Alex Jesaulenko applauding his artistry as he repeatedly soared over packs to take brilliant marks in North Adelaide's Championship of Australia win over Carlton in 1972. A talented and modest all-round sportsman, Robran also represented SA in cricket in 1971–72. Robran's brother Rodney was also a prominent footballer, his sister Julie (Francou) was an

international netballer, and his son Matthew now plays for Hawthorn in the AFL.

BW

See **FRANCOU, JULIE**.

ROCHE, DOROTHY, OAM (1928–), has lived all her life in a western Sydney suburb, and has been prominent in lawn bowls. Following her 'retirement' from tennis, she took up competitive lawn bowls in 1975. In her career she has won a State-level game of one form or another every year including Champion of Champions (singles) in 1979. In the same year she won the Alpha Romeo Sport-Star of the Year, the runners-up for that year being Ray Bryce and Doug Walters. In 1984 she was chosen to play a round-robin match with Merle Richardson against the leading male players: Roche won her game against David Bryant, then male world champion. In 1988 she captained the gold-winning team at the Melbourne World Championships, and in 1990 was granted the 'Freedom of the City of Parramatta', an honour which had been given only four times previously. She was awarded the OAM for services to lawn bowls in 1990.

LMcC

ROCHE, TONY (1945–), tennis-player, was twice ranked number two in the world behind Rod Laver. A left-hander with a fine backhand volley and a swinging serve, Roche won the French and Italian championships and was runner-up in the 1968 Wimbledon titles. He formed an overpowering doubles combination with John Newcombe: with their fine understanding they won five Wimbledon titles between 1965 and 1974 as well as four Australian, two French, one American, and one Italian championship. Unfortunately a severe shoulder injury plagued Roche throughout his career and deprived him of much greater success. He later coached Ivan Lendl and played an important role in his world ascendancy.

RC

See **Lawn Tennis**.

ROONEY, JAMES (1945–), born Dundee, Scotland, began his soccer career with spells at Peterborough and Montrose Football Clubs before his emigration to Australia in April 1968. He immediately joined Melbourne's Essendon Lions, then Sydney Prague, Apia-Leichhardt, Marconi Fairfield, Heidelberg United as player-coach, and Croydon, Melbourne. He snared the National League's inaugural Player of the Year award in 1977. The proverbial 'wee mon', Rooney's terrier-like, never-say-die qualities suited the demands of modern mid-field play. He made one hundred appearances for the national team, a number of these as captain, and scored 7 goals. Career highlights centred around the 1974 World Soccer Cup. Besides the finals, these included tense qualifying tussles against Iran in Tehran and South Korea in Hong Kong.

PM

Rorke's Drift Test. When the first two Tests of the 1914 Australia v. England rugby league series were shared, a third, and deciding, match was hastily arranged, over English protests. The 'Lions', without five of their key players because of injury, were told by their manager that they were 'playing for Right v. Wrong' and that 'England expects that every man will do his duty'. England led 9–0 at half-time but were soon hard-pressed, having lost three men injured, replacements not being permitted. With 30 minutes left, forward Albert Johnson, playing on the wing, dribbled the ball fifty metres and scored, increasing the lead to 14–0. The ten Britons, defending heroically, restricted Australia to two unconverted tries and won 14–6, regaining the Ashes, lost in 1912. As a tribute to the British team's courage in adversity, the game became known as the 'Rorke's Drift Test', after the 1879 battle when, greatly outnumbered by Zulus, British Troops won eleven Victoria Crosses.

TB

ROSE, IAIN MURRAY (1939–), born England, came to Australia at the outbreak of war in 1939. Throughout his life he was brought up on a diet which substituted natural foods for pasteurised, refined, and processed foods, and which was keyed to natural complex carbohydrates and de-emphasised fats and animal products. Former Olympic-diving gold-medallist Dick Eve gave Rose his first swimming lessons, but it was under the tutelage of Sam Herford that his world-class talents unfolded. Rose came to prominence in the 1955 Australian championships, winning the 220 and 440 yards freestyle events with a fluid stroke and four-beat kick that were to become his trademarks. In all, he was to win seven Australian championships (five individual and two team) and set fifteen world records (nine individual and six team). He won four British Empire and Commonwealth Games gold medals and four gold, one silver, and one bronze medal in Olympic competition, the highest achievement of any Australian male throughout the Games's history. In 1983 he was elected by his peers as Australia's greatest male Olympian. The 1956 Melbourne Olympic Games was the high point of Rose's career. He was victorious in the 400 and 1500 metres freestyle and the 4 × 200 metres freestyle relay. He was the first swimmer in thirty-six years to win the 400 and 1500 metres events in the same Olympics. Following the Melbourne Games he went to the University of Southern California to take up a sports scholarship. In Rome in 1960 he repeated his victory in the 400 metres freestyle, thus becoming the first and

only swimmer to win this event in consecutive Olympic Games. In the 1500 metres Rose had to settle for a silver medal, behind John Konrads, and a bronze in the 4 × 200 metres freestyle relay. Rose wanted to swim in the 1964 Games, but was unable to travel to Australia to compete in the 1964 national championships because of a movie contract, and the swimming bureaucracy refused his entry into the Olympic trials, despite his setting a world record in the 1500 metres. Rose remained in the USA, working in the television industry and managing a company manufacturing and marketing nutritional supplements.

RH and MH

See **Swimming**.

ROSE, LIONEL, MBE (1948–), was born at Jackson's Track, near Drouin, Victoria. He boxed to emulate his father and his idol, twice Australian lightweight champion George Bracken, another of the many talented Aboriginal title-holders. Rose was Australian flyweight champion in 1963 and represented Australia at the Tokyo Olympics in 1964. As a professional, he was Australian bantamweight champion from 1966 to 1969. In 1968 he became the first Aboriginal Australian to win a world title when he beat Fighting Harada in Tokyo. Rose was a fast and tough fighter, possessing sharp lefts, and was a fine counter-puncher. He was voted Australian of the Year in 1968, was offered film roles, and performed country-and-western music. Until the advent of Jeff Fenech, he had won more money than any other Australian boxer. After losing his fourth world title defence in 1969, he retired briefly, before returning as a lightweight of note. In 1975 he was beaten by Yoshiaki Numata in a world junior lightweight fight. In 1991 a television mini-series 'Rose Against the Odds' was widely acclaimed; even the serious newspapers claimed that Rose and Dawn Fraser were 'national treasures'. He had fifty-three fights, of which he won forty-two and lost eleven.

RB

See **Aboriginal Sports Foundation**; **Aborigines in Sport**; **Boxing**.

ROSEWALL, KEN ('Muscles') (1934–) was born in Rockdale, NSW, just twenty-one days and a few miles away from fellow 'whiz kid' Lew Hoad. A stylish player, Rosewall was one of the greatest players never to win Wimbledon although he reached the final on four occasions, in 1954, 1956, 1970, and 1974. After becoming Australian and French champion in 1953, when only 18, Rosewall, with Hoad, defeated the USA in the Davis Cup. Beaten by Hoad at Wimbledon in 1956, Rosewall retaliated by winning the US final a few weeks later which denied Hoad a Grand Slam. After turning professional in 1957 'Muscles' Rosewall reigned supreme in the world professional circuit, winning Wembley singles in 1957 and 1960–63. Just four months short of 40 Rosewall played in another Wimbledon final but was trounced by 21-year-old Jimmy Connors. Rosewall was more successful in the doubles, which in partnership with Hoad he had won in 1953 and 1956. He won the Australian singles title four times, the French twice, and the US twice. Rosewall lacked a powerful serve but compensated for this with his accuracy and angles. A fleet-footed and graceful player with a classical backhand and possessing a sound temperament, Rosewall was a popular player who enjoyed prolonged success.

KM-H

See **HOAD, LEW**; **Lawn Tennis**.

Rothmans Foundation, National Sport Division. In 1964 the Rothmans National Sport Foundation was established to encourage all forms of sport at a national, grass-roots level through increasing the awareness of the need for improved coaching techniques. It did not intend to embark on a programme to produce medals directly. In many ways, its establishment was an almost revolutionary step: a public company pausing in the pursuit of profits to consider the sporting community and the community at large, with no obvious commercial gain in mind. In its first twenty years the foundation's achievements included assistance to sports coaching programmes, production of coaching resources, and the appointment of full-time national coaching directors. Recently the foundation became part of Rothmans Foundation—a body wholly supported by Rothmans Holdings Ltd, which gives educational, cultural, and sporting assistance to the nation. For all that, Rothmans Foundation, National Sport Division, retains its original charter and specific purpose: 'not to groom or produce champions but to help average participants of all ages to perform better at their chosen sports.'

PC

Rothmans Medal (Rugby League) is awarded to the best and fairest player in the home-and-away matches of the Sydney premiership. First awarded to Cronulla half-back Terry Hughes in 1968, the medal is judged by referees, who allocate points on a 3–2–1 basis after each first grade match. Three players have won the medal twice: Dennis Pittard (1969, 1971), Mick Cronin (1977, 1978), and Peter Sterling (1987, 1990). The most successful club has been Parramatta, whose players have won the medal on six occasions, including four years in a row between 1976 and 1979. Only once has the medal been shared, in 1989 when Cronulla's Gavin Miller and Newcastle's Mark Sargent could not be separated. The sole hooker to win the award was Mal Cochrane of Manly in 1986,

leaving only wingers unrepresented among medal winners.

PC

Rothmans Medals (Soccer). Since 1970 the various soccer leagues have awarded Rothmans Medals to the best players in the league. The Rothmans Medal was first awarded in NSW in 1970 to the best player in the NSW State League. The inaugural winner was George Blues from Apia-Leichhardt. Between 1970 and 1987 the only dual winner was John Watkiss (Hakoah East-Sydney and then Sutherland). In 1978 there was a tie for the first time, between Terry Butler (Apia-Leichhardt) and Alan Bankhead (Arncliffe Scots). Although both players had received 27 votes, Butler was declared the winner on a count-back. From 1971 onwards the best player in the WA State League was awarded the Rothmans Medal. The only dual winner of the WA Rothmans Medal has been L. Adam (Inglewood-Kiev), who was the recipient in 1978 and 1980. Between 1971 and 1987 the Rothmans Medal was awarded to the best player in the Tasmanian State League. Dual winners of the award include Brian Davidson (Croatia-Glenorchy) in 1979–80 and Liam Monagle (Ulverstone and later Georgetown United) in 1983 and 1987. From 1985 the medal was awarded to the best player in the National Soccer League (NSL). The inaugural winner of the award was Jim Patikas from Sydney Croatia. In 1987 the Australian National Soccer League Player of the Year award was established. This award is based upon the votes of the players of the NSL for best player in the competition. It was won in its inaugural season by Frank Farina of Marconi-Fairfield. At the end of each season in the Victorian State League the Gold Medal is awarded to the best and fairest player. This award was first instituted in 1971. Dual winners include John Gardiner (George Cross), Vince Bannon (Fitzroy United Alexander and later Brunswick United Juventus) and Tommy Cumming (Essendon Croatia).

MH*

Rowing and Sculling

The mild climate, the presence of adequate rivers and harbours along which people lived and worked, and the predisposition of Australians to wager on sporting events all played a part in the development of rowing and sculling. At least as early as 1805 rowing matches between crews of visiting ships were being staged, although the first race of which we have a record occurred in 1818, when John Piper stroked a four-oared gig to victory in a race from Bradley's Head to Sydney Cove. Piper sponsored a number of crews which raced with some success during the 1820s.

From early in the history of all colonies, wagers were laid on sculling races, and cash prizes were competed for, but it was in NSW from the 1850s that professional sculling matches became a major attraction. Visits by British professionals helped raise standards, and the feats of 'cracks' like George Mulhall (first Australian champion), Richard Green, Michael Rush, and Elias Laycock all indicated that Australians could hold their own with overseas champions. Green, who had been the first to compete overseas (1863), later became a successful coach, and it was his protégé, Ned Trickett, who won the World Championship on the Thames in 1876, thus becoming Australia's first world champion in any sport. To many, the international success of Australian scullers and cricketers was proof that Australians were 'no puny, degenerate race that are reared under the Southern Cross'. Trickett duly received a massive public welcome in Sydney, was given a parade, and awarded an £850 purse. So began a remarkable period of sustained Australian excellence. Between 1876 and 1907 seven New South Welshmen held the world championship for a total of twenty-two years: after Trickett came Bill Beach, Peter Kemp, Henry Searle, Jim Stanbury, John McLean, and George Towns. Public response was enthusiastic, particularly for the feats of the Illawarra blacksmith, William Beach, and tens of thousands would treat a title match on the Parramatta or Nepean Rivers as an opportunity for a holiday. The scullers were the first Australian sporting heroes: Banjo Paterson was to liken them to 'Gladiators stalking through the degenerate Romans'.

Professional sculling did not maintain its dominant position for long. The crash of the 1890s ate into the generosity of backers, accusations of shady practices were common, and crowds switched to regularly scheduled sports such as football and horse-racing, which were also easier to watch. A few stalwarts maintained interest for some years, but although the world championship was later held by other Australians including dual Olympic winner Bobby Pearce, the professional sport was dead by the end of the 1950s. Amateur races were also held from an early date, especially at regattas such as the Hobart Regatta (1827) and Sydney's Anniversary Regatta (1837). In 1859 the Melbourne University Boat Club was the first of many strong clubs to be established over a thirty-year period, and it was through these clubs, together with the universities and the public schools, that most of the amateur development occurred.

As in other sports, intercolonial competition soon emerged. In 1863 NSW defeated Victoria in a four-oar challenge, the first inter-university race was held seven years later, and in 1878 the first intercolonial eights event was raced between Sydney's Mercantile Club and a Victorian crew. By 1902 this last event had grown into the annual interstate eight-oared championship, contested by all States. From 1920 the winning crew received the King's Cup. Of one hundred and one championships held between 1878 and 1990, Victoria won fifty-one. The men's interstate single sculling championship was first held in 1892, and annually from 1895. From 1926 the champion sculler received the President's Cup. Among the championship's most illustrious winners have been Bobby Pearce (NSW, 1927–29), Merv Wood (NSW, 1946–52, and 1955), Stuart Mackenzie (NSW, 1956–57), and Ted Hale (NSW, 1976–81). Although the first women's club, Albert Park Ladies (Victoria), was formed in 1907, and the first interstate women's races occurred five years later, rowing suffered from the social restrictions placed at that time on women in all vigorous sports. It was not until the 1970s that this sport made significant progress, with women's events beginning to enjoy a much-enhanced status at the national regatta. By the 1980s women's crews were achieving significant success overseas.

In 1912 Australian men first participated in amateur international events, at the Stockholm Olympics and at England's Henley Regatta. An early victory of historical significance was that by an AIF crew at Henley in 1919, for it was the trophy awarded by King George V for this event which later became known as the King's Cup. Despite Australia's long rowing history, its international achievements have been patchy, with some remarkably fine achievements mixed with long periods of mediocre results. Among the highlights have been Pearce's two Olympic sculling victories (1928 and 1932), Wood's Olympic sculling gold medal (1948), Mackenzie's six consecutive Henley Diamond Sculls victories (1957–62), and world championships won by Adair Ferguson (women's lightweight sculls, 1985) and Peter Antonie (lightweight sculls, 1986). World Championship victories have also included men's lightweight fours (1974, 1980 and 1981), men's eights (1986), women's junior fours (1989), and men's coxless fours (1990).

Like many other sports, during the 1980s rowing developed a much more professional approach to its organisation and preparation of crews, its search for talent, and its national administration. In this it was aided by the sport's inclusion in the Australian Institute of Sport, where talented rowers could benefit from the intensive programme offered. Also like other sports, from this period it made large strides in breaking down Australia's geographic isolation, by regularly sending many rowers overseas for international competition. As a consequence, the 1980s were by far the most successful decade of international competition enjoyed by Australia so far.

SB

See **ANTONIE, PETER; BEACH, WILLIAM;**

FAIRBAIRN, STEPHEN; FERGUSON, ADAIR; GPS Head of the River; Jack Affair; King's Cup; MACKENZIE, STUART; PEARCE, HENRY; Rowing; Intercolonial Regattas; SEARLE, HENRY; TRICKETT, EDWARD; WOOD, MERVYN.

Rowing: Intercolonial Regattas. Australia's first recorded intercolonial amateur rowing contest was a four-oar race between NSW and Victoria on the Parramatta River in February 1863. This race, won by the NSW crew, was criticised by the Victorian public because of the dubious amateur status of the NSW rowers—they purportedly included 'watermen'. Disputes over amateurism limited early intercolonial contests to club crews with compatible amateur definitions. Ironically in 1872 an intercolonial amateur fours event was held in Hobart for a cash purse of £100 and this led to a similar event in 1873 which was considered to be the first 'official' intercolonial amateur race. In 1878 the first intercolonial eight-oar race was held between NSW and Victoria. It became an annual contest held in either May or November and the focus of the rowing calendar. The four-oar contests were soon subsumed by the eights for many years. Queensland and Tasmania also competed in 1885, making the eights regatta a truly intercolonial event. SA and WA began to compete regularly in the 1890s, and from this time the regattas began to incorporate single-sculls and four-oar events. Despite the extra competition, Victorian crews dominated this era of amateur rowing. The issue of amateurism remained prominent and from 1888 the annual regattas coincided with conferences to discuss definitions of amateur status. These failed to solve the problems and controversy continued. For example, in 1895 the NSW crew refused to comply with a last-minute edict of the NSW Rowing Association not to compete against the Victorian crew. Consequently the cream of NSW rowing were ruled non-amateurs on a technicality. The main issues of contention were the inclusion of manual labourers and cash-prize winners in other sports as bona fide amateurs in rowing.

DL

ROWLEY, STANLEY RUPERT (1878–1924), a NSW athlete who was Australasian champion in the 100 and 220 yards in 1897 and 1899, was the first sprinter to represent Australia at the Olympics. At the 1900 Paris Games—the casual administration of which gravely disappointed Rowley—he ran well to gain third place in the 60, 100, and 200 metres races. Rowley also competed in the 5000 metres cross-country event as a member of the Great Britain team which won the gold medal. After retiring from competitive running Rowley served as the treasurer of the Amateur Athletic Union of Australasia from 1908 and worked in the stock and pastoral industry in Sydney until his death.

KM

Royal Federation of Aero Clubs of Australia (RFACA). The Australian Aero Club was formed in 1919 and received royal patronage in 1960 when it assumed its present title. The main role of RFACA is to promote aviation in Australia and to provide representation at all levels of government for its member clubs. It promotes sporting aviation by encouraging flying competitions on a club and inter-club basis and by holding the annual Australian Light Aircraft Championships. It also promotes record-setting flights by all powered-aircraft pilots, both amateur and professional. In 1988 it organised the highly successful Around Australia Air Race in which over a hundred aircraft competed. For pilots who do not seek competition, the federation offers a pilot-proficiency scheme and holds State and interstate flying safaris. Current membership of RFACA comprises more than sixty aero clubs in all States of Australia, a number of other aviation organisations and over eleven thousand individual members. RFACA is controlled by a council comprised of a member from each member club, which meets annually. RFACA represented all sporting aviation disciplines in Australia until 1989 through the international body, the Fédération Aeronautique Internationale (FAI). In 1984, however, separate committees were established to handle the growing number of sporting bodies and this resulted in a separate confederation in 1990 when the RFACA decided to relinquish its FAI role to concentrate its efforts on Aero Club members.

SA and IJ

Royal Life Saving Society—Australia (RLSS-A). Appalled at the number of drownings which were occurring in England, William Henry founded the British RLSS in 1891. In 1894 Henry formed a squad of six young men who toured England demonstrating methods of rescue and resuscitation which had been published in the society's first handbook. One of those young men was Frank Venning who pioneered the society in Queensland and remained a staunch member for sixty years. Soon after its establishment in England the movement spread to Australia; the first branch was formed in NSW in 1894. Actually, two branches were established in Sydney, one known as the Waverley branch and the other as the Australian; since this led to confusion the two branches amalgamated in August 1895. Branches were formed in Victoria (1904), Queensland (1905), WA and SA (1910), and Tasmania (1912). At first these branches were affiliated directly with the central executive in London, although inter-branch conferences were held periodically in

Sydney and Melbourne. Australia's geographical location, coastline, and waterways were all conducive to bathing and swimming, and public-spirited citizens established clubs and acted as lifesavers.

When the Schaeffer method of artificial respiration was first introduced in the summer of 1906–7 the government made a grant of £1000 to help finance the activities of the RLSS. It soon became evident to the society that the surf beaches presented a specific problem in supervision, so at a public meeting held during the 1908–9 season the Surf Bathers Association was formed to concentrate on matters relevant to lifesaving on ocean beaches. In December 1924 an agreement was signed between the two, now independent, lifesaving groups determining their specific areas of responsibility. Following this mutual division of interests, the RLSS continued its work on establishing lifesaving clubs within harbours, bays, and river regions and also promulgated lifesaving procedures to schoolchildren and public agencies. In 1934, at a conference in Melbourne, an Australian body was formed, then known as the Federal Council of the Society but now called the Royal Life Saving Society—Australia.

In 1952 the discontent of executive members in NSW with the methods of the London handbook (regarded as the official handbook of all Royal Life Saving Societies) and the desire of that branch to govern its own affairs led to the establishment of a breakaway organisation, the Australian Life Saving Society. This stimulated great interest throughout Australia since the new organisation was concerned with an evaluation of lifesaving procedures used elsewhere in the world, especially with the Red Cross Associations in Canada, Denmark, and the USA, and was determined to adopt methods which were modern and suitable to the Australian scene. Management in the London headquarters of RLSS was also stimulated to reassess the situation and this led to the establishment of the Commonwealth Council in 1956, with the granting of autonomy to the various national branches. This action culminated in the NSW branch integrating as an autonomous body with the Australian branch and the adoption in 1957 of the handbook prepared by the Australian Life Saving Society as the handbook of the RLSS-A. The Australian Council, having complete autonomy under the Supplemental Charter which was granted by Queen Elizabeth in 1958, deals with all matters pertaining to Australia, including items submitted to it by the States. State branches of RLSS-A compete at Australian lifesaving championships.

DR and IJ

See **Surf Lifesaving**.

Royal Melbourne Golf Club. Founded as the Melbourne Golf Club at Caulfield in 1891, this prestigious club has been influential in the development of Australian golf. Like a number of other early clubs it drew on Scottish traditions, such as a uniform consisting of a scarlet coat with gilt buttons, knickerbockers, and a Tam O' Shanter. Its inaugural professional, Richard Taylor of Hoylake, also doubled as a greenkeeper. The Melbourne Golf Club was the first site for the Australian Amateur Championship in 1894 and the next year it became the first club in Australia to be granted a royal charter. In 1898 it played host to a meeting of administrators from Melbourne, Sydney, and Adelaide which led to the formation of the Australian Golf Union (AGU). The club moved to Sandringham in 1901 and it was there in 1926 that the famous golf course architect Dr Alister Mackenzie began making modifications to what became known as the West Course. Mackenzie altered the bunkering, contoured the greens, and made undulations in the fairways, working with the 1924 Australian Open winner, Alex Russell, who subsequently designed the East Course which opened in 1932. Royal Melbourne has been the venue for a large number of major championships including the Australian Amateur (eighteen times) and the Australian Open (fifteen times). Since 1959 it has been customary to create a composite course for such championships from holes on both West and East Courses. Although the club is the best known in Australia, it has not been free from controversy; in early years two curious rulings favoured amateur winners over professional opponents. In the 1907 Australian Open, amateur Michael Scott admitted teeing off outside the markers on the 12th hole during the final round but the controlling committee of Royal Melbourne, where he was a member, ignored the infringement and Scott retained his title despite Dan Soutar's attempt to get the Royal and Ancient Golf Club at St Andrews, Scotland, to arbitrate. In an incident in 1912, again relating to an amateur playing in the Australian Open, it was alleged in written complaints from spectators that Ivo Whitton had not returned to the tee after hitting his tee shot into an unplayable lie and taking a 2-stroke penalty. The AGU decided in Whitton's favour, although the Royal and Ancient Golf Club recommended his disqualification. Controversy continued in 1987 when, during the last Australian Open staged at Royal Melbourne, there was a walk-off by players caused by a ludicrous side-hill pin-placement at the 3rd hole in the final round.

BW

See **Golf**; SCOTT, **Hon.** MICHAEL; SOUTAR, DANIEL; WHITTON, IVO.

Royal Sydney Golf Club is possibly Australia's foremost social and sporting institution. The size of the membership, the location and value of the inner-city property, the elegance of the clubhouse, the quality of the course, the grass courts and the bowling greens, the number of major tournaments 'played at Rose Bay', and the quality of its champions and administrators have produced, and sustained, both national and international reputation. Born on 2 August 1893 at Dame Eadith Walker's property Yaralla (at what is now Concord Golf Club), the club moved to Bondi, hoping for a links course towards the sea. Sandhill problems led to a turning towards the present site at Rose Bay. The present course, dating from 1909, is an old-fashioned, narrow, tight test of golf, a difficult par 72 of 6807 metres in the often windy conditions. The 426 metre 4th and 435 metre 5th are two of the best par fours in Australian golf; many rate the 211 metre 17th and 410 metre 18th as two of the best finishing holes in tournament play. The course was not designed: it evolved, with major alterations by Dr Alister Mackenzie in 1926 and Thompson Wolveridge & Associates in 1985. There are 5800 members, of whom 2100 are golfers: the rest play tennis, squash, bowls, croquet, or none of these things. A staff of 123 maintains a complex that has a turnover of $10 million a year. The club has hosted one hundred and eight major tournaments, including nine Australian Opens, five PGA titles, twenty Men's and Ladies' National Amateurs, and thirty-three Men's and Ladies' State Amateurs. In a hundred years, Royal Sydney players have won 242 major titles. In that time, members have contributed much to golf administration, especially to women's golf. Great professionals have served the club: Carnegie Clark, Dan Soutar, Fred Popplewell, J. Victor East and, in more recent times, the renowned teacher Alex Mercer.

CT

See **CLARK, CARNEGIE; POPPLEWELL, FRED; SOUTAR, DANIEL.**

Royal Tennis

Royal (real or court) tennis, as practised at its advent to the Australian colonies, was a direct descendant of the game that had been played in Europe (particularly in France, Italy, and Spain, and also in England and Scotland) probably from as early as the fourteenth century. Antecedents in turn to this game had taken a number of forms, including street games not unlike football; games in monasteries; games using the hand; games using racket substitutes such as the scanno, bracciale and paletta; games using the soft and hard ball; and finally games played with a racket and a cord (net) in an enclosed, high-walled court, using a hard ball.

This last form of the game, known simply as 'tennis', was brought to Australia by a retired London merchant, Samuel Smith Travers, who had played the game at Oxford and London's Haymarket, and elsewhere in England and France. Travers and his large family came to the

Antipodes in 1870, settling in Hobart, where he later built a court in the grounds of his residence. The court, in Davey Street opposite St David's Park, is still in use. In 1874 Travers lured an English professional, Thomas Stone, from the court at Oxford to tutor his family and others in the game. The Davey Street court was opened in 1875, the year in which Major Wingfield patented the new game of lawn tennis in England. Since 1885, when a group of players bought the court from Travers, it has been the home of the Hobart Tennis Club. The Hobart Club, the Royal Melbourne Tennis Club (founded in 1882), and the Ballarat Royal Tennis Club (founded in 1883) provide the focus of the game in Australia.

Under the initiative of the lawyer (later judge) John Burnett Box, moves began in 1881 among businessmen, lawyers, and men of property in Melbourne and the Victorian Western District (several of whom were members of the Melbourne Club in Collins Street) to build a mainland court in Melbourne. Sited at the northern end of Exhibition Street, looking out on the Exhibition Gardens, the Melbourne Tennis Club was opened in April 1882 by the Victorian Governor, the Marquis of Normanby, with Thomas Stone engaged as professional. Stone's place in Hobart was taken by Percy Finch, who continued coaching there for some years. Stone remained as professional at the Melbourne court until the Great War, being gradually replaced in the role by his son, Woolner Stone. In 1897 the club received royal patronage from Queen Victoria and became the Royal Melbourne Tennis Club. Over the next seventy years it weathered many crises of financial stringency, until in 1971 it was able to sell its prime central-city location and buy land in Sherwood Street, Richmond, to the east of the city, where a new and comfortable two-court complex with squash courts, swimming pool, club, and pro shop was completed in 1974.

The game of royal tennis in Australia has been and remains a relatively exclusive sport. The cost of building courts is very high. Those who have started clubs have generally been men of property or the professions and quite often have brought their clubs vice-regal connections. Until the 1960s royal tennis had been predominantly a male preserve, with ladies admitted as associate members, the game being considered not suited to women, played as it is with a fairly heavy racket and a hard ball. Nevertheless, women's competition is now integrated into the game, Australia producing in Judy Clarke, formerly of the Hobart Tennis Club and later of the Royal Melbourne Tennis Club, an outstanding player by world standards. She was the winner of the International Ladies' Championship in 1975, 1979, 1982, and 1985, the British Open in 1982, and the Australian Ladies' title from 1976 through to 1981 inclusive. Wayne Davies, an

Australian professional who has served at Melbourne, Hobart, Hampton Court, Bordeaux, and the New York Rackets Club, is the first Australian to win the World Men's Championship. He has held it against all challenges, at the time of writing, since 1987, when he defeated the English champion, Chris Ronaldson.

The Bathurst Cup is the royal tennis equivalent of the Davis Cup. It is currently held by England, which continues to stave off opposition from the other royal tennis nations, the USA, France, and Australia. The Cup was won by Australia in 1982 but ironically has so far never been won by France, the foster country of court or royal tennis—the game they call 'Jeu de Paume'—which has been described as being to lawn tennis what chess is to draughts for its much greater complexity and fascination.

GK-S

See **CLARKE, JUDITH**; **DAVIES, WAYNE**; **Gold Racket**; **Lawn Tennis**.

ROYCROFT, WILLIAM (1915–   ) won Australia's first equestrian Olympic gold medal in the three-day event in 1960. Winning in Rome required great courage from this Victorian farmer: on the second day of the event Roycroft and his mount, *Our Solo*, crashed heavily. Despite suffering a broken collarbone, a neck injury, and bruising, Roycroft defied the doctor's orders and rode the final section. Although he had to be lifted into the saddle and had no use of his right arm he rode faultlessly over the twelve jumps to win the gold medal. Before 1960 the tall and elegant equestrian, who used to ride to school in the foothills of the Victorian Alps, became the first Australian to win the prized Badminton Three-Day Trials in the UK. He also competed in the 1964, 1968, and 1972 Olympics as well as in the 1976 Olympics with his two sons, Barry and Wayne. Another son, Clarke, also competed in the Olympics and daughter-in-law Vicki became the first woman to win the Equestrian Grand Prix in Rome. After the Mexico Olympics Roycroft was presented with the Fédération Équestre Internationale International Silver Medal for his representation in three Olympics.

GC*

See **Equestrianism**.

Rugby League

Rugby league is a code of football in which each team consists of thirteen players and the oval-shaped ball can be handled or kicked. In 1895 a dispute about payment of working-class footballers led a group of Lancashire and Yorkshire clubs to break away from the English Rugby Union to form the Northern Rugby Football Union. Over the next eleven years the Northern Union altered the rules, eliminating two breakaway forwards from the usual union team of fifteen. In 1922 the British body became the

Rugby Football League, adopting a name used in NSW fifteen years earlier.

The split in rugby union reached Australia in 1907 when J. J. Giltinan organised a team of Sydney footballers to play visiting NZ professionals en route to England. The NSW Rugby Football League was set up on 8 August at a meeting at Bateman's Crystal Hotel, George Street, Sydney. The locals played three games against the visitors under rugby union rules. One of these Sydney pioneers, H. H. 'Dally' Messenger, joined the NZ team and toured Britain. He returned in April 1908 in time for the first competition of the new code, with nine teams competing in the league, which had been organised earlier in the year. In March a Rugby League Association was established in Queensland. At the end of the first season, Giltinan left with a team of players from both States to tour Britain. This, the first Kangaroo tour, was not financially sound and bankrupted Giltinan.

At the end of the 1909 Sydney season the league, financed by hotelier James Joynton Smith, staged a successful series of matches between Kangaroo tour members and the first Wallaby Australian rugby union team. On its 1911–12 tour of Britain the second Kangaroos, which included four New Zealanders and was captained by former Wallaby Chris McKivat, won the series, a feat not repeated for another fifty years. League in NSW and Queensland prospered and during the First World War competitions continued, whereas rugby union suspended its matches.

The rugby league organisation in NSW has traditionally been city-dominated. Although players from country districts have frequently been included in representative teams, only in rare cases have they not moved to play in Sydney. South Sydney, which won the first premiership competition in 1908, has been the most successful club, bestriding the late 1920s and, thanks partly to the famous skills of former Newcastle player Clive Churchill, the early 1950s. Balmain was strong from 1915 to 1920. Eastern Suburbs had its most successful era in the late 1930s when Dave Brown was at his remarkable peak. St George, which joined the Sydney competition in 1921, was successful in eleven straight seasons from 1956 to 1966. Among its great stars were Reg Gasnier, Johnny Raper, and Graeme Langlands. Some inner-city teams, such as Annandale, Glebe, and Newtown have dropped out of the Sydney competition. New clubs, reflecting the growing city, have been added. Manly-Warringah and Parramatta, both of which joined in 1947, became prominent in the 1970s and 1980s. The Sydney competition was extended to include Canberra and Illawarra in 1982, and Newcastle, Brisbane, and Gold Coast-Tweed in 1988. This expansion indicated the widening popularity of rugby

99 Arthur Beetson, who played rugby league for clubs in
Queensland and NSW, captained Queensland in the first
state-of-origin match in 1980.

100 The Charters Towers rugby team at an inter-town match, 1899.

101 Skiing in Australia was evident during the 1860s, although it is probable that early skiers used a pole as a brake, as illustrated in this photograph of 1897.

102 and 103 Many great Australian boxers have been Aborigines. Randell 'Ron' Richards was Australian champion in several weight divisions from 1936 to 1942, and Dave Sands won the Empire middleweight championship in 1949.

104 The Spalding Baseball Trophy, made in approximately 1894 from silver and wood, was awarded to the Melbourne Cricket Club baseball team for winning three premierships in the Victorian Baseball League.

105 Corporate signs, such as these at a football match at the MCG in 1992, illustrate how sponsorship and advertising have become an integral part of the financial infrastructure of Australian sport.

league, and the impetus was highlighted by Canberra's successive premierships in 1989 and 1990.

Two country districts of NSW deserve special mention. Newcastle took part in the first Sydney premiership and sustained a strong local competition until 1987 when it responded to the changing district demands of the game by entering a team in the Sydney league. In the south-west of the State, the Maher Cup competition among local towns was an institution from 1920 to 1971.

Rule changes have varied the code's distinctive features over the years. Perhaps the most far-reaching was the introduction in NSW in 1967 of the four-tackle rule, to combat the increasingly boring dominance of dogged forward play. The experiment was soon varied by providing for a scrum after six tackles. This became the accepted rule internationally in 1976, the same year that the value for a field goal was reduced from 2 points to 1. In 1981 differential scrum penalties were introduced and the sin bin was instituted; a minor offender could be suspended for five or ten minutes instead of being sent off for the remainder of a match. The points value for a try was increased from 3 to 4 in 1983, and scrums were eliminated after six tackles, the ball being handed to the opposing team. The league's constant adjustment of the rules has emphasised the running movement of the game and has eliminated many stoppages. The advent of television, at first for a mid-week competition in 1974, has substantially affected the administrative and playing structures of the game including the introduction of night football under lights.

Styles of play have changed. In the early years the 'no-kick rule' of South Sydney's coach Arthur Hennessy was popular. Under the influence of Duncan Thompson and Queensland in the early 1920s back-line tactics flourished. In the years soon after the Second World War there was an emphasis on forward play and strong defence, backed up by speedy wingers. The introduction of the limited-tackle rule has made 'bombs'—previously known as 'up and unders'—more frequent and strategic kicking more pronounced.

In Brisbane there was no organised competition until 1909 when Valleys, which has been the most successful club, won the first premiership. North Brisbane dominated from 1959 to 1966. As in NSW, Queensland has seen an increasing movement of top players to the metropolitan competitions, but, in a more decentralised State, teams like Toowoomba, Ipswich, and North Queensland have had periods of great strength. Toowoomba's 1924 team, 'the galloping Clydesdales', beat all comers including NSW and, in a famous victory, the touring Englishmen. The Arch Foley Shield, established

in north Queensland in 1948, is an example of regional competitions which have developed in tandem with strong district rivalries.

Queensland was slow to achieve success in its annual series of games against NSW, not winning a match until 1922. In the 1920s, when the Toowoomba trio of Duncan Thompson, E. S. 'Nigger' Brown, and Tommy Gorman were dominant, so also was their State. The comparative wealth of Sydney clubs meant that, particularly after the Second World War, Queensland continually lost players to NSW. The consequent loss of talent to the south affected interstate matches until the introduction (from 1980) of State of Origin games, inspired by Queensland's president, Ron McAuliffe. This series has now become excitingly even, although in the 1980s, when Wally Lewis, Gene Miles, and Mal Meninga shone, the northern State was the stronger.

For the first twenty years of rugby league Tom McMahon was a dominant referee, as was 'young' Tom McMahon (no relation), in the 1940s; both were known for intelligent use of the advantage rule. No referee since has been as powerful, although the controversial Darcy Lawler presided for a decade from 1954. In 1991 in-goal umpires were introduced to help determine on a fair try. There is widespread opinion that the authority of referees in the modern game has been diminished, with dissent more common as television replays subject decisions to detailed scrutiny.

Professional coaches have been a part of rugby league from its earliest days. Arthur Hennessy was an influential part of South Sydney's early success. Chris McKivat coached North Sydney to its only premierships in 1921 and 1922. Yet only after the Second World War did coaches become household names. Bob Bax took two Brisbane teams (Brothers and Norths) to great success in the period from 1955 to 1970. In the 1970s and 1980s Jack Gibson earned a reputation as a successful, if monosyllabic, team-builder ('Played strong! Done fine!'). Like many other former players and coaches, Gibson has also been prominent as a television and radio commentator, as has Rex 'Moose' Mossop, a union and league international.

Regular competition between Australia and NZ ('Kiwis') has been a feature of rugby league, except in the period between the two world wars, when only two Test series were staged, in 1919 and 1935. Test match successes were comparable until 1953, when Australia drew away, although the Kiwis won the only Test in 1971 and in the 1980s they beat Australia in several matches. Kangaroo tours to Britain have been a key feature of rugby league organisation in Australia, shaping and defining its image. British supremacy was finally ended by the 1963–64 tour of the eleventh Kangaroos. Later Kangaroos have won in 1967–68, 1973, 1978, 1982, 1986, and 1990. British tours of Australia have also been regular. Australian victories in these series were once rare. The success of the team led by Clive Churchill and coached by Vic Key in 1950 was the first time Australia had won the Ashes since its first win against a touring British team in 1920. Australia has defeated Britain in home series in 1954, 1966, 1974, 1979, and 1987. Following the 1990 Kangaroo tour of England there are signs of resurgent interest in international games. Australia first played in a demonstration game in France in 1933, and from 1938 has gone there regularly following a tour of Britain. The 1951 French visit led by the unconventional Puig-Aubert was a particular success. From 1954, a World Cup competition with teams from Australia, Britain, NZ, and France has rotated among participating countries. Australia won in 1957, 1968, 1970, 1975, and 1977.

In the 1930s there was an increase in 'poaching', as Australians like Dave Brown played in England for handsome sums. The dominance of Australia since 1970 has seen the process reversed as English players, like Queenslanders and Kiwis, have trod a path to the lucrative Sydney competition, whereas Australian coaches have made their way to England.

In any dynamic 84-year-old institution there will have been periods of administrative calm and periods of turmoil. The league's early years were shadowed by controversy over the administration of Giltinan and his treasurer, the legendary Victor Trumper, who were removed in 1909 by a 'reform team', some of whom in turn resigned in protest over the Wallaby v. Kangaroo games. But, from 1910, the NSW Rugby League experienced a period of relative tranquility, helped by the efficiency of E. R. Larkin as secretary, while Labor parliamentarian Fred Flowers exercised shrewd direction first as president and later as patron. H. H. 'Jersey' Flegg was a benevolent dictator as president from 1929 to 1960. In the Depression the code continued, with crowds willing to pay the shilling admission: in 1932 a record-breaking 70 204 saw the first Test at the SCG against Britain, but generally revenue was low between 1930 and 1945. The peak of league football's popularity, before television, was reached in W. G. Buckley's term as president from 1960 to 1973. In 1966 league was first played on Sunday at the SCG. In Queensland there was a division between Brisbane clubs and the Queensland organisation, particularly during the 1920s when rival matches were played. The breach was not really healed until 1953. Influential officials in the State have included Harry Sunderland, secretary from 1913 to 1922 and again from 1925 to 1938, and Ron McAuliffe who, as secretary, was instrumental in repairing the long split, and

who was president of the Queensland Rugby League from 1970 to 1985. The Australian Rugby League Board of Control was set up in 1924. An uneasy alliance of the two State administrations has generally seen NSW the stronger. From the 1940s league has been played in both Darwin and WA.

Rugby league in NSW suffered a decline in the 1970s, culminating in a public controversy involving its president, Kevin Humphreys. His resignation in 1983 was followed by reorganisation and the appointment of John Quayle as general manager, with the promise of a corporate management befitting the changing times. This in turn has drawn public attention to the role of sponsors, and in particular tobacco and alcohol companies, in the affairs of the sport. The 1980s saw a dramatic, television-spurred growth in the game's popularity. In Brisbane, Lang Park has been the code's major venue since 1958. Since 1990 a new football stadium has been used for league's big games in Sydney.

While there is much support in NSW and Queensland for other codes of football, since 1911 rugby league has been the most popular winter pastime in these two States, reflecting its constant adaptation to changing demographic and social conditions. In the early 1990s pop star Tina Turner has been recruited to consolidate the game's appeal to men and its attraction for women.

CC

See **Aboriginal Rugby League Test Players**; **All Golds**; **Australian Rugby Football League**; **Battle of Brisbane**; BEETSON, ARTHUR; **BROWN, DAVID**; Bulimba Cup; BURDON, ALEXANDER; BURGE, FRANK; CHURCHILL, CLIVE; **Churchill Medal**; **Clayton Cup**; **Corbett Trophy**; **Courtney International Goodwill Trophy**; **Dally M. Awards**; DAVIES, BRIAN; FLEGG, HENRY; FULTON, BOB; GASNIER, REG; GILTINAN, JAMES; **Giltinan Shield**; GORMAN, TOM; HALL, DUNCAN; HOLMAN, KEITH; HORDER, HAROLD; IRVINE, KEN; JOHNS, LESLIE; **Kangaroo Tours**; KEARNEY, KEN; LANGLANDS, GRAEME; **Lang Park**; LEWIS, WALLY; **Literature**; **Maher Cup**; McAULIFFE, RON; McKIVAT, CHRISTOPHER; MENINGA, MAL; MESSENGER, HERBERT; **Parramatta's First Rugby League Premiership**; PRICE, RAYMOND; PRIGG, WALTER; PROVAN, NORM; RAPER, JOHNNY; RAUDONIKIS, TOM; **Rothmans Medals (Rugby League)**; **Rorke's Drift Test**; **Rugby League: Ashes Victory 1950**; **Rugby League: Home Series v. Britain**; **Rugby League: Sydney Knockout Cups**; **Rugby League: Tours to New Zealand**; **Rugby Union**; **Sattler's Jaw**; SIMMS, ERIC; SMITH, Sir JAMES; **South's Spirit of 1955**; **State of Origin (Rugby League)**; STEHR, RAY; STEINOHRT, HERB;

Stephen Award; STERLING, PETER; **Strikes and Industrial Disputes**; SUNDERLAND, HARRY; **Sunderland Medal**; THOMPSON, DUNCAN; **Tied Grand Finals (Rugby League)**; **Unionism**; WEISSEL, ERIC.

Rugby League: Ashes Victory 1950. When the ninth British 'Lions' team toured Australia in 1950, a year of record rains, the hosts had not won a rugby league Test series since 1920. Great Britain won the tryless first Test 6–4, and Australia the second, 15–3. To enable the deciding match on 22 July to be played, forty tonnes of soil were spread over the sodden SCG. After a 2–2 half-time score, a copy-book Australian back-line passing movement in the sixty-fourth minute ended with lanky winger Ron Roberts, a notoriously bad handler, holding the muddy ball on his fingertips to score in the corner. The home team hung on desperately to win 5–2 and many of the delighted 47 196 spectators jumped the fence to slip and slide across the quagmire to cheer captain Clive Churchill's team and celebrate Australia's first Ashes victory for thirty years.

TB

Rugby League: Home Series v. Britain. Australia and Great Britain first played a rugby league Test in Australia in Sydney on 18 June 1910. Before a then world-record rugby league crowd of 42 000 the British won that historic match against the Dally Messenger–led home side 27–20. Messenger did his part, scoring a try and four goals. The first series involved two Tests (all subsequent series have involved three), and the British won both, beginning a dominance that lasted forty years. Before 1950, Great Britain lost a series in Australia just once, in 1920. Since the third Test of 1950, however, when winger Ron Roberts's celebrated try won Australia the Ashes on an SCG quagmire, Great Britain has succeeded only in 1958, 1962, and 1970. Australia has dominated the modern era, losing only two of the last twelve Tests. The 1979 series triumph was the first clean sweep by either nation in Australia since 1910. Australia again won all three Tests in 1984, and won the first two in 1988 before losing the third in a major upset. That shock British win, in the fifty-third Australia–Great Britain Test played in Australia, left the two countries with twenty-six wins each, with one match having been drawn.

PC

Rugby League: Sydney Knock-out Cups. In 1974 a mid-week knock-out cup competition was introduced to Sydney rugby league. The competition, the Amco Cup, involved the then twelve Sydney clubs, eight NSW country divisional sides, and Auckland. Matches were scheduled for successive Wednesday nights. The first Amco Cup began on 10 April 1974 when Easts beat Wests 22–6 at Belmore Oval, and ended on 21 August when the unheralded Western Division defeated Penrith 6–2 in the final. Since 1974 the Cup competition has continued under various sponsorships and in different formats. The Amco Cup continued until 1979. In 1980 Tooth Breweries adopted the Cup, and the competition was known as the Tooth Cup in 1980 and 1981 and the KB Cup in 1982 and 1983. In 1984 teams competed for the National Panasonic Cup, and in 1988 and 1989 for the Panasonic Cup. In 1990 the Cup was converted to a pre-season knock-out involving matches played at country venues. In 1990 Channel 10 provided the sponsorship, and in 1991 the Cup became the Lotto Challenge. The most successful club since 1974 in Cup competitions has been Balmain who won in 1976, 1985, and 1987. Easts (1975), Parramatta (1986) and Canberra (1990) are the only clubs to win the Cup and premiership double in the same season.

KC

Rugby League: Tours to NZ. Tours to NZ by Australian rugby league teams began in 1919. Before that year, NSW sides had toured in 1912 and 1913—the 1913 side being the only side, NSW or Australian, to complete a tour undefeated. Graeme Langlands (1965, 1969, and 1971) is the only player to tour NZ three times although twenty-one players have toured twice.

GF

Rugby Union
The rules of football as played at Rugby in England first appeared in written form in the 1840s and provided the basis for what became known as rugby football or (from 1871 when an organising body, the Rugby Football Union emerged) rugby union. The first rules of football to appear in Sydney were published in the annual report of the Albert Cricket Club for 1860. It is unclear to which code of football the rules actually related but an indication can be drawn from the fact that the club's annual report for 1862–63 included 'The Rules of Football as played at Rugby'. Despite claims to the contrary, the first recorded football club to be established in Sydney was the Sydney Football Club, founded in June 1865 with a strong influence from the members of the Albert Cricket Club. The club's first known game was an internal match at Hyde Park on 17 June 1865.

The absence of major suburban development in Sydney before the 1880s affected rugby's development in two ways. First, in the 1860s, apart from the early matches in Hyde Park in 1865 and a few games on the Domain in 1869, no ground was available for football in the inner city other than that at the University of Sydney, and even that appears to have been restricted. Second, when rugby clubs began to develop in the 1870s their formation was not based on a particular locality but rather on people with common backgrounds or views. This phenomenon was echoed in Queensland and in the other States when they too began to play the rugby code.

The most prominent of the first pre-suburban clubs in Sydney was the Wallaroo club, founded in 1870 mainly by ex-students from the King's School, Parramatta, and St Mark's Collegiate School, Macquarie Fields. Two of the foundation members were Richard and Montague Arnold, the former having attended Rugby in England in the 1860s. The competition that the Wallaroo club provided for the University of Sydney and the ability to play on the Sydney Common (reopened in 1869 for public use as Moore Park) enabled football to develop in the city. At the same time, private schools such as King's, Newington, and Camden College began to play the game. Clubs were also established in country centres such as Goulburn. With this development during the early 1870s, the time was ripe for the formation of a governing body and agreement on a set of rules. This occurred in 1874 with the establishment of the Southern Rugby Football Union to govern the game in the colony of NSW. The name was changed to the NSWRU in 1892.

The actual expansion of rugby football in Australia occurred in the 1880s with an intercolonial contest between NSW and Queensland played from 1882. Tours also began to take place between the two colonies and various provincial and representative teams from NZ. In 1888 a team was brought to Australia from Britain by private promoters and they played games based on both the rugby and Australian rules codes (the latter having been codified in 1859). Once the international flavour of the rugby game had been set in Sydney and Brisbane there was little chance of their clubs changing to the Australian rules or soccer.

However, the expansion of football as a popular sport was being restricted by its cosmopolitan club fixtures. What was needed was a district competition to reflect the suburbanisation of Sydney which had taken place in the 1880s and 1890s. Such a change to a local competition had already occurred in cricket in Sydney in the 1890s and had been a success in Australian rules in Melbourne. A metropolitan union was formed in Sydney in 1896 which helped the introduction of the new scheme in 1900. A minor split occurred almost immediately, with a number of mainly private-school old boys forming a separate union known as the 'City and Suburban Association', based on backgrounds and friendships rather than locality.

The major split in rugby in both Sydney and Australia occurred in 1907 with the visit of the NZ professional team on its way to England.

The new code, known as the Northern Union game and eventually called rugby league, arrived at a time when disgruntlement was rife within Sydney rugby circles. The game was no longer purely that of the private school and the middle class. Working- and lower-middle-class men wanted to play but they also wanted compensation for loss of earnings, at first for that occasioned by injuries and later for having to forgo paid work in order to play. No compromise was reached: as in Britain the middle and upper classes were happy to have the separation whereby the working person adopted a professional game while the true gentleman pursued the amateur game of rugby.

The split in Sydney was complete in 1909 when the NSW Rugby Union found that fourteen of the players from the 1908–9 Australian Rugby Tour of Britain (known as the Wallabies) had committed acts of professionalism during the latter part of the 1909 season. Attempts were made by some officials in the Metropolitan Rugby Union to settle the dispute as late as 1910 but the NSW Rugby Union did not want it resolved; it spread from Sydney to the country areas of NSW and to Queensland. The Rugby Union felt satisfied that its game was the original code and that it would survive. It arranged games against visitors including the NZ national team, the NZ Maori team, and touring students from California and Stanford Universities in America. The Rugby League countered with Test matches between the English Northern Union and domestic rugby league teams. At club level in Sydney the league moved further ahead as virtually all the star players of the era played the code.

By 1911 the NSWRU was in financial trouble, so much so that it had to sell the Epping racecourse, purchased only four years earlier in the hope of developing its own ground. The problems of the union had been compounded by the fact that in Sydney the NSW Rugby League had use in the winter of the Sydney Sports Ground as well as the SCG and the Showground. In 1914 the union secured the Sports Ground for a number of games for the first time since the split.

The game faded further from the public eye during the war years, when many clubs elected not to play, but it was restored in 1919. However, the reappearance in Queensland lasted only for that year and it disappeared until 1929. In NSW the game was initially revived in Sydney without a district competition, though in 1920 this was reintroduced and some disputes occurred as to which clubs should be eligible. Bitter at their treatment, the non-district clubs were determined to make the competition they played in worthwhile, and the president of the Mosman Club, H. Kentwell, donated a cup which signified the 'Kentwell Cup Division' of rugby in Sydney for those clubs excluded from the district competition. Another trophy, the George Burke Memorial Cup, was presented in 1924 by another Mosman official, James Burke. The non-district competition blossomed and many of those clubs eagerly awaited their chance to be promoted into the district competition, but this was not to be. In 1929 the division was complete, with the non-district clubs forming their own body known as the Metropolitan Sub-District Rugby Union and affiliating directly with the NSWRU. That division continued until the outbreak of war. It was revived after the war and suburban or subdistrict rugby developed rapidly in Sydney throughout the 1950s until its strength was somewhat diminished in 1962 with the formation of a second-division district competition. A third-division league was attempted in 1979 but was abandoned by 1987.

The 1960s also saw the formation of the Sydney Rugby Union (SRU) following a dispute between the Sydney District Clubs and those of the NSW Country Rugby Union. The SRU flourished, much to the chagrin of country officials who believed the State team should be the premier team. Tensions also developed in this era between the NSWRU and the Queensland Rugby Union (QRU) when the latter felt spurned by the NSWRU who cancelled the annual interstate fixture on the grounds that the QRU was not up to standard. Within a decade, the QRU reversed the situation, obtaining its own ground and trouncing the NSWRU team on many occasions.

It could be argued that Australian rugby has gone backwards when it is remembered that from the late 1920s Victoria was the third State in Australia supplying a number of national representatives and defeating NSW in 1929, 1933, 1935, and 1938. Also, until the mid-1960s Wallaby selection trials consisted of invitations being issued to players with the appropriate ability from all States. A national competition was attempted from the late 1960s but after eight seasons had to be abandoned because of the cost and the too predictable results.

While the Wallaby Trophy national competition may have faded, the other innovation of the late 1960s, a national schoolboys' team, has gone from strength to strength. Indeed the reason for Australian rugby's success from the mid-1970s could be attributed to the development of this scheme so that a schoolboy, no matter where he played, had a chance at national schoolboy selection through an annual carnival. While this open thinking has not flowed on to senior team selection, it has at least provided a boost for the game in the leading States as well as in those where rugby is still a minor sport.

The 1980s continued with the NSW–Queensland rivalry dominating the Australian Rugby Football Union. The NSWRU, frustrated at the success of the QRU from the mid-1970s and believing that much of the QRU's success could be attributed to its development of a football ground at Ballymore in Brisbane, attempted a similar plan at Concord Oval in Sydney's inner western suburbs. This caused Test matches to be played away from rugby's traditional home at the SCG and away from the established support of the eastern and northern suburbs. The new entrepreneurial rugby caused even further problems for the game in both NSW and Australia. Officials who had given sterling unpaid service to the game were outraged by the vast sums sunk into the Concord project and expended on administrators' fees while the game was faltering at club level in Sydney. In 1979 there were twenty-nine district clubs and sixty-six suburban clubs; within a decade that had been reduced to only twenty-three district clubs and fifty-four suburban clubs. While there had been some amalgamation of clubs, overall there had been a significant fall in the number of teams fielded.

Similarly, the development of the game in the country areas of NSW and Queensland as well as in the other States and territories of Australia has not taken place. Power and energies have been concentrated in the NSW–Queensland rivalry, which has offset any national spirit the game might have had. Despite a successful period from the late 1970s until the late 1980s, which included victories over NZ and a Grand Slam tour of Britain, Australian rugby still has to resolve the problems of professionalism and federalism in the 1990s as much as it needed to do in the 1890s. New rulings from the International Rugby Board regarding amateurism should help at the national level. The problem of developing the game at club, provincial, and State level is the challenge throughout Australia in the 1990s in the face of renewed pressure from the other football codes of Australian rules, soccer, and rugby league, as well as other new winter sports such as basketball.

TH

See **AIF Rugby Union Football Team**; **ALLAN, TREVOR**; **ARNOLD, RICHARD and WILLIAM**; **Australian Rugby Football Union**; **BONIS, EDWARD**; **BROKHOFF, JOHN**; **BURDON, ALEXANDER**; **CAMPESE, DAVID**; **CATCHPOLE, KEN**; **CERUTTI, WILLIAM**; **CONNOR, DESMOND**; **COOKE, GRAHAM**; **DAVIS, GREGORY**; **ELLA Brothers**; **FARRJONES, NICK**; **JOHNSON, PETER**; **LYNAGH, MICHAEL**; **McLEAN Family**; **MILLER, TONY**; **MORAN, HERBERT**; **POIDEVIN, SIMON**; **Rugby League**; **Rugby Union: First International Tour to Australia**; **Rugby Union: NSW v. Wales 1991**; **Rugby Union: Tour to South Africa 1933**; **SHEHADIE, Sir NICHOLAS**; **Springbok Tour 1971**; *Sydney Morning*

Herald **Best and Fairest (Rugby Union)**; THORNETT, JOHN; **Wallabies (1908–9); Waratahs Rugby Tour 1927–28**.

Rugby Union: First International Tour to Australia. An unofficial NZ side claimed the honour of being the first international rugby team to visit Australia. In 1884, eight years before the NZ Rugby Union was formed, a side, captained by W. V. Milton, a lawyer from Christchurch, and managed by co-organiser S. E. Sleigh from Otago, toured NSW. Playing in dark-blue jerseys sporting a golden fern leaf, the New Zealanders played and won eight matches with apparent ease. Throughout the tour their larger, more robust forwards laid the foundation for the victories and so began one of the great traditional contests of Australian sport.

PH

Rugby Union: New South Wales v. Wales 1991. One of the most amazing results in the long history of rugby union in Australia occurred on 14 July 1991, when NSW defeated Wales 71–8, setting several records along the way. It was the worst result ever suffered by Wales in their long, proud history, and it was NSW's highest score against any team. The 13 tries scored by NSW, and Campese's 5 tries were also records for NSW. The Waratahs led 39–0 at half-time and by the sixty-sixth minute, when NSW were reduced to fourteen men through injury, they led 65–0. Despite the inadequacies of the Welsh team, it was undoubtedly one of NSW's finest performances.

MC

Rugby Union: Tour to South Africa 1933. The Australian Rugby Union tour to South Africa in 1933 was unique in two ways. First, this was a team chosen from NSW, Queensland, and Victoria, thus being the first truly representative Australian team to make a tour of a major rugby-playing nation. Second, it was and remains the only time that a five-Test series was played between two countries. Australia played twenty-three matches, winning twelve, losing ten, and drawing one. Captained by Alec Ross, the team included such luminaries as S. Malcolm, D. Cowper, A. Hodgson, J. Kelaher, and W. Cerutti. At different stages during the tour the Australians suffered injuries and illness to major players. This led to them using Cowper, Malcolm, and Ross as captains, Ross being able to play only in the last Test due to an appendectomy. Despite these problems the Australians attempted to play the free-running style of rugby. This approach proved popular with the South African crowds. The fact that Australia was able to win two of the five internationals said much for its ability to fight back from adversity.

MC

Ryder Medal. The Jack Ryder Medal is the Victorian Cricket Association's equivalent of the AFL's Brownlow Medal and is awarded to the player voted by umpires as performing best in the Melbourne district competition. So dominant a personality in Victorian cricket that he was known as 'The King' (of Collingwood), Jack Ryder played twenty Test matches, captained Australia, and was a long-serving national selector. Appropriately the inaugural Ryder Medal was won in 1972–73 by a Collingwood cricketer, Ron Bird. Batsmen, all-rounders, and especially those with first-class experience, have been the most frequent winners of the medal. Keith Stackpole and Warren Whiteside have each won a record three medals.

DS

S

Sailing and Yachting

With so many of Australia's major cities and towns on the coast or near inland waterways, it is easy to understand why boating, cruising, and yacht-racing are some of the most popular sporting and recreational activities. The distinction between sailing and yachting is important to the sports' participants. Sailing vessels are small dinghies, steered with the aid of a centreboard, which can be raised or lowered, while yachts are larger vessels with a fixed keel. There are four distinct groups of sailing craft. The leading group, especially in terms of cost, is the offshore racing-yacht group, followed by inshore racing yachts and yachts used for a combination of inshore racing and cruising. Then there are the two off-the-beach groups of smaller and lighter sailing craft which are usually towed home by their owners. These can be loosely divided into centreboard sailing dinghies and catamaran classes.

Boating competitions have been recorded in Australia since the 1820s when races were held to celebrate special events and were generally informal. Races between longboats paved the way for the regattas which eventually led to specifically designed yachts. The first Australian racing yachts were originally English-designed fishing boats. Developed from a shallow-draft vessel with a broad beam and straight stem, these craft continued to be the prototypes for small yachts and centreboard craft until the Second World War. With the availability of low-cost materials like fibreglass and aluminium in the post-war era a greater variety of mass-produced sailing craft became possible. The modern, easy-to-sail craft have opened up the sport to a wider range and greater number of people than ever before.

The strong winds that buffet the Australian coastline all year have not hindered the popularity of ocean racing, although there were no regular events held until the inauguration of the Sydney to Hobart race in 1945. Nevertheless, Australia is one of the leading competitors in international ocean-racing events and is a regular competitor in the world's premier ocean-racing carnival, the Admiral's Cup. It is sailed off the English coast every two years and involves teams of three yachts fighting out two long and two short races. Australia first competed in 1967 when it finished second behind the British team. With the yachts *Caprice of* *Huon, Balandra,* and *Mercedes ITT,* Australia defeated Britain, by a record margin of 104 points, to win the Cup in 1969. In recent years Australia's performance in the Admiral's Cup has been disappointing.

Since 1962 Australians have also contested the world's leading match-racing event, the *America*'s Cup, with mixed success. Australia's most important ocean-racing event, the Southern Cross Trophy, is an international event conducted by the Cruising Yacht Club of Australia and the Royal Yacht Club of Tasmania. Based on the Admiral's Cup, the Southern Cross Trophy is a team event, held every two years, with three yachts representing each competing State or country. The Sydney to Hobart race is used as the fifth and final race in the event. The inaugural series was contested in 1967 and was won by a NZ team, with the NSW team placed second.

The first organised yacht races were conducted by the Victorian Yacht Club (later the Royal Yacht Club of Victoria), which was formed in 1856. The Australian Yacht Squadron (later the Royal Sydney Yacht Squadron) was formed in Sydney in 1862. The first yacht club in Tasmania was the Derwent Sailing Boat Club, founded in 1874. Queensland had a yacht club in 1866, but sailing did not prosper in that State until 1885 when the Brisbane Amateur Sailing Club was formed. SA and WA did not have organised races until the late nineteenth century due to the lack of protected waterways.

Australia's oldest centreboard-racing division is for development craft known as skiffs. The 18-footer class was developed in Australia at the turn of the century; it is the oldest skiff class still racing and the best known; it is the least restricted of any class and is known world-wide for its speed. It has also been the training ground for many of Australia's best yachtsmen. Sydney's Iain Murray sailed himself into the record books when he won his third consecutive world 18-footer crown in Sydney in 1979. International 18-footer championships have been conducted in Britain, America, and NZ as well as Australia. Other popular classes include the 16-footers and the 12-footers. Skiff-racing is the only form of sailing that is commercially sponsored, with monetary prizes and international status. Australians have won world titles in two separate classes: Sydney yachtsman Frank Tolhurst won a world title in the 5.5

metre (1976) and the E22 (1978) class while Lyndall Coxon won two women's world championships (1977 and 1978) in the Laser class. Although Australia has competed in the Olympic yachting section since 1948 it was not until 1964 that Australia captured its first gold when *Barrenjoey* won the 5.5 metre class. In 1972 Australia earned two gold medals in the Dragon and Star class.

GC*

See *America's* Cup; *Australia II*; BEASHEL Family; BERTRAND, JOHN; BETHWAITE Family; COTTEE, KAY; CUNEO, JOHN; FISCHER, SYD; FORBES, DAVID; HARDY, Sir JAMES; ILLINGWORTH, Captain JOHN; INGATE, GORDON; LEXCEN, BEN; Little America's Cup; MURRAY, IAIN; NORTHAM, Sir WILLIAM; O'DONNELL, PETER; STURROCK, ALEXANDER; Sydney to Hobart Yacht Race; TASKER, ROLLAND; WEBB, CHRIS.

SAMUELS, CHARLIE (1863–1912), born Sambo Combo at Jimbour Station, Dalby, Queensland, was originally a stockrider. At the age of 23 he ran 136 yards in 13.2 seconds, the fastest time recorded in Australian professional athletics. Credited with the startling times of 300 yards in 30 seconds flat and 100 yards in 9.1 seconds, he was considered by many 'to be the sprint champion of the world'. In 1894 the *Referee* stated that 'Samuels has, in a long course of brilliant running, established his claim not only to be Australian champion but also to have been one of the best exponents of sprint running the world has ever seen'. Though a heavy smoker and drinker, Samuels defeated three of the world's greatest sprinters—Harold Hutchens, Tom Mallone, and Ted Lazarus—over various distances. Against Lazarus, he won £90 000 for his backers. Considered a trouble-maker and a drunk, Samuels suffered the ignominies of assault and drunk-and-disorderly charges, internment at Callan Park Asylum, and finally 'removal' to Barambah, the Aboriginal penal-type settlement in Queensland, where he died at the age of 49.

CT and PT

See **Aborigines in Sport**.

Sandover Medal. Introduced in 1921 by Alfred Sandover, a leading Perth retailer, the medal is presented annually to the WA Football League's best and fairest player. The inaugural winner was Tom Outridge of Subiaco who was coincidentally an employee of Sandover. In 1984 P. Spencer (East Perth) and S. Malaxos and M. Mitchell (both of Claremont) tied for the award and as a consequence all three players received medals. Haydn Bunton of Subiaco (1938, 1939 and 1941) and Haydn Bunton junior (1962) of Swan Districts are the only father

and son, from Australian rules football, to have won the best and fairest awards in a capital city.

GC*

SANDS, DAVE (1926–52) was born David Ritchie, the fourth of six Aboriginal boxing brothers (Clem, Ritchie, George, Dave, Alfie, and Russell). An unassuming, quiet, and shy man, he was enormously popular. In the ring he was a quick, devastating puncher, winning many of his fights in the early rounds. He was Australian middleweight champion from 1946 to 1952, light heavyweight champion from 1946 to 1952, and heavyweight champion from 1950 to 1952. He also held the Australasian light heavyweight title and was Empire middleweight champion in 1949. He was the top contender for the world middleweight title in 1950, and many of the critics considered him capable of beating the two top men at the time, Randolph Turpin and the legendary Sugar Ray Robinson. He fought inconsistently overseas, was mismanaged and, like many Aboriginal sportspeople, was often homesick. He died in a truck accident at Dungog, NSW, in August 1952. He had one hundred fights, for eighty-seven wins, one draw, ten losses and two no-contests.

RB

See **Aborigines in Sport**; **Boxing**.

SARGEANT, ANNE, OAM (1957–), has done much to promote netball as a player, writer, and media commentator. She represented NSW in open interstate competition from 1978 to 1988, captaining the side in the last seven years. During these eleven consecutive years in the Australian team she played in three netball championships, where Australia won twice in 1979 and 1983 and were second in 1987. Sargeant has received many accolades and awards for her sporting excellence including induction into the Sport Australia Hall of Fame (1987), NSW Sporting Hall of Fame (1988), and the OAM (1988). In recent years she has focused on coaching, becoming an All Australia Satellite Specialist Coach in 1990.

PB and IJ

See **Netball**.

Sattler's Jaw. Determined to redress their upset loss to Balmain in 1969, South Sydney Rugby League Club qualified to play Manly-Warringah in the 1970 Grand Final. After only ten minutes' play, South's captain, prop-forward and tough-man, John Sattler, was felled by a punch from a Manly forward and suffered a double fracture of the jaw. Gasping to his winger, Mike Cleary, 'Help me up so they don't know I'm hurt', he continued his heavy involvement in the torrid game. Sattler's other team-mates learnt of his injury at half-time, when Souths led 12–6. He refused attention, returned to the field and led his team to a decisive 23–12, 3 tries to nil, victory. Only after receiving the Giltinan Shield and making a polished acceptance speech did he go to hospital.

TB

SAXBY, KERRY (1961–), walker, born Ballina, NSW, became the most prolific world-record breaker in athletic history when she set a new 3 kilometre record of 11 minutes 51.26 seconds at Melbourne in February 1991, taking her number of world bests to thirty, one ahead of the great distance runner, Paavo Nurmi. Her records have been set at distances ranging from 1500 metres to 20 kilometres, at indoor and outdoor venues, some at unofficial distances and some in mixed competition: indeed, Saxby attributes training and competing against male athletes as one reason for her success. At the time of her Melbourne victory, Saxby held existing world records in the 5 kilometres road race (20 minutes 25 seconds), 10 kilometres road (41 minutes 30 seconds), 20 kilometres road (1 hour 29 minutes 40 seconds in Sweden in 1988 when she also set a world record for the 15 kilometres split), and 1500 metres (5 minutes 50.41 seconds). Saxby also won three gold and four silver world championship medals in her career, including victories in the world indoor 3000 metres at Budapest in 1989 and the 10 kilometres road race at the 1990 Commonwealth Games. Saxby has been disqualified for losing foot contact with the track just once in a decade of competition during which she never finished outside the top five. With the addition of a walking event for females in the 1992 Games she will have her first opportunity for Olympic competition.

GC†

SCHAEFER, MANFRED (1943–), born Königsberg, Germany, is considered the leading centre-back of Australian soccer. His family emigrated to Australia when he was 12. Having played the two rugby codes in primary school, he took up soccer at high school. After joining the Bankstown club, Schaefer transferred to Budapest in 1959, for whom he went on to play over four hundred and fifty games. He made seventy-two national appearances between 1967 and 1974, including the 1974 World Cup. His defensive ability was proved against such international opposition as Brazil's Pelé and West Germany's Gerd Mueller. Upon retiring in 1975, Schaefer went on to coach St George-Budapest, Sydney Olympic, Brunswick Juventus, and Apia-Leichhardt. While he was with Olympic the club was twice winner of national cups and twice runner-up in national premierships.

GC and PK

SCHEINFLUG, LESLEY PAUL (1938–) was born in Yugoslavia of German parents. The family moved to Germany when he was 2 and emigrated to Australia in 1955. Scheinflug joined Sydney club Prague in 1957 and stayed for twelve seasons, seven of these as captain. He joined Marconi-Fairfield in 1969 as player-coach, retiring from playing in 1972. An energetic, adaptable, left mid-fielder, Scheinflug was known for his leadership qualities. He made eleven appearances in the national team in 1964–68, mostly as captain. He scored four goals for the Socceroos, one of which was Australia's first goal in a World Soccer Cup qualifying tie. His national exploits would have been greater had not FIFA banned Australia from international football from 1960 to 1963. Scheinflug's coaching career has been extensive. After Marconi came Western Suburbs, Sydney Croatia, Safeway United (Wollongong), and Brisbane Lions. Then, in the National League, Brisbane Lions (continued), Adelaide City, Marconi (twice), and Blacktown City. He was Coach of the Year while with Marconi in 1979. Club duties have been supplemented by national coaching positions. Assistant coach to Rale Rasic, then Rudi Gutendorf, Scheinflug became national coach from 1981 to 1983. He was national youth coach for various Youth World Soccer Cup campaigns from 1981 to 1991.

PM

SCOBIE, JAMES (1860–1940), born near Ararat, Victoria, first made his mark as a steeplechase jockey. He became prominent with wins in the saddle in major steeplechase races including the 1888 VRC Grand National, the 1893 Eastern and, on his own horse, *Blue Mountain*, the 1887 Caulfield Grand National. Moving from Hamilton to Ballarat he made a sensational impact as a trainer at the 1900 Victorian spring carnival, with his horses *Clean Sweep* and *Maltster* winning most of the main races. In 1912 he moved his stables to Melbourne. Scobie consistently turned out top-class winners over the next quarter-century, including three more Melbourne Cup winners. He trained nine Victoria Derby winners, the last of them, *Hua*, in 1937.

AL

SCOTT, Hon. MICHAEL, OBE (1878–1959), born London, has the distinction of being the first amateur golfer to win the Australian Open held at Botany in 1904. He won it again in 1907, amid dispute. Scott (mistakenly) drove off Royal Melbourne's twelfth outside the teeing ground, for which he should have been disqualified. Dan Soutar pursued this decision for twenty years but it was only in 1957, twenty years after Soutar's death, that golf historian Muir McLaren unearthed the Royal and Ancient Golf Club's decision in favour of Soutar. For the record, Scott was 5 shots ahead of Soutar at the finish. Scott won the Australian amateur title four times, the NSW amateur twice, and the Victorian title six times. He took the French national title twice and won the British amateur at the astonishing age of 55, the oldest man to do so. He captained Britain against America and against Australia.

CT

See **SOUTAR, DANIEL**.

SEARLE, HENRY ERNEST ('The Clarence Comet') (1866–89), professional sculler, born Grafton, NSW, was an extraordinarily talented athlete whose senior career was spectacularly brief. After five successful races against strong competition, between January and October 1888 Searle challenged Peter Kemp (Australia) for his world title. On 27 October 1888, Searle defeated Kemp by over 150 yards on the Parramatta River course. Lacking Australian challengers, Searle's only title defence was in London in September 1889, when he easily defeated the American professional champion. During the trip home, Searle contracted typhoid, dying in Melbourne in December 1889. The extraordinary public response to the death of the young hero extended throughout the colonies. A column to his memory stands at the finishing line of the old Parramatta River sculling course.

SB

See **Rowing and Sculling**.

SEDGMAN, FRANK ALLAN (1927–   ), born Mount Albert, Victoria, was one of the first Australian examples of 'power and percentage' tennis-players developed in post-war USA. A protégé of Harry Hopman, he was notable for his great speed and reflexes and decisive volleying and smashing. He was the first Australian to win the US singles, and he won the world Grand Slam doubles in 1951. He won the Wimbledon Triple Crown in 1952: the singles, doubles, and mixed doubles. He was the last to achieve this. Sedgman lost no matches in Davis Cup doubles from 1949 and was the spearhead of winning sides from 1950 to 1952. Before turning professional in 1953, Sedgman had won twenty-two Grand Slam titles in singles, doubles, and mixed doubles. In an effort to retain him as an amateur Sedgman was offered the proprietorship of a service station, but he turned professional and played, and lost, in a head-to-head contest against Jack Kramer. Sedgman proved a success in professional ranks and his long match against Pancho Gonzales at Wembley in 1956 was accounted as one of his greatest performances. Later Sedgman played successfully on the Australian veterans' tennis circuit.

GK-S

See **Lawn Tennis**.

SELLWOOD, NEVILLE (1923–62), born Queensland, was prominent as a Brisbane apprentice jockey. After riding in Townsville dur-

ing the war, he moved to Sydney and was principal rider for Maurice McCarten. In 1948–49 and 1949–50 they were the leading Sydney jockey and trainer respectively: Sellwood won the jockeys' premiership four more times. He won two Melbourne Cups, five Victoria Derbies, and three Caulfield Cups including the 1957 event on *Tulloch*. He also rode *Todman* to win the first Golden Slipper Stakes in 1957. Sellwood made several visits to Europe, and won the 1962 English Derby on *Larkspur*. Leading rider in Paris in 1962, he was killed on 7 November when his mount fell at Maison Lafitte.

AL

SHAKESPEAR, WILMA (1943–   ) began playing netball with the local Baptist Church Association in Moonee Ponds, Melbourne, and joined Aberfeldie club in her final year of high school. She was selected in the State and national team as goalkeeper in the following year, and retired from playing at the national level at the age of 23. Shakespear returned to the sport as a coach three years later and at the age of 27 became the youngest-ever national coach. She has been a part of three World Netball Championship wins: as a player in 1963, and as national coach in Jamaica in 1971 and in Trinidad and Tobago in 1979. For both world championships, Shakespear coached players who were older than her. In 1981 she became head coach of netball at the AIS (the first female to head a programme), and broke new ground in training by introducing the specialist session and the individual session to the team concept of netball. Shakespear is chairperson of the All Australia Netball Association Coaching Development Committee. In 1991 she became director of the Queensland Academy of Sport.

PB and IJ

See **Netball**.

Shannon, (1941–55), a thoroughbred racehorse and sire, won fourteen races in twenty-five starts in Sydney, and another six wins in the USA. A bay colt by *Midstream* out of *Idle Words*, he was bred at Scone in NSW and sold cheaply as a yearling to Peter Riddle who became his trainer. His early racing was disrupted by wartime restrictions, but from 4 years old he was seldom beaten. He is best remembered for losing the 1946 Epsom Handicap by a half head after being left badly at the post. At his next start he broke the Australasian record for 1 mile. In 1947 he was sold to America and, after some poor runs, found top form, equalling world records for both 9 and 10 furlongs. Retired to stud in the USA, he was again successful, siring several top-class stakes winners.

AL

SHARMAN, JIMMY Senior (1892–1965), born Narellan, NSW, on a small dairy farm, ran away at the age of 14 to become a boxer. He had an extraordinary record as a professional, winning eighty-three of his eighty-four fights, but he became more famous for his tent shows, Jimmy Sharman's Boxing Troupe. He became the Barnum & Bailey of Australian boxing. Well known as a fighter in the Riverina, he collected a troupe and pitched his tent at agricultural shows all around the country from about 1912. Many great fighters went through Sharman's tent: among them were Billy Grime, who held three Australian titles simultaneously, Frank Burns (the father of George Barnes), George Cook, Jackie Green, Tommy Uren, Mickey Miller, and Jack Hassen. Sharman had enough anecdotes to fill a book and will always be remembered for his catchcry, 'Who'll take a glove?' Jimmy Sharman Junior continued his father's work until stricter medical regulations regarding 'K.O.ed' boxers led to the demise of Sharman's troupe in 1971.

GP

See **Boxing**.

Sheaf-tossing

Competitive sheaf-tossing occurs in Europe, NZ, and Canada, but is at its most popular in Australia. The aim of sheaf-tossing is to heave a simulated sheaf over an elevated bar, using a standard two-prong pitchfork. The 'sheaf', a wheat bag filled with oaten hay, weighing 3.6 kilograms and measuring between 56 and 66 centimetres, is frequently tossed between 16 and 18 metres vertically. Strength, rhythm, and timing are important, but endurance is also necessary in an event that often lasts five hours. Included in the SA Annual Show for the first time in 1914, the event was won by S. Wait with a throw of 9.8 metres. In the 1940s the sport was dominated by the three Schwardt brothers from SA. The current Australian champion is Wesley Schache, but the highest throw of 17.4 metres thrown in 1970, belongs to Bruce Mountrey of Tasmania.

GC*

See **Country Show Sports**; **Sheep-shearing**; **Woodchopping**.

Sheep-shearing

The Australian shearing industry began shortly after the importation of sheep into NSW by Macarthur, Marsden, Cox and Riley in 1797. The removal of wool from the sheep in the early days was by using hand-held, long-bladed tong-like cutters, referred to as 'shears' or 'blades'. In 1868 J. A. B. Higham patented a mechanical shearing machine with a cutting apparatus similar to a hairdresser's comb-like clippers. It was many years before such a contraption became generally accepted. In fact it was not until 1885 that a commercial shearing machine was demonstrated by a Mr Wolseley at Dunlop Station on the Darling River. As is normal with drastic changes in any method— in this case mechanical clippers versus hand-operated blades—there was much scepticism, and therefore reluctance to change. The catalyst for the change was a competition which took place in Queensland between two groups of shearers. The machine shearers beat the blade-shearing team of six very convincingly. Machine shearing spread quickly and by 1915 most grazing properties had it installed. Because of the greater speed of mechanical clippers the size of shearing teams could be reduced. In the late nineteenth century some sheds had up to sixty shearers. Today very few have more than twenty shearers operating.

The demand by the grazier to have his shearing completed in the shortest possible time to meet the market, beat the weather, save feed, or ease a possible water shortage, caused the formation of large groups of shearers, commonly called teams. Rivalry existed between teams in an endeavour to influence the individual grazier for the right to shear in his sheds. This almost fanatical desire to outdo the other team led to three types of contests. First, there was a competition in speed and neatness between teams for the grazier's favour. Second, there was friendly rivalry between shearers within each team. The leading shearer, or 'gun' shearer, was usually the fastest in each team. Third, sometimes shearers raced against the clock instead of trying to outdo each other. As far back as the 1890s races against the clock took place. In 1892 321 sheep were shorn in a working day by a blade shearer named Howe. This tally was exceeded in the 1950s by a machine shearer named Riech in SA.

Many agricultural pursuits were displayed at country shows throughout the land. Competitions such as sheaf-tossing, calf-tying, and log-chopping were but a few. It was natural that sheep-shearing should follow. Today national competitions are conducted for substantial prize-money. Competitors are judged on a number of factors: speed, neatness, and sheep-handling ability are all considered.

WPR

See **Country Show Sports**; **Sheaf-tossing**; **Woodchopping**.

Sheffield Shield is Australia's leading domestic first-class cricket competition, in which all six States compete, with each side playing ten matches, five on their home ground and five away. The two leading States then contest a final with the choice of venue being the prerogative of the State which finishes the home and away rounds in top position. Sheffield Shield games last four days with six playing hours per day and a minimum of 96 overs to be bowled, less breaks for interruptions such as wickets falling, injuries, bad light, and rain.

The Sheffield Shield began after the donation of £150 by the Earl of Sheffield, the organiser of the English touring team to Australia in 1891–92. The Earl made the donation to further Australian cricket, and the next year the Australasian Cricket Council began the competition with three States, NSW, Victoria, and SA. In the early years these States played each other twice; Queensland was not included until 1926–27 because of the high costs of sending teams north by rail; WA did not enter the Shield until 1947–48 and surprisingly won the tournament in its first season, although it played a restricted programme, contesting only four matches to the other States' seven. Its first Shield win on an even footing was in the 1967–68 season. Tasmania was admitted to the Shield on a restricted basis in 1977–78 but gained full membership in 1982–83.

The Sheffield Shield is the grooming ground for Australia's Test players, but its spectator appeal has fallen dramatically as a result of the assault by the limited-over game. Only strong corporate sponsorship enables the State cricket associations to continue staging such games. Up to 1991 NSW has won the Shield forty times, Victoria twenty-five, and SA and WA twelve apiece. Queensland and Tasmania are awaiting their first success.

BW

SHEHADIE, Sir NICHOLAS, OBE (1926–), has been involved with distinction in almost every facet of rugby union. Sir Nicholas progressed from a 15-year-old substitute for Randwick first grade in the Sydney club competition in 1941 to become president of the Australian Rugby Football Union in 1979. In the intervening years he established a reputation as one of the best front-rowers of his era and became an institution in the Australian team for a decade. Shehadie played thirty Tests, including three as captain, after making his debut as a second-rower against the All Blacks in 1947. He had the distinction of being the first player to be selected from a touring side to play for the Barbarians at the end of the 1957–58 Wallabies' tour of the British Isles. After retiring from playing, Shehadie went on to become a first-grade referee, manager of Australian touring teams and, off the rugby front, the thirty-third Lord Mayor of Sydney. He is patron of the Randwick club.

GC†

SIEBEN, JONATHAN SCOTT (1966–), swimmer, born Ingham, Queensland, came from a working-class family which moved to Brisbane in 1977. Jon Sieben joined the Leander Club where he came under the influence of Joe King and later Laurie Lawrence. He was a member of the successful 4 × 100 metres medley relay team at the 1982 Brisbane Commonwealth Games and won a bronze medal in the 200 metres butterfly. It was at the Los Angeles Olympics in 1984 that he reached his peak when he won the 200 metres butterfly in world-record time (1 minute 57.04 seconds), beating Michael Gross of West Germany and Rafael Castrol of Venezuela. Sieben was also a member of the 4 × 100 metres medley relay team which won a bronze medal. Shoulder injuries restricted his performances before the Seoul Olympics in 1988, but he represented Australia in the 100 metres butterfly.

RH and MH

See **Swimming**.

SIMMS, ERIC (1945–), born Newcastle, NSW, was a points-scoring machine who changed the laws of rugby league. He attended Raymond Terrace High School before moving to the Sydney suburb of La Perouse. He joined South Sydney mid-season in 1965 and was a centre in that year's first-grade Grand Final. Simms played 206 first-grade games for Souths, mostly as full back, totalling 1843 points. In 1969, his 265 points broke Dave Brown's 1935 record. In the 1968 World Cup, he became the fourth Aborigine to represent Australia in the code and his 50 points in four games is still unsurpassed. He also played in the 1970 World Cup in England, scoring 37 points. Simms holds the rare sporting distinction of being so good that the rules were changed. His kicking of field goals was so consistent (19 in 1969) and so effortless (5 in one 1970 game) that their value was reduced in 1971 from 2 points to 1. Simms left Souths to join a country club, Crookwell, in 1976, retiring the following year. He is now a security officer on the Sydney wharfs.

TB

See **Aboriginal Rugby League Test Players**; **Aboriginal Sports Foundation**.

Simpson Medal, awarded by the WA Football League, is presented to the best and fairest player in all Grand Finals, carnivals, and interstate matches. The medal is named after Dr F. W. Simpson, a lifelong follower of the game, and was first won by A. Ebbs of East Fremantle in 1945. The best record of medal wins is held by South Fremantle who have been awarded seven medals from the fourteen Grand Finals in which they have played. Barry Cable, the former Perth and North Melbourne champion, has the best individual record, winning the award in 1966, 1967, and 1968.

GC*

SIMPSON, ROBERT BADDELEY, AM, MBE (1936–), cricketer, was born in Marrickville, Sydney, of Scottish immigrant parents. Initially an attacking middle-order batsman, brilliant slips field, and useful leg-break bowler, he made his debut for NSW at the age of 17 and at

19 scored 98 against the visiting Englishmen. In order to make the Test side Bob Simpson had five seasons in WA and became a no-risk opening batsman. Although he made his Test debut in 1958, a century eluded him until 1964 when he scored 311 against England at Old Trafford. Shortly before that series he had become Australian captain and had established a productive partnership with Bill Lawry. The two openers, who developed a fine understanding and realised the importance of rotating the strike, put on many fine opening stands including 382 against the West Indies at Bridgetown in 1965. Ten years after Test retirement, at 41, Simpson inspired a third-string Australian side to a 3–2 series win over India in 1977–78 when World Series Cricket recruited most of the country's best cricketers. Although his side later lost to the West Indies, they won one Test and very nearly another. In sixty-two Tests he scored 4869 runs, took 71 wickets and 110 catches. He was awarded the AM in 1978. In more recent times Simpson has been a successful manager and coach of NSW and Australia. His traditional coaching methods and emphasis on discipline played a role in the revival of Australian cricket in the late 1980s.

KM-H

See **Cricket**.

SKENE, ROBERT ('Hurricane Bob')

(1914–   ) was the first Australian to be classed as a 10-goal polo-player. He began his career in 1931 with the Australian Polo Club at Cobbitty, NSW, and took horses to India each year to play in the prestigious Indian Polo Association Championship. In 1937 Skene went to England with the Ashton brothers and they subsequently won the English Champion Cup at Hurlingham. He became the only Australian to play for England in 1939 when they met the USA in the Winchester Cup. He played again for England in Argentina in 1949. Skene joined the Indian Army in 1941, was taken prisoner at the fall of Singapore and incarcerated in Changi for more than three years. Known as 'Hurricane Bob' for his fearless riding, he was rated a 10-goal player in 1950 and retained that status for seventeen years. He won the Argentine Open Championship, the world's premier polo tournament, in 1954 and 1956. He was also US Open champion in 1952, 1958, and 1962. He was inducted into the Sport Australia Hall of Fame in 1985.

RC

Skiing

Skiing in Australia is mentioned as a sport as early as the 1861 gold rush to Kiandra. In 1909 the Kosciusko Alpine Club (KAC) was formed and a hotel opened at Sponars Creek. The following year a chalet was built at Mount Buffalo and the first KAC races were held. In 1920 the Ski Club of Australia was formed and in 1927 its president, (Sir) Herbert Schlink, organised the first crossing between Kiandra and Kosciusko on skis. In 1929 a chalet was built at Mount Buller and the following year another at Charlotte Pass, which in 1938, like many subsequent snowfield erections, was destroyed by fire. The founding of the Ski Tourers' Association in NSW by Charles Anton in 1950 led to an improved network of huts for skiers on the main range in south-east Australia. This in turn led to the opening of the Thredbo ski field in 1958. The Snowy Mountains project, from 1949 to 1956, had an important effect on development in the Australian Alps. The most important ski resorts are at Thredbo, Perisher Valley, and Guthega in NSW, Mounts Buller, Hotham, and Buffalo, and Falls Creek in Victoria, and smaller areas in Tasmania.

Australian skiers have competed in international Alpine (downhill) events since the 1952 Winter Olympic Games in Norway. In the 1969–70 season Malcolm Milne became the first Australian to win a World Cup championship race. In 1989 Thredbo was the venue for FIS (Fédération Internationale de Ski) World Cup downhill races. Nordic or cross-country skiing is also enjoyed, and national championships have been held since 1930. In the 1980s freestyle, acrobatic skiing became increasingly popular and Australians such as Kirsty Marshall have had success at international competition in this sport.

KR

See **Australian Ski Federation**; LEE, STEVEN; MILNE, MALCOLM; SMITH, CHRISTINE.

SKILTON, BOB

(1939–   ) is regarded as one of the most talented men ever to have played Australian rules football. He played his first senior game for South Melbourne in 1954 and had another 236 games for the club over the next sixteen years. He won the Brownlow Medal three times. Skilton was courageous, intuitive, and 'read' the play as well as any rover in the game. However, two skills stood out above all: his ability to evade opposing players by balking and side-stepping and his ability to kick equally well with either foot. The latter skill was remarkable in the 1950s and 1960s when most élite footballers kicked from only one side. Skilton could drop-kick the ball with pinpoint accuracy with either foot, from a standing start or on the run.

RKS

Skindiving and Spearfishing

The story of skindiving in Australia hinges on the answers to a world-wide question: what can air-breathing humans do for profit or pleasure under water without the aid of scuba equipment? The Australian coastal and riverine Aborigines and the Torres Strait Islanders were the first Australian skindivers, being adept at hunting turtles and eels under water and capable of diving to considerable depths. Skindiving since the early European settlement of Australia may have been marginally and informally influenced by this Aboriginal tradition, but much more by developments overseas, particularly in the Mediterranean. Australia, in turn, was later to influence diving techniques in the Pacific. The story of this development in skindiving techniques, sports, and pastimes in Australian waters is one of changing technology, changes in social and recreational mores, and an interweaving with practices that depend on scuba (self-contained underwater breathing apparatus).

Japanese pearl and kelp divers and Mediterranean sponge divers had been expert skindivers for centuries, but the overseas developments which resulted in the present popularity of skindiving and spearfishing in Australia stem from the 1930s, when Japanese 'goggle' divers visited Europe and introduced their sport to French swimmers who began to dive for fish using crude wooden handspears. By 1935 Corlieu had developed the first swimming fins and the skills of spearfishing had spread in a minor way to the Pacific, the USA, and Australia before the Second World War. War became a spur to invention and technology: the naval 'frogman' became synonymous with intelligence work, sabotage, and clearing of underwater obstacles; the face mask was developed to replace goggles; and before the war's end, pioneer Australian skindivers and spearfishers were experimenting with diving techniques and an array of spears—handmade and commercially made wooden bazookas, friction-trigger spears, Hawaiian sling spears—and even with dangerous means of underwater air supply such as oxygen rebreathers or regulators using beer barrels and with improvised containers filled with air. In the meantime Jacques Cousteau had been developing new techniques in the Mediterranean since 1939 and had produced an aqualung which became commercially available in Australia in the late 1940s.

As greater numbers of skindivers and spearfishers began to dive in Australian waters and on occasion clashed with anglers, those sharing an interest in diving formed the Underwater Spearfishermen's Association of NSW in 1948. The association drew up a code of ethics to circumvent the passing of legislation that might unfairly restrict the sport. In 1953 a national convention and spearfishing championships were organised in conjunction with the Australian Anglers' Association, and an inaugural meeting founded a federation at first titled the Underwater Spearfishermen's Association of Australia, later to become the Australian Underwater Federation in 1966.

The concerns of successive Federal bodies in overseeing skindiving and spearfishing coincide with the principal concerns of the sports and their participants: safety; conservation; equipment, technology, and new practices; and competition at regional, State, national, and international levels. People who fish traditionally have often imagined unfairly that those who fish under water deplete fish stocks, despite the evidence of indiscriminate overfishing from boats and shore as well as from commercial fishing and illegal netting, each of which is more damaging when set against the selectivity of spearfishing. Spearfishing in Australia has been particularly conservation-conscious and has led the world in this respect in its rules of competition and in its opposition to scuba spearfishing which does not allow a zone of retreat for fish to depths greater than the 3–5 metres at which most spearfishing without scuba is conducted. As a result, spearfishing with scuba is banned in most Australian States. Spearfishing competitions, once held from dawn to dark and allowing competitors to spear four fish of each species, have since 1957 been restricted to six hours' duration, with only one fish of each eligible species earning a score.

Expert spearfishers and skindivers can perform remarkable feats in competition. International spearfishing championships are often conducted at a depth of 30 metres or more, divers staying down and pursuing and spearing fish on the one breath for more than one and a half minutes. It is not uncommon for a national spearfishing aspirant to prospect about 10 kilometres of coastline in a six-hour period. With further moves towards conservation, the rules of national spearfishing competition were amended in 1979 to place heavier emphasis on the range of species speared and less on the weight of the fish taken. Divers have competed in underwater photography since the advent of effective underwater still cameras in the 1950s, but more recently, in a further move towards conservation, film-fishing competitions have been introduced with similar scoring systems to those for the spearing of fish, but relying on the diver photographing rather than spearing a range of fish species. Other modes of underwater competition have also developed from the basic skills of the skindiver: underwater orienteering, underwater hockey, fin swimming (which since the early 1970s has been part of the Australian National Championships and was approved as an Olympic sport in 1986) and underwater swimming, which was introduced as a 200 metres event at national level in 1975. Ladies' championships in spearfishing and underwater hockey date from the early 1960s and mid-1980s respectively.

GK-S

See **Australian Underwater Federation**.

SMITH, CHRISTINE IDRIS (1947–79), born Cooma, NSW, spent her childhood at Jindabyne, close to the ski fields. She competed in Europe and America as a junior and at 17 represented Australia at the 1964 Winter Olympics, where she finished twenty-seventh and twenty-eighth in the downhill and slalom events. Smith gave up ski racing to concentrate on interior decorating, designing a successful range of bathroom accessories.

KR

SMITH, KARAN LOUISE (née BULLOCH) (1961–) started playing netball with the Cromer Club in Manly-Warringah in 1969 at the age of 8. She first represented NSW in junior competition in 1977 and in open competition in 1979. She entered the AIS netball squad in 1981 and became a member of the Australian Open team that year. Smith was a member of the victorious Australian team at the World Netball Tournament in Singapore in 1983.

PB and IJ

Smith Medal. The Norm Smith Medal is awarded to the player voted best on the ground during the AFL Grand Final. It is named in honour of Norm Smith, a former champion player and coach. Smith played for Melbourne and Fitzroy between 1935 and 1950 and coached Melbourne, Fitzroy, and South Melbourne. As coach of Melbourne he won six premierships between 1955 and 1964. The Norm Smith Medal was first awarded in 1979, to Wayne Harmes of Carlton. Coincidentally, Harmes was a relative of Smith. Only two award winners, Maurice Rioli of Richmond in 1982 and Gary Ablett of Geelong in 1989, have not come from the side winning the Grand Final. Gary Ayres from Hawthorn won the medal twice, in 1986 and 1988.

DN

See **SMITH, NORMAN**.

Smith Memorial Medal. From 1925 until 1965 the best and fairest player in the Northern Tasmanian Football Association was awarded the Tasman Shield Trophy. In 1966 the trophy was renamed the Hec Smith Memorial Medal. It retained this name until the amalgamation of the North West Football Union and the Northern Tasmanian Football Association in 1987, when the award was replaced by the Ovaltine Medal. The only triple Hec Smith medallists (in its various forms) were C. Dennis (Scottsdale) and A. Cashion (Longford).

MH*

SMITH, NORMAN WALTER (1915–73), born Northcote, Victoria, excelled as a footballplayer, captain, and coach in a career spanning thirty-five years. With the Melbourne Football Club he played a leading role in their ten premierships over twenty-six years. He was one of the game's most notable coaches, who introduced new playing techniques such as 'decoy forward play' and 'ruck roving'. Smith started with Melbourne in 1935, was captain from 1945 to 1947, leading VFL goal-kicker in 1941 (88 goals), and played for Victoria twice. He also coached Fitzroy and South Melbourne. His name is perpetuated in the annual award of the Norm Smith Medal to the best player in the AFL Grand Final.

NS

See **BARASSI, RON**; **Smith Medal**.

SMITH, Sir JAMES JOYNTON (1858–1943) was a Sydney hotelier with one glass eye who was adept at making money from sport. He owned several racecourses, including Victoria Park which operated from 1908 to 1944. Smith financed early rugby league in Sydney, in particular the 1910 game between the first Kangaroo and Wallaby touring teams, and was patron of the NSW Rugby League from 1929 to 1943. He published the newspaper *Smith's Weekly* from 1919 to 1939 and the *Referee* and *Arrow* from 1930 to 1939.

CC

See *Referee*.

SMITH, THOMAS JOHN ('TJ') (1920–), born NSW, dominated the Sydney racing stage for more than three decades after winning his first NSW training premiership in 1952–53. Tommy Smith amassed an unbroken and unprecedented sequence of thirty-three premierships. He had a varied and difficult youth, gaining experience working in several stables but making no progress towards his ambition to be a jockey. Turning to training, he moved to Sydney in 1939 and had his first success with his horse *Bragger*, who became a consistent winner. His first major win was the 1949 AJC Derby with *Playboy*. In 1950 he appealed successfully against AJC disqualification when his horse, *Sunshine Express*, tested positive to a swab; in 1954 his mare *Tarien*, who won the AJC Doncaster, was disqualified, but Smith was exonerated. After these reverses he was virtually unstoppable, his success sealed through the achievements of the champion *Tulloch*. He built up a large stable of runners. He has trained, to date, the winners of a record thirty-five Derby races in Australia, including nine AJC Derbies. His successes include six Golden Slippers, four Caulfield Cups, two Melbourne Cups, and seven Cox Plates, three of them in succession by *Kingston Town*. In 1986 Smith floated his training business as a public company, but Tulloch Lodge Ltd became a financial failure. This coincided with his eclipse in the training premiership when he was narrowly beaten by Brian Mayfield-Smith in 1985–86. Resuming training in his own right, the resilient Smith won his thirty-fourth title in 1988–89.

AL

SMITH, TREVOR, AM (1949–   ), is regarded as Australia's greatest male hockey-player. He first played for SA in 1968 at the age of 19 and made his debut for Australia at the 1971 World Hockey Cup in Barcelona. Originally a forward, his move to centre-half after the 1976 Olympics enhanced his reputation and helped consolidate Australia's dominance in world hockey. After the 1978 World Cup in Argentina he was widely considered to be the best centre-half in hockey. In the same year he captained SA to its first Australian championship in fifty years. Smith played 176 Tests for Australia, appearing in four World Cup tournaments and two Olympics and being part of a team which won the silver medal at Montreal in 1976. In his role as play-maker, both in attack and defence, Smith redefined the position of centre-half. He was honoured by being named captain of a combined world team after the 1983 World Cup. He was awarded the AM in 1988.

RQ

SMYTH, PHIL ('The General'), AM (1958–   ), born Adelaide, the husband of Jennifer Cheesman, was a basketballer for Sturt, St Kilda, Canberra, and Australia. Smyth showed ability at an early age, and represented SA at junior and senior level on many occasions. In 1982 he joined National Basketball League (NBL) club, St Kilda, after which he moved to Canberra, with whom he played from 1983, and for whom he was the pivotal player in three NBL titles. While in Canberra, he was employed at the AIS as assistant basketball coach. Smyth was selected in NBL all-star teams between 1982–85 and 1988–89. Following overseas tours with the junior Australian team, he was a member of the senior team from 1978, playing at the world championships 1978–90, and at the Olympic Games in 1980, 1984, and 1988. He was Australian captain 1981–86, then co-captain from 1988, and up to the end of 1990 had played more games for Australia than in the NBL, largely because he did not immediately enter the fledgling league, preferring to remain with his Adelaide club, Sturt. A point guard, the 184 centimetre Smyth was one of the most gifted players to represent Australia, being a reliable shot and possessing speed, safe hands, court vision, and excellent anticipation. When these are considered with his exceptional defensive ability and his play-making role, Smyth was the complete player, and his ability was recognised in the offers he received for trials in Europe and the USA, none of which he accepted. He was awarded the AM in 1989 for services to basketball.

SB

See **CHEESMAN, JENNIFER**.

Soccer
The first recorded game of soccer in Australia was played on the afternoon of Saturday, 14 August 1880. The venue was Parramatta Common in Sydney. The teams were the King's School and an eleven that shortly after took the name the Wanderers, the first official British Association football club in Australia. The key figure in initiating the game was John Walter Fletcher, an English schoolmaster educated at Cheltenham College and Oxford. He was assisted by several others, most of whom were also public-school old boys. Men of the same background comprised the Arcadians and Coreen College, Fletcher's private-school team, both of which formed in 1881. The (NSW) English Football Association was created in 1882 and was responsible for Australia's first intercolonial matches, a NSW team visiting Victoria in 1883. The Southern British Football Association superseded this body in 1884, with the Association (knock-out) Cup beginning in 1885. The Gardiner (State knock-out) Cup, donated by Sydney businessman William A. Gardiner, replaced the Association Cup in 1888.

Correspondence between Sydney enthusiasts and Scottish contacts interstate helped the game spread to Victoria. The Anglo-Australian Football Association Football Club was formed in Melbourne in 1883. It split into the Melbourne Rovers, Prahran, Carlton, and South Melbourne clubs in 1884. The name Anglo-Australian Football Association was retained as the governing body in Victoria, which also formed in 1884. The association's secretary was Arthur E. Gibbs, a Scot who doubled as Victoria's captain versus NSW 1884–87. Under Gibbs the association in 1884 started a regular competition for the George Cup and a knock-out competition for the Beaney Cup. The latter was donated by leading Melbourne surgeon Dr James G. Beaney. Other correspondence with expatriots in Queensland led to a Scot, Andrew Rankine, forming the Rangers Football Club in Brisbane in 1883. The Scottish connection continued, with the St Andrews and Queen's Park clubs forming in 1884. They operated under the newly constituted Anglo-Queensland Football Association which established a competition in its first year of operation. The Rangers were Queensland's first champions in 1884. The game emerged in the British-populated mining district of Ipswich in 1886, and the Queensland British Football Association was established in 1889. Queensland's first representative side toured NSW in 1890.

Soccer began in WA with the formation of the Rugby and English Association Football Club in Perth in 1892. A scratch match between club members was the State's first game. The club committee was composed of a German and four Britons, one of whom was secretary-treasurer. Perth- and Fremantle-based teams were regular competitors by 1896. During the

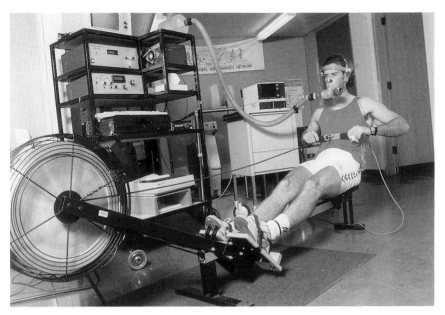

106 Nick Green, from the all-Victorian crew that won two world rowing championships in the heavyweight coxless fours event, being tested on a rowing ergometer.

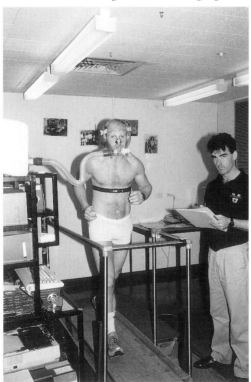

107 Champion Australian Rules footballer Gary Ablett having his fitness assessed on a treadmill.

108 On-water blood lactate measurements being made on sprint canoeist Natalie Hood to determine her anaerobic response to different intensities of effort.

109 Junior international gymnast Claire Cribbes being tested for flexibility during training by her coach Fiona Bird.

110 Australian champion weight-lifter in the 75 kilog class Damien Brown, from the Hawthorn Club in Victoria, performing a clean and jerk during an international event.

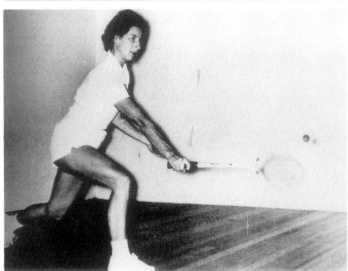

III and II2 Geoff Hunt and Heather McKay are
acknowledged as two of the greatest squash-players of
all time.

113 A swimming competition between the Randwick and Coogee Clubs, NSW, December 1898.

114 Bathing machines, such as these at Coogee, were often used in the latter years of the nineteenth century.

115 The perils of mixed bathing around the turn of the century were highlighted by the *Bulletin* in this cartoon of 1906.

116 In the past there were fewer opportunities for women to participate in swimming competitions. This carnival was held at the Adelaide City Baths in 1896.

1890s many coalminers from the eastern States flocked west with the onset of the Depression. They sought work on the goldfields and in the process established soccer clubs at Kalgoorlie, Coolgardie, and Boulder City. Coast v. Goldfields fixtures emerged soon after. Soccer began in SA in 1893. Enough enthusiasts were found at the start to form two clubs, Rangers and Pioneers. The first official game was between a combined team and HMS *Ringarooma*. Leading officials were recent British immigrants, though no one person dominated the scene. The game struggled in following seasons but gained impetus when an English Midlands firm, Holford Potteries, exported workers to establish operations in Norwood, Adelaide, in 1897. The SA British Football Association formed in 1902 with the establishment of the North Adelaide, South Adelaide, and Woodville clubs. Tasmanian soccer started in 1908 when the crew of the SS *Zealandia* staged an exhibition game on the Domain in Hobart. A week later, responding to the sailors' challenge, a small pocket of British immigrants formed a team in New Norfolk. Its leading light was retired British army colonel Joseph J. B. Honeysett. New Norfolk was followed by the Hobart Football Club, YMCA, and crews of additional visiting ships. Supported by prominent members of the military and clergy, the Tasmanian British Football Association was created in mid-1909. Soccer in what became the ACT began with the Jerrabombera Football Club. It was formed by construction workers at Canberra's Power House labour camp in 1914. At that time the district's workforce possessed numerous recent British immigrants. In mid-1914 they formed the Canberra British Football Association which included Jerrabombera, a team from Ginninderra, the Royal Military College (Duntroon), and the Canberra Football Club whose members were officers with the Department of Home Affairs which supervised the construction of Canberra.

Soccer's early link with immigrants proved to be enduring. With each new wave of immigration the game received a new influx of enthusiasts. After the initial 1880s rush had established the game, the 1900s wave revitalised earlier efforts that had flagged during the 1890s Depression. After the First World War extensive immigration from Britain throughout the 1920s took soccer to unprecedented heights, marked by capacity crowds that watched an English professional eleven tour in 1925. However the onset of the Great Depression again stifled immigration and consequently the game as well. There was a short revival in the late 1930s, typified by a second visit by an English (amateur) eleven that toured in 1937. After the Second World War came the largest influx of immigrants since the gold-rush era. But the intake was different on this occasion. The usual

British were complemented by 'displaced persons', refugees and assisted-passage migrants from all over Europe. Arriving from 1947, they turned into a flood of 'New Australians' during the 1950s and 1960s, the effect of which was profound for soccer. Right across the country the game boomed. Rates of participation and spectating soared to record levels. The two main football codes, Australian rules and rugby league, were challenged and, in some places, occasionally eclipsed.

The immigrant element complemented soccer's working-class nature. British public-school old boys may have started the game in 1880 but they were quickly replaced by blue-collar workers. In all major urban areas where soccer emerged, its principal support stemmed from industrial centres and their dormitory suburbs. Employees in the heavy manufacturing industries supplied numerous enthusiasts, as did the various branches of the transport industry and the railways in particular. The influence in shipping was also noticeable. Crews and dockside workers involved in the game were consistently found in Sydney, Adelaide, Hobart, and Perth's port of Fremantle. Albany to the south was also prominent as a site for soccer.

Mining districts were special hotbeds of the game. Queensland had the coalmines of Ipswich and West Moreton and the mineral-rich hinterlands of Maryborough and Rockhampton. NSW had the extensive coalfields of Newcastle, South Maitland, Lithgow, and Wollongong. In Victoria there were the brown coalmines of the La Trobe Valley and in SA Port Pirie. Although not a mining centre itself, Port Pirie fed off the minerals extracted at Broken Hill, its direct railway link with 'The Barrier' leading to the development of extensive smelting works. In WA there were the goldfields centred around Kalgoorlie but Geraldton's copper mines and Collie's coalmines were additional meccas for the game.

Among players, spectators, and officials, soccer has been a working-class recreation for most of its history. Like Australian rules and rugby league it has acquired a 'middle classness', but only recently and only as the population in general has become more middle-class since the 1950s. The overwhelming pattern of the game has been one of limited resources, epitomised at the grass roots by kitchen-table management committees and public-park players. Consistent with its working-class support base, soccer has seldom been concerned with amateurism. However full-time professionalism, as much as it has been sought, has only been achieved by a handful of very recent players. The highest level attained in senior ranks for most of the game's history has been part-time professionalism.

An internal factor that has helped determine the nature and direction of soccer has been the relationship between local and immigrant enthusiasts. Ever since the 1890s the game's indigenous element has always gained control of the code when either depression or war has staunched the flow of immigration. On every occasion when large-scale migration was recommenced, however, conflict has also eventually developed. Administrative splits were regular features in the two most prominent States for soccer, Queensland and NSW. Grounds, gate receipts, and player payments were the specific grievances cited, but the general issue in question centred around the sovereignty of clubs. Immigrant groups were opposed to the district system favoured by local-born officials, a system common to most codes of football in Australia but not to British football. Internal tensions were at their most explosive during the 1950s. Where before Australian and Briton shared so much, the emergence of Europeans, and especially southern Europeans, in the game added a new ingredient to soccer's formula. Yet the addition inflamed rather than eased tensions. Starting in NSW in 1957 and then spreading to all other States, the formation of (European) immigrant-controlled federations first challenged, and then quickly defeated, Australian-controlled State associations. The Australian Soccer Football Association gave way to the Australian Soccer Federation in 1961 and since then soccer's dominant pressure groups have been ethnic-based.

Turbulent times in the 1950s and 1960s highlighted tensions in society at large over the issue of immigration. The mixing of different peoples and their cultures often produced antagonism that quickly translated into chauvinism which shaded into racism. To use the pre-war term 'pommyball' was one thing, but to use the post-war term 'wogball' was qualitatively different. It smacked of prejudice. In the issue of both on- and off-field violence, something which at that time characterised European enthusiasts, soccer created a weapon which not only sapped its own strength but which was very handy for critics to use.

Yet for all of soccer's internal tensions the game did thrive, especially during the 1920s and 1950s to 1960s when junior recruitment programmes and immigration swelled numbers. NSW, the most prominent soccer State, had 150 teams in 1911, 450 teams in 1925, 721 in 1953, and 7521 teams in the peak year of 1979. Statistics for other States since 1910 are incomplete but those that are available verify Queensland as being consistently ahead of the southern and western States in terms of participants. In fact, despite the best efforts of officials in Victoria, SA, WA, and Tasmania, soccer in these States, compared to either Queensland or NSW, has been forced to rely far more on immigrant influence than local recruitment. The officials'

task has been made hard by the hold that Australian rules has had in the South and West. The administrators of Australian rules have always been extremely aggressive towards their rivals, especially in maintaining their game's hegemony over winter school sport and playing venues. Rugby league in the North and East has also been hard-nosed, but rugby union, Australian rules, and soccer actually predate league, establishing a cosmopolitan tradition that the Queensland and NSW sporting public has always maintained.

Soccer's progress for more than a century has been effectively limited by other football codes. Its success in retaining traditional patronage, aided by the process of enculturation, has allowed it to perpetuate its dominance. Yet soccer enthusiasts from 1880 have always asserted their belief that their game would one day take over. The problem was how to break into the self-generating cycle of enclosed grounds, gate receipts, crowds, player payments, attractive events, media coverage and, of late, sponsorship. The bumper crowds of the early 1960s came closest to fulfilling soccer's dreams. During the halcyon days of the NSW Soccer Federation, total crowd attendances rose from 225 000 in 1957 to 827 000 in 1964. Crowds for Sydney Grand Finals for the same period peaked at 30 158 in 1963. The major clubs in all capitals attracted overseas players with payment packages. This included illegal poaching by the Prague club in Sydney that led to FIFA, the world governing body, suspending Australia from world competition between 1960 and 1963. Other major clubs, principally Italian, Greek, or Hungarian, were Melbourne's Juventus and South Melbourne Hellas, Adelaide's Juventus and Budapest, Perth's Azzurri, Brisbane's Hellenic, and Sydney's Prague, Hakoah, Apia, and St George Budapest.

Australian soccer's international profile has never been large. An Ashes tradition has never been established despite its prominence in most other imported British sports. But World Cup ambitions began in 1966 and, after a near miss in 1970, Australia qualified for the 1974 finals in Germany. The exposure gained in the media was unprecedented for soccer and a national league was organised in 1977. In the 1980s participation numbers rose to a purported 500 000 players, placing soccer on the same level as Australian rules. However the massive number of juniors has not translated into paying spectators. With few exceptions, senior soccer during the 1980s experienced decreasing crowds. Much of this has been due to the declining patronage of ethnic clubs whose support bases have gradually dwindled with the cessation of major European immigration. At the same time, by the very nature of the ethnic flavour of senior soccer, the 'Australian' sporting public has refused to transfer its patronage from junior to senior ranks. This has much to do with the enticements of other sports but there still remains a solid rump of anti-immigrant sentiment that inhibits general public support for ethnic clubs.

Be it British or European, the immigrant element has been a catalyst for change. On most occasions the change was for the better and yet, both within and without the game, reactions against immigrant involvement have dissipated energies and effort. Soccer's progress has also pivoted on its working-class roots and its ambition to be a major code in the face of strong opposition from other games. Yet ever since 1880 the game's linchpin has unquestionably been the presence and interaction of immigrants. The game's history in Australia is mostly their story.

PM

See **ALSTON, ADRIAN**; **AROK, FRANK**; **Australian Soccer Federation**; **Australian Women's Soccer Association**; **BAUMGARTNER, LEOPOLD**; **Bradley Report**; **Crowd Disorder**; **Ethnic Influences**; **FARINA, FRANK**; **FIFA Ban on Australian Soccer**; **Fleming Medal**; **FLETCHER, JOHN**; **GEORGE, Sir ARTHUR**; **JOHNSTON, CRAIG**; **KOSMINA, JOHN**; **KRNCEVIC, EDDIE**; **MARSTON, JAMES**; **MASTERS, JAMES**; **McNABB, JAMES**; **PERKINS, CHARLES**; **QUILL, ALFRED**; **RASIC, RALE**; **ROONEY, JAMES**; **Rothmans Medals (Soccer)**; **SCHAEFER, MANFRED**; **SCHEINFLUG, LESLEY**; **Strikes and Industrial Disputes**; **WARREN, JOHNNY**; **WILLIAMS, HARRY**; **WILSON, PETER**; **World Cup Soccer Finals 1974**.

Softball

Softball began in Australia in 1939 soon after Canadian Gordon Young became the director of physical education in NSW and promoted the game in the schools. The next impetus came during the Second World War when softball was organised by US Army Sergeant William Duvernet as recreation for US nurses stationed in Victoria. In 1946 another American, Mack Gilley, introduced the game into Queensland. Softball associations were formed soon after the game had begun in each State and in 1947 Queensland issued an invitation for the first interstate championship to be played in Brisbane. NSW, Queensland, and Victoria, and a team from Ballarat participated, with Victoria winning the series. Discussions then ensued about the formation of a national softball organisation and at the second Interstate Softball Championships in Melbourne the Australian Women's Softball Council was formed, with NSW, SA, Queensland, and Victoria as founding members. WA was admitted in 1951, Tasmania in 1952, the ACT in 1961, and the NT in 1978.

The name was later changed to the Australian Softball Federation (ASF).

Australian championships are now held in strict rotation, with each State playing host in the order in which they were admitted to federation membership. Six championships are played every year: women's open (Mack Gilley Shield); women's under-19 (Elinor McKenzie Shield); women's under-16 (Ester Deason Shield); men's open (John Reid Shield); men's under-19 (Nox Bailey Shield); and the women's national club championship.

Australia became affiliated with the International Softball Federation in 1953, and has the distinction of hosting and winning the first Women's World Softball Championships in 1963 in Melbourne where teams from Japan, USA, NZ, and Papua New Guinea took part. These championships, which have become known as 'world series', have grown to where twenty-one nations played in 1990. Australia has played in all world series, being placed first in 1965 in Melbourne, fourth in 1970 in Japan, third in 1974 in the USA, fifth in 1978 in El Salvador, third in Taiwan in 1982, eighth in NZ in 1986, and third in the USA in 1990.

Softball in Australia is an amateur sport played in both summer and winter. More than fifty-eight thousand people play organised softball throughout Australia, not including school softball, where it is estimated that over a hundred and fifty thousand players participate. Softball has been played by men and boys since the late 1970s, with interstate competition for seniors beginning in February 1984 and for under-19s in 1989. The first Men's Softball World Series was held in Saskatoon, Canada, in 1988, and Australia was among the competitors.

NS* and PH-S

See **LESTER, JOYCE**; **NELSON, MARJORIE**; **YOUNG, GORDON**.

SOUTAR, DANIEL GORDON (1882–1937), born Scotland, emigrated in 1903 and won the Australian amateur golf title that year. He took the NSW Amateur in 1903 and 1904. At the end of 1904 he joined Carnegie Clark as the professional at Royal Sydney Golf Club. Clark and Soutar must be regarded as the founders of professional golf in NSW. Soutar won the Australian Open in 1905 and it is generally believed that he should have won the 1907 and 1912 Australian Opens. He twice won the Australian PGA title. Soutar was a course designer of distinction and was a successful teacher. In 1906 he published his much-admired *The Australian Golfer*. Soutar had a keen sense of humour; his advice to aspiring players was to 'Learn the Fundamentals of Golf: Swinging, Swearing and Cheating'.

CT and MP

See **Golf**; **Royal Melbourne Golf Club**; **SCOTT, Hon. MICHAEL**.

South's Spirit of 1955. After losing seven of their first ten games in 1955, South Sydney Rugby League Club had to win their next eleven games to retain the premiership they had gained two seasons before. After Souths won the first six matches comfortably, Manly-Warringah led them 7–4 at Redfern Oval until almost full time when lock Les Cowie scored in the corner to level the match. Clive Churchill, an inspiring full back but not a renowned goal-kicker, who had his wrist in a makeshift cardboard splint after breaking it in the first five minutes of the game, converted the try from the sideline for his team to win, 9–7. Without Churchill Souths won their remaining rounds and with two narrow wins in the finals they qualified to play Newtown in the Grand Final. Behind 11–7, with six minutes left, South's unyielding spirit helped them score a converted try to win 12–11, thus achieving the apparently impossible for a remarkable premiership victory.

TB

SPALDING, ALBERT GOODWILL (1850–1915), an American baseballer and sporting entrepreneur, effectively began baseball in Australia. He was an outstanding pitcher in the 1870s when baseball was rapidly replacing cricket as the major summer game in the USA and he organised the first baseball team to tour England in 1874. He became one of the important promoters and organisers of the big-business and professional game as it emerged in America in the 1870s and 1880s, and became wealthy through the sporting-goods business he established with his brother. He brought to Australia two professional baseball teams in 1888, his own Chicago team and a combined all-America side, which played exhibition matches across America and in NZ before they arrived in Sydney on 14 December. The tourists were fêted by the press, cricket authorities, and civic leaders, and large crowds watched the games in Sydney, Melbourne, Adelaide, and Ballarat before they left on 7 January 1889 for the remainder of the world tour. Exhibitions were staged in Ceylon, Italy, and France and throughout England, Scotland, and Ireland before the party returned to America. Although baseball was known and played in Australia before 1888 (mostly by Americans), Spalding's tour excited great interest among cricketers, who formed the basis of the regular teams and competitions which have existed ever since. When the first Australian team toured the USA in 1897 Spalding organised a social match in Boston between the 'Kangaroos' and former star players, and entertained the tourists at dinner—rather better treatment than they received on the rest of the tour.

BM

See **Baseball**.

SPEARS, ROBERT ADAM (1893–1950), born Dubbo, NSW, became, at Antwerp in 1920, the first Australian to win a world professional track-cycling championship. Bob Spears won his first race at Dubbo at the age of 14; in 1911 he won his first national championship over 5 miles. He made six-day racing a speciality, leaving Australia for the more lucrative US circuit in 1913. Spears won his first US title in the following year and in 1918 became all-round American pro-champion. After the First World War he returned briefly to Australia and went on to Europe where he achieved his greatest success. In a career that spanned twenty-five years, Spears won three consecutive Grands Prix de Paris, together with Grand Prix events in Denmark, Italy, and Germany. After winning the world title in 1920, he was runner-up in 1921 and 1922. He retired from racing to live in Australia after an abortive come-back in 1932. Spears died of cancer in Paris on 5 July 1950.

JS

Speed Skating

This sport is controlled by the Australian Amateur Ice Racing Council, which in conjunction with the National Ice Skating Association of Australia forms the Australian Skating Union which is affiliated to the Australian Olympic Federation. Ken Kennedy of Sydney was this country's first competitor at the Winter Olympic Games in 1936 and won British indoor titles in 1935 and 1936. States compete each June for the Duke Trophy, teams consisting of two junior men, three women and six senior men in events ranging from 500 to 3000 metres. Colin Coates represented this country in a record six Winter Olympic Games (1968–88), and his sixth place in the 10 000 metres in 1976 remains the best Games performance by an Australian. Jim Lynch dominated domestic speed skating in the 1970s, and won two titles at the 1978 International Skating Union's indoor track championships in England. Michael Richmond, from SA, won the 500 metres event at the 1981 speed-skating world short-track championships held in France.

KM

Speedway

Credit has often been given to New Zealander Johnny Hoskins for inventing the speedway form of motorcycle-racing, both in Australia and internationally. Depending on which 'authority' is consulted, this occurred in 1923, 1924, or 1925 on either a showground circuit covered in cinders or a tan exercise track for horses, though all agree that it happened at West Maitland in NSW. Hoskins certainly became a major promoter of the sport in Australia and subsequently in Britain, but clearly others were earlier in the field as Thebarton

Oval in Adelaide had a commercial quarter-mile grass track operating under lights in 1922 and there was a commercial 1 mile dirt track at Penrith in NSW two years before that. There are several earlier instances of motorcycle races on cycle tracks, racecourses, and around football and cricket grounds. It is equally clear that the sport was not an Australian invention but existed in both the USA and South Africa before its introduction to Australia. Speedcar-racing, the four-wheeled version of speedway, was launched in Australia in 1934 at Melbourne's Olympic Park and Sydney's Granville Showground. At times this, one of the most dangerous sports, rivalled horse-racing and even rugby league as a spectator sport in NSW.

JC*

See **LAWSON, AUB**; **Motorcycling**; **VAN PRAGG, LIONEL**; **WILKINSON, ARTHUR**.

SPEIGHT, JULIE (1966–), born Sydney, was the first woman track cyclist to represent Australia at the Olympics, finishing fifth in the 1000 metres sprint at the 1988 Games. She came second in the same event at the 1990 Commonwealth Games. Speight, 171 centimetres tall and weighing 63 kilograms, took up racing when she was 16. Coached by John Crouchley, she was a versatile rider who won national championships in a variety of events ranging from the 1000 metres sprint to the 50 kilometres individual road race.

RC

Sphairee
Sphairee, a miniaturised form of tennis, was developed in Sydney in 1961 by Fred Beck who wanted to devise a game which incorporated the basic elements of tennis but which would be less strenuous. The game derives its name from *sphaira*, the Greek word for ball. It can be played indoors or out of doors on a court measuring 6.2 by 2.8 metres and with a net approximately 0.6 metres high. Bats like oversized table tennis bats are used with a perforated plastic ball, 7 centimetres in diameter. The NSW Sphairee Association was formed soon after the game's inception and the first NSW championships took place in 1963, with R. B. Frost winning the men's title and N. Brown the women's. Sphairee is an ideal means of introducing children to the fundamentals of tennis while, played by experts, it is one of the fastest of all games. In the thirty years since it was introduced the game's popularity has spread and equipment is now exported to several countries including Mauritius, New Guinea, NZ, and the UK, but it is in NSW that the game has its stronghold, with over five thousand regular players.

JC*

SPOFFORTH, FREDERICK ROBERT ('The Demon') (1853–1926), born Balmain, NSW, was one of the first great overarm fast bowlers who, more than any other player, helped put Australian cricket on the map. Partnered by Harry Boyle, he took 10–20 at Lord's on 27 May 1878, demolishing a powerful MCC side and assuring the success of the tour. He is best remembered for his courageous 14–90 at the Oval Test in 1882 which enabled Australia to win its first Test in England and led to the Ashes tradition. He bowled consistently well, and was the star player on all five tours of England from 1878 to 1886. He took the first Test hat-trick in 1879. Tall and gaunt—191 centimetres and 76 kilograms—with a large nose, he was thought to be the personification of the demon and proved a fine foil and adversary for the English star W. G. Grace. Along with great stamina, pinpoint control, and well-disguised changes of pace, Spofforth was a 'thinking' bowler who made effective use of psychology to dismiss batsmen. An intense and highly motivated performer, a great presence on the field, he was always at his best in a crisis. After marriage to Phillis Cadman, daughter of a Derbyshire merchant, Spofforth settled in England. Although he played nine games for Derbyshire and club cricket for Hampstead until 1903, the demands of running a large business occupied most of his time. He was a successful tea merchant and died a wealthy man.

RC

See **Cricket**.

Sponsorship
At the outset it is important to distinguish sponsorship from patronage and subsidisation. Patronage is an altruistic activity carried out with no expectation of return other than the satisfaction of knowing that a social good is being done. A subsidy is a grant derived from national, State, or local government sources. Sponsorship, on the other hand, implies a financial outlay with some form of material return as the primary goal. The essential elements of sports sponsorship therefore are these: a sponsor makes a contribution in cash or kind, which may or may not include services and expertise, to an activity which is in some measure a leisure pursuit; the sponsored activity does not form part of the main commercial function of the sponsoring body, otherwise it becomes straightforward promotion, rather than sponsorship; and the sponsor expects a benefit in terms of publicity and product awareness.

Sponsorship has become an integral part of the financial infrastructure of Australian sport. Not only has it provided economic support to many professional and semi-professional sports such as tennis, cricket, and football, but it has also contributed to the financial infrastructure of a number of élite amateur-oriented sports like field hockey, gymnastics, swimming, and track and field. Many community and suburban sports leagues and clubs have also received significant financial support from local business houses. By the end of the 1980s a number of business corporations had negotiated multi-million dollar sponsorship agreements with sports organisations. In 1985 Ford Australia took up sponsorship of the Australian Tennis Open Championship, and guaranteed record prize-money of $2 million. A subsequent arrangement with Tennis Australia increased the prize-money to more than $2.5 million. In cricket, the Benson & Hedges Company has provided similar levels of financial support. A five-year agreement negotiated in 1984 with the Australian Cricket Board provided for an injection of $15 million into Australian cricket.

Sponsorship on this scale is new to Australian sport. For most of Australia's sporting history income came mainly from registration fees, social club activities, and gate receipts. During the 1950s and early 1960s sponsorship was scattered, and often done under the guise of benevolent grants by private individuals associated with clubs and associations. More formal sponsorship arrangements undertaken by business firms were limited to a few sports with an international focus like tennis, golf, and motor racing. Ampol Petroleum was one of the few large-scale corporate sports sponsors during this period.

While sponsorship emerged as an important funding source for sport in the 1970s, the conditions for its emergence were planted during the 1960s. The latter part of the 1960s was a period of great social change. Traditional values like the family, fidelity, loyalty, individualism, and amateurism in sport were being questioned, and Australians were looking beyond Britain for alternative cultural and social models. As far as sport was concerned, it was a time of experimentation with new coaching methods and training regimes. Scientific approaches to training gradually permeated the sporting world as new sports development models filtered in from overseas. By the 1970s club administrators and coaches demanded more time and effort from their players, and the players in turn demanded higher wages. The discovery that many sports organisations had increased their profitability impinged on the behaviour of players: they began to question the benefits they were receiving from clubs, which in turn led to disputes over transfer fees, contracts, and match payments.

At the same time the corporate world began to perceive Australian sport as an attractive vehicle for promoting and advertising their products. Articles appeared in business journals advising potential sponsors about the sports that might be suitable promotional vehicles. Sports promotion companies were consequently formed in order to act as intermediaries between business enterprises and sports associations, and to assist sports associations in publicising their sport. They became adept at advising potential sponsors about the ways in which sport could be used to achieve local publicity and goodwill, and how it could reach potential customers.

The realisation by business enterprises that sport could be used to sell products also came at a time when inflation and expanding club and player expectations created the *need* to seek out sponsors. Throughout the early 1970s Australian sport exhibited a continuing demand for better athletes, better facilities, better administrative practices, larger support staff including specialist coaches, additional medical and para-medical officers, and more effective publicity machinery. The Whitlam Labor Government of 1972–75 also supported the development of sport. It saw international sports teams as a vehicle for nationalism, and used community recreation as a means of therapeutic and preventive health as well as a form of social welfare. The Whitlam policy of expansionism in education and the arts also affected the development of sport. The commitment to funding socially beneficial programmes manifested itself in the community psyche. Bigger and better facilities were seen to be within the reach of all. An increase in spending led to an increase in expectations. But this growing demand for facilities and technology required more cash than the Federal Government could afford. Sports administrators consequently turned to the corporate sector for assistance.

By the late 1970s corporate sponsorship was providing economic support not only to the professional, mass spectator sports like international tennis, cricket, and golf, and the various State premier football leagues, but also to many amateur associations. International and interstate cricket were sponsored by the Benson & Hedges Company and Gillette respectively, the Australian Open Tennis Championships were supported by the Marlboro Company. Qantas and Telecom assisted in the conduct of the Australian Open Golf Championships, and the Victorian Amateur Athletics Association had sponsorship arrangements with Dulux Australia and the Olympic Tyre and Rubber Company.

The latter part of the 1970s and early 1980s consequently became a golden age for sports sponsorship. While on the one hand business firms were searching for new ways of upgrading their public image to balance a growing public antipathy to big business, sports leagues, associations, and clubs, at both the professional and amateur levels, were searching for extra cash to satisfy their plans for expansion and for greater local and international competitiveness. Sports sponsorship therefore provided a mutually beneficial arrangement: sport got the use of extra funds, and business got the use of an alternative advertising and promotional medium. For a number of amateur sports in particular, corporate sponsorship became an essential vehicle by which their heightened aspirations might be achieved. Amateur swimming and athletics were cases in point. The Olympic aspirations of these sports were thwarted at Montreal in 1976. Both the public and association responses were to maintain the same ambitions (i.e. Olympic and international success) and to seek sufficient financial aid to provide additional training and coaching facilities for the athletes, thereby improving performance. In 1977 the Confederation of Australian Sport, the umbrella organisation for Australian sport, published a White Paper in which it was stated that international sporting success could only be achieved with extra government funding. The drive for commercial sponsorship was also started. In January 1979 the Australian Athletic Union announced a $120 000 arrangement with the Mars Confectionery Company, and in March the City Mutual Insurance Company announced a three-year grant of $250 000 to the Amateur Swimming Union of Australia.

Another factor explaining the growth of sports sponsorship was the Commonwealth Government's prohibition of cigarette advertising on television in 1976. The three tobacco companies operating in Australia, Amatil, Rothmans, and Philip Morris, were to become the largest sponsors of sport in Australia. By 1980 business firms were directly contributing $50 million per annum to sports leagues, associations, and clubs, of which $5 million was provided by the tobacco companies.

While sports sponsorship continued to grow into the 1980s, it also drew out a number of critical reviews of its effectiveness for the sponsoring organisation. It was on the basis of a low-awareness rating that the Sydney transport company, Wards, discontinued its multi-million dollar sponsorship arrangement with the Sydney Swans football club at the end of the 1982 season. R. R. Walker, a Melbourne advertising agent and journalist, consistently argued that sports sponsorship was not cost-effective and that it failed to generate additional sales. He viewed it as good advertising money gone bad. Walker's scepticism was confirmed by a study of sports sponsorship undertaken by the Public Affairs Division of Mayne Nickless. It was concluded that since most sponsorship could deliver no more than an increase in awareness (the lowest level of marketing message), the return on funds invested would not be high. For the tobacco companies, though, sponsorship was an effective proxy for conventional advertising. During the 1981–82 Test series, Benson & Hedges gained seventy-two hours' coverage for $350 000, a fraction of the cost of conventional advertising. Similarly, in 1982 a survey of Australian football and rugby league matches during September showed that tobacco signs appeared 235 times each match, equal to fourteen and a half minutes, or 13 per cent of total viewing time.

Notwithstanding subsequent claims that sports sponsorship often constituted an ineffective form of corporate investment, sponsorship continued to grow. According to a study undertaken by the *Australian* newspaper and the Clemenger advertising agency, the most favoured sports for corporate sponsors were, in order of level of support, motor racing, golf, cricket, Australian football, rugby league, tennis, sailing, soccer, snooker, squash, bowls, surfing, and field hockey. It was estimated that by the end of the 1980s Australian business firms provided more than $150 million per annum to sports, and that tobacco companies contributed between 5 and 10 per cent of all sponsorship funds.

Sponsorship has not only added a new dimension to the financial structure of Australian sport, it has also helped to transform the structure and practice of the 'games' themselves. In cricket, a combination of sponsorship, television broadcasting, and entrepreneurial initiative led to the replacement of the five-day international Test match by the limited-over day-night game as the most popular form of the sport. A number of rule, equipment, and clothing changes were made, all predicated on the need to provide fans with exciting, colourful, free-flowing entertainment, and in a time span convenient for television stations and advertisers. The influence of corporate sponsorship and associated television broadcast rights also affected the form and structure of tennis. Not only did the method of scoring change (sudden-death tie-breakers were introduced in order to shorten the length of matches) but the traditional apparel of all white was replaced by multi-coloured dress.

The promotion of sport has now become a sophisticated marketing exercise involving both the commercial sponsor and the television broadcaster. While some business executives may see sports sponsorship as a means of rubbing shoulders with their sports heroes, it is clear that most sponsorship arrangements are viewed as an exchange process: the sports association gets the benefit of an additional source of finance, while the sponsoring organisation hopes to gain a fair return for its investment via direct support for the product, or by good corporate image and brand name exposure through either the print or electronic media.

BS

See **Sports Marketing and Management**.

Sport Australia Awards, based on a peer recognition system, were established in 1980 by the Confederation of Australian Sport and quickly became the ultimate acknowledgement of annual sporting performance for Australian sportspeople. Three gold awards are presented annually to recognise the best series of performances by a male athlete, a female athlete, and a team. Silver awards are also presented to junior athletes, administrators, coaches, the best single sporting performances, and for outstanding organisation and presentation of sporting events. Nominations from national sporting associations are voted on by two geographically separated groups of national coaches and administrators. Finalists are then considered by an academy of voters drawn from national sporting associations affiliated with the Confederation of Australian Sport. Winners are determined by first-preference votes unless a tie occurs, when second preferences are counted. The winners of the first gold Sport Australia Awards presented in 1980 were Alan Jones (motor racing), Michelle Ford (swimming), and the Australian Men's 4 × 100 metres medley relay swimming team.

GD

Sport Australia Hall of Fame was established on 10 December 1985 when 120 original members were inducted from a total of 546 nominations. By 1988 the membership had grown to 200 athletes and it continues to expand at the rate of about ten per year. Members are selected through a lengthy peer recognition system, culminating in final approval by the Sport Australia Hall of Fame Selection Committee. In 1989 the Sport Australia Hall of Fame was expanded by the inclusion of associate members selected, on the same basis as members, for outstanding achievements in roles supportive of actual participants. Initially twenty-four associate members were inducted. The Hall of Fame exists to recognise the great contribution to national prestige and pride that great sportspeople have brought to Australia. The first male and female members inducted were Sir Donald Bradman and Dawn Fraser, in recognition of their special place among Australia's greatest athletes.

GD

Sports Marketing and Management

Australians have often shown ingenuity and initiative in their ability to organise sporting events and competitions. Although the first recorded cricket match and race meeting were held as early as 1803 and 1810 respectively, it is almost certain that these were preceded by single-wicket games and match races between horse-owners. Clubs and associations soon followed in these and other sports. Such bodies took the lead in promoting intercolonial competition, which began in the 1850s with archery and rifle clubs shooting on their own butts and ranges and then transmitting the score to their opponents by letter or telegraph. Intercolonial team-games followed as transportation improved. By the 1880s colonial associations or governing bodies had been established in rugby, cricket, shooting, rowing, and Australian football. Most clubs and associations were middle-class either in origin or patronage, though other influences were in operation as works teams emerged under the aegis of private employers, public enterprise, and even trade unions. Some mass spectator events such as boxing matches were also being promoted by entrepreneurs looking for profit rather than social kudos, though generally the established sporting associations in cricket, horse-racing, and tennis were able to resist such challenges to their authority. Essentially Australian sport at the turn of the century was managed voluntarily by mainly middle-class men.

For the next seventy years the management and marketing of sport changed remarkably little. The ebb and flow in the popularity of sports were the result of changing community preferences in response to movements in population, levels of employment, and the influence of heroes and role models to which young boys and girls were attracted. The promotion of sport was left to journalists and broadcasters. Most sports were organised around a part-time 'secretary' or manager supported by a typist or clerical assistant. This 'kitchen table' sports management model dominated all Australian amateur sports and most of the professional ones. Administrative structures were simple and informal, and the organisation of major events centred around volunteer labour.

During the 1970s, however, the management and marketing of sport took on a different guise. Sport managers had become 'restless'. In Australian football, and rugby league in particular, club officials came to recognise that an increased capacity to 'buy' players was one way to achieve sporting success. This required a more systematic and sophisticated form of fund-raising, which led to the employment of full-time, paid fund-raisers. So long as the revenue gained from the employment of extra staff exceeded the cost of their employment, then it made good sporting and commercial sense to employ them. It also became obvious at this time that the commercial value of sport had been severely underused. Businesses were approached to provide sponsorship in return for naming rights, signage, and corporate entertaining facilities. By the 1980s sports marketing had become the fashionable topic of conversation among sports managers. The strong link between sport and amateurism had been broken. Sport had become increasingly professional in terms of both the payments to players and the management of sporting organisations and events. A combination of continued public support, increasing government assistance, and television broadcasts of major events set the scene for a rapid commercial expansion of sport in Australia. Whereas the annual turnover of clubs in the major football leagues in the early 1970s would have been no more than $300 000, by the mid-1980s they had reached an average of $3 million. They had become businesses and it was expected that they be managed in a professional, businesslike manner. The old-fashioned secretary had been replaced by the general manager, who in turn was supported by a marketing director, a finance director, and an executive secretary. By the end of the 1980s the marketing directors had become central to the success of large professional sports clubs, since they were responsible for the corporate client and the sale of sponsorships and corporate boxes, suites, and entertainment facilities. It had reached the stage where sports marketers had created a situation where corporate funding was the single most important revenue source for many professional sporting clubs.

Sports marketers had also been able to convince the managers of many smaller amateur-based clubs and associations that, just like the larger professional clubs, they too could realise their full commercial value by 'marketing' their sport to the corporate sector. As a result sports as disparate as field hockey, beach volleyball, weightlifting, swimming, surfing, and track and field have been able to attract the corporate sponsor. It was also clear that, as sports developed their commercial characteristics, it was necessary to employ individuals who were skilled in negotiation, planning, report-writing, financial management, and understanding complex legal arrangements and contracts. The success of sport in marketing its 'product' to the public and corporate sector therefore resulted in the need for a professional management system. The kitchen-table model had become an anachronism, a relic from a sporting era in which only enthusiasm and hard work were seen to be necessary to achieve success.

BS

See **Sponsorship**.

Sports Medicine

Sports medicine has several strands. It can mean the application of health and sports sciences to assist sportspeople to achieve excellence in athletic performance; or the use of such sciences to enable sportsmen and women, of any grade or ability, to derive optimal benefit from their participation in sport and exercise; or, more generally, the prevention and management of sports injuries.

Élite athletes were among the first to seek sports medicine advice. They were in regular need of treatment for injuries sustained simply because they were pushing their bodies to the limit. Moreover, performing as they did at the cutting edge of their particular sport, they sought information which could increase their potential and help them to gain even marginal advantages over their competitors. Hence, certainly after the Second World War, many Australian professional sports teams used the services of a team doctor, usually a 'superfan', operating in an honorary capacity. Amateurs were slower to follow, though post-war Olympic teams had medical officers appointed from doctors attending the Games in a private capacity, and in 1964 the Australian Olympic Federation decided to have medical men not only accompany the athletes but also perform pre-embarkation fitness tests. During the 1960s and 1970s most major national and State sports associations appointed medical officers and accepted the necessity of having a doctor as a member of touring parties. Today the Australian élite athlete is served by a network of medical professionals capable of providing immediate treatment and support to ensure that no injury is aggravated. Increasingly, routine medical checks are conducted by team doctors over the season and not just on match days, and sports scientists are also providing valuable data on exercise, nutrition, and mental preparation to assist in performance improvement.

Sports medicine is not confined to servicing the élite performers. As the general community increasingly began to participate in sport, there developed a need for the provision of sports medicine to a wider range of sportspeople: sport for all necessitated sports medicine for all. Although sport is health-promoting, it can also be a health hazard, and the boom in sports participation since 1960 has produced a concomitant increase in sport-related injuries. Body-contact sports inevitably mean bruises, or worse; all sports performed at high speed are inherently dangerous, with any lapse in concentration or technological failure liable to bring disaster; and then there are sports such as cricket and hockey which involve 'missiles' and 'weapons'. Some injuries are, of course, self-inflicted via the torturous regimen of daily training undertaken in the quest for endurance and improved performance. Others, particularly among weekend athletes, stem from trying to do too much too soon or aspiring to emulate sports stars while being unwilling to accept that their own sporting abilities are on the wane. Before the 1970s, most of these injured sportspeople were treated by sports trainers, men and women often ignorant of the latest methods, or by general practitioners who frequently lacked the medical knowledge specific to sports injuries. Today, however, for some there is the specialist sports medicine clinic dedicated to the treatment of injured sportsmen and sportswomen.

The earliest of these clinics in Australia were located on university campuses, generally catering for students who had been injured at weekend sports events. All of them, however, were small-scale, limited-time ventures with a restricted clientele and inadequate follow-up procedures. The major breakthrough in the provision of specialist sports medicine facilities came in the late 1960s with the opening of the Lewisham Sports Medicine Clinic which was the first of its kind in Australia in that it was staffed by specialist doctors and paramedics, all of whom had a strong interest in sports medicine. Lewisham was based on the principle that injured sportspeople had the right to expect to be seen by someone who appreciated their sports needs and how these could be attained. Thus Lewisham provided a unit for the intensive treatment of injuries caused or aggravated by athletic pursuit and for the early rehabilitation of the injured sportsperson. Others followed where Lewisham had shown the way, and the late 1970s and early 1980s saw the pace of adoption increase, especially in the commercial sector, till sports medicine clinics became an established part of the Australian sporting scene.

Australian sports medicine has adopted a multi-disciplinary approach. By the early 1970s, following the lead set in North America and Europe, many doctors were accepting that alone they could not practise sports medicine optimally and that physiotherapists and sports scientists also had a major role to play. Today doctors, exercise physiologists, physiotherapists, sports trainers, biochemists, psychologists, podiatrists, sociologists, nurses, dentists, nutritionists, coaches, and sportspeople themselves have combined their talents in a joint venture to get the best out of athletes and to encourage wide participation for health's sake.

The expansion of sports medicine and the development of a multi-disciplinary approach have both contributed to a greater stock of knowledge, both practical and theoretical. In the 1960s folklore about injury treatment abounded, particularly among sports trainers but also among medical practitioners. The lack of definitive information led to a profusion of often conflicting advice which did little for the reputation of sports medicine. Fortunately, succeeding decades have witnessed a knowledge explosion in the field of sports medicine, particularly as sports science has begun to play a more important role. Research within Australia, but mainly overseas, has produced new data and has scientifically confirmed or rejected much of the old. This has enabled the advocates of sports medicine to act as a countervailing power against the dogmatism or idiosyncrasy of sports coaches. Club doctors and physiotherapists are now less easily overruled than

they used to be as they now have the information to back their judgement. Coaches themselves have benefited from the growth of sports medicine knowledge as it has enabled some aspects of training to become less of an art and more of a science. Sportspeople have gained from advice on correct warm-up and warm-down exercises, on stretching for flexibility, on protective strapping and correct footwear, as well as on specific conditioning. There are still areas of controversy and debate but the task of the sports medicine practitioner is now more soundly based on proven knowledge.

Sports medicine has graduated from being on the fringe of orthodox medicine, facing hostility from conservative elements who regarded it almost as charlatanism or quackery, to becoming an accepted part of mainstream medicine with postgraduate courses available to doctors who wish to practise in the area. Physiotherapists, and more so sports scientists, offer specialised knowledge to sportspeople ranging from parklands athletes, participating in what can be regarded as enjoyable forms of preventive medicine, to Olympic representatives, working to the limits of their potential. Sports medicine practitioners have taken the responsibility both to encourage physical activity on the part of those whose health they feel could be improved by such involvement, whether they be young or old, male or female, able-bodied or with a disability, and to maintain the health of all those who choose to take part in sports.

WV

See **Australian Sports Medicine Federation**.

Sports Science

In order to increase the potential for success, the modern high-performance athlete is becoming increasingly dependent on scientific assistance. Principles are taken from the basic and applied sciences to provide coaches and athletes with methods and techniques that will enhance performance. Biological sciences such as applied anatomy, physiology, biomechanics, and biochemistry which in turn are based on the physical sciences of mathematics, physics, and chemistry are used to better understand responses to exercise and training and the muscular and mechanical basis of movement. In addition, behavioural science is used to analyse both the psychology of individual performers and that of the group with which they are associated.

High-performance sport requires an athlete to possess *skill, fitness, a positive mental approach* and appropriate *strategies* for meeting the demands of the contest. In more precise terms, high-level sport requires an athlete to display *skilled* movements that are *energised* by an appropriately developed level of fitness and *controlled* by a specific set of psychological skills and attributes. It is the responsibility of the coach and sports scientist to understand the relative weighting of each of these factors in a particular sport and ensure that the individual athlete is optimally prepared to meet its physical and psychological requirements.

The sport physiologist is concerned with *fitness* or the means by which sports performances are energised. This involves understanding the role that various components of fitness such as cardio-respiratory endurance, muscular endurance, speed, strength, power, and flexibility play in different sports. These fitness components can be estimated by various ergometers or dynamometers that have been designed to measure the capacities of muscle groups used in various sporting movements. There are, for example, treadmills (running), rowing, canoeing and cycling ergometers, and grip, back and leg dynamometers available for the assessment of athletes. Results of tests of the capacity and power of selected muscle groups can then be used to design appropriate training programmes. The employment of this strategy should be accompanied by a good understanding of the contribution of proper nutrition and environmental factors in achieving peak performance. For example, a high carbohydrate content in the diet is essential for facilitating recovery from hard training and for enhancing performance in prolonged efforts. It is well known that endurance performance is hampered considerably by hot conditions and by high altitude but in both circumstances there is substantial improvement following short periods of acclimatisation. Modern sport places heavy demands on athletes and often produces both acute and chronic medical problems. In recent years ailments such as stress fractures, tendonitis, and anaemia have become common among hard-training athletes. The sports physiologist is required to relate closely to the medical profession in developing ways and means of preventing and treating these problems.

Skill in sport is the focus of both the biomechanist and psychologist. The science of biomechanics is used to analyse movement by using the principles of mathematics and physics to precisely describe motion and the forces that produce it. The principal tools of the biomechanist include high-speed cameras, accelerometers, and force plates. These instruments permit detection of flaws in technique and the presence of excessive forces that might produce injury. Biomechanics has been used to describe the most appropriate sequencing of body segments in closed skills such as serving in tennis and driving in golf, to monitor ground-reaction forces while sprinting, jumping, or landing, and to design racquets, bats, clubs, shoes, and surfaces that are the most effective in terms of performance and also the least injurious. The biomechanist and applied anatomist often combine their knowledge to describe the muscle groups involved in a particular movement and the forces being generated internally in tendons and bones. By correlating internal information from the muscles (electromyography) with external dynamometry and cinematography it is possible to identify movement limitations and develop injury-prevention programmes. This has been shown in preventive programmes for lower-back injuries in fast bowlers in cricket, neck injuries in rugby-players, and knee and ankle injuries in netball-players.

The science of motor behaviour has also been applied in developing and refining sports skill. This includes applying our knowledge of the central and peripheral nervous system to understand better the role of the brain and the sensory and motor nerves in learning and controlling movement. The control of movement is particularly important in target sports such as shooting, archery, and golf where stability and steadiness are vital. Knowledge of the behaviour of the individual in learning sports skills is also important. Such knowledge involves prescribing the most appropriate environment in which to learn simple and complex skills. It involves making judgements about the distribution of practice schedules and feedback of results according to the motivation, attention span, perception, and memory of the individual. This has heightened our understanding of the development of sports skills from their very rudimentary beginnings to advanced levels where they are almost automatic; attention can then be paid to the context in which they are performed in game situations. This has implications for judging the point at which advanced technical and tactical skills should be taught in particular age and ability groups.

The controlling influence in sports performance is the mind, which determines the *mental approach* to the task. The specific skills and knowledge of a psychologist are used to analyse individual athletes in terms of their motivation, arousal, anxiety, concentration, and confidence and then prescribe an appropriate mental-skill training programme. This has proved extremely beneficial for many players in sports that require precise movements in high-pressure situations. Mental rehearsal, attentional control, and relaxation techniques now form important components of mental-skill development programmes for players in individual sports such as tennis and golf. Another area of sports psychology relates to improving behaviour within a group or team and involves the development of communication and leadership skills which enhance the overall functioning of the unit.

The roots of sports science in Australia can be traced to the early work of Professor Frank Cotton of the Physiology Department at the University of Sydney. During the 1930s he developed a connection with the famous Harvard Fatigue Laboratory in Boston, USA, and on his return to Australia his work during the 1940s and 1950s attracted the interest of prominent swimming coach Forbes Carlile and, in turn, coaches and athletes in several other sports. Most of the more recent impetus for sports science, however, came from several Australian academics who gained higher degrees, mostly from the USA and Canada, during the 1960s and early 1970s and who on their return established programmes in this subject in tertiary institutions. This was supplemented by the involvement of others who were trained within Australia by academics with a specific interest in sport who were located in physiology, psychology, physics, or engineering departments of universities.

Sports science is now taught as an applied science in several tertiary institutions throughout Australia. Graduates of these courses find employment as professional coaches, directors of coaching, fitness consultants, fitness leaders, and as sports scientists at national and State institutes of sport. Sports science also comprises the core theory programme of the national coaching accreditation scheme conducted by the Australian Coaching Council. During the past twenty years it has come from being an area of some curiosity to one that is now regarded as essential for the systematic development of the modern high-performance athlete.

FSP

See COTTON, FRANK; Applied Sports Research Programme.

Springbok Tour 1971. Undoubtedly the most controversial tour to this country by an international sporting team in Australia's history was the 1971 South African rugby union tour. To date it remains the last South African rugby team to tour Australia. Protests occurred around the country in opposition to the tour and to South Africa's apartheid policies. The demonstrations that took place were as bitter and fierce as those that took place in opposition to the Vietnam War. The Federal Government of the day placed the RAAF at the Springboks' disposal. The Queensland National Party Government declared a state of emergency so that games in Queensland could go ahead. The controversy surrounding the tour, which appeared to affect the Australian team more than the Springboks, tended to overshadow the greatness of this South African team. They played thirteen matches, including three Tests, and remained undefeated. Captained by Hannes Marais, managed by Flappie Lochner, and coached by Johan Claassen, they played effective and at times attractive rugby. The fact remains that 1971 in rugby terms is remembered for events off the field rather than on.

MC

Squash Australia. Although there was no official squash association until 1934, from 1927 many of the best squash-players engaged in *ad hoc* interclub tournament series. During 1934 a group of players decided that the pressure of local administration and the need to liaise with interstate and international organisations required the establishment of an official body, so the Squash Rackets Association of Australia (SRAA) was formed, its main purpose being the running of pennant competition between squash centres, mainly five in the Melbourne area, as well as Victorian and Australian championships for men and women. By 1936 SRAA had taken on a more national role and by 1938 eighteen clubs and associations from the Melbourne, Victorian country, NSW, and SA regions had joined. In 1936 it was decided that a separate Victorian association would look after local administration and the Squash Rackets Association of Victoria was formed during the 1937–38 season. The NSW Squash Rackets Association was established in 1937 and the first pennant competition in Sydney began in July 1939. In 1981 the SRAA merged with the Australian Women's Squash Rackets Association and became the Australian Squash Rackets Association; in 1990 the business name 'Squash Australia' was adopted. Squash Australia remains the central authority in Australia in all matters connected with the organisation of the sport and acts in the interests of both players and affiliated bodies.

LO'R and IJ

See **Squash Rackets**.

Squash Rackets

Commonly known as squash, the game is usually played as a singles competition between two players using a small hollow rubber ball and lightweight rackets on an enclosed court measuring 9.5 metres long by 6.4 metres wide. The game's origins can be traced to the English game of rackets, mentioned in Joseph Strutt's *The Sports and Pastimes of the People of England*, published in 1801. The starting point of squash, however, is acknowledged to be during the middle of the nineteenth century at Harrow school, where students waiting for their turn on the rackets court practised against the school walls. In order to preserve the school's windows from the leather rackets ball it was suggested that a squashier ball be used, hence the name 'squash'. The new ball was made from indiarubber and the rackets altered to such an extent that by 1886 squash was regarded as a game in its own right. Because of its origins and expensive facilities, the English game was mainly limited to the upper classes; in the late 1800s it spread throughout the Empire, where it remained the prerogative of the establishment. Diplomats and the military took squash to the Middle East, Asia, and the North West Frontier where members of the native populations were employed as ball boys, court attendants, and practice partners. The British dominated the game for the first seventy-five years of its existence and it has only been in the second half of the twentieth century that citizens throughout the Commonwealth have achieved similar success.

There is some argument about the origin of squash in Australia. Various authors have suggested that the earliest courts in the country were built in Melbourne, Sydney, and Brisbane; but the Melbourne Club in Collins Street is generally credited as being the first. It had two courts by 1913, when rackets courts were converted for squash. In Sydney the first courts were built about 1920 by Lt Col. Hans Bjelke-Petersen at the Bjelke-Petersen School of Physical Culture. Other courts were constructed later in the 1920s at Langridges's Gymnasium, Giles Sea Baths (Coogee), Wally Curslop's (Kogarah), and by noted sports enthusiast Dame Eadith Walker (Concord). The Prince of Wales (later the Duke of Windsor) was the first celebrity to play squash in the country. He was visiting Sydney shortly after the Bjelke-Petersen courts were opened and played on them almost daily.

Although more courts began to spring up during the 1920s and 1930s they were usually associated with private clubs or tennis clubs. By the 1930s these clubs often employed a professional. Nevertheless squash was often used as a means of attaining fitness for other sports, rather than as a game of value in itself. Thus, some early champions, for example Harry Hopman (Australian champion in 1933, 1934, and 1936) and Sir Donald Bradman (the 1939 SA champion), achieved their greatest successes and fame in other sports. The world's greatest female player, Heather McKay (née Blundell), was later to take up the game to keep fit for hockey. The national governing body of the game, the Squash Rackets Association of Australia, was formed in 1934. Although records list Australian champions for the years 1931–34, in reality these were for the Victorian championship. In 1931 the first male winner listed was F. R. Strickland, and in 1932 the first female winner was Mrs Ross Grey Smith. The first interstate match was an impromptu game held at the Royal Sydney Golf Club between Victoria and NSW in 1938. The association's headquarters were established in Melbourne, later moving to Sydney, and at present are located in Brisbane.

Although Australia's players remained isolated from international competition before the Second World War, this situation began to change after the war. Percy Pearce, perhaps one of the greatest influences on pre-war squash, coached Gordon Watson to the position of the world's third ranked professional in 1950. During the 1950s further international experience was provided by professionals from India, Pakistan and Egypt who toured the country. Such visits helped increase interest in squash. Nonetheless, élite competitive squash remained an amateur game. The number of courts in Sydney alone during the 1950s grew from twelve to three hundred and seventy. Yet English, and increasingly Pakistani, players were regarded as the world's best. When the association sent an English team to tour Australia in 1960 they remained unbeaten. The nature of the game in Australia, however, was changing. Instead of being a game restricted to the élite, the proliferation of courts was both a result and cause of the game's popularity at all community levels. This increasing pool of talent led to Australia turning the tables on their British counterparts during their 1962–63 tour of Great Britain. The team, consisting of Ken Hiscoe, Owen Parmenter, Dick Carter, Kenny Binns, Doug Stephensen, and John Cheadle, defeated Wales, England, Britain, South Africa, and Scotland. During this tour Australian squash came of age when Ken Hiscoe became the first Australian to win the British Amateur Championship, regarded as the unofficial world championship until 1967 when the first internationally recognised professional competitions were held. A similar tour to Great Britain during 1963 proved that these results were not unwarranted when Hiscoe, Carter, and Parmenter, during a period of eight days, recorded clean-sweep victories over Pakistan, England, and Britain. This began a period of more than a decade of Australian domination of international competition. Brian Boys, Cam Nancarrow, Kevin Shawcross, and two of the greatest players of all time, Geoff Hunt and Heather McKay, supplemented the successes of the first international squad. Hunt's record tally of nine British titles was broken only in 1990 by Jahangir Khan of Pakistan. McKay's undefeated record of eighteen years stands as one of the most remarkable feats in any sport. During this period she won the British Open sixteen times.

At the same time the administration of the game itself was undergoing radical developments. In 1967 the International Squash Rackets Federation (ISRF) was formed, partly because of the efforts of the Australian Vin Napier. As a result of this new organisation, official world amateur championships for both individuals and teams were instigated. Hunt won the inaugural individual title and Australia the team event. In 1973 the International Squash Players' Association was formed; its first president was Ken Hiscoe. As in tennis, the call to professionalism was becoming strong at this time, and although the ISRF held out against the tide, it was obvious that the world's best were leaving the amateur ranks. By 1976 the ISRF capitulated and the world's first open championship was held; McKay won the women's title and Hunt the men's. Since 1980 all squash competitions have been open to both amateurs and professionals.

The 1980s saw Australia slip from its position as the world's leading squash country, although it has remained a dominant force. In 1989 it won the world team championship 3–0 over Pakistan. Rodney Martin, Chris Dittmar, Chris Robertson, Rhonda Thorne, and Vicki Cardwell have achieved international success. In 1985 the establishment of the AIS in Brisbane with Geoff Hunt as head coach and later Heather McKay as second coach was a significant move to develop the talents of prospective champions. On a less competitive level there are at present 650 000 regular players in Australia. Although an estimated 50 per cent of these are professional or skilled workers, the game remains available to the average Australian.

KT

See **BELSHAM, VICTOR; CARDWELL, VICKI; CARTER, DICK; DITTMAR, CHRIS; HISCOE, KEN; HUNT, GEOFF; MARTIN, RODNEY; McKAY, HEATHER; NANCARROW, CAMERON; Squash Australia; THORNE, RHONDA; WALKER, PATRICIA**.

Stadiums Limited was formed in 1913 by sportsman Reginald 'Snowy' Baker and a few businessmen to promote boxing at the Rushcutters Bay Sydney Stadium. John Wren purchased most of Baker's shares in 1915 and his family still dominated the company in the 1970s. Stadiums Limited monopolised boxing promotion in the east-coast capitals for fifty years. With Richard Lean as general manager, the company earned a tough reputation. It acted as match-maker and promoter, controlling the destiny of boxers and managers alike. Only one boxer, Jimmy Carruthers, ever extracted more than 25 per cent of the take. The careers languished of those who fell foul of Lean. Boxing unions and controlling bodies were anathema to Stadiums Limited, which successfully quashed all attempts to establish them. Boxing was less innovative, less regional, and more dangerous under Stadium's monopoly, but the company paternally looked after its own. Amidst a decline in boxing, it promoted its last fight in 1975 and now leases out Festival Hall in Melbourne and Brisbane for various entertainments, including boxing.

RB

See **BAKER, REGINALD; McINTOSH, HUGH**.

STAMPFL, FRANZ (1918–), Viennese-born athletics coach, pioneered and popularised interval training which involved repetition running interspersed with timed, active recovery periods. Stampfl gained an international reputation through his association with British runners Roger Bannister, Chris Chataway, and Chris

Brasher during the early 1950s. A suave and intelligent man, he was invited to Melbourne in 1955 to coach at the University of Melbourne and to assist the Victorian track and field team. He quickly made his mark by coaching Merv Lincoln and 1968 Olympic gold-medallist Ralph Doubell. Stampfl's training methods, although very successful, were often criticised, particularly by rival coach Percy Cerutty, for being too mechanistic and regimented. In 1985 Stampfl became a quadriplegic when his car was hit from behind when stopped at a red light, but he continued coaching from a wheelchair.

RKS

See **CERUTTY, PERCY**.

State of Origin (Rugby League). The concept of State of Origin matches was developed in 1980 in response to a series of lopsided interstate contests where players were chosen to represent the State in which they were playing. The wealthy Sydney-based clubs had enticed many Queenslanders south, effectively weakening the northern State. The first match at Lang Park, Brisbane, attracted a capacity crowd and success of the concept was ensured by two factors: Queensland's emphatic 20–10 win and the fact that Parramatta team-mates, but opponents that evening, Arthur Beetson and Michael Cronin, were involved in a fight. As interest in the series grew so too did the fanaticism of the players and the crowds. Fighting on and off the field became common. Insults were traded: NSW were labelled 'cockroaches' and Queensland 'canetoads'. NSW did not record its first series win until 1985 and by then rivalry was so intense that it affected the Australian team's NZ tour later that year. In 1986 the Australian Rugby League took over the promotion, insisting on a code of player behaviour. So far the series has been dominated by Queensland. It has produced a controversial figure in referee Barry 'the Grasshopper' Gommersall and it has been graced by the talents of Wally Lewis who played throughout the decade.

RA

STAUNTON, ROBERT ERIC, OAM (1936–90), born Sydney, was a basketball administrator. He played, coached, and refereed to State level, but his main contribution to basketball came in his commitment to junior development and tireless administrative work, both in Australia and internationally, in which he held an extraordinary number of positions. In 1978 Staunton became first executive director of the Australian Basketball Federation, and in 1987 received the OAM for services to basketball. He also managed the Australian Olympic team in 1976 and 1980. Bob Staunton was a model administrator and earned much respect for his enormous capacity for work, his meticulous eye for detail, and his loyalty. There is wide agreement that Staunton's work helped immeasurably in pushing basketball to the forefront of Australian sport in the 1980s.

SB

Stawell Gift. The premier event of the Stawell Athletic Club is the world's oldest and Australia's most famous professional foot-race. First run in 1878, in front of 2000 spectators, the £24 first prize was collected by 24-year-old farmer W. O. Millard. He had started from a handicap of 8 yards and won in a time of 12.75 seconds. Since 1878 the Stawell Gift meeting has been held annually over the Easter weekend, except for the war years 1942–45. The race was run over 130 yards until 1973, when the distance was changed to 120 metres. The Stawell Gift has always been held at precisely 3.15 p.m. and it has never been postponed because of inclement weather.

GC*

St Bernard's Disqualification. In 1988 the Victorian Amateur Football Association (VAFA) faced an interim injunction obtained in the Victorian Supreme Court by a member club, St Bernard's Collegians. This action effectively challenged the self-disciplinary authority of the VAFA and sporting organisations in general. St Bernard's instituted proceedings after the VAFA fined, suspended, and relegated the club for offering payments to a prospective recruit, Terry Young, who was then playing for the Fawkner club. Although St Bernard's claimed that Young had not been approached by a club official but by a private individual, their application was eventually unsuccessful.

DS

STEHR, RAY (1913–83), born Sydney, established a reputation as one of the toughest front-row rugby league forwards of his era. After making his first-grade debut for Eastern Suburbs in 1929 when only 16, he did not retire until 1946. Stehr played eleven Tests for Australia and made two Kangaroo tours, in 1933–34 and 1937–38. His clashes with the English forwards in the 1936 home series were legendary. He was sent off in both the second and third Tests against Great Britain—the only Australian player ever sent off in two Tests in a single series against Great Britain. After retirement he was president of Eastern Suburbs and acted as an agent for English clubs interested in obtaining Australian players. He was elected to the NSW Hall of Champions in 1983.

MC

STEINOHRT, HERB (1899–1985), born Pittsworth, Queensland, lived his adult life at Toowoomba. Tall, rangy, a rugby league second-row and prop-forward of great strength and resilience, he played over a hundred games for Toowoomba. Steinohrt is one of Queensland's most capped players, representing that State from 1925 to 1933; he also played for Australia in nine Tests between 1928 and 1932. His captaincy in 1932 included a win in the 'Battle of Brisbane' Test. His coaching ranged from decades of work with schoolboy teams through to Queensland coach and Australian selector. Despite his ruggedness, he was never sent off the field. His biography by Jim Sweeney was called *The Gentle Clydesdale* (1975).

SJR

See **Battle of Brisbane**.

STELLIOS, BASILIOS ('Bill') (1959–   ), born Sydney, was a notable weightlifter who took up the sport when he was 12, setting records in age-group competitions from 14 years onwards. In his first major Australian representation at the 1978 Commonwealth Games, Bill Stellios won a gold medal in the 67.5 kilogram class. Following an eleventh place at the 1980 Olympics he defended his Commonwealth Games title at Brisbane in 1982. This time though he had to be content with a silver medal, being narrowly defeated by David Morgan of Wales. Placed seventh in the 75 kilogram class at the 1984 Olympics, he ended his international career with yet another gold medal at the 1986 Commonwealth Games.

MN

Stephen Award. Ken Stephen was a former South Sydney and Balmain rugby league five-eighth and long-time NSW Rugby League secretary and administration manager who died in July 1988. The Ken Stephen Citizenship Award was introduced after his death to commemorate his contribution to rugby league, and is awarded annually to a Sydney premiership player in recognition of that player's service to the game and the community. The medal was first won by the then NSW and Balmain captain Wayne Pearce. Subsequent winners have been St George's Aboriginal winger Ricky Walford in 1989 and Illawarra's Michael Bolt in 1990.

PC

STEPHENSON, JAN (1951–   ), born Balmain, Sydney, was the first Australian female golfer to win more than $1 million in prize-money. As a teenager she was helped by Norman von Nida. At 18 she appeared in Australia's Tasman Cup team. When she missed selection in the Espirito Santo World Amateur Teams Golf Championship, she criticised the selectors. After turning professional in 1972 she earned more than $20 000 in her first season and decided to base herself in America. She won the Sara Coventry Naples Classic and the Birmingham Classic in 1976 and the Australian Women's Open in 1977. In 1981 she set a record for the US circuit when she returned a score of 198—18 under par—for the 54-hole Mary Kay Classic.

She reached her peak in the next few years when she won prestigious US tournaments: the 1982 PGA Ladies' Championship and the 1983 Ladies' Open Championship. In recent years Stephenson has augmented her income by designing golf courses in America and Japan.

GC*

See **Golf**.

STERLING, PETER ('Sterlo') (1960–), born Queensland, was Australia's top rugby league half-back during the 1980s. After playing his early football in Wagga, he was spotted by Parramatta as a schoolboy and was a pivotal member of that club's Sydney first-grade premiership-winning teams of 1981, 1982, 1983, and 1986. He toured with the unbeaten Kangaroo teams of 1982 and 1986, and played several seasons with Hull in England. A dual winner of the Rothman's Medal for best and fairest footballer (in 1987 and 1990), 'Sterlo' was a short but tough half-back, adept at kicking and passing, with instinctive ability to 'read' the play. His brilliant skills, likeable personality and long fair hair made him one of the code's most popular players.

CC

STEWART, IAN HARLOW (1943–), born Queenstown, Tasmania, is one of the all-time great players of Australian football. Between 1963 and 1975 he played 205 VFL games with St Kilda (128 games) and Richmond (77 games). He is one of a small group of élite players who has won the Brownlow Medal on three occasions; in 1965, 1966 (both with St Kilda), and in 1971 (with Richmond). Playing in the centre, Stewart, who was 179 centimetres tall and weighed 79 kilograms, was a brilliant reader of play who gathered many possessions and was an excellent disposer of the ball, setting up opportunities for team-mates downfield. He coached South Melbourne from 1976 to 1977 and from 1979 to 1981, and Carlton briefly in 1978 for a total of 117 games, recording fifty-one wins, sixty-five losses, and one draw.

BD

St Kilda's Premiership (1966). It was two and a half minutes into time-on in the last quarter, with the scores tied. Seventeen-year-old Barry Breen grabbed the ball from a ball-up on the St Kilda half-forward line and miskicked the ball towards goal. It bounced through for a point. St Kilda managed to hold on, with Bob Murray marking strongly across the half-back line in the last seconds of the game. St Kilda had won its first premiership after sixty-nine years in the VFL. Supporters alternated between cheering and crying tears of joy. The Saints had traditionally been the joke of the VFL, 'winning' eighteen wooden spoons by 1955, and having played in the finals only five times by 1960. During the 1960s St Kilda assembled a team of talented and dedicated players. In 1961 and 1963 they were defeated in the first semifinal, and lost the 1965 Grand Final. In 1966 they provided supporters with their most memorable moment with a hard-fought, one-point win over Collingwood.

BD

STRICKLAND, SHIRLEY (later de la HUNTY), MBE (1925–), born Guildford, WA, developed an interest in a 'new-fangled' race, hurdling, while attending Northam High School. While studying at the University of WA she won the State and Australian sprint and hurdles titles. Further coaching from Betty Beagley, Frank Preston, and Austin Robertson, combined with Strickland's natural ability, mastery of techniques, and dedication, saw her become the first Australian woman to win track and field medals at the Olympics. She came third in the 80 metres hurdles and the 100 metres sprint and collected a silver medal in the 4 × 100 metres relay team at London in 1948. She next won the hurdles and came second to Marjorie Jackson in both sprints at the 1950 Auckland British Empire Games. In 1952, as Shirley de la Hunty, she took out a bronze medal in the 100 metres but won her main event, the 80 metres hurdles, at the Helsinki Olympics. She set world-record times—11 seconds and 10.9 seconds—on successive days. During a tour of Europe in 1955 de la Hunty established a world record for the 100 metres (11.3 seconds) and was a member of an Australian relay team that set six world records. She received the Helms Award in 1956. Retaining her hurdles title in 1956, she became the first woman athlete to successfully defend an Olympic title. She won a second gold medal as a member of the sprint relay team. Awarded the MBE in 1951, de la Hunty has championed junior competition since retirement.

JAD

Strikes and Industrial Disputes
The organisation and presentation of sporting competitions necessarily involves the interaction of players and administrators. While they may have common interests and objectives, such as sharing 'a love of the game', they are nonetheless involved in an authority relationship concerning decisions made in their sport. Players and administrators often have different goals and objectives, and differ over methods of conducting and playing a sport. In most cases differences are quickly and easily resolved through discussion and compromise; occasionally they prove more intractable, and there may be threats to use, or actual use of, strikes and industrial conflict. So far, however, Australian team sports have had little experience of this kind.

Conflict is likely to arise in three areas:

117 Technological advances have improved the efficiency of preparing facilities and venues. The MCG staff utilised 'Dolly' in preparing pitches in 1920.

118 The southern end of the Hill at the Sydney Cricket Ground during the First Test of 1903.

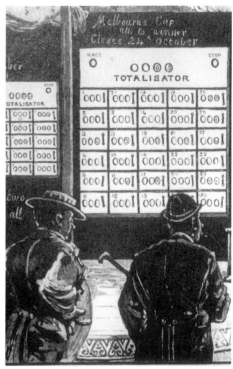

119 A technological development in the racing industry was the 'totalisator'.

120 Technology in lighting allowed a night football match to be played on the MCG in 1879.

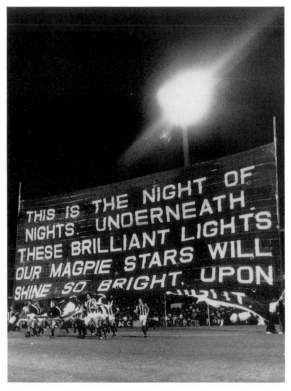

121 The first night football match at the MCG this century was played on 29 March 1985 between Collingwood and North Melbourne.

the formation of rival or breakaway competitions, team–administrator disputes, and player association–league disputes. There have been three examples of breakaway or rival competitions being formed after disputes between players and administrators. The first occurred when players deserted the (amateur) rugby union code to form the (professional) NSW Rugby League in 1908 after disputes over payments for lost time from work, expenses, and injuries. The other two examples occurred in cricket. Following a period of tension between players and the Australian Cricket Board (ACB) in the 1970s, Australia's leading players signed lucrative contracts with media magnate Kerry Packer to play for World Series Cricket in 1977. Peace was restored when the ACB granted Packer exclusive rights to televise Test and other international games. Eight years later many of Australia's prominent cricketers contracted to play two series in South Africa in 1985–86 and 1986–87 in defiance of a ban imposed by the ACB and the International Cricket Conference.

Cricket is also prominent in many of the clashes which have occurred between teams and administrators. In 1884–85 many of Australia's most accomplished cricketers refused to play Test matches against a touring English team because of differences over match payments. In 1912 six players refused to tour England because they disagreed with the choice of the manager by the ACB. This was the tip of the iceberg of a wider struggle between players and administrators, with added fissures engendered by interstate rivalry, concerning the issue of power and control within Australian cricket at the beginning of the twentieth century. During the 1936–37 series against England, players Bill O'Reilly, Stan McCabe, Chuck Fleetwood Smith, and Leo O'Brien were called before the ACB to discuss issues pertaining to their attitude to the game. Nothing actually ensued from these discussions. The episode, however, seems to have been symptomatic of sectarian tensions between Masons and Catholics which were a feature of Australian cricket for a time. On the 1969–70 double tour to India and South Africa players refused to agree to an extra fifth Test on the South African leg when their request for an additional payment of $500 was turned down by the ACB. In his capacity as Australian captain, Ian Chappell made unsuccessful representations to the ACB to increase payments to players. During the 1974–75 series against England there were suggestions that strike action was in the air unless player payments were increased. In 1976 the SA Sheffield Shield side decided to hold a strike—albeit a short-lived one—over the selection of a team to tour the eastern States. Players and the ACB also had problems over contracts before a tour to the West Indies in 1984.

Other examples of team–administrator disputes can be found in soccer and the VFL. In 1974 the Socceroos threatened strike action over inadequate pay for a warm-up match against an overseas side during their preparations for the World Cup. Hawthorn's VFL players threatened to strike in 1980 over payments to non-contract players. In the following year South Melbourne players threatened strike action in an effort to pressure their club to relocate to Sydney. They believed that such a move would help to ensure that they received match payments owed to them by South Melbourne. Several player associations have found it difficult to gain recognition and develop a bargaining relationship with the controlling bodies of their respective sports: the Australian Football Players' Union formed by VFL and VFA players in 1955; an abortive players' association formed in the SA National Football League in 1974; the Professional Cricketers Association between 1979 and 1982; and the WA Football League Players' Association between 1979 and 1986. In 1974 the VFL Players' Association threatened strike action when the VFL rescinded the ten-year rule which enabled players with ten years of service with a club to seek employment with other clubs, free of the encumbrance of the transfer system. The VFL did not back down and duly rescinded the rule; the players' association did not act on the threat. In late 1980 and early 1981 the VFL withdrew its recognition of the players' association, but a threat by Essendon and Fitzroy players not to play in the opening round of the night competition resulted in the VFL backing down and agreeing to recognise the organisation again. In 1990 the (then) AFL Players' Association again challenged the AFL's authority, this time as a result of problems in negotiating changes to the standard player contract. At the end of 1989, and into 1990, the relationship between the Association of Rugby League Professionals and the NSW Rugby League deteriorated over the latter's decision to introduce a draft to allocate players between clubs. The players' association, in 1990, mounted a challenge before the Federal Court of Australia to test the legality of that draft.

BD

See **Restraint of Trade**; **Unionism**.

STURROCK, ALEXANDER ('Jock'), MBE (1915–), was the first yachtsman to represent Australia at the Olympics when he and Len Felton finished seventh in the Star class in the 1948 Games. He took part in the next three Olympics, achieving third in the 5.5 metre class in 1956, and carried the Australian flag at the 1960 Olympics. Sturrock, who won his first yachting championship at the age of 12, achieved fame when he skippered *Gretel* in the 1962 *America*'s Cup. Although defeated four to one by *Weatherly, Gretel*'s victory in the second race was the first by a challenger since 1934. He also skippered the next America's Cup Challenge, *Dame Pattie*, in 1967. Sturrock was a very versatile yachtsman who won well over four hundred championship races. He won his first Australian championship in 1932 in the 12-foot Cadet dinghy *Monsoon*. At 18 he helped start the International Star Class in Australia. The first three Star-class yachts were built in the Sturrock family timberyard in Melbourne and Sturrock won the first eight national championships (1935–47). He was Australian Dragon-class champion in 1953–54, 1954–55, and 1955–56; Australian 5.5 metre champion in 1956 and 1959, and 6 metre champion in 1946, 1947, and 1949. He also won the Melbourne to Sydney 600-mile handicap in 1962. Sturrock was named Australian of the Year and Australian Yachtsman of the Year in 1962. He was awarded the MBE in 1975 and inducted into the Sport Australia Hall of Fame in 1985.

RC

SUNDERLAND, HARRY (1889–1964), was secretary of the Queensland Rugby League from 1913 to 1922 and from 1925 to 1938, when he became manager of the Wigan club, as well as becoming a journalist and broadcaster. He was co-manager of three Australian teams to tour England, and a member of the Australian Rugby League Board of Control from 1925 to 1939. His initiatives were mainly responsible for establishing the code in France. Sunderland's self-assured, energetic, and sometimes abrasive pursuit of his expansionist goals earned him the sobriquet of 'the Little Dictator'. His activities, in which his own journalistic and commercial interests were mixed with his administration, provoked much controversy in Queensland, but established rugby league as the State's premier winter sport. He lived in England from 1938 until his death in Manchester on 15 January 1964.

SJR

See **Rugby League**; **Sunderland Medal**.

Sunderland Medal. The Sunderland Memorial Medal awarded to the best Australian player in each home Test rugby league series was won first by Johnny Raper against France in 1964. Billy Smith received the next two medals against Britain in 1966, and NZ in 1967, after which it was decided to restrict the award to England–Australia clashes in Australia. Subsequent winners have been Ron Coote 1970, 1974, Ray Price 1979, Wayne Pearce 1984, and Wally Lewis 1988. The medal honours Harry Sunderland, a major figure in rugby league development. England also commemorated his contribution to rugby league in 1965 by insti-

tuting the Sunderland Trophy for the Man of the Match in each year's premiership final.

TB

See **SUNDERLAND, HARRY**.

Surf Life Saving Association of Australia. Around the turn of the century surf bathing began to grow in popularity in Australia and with this came the increased risk of drowning. Groups of bathers began to form clubs such as the Bronte Life Saving Brigade (1903) and the Bondi Surf Lifesaving Club (1906) to help protect and rescue weaker swimmers. In October 1907 the surf-bathing clubs formed an umbrella organisation under the name of the Surf Bathing Association of NSW (SBANSW) to achieve central control over the clubs, formulate and develop rescue methods, and lobby the government for official recognition of the sport. In 1911 the NSW Government appointed a Surf Bathing Committee to examine the sport. In 1920 the SBANSW changed its name to the Surf Life Saving Association of NSW and in 1923 this association became a national body, the Surf Life Saving Association of Australia (SLSAA), adopting as its motto in 1932 'vigilance and service'. The basic proficiency standard in lifesaving techniques for club members, the Bronze Medallion, was introduced in 1910 and is still the basic qualification required to perform rescues. Although the humanitarian aspects of lifesaving are important to the association, a major attraction for its membership are the sporting events and carnivals which culminate in the annual SLSAA championships.

GS and IJ

See **Surf Livesaving**.

Surf Lifesaving

During the eighteenth century the English aristocracy was alerted by medical practitioners to the health-giving and therapeutic properties of cold-water bathing. Under aristocratic patronage the middle classes adopted bathing as a healthy pastime and developed it as a sport (i.e. swimming). During the nineteenth century evangelically inspired factions, following the puritans, campaigned against what they deemed morally offensive and socially subversive behaviour, including bathing in public view. Thus bathing's social acceptance was confined to enclosed baths (both sea and fresh water), or from horse-drawn bathing machines (sea water), where public display could be monitored and controlled.

In Australia, official ordinances regulated public behaviour. In 1838 for example, the NSW Government passed legislation prohibiting bathing in waters exposed to public view between 6 a.m. and 8 p.m. These restrictions brought moralists into conflict with those for whom promenading and open bathing were natural pleasures and with other middle-class factions who sought control of public places, such as beaches, for their own social and financial interests. At the turn of the century many viewed surf bathing against a background of urban squalor and bubonic plague and the inevitability of war: 'The stinging spray of the surf' and 'the glowing sun' were 'supreme builders of health and bodily pride', 'helping to build up a race of fine young hard Australians'. Property-owners, land speculators, and a myriad of small businessmen such as food, transport, souvenir and entertainment vendors, welcomed surf bathing as 'a commercial Godsend'. 'But for prudishness and false modesty,' wrote one observer, 'the waves breaking on the sands might have been rolling sovereigns into the pockets.' They saw surf bathing as simply another aspect of development and progress conducive to swelling the populations in seaside suburbs and towns.

These factions challenged repressive beach-bathing laws. In October 1902 William Gocher, proprietor and editor of the *Manly and North Sydney News*, publicly defied the law and bathed during daylight hours at Manly. Police Inspector-General Fosbery refused to prosecute Gocher and the law became obsolete. The right to bathe in public view was won but the struggle for control of the beach was not over. First, moralists resolved to protect 'the common standards of propriety that prevail among civilized nations'. They directed attention to bathers' costumes, 'loitering' on the beach after bathing, the 'sun bath' (a practice described as reducing humans to 'the same level as dogs'), and mixed bathing. Second, governments and municipal councils were ambivalent towards surf bathing, in some cases dismissing it as a fad, and were unwilling to finance public dressing sheds, safety equipment, and lifeguards. Surf bathers formed informal 'dressing shed syndicates' and life-saving patrols and in October 1907, in response to the NSW Government's proposed new costume restrictions, about a dozen clubs formed the umbrella Surf Bathing Association of NSW (SBANSW). Its objects were to provide better facilities for surf bathers, institute improved lifesaving methods and aids, and provide rules for the proper conduct of surf bathers.

If surf bathing was founded on social resistance to repressive forms of control, the class structure and aims of the SBANSW quickly ensured the sport's official sanction under its auspices. John Lord, the association's president, was appointed chairman of the government's Surf Bathing Committee directed to inquire into the sport in 1911. Lord's successor, Charles Paterson, was also a member of the four-man committee. The government adopted virtually all the committee's recommendations. The SBANSW opposed free dressing areas for surf bathers who, it said, should pay for all facilities including equipment and beach accommodation used by volunteer lifeguards. It endorsed neck-to-knee bathing costumes and described the sun bath as 'objectionable' and said it should be restricted to special enclosures. Affiliated clubs were structured around rational forms of masculinity and ruggedness based on military organisation, discipline, precision, and drills.

The survival of the SBANSW was due to its assumption of 'duty of care' for surf bathers. The association defined itself not as a sporting organisation but as a humanitarian and volunteer safety service and, consistent with this image, changed its name in 1920 to the Surf Life Saving Association (SLSA). The SLSA reinforced its self-imposed responsibility by highlighting rescues performed by lifesavers (as of October 1990 members had undertaken 344 678 rescues) and by the adoption of the motto 'Vigilance and Service' and the maxim 'No lives lost while patrols on duty'. If assumption of 'duty of care' increased the SLSA's status and financial assistance from governments well aware that voluntary organisations frequently provide the most cost-effective services, it also exposed the association to the risks and expense of public liability.

The SLSA has been unable to reconcile the fundamental contradiction of the lifesaver as a sportsperson. It has provided over a hundred athletes to Australian Olympic teams and its annual Australian Championships surpass the Commonwealth Games in terms of number of competitors. The sporting image of the lifesaver is deliberately fostered by the SLSA and used to raise public monies and entice commercial sponsorship. Officially competition provides members with the means to practise and develop lifesaving skills, but many members and clubs regard lifesaving sport as the end rather than the means.

The development of the Ironman Grand Prix circuit during the 1980s exacerbated the lifesaver/athlete contradiction. Large corporate sponsorships and massive media attention given to the Ironman do not rest easily with the SLSA's carefully nurtured image of a voluntary humanitarian organisation dependent upon government assistance (the Federal grant for 1988/89 was over $1 million). The SLSA's ruling body, the National Council, proposes to divide lifesaving into distinct sporting and rescue divisions, but it is doubtful whether this will resolve the problem at club level.

The SLSA has provided a positive contribution to making Australian beaches safer. Its future, however, is by no means assured. As a safety service it faces challenges from many sources, while the formation of the rival Ironman circuit is evidence of the tensions between the members and the National Council.

DB

See **Black Sunday**; **Ironman**; KENNY, GRANT; LEECH, GUY; MORRISON, DONALD; NEWBIGGIN, BOB; **Surf Race Champions**.

Surf Race Champions. The senior surf race is the lifesaving movement's most prestigious event and one of the oldest. It was won first by J. G. Brown in 1915. The race's status derives from its long tradition and its association with many of Australia's best swimmers. Lifesavers who have won the senior surf race and represented Australia in the Olympic Games include Ernest Henry, Noel Ryan, Jon Donohoe, Graham White, Max Metzker, Graeme Brewer, Ron McKeon, and Paul Moorfoot. White and Bob Newbiggen both won the event four times. The race starts on the beach about 5 metres from the water's edge. The competitors sprint into the surf and swim about 200 metres to a line of seven buoys anchored parallel to the beach and spread over approximately 35 metres. They swim behind the buoys and then back to the shore, always on the lookout for the wave that will deliver them to the shallows. The finish line is on the sand about 15 metres from the water's edge. The conditions of the race, including position at the start, the location of channels and rips, and the form and duration of waves, introduce a significant luck factor in separating winners from losers.

DB

See NEWBIGGIN, BOB.

Surfboard Riding World Championship 1964. The first officially recognised World Surfboard Championship was held at Manly on 16 and 17 May 1964. More than two hundred competitors, including some from the UK, US, South Africa, France, and NZ saw Australian surfers awarded both world titles. A crowd of 60 000 spectators witnessed the 19-year-old Bernard 'Midget' Farrelly win the men's world title as well as the Australian senior men's title, while Phyllis O'Donnell won the women's world and Australian titles. A third title contested at the championship was the Australian junior men's event, won by Robert Connolly of South Bondi.

GC*

See **Surfing**.

Surfing

Australian surfboard riding developed after South Sea Islander Tommy Tanna introduced body surfing at the turn of the century. Alick Wickham fashioned a board from a length of driftwood, while in 1912 C. D. Paterson brought a genuine redwood 'alaia' surfboard from Hawaii, but no one could ride it. Duke Kahanamoku, the famous Olympian, visited Australia in 1915 and made a board from sugar pine which he rode at Freshwater. Isabel Letham, still a Freshwater club member in 1991, was the first Australian female surfer as she rode tandem with him that day. He gave his board to Claude West, a 15-year-old who was Australia's first surfboard champion (1915–24). West also used his board, as still happens today, to make rescues. The first highly successful hollow board was built in the 1920s by American Tom Blake who won the 1930 Hawaiian championship with it. The hollow board was popular lifesaving equipment in the USA. In Australia, the early emphasis was on designing for speed rather than manoeuvrability. In America, board design also took paddling and better wave-riding into account. Frank Adler of Maroubra introduced the hollow board to Australian surf club competition in 1934. The surf ski was invented by the Australian G. A. Crackenthorp at this time and by 1937 was adopted as standard lifesaving equipment by the SLSA (Surf Life Saving Association, established 1907). In the 1930s surfboard competitions in Australia were either a race or a display, depending on conditions on the day. Generally, the surfboard was frowned on by officials of the surf lifesaving movement because they believed it was undermining the established reel-and-belt method of rescue.

The Second World War broke the communication barrier that had seen Australian surfing develop largely independently of American influence. The early 1950s saw the arrival, with surfing actor Peter Lawford, of the lightweight balsawood Malibu board pioneered by Bob Simmons in the USA. Such boards, also called 'zip boards', meant increased manoeuvrability and also meant that surfers no longer needed to store heavy boards at beach clubhouses. Eventually Simmons worked with polyfoam and fibreglass, but the name Malibu (after a beach where it was tested) remained attached to the lightweight board. The adoption of these boards by Australian surfers was accelerated after 1956 when a team of American lifeguards invited to Australia during the Olympic Games by the SLSA gave an exhibition of Malibu-riding at local beaches. Within weeks hollow plywood copies were being made in Australia. By 1959 1 500 Malibus a year were produced in Australia and by 1962 this had grown five times over. Also in 1956, Hobie Alter and Dave Sweet, two Californians, produced the first boards made from polyurethane—light enough for both men and women to carry them.

Though the first International Surfing Championships were held at Makaha in Hawaii in 1954, Australians did not compete until 1961. Throughout the late 1950s and early 1960s in both Australia and the USA board-riders were considered 'low-class' and mildly subversive. In Australia technological advances, improved transport, and greater consumerism were influential in the spread of surfing. For a short time in the early 1960s two youthful factions developed: the 'Rockers' from the suburbs despising the 'Surfies' from the beaches. Larrikinism and the Surfie v. Rocker clashes saw many theatres close their doors to surfing movies in the early 1960s.

By 1967 Australian surfboard design and riding techniques had moved ahead of the Americans. The 'inside the curl' style was to take Australia to the front in world surfing. From the static stand-up style, surfing developed through turning and classic (functional) styles to nose riding and the modern Australian 'power' method, and then emphasis on tube riding.

Before 1964 the Hawaiian Makaha contest was considered the unofficial world championship. It was won in December 1963 by Australian Bernard 'Midget' Farrelly. In 1964 Farrelly won the inaugural World Amateur Men's Surfing Championships organised by Bob Evans at Manly, while another Australian, Phyllis O'Donnell, won the women's event. The World Amateur Championships were not held in the years 1973–77, and from 1970 to 1975 the Smirnoff contest in Hawaii was considered the unofficial world professional surfing championship. In those years Robert 'Nat' Young (1970), Paul Neilsen (1971), Ian Cairns (1973), and Mark Richards (1975) won the event. In 1976 Peter Townend from Australia won the first IPS (International Professional Surfers) Men's Professional World Championship, and Mark Warren won the Smirnoff contest.

In both amateur and professional contests, Australia's record is outstanding. Since the Makaha event in December 1962, Australian achievements include the 1966 Amateur World Champion, Nat Young, and Men's Professional Championship winners Wayne Bartholomew (1978), Mark Richards (1979–82), Tom Carroll (1983–84), Damien Hardman (1987), and Barton Lynch (1988). Jenny Gill (1982), Connie Nixon (1986), Pauline Menczer (1988), and Kathy Newman (1990) have been Women's World Amateur Champions. Mark Scott (1980) and Mark Sainsbury (1986) were winners of the Men's Amateur Championship, and Damien Hardman was Junior World Champion in 1984. In the women's professional ranks Pam Burridge became Australia's second world champion at the Billabong contest at Hawaii's Sunset Beach in December 1990. The previous year Wendy Botha (originally from South Africa, now a naturalised Australian) had won. Both Burridge and Jodie Cooper have been consistently placed in World Championship events. Gail Couper was five times Australian champion in the 1960s and 1970s.

The IPS, which was set up in 1976, was disbanded in 1982 and replaced by the Association of Surfing Professionals (APS) led by Ian Cairns. A world tour operates today. Contests are rated according to how much money they carry. The ASP rule book states: 'The surfer who executes the most radical functional manoeuvres in the most critical part of the biggest or best waves over the longest distance shall be deemed the winner.' Since 1982 style has diminished in importance. The single most controversial criterion is the length of the wave.

Australia has a well-developed contest system. The man-on-man system was devised by Peter Drouyn and was introduced in 1977 to international competition. A major coaching programme is being developed and Australia has been at the forefront of design in recent years. From 1968 boards got shorter and lighter. Bob McTavish, George Greenough, and Nat Young cut the length of Malibus and introduced 'V bottoms'. In the modern surfboard, noses and tails are generally thin. The single fin was replaced with a twin fin on boards built locally by Americans Tom Hoye and Geoff McCoy in 1973. This enabled radical direction changes, and in 1981 Simon Anderson designed the three-fin 'thruster' to give more thrust out of a turn. Glen Winton of Australia was responsible for the successful four-fin design.

Sponsorship has greatly assisted surfing, which is seen by many as more a way of life than a sport. Today most of Australia's top performers work in the industry as manufacturers, designers, and shapers. Surfing reflects some of the latest technology, with radio helmets capable of picking up FM radio and transmissions from the coach on the beach. Surfing on a board is also the domain of the longboarder, kneeboarder, and the windsurfer. Says Barton Lynch, 'Every successful surfer thinks, controls what's going on in their minds. Pure ability will only take you so far, then your head has to take you the rest of the way.'

CD

See **Australian Surfriders Association**; **Bell's Beach**; CARROLL, TOM; FARRELLY, BERNARD; O'DONNELL, PHYLLIS; RICHARDS, MARK; **Surfboard Riding World Championship 1964**; YOUNG, ROBERT.

SUTTON, GARY (1955–), born Moree, NSW, later settled in Sydney. He enjoyed success in both amateur and professional cycling and at the peak of his career, won the 1980 World Amateur Cycling Championship in the 50 kilometres points-score event at Besançon, France. In addition to four other medals in world championship events, Sutton also won forty-two Australian national titles and competed in two Olympics (Munich and Montreal) and two Commonwealth Games (Christchurch and Edmonton). Sutton won his first major race at 13 years of age and his first national junior road title in 1971. At the 1976 Olympics he finished sixth in the 4000 metres individual pursuit. His Commonwealth Games performances yielded gold, silver, and bronze medals and he went on to compete in eleven world cycling championships. His professional career began in 1981 and his wins included most of the major Australian races. He retired briefly in the mid-1980s, but returned to professional cycling in 1988. At the age of 34 Sutton was narrowly beaten to take a silver medal over 50 kilometres in the 1989 World Championships in Lyons. He retired again in late 1991. He was appointed NSW State cycling coach in April of the same year.

JS

SUTTON, HARVEY (1882–1963), born Bendigo, Victoria, was an outstanding medical doctor and athlete. While working at a London hospital, he represented Australia as an 800 metres runner in the 1908 Olympics. After distinguished service with the AIF during the First World War, Sutton joined the NSW Education Department. There he was a vigorous promoter of public health and sanitary housing. Sutton co-founded Health Week in 1921. During the 1920s and 1930s this annual event encouraged people to eat a healthy diet and made the sometimes controversial link between physical activity and mental stability. Harvey Sutton also established the School of Tropical Medicine at the University of Sydney.

SC

Swimming

The dawn of the modern age of competitive swimming in Australia came on 14 February 1846, at the 'Gentlemen's Baths' of Thomas Robinson, situated in Woolloomooloo Bay, near the Domain in Sydney. Two swimming events were held: a 440 yards open race and a 100 yards race for juveniles. Although these events represented the first official swimming races in Australian history, they obviously did not herald the beginning of swimming in the Antipodes. Long before the early settlers of the colony of NSW risked drowning or a shark attack, the Aborigines had enjoyed the pleasures and harvested the fruits of the sea, lakes, and rivers of their native land.

The first land grant to build public baths was gazetted on 17 December 1829, but it took ten years for Thomas Robinson to build his floating baths, one for ladies and one for gentlemen, in Woolloomooloo Bay. It was in such public baths that the sport of competitive swimming blossomed in Australia. In 1861 the NSW champion, Joseph Bennett, challenged and defeated the Victorian champion, Stevens, over 200 yards. The race was swum at Captain Kenney's Bathing Ship at St Kilda. The winners of such races won handsome prizes; in fact the

Champion's Cup of Victoria was valued at £30 in 1861. In 1877–78 an English swimmer, Miss Elphinstone Dick, taught and coached 300 ladies and children at Kenney's Baths, St Kilda. The most famous teacher of swimming of the period was 'Professor' Frederick Cavill, who taught swimming at the Lavender Bay Baths in Sydney. He was the father of six boys and three girls, and all his sons became swimming champions. Apart from their personal achievements, the Cavill family made a major contribution to the development of Australian and world swimming by developing and popularising the Australian crawl stroke and the double-arm breast-stroke, now known as the butterfly stroke. The advent of the Australian crawl was soon to revolutionise sprint swimming throughout the world. The stroke was developed by Dick (Richmond) Cavill, who had seen Alick Wickham, a young Solomon Islander, using it in Sydney.

By the end of the century swimming clubs were a feature of the main Australian cities and of many country towns. In 1888 the Sydney Bathing Company opened an indoor swimming pool in Pitt Street called the 'Natatorium'. By 1890 the Natatorium had been the scene of club events and professional challenges involving such swimmers as W. J. Gormly and George Meadham. Many clubs began to restrict their membership to amateur members, though some retained their professional coaches-cum-champions. In 1892 the NSW Amateur Swimming Association (NSWASA) was formed, and two years later it staged the initial Australasian championships in NZ in conjunction with the NZASA. NSW swimmers totally dominated the Australasian championships until 1905, when for the first time a swimmer from another State, P. Matson from WA, won an event, the inaugural 220 yards breast-stroke title.

In 1899 Australians experienced international success when two of Fred Cavill's protégés, Freddie Lane and Jack Hellings, had an impressive campaign in England. Lane's success continued at the Paris Olympics in 1900, where he won Australia's first Olympic gold medals for swimming. Using his own version of the trudgen stroke, Lane won the 200 metres freestyle and the 200 metres obstacle race. In 1905 Australian swimmers held all the world records for the recognised men's events: Alick Wickham for 50 yards and Dick Cavill and Cecil Healy shared the 100 yards title. All other records belonged to the sensational Barney Kieran.

Australian women were also gaining recognition in the world at this time. Annette Kellerman secured considerable notoriety for her progressive attitude and for her daredevil acts and feats of distance swimming. In 1906, the Ladies' Amateur Swimming Association of NSW held its championships behind locked doors, men not being allowed as spectators. While Kellerman gained fame through her somewhat vaudevillian feats, Fanny Durack and Mina Wylie became the two leading female amateur swimmers of the pre-war era. As Australian swimmers prepared themselves for the 1912 Stockholm Olympics it seemed as though they would totally dominate the pool. At Stockholm Durack won gold in the 100 metres freestyle (using the trudgen stroke) and Mina Wylie gained the silver medal in the only individual swimming event for women on the programme. The other gold medal won by Australasia at Stockholm also went to the swimmers. The men's 4 × 200 metres freestyle relay team of Leslie Boardman, Malcolm Champion (a New Zealander), Harold Hardwick, and Cecil Healy won in a new world record time.

One of the golden eras of Australian swimming began in 1912 when William Longworth asserted his dominance. Longworth won every NSW and Australian freestyle title from 100 yards to 1 mile. He repeated this feat (with the exception of the 100 yards) in both 1913 and 1914. Bill Longworth used the crawl stroke, the style Fanny Durack had adopted so successfully (she set eleven world records). The modern era of Australian competitive swimming had truly begun. After the war, the next international sporting challenge Australian swimmers faced was the 1920 Antwerp Olympics. These Games heralded the revival of Frank Beaurepaire's 'amateur' career; after being declared a professional before the 1912 Games, he was reinstated and won a silver medal at Antwerp in the 4 × 200 metres relay and a bronze in the 1500 metres freestyle.

Early in 1923 Australian swimming was rocked when a 15-year-old schoolboy named Andrew Charlton defeated Frank Beaurepaire in a 440 yards freestyle race at the Manly Baths in Sydney. Thus began the career of 'Boy' Charlton, who came to the attention of the Australian public. Charlton was an automatic selection for the 1924 Olympics in Paris. He also competed in two further Olympics, in 1928 and 1932. Other Australian successes at the 1932 Los Angeles Games were Clare Dennis who won the 200 metres breast-stroke, and Philomena Mealing, who gained silver in the 100 metres backstroke event.

For the next fifteen years Australian swimming appeared to have lost its competitive edge. But although Australia gained only two silver and two bronze medals in the pool at the London Olympics in 1948, it seemed that the standard of domestic swimming was rapidly improving. Forbes Carlile had been appointed coach to the Olympic squad the year before, and it was his influence which led Australia to its next Olympic gold. At Helsinki in 1952 John Davies, one of the new breed of Australians who swam and studied at US universities, won the 200 metres breast-stroke event using the butterfly stroke and a frog kick.

The Helsinki Games were far from successful for Australian swimmers, and after their mediocre efforts national coaches began to apply the scientific methods of training and conditioning suggested by the research of Professor Frank Cotton of Sydney University. Cotton, assisted by Forbes Carlile, developed methods of training that were put into practice by Carlile, Sam Herford, Harry Gallagher, and Frank Guthrie to prepare the Australian swimmers for the Melbourne Olympics in 1956. The results were the most outstanding in Australia's swimming history: a total of fourteen medals, eight gold, four silver and two bronze. The Melbourne Olympics placed Australia back at the top of the swimming world. During the four years after these Games, however, there was a slight decline in Australian swimming standards, though the world-record performances of John and Ilsa Konrads were noteworthy. In Rome in 1960, Dawn Fraser, Murray Rose, and David Theile repeated their victories in the 100 metres and 400 metres freestyle and 100 metres backstroke respectively, John Konrads was victorious in the 1500 metres and John Devitt won a controversial decision in the men's 100 metres freestyle. Australian swimming officialdom's ability to precipitate controversy was again in evidence in 1964. Before the Tokyo Games the Australian Swimming Union (ASU) refused to allow Murray Rose (who had just broken the world 1500 metres record) to swim in the Olympic trials. Rose's exclusion was soon forgotten in the wake of Dawn Fraser's ten-year suspension that had been incurred as much by her anti-establishment attitude as by her alleged flag-stealing antics, despite having won the gold medal in the 100 metres for an unprecedented third time.

In 1966 Australian swimmers dominated the British Empire and Commonwealth Games events in Jamaica and it appeared that the national swimming team was ready to challenge the USA at the Mexico Olympics. This did not eventuate, but Michael Wenden proved that Australia could continue to produce champions when he broke the world record to win the 100 metres freestyle event and beat the great Don Schollander to win the 200 metres freestyle.

The results of the 1970 Edinburgh British Commonwealth Games foreshadowed a boom period for Australian swimming. The next two years were spent preparing the team for the Munich Olympics. The ASU sent them on a world tour, competing in Europe, the USA, and NZ. Their performances indicated that the men might end the dominance of the Americans. However it was the women, led by Shane Gould (three gold, one silver, and one bronze), who upheld Australia's swimming honour at Munich. The 1972 Olympics produced Australia's greatest team performance since the heady days of 1956. Much of the success was due, in part, to the directorship of head coach Don Talbot.

The advance of the Eastern bloc countries and a resurgence in American swimming saw Australia's high hopes for success at the Montreal Olympics dashed, with only a single bronze medal being won by Stephen Holland in the 1500 metres freestyle. On 25 January 1981 the AIS was opened in Canberra. The disappointing performances by Australian athletes at the 1976 Olympics and an analysis of overseas programmes and government involvement in sport made it clear that central government funding was vital if Australian sport in the future was to compete in the world arena. The boycott of the Moscow Games by the USA and many other Western nations allowed the Eastern bloc to dominate the 1980 Olympics; nevertheless, Australian swimmers gained seven of the country's nine medals.

The early 1980s once again resounded to the faux pas of Australian swimming officialdom. Michelle Ford, a 19-year-old dual Olympian, fell foul of the ASU largely because she resented being treated, as she said, 'like a 13-year-old', and Neil Brooks, once called 'the male Dawn Fraser', also clashed head on with team officials before the Commonwealth Games in Brisbane in 1982. The 'Mean Machine', the men's 4 × 100 metres freestyle relay team, performed valiantly at the Los Angeles Olympics in 1984, getting a silver medal. Indeed, the swimming teams dominated the medal tally for the Games, winning one gold, five silver, and six bronze medals. Jon Sieben's world record in winning the 200 metres butterfly was the Australian highlight of the Games.

As with all Australian sport, swimming in the late 1980s was influenced by the forces of commercialism. Leading swimmers, who have always had a very high media profile, became heavily involved in sponsorship. The impact of the AIS intensified, as did the efforts of the satellite squads under such coaches as Laurie Lawrence, Bill Sweetnam, and Joe King. The Seoul Olympics in 1988 were moderately successful, with Duncan Armstrong's efforts raising the Australian flag at the pool.

The 1990s began on a comparatively high note for Australian swimming at the Commonwealth Games held in Auckland, but the media hyperbole and exposure surrounding the selection of the team and the performances of 'Super Mum' Lisa Curry-Kenny detracted from the overall quality of the team's performance. Although Australia dominated the other Commonwealth nations, only the swims of two young Queenslanders, Glen Houseman and

Kieran Perkins, could have been considered world-class. Hayley Lewis's outstanding performances at the 1991 World Championships in Perth reinforced her potential as an Olympic medallist in Barcelona. In general, swimming could be claimed as Australia's most successful international sport. Since 1900, when Freddie Lane won the country's first gold medal in the water, Australians, both male and female, have maintained a high standing among the major swimming nations of the world.

RH, MH, and PH

See **ARMSTRONG, DUNCAN**; **AUSSI Masters Swimming**; **Australian Swimming**; **Bathing Costumes Controversy**; **BEAUREPAIRE, FRANK**; **BERRY, KEVIN**; **CARLILE, FORBES**; **CAVILL Family**; **CHARLTON, ANDREW**; **COOPER, BRADFORD**; **COTTON, FRANK**; **CRAPP, LORRAINE**; **DAVIES, JOHN**; **DENNIS, CLARE**; **DEVITT, JOHN**; **DURACK, SARAH**; **FORD, MICHELLE**; **FRASER, DAWN**; **GALLAGHER, HARRY**; **GOULD, SHANE**; **HARDWICK, HAROLD**; **HENRICKS, JON**; **KELLERMAN, ANNETTE**; **KIERAN, BERNARD**; **KONRADS, JOHN**; **LANE, FREDERICK**; **LAWRENCE, LAURIE**; **LEWIS, HAYLEY**; **MARONEY, SUSAN**; **McCLEMENTS, LYN**; **NEALL, GAIL**; **O'BRIEN, IAN**; **RENFORD, DES**; **ROSE, IAIN MURRAY**; **SIEBEN, JONATHAN**; **TALBOT, DON**; **TAYLOR-SMITH, SHELLEY**; **THEILE, DAVID**; **WENDEN, MICHAEL**; **WHITFIELD, BEVERLEY**; **WINDLE, ROBERT**.

Sydney Cricket Ground (SCG), three kilometres south-east of the city centre, is part of land formally approved in May 1852 for use by the military as a garden and cricket field. It was known at first as the Garrison Ground, then the Military and Civil Ground from the mid-1860s. The first reported cricket match was played on 15 February 1854, and horse-racing and athletics also took place there. The NSW military commander, Colonel Richardson, exercised influence over the use of the ground during the 1870s and favoured his cricket club over others. This situation led to agitation by the NSW Cricket Association, headed by Richard Driver, to gain control of the ground. They were successful, and on 3 August 1877 the Governor dedicated the 'Association Ground', first as a cricket ground and second for any other public amusement or purpose, with control by three trustees. After an extensive improvement programme, the first match, the final of the Civil Service Challenge Cup, was played on 25 October 1877. The initial first-class match there was between NSW and Victoria in February 1878, and the first Test match began on 17 February 1882. During the period to 1914, extensive use of the ground was made by other sports, especially athletics, tennis, baseball, football, and cycling.

The Sydney Cricket Ground, its official name since 1894, was not controlled by the cricket association, but by the SCG Trust which allowed other sports to operate, sometimes at the expense of cricket. This situation had been a point of regular dispute since 1877. From 1914, the other major sports at the SCG have been rugby union, rugby league, soccer, and, latterly, Australian rules. The 1938 British Empire Games were also held at the SCG. Ned Gregory constructed the original scoreboard (a wonder in its day) in 1896 and the concrete scoreboard on the Hill began operation in 1924. The Doug Walters Stand now obscures it, and scores have been displayed on an electronic board since 1983. In 1878 the only stands were the original Brewongle Stand and a small members' pavilion. Grandstand development continued, the 1980s being the most active period with improvements such as the Bill O'Reilly Stand featuring corporate boxes. The ground capacity now is 40 000, reduced from 78 000 for a rugby league Grand Final in 1965. Areas like the legendary Hill (home of 'Yabba'), formerly accommodating a large crowd, have been reduced by grandstand development. World Series Cricket, promoted by Kerry Packer, led to the first night game being played in 1978, and this has continued to be the most popular version of cricket at the ground. The SCG has been the focus for important sporting events in NSW since 1877, but recent venue developments by other sporting bodies have left cricket and Australian rules as the only sports now regularly played there.

SG

See **Crowd Disorder**; GASCOIGNE, STEPHEN; NOBLE, MONTAGUE.

Sydney Morning Herald **Best and Fairest (Rugby Union) Award** was first instituted in 1976. It is an award for the player judged to be the best and fairest over the normal competition rounds, in first grade, in the Sydney rugby union competition. Points are awarded on a three, two, one basis by judges delegated to each game. The judges are usually ex-players or ex-journalists. In the early years of the competition the winners were given a trophy and their club received a cup which was retained for one year. Now a cash prize is awarded which goes to the player's club. The most successful club is Western Suburbs whose players have won the award on five occasions. Three men have each won the award twice: Geoff Richards (Eastern Suburbs) 1978 and 1982, Grant Andrews (Warringah) 1979 and 1980, and Fetaiaki Langi (Western Suburbs) 1987 and 1988.

MC

Sydney to Hobart Yacht Race, along with the Bermuda and Fastnet races, is one of the three major offshore races in the world. In-augurated in 1945, the race was the idea of Captain John Illingworth RN, commander of the Cruising Yacht Club of Australia. The club had agreed to stage a pleasure cruise from Sydney to Hobart but, on the recommendation of Illingworth, the cruise was organised as a racing event. Illingworth's *Rani* took out the line and handicap honours, from a field of nine yachts, in 6 days 14 hours and 22 minutes. Always starting on Boxing Day, the race is open to yachts of all sizes. The race starts in Sydney Harbour, then the yachts follow the sheltered NSW shore, cross Bass Strait, run down the east coast of Tasmania and sail up the River Derwent. Heavy gales are common as the yachts cross Bass Strait, in contrast to the windless final leg encountered in the River Derwent. In 1977, 58 of 129 starters and in 1984, 105 of 152 starters were forced to retire due to severe gales. Since 1967 the Sydney to Hobart race has formed part of the Southern Cross Series. In the 1980s it became an object of legal betting, with the Tasmanian TAB operating a double on the line honours and handicap winners. In the same decade the race became more commercial, with its sponsor's name (currently Hitachi) appearing in the race's official title.

GC*

See **ILLINGWORTH, JOHN**.

Sydney to Melbourne Run. The ultra-marathon from Sydney to Melbourne sponsored by the Westfield shopping centres was an immediate sensation from its first running in 1983. The concept of a race over 875 kilometres, taking between five and six days, was challenging enough, but when the inaugural winner from eleven starters was a 61-year-old farmer who trained in 'gum boots', a sporting legend (Cliff Young) and a classic race were born. In subsequent years the race distance increased to over 1000 kilometres as different routes were tried. Nevertheless the average speed of the winner also increased, from Cliff Young's 6.04 km/h in 1983 to the 8.25 km/h of Yiannis Kouros in 1989. The field size also increased gradually to forty-three in 1988 although in most years only about half of the competitors have completed the event. The second, third, and fourth running of the annual event each had different winners, despite the media and general public's wish that Cliff Young could repeat his 1983 success. By 1987 it had become clear that this would never happen because the race had produced another hero—the Greek champion Yiannis Kouros, who repeated his 1985 victory. Kouros proved to be unbeatable in the event. In 1985 he won by a margin of 24 hours; in 1987 the margin was 26 hours. His dominance resulted in a rule change in 1988 whereby Kouros was handicapped to begin 12 hours behind the rest of the field. This reduced his winning margin to only 16 hours and to 11 in 1989. In 1990 an 8-hour handicap and a virus narrowed the margin to almost 10 hours. Kouros, like Cliff Young, provided material for the media, ensuring prominence for the race, but his dominance of the event has also threatened to destroy it. In 1991 his decision not to contest the race (officially) reduced the media coverage despite a record prize of $100 000. Reduced coverage has in turn caused the sponsor to consider withdrawing from the event from 1992.

JO'H

See **YOUNG, CLIFF**.

Synchronised Swimming
This sport is a discipline of swimming and has its technical rules laid down by the Fédération Internationale de Natation Amateur (FINA). Competitions are divided into two sections, figures and routines, and there are three events: solo, duet, and team (eight swimmers). Routines are swum to music and judged using separate scores on technical merit and artistic impression. Synchronised swimming as a sport evolved from the effortless swimming and floating water patterns of water ballet which is enjoyed by people of all ages around the world. At the turn of this century 'water shows' were popular and developed into a sport in Canada and the USA. The development of the sport in Australia has been slower than in the countries of its origin. Europe and North America traditionally built indoor heated pools but this was not the case in Australia, especially in the country centres. However, one of the most influential exponents of what has become known as synchronised swimming was Australian Annette Kellerman whose film-biography, featuring Esther Williams as Kellerman, also gave impetus to its development when it was released under the title *Million Dollar Mermaid* in the late 1950s.

In the early 1960s the Amateur Swimming Union of Australia (ASUA) was asked by FINA to add synchronised swimming as a fourth discipline of swimming. The ASUA established a synchronised swimming subcommittee and from 1964 people in the various States who were interested in working within synchronised swimming did their best to solve the mysteries of figure performance (then called 'stunts') and to conduct teaching programmes and competitions. State and national championships have been conducted annually since that year. After the restructuring of ASUA in 1985, when it became Australian Swimming Incorporated (ASI), the synchronised swimming subcommittee was advised to become independent, as diving and water polo had done previously. In November 1985, Australian Synchronised Swimming (ASS) became autonomous and affiliated with ASI.

Ten countries competed in the First World Synchronised Swimming Championships in Belgrade in 1973; Australia entered one swimmer and was placed sixth. World championships have been held every four years since then, Perth hosting them in 1991 with twenty-one countries participating. Following this championship Australia was ranked fifteenth. Australia has also competed regularly in the Pan-Pacific competitions which are held every two years. Since 1984, when synchronised swimming was included in the Olympic Games in Los Angeles, the sport has developed greatly.

CP, RK*, and IJ

See **KELLERMAN, ANNETTE**.

T

Table Tennis

The sport began as a parlour game in Victorian homes in England, the equipment used being mostly improvised and home-made. The main technical improvement was the introduction of a light, hollow ball. Parker Brothers adopted the familiar trade name Ping Pong, which derived from the sound the ball makes: 'ping' when the ball hits the bat, and 'pong' when the ball hits the table. The game was popular in Central Europe by 1905, but had been introduced to Japan, China, and Korea even earlier than this. After a period of decline the game was revived in England and Wales in the early 1920s. Table tennis is first known to have been played in Australia in Adelaide as early as 1898. In 1933 all States combined to form the Australian Board of Control, and also in this year the first Australian titles were held in Melbourne. Australia was affiliated with the world body in 1936, and officially became the Australian Association the following year. As a world body member Australia could then compete in international events, and in 1940 a team was sent to the Pan-Pacific Tournament in Tokyo. The world competition was attended for the first time in 1954 in Wembley, England. Table tennis joined the Olympic Games as an official event in 1988.

RL*

Taekwondo

Taekwondo, a Korean martial art which is over two thousand years old, literally means 'way of the hands and feet'. It was introduced to Australia in the early 1970s and is now a widely practised martial art and international sport with the status of having been included as a demonstration sport at both the 1988 (in which Australia competed) and 1992 Olympic Games. The Australian Taekwondo Association (ATA), the only Australian affiliate of the World Taekwondo Federation (WTF), regulates and promotes taekwondo in Australia and regularly conducts Australian championships, referee seminars, and coaching courses; it also participates in the National Coaching Accreditation Scheme. Australian Taekwondo Union championships for members of both the ATA and the ATF (Australian Taekwondo Federation) are also held at various State venues. Competitions generally include separate divisions in 'sparring' for men and women; 'poomse', a series of precise sparring techniques which call for balance and co-ordination, in which men and women of the same rank compete together; and 'breaking' of wood by various methods (using either the hand or foot). Australia has competed regularly at the Asian Taekwondo Regional Championships against countries and territories from the Asian and Oceanic regions. In 1976 the second championship was held in Melbourne. The seventh competition, held in Darwin in 1986, was the most successful tournament for Australia which collected three gold medals (two of them to women), four silver, and five bronze. This was the first international taekwondo championship in which protective headgear was made compulsory. Since then, domestic and international competition under the WTF has followed these guidelines.

GL and MR

TALBOT, DON (1934–) has made a unique contribution to world swimming, having headed both the Australian and Canadian national teams. As head coach of Australian teams between 1958 and 1972, he coached many notable swimmers including John and Ilsa Konrads. His efforts in the late 1970s took the Canadian team to the forefront of world swimming. He was appointed founding chief executive of the AIS in 1980. In 1989, after a further period in Canada, he returned to Australia to coach the national team.

PH

See **Swimming**.

TALLON, DON (1916–84), born Bundaberg, Queensland, was possibly the most skilful wicket-keeper in Australian cricket history. Tallon played his first major representative game for a Queensland country eleven in February 1933, and in December of that year made his first-class debut for Queensland. In the 1938–39 season he equalled two world records by claiming twelve dismissals in a match, and seven in an innings. He made his Test debut against NZ in 1945–46 and, until 1948, continued to set new standards in wicket-keeping excellence. He toured England twice and played the last of his twenty-one Tests in 1953. He died in Brisbane on 7 September 1984.

RF

TASKER, ROLLAND LESLIE (1926–), a Perth accountant turned sail-maker, was the first Australian to win a world championship in yachting and was also the first Australian, along with Jock Sturrock, to win an Olympic medal in this sport. Rolly Tasker began sailing with Vee Jays and 16-foot skiffs. He then moved to Sharpies and won 180 events, including a number of national titles. He later raced in the Flying Dutchman class. Tasker built his own boats, made his own sails and designed his own fittings. With crewman John Scott, he was unlucky not to win the 12 metre Sharpie class at the 1956 Olympics. After an unfortunate disqualification in the final race he had to settle for the silver medal after a count-back. In 1958 Tasker won the world championship in the Flying Dutchman class in Austria and came second in the event at Florida in 1962. In 1959 he finished third in the World Dragon class in Italy. After competing in the 1960 Olympics, he crewed on *Gretel* in the 1962 *America's* Cup challenge. Tasker was a versatile yachtsman who won the B Class World Catamaran Championship in Melbourne in 1966 and competed successfully in ocean racing in his self-designed craft, *Siska*. He later became one of the world's largest manufacturers of sails.

RC#

Tasmanian International Velodrome at Launceston has, since opening in 1985, rapidly established itself as a first-class venue, capable of staging most types of cycling events. The main feature of the facility is the 286 metre board track, which was ratified in 1986 by the Union Cycliste Internationale, which thereby recognised its international standard and sanctioned its use for world-record attempts. Later it was also accepted into the prestigious Union Internationale de Velodromes. Numerous championships have been conducted at the velodrome, including the Tasmanian amateur titles (1985), the Australian amateur championships (1985 and 1986), the Australian Masters games (1987) and the Australian professional championships (1988). Internationally, the venue has hosted the Oceania Cycling Championships (1989), World Series Cycling (1986, 1987, and 1988), and World Championship Cycling (1989) which featured Stephen Pate and Martin Vinnicombe who collectively established four world records. Tasmanian Danny Clark, the internationally renowned 6-day rider, has competed at the venue in 6-day and madison races, and has had a concourse at the velodrome named after him. In 1988 the Tasmanian International Velodrome was retitled the 'Silverdome' in an attempt to promote its multi-functional capabilities. Since opening, the Silverdome has provided facilities for numerous indoor sports in addition to hosting conferences, exhibitions and public entertainments. The Silverdome has given Australian cyclists a world-class venue and in doing so has greatly facilitated the development of track cycling in Australia as well as its international reputation.

DRS

Tassie Medal. The Eric Tassie Medal was first awarded in 1937 to the fairest and best player in the Australian National Football Council Carnival series, played from 1908 to 1972 between the various States. Tassie was a distinguished administrator who filled executive positions with the Norwood Football Club, the SA Football League and the Australian National Football Council between 1919 and 1934. The formation of the National Football League in 1975 led to the discontinuance of the Tassie Medal. In 1979 the award was revived. It is now presented to the best player in the State of Origin championships, as decided by umpires' votes.

MH*

TAYLOR, MARSHALL W. ('Major') (1878–1932), an American sprint cyclist, was the first great international black athlete. He was also the highest-paid sportsman of his era (he turned professional in 1896), at the time when cycling was the pre-eminent and most lucrative international sport. He broke the racial sporting barrier in cycling in numerous countries, including Australia. He toured 'down under' in 1902–3 and 1903–4, where the Sydney One Thousand, the richest cycle race in the world (£750 for the winner of the mile race) was held. His second tour included three white Americans who intensely disliked him. They were driven by professional ego and racial antipathy. The result was an American racial battle fought out on Australian cycle tracks. It saw bitter, vindictive, yet spectacular riding, before the largest crowds in Australian cycling history. Numerous world and Australian records fell, and the season ended up in the NSW Supreme Court, where the winner of the Sydney One Thousand took a year to be decided. Major Taylor retired in 1910, and died in obscurity.

JF

See **Ethnic Influences**; WALKER, DON.

TAYLOR, VALERIE MAY (née HUGHES) (1935–), born Sydney, is the outstanding Australian woman exponent of spearfishing, scuba-diving and still and movie underwater photography. She often works in partnership with her husband Ron Taylor. Valerie Taylor first began swimming in the late 1940s as therapy to help regain the use of her legs after suffering poliomyelitis in childhood. She began diving in the Port Hacking district of NSW in the mid-1950s as a member of the St George Spearfishing Club, at the same time working as an actress and television scriptwriter. She became Australian woman champion in spearfishing and scuba-diving during the 1960s.

From the early 1960s, however, she and her husband (an Australian and world spearfishing champion) began concentrating on the filming of spectacular underwater action for print features, film, and television. This has led to their contribution to such productions as *Shark Hunters* (1963), *Blue Water: White Death* (1969–70), *Barrier Reef* (1970–71), *Jaws* and *Orca* (1974), *Blue Lagoon* (1980) and *Wreck of the Yongala* (1982), as well as to Valerie's photographic features in *National Geographic, Stern, Reader's Digest, Life* and other magazines. It has also led to her consultancies as adviser to the Belgian Scientific Expedition to the Great Barrier Reef (1967) and as representative of the Minister for the Environment on the NSW Pollution Control Commission (1977–78). In 1981 Taylor became the first woman photographer to win the NOGI award for the Arts (Photography) of the Underwater Society of America.

GK-S

TAYLOR-SMITH, SHELLEY (1961–   ), born Perth, is a long-distance swimmer. After joining the Surat Hill Swim Club at the age of 6 she became a successful age-group swimmer at the State and national level. A turning point occurred when she won a scholarship to the University of Arkansas, graduating in physical education. Her coach Sam Freas, who observed how much faster she swam in open water, helped her development as a marathon swimmer. Taylor-Smith broke the women's 4 mile record in 1983. She was the first woman to finish at the Seal Beach 25 kilometres swim in 1985 and then won the Manhattan Island swim four times, gaining the record for that event; she also won the Australian marathon title from 1988 to 1990. The high point of her career was victory in the women's world marathon championship in her home town, Perth, in 1991.

RH and MH

Technology
Many of the technological changes which occurred throughout the nineteenth century transformed the pastimes and games of Australians into sports. Although the origins of many pastimes were rural, the urban-industrial social environment brought about by technological changes facilitated their development to the stage where there were State, national, and international governing bodies of sport within the first decades of the twentieth century. Civic and colonial pride in the achievements of sporting teams and athletes became more evident as the century progressed. The emancipation of women had its beginnings in the urban-industrial environment and the use of sport to advance their claims towards social freedom was evident, especially in tennis and cycling.

As transportation became cheaper, faster, and more comfortable following the advent of the steamboat and steam locomotive, sporting enthusiasts travelled more frequently to other towns and cities. The introduction of tramways made travel within urban centres more convenient, and this resulted in a greater number of spectators at sporting events. The more efficient printing industry, and better means of communication by telegraph, oceanic cable, telephone, and photography enabled the editors of the periodical press to include many more items of sporting interest in their columns. Newspapers served increasingly as the medium for directing, and reflecting, public opinion on matters pertaining to sport, as well as informing readers of forthcoming events and the latest sporting results from many parts of Australia and other countries. The postal system, the press, telegraph, and telephone were used to arrange sporting excursions and competitions.

The equipment for physical activity, and the activity itself, were interdependent variables; changes within one subsequently created a necessary, or at least a desirable, change in the other in order to facilitate the continued development of the sport. Many of the changes in sporting equipment were gradual and involved only minor refinements; others were more distinct and were regarded as inventions worthy of patent, and sometimes necessitated changes to playing rules. An example was the changes made in baseball following the introduction of the catcher's glove or mitt. Before this innovation the catcher had to stand far beyond the batter in order to catch the pitched ball after the first bounce. The protection the glove offered enabled the catcher to stand directly behind the batter, thereby improving the skill, speed, and spectacle of the sport.

Golfing equipment also illustrates the relationship between the technology and playing rules and techniques. Whittled sticks gave way to specially designed clubs, and these were given names which tended to reflect the quality and nature of the courses on which they were used, such as mud spoon, sand and track irons, and driving putter. Changes in golf sticks were usually the result of changes in the type of ball in use. Golf balls until the 1880s were 'featheries' which were hand-made by compressing boiled goose feathers inside a leather cover. As the materials dried, the leather shrank and the feathers expanded, forming a hard ball capable of being driven 150–170 metres. But featheries could withstand neither the blows of clubs nor the rigours of the ground very well and gutta-percha balls or 'gutties', which were smooth, solid, and more durable, became an ideal substitute. It was soon found by the users of the guttie that an older, niched, and marked ball travelled further in flight than a new smooth one, and a pattern of dimples and raised bumps was soon introduced as part of the manufacturing process. The most important development in the manufacture of the golf ball, however, was the rubber ball wound with thread, introduced about the turn of the century; this ball was so lively and travelled so far that golf courses had to be enlarged. In order to utilise the better balls to the greatest extent, corresponding changes had to be made in golf clubs. These relationships between length of courses, quality of balls, and type of clubs have, of course, continued throughout the twentieth century with a far greater use of synthetic materials. The more efficient techniques of manufacturing not only resulted in sporting goods becoming cheaper and more available to the public but also helped to standardise the equipment for use in competition.

Many sports facilities were also improved: grounds, tracks, fields, rinks, and gymnasia were transformed into more appropriate venues for athletes to demonstrate their skills, and towards the end of the century, full- and part-time curators and groundskeepers were employed to maintain them.

A major innovation in horse-racing equipment towards the end of the nineteenth century was the use of a starting barrier. For most of the century horses had been lined up behind a mark on the track and the signal to start was a vocal 'away', a flag, or a horn. This procedure was far from satisfactory and the invention in Australia of a 'starting machine' was greeted with enthusiasm. Messrs Johnstone and Gleeson developed a screen or barrier of eight light ropes stretched parallel to each other at intervals of a few inches. The ropes were attached to a wire running to a pulley machine operated by the starter. Further improvements followed; in particular barrier stalls, built of steel with padding to protect the horses, were introduced to Australia in 1947. They spaced runners evenly across the track and gave the starter a clear view of all the horses. When the starter's button was pressed the gates in front of each horse opened simultaneously. As with the earlier starting machine, this gave all horses the chance of a fair start, a vital contribution to the racing and gambling industries of Australia.

Technological changes in communications have been transforming influences on sport. Apart from the rise of the sports reporter in the print medium, radio has brought a dimension of 'being there' since the early horse-racing, cricket, and football broadcasts of the 1920s. An example of an ingenious use of technology was the 'synthetic Tests' by the ABC in the 1934 cricket series between England and Australia in England. 'Ball-by-ball' descriptions were given from the ABC's studios in Sydney upon receipt of short descriptive telegrams sent approximately five minutes apart from the cricket grounds in Britain. A team of cricket commentators in the studio described play as if they were live spectators, using sound effects such as a pencil tapped against a piece of wood to simulate the bat striking the ball. Today of course not only can the home viewer enjoy the benefits of television coverage but spectators at major sporting grounds such as the Melbourne and Sydney Cricket Grounds, and VFL Park at Waverley, Victoria, have scoreboards which serve as giant television screens providing live coverage, scores, player and match statistics and historical facts, replay highlights and, of course, commercials and advertisements. The extent of the influence of communications technology on sport is apparent when one considers that in 1900 one either had to be at a sporting event, read about it in the press, or talk to someone who had been there. Today we have the live television coverage of the 1992 Olympics in Barcelona brought about by satellite, along with features such as instant replay, slow-motion, split-screens, and miniscule cameras in strategic locations.

IJ

See **Golf**; HENSELL, WILLIAM; **Media**.

Tennis Australia

The Australasian Lawn Tennis Association (ALTA) was formed at a meeting held in September 1904. Its inception arose from a resolution by the NSW Lawn Tennis Association to invite representatives from each State and NZ to discuss the formation of a national organisation so that these two countries could compete as one nation in the Davis Cup and to institute and hold the Australasian Championships. NZ and all states except WA were represented. NZ later wished to be regarded as a separate tennis nation and withdrew its affiliation in 1922. ALTA continued to function as the Australasian body until 1926 when the title was changed to the Lawn Tennis Association of Australia (LTAA). The former winner of Wimbledon and great Davis Cup player, (Sir) Norman Brookes, was appointed president, a position he held for twenty-nine years until 1955. Following the approval of 'open tennis' in 1968 it was necessary to change administrative procedures within the LTAA. The first full-time executive director was appointed in 1975, Davis Cup director in 1974, tournament director in 1976, and national coach in 1980. The president's position became full-time in 1982. In 1986 the organisation adopted the new title of Tennis Australia.

MD and IJ

See **Lawn Tennis**.

Tennis: Élite Players since 1930. Between 1933, when Jack Crawford won Wimbledon, and 1987 when Pat Cash performed the same feat, Australia produced some of the world's best male tennis-players. Frank Sedgman and Lew Hoad were both powerful serve-and-volley players who inspired the public in the golden fifties. Ken Rosewall, with a superb backhand, teamed with Hoad in the Davis Cup and won every major title (except Wimbledon) over a period of twenty years. Left-hander Rod Laver, with an all-round game, was victorious in the first Open Wimbledon in 1969, the year of his second Grand Slam. John Newcombe and Roy Emerson had fine records in major events, including five Wimbledon crowns between 1964 and 1971. Ashley Cooper (1958) and Neale Fraser (1960) also managed to win Wimbledon. This title eluded Ken McGregor, Fred Stolle, and Tony Roche who nevertheless all reached a Wimbledon final and had high international rankings. Australians, too, had a reputation for fine doubles play. John Bromwich (a runner-up in singles at Wimbledon in 1948) and Adrian Quist were perhaps the greatest, but some critics suggest Newcombe and Roche were their equals.

Most experts agree that Margaret Court (Smith) has been the best female tennis-player produced in Australia. In the twelve years to the end of 1973 Court, with her powerful serve-and-volley game, won twenty-four Grand Slam singles titles. The only other Australian woman to win Wimbledon was Evonne Cawley (Goolagong), who was noted for her exhilarating tennis. Other Australians to achieve a measure of success on the modern circuit have been Lesley Bowrey (Turner), Robyn Ebbern, Jan Lehane (O'Neill), Judy Tegart, Helen Gourley (Cawley), Leslie Hunt, Karen Krantzcke, Kerry Reid (Melville), and Diane Fromholtz (Ballestrat). They were preceded by Lorraine Coughlan (Robinson), Mary Reitano (Carter) and Beryl Penrose who all held the nation's number one ranking. Before the circuit days Joan Hartigan won three Australian Opens in the 1930s. Thereafter, until the early 1950s, Nancye Bolton (Wynne) was Australia's 'first lady of tennis' with twenty Open titles. On ten occasions she teamed with Thelma Long (Coyne) to win the national doubles. Two others with long careers were Nell Hopman and Mary Hawton. In the 1970s and 1980s Wendy Turnbull also enjoyed many years as one of Australia's top-ranked players. She has shared Elizabeth Smylie's (Sayers) distinction of winning Grand Slam doubles titles.

HCJP

See **Lawn Tennis**.

Tennis: Open Champions before 1930. Australia's most celebrated tennis-player before the First World War was Norman Brookes, the Wimbledon singles champion in 1907 and 1914.

He was rarely able to compete in the Australasian Open, but in 1911 he won the title by defeating Horrie Rice (the 1907 winner). Gerald Patterson was another to win two Wimbledon crowns and capture one Australian Open. In 1927 he scored over Jack Hawkes, the previous title-holder. Before 1930 the player with the best record in the Open was J. O. Anderson, who had three wins in the mid-1920s. Rod Heath who won the inaugural Open in 1905 was also champion in 1910. Another player with two wins was Pat O'Hara Wood (1920 and 1923). His brother Arthur had been the victor in 1914 before losing his life during the war. This fate also befell the great New Zealander Anthony Wilding who gained the title in Christchurch (1906) and Perth (1909). Ernie Parker (1913) and Rice Gemmell (1921) had wins against weak fields in Perth. Frenchman Jean Borotra (1928) was possibly the most notable overseas player to gain the title. The first two women's titles, in 1922 and 1923, were won by Mall Molesworth. But the champion of the 1920s was Daphne Akhurst with five crowns between 1924 and 1930. Sylvia Lance defeated Esna Boyd in the 1924 final. Boyd won in 1927 but is particularly remembered for the six occasions on which she was runner-up.

HCJP

Tennis: Open Championship. In 1924 the Australian Open was designated as a 'national event' by the International (Lawn) Tennis Federation and was later regarded as having 'Grand Slam' status. The inaugural Australasian Open, as it was known until 1927, was held in Melbourne during 1905 with seventeen entrants. Twice (1906 and 1912) the event was played in NZ and until 1972 its venue was rotated around the State capitals (except Hobart) and held at various times of the year. Thereafter, Melbourne has been the home of the Open, with the surface being changed from grass to rebound ace when in 1987 the event was moved from Kooyong to the new National Tennis Centre at Flinders Park. Not until 1922 were ladies' singles and doubles included in the championship. At first the Open was strictly an amateur event with no seedings. From 1924 some travelling expenses were permitted but professionals could not compete until 1969. Now the prize-money is considerable, with the event being underwritten by sponsorship and television contracts.

HCJP

Tenpin Bowling
The first bowling centre in Australia was established in Glenelg, SA, in 1960. The inaugural Australian championships were held in Sydney in 1962 under the control of the Australian Tenpin Bowling Congress (ATBC). Masters events for men began in 1963, and for women

the following year. Wollongong's Joe Velo was the first person to bowl a perfect score in a sanctioned tournament, a feat he achieved in an ATBC event in 1963. Velo was prominent in domestic men's competition from 1960 to 1980, while Ruth Guerster of Melbourne dominated the women's game between 1966 and 1980.

KM*

See **Australian Tenpin Bowling Congress**.

The Barb (1863–88), a jet-black thoroughbred racehorse by *Sir Hercules* out of *Fair Ellen*, was the winner of sixteen races from twenty-one starts in NSW, Victoria, and Tasmania including the 1866 Melbourne Cup, the Australian Jockey Club Derby, and the Australasian Champion Sweepstakes. Bred at Kelso in NSW by George Lee, *The Barb* was sold as a yearling to John Tait and was trained and often ridden in races by James Ashworth. His greatest performance was the second of his two successive Sydney Cup wins. His handicap weight of 10 stone 8 pounds remains the record weight carried to victory in the race. He was retired to the stud in 1869, but met with little success.

AL

THEILE, DAVID EGMONT (1938–) is the only Queensland swimmer to win consecutive Olympic gold medals, and the only Australian to have won the Olympic backstroke event. He accomplished these feats while a medical student at the University of Queensland. At the 1956 Melbourne Games he won the 100 metres backstroke, and in the 1960 Rome Olympics he repeated this success as well as receiving a silver medal in the 4 × 100 metres medley relay. The key to Theile's success was that he was a thinking swimmer who consistently analysed not only his own technique but also his opposition's. He used the 'S' arm-pull, while most swimmers of the period used the straight arm-pull. His turn was considered controversial as he used his own variation of the tumble turn. He found that it was more natural for him to touch with the arm curved slightly round the top of his head rather than straight back. He turned over the opposite shoulder, whereas in the conventional turn the swimmer turned over the same shoulder as the hand that touched. In the 1956 Games he did not use the turn until the final, thus not giving the judges an opportunity to debate its legality. Theile had the perfect build for the 100 metres backstroke. He was 1.9 metres tall, with a lean, well-proportioned, and muscular physique. Now a prominent Brisbane surgeon, he is honoured by the David Theile Swimming Pool at the University of Queensland.

RH and MH

See **Swimming**.

THOMPSON, DUNCAN (1895–1980), born Warwick, Queensland, and represented Queensland at rugby league in 1915. He captained NSW from 1920 to 1923 and played for North Sydney, who were premiers in 1921 and 1922, before returning to Toowoomba and Queensland for their dominant seasons in 1924–25. He played in nine Tests from 1919 to 1924. A slight, imaginative half-back, he later attracted many players and future coaches to Toowoomba as he coached that city's team to Bulimba Cup success from 1951 to 1956: he called his formula 'contract football'. Mick Madsen said that he 'taught forwards how to think'.

SJR

See **Rugby League**.

THOMPSON, JOHN MAITLAND (1902–86), caver, was born at Moonee Ponds in Victoria. He was a former sailing-ship master who left the sea 'when they put engines in them', and became harbour master at Ceduna and later at Port Adelaide in SA. At Ceduna he became interested in the caves of the Nullarbor Plain, and led many expeditions there between 1935 and 1955. He adapted his ocean-going navigational skills to locating himself on the Nullarbor and explored over one hundred and sixty caves there.

EH-S

See **Caving**.

THOMPSON, RAELEE (1945–), fast bowler, born Victoria, represented Australia between 1972 and 1984–85 in sixteen Tests and was, at the time, Australia's most internationally represented female cricketer. As a member of the 1976 Australian team to tour England, she took part in the first women's international match to be played at Lord's. She finished this series as Australia's chief wicket-taker. Not surprisingly, she cites the historic 1984–85 Jubilee Test series against England as the most memorable of her career. It was in the final Test at Bendigo that she achieved the hitherto elusive bag of five wickets in an innings, taking 5–33 off 28 overs. She also topped the bowling averages for the series.

LR

THOMPSON, W. B. (1906–45), born Sydney into a middle-class family, was Australia's greatest pre-war racing driver. He was racing a Bugatti at 21 and won his first Australian Grand Prix (AGP) two years later. Bill Thompson's careful preparation and forceful but brilliantly consistent driving brought not only three AGP victories (1930 and 1932 in a T37A Bugatti and 1933 in a Riley Brooklands) but also two close second placings (1934 and 1935 in an MG Magnette) before he effectively retired. He died in an aircraft accident near the Marshall Islands on 12 February 1945.

GH

122 Edward Trickett, a professional sculler, was the first Australian to win a world title in any sport when he beat Joseph Henry Sadler on the Thames River, London, on 27 June 1876.

123 Len Sheppard, who has been water skiing for thirty years, won the World Disabled Water Skiing championship in slalom (leg amputee division) in 1987 and 1991.

124 The rules of several sports appear to permit actions
which would otherwise be considered as assault, so it is
not surprising that incidents in contact sports sometimes
spill over into violent conflict.

125 John Greening of Collingwood was struck behind
play early in the first quarter of the VFL Round 14 match
in July 1972. He was in a coma for twenty-four hours and
unconscious for days.

THOMSON, PETER, MBE (1929–   ), born Melbourne, has an incomparable record in golf as a player, administrator, course designer, journalist, and broadcaster. In 1948 he won the Victorian Amateur before turning professional in 1949. He won the Australian Open in 1951, 1967, and 1972 and the NZ Open nine times. Other victories included the NZ professional, the British match play, the Victorian match play, the Ampol, Pelaco, and Speedo events. With Kel Nagle he won the Canada Cup in 1954 and 1959. His first American tournament victory, the Texas Open, meant beating Cary Middlecoff and Gene Littler in a play-off. His greatest triumph was to have won five British Opens, a feat which puts him ahead of the next best tally of 'majors' won by an Australian, the two victories of David Graham. Thomson won in three successive years—1954, 1955, and 1956 —and again in 1958 and 1965. This last victory was his most memorable: he beat Jack Nicklaus, Arnold Palmer, Gary Player, and Tony Lema. An educated man (he trained as an industrial chemist), he is literate, articulate, and learned. He is also modest. He has contributed much of his wisdom as president of the Australian PGA. His firm, Thomson Wolveridge & Associates, has built many fine courses and refurbished, among others, Royal Sydney in the 1980s. His lowest Australian score was 262; in 1962 he recorded 275 at the old St Andrews course; at the 1959 Pelaco in Victoria he had five successive rounds under 70: yet he claims he was never a good putter!

CT

See **Golf**.

THORNE, RHONDA (later SHAPLAND) (1958–   ), born Queensland, is one of three Australian women to have won the World Squash Open Championship, taking the title in Toronto in 1981. She also won the Australian women's Open title in the same year. She again reached the final of the world championships in 1982 but this time lost to fellow Australian Vicki Cardwell. Thorne first represented Australia as a junior from 1974 to 1976. She was a member of the Australian Open team in 1977–83 and its captain from 1981 to 1983. She was named Queensland Sportswoman of the Year in 1984.

KT

See **Squash Rackets**.

THORNETT, JOHN, MBE (1935–   ), and **RICHARD** (1940–   ) are members of one of Australia's great sporting families. John, Dick, and Ken (who represented Australia in rugby league), were powerfully built and possessed of great ball-handling skills, which they also used to effect playing water polo. As an inspirational captain in rugby union, playing at second row or front row, John advocated hard but fair play and set a fine example of his philosophy during eight overseas tours and thirty-seven Tests. Thornett led Australia in sixteen Tests between 1962 and 1967 when Australia drew 2–2 in the series with South Africa, defeated England 18–9 in 1963, the All Blacks 20–5 in 1964, and recorded two wins over South Africa in 1965. John Thornett played fourteen seasons of first-grade football, first with Sydney University and later with Northern Suburbs, where he coached on retirement. The youngest of the brothers, Dick, is one of the few sportsmen to represent his country in three sports. After competing for Australia in water polo at the 1960 Rome Olympics he went on to appear in eleven rugby union Tests against Fiji, France, NZ, and South Africa, and then pursued a career in rugby league, playing a further ten Tests. At 104 kilograms, the big Randwick second-rower was a feared runner with the ball and was renowned for his strength in rucking and mauling.

GC†

THURGOOD, ALBERT JOHN (1874–1927) had a profound impact on Australian football with his fine athleticism, speed, high marking, and long, accurate kicking in a career lasting from 1892 to 1906 but effectively shortened to eight years due to the VFL's refusal to grant him a permit to play and a serious leg injury. 'Albert the Great', as he was known, was the first outstanding goal-kicker even though he played mainly at ruck and half-forward. His yearly tallies of 56, 64, (a record), 63, 53, and 27, as well as match tallies of 12 (v. Richmond), 9 (v. North Melbourne), and 15 (v. West Perth) were sensational for that era. He first played for Essendon (VFA), then transferred to Fremantle (1895–97), before returning to Essendon (VFL) but was forced to stand down for nearly two seasons. He played a key role in Essendon's run of premierships at the turn of the century.

NS

Tied Cricket Tests. In the history of Test cricket there have been only two tied Tests: the first occurred in Brisbane on 9–14 December 1960 during the series between Australia and the West Indies in a match which set the pattern for what has been widely regarded as the finest series yet played in Australia. Coming into the match the form of the West Indies had been disappointing. They had won only one first-class game and had suffered an innings defeat at the hands of NSW. Batting first, the visitors were inspired by a sparkling innings from Sobers (132) who was well supported by Worrell (65), Solomon (65), and Alexander (60). Nevertheless their first innings total of 453 was eclipsed by Australia's 505 which included significant scores by O'Neill (181), Simpson (92), and McDonald (57). With a second innings score of

284 the West Indies set Australia 232 to win with the luxury of a day's batting. After an early collapse, Davidson (80) and Benaud (52) turned the match in favour of the home side. With one over remaining Australia required 6 runs with 3 wickets in hand. Hall had Benaud caught at the wicket then dropped Grout, who was out the next ball seeking a match-winning run. Meckiff was then dismissed by a Solomon throw from square leg and pandemonium broke loose, not least in the ABC broadcast booth where confusion reigned over the final result.

No less exciting was the second tied Test which transpired in Madras in September 1986 when India met Australia in the 1052nd Test match. Australia won the toss, batted, and controlled the first three days. A double century from Jones and centuries from Boon and Border resulted in a first innings total of 7 declared for 574. In reply India avoided the follow-on, with Kapil Dev scoring 119 out of a total of 397. In 49 overs on the fourth day Australia scored 170 runs for 5 wickets to set India 348 runs to win, off a minimum of 87 overs on the last day. Gavaskar scored 90 to put India in a strong position at 251 for 4 wickets. Scenting a strong chance of victory, India continued to score freely until, with 30 balls remaining, India required just 18 runs. Bright struck three times, leaving India 4 runs to win off 8 balls. When Matthews had the last batsman, Maninder, leg-before on the penultimate ball the scores were even and the cricket world's second tied Test had taken place.

RA and GC*

Tied Grand Finals (Rugby League). The 9–9 draw between Parramatta and St George at the SCG on 17 September 1977 was the first-ever tie in a Sydney Rugby League Grand Final. Earlier, when Newtown and South Sydney drew 4–4 in the last game of 1910, there was no provision for a Grand Final and Newtown were awarded the premiership, being 1 point ahead of Souths on the competition table. In the 1977 game, a Parramatta try in the corner three minutes from full time evened the score 9–9, but champion goal-kicker Michael Cronin could not convert to win the title. Twenty minutes' extra time did not change the score. In the following Saturday's replay, St George over-powered Parramatta to win 22–0. Remarkably, the 1978 Grand Final between Manly-Warringah and Cronulla-Sutherland also ended in a tie 11–11, and Manly won the Tuesday replay 16–0.

TB

Tied Grand Finals (VFL). There have been two tied Grand Finals in the VFL, 1948 and 1977. In 1948 Essendon had finished the home-and-away series three games clear of second-placed Melbourne and had also beaten them in the second semifinal. In an appalling display of

inaccuracy, however, Essendon was lucky to escape with a tie from a match they should have won easily. The final scores were Essendon 7–27–69, Melbourne 10–9–69. In the replay, Melbourne led all day, defeating Essendon by 39 points. Collingwood finished last in 1976, but under their new coach Tom Hafey they topped the ladder in 1977. North Melbourne had lost the qualifying final and had already played three finals matches before the Grand Final. Both sides were missing top players: North had lost Keith Greig to injury and Collingwood's Phil Carmen had been suspended. In the first Grand Final to be televised live in Victoria, strong play by Collingwood and inaccuracy by North had given Collingwood a 27-point lead at three-quarter time. In the final quarter a revitalised North Melbourne kicked 5 goals to Collingwood's 1, but that one goal, kicked by Ross 'Twiggy' Dunne in the final minute of play, levelled the score at 76 points each. North Melbourne won the replay, after having played five consecutive finals matches to win its second premiership.

DN

Titus Award. In 1977 the VFL decided to institute an award for the recognition of men who had given outstanding service to their club and contributed to the advancement of Australian rules football. The first recipient was W. J. 'Skinny' Titus. During a playing career which lasted from 1926 until 1943 Titus played 294 games and kicked 970 goals. In 1940 Titus was the leading VFL goal-kicker, with 100. After coaching Richmond in 1965 Titus continued for many years as a club administrator. After his death in 1977 it was decided to rename the trophy the W. J. Titus Award in his honour.

MH*

TODD, JOHN (1938–), born Manjimup, WA, was a left-footed rover who won the Sandover Medal at the age of 17 in his first year of senior Australian football, playing for South Fremantle. He played one hundred and thirty-two senior and nine State games before he retired as a player due to injury. For twenty-two of the next twenty-six years he was coach of South Fremantle, East Fremantle, and Swan Districts (leading them to three successive premierships from 1982 to 1984). He was also the inaugural coach of the West Coast Eagles, taking them to the finals in his second year. Later he returned to Swan Districts, winning another flag in 1990.

WPR

Touch

Touch football has its origins in training routines adopted by rugby union and league sides in Sydney during the early 1960s, spreading to outdoor social gatherings, school playgrounds, and inter-office challenges. There were wide interpretations of rules, no true referees, and games of up to thirty a side played on any convenient open space. The first recognised competition began with the formation of the South Sydney Touch Football Association and was played at Pioneer Park, Malabar, in 1968. By the time the NSW Touch Football Association was established in 1972 there were six affiliated bodies with 1500 players. The ACT association was formed in 1975, followed by Victoria (1976), SA (1978), Queensland, Tasmania and the NT (1979), and WA (1980). Rule interpretations varied from State to State until the formation of the Australian Touch Football Association (ATFA) in November 1978, when the laws governing the NSW game were largely adopted. Women have played touch since its earliest days. Partly to encourage this, at its meeting in September 1981 ATFA took a number of steps to disassociate itself from what it perceived to be its macho image, including dropping 'football' from its title and introducing a smaller ball.

The first national championships, held in December 1980, were dominated by NSW, a trend which continued through the decade until 1989 when Queensland, with wins in five of the eight divisions, indicated a challenge to that supremacy. Australia is still largely unchallenged in the international arena. Since playing the first official Test match against NZ in Melbourne on 23 February 1985 it has suffered just one defeat, winning men's, women's, mixed, and masters divisions at the first World Cup, on the Gold Coast in 1988. For the second competition, in Auckland in December 1991, the divisions were increased to six, the original masters category being divided into senior men (over-30) and masters (over-35); senior women (over-27) was also added. It was in this latter competition that the Australians suffered defeat for the first time, being beaten 4–3 by NZ after extra time in the final.

The Australian Touch Association has well over a hundred thousand registered players, but believes there are as many again in unaffiliated competitions, while up to half a million children play at school.

GC

Touring Car Championship. The life-blood of Australian motor sport, the Australian Touring Car Championship, can be traced back to 1960 when it was based on a single race. The inaugural championship was held at Orange, NSW, when 7000 spectators turned out to see the British-built Jaguar of David McKay reach speeds of 200 km/h to win the 20-lap race. For the next eight years the championship was held on different tracks around Australia, Pete Geoghegan being the most successful driver

with four championship wins driving Jaguars. In 1969 the championship was expanded to incorporate five races in five different States. Since then no one driver or car has dominated the championship, although for a decade GMH and Ford vehicles were unbeatable until the BMW of Ian Richards saw European cars leave their mark on the championship series in 1985.

GC*

Trampolining
Australians began trampolining in the late 1940s, the trampoline having been developed by George Nissen in America earlier in the decade, but it was not until 1959 that the governing body of world gymnastics, the Fédération Internationale Gymnastique, approved rebound tumbling as a special event for all member organisations. Queensland, NSW, and Victoria formed State organisations in 1963 and the Australian Trampoline Sports Union (ATSU) was formed in November of that year; SA affiliated later, Tasmania in 1970 and WA in 1984. The first Australian championships were held in 1964 at North Sydney High School gymnasium. The entrants comprised ten senior men, seven senior women, twelve junior women, and eighteen junior men. The first world championships were held in London in March 1964. Don Viney from Victoria created controversy by taking over his own string bed; at first he was regarded as a professional and then a non-amateur. He was eventually allowed to bounce but was quickly eliminated from competition. The woven-string bed has gained popularity domestically over the years, but is not in widespread use overseas so Australians still have to make adjustments when they travel to foreign competitions where they generally compete on woven quarter-inch web beds. Australians have competed in all world championships since 1964. In 1971 synchronised trampolining was introduced into competition, and in 1976 the double-mini made its appearance. Australians have dominated the world championships in the latter event, with Brett Austine winning in 1982, 1984, and 1986, and Adrian Wareham claiming the title in 1988 and 1990. Elizabeth Jensen and Lisa Newman-Morris finished first and second in the women's double-mini world championship in 1988, and reversed their placings in 1990. At present the Australian championships have events in trampoline, synchronised trampoline, double-mini trampoline, and tumbling. Age categories include sub-juniors (under-13), juniors (under-16), and seniors (over-16). There are approximately two thousand competitive members around Australia, with many others doing classes just for fun.

KM*, MT, and IJ

Triathlon
The first triathlons were conducted a little over

a decade ago in San Diego on the American west coast. They caught the attention of the sporting world after the world-wide publicity of the Hawaiian Ironman Triathlon—a combination dreamt up by John Collin of a 3.8 kilometre swim, a 180 kilometre bike ride and a 42.2 kilometre run. At about the same time triathlons were introduced to Australia, the first event being conducted at West Lakes in SA. Since their introduction in Australia, triathlons have developed from an 'anything-goes-just-as-long-as-you-finish' situation to a highly organised and well-controlled sporting event. The distances vary greatly, with some events catering mainly for beginners, others for the serious athlete. The calendar of events is very full during the season, November to March. Most competitions are sanctioned by the controlling State association which is affiliated with the national organisation, the Triathlon Federation of Australia. These associations were formed to ensure that the rules are administered at events and that these are conducted in a professional and safe manner.

At present Australians rate highly in world rankings, consistently finishing in top placings in world championships and in the Hawaiian Ironman each year. In the 1990 world championships held in Orlando, Florida, Australians Greg Welch, Brad Beven, and Stephen Forster finished first, second, and third in the men's individual events, and Australia won the junior men's and junior women's teams competitions. There are about five thousand registered members of associations in Australia with about twenty thousand participants in the sport.

BJ

See **WELCH, GREG**.

TRICKETT, EDWARD (1851–1916), born Sydney, was a professional sculler. After winning the Australian sculling championship in 1875, Trickett travelled to London, and on 27 June 1876 earned his special place in sporting history by becoming the first Australian to win a world title in any sport. Sydney's delirious welcome to him on his return was marked by the presentation of a publicly subscribed purse of £850. Trickett successfully defended his world title twice but lost it in 1880 to the Canadian Ned Hanlan. He rowed a few more races as Australian champion, but never again reached the heights of 1876–79.

SB

See **Rowing and Sculling**.

Trugo

Trugo is a little-known, uniquely Australian sport which evolved from a lunch-time game played by workers at Melbourne's Newport Railway Yards in the 1920s. It is still played almost exclusively in Melbourne and its geographic spread is limited to a handful of origi-

nally working-class inner suburbs. Under the constitution and rules of the Victorian Trugo Association, players must be aged 60 years and over or qualify as bona fide pensioners. It is played by both men and women. There is some dispute about the origin of the name. One version holds that it is derived from an early player exclaiming his hit to be a 'true go', meaning a straight shot through the goals. Others say it derives from the initials 'TG', those of Tom Greaves, one of the earliest exponents of the game at the Newport Railway Yards and the acknowledged 'father' of trugo.

The game is akin to a cross between croquet and lawn bowls. It is played on 30 metre lawn courts, in individual contests or by teams of up to eight players hitting small rubber disks (or 'wheels') down the court with wooden mallets, aiming at goal-posts set at opposite ends of the court. The rubber rings—11 centimetres in diameter, 4 centimetres thick, with a hole in the centre—were originally the discarded buffer washers from railway carriages, although they are now specially manufactured for the game. The first organised game is believed to have been played at Yarraville in 1925. The first club was formed soon after at Yarraville with financial support from local business houses. By the 1930s clubs were formed in the inner suburbs of Newport, South Melbourne, and Port Melbourne, and also at Preston. Clubs were later established at Ascot Vale, Coburg, Prahran, and Brunswick. By the mid-1980s the Victorian Trugo Association comprised twelve clubs and three hundred regular competitors. Interclub competition matches are played from August to April, while intraclub games are played throughout the year. Male players conventionally hit the rings in a backwards between-the-legs movement known as 'tunnelling'. Female players more often address the rings side-on, in a similar fashion to croquet. This is referred to as 'side-swiping'. The wooden mallets are individually weighted for each player. Women's matches are played on a shorter 21 metre pitch.

JS

TRUMBLE, HUGH (1867–1938), born Melbourne, was considered the greatest spin bowler of the so-called golden age of Australian cricket. His solemn, scholarly appearance was reflected in his approach to his sport. English Test player and writer C. B. Fry believed Trumble to be 'the most observant and acute judge of the game, a perfect master of the whole art'. The tall, angular, orthodox off-break bowler took a hat-trick in 1901–2 and again in 1903–4, both times against England at the MCG. Trumble took 141 wickets at 21.78 in thirty-two Tests, and took 5 wickets or more sixty-nine times in his first-class career. He captained Australia twice during the 1901–2 season. Trumble became secretary of the MCC in 1911 and served in that position for twenty-seven years until his death.

DM

See **Cricket**.

TRUMPER, VICTOR THOMAS (1877–1915) was the crown prince of cricket's golden age and possibly the most dashing batsman of all time. Trumper's birthplace is unknown as no birth certificate exists. He played with distinction at Crown Street School and was the first to score 1000 runs in Sydney grade cricket, in 1897–98. By hitting 292 not out against Tasmania in 1898 he became the first to make 100 runs before lunch in a first-class match in Australia. On his first tour of England in 1899 he hit a match-winning innings of 135 not out at Lord's in his second Test and became the first Australian to score a triple century in England, making 300 not out against Sussex. In 1902 the English saw him achieve cricketing immortality, hitting eleven centuries in one of the wettest summers. He made 2570 runs at an average of 48.49. During the Manchester Test Trumper became the first cricketer to score a century before lunch on the first day of a Test. Trumper hit a memorable 185 not out at Sydney during the 1903–4 series. He did not maintain the majesty of 1902 on the 1905 and 1909 English tours but crowds continued to turn up to see him bat. His genius resurfaced in 1910–11 when he amassed 661 runs at an average of 94.43 against the South Africans. Statistics do not convey the audacity and inventiveness of Trumper. Johnny Moyes wrote that 'he opened the windows of the mind to a new vision of what batting could be . . . He was the originating genius of a new outlook in batsmanship.'

PS

See **Cricket**.

Tulloch (1954–69), by *Khorassan* out of *Florida*, was one of the greatest Australian thoroughbred racehorses. He won thirty-six races and was only once unplaced in fifty-three starts. Bred at Trelawney Stud in NZ, the bay colt was sold cheaply as a yearling to Sydney trainer Tommy Smith who subsequently sold him to A. E. Haley. *Tulloch* performed well enough as a 2-year-old, but as a 3-year-old was almost unbeatable: his fourteen victories included the AJC Derby in race-record time, the Caulfield Cup (where he set an Australian record), the Victoria Derby, and the Queensland Derby. Yielding to public concern, he was withdrawn from the Melbourne Cup where he had been heavily handicapped. After the autumn of 1958, *Tulloch* contracted a severe virus and did not resume his racing career until March 1960. To the delight of the large Flemington crowd, he won the Queen's Plate. He won his remaining four races that autumn, and was again in peak form in the spring, winning the W. S. Cox Plate in Australian-record time. After his seventh place in the 1960 Melbourne Cup carrying 10 stone 1 pound to *Hi Jinx*, his jockey, Neville Sellwood, was condemned for allowing him too long at the tail of the field. In his final season, autumn 1961, he won several races and was second in the Sydney Cup. His farewell was before an ecstatic crowd at Eagle Farm where he won the Brisbane Cup. Retired to stud, *Tulloch* was regarded a failure, though one daughter, *Valide*, won the SA Oaks.

AL

TURNER, CHARLES THOMAS BIASS ('Terror') (1862–1944), born Bathurst, NSW, was a bowler who took 101 wickets at 16.53 in seventeen Tests against England between 1886 and 1895, including 5 or more wickets in an innings eleven times. Of medium height, Turner bowled with a front-on action at a lively medium pace, combining meticulous accuracy on good wickets with a full repertoire of sharply lifting off-breaks, leg-cutters, and top spinners when the pitch was helpful. He took 678 wickets on three tours to England, forming a deadly combination with the left-arm spinner J. J. Ferris in 1888 and 1890. Turner's haul of 106 wickets in the 1887–88 Australian season has never been surpassed. Turner was Spofforth's successor as Australia's strike bowler. His nickname, 'Terror', evokes the effect he had on a generation of batsmen.

WF

TURNER, LESLEY (1942–), born Sydney, was a member of a well-known tennis family. She later married Bill Bowrey who won the Australian Open in 1968. The Australian open title eluded Turner although in 1964 and 1967 she was runner-up. Her game was stylish and sound including an accurate serve and neat volley. She eventually won thirteen Grand Slam events including two French singles titles. The second, in 1965, thwarted Margaret Court's Grand Slam. In partnership with Court she won the 1964 Wimbledon doubles. When Australia's inaugural Federation Cup team was chosen in 1963 Lesley Turner was a member.

HCJP

U

Underarm Bowling Incident. On 1 February 1981 Australia played NZ in the third final of the Benson & Hedges World Series Cup at the MCG. Australia scored 235, and with the last ball to be bowled, NZ required a six to win the match. In an excess of caution, the Australian captain, Greg Chappell, instructed his brother Trevor to bowl an underarm 'grubber' to the NZ number ten batsman, Brian McKechnie. McKechnie made no attempt at the impossible task of scoring a six, and then threw his bat towards mid-wicket in justifiable pique. The incident caused a furore and soured relations between the two countries. Subsequently, the rules of the competition were changed to proscribe underarm bowling.

JNT

Unionism

When the players of professional team-sports mix together socially after games, or on tour, their conversations will sometimes turn to issues associated with the terms and conditions of employment. They will discuss such things as pay and remuneration, injuries, medical benefits, insurance, and the various labour-market rules which leagues and clubs have instituted to control and regulate their employment. Most sports have made use of systems of maximum wages to restrict the earnings of players. In addition, zoning and transfer systems have often bound players to a particular club during their playing life so that they cannot move to another club without the permission of their 'owning' club, which of course restricts their economic freedom. During these conversations someone might suggest that they should form a union or players' association to improve their lot. In trying to both attract potential members and develop a bargaining relationship with leagues and clubs, players have generally preferred to use the term 'association' rather than 'union' to avoid the impression of being militant or confrontational.

It is one thing to talk about forming a players' association or union, and another to possess the organisational verve to bring such a body into being. Over the years different generations of soccer-players have spoken about the need to form an association, but so far Australian soccer is unique in having had no experience of a players' association. VFL players have periodically expressed a desire to unionise, for example, in 1913, 1931, and 1944. In 1952–53 rugby league's Kangaroos discussed the possibility of forming a union to defend and advance the rights and interests of rugby league players.

The first two attempts to unionise players occurred in Australian rules football in the Victorian competitions, over forty years apart. In 1914 a Victorian Footballers' Council was formed to provide members with retirement, accident, and illness benefits, but it collapsed with the advent of war. In 1955 former St Kilda player Tom McNeil sought to organise VFL and VFA players into the Australian Football Players' Union after an overseas trip where he had come into contact with a number of European soccer-players' unions. The union managed to attract only 178 adherents, or 20 per cent of the potential membership, and had difficulties getting recognition from both the VFL and the VFA. It folded in early 1956 after an unsuccessful attempt to obtain registration as a trade union under the (Commonwealth) Conciliation and Arbitration Act.

The 1970s saw many attempts at creating players' associations, in six different sporting competitions. The cause of this proliferation was the increased professionalisation of sport in the 1970s, and the associated demands and pressures placed on players. At the end of 1973 Essendon player Geoff Pryor started moves to form the VFL Players' Association, which in 1989 changed its name to the AFL Players' Association. Since its formation the association has represented 60–70 per cent of footballers, having had problems recruiting members from the North Melbourne, Geelong, Richmond, and Brisbane Bears clubs. At various times it has flirted with the idea of affiliating with the Australian Council of Trade Unions (ACTU) or seeking registration as a trade union. The association has been recognised by the AFL and negotiates with them over the employment of footballers. At the beginning of the 1981 season the threat of strike action was used to dissuade the VFL from withdrawing recognition of the association. There was also threatened strike action in 1990 following difficulties in negotiating changes to standard player contracts. Since the early 1980s the affairs of the association have been guided by the executive director, Peter Allen.

In 1974 South Adelaide captain Bob Keddie tried to form a players' association among players of the SA National Football League. A former Hawthorn player, he had links with the

VFL Players' Association. Despite some initial enthusiasm, his attempt was unsuccessful. Western Australian Ian Miller played with Fitzroy in the VFL in the late 1970s and was a member of the VFL Players' Association. After returning to the West he formed the WA Football League Players' Association in 1979. It did not have many problems in enrolling players as members but it did find it difficult to develop a bargaining relationship with the WA Football League and to secure concessions from them. The association collapsed with the entry of the West Coast Eagles into the VFL at the end of 1986. In 1990 there was an attempt to revive the WA Football League Players' Association under the leadership of East Perth player Glenn Bartlett, who had been a trade union official with the Federated Clerks' Union.

In the early and mid-1970s Australia's leading cricketers believed that they were inadequately compensated for the time they devoted to cricket, and that the Australian Cricket Board (ACB) did not take account of their needs and interests when making decisions. Under the leadership of Ian Chappell, the players felt that their position would be enhanced by forming a players' association. During the mid-1970s they had discussions with Bob Hawke, president of the ACTU. With the advent of World Series Cricket in 1977 the players formed the Professional Cricketers Association of Australia. Kerry Packer provided a $10 000 loan to help it become established. In early 1979 the Cricketers Association was registered under the NSW Companies Act. After the 1979 agreement between Packer and the ACB, the Cricketers Association sought to expand its membership to ACB players. Membership exceeded sixty, or about 75 per cent of regular first-class cricketers. The association was constrained mainly by the problem of having a small membership, evenly distributed across six States, in a continent as large as Australia. In addition, the ACB's use of a player representation system in a cricket subcommittee, and the appointment of a co-ordinator to act as an intermediary between the ACB and players, frustrated the association's attempts to be recognised by the ACB. The Cricketers Association was moribund by 1982 and was officially wound up in 1988.

At the tail-end of the 1978 season the idea of a players' union in the Brisbane rugby league competition was mooted but no such body was formed. In NSW, however, there were developments. During 1974 there had been talk of forming a players' association in the NSW Rugby League, on similar lines to the VFL Players' Association. John McQuaid of the Australian Theatrical and Amusement Employees' Association argued that players would benefit from being covered by an award of an industrial tribunal. But it was not until 1979

that a players' association emerged, when a group of players, former players, coaches, and professionals (accountants, lawyers etc.) formed the Association of Rugby League Professionals. With the election of coach Jack Gibson as president in 1980, the association grew and developed. It was registered under the NSW Trade Union Act in 1980, and the Industrial Arbitration Act in 1984. It has generally enjoyed high membership levels, in 1990, for example, having 873 members, or 96 per cent of players. Notwithstanding some initial problems, it has gained recognition from the NSW Rugby League; it has been involved in negotiations over a wide range of issues, and has gained representation rights on various committees operated by the league. In 1989 and 1990 relationships soured over the Rugby League's proposal to introduce a draft system to allocate players between clubs. Disquiet among players resulted in a change of leadership, with Kevin Ryan replacing John Adam as president and the start of proceedings to challenge the legality of the draft before the Federal Court of Australia. In 1989 players in the National Basketball League formed the Basketball Players' Association of Australia. Led by players Larry Sengstock, Damian Keogh, Wayne Carroll, and Phil Smyth, this has achieved a 70 per cent membership coverage (approximately one hundred and twenty members) and has had positive responses on recognition from the National Basketball League.

Player associations meet a number of problems in developing themselves as organisations and acquiring the wherewithal to pursue their various goals. Of the nine attempts to form player associations or unions only three have survived: the Australian Football League Players' Association, the Association of Rugby League Professionals, and the embryonic Basketball Players' Association of Australia. They are plagued by a number of serious problems. First, their members have a short playing life: only a very small number of highly skilled players last ten years or more, and/or are still playing in their thirties. The constant turnover of members means problems in continuity and in costs associated with educating new members in the association's needs or rationale. Second, membership is small, in some cases very small: the maximum membership for the Association of Rugby League Professionals is 912 (16 teams by a 57-player roster), 780 for the AFL Players' Association (15 by 52), and 168 for the Basketball Players' Association of Australia (14 by 12). The Professional Cricketers Association of Australia had a maximum membership of 67. Third, all player associations had, or have, low membership subscriptions. The WA Football League Players' Association initially had a membership fee of $10 for senior players (less for juniors), which it later increased to $12. The cricketers set their membership fee at $25, the basketball players $20, the rugby league players $20, and in 1990 Australian rules footballers set membership subscriptions at $75. The associations have attempted to supplement their income by sponsorships or product endorsements, and have also negotiated deals to enable members to receive services free of charge or at a discount. Fourth, low membership and low subscription levels translate into low incomes which reduce the ability of player associations to provide services for members and defend and advance their rights and interests. Fifth, because of low income, player associations have experienced leadership problems. They have not generated enough revenue to employ staff who would devote all their time and energies to the needs of players and their associations. Players have either performed these functions themselves on top of their commitments as players, or they have relied on former players and/or others to do honorary work. For example, John Adam and Kevin Ryan, both former rugby league players, have looked after the affairs of the Association of Rugby League Professionals in addition to working in busy legal practices.

Player associations have two main activities: they provide services and advice to members, for example on medical and financial matters; and they negotiate with their respective leagues on the provisions contained in standard player contracts and/or the terms and conditions which govern the employment of members. They have tended to react to events, rather than initiate action. In doing so, however, those associations which have survived and had some longevity have forced their respective leagues and clubs to pay greater attention to the needs and interests of players.

BD

See **CHAPPELL Family**; COVENTRY, SYD-NEY; **Strikes and Industrial Disputes**.

V

VAN PRAAG, LIONEL (1908–87), born Sydney, was the first winner of the World Speedway Championship at Wembley, London, in 1936 and was one of the toughest characters in the sport, surviving multiple crashes and injuries. He began racing at Sydney's Wentworth Park speedway and by 20 was SA champion and world speed record-holder for 400 metres. Signed up for Wembley in 1931, he was an immediate success. He regularly represented Australia in Test matches and also promoted the sport at the Sydney Sportsground in the late 1940s. He was a renowned aviator, flew for the RAAF in the Second World War, and won the George Medal for gallantry. His son Barry took up speedway in the 1960s but an accident in 1973 left him a quadriplegic. Van Praag died in Brisbane on 19 May 1987.

PW*

Veterans

Although recent years have seen a boom in veterans sport in Australia, sporting activity among the older age groups is nothing new. Many people have been active in sport continuously from youth to old age. Certain sports such as bowls and golf have always been associated with older people, particularly men, and have provided regular activity for this age group. Veterans have continued to play cricket, particularly in lower grades, into their sixties and football too has had its devotees active until their fifties. In athletics, distance runners have graduated from the mile race to the 3 and 6 mile runs as they aged and then to the marathon. Tennis has always had players across the whole age spectrum.

In the post–Second World War era there has been an explosion in knowledge of the physiology of ageing. This has led to greater interest in the older population and its performance criteria and as a result a singling out of this group for competitive purposes. This happened particularly in athletics and swimming where times can be measured. One result was the development of veterans athletics in all States, with local and national championships. At international meetings older Australian athletes have performed well and have broken world records in winning their events, the runner George McGrath, for one, being a regular record-breaker at successive games in 5000 and 10 000 metres events. Masters swimming associations have attracted many former Olympians and have provided an impetus for the winter 'iceberg' clubs to train and improve their performance.

Other sports have also initiated their veterans sections. Veterans tennis, for example, has developed in keeping with world movements. The objects of the Veterans' Lawn Tennis Club of Australia, founded in 1970, were to encourage those who had reached the age of 45 to continue playing tennis in 'the spirit in which it was first played—for the love and enjoyment of the game'. Another aim was to promote veterans competitions at State, national, and eventually international level. A schedule of tournaments was organised and a ranking system developed. Later, the age limit was lowered to 40 years of age. International team matches in varying age divisions are now held annually. In the most recent series Australia won the men's singles over 55 and 65, and the men's doubles over 45, 60, and 65 and the women's doubles over 50. In the individual trophy Bob McCarthy has maintained his singles dominance in his age group for the last six years. Veterans rowing is growing and national and local regattas are held, though, to date, world titles have eluded our oarsmen. Bodybuilding is attractive to some mature-aged males wishing to tone up their bodies. There have been national and State titles and these are being attended by increasing numbers. Water skiing, both barefoot and on skis, caters for veterans, with a special division for those over 40. The 'Golden Oldies' has provided for the older person to play rugby union at a competitive international level with the rules modified to allow for age. Seniors golf is booming, with international, national and State tournaments, at which Bruce Crampton and Kel Nagle have been outstanding. Veteran cyclists compete regularly in State and national events. In several sports, including archery, angling, tenpin bowling, motor-boat racing, and shooting, veteran performers participate against younger competitors. Equestrian events too attract all ages, with older competitors filling many first places. Sailing also is for all ages and an Olympic gold medal was won by veteran Bill Northam at Tokyo. Snooker produced Eddie Charlton in the champion ranks at a mature age.

The recent explosion in participation in physical activity by veterans has led to more interest being taken in training along correct lines. The result has been a greater number of people increasing their enjoyment of life and gaining in physical fitness, which improves their chances of avoiding heart disease and the diseases of inactivity. Better control of blood pressure also reduces the need for medication. Unfortunately the most recent 'Golden Oldies' rugby union tournament resulted in some fatalities, thus emphasising the need for proper preparation for all mature-aged athletes who wish to take part in strenuous activity: age will not necessarily reduce the intensity of competition.

The greatest benefit from veterans sport has been the realisation that life does not end at 40. With regular training and appropriate competition, sport can be fun throughout life and this idea has broadened the outlook of many mature-aged people. The psychological and health benefits of such activity might well permeate the whole community to the benefit of all.

APM

See **Masters Games**.

VFL Grand Final 1946. Essendon spectacularly defeated Melbourne 22 goals 18 behinds to 11 goals 9 behinds due mainly to a scoring spree in the third quarter. Early in the game 'the Dons' quickly found themselves 5 goals down but by the end of the first quarter had fought to within 7 points of Melbourne. In the second term the teams produced an enthralling contest as 'the Demons' battled to a lead of 3 points. The third term surprised everyone as Essendon added goal after goal to establish an amazing total of 11 goals 8 behinds for the quarter, still an unequalled finals record. The Dons then held on to their 10-goal lead for the 1946 flag.

GC*

VFL Park, Waverley, was born out of the commercial expansion of Victorian football in the 1960s. Throughout a controversial history it has struggled for full acceptance from governments and the community. As commercial considerations increased in importance for the VFL, so too did its frustration with the financial arrangements for the lucrative finals matches played at the MCG. In 1962 the VFL bought 212 acres of land for a stadium of its own, twenty-five kilometres south-east of Melbourne. VFL Park, however, lacked the MCG's centrality and proximity to public transport. Its open stand design was also criticised for affording less atmosphere than the MCG; as well, its spectator capacity was limited to 76 000 by the Victorian Health Department, whereas the MCG could comfortably accommodate over ninety thousand. The VFL always intended eventually to stage the Grand Final, one of Victoria's premier sporting events, at VFL Park. Their announcement that the 1984 Grand Final would be played at Waverley triggered extensive debate, but the Cain Labor Government intervened to ensure that the game remained at the MCG in line with popular opinion. Ironically, VFL officials were forced to find other uses for their specialist football stadium to service loans and help dispel the public perception of the venue as a white elephant. One of these activities was World Series Cricket, in itself of great historical significance to cricket's development, including the first night-cricket match in 1978. More recently, the AFL has tentatively looked to establish a 'home' club at the ground. The building of VFL Park eventually proved to be a successful means for the VFL to secure greater financial returns from its lucrative finals matches. This outcome reflects poorly on VFL–government relations, however, in that the VFL was only able to achieve its aims in a most confrontational and expensive manner.

DS

Victorian Amateur Football Association (VAFA) celebrates its centenary in 1992. Despite being an 'amateur' body, a feature of the VAFA's growth has been a professionalism which has allowed it to prosper when other competitions have foundered. L. A. Adamson, a vigorous proponent of 'Muscular Christianity' and the VAFA's second president, gave it many of its initial ideals, especially the notion of the 'purity' of amateur sport. Some early teams were associated with VFL clubs but most clubs now represent either suburban districts or the players' previous schools. Milestones in its development were the establishment of a weekly *Record*, representative matches, under-age sections, media involvement, long-term occupation of Elsternwick Park as the VAFA's playing and administrative centre, marketing and sponsorship activities, banning of alcohol at matches to attract family involvement, and the appointment of a full-time general manager. Relegation and promotion of teams from the seventeen sections has been a major feature of the amateur competition, along with umpires' disciplinary power to 'order off' players. Defining and monitoring amateur status has probably been the VAFA's most difficult continuing issue. The VAFA's long-term well-being now seems assured, and over ten thousand players are registered. Almost inadvertently, amateurism provided benefits greater than assuring the code's 'purity', by enhancing VAFA clubs' financial viability.

DS

See **Amateurism**; **St Bernard's Disqualification**.

Vigoro

Vigoro was introduced into Australia by an Englishman, John George Grant, who gave a demonstration of the sport at the Carlton Cricket Ground about 1908. His efforts to promote the game were not successful, and Grant returned to England for ten years, after which he once again attempted to bring the game to Australia. This time, he found a receptive audience in Sydney among girls leaving school, and in 1919 the first vigoro association was formed in NSW. The game's rules and equipment are copyright, which on Grant's death passed to Mrs R. E. Dodge, first president of the vigoro association; on her death in 1973 the copyright passed to her daughter. Vigoro is similar to cricket in having stumps, but the bats are shaped like canoe paddles and there are twelve not eleven players in each team. Two bowlers bowl alternately from the same end using different-coloured balls. If the batter hits the ball outside the crease then a run must be attempted. It is thus a much faster game than cricket. It is played in the summer in Tasmania, Queensland, and NSW (where it is also a winter game). The All Australian Association was formed in 1932, and the game remains solely under the control of women. Vigoro is strongest in north Queensland, where it is played in primary schools, and this is reflected in the State's domination of the interstate junior (under-18) team championship, the Dodge Junior Cup, and, since 1980, real success at the interstate grade one team level. The All Australian tournament now has a veterans competition.

KM*

See **Cricko**.

Violence by Players

On-field violence, between participants as distinct from between spectators, has been a feature of many Australian sports throughout their organised history. A nineteenth-century commentator wrote: 'Football in Victoria is no child's play, and some of its votaries would undoubtedly take high honours at Donnybrook in a free fight, to judge from the combative qualities displayed when only a Rugby ball is the subject of dispute.' The rules of several sports appear to permit actions which in other contexts would be considered assault upon the person, so it is not surprising that incidents in contact sports in particular sometimes spill over into violent conflict between players. Violence is not restricted to these sports and some of the apparently more sedate non-contact pursuits, including cricket and tennis, have had well-reported clashes between contestants. Most matches, even in contact sports, end without incidents being reported in the media, or indeed without incidents which result in the attention of the disciplinary bodies of the various codes. Some of the spectacular exceptions in recent years, such as the prolonged brawl in the 1990 AFL Grand Final between Collingwood and Essendon, or the encounter between Dennis Lillee and Javed Miandad in a Test match in November 1981 between Australia and Pakistan, involve more ritual posturing than actual

physical injury. Other incidents have resulted in injury and legal intervention, by the police or by injured parties. The Leigh Matthews–Neville Bruns fracas in Australian rules in 1985 and the Darryl Brohmann case in rugby league in 1983 were widely publicised, with the police taking action in the former, following strong media pressure, and the injured party suing in the latter and eventually receiving an out-of-court settlement, reputed to have cost the other party $200 000. These cases did not set major legal precedents and indeed cases of manslaughter against sportsmen held responsible for the death of fellow players date back at least to 1878 in British law, which continues to set the framework in which many Australian decisions are taken.

Though there are no convincing statistics to prove the matter, it appears that levels of physical violence in sport have declined. Most football codes have outlawed violent forms of tackling or bodily contact, such as the spear tackle in rugby league, raking a player off the ball with studs or stamping in rugby union, shirt-fronting in Australian rules, and tackling from behind in soccer. Early sports reports carried accounts of death or serious injury resulting from violent on-field incidents, and while media coverage of the major sports has expanded and the numbers involved have grown, it would appear that such reported incidents have become rarer. There has been some speculation that the periods immediately following the two world wars saw an increase in on-field and off-field violence in Australian rules football, but no indication whether this was typical of all sports or even any convincing evidence that it was true of football. The bloody Grand Final of 1945 between Carlton and South Melbourne, said to be the roughest game of Australian rules football ever played, has achieved legendary status, but can hardly be regarded as the norm for that era.

Since it appears that many contact sports have speeded up, partly as participants have become fitter and partly because of media and spectator demands, the occasions for violent collisions between players has probably increased, yet there is little evidence to support a widespread popular belief that levels of on-field violence in sport have risen recently. In those sports which do maintain information on reported incidents, the record is ambiguous, with some indications of a decline in the rate of incidents per player, even if sometimes there is an increase in the absolute number of such incidents. Even here it is difficult to make categorical statements, since closer analysis of reported incidents shows that many are for technical breaches of the laws of the game rather than physical violence directed towards opponents or officials. On the other hand, in many sports it is quite clear that many incidents pass unreported by officials and media, even though they involve on-field violence.

Comparisons of on-field violence between Australia and other countries are made difficult by the lack of relevant statistical data. In soccer, at National League level, the numbers of cautions and sendings-off in Australia tend to be lower than in say, Scotland, but once again it is difficult to say how many of these offences relate to violent conduct and how many to technical breaches of the rules or dissent. Similar problems occur in trying to compare rates of violence between sports, though a start has been made in research in this area, involving both quantitative data and the analysis in depth of particular incidents. Changes in rules, or the stringency with which they are applied, often in response to outside stimuli, play havoc with comparative data. Often what one sees is changes in reporting and enforcement procedures rather than changes in the level of the offences or violence of which they are taken to be a measure.

Not all examples of on-field violence are confined to the players. Attacks on officials are relatively rare and usually subject to severe punishment, with lifetime playing bans often being imposed. Badgering and abuse of officials is much more common, as is verbal violence towards other players—'sledging'—in many sports. There are reported incidents of officials attacking players in junior and country sport, though this happens rarely at higher levels where trained officials are more likely to be in control.

It is a nice question whether action which causes injury within the rules of the game should be considered violent or not. If a player suffers a broken leg in the course of a legitimate tackle is that more or less violent than a punch thrown in defiance of the code of the game, but which does not result in lasting physical injury? There is a well-known legal shibboleth that 'no rules or practice of any game whatever can make that lawful which is unlawful by the law of the land', but much turns on the context in which this statement is applied. It is widely accepted that participation in sport involves acceptance of the risk of injury within the laws of each particular game, but the notion that an injury sustained as a result of a breach of the law may result in civil action is still resisted by many involved in Australian sport.

Connections between violence on and off the field have been discussed in academic and media circles for many years with few firm conclusions. There is little support now among psychologists for the notion that witnessing on-field violence acts cathartically to release tensions in the spectators. There have been occasions when those within, or associated with, particular sports have encouraged or condoned on-field violence as a means of attracting crowd or television audience support, though there is countervailing evidence that some sports have seen an increase in support as they have (and been promoted as having) overcome problems associated with on- and off-field violence.

Male codes of aggression and courage help to explain the continuance of violence associated with sport in Australia, as they do elsewhere, but female sports, such as netball and hockey, also report concerns with on-field violence. Imitations of male stereotypes cannot be wholly responsible. Changes in social attitudes to violence have brought to the fore many elements of sport which were previously accepted or ignored by those engaged in the various games. It is likely that in future sports will come under even closer scrutiny in terms of their attitudes to violence on the field of play, with the claim to a special status beyond the law being further challenged.

RH†

See **Gender**; **Law**.

Volleyball

The beginnings of volleyball in Australia can be traced to the 1920s although at this stage it was not regarded as a competitive sport but one rather more along the lines originally intended by its American inventor in the 1890s, William Morgan, who considered it to be an entertaining recreational activity. It is probable that volleyball was introduced into Australia during the First World War by servicemen who had learned the game through contacts with their American counterparts in Europe. The influx of immigrants from European countries after the Second World War, particularly the Baltic states of Lithuania, Latvia, and Estonia, gave added impetus to the sport and in the 1950s volleyball associations were formed in Sydney, Melbourne, and Adelaide.

In the early 1960s Eddie Engels from Sydney introduced the idea of a national competition and a national sporting body to those administering competitions in Sydney, Melbourne, and Adelaide. As a result the first National Cup was played at Melbourne's Albert Park Centre in 1962. Men's teams from Adelaide, Sydney, and Melbourne took part and the Victorian team was the first to win the 'Australian' championship. In 1963 the first national volleyball body was founded in Adelaide. Three State representatives—Graham Cox from Victoria, Wally Lebedew from SA, and Guido Lacis from NSW—came together to promote volleyball nationally and founded the Australian Volleyball Federation (AVF). From that date it was decided that championships would be held annually with State capitals hosting the competition in rotation. Women took part in the volleyball championships for the first time in 1965 when Melbourne again hosted the Cup. The SA team emerged as a major force in women's volleyball, winning not only the first premiership, but also another eleven titles in the ensuing fourteen years.

The 1970s saw both expansion and structural changes in volleyball. All States joined the AVF by the end of the decade (the NT affiliated in 1983); age grouping became necessary with the introduction of the Australian Junior Championships (under-20 State teams) in 1976. This decade also witnessed the granting of financial assistance to administrators and players. By the early 1970s a new generation of volleyball-players had emerged. Children of 'new Australians' who had played with their parents in clubs now played in junior competition. The young people's interest in and enthusiasm for volleyball meant that the game became popular in schools. An additional factor influencing the acceptance of volleyball was the change in the educational philosophy of sport and physical education. Teachers searched for non-contact sports, games which not only demanded great skill and intelligence but also developed teamwork and social skills; volleyball met these criteria and rapidly became one of the biggest secondary-school sports across the country.

From 1973 onwards volleyball, together with other sports, entered a new era of government intervention. The incoming Federal Labor Government honoured its election promise to give financial support to sport and awarded the first grant to volleyball. This money was used to stage the initial Oceania Volleyball Championships in Sydney in 1973. Both the Australian senior men's and women's teams won the inaugural championships, beating New Caledonia and Tahiti respectively. Government funding marked the beginning of the professionalisation of volleyball; paid State and national executive directors together with committees of volunteers and honorary members directed and administered the sport from then on. Professional coaches were also attracted from overseas to cater for the demand Australia could not meet at that time. Some grants received from the Federal and State Governments were earmarked for special purposes. For example, Victoria employed the first professional coach, Tomas Santamaria (1978), NSW engaged the first paid executive director, Peter Epov (1979), and the Australian Volleyball Federation hired its first national executive director, John Ostenmeyer, in 1979.

The 1980s saw an expansion of all associations and competitions. The State and national executive directors created the National Volleyball League which existed between 1981 and 1985. Amateur players had to carry the enormous costs of commuting between capital cities.

Eventually the tyranny of distance led to the discontinuation of the national league. Other attempts to expand the competition were much more successful. Many new clubs and associations were formed around Australia, including the Eastern Metropolitan Volleyball Association in Melbourne. From its first annual general meeting in December 1980 it grew from a strength of under thirty teams to over one hundred and fifty teams by 1990. Nationally the AVF manages about six hundred thousand volleyballers across Australia.

The rapid growth and development of volleyball throughout Australia since the 1950s shows that it is no longer solely an ethnic sport. It has increased in both popularity and status. It is played in the city and the country, by men and women, in schools and at social gatherings. It is played at amateur level and as part of the élite players' programme offered by the AIS. It has become so popular that in 1990 the Australian men's team gained admission to the AIS as part of the national élite players' promotion programme. Government grants provide facilities and scholarships to players as well as to coaches to foster top-level competition in volleyball. Australian players and officials are also involved in international volleyball; for example, Eric Hayman has been a member of the Victorian Olympic Council as well as a vice-president of the Asian Volleyball Confederation's Central Zone in which Australia participates.

Two crucial factors in the growth of volleyball have been the high level of interest and enthusiasm shown by players and supporters and the willingness of so many people to volunteer their labour to further the progress of the sport. More recently, government funding and corporate sponsorship have enabled administrators to provide better facilities, offer more professional training and procure administrative support, all of which have assisted the development of the sport.

IF and KB

See **DANSIE, SUE; FOOT, ROBERT; HAYMAN, ERIC; LACIS, GUIDO; LEBEDEW, WALKIRI.**

VON NIDA, NORMAN GUY (1914–), born Sydney, was a colourful golf personality of the late 1940s and 1950s. He won the Australian Open three times, the Australian PGA title four times, and the McWilliams Wines event three times, as well as winning twelve tournaments in Britain. He learned to play golf after moving to Brisbane as a young man. While caddying at Royal Brisbane Golf Course, he picked up many golfing ideas by closely observing the best players. A small, lightly built man with a fondness for black berets, Von Nida was plagued by illness and eventually retired due to a bad back. He was known for his generosity to younger players. He was club professional at Royal Selangor Golf Club, Malaysia, for three years from 1976.

GC*

See **Golf**.

VOUKELATOS, NIKOS (1963–), born Sydney of Greek parents, is a weightlifter who won back-to-back Commonwealth Games gold medals: in Brisbane in 1982 in the 52 kilogram class and then at the 1986 Edinburgh Games in the 56 kilogram class. In 1982 Voukelatos won Australia's first gold medal of the Games and in the process became the youngest-ever Commonwealth Games weightlifting champion. He dominated Commonwealth and Australian weightlifting in 52 and 56 kilogram classes for more than a dozen years.

MN

W

Wakeful (1896–1923), a thoroughbred race-horse and broodmare, was the best of many fine mares bred by William Wilson at St Albans Stud in Geelong. On Wilson's death in 1900 the unraced mare was sold to G. L. McDonald. Under trainer H. Munro, she raced first as a 4-year-old and after two starts in the spring she won three of the most important sprints on the calendar—the Oakleigh Plate, the Newmarket Handicap, and the AJC Doncaster—before running third in the 2 mile Sydney Cup. This versatility remained a feature of her career: at 5 years of age her wins ranged from 1 to 3 miles. She lost the Caulfield Cup by a half-head, and won the Sydney Cup of 1902 carrying a record weight of 9 stone 7 pounds in a race-record time. As a 6-year-old, and restricted chiefly to weight-for-age racing, she won ten top-class races at Randwick, Flemington, and Caulfield. In her final season, as a 7-year-old, she won three races, including the VRC Melbourne Stakes for the third time, but her greatest performance was her last, in defeat, in the 1903 Melbourne Cup. Her little jockey, the young Frank Dunn, carrying saddle bags filled with lead to bring his weight to the allotted 10 stone, had miscalculated and had taken the mare to the front too far from home. *Wakeful* remained in the lead until beaten in the last moments by the lightly weighted *Lord Cardigan*. At stud she produced ten foals, including the Oakleigh Plate and Futurity winner *Blairgour*, and *Night Watch*, who won the 1918 Melbourne Cup.

AL

WALKER, DON (c.1874–?), born Canada, came to Australia in 1879 at the age of 5. By 1899 he had been placed in the top three at the Australian Cycling Championships for twelve years. His greatest season was in 1902 when he was Australian champion and held numerous records. When the American and world sprinting champion, Arthur Zimmerman, came to Australia in the mid-1890s, Walker was one of only three riders to defeat him. 'Major' Taylor, the black American champion, who raced and defeated every significant US and international rider over a fifteen-year career, ranked Don Walker as one of the ten best foreign riders he ever faced. Taylor found it difficult to compare Walker with the Continental riders' styles, but felt that none of the Europeans would have survived those 'tearing, pace-changing races' that Walker rode so brilliantly. Walker occasionally defeated the Major during Taylor's two Australian tours in 1902–4. He accompanied Taylor to the US in 1904, where he rode to mixed success before returning to Australia. He worked for Dunlop, in Melbourne, after retirement.

JF

See **TAYLOR, MARSHALL**.

WALKER, PATRICIA ('Jean') (née DUMBRELL), OAM (1929–), squash administrator, also represented NSW from 1960 to 1966 and Australia in 1964 as a player. As president of the NSW Women's Squash Racquets Association from 1961 to 1963 she fought for changes in selection procedures following the shock omission of Heather McKay. Walker was president of the Australian Women's Squash Rackets Association from 1964 to 1977. During that time she argued that there was nothing inherently wrong in athletes receiving prize-money. Walker also campaigned for an official world title in addition to the British title, then an unofficial world crown. She began negotiations during a 1971 tour, when managing the Australian team. Her proposals were accepted and the first Women's World Squash Championships were held in Brisbane in 1976.

KT

Walla Walla (1922–?) a pacer, was so famous for giving away big starts and making up ground from a seemingly impossible handicap that he was responsible for a popular trotting phrase 'further back than *Walla Walla*'. Unraced until he was 6, when he won at Gunning in 1928, he reached his peak at 9 and recorded fast times into his thirteenth year. In 1933 he ran the mile in 2 minutes 6 seconds from a standing start, breaking the Australian record, and a year later he clocked 2 minutes 4 seconds to create a world record. Despite a handicap of 180 yards he was successful at Harold Park over 12 furlongs. His longest handicap was 288 yards when he finished third at Goulburn in 1929. *Walla Walla* was a natural pacer who often ran without hobbles. He sired 158 winners at stud; *Radiant Walla* and *Wirra Walla* were the most prominent.

GC*

Wallabies 1908–9. In 1908–9 the Australian rugby team toured England and Wales. On board ship, after docking in Plymouth, they decided to assume the title 'Wallabies'. Captained by Dr H. M. Moran, they won twenty-five of their thirty-one matches including the 1908 Olympic title. After losing, controversially, to Wales and two further defeats in Wales, the Wallabies rallied to win the inaugural Test against England 9–3. This victory, Australia's first in a Test, served to vindicate the Wallabies who throughout the tour had received considerable criticism from the British press and English rugby officialdom.

PH

Wander Medal. The best and fairest award in the North West Football Union in Tasmania was inaugurated in 1923 as the Cheel Medal. This award was replaced in 1930 by the Wander Medal, presented by the Wander company. In 1987, with the amalgamation of the North West Football Union and the Northern Tasmanian Football Association, the award was replaced by the Ovaltine Medal. The only triple Wander-medallist was D. Baldock (Latrobe and East Devonport) while dual winners include W. Berryman (Devonport), R. Hickman (Latrobe), J. Jillard (Latrobe), and R. Smith (Penguin and Wynyard).

MH*

War

For peoples of British backgrounds particularly, war was often seen as an imperial adventure, exciting, dashing, and honourable. The qualities esteemed and developed in the English public schools had their place on the battlefield and the schools themselves saw it as their mission to prepare young men to fight. Sport was an important training ground in these schools, both for life and for war. This sense of purpose for games was transferred to Australia and developed. Sport came to dominate the life of the colonies that the 'better classes', even in the better schools, needed a higher justification to explain away their obsession. Sport would teach valuable lessons about loyalty, co-operation, commitment, and perseverance.

When Australians went to war in the nineteenth century they used the language of sport to explain their experience. War would be their test; like the increasingly frequent cricket matches with England, war would show if the British spirit had been successfully transferred to Australia or whether, on the contrary, there had been a deterioration of spirit and character in the harsher and less refined circumstances of the colonies. Australians approached war with some anxiety, aware of the importance of the test and alert for any signs of weakness. This concern to pass the test of war provided a

significant part of the motivation at Gallipoli, and the parallels between sport and war were frequently drawn by the Anzacs. Writing to his parents before the landing, a Victorian expressed a sense of satisfaction that he and his mates would go into action just as the football season was about to start in Melbourne. It pleased him that the two campaigns, both for a flag, would kick off at roughly the same time.

Officers constantly used sporting language to encourage and motivate their men. Sport provided images that soldiers could understand and, if war was a game, then losses could be accepted with some equanimity. The Turk, at first despised as lacking in spirit and a proper attitude, soon proved himself to be a good sport and became popular with the Australians. This part of a wider world war was on such a small scale, so intimate, that the opposing forces could engage in the duels characteristic of sport. Individual snipers delighted in showing their prowess and mastery, and great play was made of the ability to throw and return bombs between the two lines of troops. When the Australians wanted to show just how normal things were at Gallipoli, in the greatest possible conflict with reality, they staged a cricket match on 'Shell Green'. The match was meant to fool the Turks into accepting the permanence of the Anzacs' presence but the 'players' were at their game only for a few minutes at a time before Turkish shells scattered them.

Charles Bean, the Australian official correspondent and later war historian, used sporting imagery in his own writing in the early phases of the First World War. As a British public schoolboy, and a colonial, Bean accepted without hesitation that sport was a metaphor and an exemplar for life. Touring the battlefields in July 1916, shortly after the Australians had gone into action in France, Bean found that the Australians had done well. 'One's heart was lightened,' he wrote, 'as it is when one arrives at a cricket match and finds that your own team has got a real good start on the other side. Clearly we had taken Fricourt.' Bean quickly learned that in France war was not a game. Two mighty armies opposed each other and there was no room for individual duels or the personification of the enemy. Here all was artillery, with ground troops following up. Bean's sporting imagery gave way to a more brutal language, almost purpose-built for war, which tried to make sense of the mind-numbing statistics. When Australians went to war again in 1939, to continue what it seemed had only been interrupted in 1918, it was always with the knowledge of the Anzacs and the horror of the western front before them. War had produced heroic behaviour and Australians had won their place among the best of the world's soldiers, but war could no longer be seen as a game, as an

126 During both World Wars sporting fixtures were restricted, including football in the 1940s.

127 With the slogan 'Enlist in the Sportsmen's 1000', the Victorian Sportsmen's Recruiting Committee relied heavily on the close relationship between sport and war.

The Inaugural
GOLDEN GUM BOOT AWARD
Presented to
CLIFF YOUNG
by
NETWORK 10
June 13 1983
for
REMARKABLE ATHLETIC ACHIEVEMENT

128 Cliff Young helped to popularise ultra-marathon
running when he won the Sydney to Melbourne race in
1983, especially when it was reported that he trained
in gumboots.

adventure, and few later war correspondents would write as naively as Bean had once done. The First World War had altered a nation's understanding of war.

At the same time sport itself had changed, partly under the pressure of war. The notion of sport as a metaphor for life gave place to sport as exercise for some, as business for others. When war had broken out in 1914, those who saw sport as a training for life expected that sportsmen, now that the real test was at hand, would abandon their games so that they and the nation of spectators would not be distracted from the main game. These people called for the abandonment of adult matches, believing that all fit young men would want to volunteer to serve anyway, and proposed calling off schoolboy conflicts to show that the nation was serious in its devotion to war. Others, more normally found in the working classes, who had not seen sport as much more than a diversion from the grind of daily existence, and did not need to dress sport in metaphorical clothes, could see no point in the abandonment of matches, even if there was a war on. There was a bad-tempered debate throughout Australia during the years of the First World War about the continuance of sport. This became even more hysterical as, under the pressure of the conscription campaigns, the nation split into two classes—the 'patriots' and the rest.

While more middle-class sporting associations like those responsible for rugby union, cricket, and tennis simply abandoned all competition, in other sporting bodies the split was more obvious. The VFL, for example, debated the issue throughout 1915, without agreement. In 1916 only the four most obviously working-class clubs—Collingwood, Fitzroy, Richmond, and Carlton—continued in the competition. They played each other three times before each, naturally, won a place in the finals. Some sporting bodies, while they may have passed their self-imposed test of patriotism, never recovered from the collapse of their competition during the war years. The VFA, for one, gave up games in 1915 until the end of the war and never again seriously challenged the VFL for football dominance in Victoria.

By 1939 sport was seen to have less of a nation-building role in the minds of most Australians and there was no great agitation for the abandonment of games. International competition was suspended again, of course, and many who may have represented Australia and come into their years of greatest dominance were forced to abandon their hopes and expectations. Because sportsmen were of an age to enlist, however, and could normally pass the fitness tests, many of them also gave up their domestic careers. In that sense, war was a crueller blow for sportsmen than for others, who might resume their careers, perhaps with improved prospects, at the end of the war. Sportsmen might find that their skills were lost or that their age, after the war, was against them.

In 1939, and for the wars beyond, few spoke of war as a test of national character and few would seek to draw the parallels between sport and war. Increasingly sport was seen as an end in itself, not as a training ground for values and virtues, and war was recognised as an evil with a language all its own. By becoming self-confident in sport and in war, Australia had broken the connection—at best tenuous—between them.

MMcK

See **Nationalism**.

Waratahs Rugby Tour 1927–28. This rugby union team was one of the earliest great touring sides. Named after the emblem of the only State in Australia at the time with an organisational structure for rugby, NSW, it mainly contained players from Sydney-based clubs. The two exceptions were Tom Lawton from Brisbane and Syd Malcolm from Newcastle. Captained by the legendary A. C. 'Johnnie' Wallace, the team played a brand of rugby that has never been forgotten—fast, open, and exciting. The ability to run the ball from any position on the field and in any situation led them to scoring tries that long remained in the memory of those who watched them play. The side played thirty-one matches in the British Isles and France, winning twenty-four, drawing two, and losing only five. Immortal figures in the side included A. C. Wallace, C. Towers, T. Lawton, S. Malcolm, S. King, and J. W. Breckenbridge. This tour had an interesting sidelight almost sixty years later when in 1986 the Australian Rugby Football Union retrospectively granted full Australian Test status to those players who appeared in the five internationals, recognition they so well deserved.

MC

WARBY, KEN, MBE (1939–), became the fastest man on water on 20 November 1977 when his jet-powered hydroplane, *Spirit of Australia*, averaged 464 km/h at Blowering Dam, near Tumut, to eclipse the world record of American Lee Taylor. Less than twelve months later Warby broke his own record when he averaged 511.11 km/h, reaching 529 km/h on the return run. Warby was the first to design, build, and drive his own boat to a world record. He was also the first Australian to hold an unlimited speed record. He was inducted into the Sport Australia Hall of Fame in 1985.

RC

WARILD, ALAN THOMAS (1956–), born Sylvania, NSW, developed a particular interest and skill in ultra-lightweight equipment for exploration of deep caves, thus enabling him to be one of the only people to undertake solo descents of many of the world's deepest caves. He has led many major expeditions, particularly to Mexico.

EH-S

WARREN, JOHN NORMAN, MBE (1943–), born Randwick, Sydney, was Australia's favourite soccer-player. At the age of 5 he played in the Botany Methodist under-12s. At 16 he made his senior debut for Canterbury Marrickville, coached then by Joe Vlasits. In 1963 he joined St George and, apart from a short stint with Stockport County in England (1968–69), stayed with the Saints till his retirement in 1974. Altogether Warren represented Australia sixty times, forty-four of them at full international level. A competitive mid-fielder with splendid ball control, Warren played for Australia from 1965 to 1974, serving as captain from 1967 to 1971. Battling back from a bad knee injury sustained in 1971, he played in the 1974 World Cup finals, eventually making a total of sixty-two national appearances. After retirement Warren coached St George in 1975 and newly formed National Soccer League club Canberra City from 1977 to 1978. In more recent times he has concentrated on business interests associated with soccer, including journalism, marketing, and nation-wide coaching clinics. Warren was awarded the MBE in 1973, and in 1990 the National Soccer League named its Player of the Year award after him, in recognition of his services to Australian soccer.

GC, MH* and PM

Warrnambool Grand Annual Steeplechase is the longest horse race in Australia. It was first run in 1872 but not given its current name until 1895. The 5500 metres steeplechase with its thirty-three fences is a gruelling test of jumping and staying ability as well as courage of both horse and rider. In 1909 and 1934, all ten starters either fell or balked. Only two started in 1892 and the sixteen in 1949 and 1953 were the largest fields. Horses run right-handed for most of the chase and finish the left-handed way. They leave the course proper to race twice through Brierly and Granters Paddocks and jump three road-doubles. The last double, Tozer Road, evokes the history of the sport, the course, and the club. Francis Tozer raced horses at the first meeting in Warrnambool held in 1848 and was one of the founders of the Warrnambool Racing Club in 1868. This aptly named race has a stature which far exceeds its $57 500 prize-money.

WAE

Water Polo
Following closely behind the establishment of competitive swimming, the first water polo game in Australia is reported to have been played in Sydney in the late 1880s. NSW and Victoria began competing for the Regal Cup in 1922–23, and the open men's championship for State teams was inaugurated in 1948 with Victoria, Queensland, and NSW involved; in 1964 all six States participated for the first time. National championship open competition for women began in 1975, and in 1986 the Australian team became the first official women's world champions. The sport's record for longevity is held by Peter Montgomery of NSW who competed at four Olympic Games (1972–84). Prominent players Roger Cornforth and Dick Thornett also represented Australia at rugby union, with Thornett additionally playing rugby league at international level.

KM*

See **THORNETT, RICHARD**.

Water Skiing
Hen and Chicken Bay on Sydney Harbour was the location in 1934 for Ted Parker of Earlwood to become the first Australian to successfully ski on water. Parker wore skis modelled on photographs in the American magazine *Popular Mechanics* and was towed by a 3-point hydroplane with a 22-horsepower Johnson outboard motor. It is estimated that more than a million Australians have water-skied at some time in their lives and more than sixteen thousand are involved in competitive water skiing in its different varieties. Water skiing progressed slowly after that auspicious day in 1934 due mainly to the lingering effects of the Depression and the war. Fuel was rationed and its use was for essential services only; it also became difficult to obtain basic materials to build leisure craft. Once rationing of essential commodities was relaxed there was a strong demand for recreational boats; an added feature was that the Department of Defence was disposing of surplus military hardware of all kinds, including Ford and Chrysler engines which, with some marine modifications, could be used as excellent speedboat motors for the cost of as little as £5 at auction for a brand-new Ford V8 still in its crate.

It is generally agreed that water skiing began as a sport in Australia with Sydney photographer Reg Johnson inviting his friends and associates for skiing parties on the Hawkesbury River. Competition water skiing started on Lake Parramatta in 1951 and the first Australian championship was held in Penrith in 1952. The Australian Water Ski Association (AWSA) was formed in NSW in 1951 with Bill McLaughin, an early enthusiast and instigator of the first competition water skiing event, as president. When skiers from other States came to the first Australian Water Ski Championships it was decided that each State would form its own association to promote and assist the sport; the next year the Australian Water Ski Association split from the NSW association. Following AWSA's formation in 1953, Australians took part in the international championship held in Toronto, Canada, and Australia has competed at every world championship since 1957.

In those early years competitions were for tournament skiing only as the World Water Ski Union (WWSU) recognised only trick, jump, and slalom as legitimate water skiing. However, by 1969 barefoot skiing and ski racing had been accepted by AWSA and prompted by Australia's example the WWSU added competition barefoot skiing in 1972 and ski racing in 1978. The first Australian to have skied barefoot was Doug Leversha who amazed spectators with this feat in 1955. Barefooting became organised formally in March 1960 with the establishment of the Australian Barefoot Water Ski Club at Sackville, near Windsor—entry qualification was to have skied barefoot for at least 60 seconds. Australia hosted the first World Barefoot Ski Championships in 1977 on the Molonglo River near Canberra; Australia has competed at every world championship since.

The annual Hawkesbury Bridge-to-Bridge International Ski Race Classic, which has been held since 1961, is the world's longest and fastest. The distance from Dangar Island (near Brooklyn Bridge) to the finish at Governor Phillip Park, Windsor, is 114 kilometres. The event attracts more than sixteen hundred competitors. An Australian, Christopher Massey, has held the world record for speed on water skis—230.26 km/h—achieved on the Hawkesbury River at Windsor in March 1983.

MBW and IJ

See **COCKBURN, BRUCE**.

WATERS, WILLIAM FRANCIS (1897–1968), born Traralgon, Victoria, was prominent as a bushwalker and ski tourer. He was a member of the scout movement from 1908 until his death, and for much of that time, from 1930 to 1965, was Commissioner for Rovers. He was also a leading member of the Melbourne Amateur Walking and Touring Club, holding office at various times as secretary, chief trip organiser, and president. But most importantly, he was an untiring walker and skier, with a talent for enthusing others, and introduced many thousands to both sports.

EH-S

WATSON, KENNETH BROUGHTON (1919–), born Melbourne, was a basketball administrator and coach. He began playing basketball in the 1930s, making the Victorian team in the following decade, but his main contribution came through administration and coaching. As secretary of the Victorian Basketball Association from 1940 to 1985, he worked tirelessly, helping to lay a firm foundation for the sport in Victoria, long regarded the centre of the sport in Australia; he also served as secretary of the Australian Basketball Union from 1953 to 1963. His wife Betty was also very active in basketball administration during this time. Watson coached the Australian men's Olympic team in 1956 and 1968, and also coached the Melbourne Tigers for many years. In the 1970s and 1980s he was a remarkably successful coach of club junior teams.

SB

WEBB, CHRIS (1866–1948) was the racing name of Henry Christopher Wagg, the greatest skipper of Australian 18-footer yachts in the period from 1891 to 1940. He won the inter-colonial 'eighteen' trophy in Brisbane in 1897, and national championships (variously titled) in 1908 (Perth), 1909 (Sydney), 1910 (Perth), 1912 (Sydney), 1914 (Perth), 1924 (Sydney), 1925 (Perth), and 1927 (Sydney); he contested his last Australian championship in 1937. Webb's success as a helmsman stemmed from unsurpassed knowledge of rigging and trimming and, especially on his home territory, Sydney Harbour, local tides and conditions. For most of his sailing career he worked as a night watchman for Sydney Ferries Limited.

CC

Weightlifting
Conducted in ten weight divisions ranging from under 52 kilograms to over 110 kilograms, competitive weightlifting is judged on the total weight raised by each lifter's best attempt in the snatch, and the clean and jerk. Championships in Australia began in 1945, and Charles Henderson of NSW won twelve titles between 1951 and 1968 (including ten in a row at bantamweight and two later at featherweight). Australian teams have enjoyed success in Commonwealth Games competition, particularly in 1978, 1982, and 1986. Dean Lukin claimed the country's only Olympic gold medal in weightlifting when he won the superheavyweight division in Los Angeles in 1984.

KM*

See **BARBERIS, VERDI**; **KABBAS, ROBERT**; **LUKIN, DEAN**; **STELLIOS, BASILIOS**; **VOUKELATOS, NIKOS**.

WEINDORFER, GUSTAV (1874–1932), born Spittal, Austria, emigrated to Melbourne in 1900 and became an active member of the Victorian Field Naturalists' Club. He moved to Tasmania in 1905 and married Kate Cowle. They began farming, and pioneered walking in the Cradle Mountain area of Tasmania, later building Waldheim Chalet there. After his wife's premature death in 1916, Weindorfer sold the farm and lived at Cradle Mountain.

More than anyone else, he was responsible for making the area a mecca for walkers.

EH-S

WEISSEL, ERIC (1903–72), born Cootamundra, NSW, was a rarity among Australian rugby league players in that he played all his football outside a metropolitan area, in southern NSW, where he took part in the Maher Cup competition from 1921 to 1939. He also played for Australia, making his debut in the second Test against Great Britain in 1928, before he represented NSW. He played eight Tests for Australia and toured with the 1929–30 Kangaroos. His most famous performance was in the 1932 'Battle of Brisbane' when, despite a bad ankle injury, he made a long break to set up a match-winning try against Great Britain. A five-eighth and an accomplished kicker off either foot, he had a reputation for fair play.

MC

See **Battle of Brisbane**.

WELCH, GREG (1965–), born Bangor, Sydney, is a lightly built triathlete—58 kilograms and 166 centimetres—who came second in the 1991 unofficial world triathlon championship, the legendary Hawaiian Ironman Triathlon. Before that Welch became the 1988 world 2 kilometres beach sprint champion and the 1990 world Olympic-distance triathlon champion. He also holds the world record in the Hawaiian Triathlon in two different age groups and in 1991 the US long-course half-Ironman title. Welch is a dedicated and versatile athlete who is also a State-level squash-player and won a half-marathon in San Diego in 1991. Because he has settled in America, competing the year round in various events, his achievements have not been fully appreciated in Australia.

RC

See **Triathlon**.

WENDEN, MICHAEL VINCENT (1949–), born Burwood, Sydney, came from a working-class family. His swimming potential was soon realised by coach Vic Arneil who was an advocate of sprint work rather than the endurance work supported by Don Talbot and Forbes Carlile. He was the first 14-year-old boy to swim under 60 seconds for the 100 metres, recording 58.6 seconds and, while still a junior, he swam an Australian record of 54.2 seconds. In the 1966 Jamaica British Empire and Commonwealth Games, Wenden won three gold medals, in the 110 yards freestyle and as a member of the 4 × 110 yards and the 4 × 220 yards freestyle relays. He was successful again in the 1968 Mexico Olympic Games, where he won the 100 and 200 metres freestyle, and achieved a silver in the 4 × 200 metres freestyle relay. In the 1972 Munich Games, Wenden

secured a fourth and two fifth places. He remained dominant in the British Commonwealth Games, winning four gold medals in 1970 in Edinburgh (100 and 200 metres freestyle, and 4 × 100 and 4 × 200 freestyle relays) and one silver in the 4 × 100 metres medley relay. He was not as successful in the 1974 Christchurch Games, but won gold in the 100 metres freestyle and the 4 × 200 metres freestyle relay, silvers in the 4 × 100 and the 4 × 200 metres freestyle relay, and a bronze in the 4 × 100 metres medley relay. Wenden collected a total of four Olympic medals, eleven Commonwealth Games records, and won eleven individual and sixteen team national titles. Since his retirement, he has worked hard to put back into swimming as much as he received from it.

RH and MH

See **Swimming**.

Western Australian Cricket Association Ground. The WACA holds a unique place in Australian sporting history. It is the only major sporting venue in the country owned by its controlling body. The reasons for this ownership stem from the last century. In 1889 the officials of the WACA, headed by its president, J. C. H. James, and executive members G. Parker and A. Lovekin, approached the Governor of WA, Sir Frederick Broome, about the possibility of obtaining an area of land which they could develop exclusively for cricket. Broome recommended that the 'Southern Portion of Perth Reserve 27A be leased to the Association for 999 years'. Work began on ground development and the area was fit to use for cricket on 3 February 1894. Earlier that year a certificate of title for the lease was issued to the trustees.

Although the area was developed as a cricket ground it has not been used exclusively for that sport; indeed, it has hosted many other attractions. In 1895 football was played there and the Perth Football Club used the WACA as its home venue from 1900 to 1958. The WA football Grand Final was played there in 1913 before a crowd of 14 000. In 1913 a perimeter track and electric lights were erected around the ground for the purpose of night trotting. In 1929 the WACA sold part of its ground to the Trotting Association who moved to their newly developed track adjacent to the cricket ground. On 22 February 1922 the 999-year lease was converted to a freehold title, giving the ground to the cricket association. In 1930 the perimeter track was leased to the Perth Speedway Company for use in motorcycle-racing. This venture did not last long and the speedway fence and lights were removed in 1935, and a new boundary fence was put up. Another sport to occupy the WACA was baseball. In 1938 the Claxton

Shield interstate competition was played there. Later in 1954 three 80-foot light towers were erected for night baseball. The conversion of baseball to a summer sport saw it disappear from the ground in 1964.

A visit from the Indian soccer team took place in 1938 and matches were played at the WACA. While the baseball lights were still operative, international soccer matches were played before large crowds. A move by WA to host a cricket Test match in 1938 led to major development of the WACA ground in order to accommodate the event. The old light towers were removed, a new stand was built, and other changes took place. The first men's Test match in Perth took place on 11 December 1970, and the public response produced 84 000 spectators. The ground and its practice facilities were regarded as the best in Australia. This was a tribute to the long-time curator, Roy Abbott. Today the WACA is a fixture on the Test match circuit. Further modernisation took place in the 1980s in an endeavour to make the WACA a world-class venue. The ambitious programme had a total expenditure estimate of $45 million. New stands, six modern light towers to cater for night cricket (and other sports as well), new entrance gates, a restaurant, and new offices were all part of the project. On 10 October 1986 the first night-cricket match was played, an interstate McDonald's Cup match between WA and Victoria. In recent times the WACA has become one of the major night venues for the AFL, although night football was tried in the early 1960s without success. Other sporting events which have been contested at the WACA include rugby league games, international and interstate hockey matches, private schools interschool athletics up to 1962, and the 1990 World Lacrosse Championships.

As well as sporting events, some interesting functions have taken place at the WACA. In 1919 Sir Norman Brearly, the famous aviator, used the ground as an aerodrome. During the Second World War the main buildings were commandeered by the military. In 1962 Prince Philip, Duke of Edinburgh, presented the Queen's Regimental Colours to the First Royal WA Regiment. Some musical pop concerts have also been staged at the ground.

WPR

White Hope, by *Such a Mark* out of *Game 'Un*, was a greyhound, purchased from England in 1912 by H. Victor Roye. A brindled-and-white dog of about 65 pounds, *White Hope* had an impressive ancestry which included dogs such as *Fiery Furnace*, *Under the Globe*, *Sir Sankey*, and *Young Fullerton*. Observers commented on *White Hope*'s lack of looks, but this had no effect on his potency, and his influence on Australian blood lines was immense. He sired five winners of the Australian Waterloo Cup and his progeny won every important Australian race.

TGP

WHITEFORD, DOUG (1915–79), born Melbourne, was a racing driver. A skilled motor engineer, he was said to be able to use his left and right hand simultaneously to perform different tasks. It was somehow appropriate for a man whose way of life seemed to allow no middle ground; some people venerated him, others found him abrasive. Nonetheless he was widely respected: he presented himself and his cars immaculately and was a formidably hard competitor. He won three Australian Grands Prix in four years (1950, 1952, and 1953) and would undoubtedly have achieved even more given better resources. He kept racing until 1976, and died on 25 January 1979.

GH

WHITFIELD, BEVERLEY JOY (1954–), born Shellharbour, NSW, was a swimmer who came from a close-knit working-class family. She was taken every weekend to Sydney to be coached by Terry Gathercole and travelled to Texas for six months in 1969 when Gathercole accepted a coaching position there. In her total career Whitfield won eight individual Australian championships (100 and 200 metres breaststroke) and two relay championships (4 × 100 metres medley relay, twice). At the 1970 Edinburgh British Commonwealth Games she achieved gold medals in the 100 and 200 metres breaststroke and was a member of the successful 4 × 200 metres medley relay. It was at the 1972 Munich Olympics that she gained sporting immortality, winning a gold medal in the 200 metres breaststroke. Like Gail Neall, her victory came from lane 7.

RH and MH

WHITTEN, TED (1934–) grew up in the western suburbs of Melbourne and played all his football with Footscray in the VFL. He was a football prodigy, playing his first senior game with the club in 1951, at the age of 17. Whitten went on to become one of the most respected and skilful players in modern football; a combination of style, aggression, and skill made him one of the most complete footballers. He played in 321 games and one premiership side. He is credited with inventing the flick pass, which was a form of handpass in which the ball was 'slapped' with the palm of the hand as the elbow quickly extended, enabling the ball to be passed quickly in any direction. It proved so successful that other clubs questioned its legality and it was later banned. Whitten later coached Footscray with moderate success and promoted interstate football.

RKS

WHITTON, IVO HARRINGTON (1893–1967), born Melbourne, was the dominant figure in Australian golf from just before the First World War until his term as a member of the Royal and Ancient Rules Committee in 1953. He won the first of his five Australian Opens in 1912. His last major victory was the Queensland amateur in 1933. In 1920 he won the prestigious Helms Award as Australia's Athlete of the Year; his handicap was then an unbelievable plus eight. His fifth Open, at Kensington in 1931, was a tremendous achievement: eight behind going into the last round, he shot 72 in a howling gale. In his career he won five Australian Opens as an amateur, five Victorian amateurs, three Queensland amateurs, one NSW, two Australian amateurs, and a Queensland Open. Whitton served on the St Andrews Committee that unanimously abolished the 'stymie' in match play. Perhaps he recalled losing to Len Nettlefold in the 1926 Australian amateur: on the final green Nettlefold laid him a full stymie; in going for the hole he knocked the Tasmanian's ball into the cup!

CT

WILKINSON, ARTHUR GEORGE ('Bluey') (1911–40) was Australia's second Speedway World Champion, winning at Wembley in 1938. Beginning racing at Bathurst Sportsground in 1927 he was brought to Sydney where he lost to Van Praag in the NSW championship. Public subscriptions enabled Wilkinson to travel to London in 1929 where he secured a contract with West Ham. Establishing himself in the Australian Test team he was the only rider to secure maximum points in all five Tests in 1930. After 1938 Wilkinson became a promoter at Sheffield. He rode only once more, at a 1939 charity meeting, when he twice beat English champion Arthur Atkinson and broke the West Ham speedway record. Returning to Australia to enlist in the RAAF, he was killed instantly on 27 July 1940 when his motorcycle smashed into a truck.

PW*

WILLIAMS, FOSTER NEIL (1922–), born Quorn, SA, was one of four brothers to play league football. Playing for West Adelaide Williams made his league debut at the late age of 24 but reserved his greatest successes for Port Adelaide whom he led to nine premierships between 1950 and 1965, including five in a row (1954–58) as captain-coach. Williams's method was based on pace and aggression, long kicking, and players dashing to the fall of the ball or what he once described as 'a minimum approach to goal with maximum body power'. More than anyone else Williams also created the Port Adelaide spirit which has made the club dominant in post-war football. Williams played thirty-five matches for SA and coached the side

on numerous occasions. Three of his sons, Mark, Anthony (deceased), and Steven, have been prominent league footballers, and his daughter Jenny is an international lacrosse player. He is honoured by the Fos Williams Medal for the best SA player in an interstate game, which was presented for the first time in 1981.

BW and MH*

WILLIAMS, HARRY (1951–), born Sydney, was the first (and so far only) Aborigine to play soccer for Australia. At the age of 8 he began playing with the St George juniors. After making his senior debut for Western Suburbs, he transferred to the St George club. Recognising his speed and overlapping abilities, coach Frank Arok switched him to left full back where he was an instant success. Williams was a member of the 1974 World Cup squad, coming on as a substitute in the final game. From then on he became a Socceroo regular, starring in the unsuccessful 1978 World Cup qualifying campaign. Injury and study commitments resulted in his retirement from international soccer at 27. In all, he played seventeen full internationals and twenty-six other representative games for Australia. He did continue playing for Canberra City and Inter Monaro until 1990. He became a senior public servant and in 1990 assumed responsibility for the sports portfolio in the newly created Aboriginal and Torres Strait Island Commission.

GC

See **Aborigines in Sport**.

WILLIAMS, HARRY LLEWELYN (1915–61), born Melbourne, was a golfer of great potential. Gene Sarazen's opinion was that he was the world's greatest left-hander, with a future in world golf. The American wanted to take him to the USA, an offer he declined. He won the Australian amateur at the age of 16 at the Australian Golf Club, where he was to win it again in 1937. He was five times Victorian amateur champion. When he and Jim Ferrier were both 16 they played a series of matches: Williams won the first seven of them. Most critics saw him as potentially Australia's greatest golfer of all time. His father died in 1933, and thereafter his interest in golf declined. He virtually quit golf at the age of 24. A strange relationship with his mother, gambling, and depression, saw him commit suicide, penniless, aged 46.

CT

WILLIAMS, MERVYN (1901–80), born Maryborough, Queensland, boxed as a schoolboy, rising through the amateurs and 'pros' to be Queensland middleweight champion in 1922. On retirement he worked in Melbourne as a bread-carter then refereed for Stadiums Limited. A controversial decision in the 1940s channelled him into boxing journalism for the next thirty years. Much respected, Williams rose to edit the *Sporting Globe*. He co-compered *TV Ringside* with Ron Casey after 1968 where his colourful phraseology became legendary, one famous quip being 'he had less chance than a crippled prawn in a flock of seagulls'. Williams delighted in being director of the *Herald and Weekly Times* Royal Children's Hospital Appeal (1960–64).

RB

See **Boxing**.

WILLS, THOMAS WENTWORTH (1835–1880), cricketer, born Molonglo Plains, NSW, lived in the Port Phillip District (now Victoria) from the age of 4. He was an outstanding sportsman and was known as the 'W. G. Grace of Australian cricket'. He instigated Australian rules football, and in its earliest years was a great exponent of that sport. In his teens he was a pupil at Rugby in England where he was dux of his class, was captain of the school eleven, and excelled at football. He played cricket with Kent, Cambridge University, Marylebone, and United Ireland. Returning to Victoria, he was an automatic choice for the intercolonial cricket team of 1857, and was captain in the following seasons. In 1861 his father Horatio persuaded him to join an overland party to establish a pastoral property inland from Rockhampton at Cullinlaringo. There the local Aborigines massacred nineteen of the party, leaving Thomas as one of the two survivors. After this shattering experience Wills resumed his sporting career in Victoria, and in 1866–67, as coach of the Aboriginal cricket team, laid the foundations for their successes in England in 1868. In first-class cricket Wills scored 602 runs (average 12.28) and took 121 wickets (average 10.07). In 1857–58 he was secretary of the MCC, about which time he wrote his now famous letter suggesting that cricketers keep fit by playing a game like football in winter, and by 1859 the first rules of Australian football had been devised. The traumatic experience of 1861 eventually took its toll when Wills committed suicide in tragic circumstances in 1880.

RH*

See **Aborigines in Sport**; **Australian Rules Football**.

WILSON, BETTY (1921–), born Melbourne, has been described as the greatest all-rounder Australian women's cricket has produced, and is widely recognised as the most outstanding female player of any era. In the course of her impressive eleven-Test career she was the first Australian woman to make a Test century, accumulated 862 runs (including three centuries and three half-centuries), took 68 wickets, and held ten catches. She first came to the attention of the Collingwood club after

stylishly returning several balls from the boundary at Mayor's Park, Clifton Hill, when she and her father had stopped to watch a match in progress. This promising beginning was jeopardised when, after being hit while batting, council officials tried to have her removed from the side. She was then aged 10. She honed her extraordinary batting style and intricate footwork, and developed an extensive repertoire of strokes with backyard practice sessions. Using a cricket ball suspended from the clothes-line in a pair of her mother's discarded stockings, she worked on her strokeplay. Bowling at a solitary lamp post might perhaps account partly for her versatility as a bowler. In a career studded with spectacular performances possibly her finest achievement came during England's 1957–58 tour. After a disastrous start—Australia was all out for 38—she proceeded to humble the English line-up. Using her spin bowling to devastating effect she proceeded to take 7–7: this included a hat-trick, the only one in women's Test cricket. In a fitting tribute to this outstanding sportswoman, she was among the first inductees into the Sport Australia Hall of Fame.

LR

See **Cricket**.

WILSON, PETER (1948–), born Newcastle, England, learned his football in the north-east and first signed for Middlesborough. Unable to crack the first team he emigrated to Australia, signing for South Coast United (Wollongong) in 1968. Moves followed, with Marconi, Safeway United (Wollongong), Western Suburbs, and finally Apia-Leichhardt enlisting his services. Wilson started his career as a full back but later moved to sweeper. Between 1970 and 1979 he made 115 appearances for the national team, becoming the most capped Australian player ever. He captained Australia from 1971, including during the 1974 World Soccer Cup finals. Tall, domineering in the air but also an accurate distributor of the ball, Wilson's toughness did not endear him to referees. However, the same toughness ensured few opponents ever got the better of him. It was a measure of the man who worked in the Wollongong mines even while playing for Australia.

PM

WINDLE, ROBERT (1944–) was one of the most versatile male swimmers Australia has produced. In the Olympic Games he swam the 100, 200, 400, and 1500 metres events, and in Australian championships he was successful over 220, 440, 880, and 1650 yards. In all, he won nineteen Australian championships and six British Empire and Commonwealth Games medals (four gold, one silver, and one bronze). He was selected for three Olympic Games (1960, 1964, and 1968), earning a gold medal in the 1500 metres freestyle and a bronze in the

4 × 100 metres freestyle relay in Tokyo; in 1968 at Mexico City he won a silver in the 4 × 200 metres freestyle relay and a bronze in the 4 × 100 metres freestyle relay.

RH and MH

Windsurfing

The sport originated in California in the 1960s, and by 1976 Greg Kelly and Roger Dulhunty had opened a business in Sydney importing American sailboards. They gained a licence to manufacture their own boards the next year under the trademark Windsurfer. National championships began in 1977, with four weight divisions in which women and men compete together. Australians entered the world championships in Italy in the same year, with Greg Hyde finishing fourth in the lightweight division and Kevin Wadham fifth in the medium heavyweights. Australia's first world champion windsurfer was Grant Long of Newcastle, who won the heavyweight division in the Bahamas in 1980. The sport is controlled nationally by the Windsurfer Class Association of Australia.

KM*

WINTER, ANTHONY WILLIAM ('Nick')

(1894–1955), born Brocklesby, NSW, was a triple jumper who produced a world-record leap of 15.525 metres in the hop, step, and jump to win the event at the 1924 Olympics. Described as a 'devil-may-care Australian', he was a popular champion. The son of a fettler, who was a labourer before enlisting in the AIF in 1915, he became a fireman after the war. He was tall and slender, ambidextrous and double-jointed, and played most sports including team-games as well as tennis, golf, and wrestling. As a member of Botany Harriers, and then of South Sydney and Western Suburbs amateur athletic clubs, he competed successfully in the high jump and hurdles, but excelled at the triple jump and created an Australasian record of 14.503 metres in 1919. Winter was included in the 1928 Olympic team but failed to qualify for the final. He became a skilled billiards player, who revelled in trick shots, and finished runner-up in the State championships in 1927. Winter later ran a billiard saloon in George Street, Sydney.

IJ

See **Athletics**.

WINTER, JOHN A. (1924–), born Perth,

was the first Western Australian to win an Olympic gold medal and the only Australian to win a medal in the high jump. He was educated at Scotch College where he showed great leaping skill and was often seen practising with a pogo stick or jumping over a clothes-line. War service interrupted his athletic career but enabled him to study jumping styles of the day, including the eastern cut-off technique, which he mastered. He broke the Australian high jump record in 1947 and won the Australian title in 1947 and 1948. Competing against more fancied opponents in the London Olympics he had to suffer the pain of a back injury and fading light but was able to summon reserves of strength and soar over the bar at 1.98 metres to win the event. He also won the high jump at the 1950 British Empire Games in Auckland.

WPR

See **Athletics**.

Women's Cricket: First Test. The first cricket Test match for women was played at the Brisbane Exhibition Ground from 28 to 31 December 1934. Betty Archdale led the English side and Margaret Peden was the Australian captain. Perhaps overwhelmed by the occasion, Australia scored only 47 in their first innings, with vice-captain Kath Smith (25) scoring more than half the runs. Australia improved in their second innings to reach 138 but England (154 and 1–34) won the Test easily. The match was dominated by the English all-rounder Myrtle Maclagan, (72 and 7–10) but Australian off-spinner Ann Palmer (7–18) performed well with the ball. The aggregate crowd for three days was 9000. England also won the second Test which was played at the SCG while the third Test at the MCG was drawn. The 1934–35 tour took place as a result of the bold initiative of the Australian Women's Cricket Council which, when it only had 14s 8d in the bank, invited English women to tour. The tour proved a financial success and generated much publicity for women's cricket. The Australian women toured England for the first time in 1937.

RC

Women's World Cup Hockey. The Australian Women's Hockey Association (AWHA) was a foundation member of the International Federation of Women's Hockey Associations (IFWHA) in 1927 and Australian women were represented at the IFWHA conference tournaments, staged every four years between 1953 and 1979. The other controlling world hockey body, the Fédération Internationale de Hockey (FIH) organised the first Women's World Cup in 1974, and when the AWHA affiliated with the FIH in 1981, it became eligible to send a team to the World Cup. At the fourth World Cup in 1981 in Buenos Aires, Australia finished in fourth place. They won a bronze medal in Kuala Lumpur in 1983 and came sixth in Amsterdam in 1986. Between 1974 and 1986 the World Cup titles were shared between West Germany and the Netherlands. Twelve women's hockey nations took part in the seventh FIH Women's World Cup tournament held at the NSW State Sports Centre at Homebush from 2 to 13 May 1990. The Australian team, captained by Sharon Buchanan, defeated Korea 2–1 in extra time in the semifinal. The 1988 Olympic gold-medallists then met the current World Cup champions, the Netherlands, in the final. The Dutch team won their fourth World Cup title when they defeated Australia 3–1.

MS

WOOD, MERVYN, LVO, MBE, QPM

(1917–), amateur sculler, was one of Australia's most durable sporting champions. He rowed in the eights at the 1936 Olympics, but it was in sculls that he became prominent, winning the Australian championships from 1946 to 1952 and again in 1955. His Olympic performances included first place in the single sculls in 1948, second in the same event four years later, and third place in the double sculls in 1956. At the British Empire and Commonwealth Games he was champion in both the single and double sculls in 1950, a member of the winning double sculls and coxed fours in 1954, and was second in the double sculls in 1958; he also won the Henley Diamond Sculls in 1948 and 1952. He was later NSW Police Commissioner. He was awarded the MBE in 1957 for services to Australian sport.

SB

See **Rowing and Sculling**.

Woodchopping

This sport involves both the felling of trees and splitting of timber and is one in which Australians have excelled in world competition. The first recorded domestic contest was in Tasmania in 1874, and a tournament in Latrobe, Tasmania, in 1891 offered prize-money of $2000; the United Australasian Axemen's Association emerged shortly after. Legendary names in the sport include Mannie McCarthy, who competed in his 58th Sydney Show at the age of 78 in 1980; the Youd brothers from Tasmania, three of whom have held a world title and several world records; and Victorian Jack O'Toole who won twenty-four world championships from 1947. Experience rather than youth is an advantage for competitors, and handicapping in various events produces exciting finishes. The Sydney Royal Easter Show is the premier competition in Australia.

KM*

See **Country Show Sports**; **FOSTER, DAVID**; **Sheaf-tossing**; **Sheep-shearing**; **Woodchopping Monument**.

Woodchopping Monument. The beginnings of competitive chopping, a long-time feature of Australian carnivals and agricultural shows, are commemorated at Ulverstone in Tasmania. It was there that the first recorded chopping contest took place in 1874 between Tasmania's Joseph Smith and Victoria's Jack Biggs. To mark the occasion a plaque has been placed on the site where the wager was laid which led to

that contest. The unusual monument is shaped like a sawn section of a dice, with slots cut in the sides as if an axeman had begun to cut through. The plaque, which is floodlit at night, was unveiled by the warden of Ulverstone, W. H. Brand, on behalf of the Australian Axemen's Association.

GC*

See **Woodchopping**.

WOODFULL, WILLIAM MALDON, OBE

(1897–1965), was one of the greatest and most respected captains in Australian cricket. A man of Christian principles, strong moral fibre, and physical courage, whose handling of the 'bodyline' crisis was faultless, he was a solid opening batsman whose defence was close to impregnable. In Test matches and for Victoria, he featured in many notable opening partnerships, mainly with Ponsford. In thirty-five Tests he scored 2300 runs, at an average of 46.00, including seven centuries and a highest score of 161 as well as carrying his bat on two occasions against England. He was the only Australian captain to regain the Ashes twice in England. In all first-class matches he scored a total of 13 392 runs, averaging 64.99. Woodfull was a leading educationalist in Victoria.

RH*

See **Bodyline**.

WOODS, DEAN, OAM (1966–), born

Wangaratta, Victoria, came from a cycling family. Dean and his brother Paul received strong support from their parents, who had taken part in club-level cycling. Woods was tall and slender (180 centimetres and 73 kilograms) for a cyclist but had powerful thighs. In 1983 he won the Australian junior titles in the 3000 metres individual pursuit and thirty kilometres points-score event; later at the world junior championship in NZ he won the individual pursuit and came second in the points race. After performing well in the 1984 Australian championships, he was selected for the 1984 Olympics. At Los Angeles he had to race on a borrowed bike because his only cycle had broken at training. Woods narrowly missed a bronze medal in the 4000 metres individual pursuit but, partnered by Michael Grenda, Kevin Nichols, and Michael Turtur, he won a gold medal in the 4000 metres team pursuit. Woods was successful at the 1986 Commonwealth Games, winning a gold medal in the 4000 metres individual pursuit and 4000 metres team pursuit and a silver in the 20 kilometres scratch race.

RH and MH

WOOTTON, FRANK (1894–1940), cham-

pion English jockey, was born in Australia, the eldest son of racehorse-trainer Richard Wootton. At the age of 13 he accompanied his family first to South Africa and then to England. By the time he was 21 Wootton had ridden 882 winners in England and was leading jockey for four successive seasons, 1909–12. His career was interrupted by the war, and increasing weight forced him to restrict his later riding to hurdle races. In 1915 Richard Wootton returned to Australia, and in 1933 Frank also returned. His younger brother, Stanley, also rode in England, and later became a noted trainer. Stanley also had breeding interests in Australia and in 1951 sent out the stallion *Star King* (renamed *Star Kingdom*), who made a spectacular contribution to Australian bloodstock.

AL

World Cup (Cricket). The World Cup is a one-day cricket competition. Each team is permitted to bat for 50 overs: no bowler is allowed more than 10 overs. The competition began in 1975 and has been played subsequently at intervals of approximately four years. The first three competitions were held in England, but in 1987, with some trepidation, the International Cricket Conference acceded to a joint request from India and Pakistan to host the competition on the subcontinent. In February–March 1992 the World Cup was jointly hosted by Australia and NZ, with Pakistan beating England in the final. The competition was to be made up of eight teams, comprising the seven countries which have full membership of the International Cricket Conference (i.e. have Test status), plus an associate-member country, but political developments in South Africa enabled a team from that nation also to be included. A competition among associate members is played some months beforehand to determine which country will occupy this position. Australia has performed with mixed fortunes. It reached the final at Lord's in 1975, losing to the West Indies by a mere 17 runs, after five Australian batsmen had been run out. In 1979 Australia's performance was less distinguished, as it failed to reach the semifinals, lost two preliminary matches and managed to beat only Canada. In 1983 Australia also did poorly, suffering the indignity of a defeat by 13 runs at the hands of Zimbabwe. However in 1987, Australia performed magnificently. Unexpectedly reaching the final, at Eden Gardens, Calcutta, before a vast crowd, Australia, led by Allan Border, beat England by 7 runs in a tense finish.

JNT and BW

World Cup Soccer Finals. Australia's only appearance in the World Cup finals occurred in 1974. After qualifying from the South Pacific zone by finishing top of a group including Iraq, NZ, and Indonesia, Australia had to defeat Iran and South Korea to ensure its place in the finals. During the finals in West Germany the Australian side failed to win a game, losing 2–0 to East Germany in Hamburg, 2–0 to West Germany, also in Hamburg, and drawing 0–0 with Chile. The Australian team's effort at the 1974 World Cup compared favourably with other underdogs, such as Zaire, who were beaten 9–0 by Yugoslavia, and Haiti, who went down to Poland 7–0. The 1974 side was coached by Rale Rasic, who was born in Yugoslavia and settled in Australia in 1966. Before being appointed the national team coach, Rasic was in charge of Melbourne HSC, St George Budapest, Marconi, and Pan Hellenic. After the 1974 World Cup, Rasic took over as coach of Adelaide City in the National League.

MH*

World Series Cricket is the name of a limited-overs international cricket competition (popularly known as one-day cricket) played in Australia each summer. The competition involves three international sides: Australia and two visiting international sides. After a series of preliminary rounds, in which each country plays the other in four or even five games, a best-of-three final between the two leading sides is played off in February. World Series Cricket has become the most visible form of cricket in each Australian summer. Day–night games played in Sydney, Melbourne, and Perth have proved a popular and convenient innovation. The name World Series Cricket originally applied to an unofficial international cricket competition sponsored by PBL Marketing from 1977 to 1979 when Kerry Packer's competition ran in opposition to the official matches run by the ACB. Following the agreement between PBL Marketing and the ACB in 1979, World Series Cricket became the name of the official limited-overs competition. Limited-overs cricket has been played in Australia since the 1969–70 season when the six States of Australia, as well as NZ, played in a knock-out competition which involved only six games. The potential popularity of this form of cricket was demonstrated in 1970 when 46 000 people attended a hastily organised match at the MCG after the first three days of a Test match had been washed out. A full-scale competition was not introduced until 1977.

RC

See **Cricket**.

WORRALL, JOHN (1863–1937), born Leviathan Reef, outside Maryborough, Queensland, was a Test cricketer, Australian rules footballer, and successful coach in both sports; he later became a respected sporting journalist with the *Australasian*. A rover with the newly formed Fitzroy club from 1884 to 1893, he captained the side for five seasons. He was 'Champion of the Colony' in 1887 and 1890. After transferring to Carlton as manager-coach he led the club to a hat-trick of premierships (1906–8).

He later coached Essendon to successive premierships in 1911–12. A forceful right-hand batsman, Worrall played eleven Tests for Australia and was also a useful off-spin bowler for Victoria. An outstanding player and coach in Melbourne district cricket, his innings of 417 not out for Carlton stood as the highest individual score in senior cricket until 1902. Worrall also played for Fitzroy Bohemians, East Melbourne, Hawksburn, and South Melbourne. It has been claimed by some that Worrall was the journalist who coined the word 'bodyline'.

SB*

See **Bodyline**.

WRAY, LEONORA (1886–1979), born East Maitland, NSW, is in many ways the cornerstone of women's golf in Australia. Leo Wray won her first major title in 1906, the NSW title, with a mere five clubs in her bag. She won the Australian national title in 1907 and 1908. Then followed typhoid fever, which ended her golf for ten years. Remarkably, she won the Australian title again in 1929. In all, she won three national titles and four NSW titles, the first in 1906, the last in 1930. With Una Clift, Wray made women's golf what it is today. She was a delegate to Melbourne in 1921, at which meeting the Australian Ladies' Golf Union was formed. She and Clift established a junior girls' coaching scheme, two of whose graduates were Joan Hammond in the 1930s and Pat Borthwick in the 1950s and 1960s. In 1950 she captained and managed the Australian team to England and a year later was made a life member of the NSW Ladies' Golf Union.

CT and MP

See **Golf**.

WREN, JOHN (1871–1953), born Collingwood, Melbourne, was a famous sports promoter, gambling entrepreneur, and racehorse-owner. He first became prominent in the 1890s as the proprietor of an illegal totalisator in Collingwood. With proceeds from the tote, Wren took an interest in other sports. He won handsomely from the 1901 Austral Wheelrace. In 1904 he bought the racehorse *Murmur* which won the Caulfield Cup, encouraging him to buy more horses. The following year the VRC disallowed the entry of Wren's horses to its meetings on the grounds that he was conducting an illegal gambling business. Closing his tote in 1907, Wren entered a partnership with Benjamin Nathan to buy three Melbourne racecourses which conducted pony races and trotting that were not under VRC control. Ruling these courses with a firm hand, Wren gained a reputation for honest racing. In 1910 he extended his operations to Brisbane and in 1912, to Perth. At the same time, Wren was developing his interest in promoting boxing. In 1914 he bought the Newtown Olympia in Sydney as a boxing sta-

dium, and at the end of the First World War built the West Melbourne Stadium. His organisation became the major boxing promoter in Australia, and professional wrestling was added to this in the 1920s. After 1918 he expanded his sporting promotions to motor racing, building the Motordome in Melbourne in 1920.

In the 1920s, sensing growing political opposition to him generally and to private racecourse ownership in particular, Wren moved to distance himself from control of his racecourses. By the end of the Second World War government reforms concluded that process. Wren's influence in Australian professional sport remains open to speculation, fuelled by the publication of Frank Hardy's novel *Power Without Glory*, which was the subject of an unsuccessful action for criminal libel. Beyond dispute is that Wren made a great fortune from his various sporting enterprises and that he had a reputation as a sporting philanthropist. He was a keen supporter of the Collingwood Football Club and died the day after attending their 1953 Grand Final win.

AL

See **Boxing**; **Harness Racing**; **Horseracing**; **Stadiums Limited**.

Wrestling

Wrestling bouts between European settlers are recorded early on in Australia's history, in particular between soldiers and convicts and on the goldfields. These were often conducted in the styles of wrestling native to English counties, for example, 'Cumberland Style'. Wrestling was administered as a sport from 1911, the year of the first national championships, by the Australian Amateur Boxing and Wrestling Union. Australian and State championships in boxing and wrestling were conducted together, usually biennially. A number of competitors won national and/or State titles in both sports. Most of the championships before 1956 were conducted in boxing rings rather than on the wrestling mats specified in the international rules. In 1952–53, with the prospect of the Melbourne Olympics looming, the sports of boxing and wrestling separated at national level and the Australian Amateur Wrestling Union (AWU) was formed. The States followed, Victoria in 1952, Queensland in 1959, and NSW in 1960. Since the formation of the AWU, national championships have been conducted annually in freestyle wrestling in an open division, national championships for juniors (15–20-year-olds) being held for the first time about 1969 and for schoolboys in 1977. In 1990, the official FILA (Fédération Internationale de Lutte Amateur) age and weight categories for juniors (17 to 18 years) and seniors (19 to 20 years) were used for the first time in the national championships. National Greco-Roman championships for seniors were conducted for the first time in 1956 and annually after that until 1963 when the decision was made to abandon national titles in this style of wrestling.

Australia first entered wrestlers in the Olympic Games in 1924 and has entered all Olympic freestyle competitions since, though not in all divisions. Australia's first Olympic wrestling medal, a bronze, was won by Eddie Scarf in the light heavyweight division in 1932. In 1948 Dick Garrard won a silver medal in the lightweight and Jim Armstrong a bronze in the light heavyweight division. Australia has competed in all Commonwealth Games wrestling meets, and in 1978 Zsig Kelevitz won a gold medal in Edmonton. Australian wrestlers first entered the World Freestyle Wrestling Championships in 1954, and have become more competitive with increased funding. Wrestling for women was included in the 1989 FILA World Championships for the first time, and Australia entered one competitor. Before 1989, participation by females was mainly restricted to pre-pubescent girls participating in youth club training and occasional competitions. Over the last forty years the base for the development of Australian wrestling has been in organisations such as the Police Citizens Youth Clubs. In 1982, in a move to improve the administration of the sport, National Coaching Accreditation Schemes at Levels I and II were introduced, and in 1984 a professional executive director and development officer was appointed. Promotional programmes such as the 'Life. Be In It!' *Come 'n Try Wrestling* booklets and the Aussie Sport mini wrestling programmes were devised.

In the face of legal actions taken in 1987 against the unincorporated national body by individuals in Victoria and the Victorian Wrestling Association, and with legal aid denied to the AWU, all office-bearers resigned. The disgruntled State bodies created a new Australian Wrestling Federation Incorporated (AWF) and were provisionally granted FILA membership which was later withdrawn. In 1987 both the remnants of the AWU and the AWF conducted their own national championships. Repercussions from these events included reduced funding from the ASC and the loss of professional staff. As of 1990 the Australian Wrestling Union Inc. now has State associations in Queensland, NSW, Victoria, Tasmania, SA, WA, and the ACT, and the level of development is making a recovery after the events of 1987.

RM

See **GARRARD, DICK; MILLER, WILLIAM**.

WYNNE, NANCYE (later BOLTON) (1918–), born Melbourne, was widely regarded as the 'First Lady of Australian tennis' from the late 1930s until the early 1950s. Particularly in combination with Thelma Long she was a formidable doubles-player. Tall, with a powerful service and hard-hitting forehand, she lost to Alice Marble in the 1938 US Open final. The outbreak of war, in which her husband was killed, probably thwarted her rise to international greatness. Nevertheless after the war, as Nancye Bolton, she achieved world number four ranking and eventually gained twenty Australian titles with her sixth singles crown coming in 1951.

HCJP

See **Lawn Tennis**.

Y

'Yabba' see GASCOIGNE, STEPHEN.

YOUNG, CLIFF (1922–   ) helped to popularise the 875 kilometres Sydney to Melbourne ultramarathon when he won the event in 1983. Before that he was an obscure potato farmer from Beech Forest in Victoria. Given his age (he was 61 in 1983), his shuffling style of running in long pants which ballooned around his thighs, and his habit of training in gumboots, Young—epitome of the Aussie battler—became an instant celebrity. A vegetarian, non-smoker, and teetotaller, Young ran in a further five ultramarathons after 1983. He also competed in the gruelling Marathon to Athens race in 1983 where he finished seventy-fourth.
RP
See **Sydney to Melbourne Run**.

YOUNG, ROBERT ('Nat') (1950–   ), born Collaroy, Sydney, along with 'Midget' Farrelly helped to extend the popularity of surfing in the 1960s. When he won the world championship at Ocean Beach, San Diego, in 1968 Young was the first world champion who was not a native of the host country. The 18-year-old pioneered a whole new technique of surfing. He replaced the conventional and accepted smooth, fluid, and flowing style with a more high-speed aggressive surfing technique featuring rapid-fire changes of direction and flashy arcs and he became known as 'The Animal'. Young had achieved prominence when he won the 1963 Australian title and dominated the Bell's Beach Championship, winning it four times between 1966 and 1970; he was Australian men's champion three times between 1966 and 1969, and won the Smirnoff World Pro Championships in 1970. With the advent of Malibu boards Young dropped out of the world surfing circuit but returned to win the first world seniors' championship in 1987. Angry about beach pollution, he polled well as an independent in the blue-ribbon Liberal seat of Pittwater in 1986. He was inducted into the Australian Surfing Hall of Fame in the same year.
RC
See **Surfing**.

YOUNG, Sir JOHN (1827–1907), born Kent, England, the architect of Australian lawn bowls, personified the traits of nineteenth-century lawn bowls: he was affluent, a subscriber to middle-class values, and white Anglo-male.

Young emigrated to Melbourne in 1855, and thence to Annandale, Sydney, in 1859 where he constructed a bowls green on his property, Kentville, in 1876. Having purchased substantial parts of Annandale as a speculative venture, Young used his green as one of his promotions, transporting would-be purchasers to Kentville to enjoy a few 'ends'. Young helped to standardise and popularise lawn bowls in Australia and overseas. He started intercolonial lawn bowls matches; the first, between Victorian and NSW teams, was played at Kentville in 1880. He also formed the world's first lawn bowls association, the NSW Bowls Association. Indeed, such was Young's passion for organisation that in collaboration with Charles Wood (president of the Victorian Bowls Association), and the Earl of Jersey, he later helped to establish the Imperial Bowling Association in England in 1899. An Australasian team, including Young, toured and played British teams in 1901. Young's influence in Sydney society was considerable. His political activities included eleven years on the Sydney Municipal Council, and he was Lord Mayor in 1886. A draftsman by profession, Young designed a number of prominent city buildings including the Redfern Mortuary Station. He died on 27 February 1907 and was buried in Waverley Cemetery, Sydney.
LMcC
See **Lawn Bowls**.

YOUNG, WILLIAM GORDON (1904–74), born Guelph, Canada, graduated from Springfield College, USA, in 1927. After appointments in the YMCA and in physical education at the University of Western Ontario he became director of physical education in NSW in 1938. He organised annual holiday camps for primary-school teachers at Brookvale Oval. In order to spread physical education Young formed a 'flying squad' of twelve men and women who took in-service training to the state classrooms, demonstrating physical education lessons in primary schools. As an executive member of the National Fitness Council, Young was instrumental—even driving the bulldozer himself—in the construction of appropriate camp sites. He was awarded life membership of the Australian Physical Education Association (now ACHPER) in 1968.
IJ
See **Softball**.

BIBLIOGRAPHY ON THE HISTORY OF SPORT IN AUSTRALIA

Greg Blood

THIS SECTION aims to complement information contained in the Companion. Readers will find that this section provides them with information resources on Australian sport that can be used to follow up sports and topics in the *Companion* in more depth. Many library collections and information databases were used to compile the following bibliography.

Library collections that were used included the National Library of Australia, Melbourne Cricket Club, University of Canberra and the National Sport Information Centre. Information databases that were used included the Australian Bibliographic Network (ABN), Australian Public Affairs Information Service (APAIS), SPORT Database, and the LEISURE Database. The bibliography also relied heavily on contributors to the *Companion*.

Due to space restrictions it was decided to omit certain types of information including journal articles. To overcome this deficiency in the bibliography it was decided to outline the major collections and information databases where this information can be found.

Library Collections

There are many good sports collections in both public and private libraries in Australia. The following libraries have good Australian sports collections:

National Library of Australia has the most comprehensive collection on Australian sport due to its policy on collecting all material published in Australia or about Australia.

Melbourne Cricket Club Library has good collections on cricket, tennis, and Australian football. The extensive Pat Mullins cricket collection is housed in this library.

National Sport Information Centre has been comprehensively collecting Australian sport information since 1988. The Centre also has good historical collections on athletics, boxing and the Olympic Games.

Other good sports collections are located in State Libraries, University of Canberra, Victoria University of Technology and University of SA. For other collections refer to **Guide to Sports Collections in Australia** published by the National Sport Information Centre.

Information Databases

Information databases available online and CD-ROM provide very fast access to information. The following databases contain information on Australian sport:

SPORT Database is the most comprehensive database on sport and includes sports history books, journal articles, theses and conference papers published in Australia and overseas.

AUSPORT Database comprehensively includes information on Australian sport published since 1988.

APAIS produced by the National Library of Australia includes a wide range of periodical and newspaper articles, scholarly journals, and conference papers in the social sciences area including sport.

LEISURE produced by Footscray Institute of Technology covers Australian sport information for the period 1980 to 1988. AUSPORT Database continues the coverage of the LEISURE Database.

Australian Historic Records Register produced by the National Library of Australia is a comprehensive list of over 3500 records held by individuals, families, community organisations, and businesses around Australia. The register contains many records on sport.

Australian Bibliographic Network (ABN) operated by the National Library of Australia provides access to books, journal titles, conference proceedings, theses, and audiovisual material held in Australian libraries. Library locations for the majority of items listed in the bibliography can be found using ABN.

Access to these databases is available through the National Library of Australia, State Libraries, university libraries, public libraries and specialist libraries such as the National Sport Information Centre.

Bibliography Guidelines

As previously mentioned it was not possible exhaustively to list all information on the history of sport in Australia. We have used the following guidelines in preparing the bibliography:

- Books, government reports and theses only have been included due to space limitations. Many contributors to the Companion used journal articles and conference papers to support their contribution. This information can be located from the above-mentioned information databases.
- Material omitted includes journal articles, conference papers, newspaper articles, programmes, films, videotapes and audiocassettes.
- Books on the general history of a sport have not been included unless there was substantial information on Australian sport.
- The latest edition only has been listed. Books such as *Australian Sporting Records* have many editions.
- Due to the proliferation of books on cricket it was decided not to include most biographies, autobiographies, individual tours and club histories.
- Several of the contributors to the Companion used general history works to support their contribution. These general history works have not been included.

GENERAL

Andrews, Malcolm. *Encyclopedia of Australian sport*. Sydney, Golden Press, 1979

——. *Great Aussie sports heroes*. Sydney, Lilyfield, 1986

——. *More great Aussie sports heroes*. Sydney, Lilyfield, 1987

——. *101 Australian sporting heroes*. Sydney, Child & Associates, 1990

Armstrong, Thomas M. Sport and the Sydney daily press, 1850–1900. BHMS (Honours), University of Queensland, 1982

——. Sport as public policy, 1972–1985. MHMS, University of Queensland, 1985

——. Gold lust, federal sports policy since 1975. Ph.D., Macquarie University, 1988

Arnold, Trevor. Sport in colonial Australia. Ph.D., University of Queensland, 1979

Australia. Dept of Sport, Recreation and Tourism and ASC. *Australian sport: a profile*. Canberra, Australian Government Publishing Service (hereafter AGPS), 1985

Australia. Parliament. House of Representatives. Standing Committee on Expenditure. *The way we p(l)ay: Commonwealth assistance for sport and recreation*. Canberra, AGPS, 1983

Australia. Parliament. House of Representatives. Standing Committee on Finance and Public Administration. *Going for gold: the first report on an inquiry into sports funding and administration*. Canberra, AGPS, 1989

——. *Can sport be bought? the second report of an inquiry into sports funding and administration*. Canberra, AGPS, 1989

ASC. *A decade of champions*. Canberra, AGPS, 1988

Australians in sport. Melbourne, Cassell, 1974

Baka, Richard. *Similarities between Australian and Canadian government involvement in sport*. Melbourne, Dept. of Physical Education and Recreation, Footscray Institute of Technology, 1983

Blanch, John. *Australian sporting records*. 8th edn, Sydney, Bantam Books, 1988

Cadigan, Neil, et al. *Blood, sweat & tears: Australians and sport*. Melbourne, Lothian, 1989

Cashman, Richard and McKernan, Michael (eds). *Sport in history: the making of modern sporting history*. Brisbane, University of Queensland Press, 1979

——. *Sport, money, morality and the media*. Sydney, University of NSW Press, 1981

Collins, Bill, Aitken, Max and Cork, Bob. *One hundred years of public school sport in New South Wales, 1889–1989*. Sydney, NSW Dept. of School Education, 1990

Colwell, B.J. The British sporting heritage on colonial Australia and Canada: societal influences on the development of the organizational structure for sport. MHMS, University of Queensland, 1980

Connellan, Mark. The ideology of athleticism, its antipodean impact, and its manifestation in two Catholic schools. B.Ed. (Honours), University of Sydney, 1985

Cumes, James. *Their chastity was not too rigid: leisure times in early Australia*. Melbourne, Longman Cheshire, 1979

Daly, John. *Elysian fields: sport, class and community in colonial South Australia 1836–1890*. Adelaide, J. Daly, 1982

——. *Quest for excellence: the AIS in Canberra*. Canberra, AGPS, 1991

——. Sports, class and community in colonial South Australia. Ph.D., University of Illinois, Urbana-Champaign, 1978

Dudley, Robert P. A history of sport in the Moreton Bay District 1842–1872. Ph.D., University of Queensland, 1989

Dunstan, Keith. *Sports*. Melbourne, Sun Books, 1981

Ferguson, D.J. Play for a purpose: sport and Sydney society 1900–1914. B.A. (Honours), University of NSW, 1979

Goddard, G.H. *Soldiers and sportsmen*. London, AIF Sports Control Board, 1919

Goldlust, J. *Playing for keeps: sport, the media and society*. Melbourne, Longman Cheshire, 1987

Gordon, Harry. *Young men in a hurry: the story of Australia's fastest decade*. Melbourne, Lansdowne, 1961

Heads, Ian. *Backpage of sport: Australia's greatest sporting moments*. Sydney, Lester-Townsend, 1989

Heads, Ian and Lester, Gary. *200 years of Australian sport: a glorious obsession*. Sydney, Lester-Townsend, 1988

Howard, Bruce. *A nostalgic look at Australian sport*. Adelaide, Rigby, 1978

——. *The proud Australians: more than a century of sport*. Adelaide, Rigby, 1978

Howell, Reet and Howell, Max. *The genesis of sport in Queensland*. Brisbane, University of Queensland Press, 1992

——. *History of Australian sport*. Sydney, Shakespeare Head, 1987

Inglis, Gordon. *Sport and pastime in Australia*. 2nd edn, London, Methuen, 1912

Jacques, Trevor and Pavia, G. *Sport in Australia: selected readings in physical activity*. Sydney, McGraw-Hill, 1976

Kearney, Neil. *Tasmania's greatest sportsmen*. Launceston, Foot & Playsted, 1977

Kino, Brian. *The carnivals: a history of Jewish amateur sporting contests in Australia, 1924–1974*. Melbourne, York Press, 1974

Lawrence, Geoffrey and Rowe, David (eds). *Power play: essays in the sociology of Australian sport*. Sydney, Hale & Iremonger, 1986

Lord, David. *Best last ten years in Australian sport*. Kurralta Park, SA, H. Frost, 1978

Mandle, William. *Winners can laugh: sport and society*. Melbourne, Penguin, 1974

McKay, Jim. *No pain, no gain? Sport and Australian culture*. Sydney, Prentice Hall, 1991

O'Keefe, D. and Atkinson, A. *Competitors: the sports experience, Australian sporting photographs 1950s to 1980s*. Sydney, D. O'Keefe, 1984

Powers, J. and Suter, V. *Australian sports heroes*. Melbourne, Nelson, 1982

Report of the Australian Sports Institute Study Group. Canberra, AGPS, 1975

Rowe, David and Lawrence, Geoffrey. *Sport and leisure: trends in Australian popular culture*. Sydney, Harcourt Brace Jovanovich, 1990

Rothmans National Sport Foundation. *Twenty years of achievement 1964–1984*. Sydney, The Foundation, 1984

Sharp, Martin. Sporting spectacles: cricket and football in Sydney, 1890–1912. Ph.D., Australian National University, 1986

Shepherd, Jim. *Australian sporting almanac*. Sydney, Hamlyn, 1974

——. *Encylopedia of Australian sport*. Adelaide, Rigby, 1980

——. *Great moments in Australian sport*. Sydney, Angus & Robertson, 1988

——. *Winfield book of Australian sporting records*. Adelaide, Rigby, 1981

Smith, Terry. *The Champions: Australia's sporting greats*. Sydney, Angus & Robertson, 1990

Stoddart, Brian. *Saturday afternoon fever: sport in the Australian culture*. Sydney, Angus & Robertson, 1986

Unstead, R. and Henderson, W. *Sport and entertainment in Australia*. London, Black, 1976

Vamplew, Wray. *Sport and colonialism in nineteenth century Australia*. Adelaide, Australian Society for Sports History, 1986

Whitington, R. *Great moments in Australian sport*. Melbourne, Macmillan, 1974

Wide World of Sports. *Australian sporting hall of fame*. Sydney, Angus & Robertson, 1984

Wilkinson, J. *Famous Australian sports pictures*. Melbourne, Currey O'Neil, 1982

ABORIGINES
Blades, Genevieve. *Australian aborigines, cricket and pedestrianism: culture and conflict, 1890–1910*. B.H.M.S. (Honours), University of Queensland, 1985

Harris, Bret. *The proud champions: Australia's aboriginal sporting heroes*. Sydney, Little Hills, 1989

Salter, M. A. *Games and pastimes of the Australian aboriginal*. M.A., University of Alberta, 1967

Tatz, Colin. *Aborigines in sport*. Adelaide, Australian Society for Sports History, 1987

AERONAUTICAL SPORTS
Ash, Allan. *Gliding in Australia*. Hawthorn, Vic., Hudson, 1990

Gwynn-Jones, T. *The air racers: aviation's golden era 1909–1936*. Sydney, Lansdowne, 1983

Mitchell, Marion and Smith, Julie. *Ballooning in South Australia, 1871–1983*. Greenacres, SA, South Australian Balloon & Airship Club, 1983

Potter, Moss. *On top of the world*. Waikerie, Waikerie Gliding Club, 197-?

Rodgers, Helene. *Early ballooning in Australia*. Melbourne, Set & Forget Press, 1989

AUSTRALIAN FOOTBALL
Agars, Merv. *Bloods sweat and tears: West Adelaide Football Club, 1877–1987*. Adelaide, West Adelaide Football Club, 1987

Atkinson, Graeme. *3AW book of footy records: all the great players, matches, goals, kicks, brawls and sensations from more than 100 years of Aussie rules in Australia*. Melbourne, Matchbooks, 1989

——. *The complete book of VFL finals: from 1897 to the present*. Rev. edn, Melbourne, Five Mile Press, 1989

Australian rules 100 greatest players. Sydney, Murray, 1978

Aylett, Alan and Hobbs, Greg. *My game: a life in football*. Melbourne, Sun Books, 1986

Bartrop, Paul R. *Scores, crowds and records: statistics on the Victorian Football League since 1945*. Sydney, History Project Incorporated, 1984

Blainey, Geoffrey. *A game of our own: the origins of Australian football*. Melbourne, Information Australia, 1990

Buggy, Hugh and Bell, Harry. *The Carlton story*. Melbourne, Eric White Associates, 1958

Christian, Geoff. *The footballers, from 1885 to the West Coast Eagles*. Rev. edn, Perth, St George Books, 1988

Clonard, Derby. *Jubilee: fifty years history of Richmond Football Club*. Melbourne, Roberts, 1934

Coward, Mike. *Red and blue blooded*. Adelaide, K.B. Printing, n.d.

Delbridge, N. *The Bulldog book: sons of the 'Scray (1883–1983)*. Melbourne, All Graphic Industries, 1983

Dowling, Gerard P. *The North story*. Melbourne, Hawthorn Press, 1973

Dunn, John and Main, Jim. *Australian football: an illustrated history*. Melbourne, Lansdowne Press, 1974

Dyer, Jack and Hansen, Brian. *Captain Blood*. London, Paul, 1965

——. *The wild men of football*. Melbourne, Southdown Press, 1968

Fiddian, Marc. *The pioneers*. Melbourne, VFA, 1977

——. *The roar of the crowd: a history of VFA Grand Finals*. Melbourne, VFA, 1987

Fitzgerald, Ross and Spillman, Ken. *The greatest game*. Melbourne, William Heinemann, 1988.

Gillett, R. A. Where the big men fly: an early history of Australian football in the Riverina region of N.S.W. B.Litt., University of New England, 1983

Glossop, Mathew. *East Perth 1906–1976*. Perth, M. Glossop, 1976

Gordon, Harry. *The hard way: the story of Hawthorn Football Club*. Sydney, Lester-Townsend, 1990

Gordon, Kerrie and Dalton, Alan. *Too tough to die: Footscray's fightback 1989*. Melbourne, Footscray Football Club, 1990

Hansen, Brian. *Tigerland: the history of the Richmond Football Club from 1885*. Melbourne, Richmond Former Players and Officials Association, 1989

Harrison, Henry. *The story of an athlete: a picture of the past*. Melbourne, Alexander McCubbin, 1924

Hart, Royce. *The Royce Hart story*. Melbourne, Nelson, 1970

Hewart, Tim. *The Blues: a history of Carlton Football Club*. Melbourne, Carlton Football Club, 1982

Hobbs, Greg. *125 years of the Melbourne Demons: the story of the Melbourne Football Club 1858 to 1983*. Melbourne, Melbourne Football Club, 1984

——. *Richmond: the home of the Tigers*. Melbourne, Richmond Football Club, 1981

Hobbs, Greg and Sheehan, Mike. *The VFL hall of fame: the greats of Victorian football*. Melbourne, Herald and Weekly Times, 1981

Hutchinson, Col. *Cats' tales: the Geelong Football Club, 1897-1983*. Geelong, Geelong Advertiser, 1984

Hutchinson, Garrie. *From the outer: watching football in the 80s*. Melbourne, Penguin, 1984

——. *The great Australian book of football stories*. Melbourne, Currey O'Neil, 1983

Lane, Christopher. The premiers: Norwood Football Club, 1878–1889. B.A. (Honours), University of Adelaide, 1987.

Lee, Jack. *Old Easts 1948–1975*. Perth, Reeds Printing, 1976

Mancini, A. and Hibbins, G. M. (eds). *Running with the ball: football's foster father*. Melbourne, Lynedoch, 1987

Maplestone, Michael. *Flying high: the history of the Essendon Football Club*. Melbourne, Essendon Football Club, 1983

——. *Those magnificent men 1897–1987*. Melbourne, Essendon Football Club, 1988

McLean, A. R. *100 years with the Magpies: the story of the Port Adelaide Football Club 1870–1970*. Adelaide, Letterpress, 1970

Mullen, C. C. *History of Australian rules football*. Melbourne, 1958

Nicholls, John and McDonald, Ian. *Big Nick*. Melbourne, Sparks, 1977

Oakley, Barry. *A salute to the Great McCarthy*. Melbourne, Penguin, 1971.

Pinchin, Ken and Leeson, Allan. *A century of Tasmanian football 1879–1979*. Hobart, Tasmanian Football League, 1979

Pollard, Jack. *High mark: the complete book of Australian football*. 2nd edn, Sydney, Murray, 1967

Powers, John. *The coach: a season with Ron Barassi*. Melbourne, Thomas Nelson, 1978

Richards, Lou and McDonald, Ian. *Boots and all*. London, Paul, 1963

Rodgers, Stephen. *Toohey's guide to every game ever played: VFL results 1897–1982*. Melbourne, Currey O'Neil, 1983

Sandercock, Leonie and Turner, Ian. *Up where Cazaly? The great Australian game*. London, Granada, 1981

Sheehan, Mike (ed.). *Backpage, great headlines of Australian football*. Sydney, Lester-Townsend, 1990

Sheedy, Jack and Farrell, Darcy. *My football life*. Perth, J. Sheedy, 1969

Stewart, Bob. *The Australian football business: a spectator's guide to the VFL*. Sydney, Kangaroo Press, 1983

Stremski, Richard. *Kill for Collingwood*. Sydney, Allen & Unwin, 1986

Sutherland, Mike, et al. *The first one hundred seasons: Fitzroy Football Club, 1883–1983*. Melbourne, Fitzroy Football Club, 1983

Taylor, E. C. H. *100 years of football: the story of the Melbourne Football Club, 1858-1958*. Melbourne, Wilke, 1958

Taylor, Kevin. *The Sydney Swans: the complete history, 1874–1986*. Sydney, Allen & Unwin, 1987

Western Australian football history, 1885–1971. Perth, Pelpel Co., 1971

Whimpress, Bernard. *The South Australian football story*. Adelaide, SA National Football League, 1983

Wood, John. *Gentleman Jack: the Johnny Cahill story 1958–82*. Adelaide, J. & W. Wood, 1982

——. *S.A. Greats: the history of the Magarey Medal*. Adelaide, J. & W. Wood, 1988

BASKETBALL
Basketball in New South Wales: a history 1938 to 1988. Sydney, NSW Basketball Association, 1988

Maher, Tom and Howell, Stephen. *Coast to coast: the challenge of basketball*. Melbourne, Houghton Mifflin, 1990

Nagy, Boti. *High flyers: women's basketball in Australia*. Melbourne, Sun Books, 1990

BILLIARDS
Ricketts, A. *Walter Lindrum: billiards phenomenon*. Canberra, B. Clouston, 1982

BOXING
Australia. *Interdepartmental Committee of Inquiry into Boxing and Other Combat Sports. Report*. Canberra, AGPS, 1976

Corris, Peter. *Lords of the ring*. Sydney, Cassell, 1980

Doherty, William J. *In the days of the giants: memories of a champion of the prize-ring*. Sydney, George Harrap, 1931

Famechon, Johnny. *Fammo*. Melbourne, Sun Books, 1971

Ferry, F.J. *The life story of Les Darcy: late middleweight champion of the world*. Sydney, F.J. Ferry, 1937

Gattellari, Rocky. *The rocky road*. Melbourne, Heinemann, 1989

Jeffries, C. *Famous fights at the Stadium*. Sydney, Platypus Press, 1914

Kieza, Grantlee. *Australian boxing: an illustrated history*. Sydney, Gary Allen, 1990

Kieza, Grantlee and Muszkat, Peter. *Fenech, the official biography*. Sydney, Lester-Townsend, 1988.

Mitchell, Ray. *Fighting Sands*. London, Horwitz, 1965

——. *Great Australian fights*. London, Horwitz, 1965

Read, Jack. *Griffo: his life story and record*. Sydney, Fine Art Publishers, 1926

——. *Read's Australian boxing records*. Sydney, Invincible Press, 1947

Rose, Lionel. *Lionel Rose: Australian, life story of a champion*. Sydney, Angus & Robertson, 1969

Rule, Andrew. *Rose against the odds: the Lionel Rose story*. Kilmore, Vic., Floradale Productions, 1991

Ryan, Max. *Two champs from Narrabri*. Tamworth, Peel Valley Printery, 1988

Swanwick, Raymond. *Les Darcy: Australia's golden boy of boxing*. Sydney, Ure Smith, 1965

Truslove, Charlie. *The great fight way*. Perth, Patersons Press, 193–?

Solar Plexus. *The Darcy story: from blacksmith's apprentice to world's champion boxer*. Sydney, New Century Press, 1919

Vic Patrick—the champ. Sydney, Consolidated Press, 1946

Will, Beverley. *Fighter lady*. Melbourne, Franklin Carrack, 1974

CANOEING

Morrison, Joan. *The challenge of canoeing*. Series 1—slalom and wildwater in NSW and Australia. Australia, 198–?

COMMONWEALTH GAMES

Blanch, John and Jenes, Paul. *Australia's complete history at the Commonwealth Games*. Sydney, John Blanch, 1982

Moore, Katharine E. The concept of British Empire Games: an analysis of its origin and evolution from 1891 to 1930. Ph.D. University of Queensland, 1986

Tunstall, Arthur. *Australia at the Commonwealth Games 1911–1990: XIV Commonwealth Games Auckland.* Sydney, Australian Commonwealth Games Association, 1990

University of Queensland, Australian Studies Centre. *The 1982 Commonwealth Games: a retrospect.* Brisbane, The Centre, 1982

CRICKET

Atkins, Jack. *Hanson Cater: 'Australia's undertaker wicketkeeper'.* Sydney, Waverley Historical Society, 1976

Benaud, Richie. *Benaud on reflection.* Sydney, Collins, 1984

———. *Lights, camera, action: an illustrated history of the world series.* Melbourne, Hamlyn, 1990

Bose, Mihir. *Keith Miller: a cricketing biography.* London, Allen & Unwin, 1980

Bouwman, Richard. *Glorious innings: treasures from the Melbourne Cricket Club.* Melbourne, Hutchinson, 1987

Bradman to Border: a history of Australia-England test matches from 1946. Sydney, ABC Enterprises, 1986

Bradman, Donald. *The art of cricket.* Rev. edn, Sydney, Hodder and Stoughton, 1984

———. *Farewell to cricket.* London, Hodder & Stoughton, 1950

Brayshaw, Ian. *Cricket west.* Perth, Transgraphics, 1979

Cardwell, Ronald. *The A.I.F. cricket team.* Sydney, R. Cardwell, 1980

Cashman, Richard. *'Ave a go, yer mug! Australian cricket crowds from larrikin to ocker.* Sydney, Collins, 1984

———. *Australian cricket crowds: the attendance cycle daily figures 1877–1984.* Sydney, History Project Incorporated, 1984

———. *The 'Demon' Spofforth.* Sydney, NSW University Press, 1990

Chapple, S. G. *50 years of cricket in Tasmania's North East.* Launceston, S. G. Chapple, 1985

Cricket, a pictorial history of Australian test players. Melbourne, Garry Sparke, 1982

Crowley, Brian. *A cavalcade of international cricketers: more than 1500 test players.* Melbourne, Macmillan Australia, 1988

———. *A history of Australian batting, 1850–1986.* Melbourne, Macmillan, 1986

———. *A history of Australian bowling and wicket-keeping, 1850–1986.* Melbourne, Macmillan, 1986

———. *The springbok and the kangaroo: a complete history of South Africa versus Australia at cricket.* Johannesburg, Blue Crane Books, 1967

Derriman, Philip. *The grand old ground: a history of the Sydney Cricket Ground.* Sydney, Cassell Australia, 1981

——. *True to the blue: a history of the New South Wales Cricket Association.* Sydney, Richard Smart Publishing, 1985

Dundas, Ross. *Highest, most and best: Australian cricket statistics 1850–1990.* Sydney, Angus & Robertson, 1990

Dunstan, Keith. *The paddock that grew: the story of the Melbourne Cricket Club.* 3rd edn, Sydney, Hutchinson Australia, 1988

Egan, Jack. *The story of cricket in Australia.* Melbourne, Macmillan, 1987

Fingleton, Jack. *Batting from memory.* London, Collins, 1981

Forsyth, Christopher. *Pitched battles: the history of the Australia–England test wars.* Rev. edn, Melbourne, Widescope, 1978

Foskett, Alan. *Cricket in the ACT 1922–1969: some information and highlights.* Canberra, Alan Foskett Consultancy Services, 1989

Frith, David. *Archie Jackson: the Keats of cricket.* Rev. edn, London, Pavilion, 1987

——. *Australia versus England: a pictorial history of every test match since 1877.* Updated 7th edn, Melbourne, Viking O'Neil, 1990

——. *England v Australia test match records 1877–1985.* London, Willow, 1986

Giffen, George. *The golden age of Australian cricket.* Melbourne, Currey O'Neil, 1982

——. *With bat and ball.* London, Ward Lock, 1898

Harte, Chris. *The history of the Sheffield Shield.* Sydney, Allen & Unwin, 1987

——. *SACA: the history of the South Australian Cricket Association.* Adelaide, Sport Marketing (Australia), 1990

Hordern, Herbert V. *Googlies: coals from a test-cricketer's fireplace.* Sydney, Angus & Robertson, 1932

Hutcheon, E.H. *A history of Queensland cricket.* Brisbane, 194-?

Iredale, Frank. *33 years of cricket.* Sydney, Beatty Richardson, 1920

McGilvray, Alan. *McGilvray: the game is not the same.* Sydney, ABC, 1985

McHarg, Jack. *Stan McCabe: the man and his cricket.* Sydney, Collins, 1987

Mailey, Arthur. *10 for 66 and all that.* London, Phoenix House, 1958

Millbank, S. I. S.A.C.A., cricket and South Australia: 1871–1914. BA (Honours), Flinders University of SA, 1981

Montefiore, David. *Cricket in the doldrums: the struggle between private and public control of Australian Cricket in the 1880s.* BA (Honours) University of NSW, 1989

Moody, Clarence. *South Australian cricket: reminiscences of fifty years.* Adelaide, W. K. Thomas, 1898

Moyes, A.G. *Australian cricket: a history.* Sydney, Angus & Robertson, 1959

——. *A century of cricketers.* Sydney, Angus & Robertson, 1950

Mulvaney, D. and Harcourt, Rex. *Cricket walkabout.* 2nd edn, Melbourne, Macmillan, 1988

Noble, Monty. *The game's the thing.* London, Cassell, 1926

Page, Roger. *A history of Tasmanian cricket.* Hobart, Government of Tasmania, 1957

Pollard, Jack. *Australian cricket: the game and the players.* Rev. edn, Sydney, Angus & Robertson, 1988

——. *The Bradman years: Australian cricket 1918–1948.* Sydney, Angus & Robertson, 1988

——. *The pictorial history of Australian cricket.* 3rd edn, Sydney, Hodder & Stoughton, 1989

——. *The formative years of Australian cricket 1803–1893.* Sydney, Angus & Robertson, 1987

——. *The turbulent years of Australian cricket 1893–1917.* Sydney, Angus & Robertson, 1987

Robinson, Ray. *On top down under: Australia's cricket captains.* 2nd edn, Sydney, Cassell, 1981

Rosenwater, Irving. *Sir Donald Bradman: a biography.* London, Batsford, 1978

Scott, Jas. *Early cricket in Sydney, 1803 to 1856.* Sydney, NSW Cricket Association, 1991

Sharp, Martin. Professionalism and commercialism in Australian cricket during the 1930s: the origins of the cricket revolution. BA (Honours), University of NSW, 1981

Sharpham, Peter. *Trumper: the definitive biography.* Sydney, Hodder & Stoughton, 1985

Sissons, Ric and Stoddart, Brian. *Cricket and Empire: the 1932–33 bodyline tour of Australia.* Sydney, Allen & Unwin, 1984

Smith, Rick. *Prominent Tasmanian cricketers: from Marshall to Boon.* Launceston, Foot & Playsted, 1985

Smith, Sydney. *History of the tests: record of all test cricket matches played between England and Australia 1877 to 1946*. Sydney, Australasian Publishing, 1946

Stobo, Richard. Cricket and Australian nationalism in the 19th century. BA (Honours), University of Sydney, 1987

Stokes, Edward. *Australian test cricket facts, 1946–1978*. Sydney, Ure Smith, 1979

Torrens, Warwick. *Queensland cricket and cricketers, 1862–1981*. Brisbane, W. Torrens, 1982

Trumble, Robert. *The golden age of cricket: a memorable book of Hugh Trumble*. Melbourne, R. Trumble, 1968

Webster, Ray (compiler) and Miller, Alan (editor). *First-class cricket in Australia, vol. 1 1850–51 to 1941–42*. Glen Waverley, Vic., Ray Webster, 1991

Whimpress, Bernard and Hart, Nigel. *Adelaide Oval test cricket 1884–1984*. Adelaide, Wakefield Press and the SA Cricket Association, 1984

Whitington, R. S. *Australians abroad: Australia's overseas test tours*. Melbourne, Five Mile Press, 1983

——. *An illustrated history of Australian cricket*. Rev. edn, Melbourne, Currey O'Neil, 1987

Whitington, Richard M. *The quiet Australian: the Lindsay Hassett story*. Melbourne, Heinemann, 1969

Williams, R. and Smith, R. (eds). *To celebrate a century of Northern Tasmanian Cricket Association 1886–1986*. Launceston, Foot & Playsted, 1986

Woods, Sammy. *My reminiscences*. London, Chapman Hall, 1925

CRICKET (INDOOR)
Cosier, Gary and Smithers, Patrick. *Indoor cricket: the history, the rules, and how to play the game*. Melbourne, Five Mile Press, 1986

CRICKET (WOMEN'S)
Butcher, Betty. *The sport of grace: women's cricket in Victoria*. Melbourne, Sports Federation of Australia, 1984

Cashman, Richard and Weaver, Amanda. *Wicket women: cricket & women in Australia*. Sydney, NSW University Press, 1991

Frost, Lenore. *Donex Ladies Cricket Club record club, 1945–46 to 1984–85*. Melbourne, L. Frost, 1986

Hawes, Joan. *Women's test cricket: the golden triangle, 1934–1984*. Sussex, Book Guild, 1987

Joy, Nancy. *Maiden over: a short history of women's cricket and a diary of the 1948–49 test tour to Australia*. London, Sporting Handbooks, 1950

Papasergio, Clare and Moy, Janice. *The History of women's cricket in Western Australia*. Perth, Imperial Printing, 1990

Western Australian Women's Cricket Association. *Australia vs. England: women's test cricket, fifty years.* Perth, The Association, 1985

CROQUET
Dettman, Dorothy. *Hoop & roquet: a history of the Northern District Croquet Association.* Kyneton, Vic., D. Dettman, 1991

Dickinson, Winifred. *A history of the Australian Croquet Council 1949 to 1986.* Port Macquarie, NSW, W. Dickinson, 198–?

Hooper, Max. *Croquet history: mainly Australia, especially New South Wales.* Sydney, M. Hooper, 1991

Ridley, Joyce. *A history of croquet in Victoria, 1866 to 1980.* Melbourne, J. Ridley, 1980

CYCLING
Fildon, Paul. *Murray's guide to cycling.* Sydney, Murray, 1980

Fitzpatrick, J. *The bicycle and the bush: man and machine in rural Australia.* Melbourne, Oxford University Press, 1980

Madden, Ray. How delightful is the sensation: women and cycling in the 1890s. BA (Honours), University of NSW, 1983

Mockeridge, Russell and Burrowes, John. *My world on wheels.* London, Paul, 1960

Opperman, Hubert. *Pedals, politics and people.* Sydney, Haldane, 1977

DRUGS IN SPORT
Australia. Parliament. Senate Standing Committee on Environment, Recreation and Arts. *Drugs in sport: an interim report.* Canberra, AGPS, 1989

———. *Drugs in sport: second report.* Canberra, AGPS, 1990

Australian Sports Medicine Federation. Drug Control Committee. *Survey of drug use in Australian sport.* Melbourne, The Federation, 1983

Donald, Ken. *The doping game.* Brisbane, Boolarong, 1983

EQUESTRIAN
Boillotat, Sally. *Polocrosse: Australian made, internationally played.* Sydney, Belcris Books, 1990

Conquest, R. *Dusty distances: yesterday's Australia.* Adelaide, Rigby, 1978

Couch-Keen, Glenda. *Equestrienne Australis: the story of Australia's horsewomen.* Springton, Sidesaddle Association of SA, 1990

Hayes, Mark D. *The origin of the rodeo in Australia.* Longreach, Queensland, Australian Stockman's Hall of Fame, 1984

Poole, Peter. *Rodeo in Australia.* Adelaide, Rigby, 1977

GAMBLING
Caldwell, Geoff, et al. *Gambling in Australia.* Sydney, Croom Helm, 1985

O'Hara, John. *A mug's game: a history of gaming and betting in Australia*. Sydney, NSW University Press, 1988

——. Gaming and betting in Australia 1788–1983. Ph.D., University of New England, 1985

GOLF

Alenson, John. *Ten decades, 1882–1982: a story of the events which go to make the history of 100 years of the Australian Golf Club*. Sydney, Australian Golf Club, 1982

Barnaby, James W. *The history of the Royal Melbourne Golf Club, 1941 to 1968*. Melbourne, Royal Melbourne Golf Club, 1972

Bell, Clarrie. *Eighty golfing years: a history of North Adelaide Golf Club*. Adelaide, North Adelaide Golf Club, 1985

Branson, V. *Kooyonga: the story of a golf club*. Adelaide, Kooyonga Golf Club, 1983

Ellis, Alexander D. *The history of the Royal Melbourne Golf Club, 1891 to 1941*. Melbourne, Robertson & Mullens, 1941

Innes, David J. *The story of golf in New South Wales, 1851–1987*. Sydney, NSW Golf Association, 1988

Lee, Jack. *Royal Perth: the history of Royal Perth W.A.'s first golf club, founded in 1895*. Perth, J. Lee, 1978

Johnson, Joseph. *The Royal Melbourne Golf Club: a centenary history*. Melbourne, Royal Melbourne Golf Club, 1991

Mansfield, Garry. *A history of golf in Victoria*. Melbourne, Victorian Golf Association, 1987

McLaren, Muir. *The Australian and New Zealand golfer's handbook*. 6th edn, Sydney, Reed, 1980

Norman, Greg and Lawrence, Don. *My story*. London, Harrap, 1983

Owen, William. *A short history of the Royal Sydney Golf Club*. Sydney, Royal Sydney Golf Club, 1949

Perry, Phyllis. *From green to gold: the first fifty years of the Australian Ladies Golf Union*. Melbourne, Australian Ladies Golf Union, 1976

Phillips, Murray. A history of the Brisbane Golf Club. BA (Honours), University of Queensland, 1986

Pollard, Jack. *Australian golf: the game and the players*. Sydney, Angus & Robertson, 1990

Ramsey, Tom. *25 great Australian golf courses and how to play them*. Sydney, Rigby, 1981

Ridgway, Marjorie A. *South Australian golf, 1869–1970*. Adelaide, SA Ladies' Golf Union, 1972

Saunders, P. Not a game but a way of life: some aspects of the effect of social change on the game of golf in Australia, with particular reference to South Australia. BA (Honours), Flinders University of SA, 1980

Smith, Terry. *Australian golf: the first 100 years*. Sydney, Lester-Townsend, 1982

——. *The complete book of Australian golf*. Rev. edn, Sydney, ABC, 1988

Soutar, D. *The Australian golfer*. Australia, E. W. Cole, 1908

Tatz, Colin and Stoddart, Brian. *The Royal Sydney Golf Club: the first hundred years*. Sydney, Allen & Unwin, forthcoming

Tresider, Phil. *Great days of Australian golf*. Sydney, Ironbark Press, 1990

Williams, Stewart H. *The test of time: the history of the Kingston Heath Golf Club*. Melbourne, Macmillan, 1981

GREYHOUND RACING
Stearn, Duncan. *The ultimate accolade: the New South Wales Greyhound of the Year award 1965–1985*. Sydney, Dunlor Publications, 1986

HARNESS RACING
Agnew, Max. *Australia's trotting heritage*. Mitcham, Vic., Standard Bred Publications, 1977

——. *Silks and sulkies: the complete book of Australian and New Zealand harness racing*. Sydney, Doubleday, 1986

——. *The George Gath story*. Melbourne, Hunters Publications, 1987

Bisman, Ronald and Strong, Tayler. *The Interdominions: saga of the champions*. Auckland, Moa Publications, 1975

Brown, Greg. *One hundred years of trotting 1877–1977*. Sydney, Whitcombe & Tombs, 1981

Dullard, V. *Globe Derby's greatness*. Melbourne, Wellham Printing, 1942

Ford, Peter. *Halwes, Australasian pacing champion*. Hobart, Libra Books, 1985

Goffin, Graham. *Globe trotters: pacesetters of harness racing*. Melbourne, Hanwards Publications, 1978

——. *Paleface Adios, the living legend*. Melbourne, Harness Racing Publications, 1982

Jenkins, Ron. *Great trotters*. Sydney, Pollard, 1974

——. *P. J. Hall: a famous name in trotting*. Sydney, Lautoka, 1977

Porter, Kim. *The Australian trotter and pacer*. Clare, S. Aust., K. Porter, 1969

The people's heritage: playground of the people governed by the people, for the people. New edn, Perth, WA Trotting Association, 1944

HOCKEY

Browne, Fred. *The game that grows*. Perth, 1960.

Fildon, Paul G. *Murray's guide to hockey*. Sydney, Murray, 1978

Hodges, Lena and Dive, Molly. *A history of the New South Wales Women's Hockey Association 1908–1983*. Sydney, The Association, 1984

McLeary, Ailsa. *Elsternwick Hockey Club 1905–1990: a history*. Melbourne, 1990

Miller, Clary. *Hockey's grand slam*. Perth, AGGISS Sports Promotions, 1988

South Australian Hockey Association. *Seventy fifth anniversary souvenir 1903–1978*. Adelaide, The Association, 1978

Tronson, Mark. *Australia's World Cup Hockey 'gold medal' victory*. Wallacia, NSW, International Field Hockey Publishing, 1986

——. *Hockey champions*. Wallacia, NSW, International Field Hockey Publishing, 1986

HORSE-RACING

Ahern, B. *A century of winners: the saga of 121 Melbourne Cups*. Brisbane, Boolarong Publications, 1982

Barrie, Douglas. *Turf cavalcade: a review of one hundred and fifty years of horse-racing in Australia, and of the Australian Jockey Club's hundred years at Randwick*. Sydney, AJC, 1960

Barrie, Douglas and Pring, Peter. *Australia's thoroughbred idols*. Penrith, NSW, Discovery Press, 1973

Benson, Margaret. *Tommy Woodcock (the story of Australia's most remarkable trainer)*. Melbourne, Shenley Publications, 1978

Boulter, Richard. *Forty years on, the Sydney Turf Club: a history of the first forty years (1943–1983)*. Sydney, Sydney Turf Club, 1984

Brassel, Stephen. *A portrait of racing: horseracing in Australia and New Zealand since 1970*. Sydney, Simon & Schuster, 1990

Brennan, Allan. *The life story of jockey Jim Pike*. Sydney, Jackson & O'Sullivan, 1933

Brown, Joe. *Joe Brown's autobiography: just for the record*. Sydney, ABC, 1984

Bryant, Bert and Phillipson, Neill. *The Bert Bryant story*. Adelaide, Rigby, 1978

Burke, J.S. Some aspects of early Sydney horseracing: 1810–1918. BA (Honours), University of NSW, 1980

Carter, Isabel. *Phar Lap: the story of the big horse*. Melbourne, Lansdowne, 1964

Cavanough, Maurice. *The Caulfield Cup*. Sydney, Pollard, 1976

——. *The Melbourne Cup 1861–1982*. Melbourne, Currey O'Neil, 1983

Clonard, Derby. *Victorian turf cavalcade: 1836–1936*. Melbourne, Page Printing, 1936

Collins, James. *Lightning Phar Lap, the Australian wonder horse*. Brisbane, Read Press, 1932

Contos, Mick. *Born to ride, the Kevin Langby story*. Sydney, Lester-Townsend, 1988

De Lore, Brian. *Famous winners of the Australian turf*. Sydney, View Productions, 1984

Doyle, Con and Howard, Peter. *Silks and thoroughbreds: the Con Doyle story*. Toowoomba, Qld., Darling Downs Institute Press, 1988

Fiddian, Marc. *Winners galore: the Better Boy story*. Carrum Downs, Vic. Range View Stud, 1983

Fiddian, Marc and Ryan, Ray. *Behind the glasses*. Pakenham, Vic., Pakenham Gazette, 1990

Freedman, Harold and Lemon, Andrew. *The history of Australian thoroughbred racing*. vol. 1: *The beginnings to the first Melbourne Cup;* vol. 2: *The golden years from 1862 to 1914*. Melbourne, Southbank Communications, 1990

Gould, Nat. *On and off the turf in Australia*. London, Routledge, 1895

Greenwood, G. *Gloaming: the wonder horse*. Sydney, New Century Press, 1927

Griffiths, Samuel A. *A rolling stone on the turf*. Sydney, Angus & Robertson, 1933

——. *Turf and heath: Australian racing reminiscences*. Melbourne, A. H. Massina, 1906

Haitana, Hayden. *Fine Cotton & me: the confessions of Hayden Haitana*. Sydney, Angus & Robertson, 1986

Helgeby, S. Sport and festival: horse-racing in NSW, 1850-1870. BA (Honours), Australian National University, 1984

Henry, J. *The racing career of Tom Hales, Australia's premier horseman*. Melbourne, 1901

Hickie, David. *Gentlemen of the Australian turf: their bets, their bankrolls, their bankruptcies*. Sydney, Angus & Robertson, 1986

Higgins, Roy and Vine, Terry. *The professor*. Melbourne, Caribou Publications, 1984

History & growth of the South Australian Jockey Club. Adelaide, The Club, 1955

Hobson, Warwick. *Racing's all-time greats*. Sydney, Thoroughbred Press and Horwitz Grahame, 1986

——. *The story of the Golden Slipper Stakes*. Gosford, NSW, Horse-Racing Publishing, 1984

Hynes, Matt. *The Melbourne Cup down the years: champions from 1861 to 1950*. Adelaide, Hynes, 1950

Johnstone, Rae. *The Rae Johnstone story*. London, Paul, 1958

Lang, William, Austin, Ken and McKay, Stewart. *Racehorses in Australia*. Sydney, Art in Australia, 1922

Lillye, Bert. *Backstage of racing*. Sydney, Fairfax, 1985

Knight, Lorin. *Scobie*. Bognor Regis, New Horizon, 1983

McGill. J. *Historical happenings and incredible incidents of the Queensland turf*. Brisbane, 1963

Mitchell, H. *Victoria's greatest races*. Melbourne, British and Australasian Publishing Service, 1924.

Montgomerie, Bruce. *Bart, the story of Bart Cummings*. Sydney, Watermark Press, 1988

Morris, A.P. *A story of courage: 'Flight', Australia's greatest stake-winning mare*. Sydney, 1948

Noud, Keith. *Courses for horses*. Brisbane, Boolarong for Brisbane Amateur Turf Club, 1989

Oliver, W. *From then—till now: a historical review of the Tasmanian Turf Club, racing identities, racehorses and courses*. Hobart, W. Oliver, 1987

Penton, N. *A racing heart: the story of Australian turf*. Sydney, Collins, 1987

The Perth Cup at Ascot: 100 years. Hampton, Vic., Magazine Art for the WA Turf Club, 1986

Poliness, G. *Carbine*. Sydney, Waterloo Press, 1985

Pollard, Jack. *Australian horse racing*. Sydney, Angus & Robertson, 1988

——. *The pictorial history of Australian horse racing*. Rev. edn, Sydney, Hodder & Stoughton, 1989

Pring, Peter. *Major Australian races and racehorses 1960–1980*. Sydney, Thoroughbred Press, 1980

——. *Peter Pring's great moments in Australian racing: from Phar Lap to the present day*. Sydney, Thoroughbred Press, 1978

——. *The Star Kingdom story*. Sydney, Thoroughbred Press, 1983

Scobie, James. *My life on the Australian turf*. Melbourne, Speciality, 1929

Sewell, W.B. *The romance of racing in South Australia*. SA, W. Sewell, 1970

Sigley, Bill. *Mighty Bernborough: the story behind the legend*. Brisbane, Boolarong, 1990

Spinty, Jack. *Phar Lap*. Sydney, New Century, 1932

That horse—Bernborough. Sydney, Consolidated Press, 1946

Tip and Tony. *The life, adventures, and sporting career of Joe Thompson: the king of the ring*. Melbourne, America Publishing, 1877.

Tomlinson, Jenny. *Born winners, born losers: a history of thoroughbred breeding and racing in Western Australia since 1833*. Perth, Reeve Books, 1990

Townsend, Helen. *Phar Lap: a pictorial history*. Sydney, Lansdowne, 1983

Turf men and memories: sketches of the careers of leading Australian trainers, jockeys and sporting identities, pen pictures of Carbine and Trafalgar. Melbourne, Thomas Smart, 1912

White, R. *Courses for horses: the story of Victorian and Riverina race courses*. Melbourne, Five Mile Press, 1985

Wilkinson, Jack and Grant, Warren (eds). *Great Australian turf pictures*. Melbourne, Sun Books, 1976

Wilkinson, Michael. *The Phar Lap story*. Sydney, Budget Books, 1983

Woodcock, Tommy. *Tommy Woodcock 1905–1985: the life story of Tommy Woodcock, horseman, best friend to Phar Lap and Reckless*. Melbourne, Greenhouse, 1986

HUNTING
Daly, John. *The Adelaide Hunt: a history of the Adelaide Hunt Club, 1840–1986*. Adelaide, Adelaide Hunt Club, 1986

Nagel, Maureen. Hunting and other sport in Australian paintings 1788–1900. BHMS (Honours), University of Queensland, 1987

Ronald, Heather B. *Hounds are running: a history of the Melbourne Hunt*. Kilmore, Vic., Lowden, 1979

LAW
Healey, Deborah. *Sport and the law: a guide for people involved in sport*. Sydney, NSW University Press, 1989

Kelly, G. Maurice. *Sport and the law: an Australian perspective*. Sydney, Law Book, 1987

Pannam, Clifford Leslie. *The horse and the law*. 2nd edn, Sydney, Law Book, 1986

LAWN BOWLING

Guiney, Cyril. *Centenary: the history of the Royal New South Wales Bowling Association, 1880–1980*. Sydney, The Association, 1980

Henshaw, John and Glenn, Ord. *The first one hundred years of the Royal Victorian Bowls Association 1880–1980*. Melbourne, The Association, 1979

Hoey, Tom. *Bowls the Australian way*. Melbourne, Lansdowne, 1974

McCarthy, Lovella. Testing the bias: sex, class and lawn bowls. BA (Honours), University of NSW, 1985

Morelle, Lettie. *The first fifty years: a brief history of the growth and development of the Queensland Ladies' Bowling Association, 1930 to 1980*. Brisbane, The Association, 1980

Pollard, Jack. *Lawn bowls: the Australian way*. Melbourne, Lansdowne, 1962

MOTOR SPORTS

Bartlett, Kevin and Shepherd, Jim. *Big rev Kev*. Sydney, Lansdowne, 1983

Blanden, John. *A history of the Australian Grand Prix*. Belair, SA, Museum Publishing, 1981

Brabham, Jack. *When the flag drops*. London, Kimber, 1971

Brock: the man, the machines, the legend. Sydney, Australian Consolidated Press, 1988

Cox, Don and Will Hagon. *Australian motorcycle heroes, 1949-1989*. Sydney, Angus & Robertson, 1989

Green, Evan. *Evan Green's world of motor sport*. Sydney, Summit Books, 1977

Hanrahan, Bryan. *Motor racing the Australian way*. Melbourne, Lansdowne, 1972

Harding, Mike. *The racing history of Fords and Holdens*. Sydney, View Productions, 1986

Hartgerink, Nick. *Gardner, a dream come true*. Sydney, Hutchinson Australia, 1989

Hassall, David. *The Peter Brock story*. Melbourne, Garry Sparke, 1983

Hoskins, John. *Roarin' round the speedways: the story of speedway racing*. London, McCorquodale, 1930

Howard, Graham and Wilson, Stewart. *Australian touring car championship: 30 fabulous years*. Rev. edn, Sydney, Chevron Publishing, 1986

Jones, Alan and Botsford, Keith. *Driving ambition*. London, Paul, 1981

Kennedy, Alan. *Australia's greatest months of motorsport*. Sydney, Fairfax, 1987

Naismith, Barry. *The Jim Richards story*. Melbourne, Garry Sparke, 1986

The official 50-race history of the Australian Grand Prix. Sydney, R & T Publishing, 1986

Pollard, Jack. *One for the road*. 2nd edn, Sydney, Pollard Publishing, 1974.

Shepherd, Jim. *A history of Australian motor sport*. Sydney, Sportsbook, 1980

Simpson, Ray. *Australian motor racing in the 1980s*. Sydney, View Productions, 1986

——. *Australian touring car racing*. Sydney, View Productions, 1987

Tuckey, Bill. *Australia's greatest motor race, the complete history*. Sydney, Lansdowne, 1981

——. *The book of Australian motor racing*. Sydney, Murray, n.d.

——. *The rise and fall of Peter Brock: the motor industry crash that shocked Australia*. Melbourne, Greenhouse Publications, 1987

Tuckey, Bill and Jacobson, Mike. *Dick Johnson, the real story of a folk hero*. Sydney, Chevron, 1989

Wilson, Stewart. *Ford: the racing history*. Sydney, Chevron, 1989

Wilson, Stewart, et al. *Holden: the official racing history*. Sydney, Chevron 1988

NETBALL
All Australia Netball Association. *Golden jubilee souvenir booklet, 1927–28 – 1977–78*. Sydney, The Association, 1978

Edman, Donna. The commercialization of women's sport: netball as a case study. BA (Honours), University of NSW, 1986

Hyland, Deirdre. *'Little Anne': a biography of Anne Clarke, B.E.M*. Sydney, NSW Netball Association, 1987

Jobling, Ian and Barham, Pamela. *Netball Australia: a socio-historical analysis*. Brisbane, I. Jobling and P. Barham, 1988

OLYMPIC GAMES
Atkinson, Graeme. *Australian and New Zealand Olympians: the stories of 100 great champions*. Melbourne, Five Mile Press, 1984

Blanch, John and Jenes, Paul. *Australia at the modern Olympic Games*. Sydney, John Blanch Publishing, 1984

Dent, William. Australia's participation in the Olympic and British Empire Games, 1896–1938. MA, University of New England, 1987

Donald, Keith and Selth, Don. *Olympic saga: the track and field story, Melbourne 1956*. Sydney, Futurian Press, 1957

Howell, Reet and Howell, Max. *Aussie gold: the story of Australia at the Olympics.* Brisbane, Brooks Waterloo, 1988

Lester, Gary. *Australia goes to the Olympics 1896–1980.* Sydney, Magazine Promotions Australia, 1980

May, Norman. *Gold! gold! gold!* Sydney, Horwitz Grahame, 1984

Official report of the Organising Committee for the Games of the XVI Olympiad, Melbourne 1956. Melbourne, Government of Victoria, 1956

Olympic Games Melbourne 1956. Sydney, Colorgravure, 1956

PHYSICAL EDUCATION

Kentish, G. *Fritz Duras: the father of physical education in Australia.* Adelaide, ACHPER Publications, 1984

ROWING

Bennett, Scott. *The Clarence Comet: the career of Henry Searle 1866–89.* Sydney, Sydney University Press, 1973

Gorman, Francis. *Rowing at Riverview: the first hundred years, 1882–1982.* Sydney, St Ignatius' College, 1983

Jacobsen, Alan. *Australia in world rowing: the bow-waves and strokes.* Melbourne, Hill of Content, 1984

Jeffreys, Ralph S. *Fremantle Rowing Club: the first one hundred years, 1887–1987.* Fremantle, Fremantle Rowing Club, 1987

Kavanagh, Merle. *On these bright waters: a centennial history of Leichhardt Rowing Club, 1886–1986.* Sydney, Leichhardt Rowing Club, 1986

Lang, John. *The Victorian oarsman with a rowing register, 1857–1919.* Melbourne, A.H. Massina, 1919

Leicester, Andrew. *A history of rowing in the Athletic Association of the Great Public Schools of New South Wales.* Sydney, The Kings School, 1978

McSwan, Eleanor. *Champions in sport, Henry Searle and Chimpy Busch.* Maclean, NSW, Maclean District Historical Society, 1973

Negus, Guy. *Western Australian Rowing Club Inc. 1868–1968.* Perth, WA Rowing Club, 1990

1910–1979 rowing, a history of AHS. Adelaide, Adelaide High School, 1980

Rickards, Field. *Rowing in Victoria: the first 100 years of the Victorian Rowing Association, 1876–1976.* Melbourne, Victorian Rowing Association, 1976

200 years of rowing: commemorative programme. Sydney, Australian Rowing Council, 1988

Wetherell, H. *A short historical sketch of the Commercial Rowing Club.* Brisbane, Commercial Rowing Club, 1945

RUGBY LEAGUE

Andrews, Malcolm. *Rugby league heroes*. Sydney, Horwitz, 1982

——. *Rugby league, the greatest game of all*. Sydney, Horwitz, 1983

Armstrong, Geoff. *The greatest game of all: a celebration of rugby league*. Sydney, Ironbark Press, 1991

Field, W. T. Sport, war and society: a study of St. George District Rugby League Football Club 1939–1945. BA (Honours), University of NSW, 1981

Grand finals: Sydney rugby league's greatest moments. Sydney, Murray, 1978

Greenwood, Geoff. *Australian rugby league's greatest games*. Sydney, Murray, 1978

——. *Australian rugby league's greatest players*. Sydney, Murray, 1978

Haddan, Stephen. *The Power's bitter history of N.S.W. rugby league finals*. Norman Park, Qld., S. Haddan, 1991

Harris, Bret. *The Best of both worlds: the Michael O'Connor story*. Melbourne, Macmillan, 1991

Heads, Ian. *Local hero: the Wayne Pearce story*. Sydney, Ironbark Press, 1990

——. *March of the dragons: the story of St. George Rugby League Club*. Sydney, Lester-Townsend, 1989

——. *The history of Souths, 1908–1985*. Sydney, Hoffman-Smith, 1985

——. *The story of the Kangaroos*. Sydney, Lester-Townsend, 1990

Howell, Max and Howell, Reet. *The greatest game under the sun: the story of rugby league in Queensland*. Brisbane, L. I. Bedington, 1989.

Lester, Gary. *Berries to Bulldogs*. Sydney, Lester-Townsend, 1985

——. *The Bulldog story: a history of the Canterbury-Bankstown Rugby League Club*. Sydney, Playwright Publishing, 1991

——. *The story of Australian rugby league*. Sydney, Lester-Townsend, 1988

Lovett, Neil. *Footy manual: a historical and coaching guide of the Illawarra Steelers*. Wollongong, Illawarra District Rugby League Football Club, 1988

Macdonald, John. *Big Mal: the inspiring story of Mal Meninga*. Sydney, Lester-Townsend, 1990

Masters, Roy. *Inside league*. Sydney, Pan Books, 1990

McGregor, Adrian. *King Wally: the story of Wally Lewis*. Brisbane, University of Queensland Press, 1987

Messenger, Dally. *The master: the story of H.H. 'Dally' Messenger and the beginning of Australian rugby league*. Sydney, Angus & Roberston, 1982

Mortimer, Steve and Tasker, Norman. *Top dog, the Steve Mortimer story.* Sydney, Hutchinson Australia, 1988

Pollard, Jack. *Rugby league, the Australian way.* Rev. edn, Melbourne, Lansdowne Press, 1970

Price, Ray and Cadigan, Neil. *Perpetual motion.* Sydney, Angus & Robertson, 1987

Ryan, Ronald. The history of rugby league football in Australia. MA, California State University, Long Beach, 1978

Scott, Edmond. The development of rugby league in Brisbane. MHMS (prov.), University of Queensland, 1985

Smith, Robert. *The sea eagle has landed: the story of Manly-Waringah Rugby League Club.* Sydney, Sea Eagles Marketing, 1991

Walsh, Ian and Willey, Keith. *Inside rugby league.* Sydney, Horwitz, 1968

Whelan, Col and Heads, Ian. *Days of glory: ten years of the Winfield Cup.* Sydney, Ironbark Press, 1991

Whiticker, Alan. *The history of the Balmain Tigers.* Sydney, Sherborne Sutherland Publishing, 1988

Whiticker, Alan and Anderson, Greg. *The history of the North Sydney 'Bears'.* Sydney, Sherborne Sutherland Publishing, 1988

RUGBY UNION
Bickley, W. *Maroon: highlights of one hundred years of rugby in Queensland, 1882–1982.* Brisbane, Queensland Rugby Union, 1982

Fihelly, Michael J. *Century of rugby football, 1824–1924.* Brisbane, Rawlings, Mullins & Co., 1924

Harris, Bret. *The marauding maroons.* Sydney, Horwitz, 1982

Harris, Stewart. *Political football: the Springbok tour of Australia, 1971.* Melbourne, Gold Star, 1972

Hickie, Tom. *The game for the game itself! The development of sub-district rugby in Sydney: in remembrance of every person who has administered, played for or supported a sub-district rugby club.* Sydney, Sydney Sub-district Rugby Union, 1983

Horton, Peter A. A history of rugby union football in Queensland 1882–1891. Ph.D., University of Queensland, 1989

Poidevin, Simon and Webster, Jim. *For love not money: the Simon Poidevin story.* Sydney, ABC, 1990.

Pollard, Jack. *The Australian rugby union: the game and the players.* Sydney, Angus & Robertson, 1984

Price, Maxwell. *Wallabies without armour.* Sydney, Reed, 1970

Steer, Mark. *The whole world watched: anti-apartheid, Queensland, Australia, 1971.* Brisbane, K. Howard, 1971

Wilkins, Phil. *The highlanders: the first 50 years of the Gordon Rugby Football Club.* Sydney, Gordon Rugby Club, 1986

SKIING

Beatty, Bill. *The white roof of Australia.* Melbourne, Cassell, 1958

Bennett, Donald. *Hotham horizon, the Alpine Club of Victoria: a reminiscence.* Melbourne, D. Bennett, 1987

Cross, Wendy and Beilby, Peter. *Australian skiing: a complete handbook.* Melbourne, Four Seasons, 1983

Hull, Mick. *Mountain memories: sixty years of skiing.* Melbourne, MH Books, 1990

Kaaten, Sverre. *52 years of skiing in Australia through Norwegian eyes.* Sydney, David Boyce Publishing, 1981

Lloyd, Janis. *Skiing into history 1924–1984.* Melbourne, Ski Club of Victoria, 1985

Sheridan, L. *Shes and skis: golden years of the Australian Women's Ski Club 1932– 1982.* Melbourne, Australian Women's Ski Club, 1983

Stephenson, Harry. *Skiing the high plains: stories of the exploration of Victoria's snowfields.* Melbourne, Graphic Books, 1982

Walkom, Rick. *Skiing off the roof: the Kosciusko Chalet at Charlotte Pass and its place in history.* Pokolbin, NSW, Arlberg Press, 1991

SOCCER

Baumgartner, Leo. *The little professor of soccer.* Sydney, Marketing Productions, 1968

Grant, Sid. *Jack Pollard's soccer records.* Sydney, Jack Pollard, 1974

Johnston, Craig. *Walk alone: the Craig Johnston story.* Sydney, Collins Australia, 1989

Mosely, Phil. A social history of soccer in N.S.W., 1880–1956. Ph.D., University of Sydney, 1987

Olivier-Scerri, Gino. *Encyclopedia of Australian soccer 1922–88.* Sydney, Showcase Publications, 1988

Warren, Johnny and Dettre, Andrew. *Soccer in Australia.* Sydney, Hamlyn, 1975

SPHAIREE

Beck, Frederick. *The game of sphairee: strokes, tactics, history.* Sydney, Cheiron Press, 1981

SPORTS MEDICINE

Vamplew, Wray. *A healthy body: the Australian Sports Medicine Federation 1963–1988*. Canberra, Australian Sports Medicine Federation, 1989

SURF LIFE SAVING

Galton, Barry. *Gladiators of the surf: the Australian Surf Life Saving Championships, a history*. Sydney, Reed, 1984

Harris, Reg S. *Heroes of the surf: fifty years history of Manly Lifesaving Club*. Sydney, Manly Lifesaving Club, 1961

Haylock, Gretta. *History of swimming and lifesaving at Seacliff: a record of all major awards and achievements made by members during the past 50 years, 1930–1980*. Adelaide, G. Haylock, 1980

Jaggard, Edwin A. *A challenge answered: a history of surf lifesaving in Western Australia*. Perth, Surf Lifesaving Association of Australia, WA State Centre, 1979

——. *The premier club: Cottesloe Surf Life Saving Club's first seventy-five years*. Perth, Cottesloe Surf Life Saving Club, 1984

Winders, J.R. *Surf life saving in Queensland*. Brisbane, Queensland State Centre of the Surf Life Saving Association of Australia, 1970

SURFING

Cassidy, Graham and Luton, Geoff. *Greats of the Australian surf*. Sydney, Lester-Townsend, 1989

Farrelly, Midget. *This surfing life*. Adelaide, Rigby, 1965

Margan, Frank. *A pictorial history of surfing*. Sydney, Hamyln, 1970

Maxwell, C. Bede. *Surf: Australians against the sea*. Sydney, Angus & Robertson, 1949

Pearson, Kent. *Surfing subcultures of Australia and New Zealand*. Brisbane, University of Queensland Press, 1979

Wilson, Jack. *Australian surfing and surf life saving*. Adelaide, Rigby, 1979

Young, Nat and McGregor, Craig. *The history of surfing*. Sydney, Palm Beach Press, 1988

SWIMMING

Bennett, Scott. *The Clarence Comet: the career of Henry Searle, 1866–89*. Sydney, Sydney University Press, 1973

Cecil Healy in memoriam. Sydney, John Andrew, 1920.

Clarkson, Alan. *Lanes of gold: 100 years of the NSW Amateur Swimming Association*. Sydney, Lester-Townsend, 1989

Fromholtz, Laurence. *The Sobraon Wonder: a biography of Bernard Bede (Barney) Kieran*. Wagga Wagga, NSW, L. Fromholtz, 1991

Gordon, Harry and Fraser, Dawn. *Dawn Fraser*. Melbourne, Circus, 1965

Gould, Shane. *Swimming, the Shane Gould way*. Sydney, Oak Tree Press, 1972

Hamill, Alex. *1884–1984, celebrating a centenary—Balmain Swimming Club*. Sydney, Balmain Swimming Club, 1984

Knox, Ken. *The Dawn of swimming*. London, Stanley Paul, 1962

Lomas, Graham. *The will to win: the story of Sir Frank Beaurepaire*. London, Heinemann, 1960

Philip, George B. *Sixty years' recollections of swimming and surfing in the Eastern Suburbs*. Sydney, G. Philip, 1940

Raszeja Wood, Veronica. *A decent and proper exertion: the rise of women's competitive swimming in Sydney to 1912*. BA (Honours), University of NSW, 1990

Rose, Eileen. *The torch within*. Garden City, NY, Doubleday, 1965

TENNIS
A century of Queensland: tennis centenary 1888–1988. Brisbane, Sunshine Publications, 1988

Austral. *Lawn tennis in Australasia*. Sydney, Edwards Dunlop, 1912

Coombe, D.C. *A history of the Davis Cup*. Sydney, Australasian, 1949

Court, Margaret. *Court on court: a life in tennis*. New York, Dodd Mead, 1975

Deacon, William. The influence of Harry Hopman on Australian tennis. BA (Honours), University of Queensland, 1985

Fraser, Neale and McDonald, Ian. *Power tennis*. London, Stanley Paul, 1962

Garnett, Michael. *A history of royal tennis in Australia*. Melbourne, Historical Publications, 1983

Goolagong, Evonne and Collins, Bud. *Evonne*. London, Hart-Davis Mac-Gibbon, 1975

Greenwood, Geoff. *The golden years of Australian tennis*. Sydney, Murray, 1977.

Hoad, Lew and Pollard, Jack. *My game*. London, Hodder & Stoughton, 1958

Hogan, Ashley. *Is there any prize money?* Sydney, Lilyfield, 1987

Hopman, Harry. *Aces and places*. London, Cassell, 1957

Johnson, Joseph. *Amazing grace: the story of the Grace Park Lawn Tennis Club 1889–1989*. Melbourne, Grace Park Lawn Tennis Club, 1989

———. *Grand slam: the story of the Australian open tennis championships*. Melbourne, Courtney Books, 1985

Kinross-Smith, Graeme. *The sweet spot: one hundred years of life and tennis in Geelong, a centenary history of the Geelong Lawn Tennis Club.* Melbourne, Hyland House, 1982

Laver, Rod and Collins, Bud. *The education of a tennis player.* London, Pelham, 1971

Mathews, Bruce. *Game, set and glory: a history of the Australian tennis championships.* Melbourne, Five Mile Press, 1985

——. *Pat Cash: my story.* London, Macdonald, 1988

McLean, Ron. *Country cracks: the story of N.S.W. country tennis.* Gunnedah, NSW, R. McLean, 1984

Meltzer, Paul. *Great players of Australian tennis.* Sydney, Harper and Row, 1979

New South Wales Centenary 1895–1985. Sydney, NSW Tennis Association, 1985

Newcombe, John. *Bedside tennis.* New York, St Martin's Press, 1983

O'Farrell, Virginia. Open tennis: the Australian debate 1955–1975. BA (Honours), University of NSW, 1982

Pails, Dinny. *Set points.* Sydney, Currawong, 1952

Quist, Adrian and Egan, Jack. *Tennis, the greats, 1920–1960.* Sydney, ABC, 1984

Rowley, Peter and Rosewall, Ken. *Ken Rosewall: twenty years at the top.* London, Cassell, 1976

Smith, Margaret and Lawrence, Don. *The Margaret Smith story.* London, Stanley Paul, 1965

Stolle, Fred and Wydro, Ken. *Tennis down under.* Bethesda, Md., National Press, 1985

Trengove, Alan. *The story of the Davis Cup.* Melbourne, Stanley Paul, 1985

Whitington, Richard. *An illustrated history of Australian tennis.* New York, St Martin's Press, 1976

Yallop, R. *Royal South Yarra Lawn Tennis Club: 100 years in Australian tennis.* Melbourne, Currey O'Neil, 1984

TENPIN BOWLING
Australian tenpin bowling. Melbourne, Bowlers World, 1988

TRACK AND FIELD
Australian Athletic Union. *Australian athletics at 'the Games'.* Melbourne, The Union, 1983

Blake, Jim. *100 Stawell Gifts, Stawell Athletic Club 'ever foremost': official history.* Stawell, Stawell Athletic Club, 1981

Boyle, Raelene and Craven, John. *Rage Raelene, run*. Melbourne, Caribou, 1983

Branagan, David F. *From time to time: a history of the Sydney University Athletic Club, 1878–1978*. Sydney, The Club, 1978

Brown, Les and O'Donoghue, Les. *One hundred Bay Sheffields*. Adelaide, L. J. Brown, 1987

Bull, Joe. *The spiked shoe*. Melbourne, National Press, 1959

Cerutty, Percy W. *Sport is my life*. London, Stanley Paul, 1966

City to surf: Australia's run of the year. Sydney, Fairfax Library, 1986

Clarke, Ron and Trengrove, Alan. *The unforgiving minute*. London, Pelham, 1966

Cuthbert, Betty and Webster, Jim. *Golden girl*. London, Pelham, 1966

Elliott, Herb and Trengove, Alan. *The golden mile*. London, Cassell, 1961

Gould, Nell. *Women's athletics in Australia: official history of the Australian Women's Amateur Athletic Union*. Sydney, MGA Publications, 1972

Kelly, Graeme. *Mr controversial: the story of Percy Wells Cerutty*. London, Stanley Paul, 1964

Kelly, William. *The South Australian Amateur Athletic Association: a history, 1867–1973*. Adelaide, The Association, 1973

Lenton, Brian. *Off the record*. Canberra, Lenton, 1981

Maher, John J. *Official history of the Stawell Athletic Club, 1877–1937*. Stawell, The Club, 1937

Mason, Percy. *Professional athletics in Australia*. Adelaide, Rigby, 1985.

100 years of the NSW AAA. Sydney, Fairfax Library, 1987

Ross, John. Pedestrianism and athletics in England and Australia in the nineteenth century: a case study in the development of sport. BHMS (Honours), University of Queensland, 1984

Waddell, Peter. *A history of Australian race walking: part 1*. Canberra, P. Waddell, 1990

TRUGO
Victorian Trugo Association. *Over fifty years of trugo*. Melbourne, The Association, 1984

VIOLENCE
Cunneen, Chris, et al. *Dynamics of collective conflict: riots at the Bathurst Bike races*. Sydney, Law Book, 1989

Pickard, Pauline. An investigation of crowd behaviors in selected Australian sports, with particular emphasis on violence, aggressive behavior and facilities. Ed. D., Boston University, 1990

Sport and Recreation Ministers' Council. *Violence in sport.* Canberra, The Council, 1985

Vamplew, Wray. *Sports violence in Australia: its extent and control.* Canberra, ASC, 1991

WATER SKIING

Wansey, Michael. *In search of gold: the Australian Water Ski Association 1990 five year sports development plan.* Canberra, Australian Water Ski Association, 1990

Wing, B. *Water skiing in Australia.* Sydney, B. Wing, 1982

WEIGHTLIFTING

Gill, Trevor. *The world on my shoulders, from fishing for tuna to lifting for gold: the Dean Lukin story.* Melbourne, Penguin, 1985

WOMEN

Mitchell, Susan and Dyer, Ken. *Winning women: challenging the norms in Australian sport.* Melbourne, Penguin, 1985

Randall, L.M. A fair go? Women in sport in South Australia 1945–1965. BA (Honours), Flinders University of SA, 1986

Stell, Marion. *Half the race: a history of women in Australian sport.* Sydney, Angus & Robertson, 1991

WOODCHOPPING

Beckett, R. *Axemen stand by your logs.* Sydney, Lansdowne, 1983

YACHTING

Bonnitcha, Frank. *A history of 16ft skiffs in N.S.W. 1901–1989.* Sydney, NSW 16ft Skiff Association, 1990

D'Alpuget, Lou. *Yachting in Australia: from colonial skiffs to America's Cup defence.* Sydney, Collins, 1986

Ferris, J.H. *The long hard beat: a history of the Royal Melbourne Yacht Squadron.* Melbourne, Royal Melbourne Yacht Squadron, 1990

Fry, Peter. *Bluewater Australians: the Australian experience in ocean sailing.* Sydney, ABC, 1987

Goddard, R. *A century of yachting: a record of a great sport 1837–1937.* Sydney, R. Goddard, 1937?

Lester, Gary and Sleeman, Richard. *The America's Cup: 1851-1987: sailing for supremacy.* Sydney, Lester-Townsend, 1986

Neale, R. *Jolly dogs are we: the history of yachting in Victoria 1838–1894.* Mont Albert, Vic. Landscape Publications, 1894

Ross, Bob. *The sailing Australians*. Adelaide, Rigby, 1973.

Stannard, Bruce. *The triumph of Australia II: the America's Cup challenge of 1983*. Sydney, Lansdowne Press, 1983

Stephensen, Percy. *Sydney sails: the story of the Royal Sydney Yacht Squadron's first 100 years (1862–1962)*. Sydney, Angus & Robertson, 1962

Webster, Edwin. *A hundred years of yachting*. Hobart, J. Walch, 1936

KEY TO AUTHORS

AB	Alf Batchelder	ES	Edmond Scott
AB*	Anne Bremner	ES*	Erica Sainsbury
AB†	Alex Barter	FM	Frances Millane
AL	Andrew Lemon	FM*	Frank Mines
AM	Andrew Moore	FSP	Frank S. Pyke
AM*	Al Mewett	GB	Greg Blood
AMJ	Anne Marie Jonas	GB*	George Biggs
AN	Alan Newman	GB†	Geoff Bassingthwaighte
AP	Alice Paul	GC	Graham Cooke
AP*	Andrew Paul	GC*	Gerald Crawford
APM	Anthony P. Millar	GC†	Graham Croker
AW	Amanda Weaver	GC#	Greg Campbell
BB	Brierly Bailey	GD	Garry Daly
BC	Ben Crowe	GF	George Franki
BC*	Ben Calver	GFT	George F. Tillotson
BD	Braham Dabscheck	GH	Graham Howard
BJ	Brian Jackson	GH*	George Hay
BK	Bill Keir	GK-S	Graeme Kinross-Smith
BM	Bruce Mitchell	GL	Glen Lee
BN	Bede Nairn	GL*	Glynn Lawry
BS	Brian Stoddart	GL†	Geoff Lawrence
BS*	Bob Stewart	GM	Gloria Murgey
BS†	Bruce Smith	GN	Geoff Nash
BW	Bernard Whimpress	GP	Gary Parker
CC	Chris Cunneen	GR	Gerard Roe
CC*	Chris Collins	GS	Greg Smith
CD	Chris Dunshea	GW	Gerald Walsh
CF	Catherine Fox	HCJP	Harry C. J. Phillips
CH	Christiaan Hobson	HK	Helen Keane
CH*	Col Hutchinson	HR	Heather Reid
CJF	Christopher John Fleming	HS	Hank Stanley
CP	Colleen Parker	IC	Ian Curedale
CS	Christopher Spence	IF	Imke Fischer
CT	Colin Tatz	IF*	Ian Fowler
CY	Carolyn Young	IH	Ian Harriss
DA	Daryl Adair	IJ	Ian Jobling
DB	Douglas Booth	IJ*	Ian Jarman
DC	Don Cox	IM	Ivan Martin
DH	Dierdre Hyland	IMcD	Ian McDonald
DH*	David Hogg	IW	Ivan Wingate
DH†	Dave Headon	JAD	John A. Daly
DJ	David Jenkin	JC	Jak Carroll
DJ*	Dan Joyce	JC*	Janice Cameron
DL	David Lane	JD	Julie Draper
DMcL	Donald McLeish	JF	Jim Fitzpatrick
DM	David Montefiore	JFR	J. Rodgers
DM*	Dene Moore	JG	John Gibney
DN	Dave Nadel	JM	Joan Morison
DR	Daphne Read	JMcC	John McCoy
DR*	David Rowe	JMcH	Jack McHarg
DRS	Donna Rae Szalinski	JNT	J. Neville Turner
DS	David Southgate	JO'H	John O'Hara
EB	Ed Biggs	JP	Jocelyn Polley
EH-S	Elery Hamilton-Smith	JS	John Schauble
EJ	Ed Jaggard	JS*	Jeffrey Slatter
EM	Elaine Murphy	KB	Ken Breen
EP	Eric Panther	KC	Kris Corcoran

KD	Kim Dickson	RB	Richard Broome
KM	Katharine Moore	RB*	Richard Baka
KM*	Katharine Moore (with	RB†	Roma Brideoake
	information supplied by	RC	Richard Cashman
	relevant association)	RC*	Raymond Cher
KM-H	Kersi Meher-Homji	RC†	Ray Crawford
KO'B	Kitty O'Brien	RC#	Richard Cashman (drawing from
KR	Kerry Regan		the works of Lou d'Alpuget)
KS	Karin Sheedy	RF	Ric Finlay
KS*	Kery Staples	RF*	Richard Fotheringham
KT	Kristine Toohey	RG	Robin Grow
KT*	Kevin Thompson	RH	Reet Howell
KT†	Kate Tierney	RH*	Rex Harcourt
KW	Ken Winsor	RH†	Roy Hay
LB	Lois Bryson	RJP	Robert J. Paddick
LC	Lorraine Carlton	RK	Roy Kirkby
LMcC	Louella McCarthy	RK*	Roz Keeble
LM	Les Murray	RKB	R. K. Burns
LO'R	Lynnette O'Reilly	RKS	R. K. Stewart
LR	Leonie Randall	RL	Rob Lynch
MB	Mark Buhagiar	RL*	Rod Lindroth
MBW	Michael B. Wansey	RM	Reg Marsh
MC	Michael Christie	RO	Roslyn Otzen
MD	Mike Daws	RP	Rosemary Phillips
MF	Mimi Frost	RQ	Roderic Quinn
MH	Max Howell	RR	Rae Reid
MH*	Mark Harris	RS	Richard Stremski
MK	Margaret Killin	RS*	Rosalie Stewart
ML	Marie Little	RW	Roy Ward MLC
MMcK	Michael McKernan	SA	Shirley Adkins
MN	Michael Noonan	SA*	Stuart Alldritt
MP	Murray Phillips	SB	Scott Bennett
MR	Marlene Ryzman	SB*	S. Bird
MS	Max Solling	SC	Shane Cahill
MS*	Martin Soust	SG	Stephen Gibbs
MT	Melanie Tonks	SJ	Steve Jones
MV	Marie Van Der Klooster	SJR	S. J. Routh
MW	Martin Whiteley	SN	S. Nagae
MW*	Max Walters	SW	Sue Webb
NS	N. Sowdon	TA	Tom Armstrong
NS*	Narelle Stafford	TB	Tom Brock
PB	Pamela Barham	TB*	Thomas J Bergin
PB*	Peggy Browne	TC	Tom Cuddihy
PC	Peter Corcoran	TD	Tom Dunning
PD	Philip Derriman	TGP	T. G. Parsons
PH	Peter Horton	TH	Tom Hickie
PH-S	Pauline Harvey-Short	TM	Tom Miller
PJ	Paul James	TM*	Toby Miller
PJ*	Paul Jenes	TMcC	Tom McCullough
PK	Peter Konsto	TN	Tony Narr
PM	Phil Mosely	TR	Tony Robinson
PMcM	Peter McMenamin	VJ	Val Johnston
PP	Peter Poole	VO'F	Virginia O'Farrell
PS	Peter Sharpham	VRW	Veronica Raazeja Wood
PT	Paul Tatz	WAE	Warren A. Ellem
PW	Peter Williams	WF	Warwick Franks
PW*	Peter White	WPR	W. P. Reynolds
RA	Rod Allan	WV	Wray Vamplew
RAA	R. A. Abbott		

SOURCES OF ILLUSTRATIONS

The illustrations in this publication are reproduced with the permission of many individuals, institutions and associations. In some cases ownership of copyright of photographs used in this book could not be traced and in such cases it is regretted that acknowledgement could not be given.

1. H. A. Godson Collection, State Library of South Australia. Photograph 28A/14. It is probable that the photograph was taken by George Taplin, missionary at Point Macleay from 1859 to 1879. The bowler is apparently about to attempt a round-arm (horizontal to the shoulder) delivery.
2. Melbourne Cricket Club Library.
3. D. Hall, Dalby, Queensland. Private collection.
4. Mullett family, Drouin, Victoria. Private collection.
5. *Australian Soccer Weekly*.
6. *Advertiser*, Adelaide; photographer, Sam Cheshire.
7. Australian Gallery of Sport and Olympic Museum. The Briscoe Trophy was lost and then discovered, dirty and blackened, in a South Melbourne antique shop by Harry Duncan, a former president of the Albert Park Rowing Club. It was subsequently donated to the National Trust of Australia (Victoria) for display at one of its properties. It is on loan to the Australian Gallery of Sport and Olympic Museum from Mr T. Warburton.
8. *Australian Sketcher*, 8 July 1876. National Library of Australia, Canberra.
9. Mitchell Library, State Library of New South Wales.
10. Mitchell Library, State Library of New South Wales.
11. 'The *Sun* Superun', 11 April 1990. Herald & Weekly Times, Melbourne; photographer, Donna Todd.
12. Australian Gallery of Sport and Olympic Museum.
13. Australian Gallery of Sport and Olympic Museum.
14. Australian Gallery of Sport and Olympic Museum; photographer, Carolyn Dew.
15. Australian Gallery of Sport and Olympic Museum; photographer, Carolyn Dew.
16. *Australasian Sketcher*, 27 July 1883.
17. Arthur Streeton, *The National Game (1889)*. Oil on cardboard 11.8 × 22.9 cm. Art Gallery of New South Wales.
18. S. T. Gill, *McLaren's Boxing Saloon, Main Road, Ballarat* (1854), watercolour. Mitchell Library, State Library of New South Wales.
19. Australian Gallery of Sport and Olympic Museum.
20. Australian Gallery of Sport and Olympic Museum.
21. Source not known.
22. *Canberra Times*; photographer, Peter Wells.
23. Australian Gallery of Sport and Olympic Museum; photographer, Erin O'Brien.
24. Melbourne Cricket Club Museum.
25. *Australasian Sketcher*, 8 July 1876. National Library of Australia, Canberra.

26. *Snowy Baker's Magazine*, 6 April 1912.
27. Aboriginal and Torres Strait Islander Commission.
28. Ian Jobling, private collection; source not known.
29. Mitchell Library, State Library of New South Wales.
30. *Courier-Mail*, 27 November 1936.
31. Reproduced by courtesy of the *Sydney Morning Herald*.
32. Herald & Weekly Times, Melbourne.
33. Reproduced by courtesy of the *Sydney Morning Herald*.
34. Ian Jobling, private collection; source not known.
35. Herald & Weekly Times, Melbourne.
36. Source not known.
37. *Australasian Sketcher*, 12 August 1882.
38. La Trobe Collection, State Library of Victoria.
39. Mortlock Library of South Australiana, State Library of South Australia. SSL:M:B11915
40. Melbourne Cricket Club Museum. Stephenson's tour was sponsored by Melbourne caterers, Messrs Spiers and Pond, whose Cafe de Paris in Collins Street can be seen in the background.
41. Henry Burns, *The First International Cricket; H. H. Stephenson's All England Eleven versus the Victorian Eighteen, Melbourne Cricket Ground, 1 January 1862*. Watercolour. Melbourne Cricket Club Museum.
42. John Oxley Library, Queensland.
43. Australian Gallery of Sport and Olympic Museum.
44. *Queenslander*, 16 February 1933.
45. Australian Gallery of Sport and Olympic Museum.
46. Bradman Museum, Bowral, New South Wales; photographer, M. Hutchinson, D.E.M. Architects.
47. Bradman Museum, Bowral, New South Wales; photographer, M. Hutchinson, D.E.M. Architects.
48. Australian Gallery of Sport and Olympic Museum; donor, Rupert Bates.
49. La Trobe Collection, State Library of Victoria.
50. Australian Gallery of Sport and Olympic Museum; donor, The Hon. Maurice O'Sullivan.
51. Courtesy of Memphis Shelby County Public Library and Information Center, Memphis, Tennessee. It should be noted that Darcy's date of birth is incorrectly listed on the death certificate as 1896. Photograph, Katharine Moore, private collection.
52. Melbourne Theatre Company's production of David Williamson's *The Club*, first performed on 24 May 1977 at Russell Street Theatre; directed by Rodney Fisher and designed by Shaun Gurton. Actors (from left): Terence Donovan, Frank Wilson, Harold Hopkins. Photographer, David Parker.
53. Cuthbert Charles Clarke, *The Caledonian Games* (1861). Pen and wash drawing. La Trobe Collection, State Library of Victoria.
54. Reproduced by courtesy of the *Sydney Morning Herald*.
55. Herald & Weekly Times, Melbourne.
56. Reproduced by courtesy of the *West Australian*.
57. Australian Paralympic Association; photographer, Rick Lodge.

58. Special Olympics Australia.
59. Photographer, Simon Gillett.
60. ACHPER (Qld) Women in Sport Special Interest Group and Women's Sport Promotion Unit, Australian Sports Commission.
61. Herald & Weekly Times, Melbourne.
62. Colin Laverty (1983), *Pastures and Pastimes: An Exhibition of Australian Racing, Sporting and Animal Pictures of the 19th Century*, Gardner Printing Co. (Vic.) Pty Ltd, Mitcham. Private collection.
63. Photographer, Ian Jobling. Private collection.
64. *Australasian Sketcher*, 26 October 1878.
65. *Australasian Sketcher*, 23 July 1881.
66. *Illustrated Australian News*, 24 March 1875.
67. John Rae, *A Game Like Hockey in Hyde Park, Sydney*. Mitchell Library, State Library of New South Wales.
68. Mortlock Library of South Australiana, State Library of South Australia. SSL:M:B7596
69. *Australasian Sketcher*, 8 July 1882.
70. Photographer, Ian Jobling. Private collection.
71. Melbourne Cricket Club Museum.
72. Herald & Weekly Times, Melbourne.
73. *Town & Country Journal*, 14 May 1887.
74. Herald & Weekly Times, Melbourne.
75. Australian Gallery of Sport and Olympic Museum.
76. Australian Gallery of Sport and Olympic Museum; photographer, Carolyn Dew. With thanks to HSV7.
77. Courtesy of *Rugby League Week*.
78. Ian Jobling, private collection; source not known.
79. Ian Jobling, private collection; source not known.
80. Australian Gallery of Sport and Olympic Museum; photographer, Erin O'Brien.
81. British Olympic Association, Olympic Report, 1908. Ian Jobling, private collection.
82. Ian Jobling, private collection; source not known.
83. Ian Jobling, private collection; source not known.
84. Mitchell Library, State Library of New South Wales and Australian Gallery of Sport and Olympic Museum.
85. Australian Gallery of Sport and Olympic Museum; donor, Mrs Violet Stedman.
86. Australian Gallery of Sport and Olympic Museum; donor, Mrs M. McKay, Carrum, Victoria.
87. Australian Gallery of Sport and Olympic Museum.
88. Australian Gallery of Sport and Olympic Museum; Ian Beaurepaire Collection.
89. Australian Gallery of Sport and Olympic Museum.
90. Australian Gallery of Sport and Olympic Museum.
91. Australian Gallery of Sport and Olympic Museum; photographer, Koh Eng Tong.
92. *Pix*, 24 November 1956. Australian Consolidated Press.

93. Herald & Weekly Times, Melbourne.
94. Australian Gallery of Sport and Olympic Museum; Olympic Report, 1956.
95. Aboriginal and Torres Strait Islander Commission.
96. Museum of Victoria.
97. *Australasian Sketcher*, 27 November 1880.
98. Ian Jobling, private collection; source not known.
99. Courtesy of *Rugby League Week*.
100. *North Queensland Register*, 26 September 1904.
101. National Library of Australia, Canberra.
102. Alick Jackomos, Melbourne. Private collection.
103. Associated Press.
104. Melbourne Cricket Club Museum.
105. Australian Gallery of Sport and Olympic Museum; photographer, Carolyn Dew.
106. Victoria University of Technology, Footscray campus.
107. Victoria University of Technology, Footscray campus.
108. Victorian Institute of Sport.
109. Victorian Institute of Sport.
110. Victorian Institute of Sport.
111. Tim Pike, Sporting Prints, England.
112. *Age*, Melbourne.
113. Mitchell Library, State Library of New South Wales.
114. National Library of Australia, Canberra.
115. Courtesy of the *Bulletin*.
116. State Library of South Australia.
117. Melbourne Cricket Club Library.
118. Philip Derriman, *The Grand Old Ground: A History of the Sydney Cricket Ground*. Cassell Australia, Sydney, 1981.
119. *Australasian Sketcher*, 18 November 1882. The Sportsman's Club of Melbourne rented the Apollo Hall in Bourke Street during race week in November 1882 and placed a 'tote' there because, as the *Australasian Sketcher* reported, it 'was much in request amongst a certain class of the community who place no great faith in the bookmakers'.
120. *Illustrated Australian News*, 30 August 1879. This was the first commercial use of electricity in Victoria. A reporter said: 'It was quite a spectacle but spoilt by players going out of sight in the dark patches'.
121. Herald & Weekly Times, Melbourne.
122. Reproduced by courtesy of the *Sydney Morning Herald*.
123. Len Sheppard and Australian Gallery of Sport and Olympic Museum.
124. *Sporting Globe*, 9 June 1967. Rugby league match between South Sydney and Balmain at the Sydney Sports Ground.
125. Herald & Weekly Times, Melbourne.
126. Herald & Weekly Times, Melbourne.
127. Artist unknown, *Which? Man you are Wanted: in the Sportsmen's 1000*. Colour lithographic poster 100 × 72 cm. Australian War Memorial (V5005).
128. Australian Gallery of Sport and Olympic Museum; photographer, Erin O'Brien.

ACKNOWLEDGEMENTS

The members of the Australian Society for Sports History (ASSH), and especially the editors of *The Oxford Companion to Australian Sport*, are grateful that the photographers, museums, libraries, newspapers and magazines listed below, willingly co-operated in the production of this publication by permitting the inclusion of illustrations. On behalf of the ASSH, I particularly thank those who generously waived the fees normally associated with permission to reproduce photographs. I am personally indebted to Thomas McCullough and Gregor McCaskie, of the Australian Gallery of Sport and Olympic Museum, and Susanne Motherwell, of the Herald & Weekly Times, for their assistance and advice.

Ian Jobling
Co-Editor and
Co-ordinator of Illustrations

Aboriginal and Torres Strait Islander Commission
Advertiser, Adelaide
Age, Melbourne
Art Gallery of New South Wales
Associated Press
Australian Consolidated Press
Australian Council for Health, Physical Education and Recreation
Australian Gallery of Sport and Olympic Museum
Australian Paralympic Association
Australian Soccer Weekly
Australian Sports Commission
Australian War Memorial
Bradman Museum
Canberra Times
Sam Cheshire
Courier-Mail, Brisbane
Philip Derriman
Carolyn Dew
John Fairfax & Sons
Simon Gillett
D. Hall
Herald & Weekly Times
M. Hutchinson, D.E.M. Architects
Ian Jobling
Koh Eng Tong
Katharine Moore
La Trobe Collection, State Library of Victoria
Alick Jackomos
Colin Laverty

Rick Lodge
M. McKay
Melbourne Cricket Club Library
Melbourne Cricket Club Museum
Melbourne Theatre Company
Mitchell Library, State Library of New South Wales
Mullett family
Museum of Victoria
National Library of Australia
The North Queensland Newspaper Company Limited
Erin O'Brien
John Oxley Library
David Parker
Len Sheppard
Tim Pike, Sporting Prints, England
Rugby League Week
Special Olympics Australia
State Library of South Australia
Sydney Morning Herald
Paul Tatz and Colin Tatz
Donna Todd
Victoria University of Technology, Footscray campus
Victorian Institute of Sport
Peter Wells
West Australian, Perth